The Blue Guides

The Baptistery, Parma

Please write to us with your suggestions and corrections for the next edition of the guide. Writers of the best letters will be awarded a free Blue Guide of their choice.

If you would like to be included on our mailing list for information about Blue Guides, please write to us at Freepost, A & C Black (Publishers) Ltd, Cambridgeshire, PE19 3EZ

Northern Italy

From the Alps to Bologna

Alta Macadam

BLUE GUIDE

A&C Black • London
WW Norton • New York

Tenth edition 1997; reprinted December 1998

Published by A & C Black (Publishers) Limited
35 Bedford Row, London WC1R 4JH

A CIP catalogue record of this book is available from the British Library.

ISBN 0-7136-4294-7

Published in the United States of America by
WW Norton and Company, Inc
500 Fifth Avenue, New York, NY 10110

Published simultaneously in Canada by
Penguin Books Canada Limited
10 Alcorn Avenue, Toronto
Ontario M4V 3B2

ISBN 0-393-31745-5 USA

The author and the publishers have done their best to ensure the accuracy of all the information in Blue Guide Northern Italy; however, they can accept no responsibility for any loss, injury or inconvenience sustained by any traveller as a result of information or advice contained in the guide.

Alta Macadam has been a writer of Blue Guides since 1970. She lives in Florence with her family (the painter Francesco Colacicchi, and their children Giovanni and Lelia). Combined with work on writing the guide she has also been associated with the Bargello Museum, the Alinari photo archive, and Havard University at the Villa I Tatti in Florence. As author of the Blue Guides to Northern Italy, Rome, Venice, Sicily, Florence, Tuscany and Umbria she travels extensively in Italy every year to revise new editions of the books.

Cover picture: view of Lago Maggiore. Tony Stone Images/Shaun Egan.
Title page illustration: Tempio Malatestiano, tomb of Isotta degli Atti, wife of Sigismondo Malatesta.

Printed in Great Britain by Redwood Books Ltd, Trowbridge, Wiltshire.

Contents

Piedmont 187

Valle d'Aosta 227

Liguria 240

Veneto 272

Emilia Romagna   401

Maps

Atlas of Northern Italy *at the end of the book*

Ground plans

Introduction

Northern Italy comprises a vast area from the Alps down through the wide Po valley to Emilia Romagna at the foot of the Apennines. It stretches west through Liguria to the French border, and east along the Adriatic coast to Trieste, now on the Slovenian frontier. It includes some of the most important historic cities of Italy, such as Milan, Turin, Genoa, Venice, Padua, Verona, and Bologna, all with remarkable art treasures, and numerous beautiful small towns such as Ferrara, Vicenza, Mantua, and Bergamo. It also takes in the famous lakes of Garda, Maggiore, and Como. The Veneto region is well known for its numerous country villas. Romagna includes Ravenna, with its splendid Byzantine mosaics.

Detailed practical information has been supplied throughout the text, with information offices, car parks, local transport, a careful selection of hotels and restaurants (the smaller ones, often family run, and in fine positions, have been favoured), cafés, picnic places and annual festivals. There are excellent roads now all over the north of Italy, but the area can also be visited with great ease by public transport.

This is a region of the country which has for centuries been traversed by travellers on their way south (particularly to Rome) and by invading armies over the great Alpine passes. It has numerous areas of the greatest interest and some beautiful countryside. Places less well known but well worth a visit include the small towns of Castiglione Olona and Sabbioneta in Lombardy, Orta San Giulio on the Lago d'Orta, the delta of the Po, Bassano del Grappa in the Veneto, Udine, Cividale and Pordenone in the Friuli, and Parma in Emilia.

This tenth edition of *Blue Guide Northern Italy* has been totally rearranged on a strictly regional basis, with separate chapters for the most important towns, and their provinces. The guide now takes in the regions commonly considered to cover northern Italy: Lombardy, Piedmont, Valle d'Aosta, Liguria, Veneto, Friuli-Venezia Giulia, Trentino-Alto-Adige, and Emilia Romagna.

Acknowledgements

Numerous friends in Italy greatly assisted the author during the preparation of the text with specialised information. These include Pietro Marani, Angela Passigli, Flaminia Montanari, Stefano De Martino, Medardo Pellicciari, and Françoise Chiarini.

The local tourist boards all over northern Italy were extremely helpful and generous to the author during her travels. Particular thanks go to the following. In Lombardy: the directors of the APT of Milan, Lodi and Pavia; Rag. Lorenzo Sambiagio for his help on Isola Bella and Isola Madre on Lago Maggiore; Dott. Raffaele Montagna and Sig. Lamberto Ruffini of the APT del Varesotto; the director of the APT di Como; Signora Rosangela Massazza of the APT del Lecchese; Dott. Giampietro Benigni of the APT di Bergamo (and in particular Liliana Moretti); Prof. Maurizio Benzola of the APT del Bresciano; Rag. Mario

Gaiardi of the APT del Cremonese; and Dott. Franco Pellegrini of the APT del Mantovano.

In Piedmont: Signora Maria Grazia Purghè of the APT di Novara, and Dott. Burgner of the APT del Lago di Orta. In the Valle d'Aosta: Dott. Giorgio Boglione and Sig. Maurizio Di Stasi of the Assessorato del Turismo. In Liguria: Rag. Antonio Fazio of the APT of Genova.

In the Veneto: Dott. Stefano Marchioro of the APT di Padova (and in particular Sig. Zancopè); Sig. Sestilio Marcheselli of the APT of Rovigo; Sig. Pierluigi Tumiati of the APT del Vicentino (who was extremely kind and helpful); Dott.ssa Antonella Leonardo of the APT di Verona (and Sig. Benigno Barzoi on the Lago di Garda).

In Friuli-Venezia Giulia: Dott. Franco Richetti of the Azienda Regionale. In Trieste, Paolo de Gavardo of the APT; at Udine Dott.ssa Mizzau; at Gemona and Venzone Sig. Persello; at Pordenone Dott. Vannes Chiandotto (and in particular Cristina Paolin).

In Emilia Romagna: the Ufficio Informazione e Accoglienza Turistica of Bologna; the Assessorato Turismo della Provincia di Ferrara; Dott. Gabriele Annoni of the Assessorato Turismo della Provincia di Parma; Luigi Buzzani of the Amministrazione Provinciale of the Ufficio Turismo di Piacenza; Dott. Walter Verlicchi of the Servizio Turismo of the Provincia di Ravenna (with particular thanks to Elisabetta Antognoni), and Sig. Gian Francesco Donati of the Azienda di Informazioni Turistiche della Provincia di Rimini (and Isabella Amaduzzi).

How to use the Guide

The guide is divided into the eight regions of northern Italy. Within each region are **chapters** devoted to the main towns and their immediate environs, and to each province, or to an area known for its distinctive landscape (such as the lakes). The sections dedicated to the major towns are organised into a number of walking itineraries, with separate descriptions for the major monuments and museums.

An exhaustive section at the beginning of the book lists all the **practical information** a traveller is likely to need in preparation for a visit to northern Italy and while on the journey. This information, which includes public transport, is integrated with specific details at the beginning of each chapter and at the beginning of the description of each town. Information has been given both for those who visit the area by car and those who travel by public transport.

A small selection of **hotels** is given throughout the text, with official star ratings to give an indication of price. Hotels are almost always marked with clear signposts in towns and on roads. For further information, see under 'Accommodation' in the Practical Information section.

Restaurants have also been indicated throughout the book, and these have been divided into three categories which reflect price ranges in 1997: **'A'** indicates expensive luxury-class establishments; **'B'** is for first-class but slightly cheaper restaurants; and **'C'** for simple, but excellent value *trattorie* and *pizzerie*. For further information, see under 'Restaurants' in the Practical Information section.

The **most important monuments or works of art** in northern Italy have been highlighted in bold capital letters throughout the text, and **asterisks** are used to indicate places or works of art which are particularly beautiful or interesting. The **highlights** section on pages 13–14 singles out the major places of interest in the region which should not be missed.

All **churches** are taken as being orientated, with the entrance at the west end and the altar at the east end, the south aisle on the right and the north aisle on the left.

In the larger towns all the main monuments have been keyed (i.e. Pl. 2) in the text against the double page **town plans** which are gridded with numbered squares. On the ground plans of museums, figures or letters have been given to correspond with the description in the text.

The **local tourist boards** (in most regions called Azienda di Promozione Turistica, shortened to APT) are usually extremely helpful and it is only through them that it is possible to secure up-to-date information on the spot about opening times and accommodation. The eight Regional offices have been listed with their telephone numbers on page 18, and the local information offices are listed at the beginning of each chapter and in each town. On the town maps they are marked with **i**, the symbol which is used on local signposts throughout Italy.

Opening times of museums and monuments have been given throughout the text (i.e. 9–14: fest. 9–13), with the abbreviation 'fest.' indicating times for Sundays and holidays. However, opening times vary and often change without warning, so it is best to consult the local APT about up-to-date times on your arrival. For further information, see p 30. Almost all churches close at 12 and do not reopen again until 15 or 16 or even 17.

Although detailed town plans are provided, every traveller to northern Italy whether driving or using public transport, will also need large scale **maps** of the area: the best are those produced by the TCI (details on p 22).

Abbreviations used in the guide:

APT   Azienda di Promozione Turistica (official local tourist office)
C   century
CAI   Club Alpino Italiano
FAI   Fondo per l'Ambiente Italiano (founded in 1975 on the model of the British National Trust)
fest.   *festa*, or festival (i.e. holiday)
FS   Ferrovie dello Stato (Italian State Railways)
IAT   Information office of APT
Pl.   plan
TCI   Touring Club Italiano

Highlights

Lombardy. Milan is one of the most interesting cities in Italy, with a splendid Gothic cathedral, the Brera gallery containing a superb collection of paintings, Leonardo da Vinci's famous fresco of the Last Supper, the Scala theatre, renowned for opera, and numerous museums (including the delightful Poldi Pezzoli), and churches (notably Sant'Ambrogio, San Satiro, Sant'Eustorgio, and San Lorenzo Maggiore).

Near Milan is the Certosa di Pavia, important for its 15C works. The Italian lakes have been visited for centuries for their beautiful scenery: on Lago Maggiore the charming Isole Borromei have lovely gardens; on the Lago di Como, the most attractive towns are Como itself, Bellagio, and Varenna, and there are fine gardens on its shores. Perhaps the most beautiful lake of all is the Lago di Garda, with the spectacular Roman villa at Sirmione.

Mantua is a lovely old town, famous for its huge Palazzo Ducale with its frescoes by Mantegna, and for the handsome Palazzo Te. The upper town of Bergamo is particularly well preserved with some important art treasures, and Cremona is a pleasant city. Brescia has interesting Roman and Lombard remains. The small towns of Castiglione Olona, with its Renaissance works, and Sabbioneta, laid out in the 16C, are of the greatest interest. There are important prehistoric rock carvings in the Valle Camonica.

Piedmont. Turin, one of the largest towns in Italy, has a 17C–18C aspect and some very fine museums (including an important Egyptian collection), and grand Savoy residences on the outskirts. Novara is a pleasant 19C town. On the picturesque Lago d'Orta is the charming, well preserved village of Orta San Giulio. The Langhe and Roero districts, famous for their vineyards, have pretty landscapes.

Valle d'Aosta. Aosta has some important Roman remains, and throughout the valley are castles, many of which can be visited. The Gran Paradiso national park has fine mountain scenery.

Liguria. Genoa is a historic city with fine palaces and magnificent art collections. The peninsula of Portofino is particularly beautiful, and in the gulf of La Spezia is the picturesque village of Portovenere. The most unspoiled part of the coast is the Cinque Terre, with a series of delightful little remote villages in spectacular scenery.

Veneto. Apart from the world-famous city of Venice, the Veneto includes Verona, a particularly beautiful city with fine churches and piazze, and a celebrated Roman amphitheatre. The lively university town of Padua has interesting monuments including important frescoes by Giotto, and the town of Vicenza, laid out by the great 16C architect Palladio, is unusually well preserved. All over the Veneto are splendid country villas, some built in the early 16C by Palladio, others by 17C and 18C architects. Attractive small towns include Treviso and Bassano del Grappa. Montagnana and Cittadella have very well preserved walls. The area around the Delta of the Po has a remarkable landscape, and there is fine mountain scenery in the Dolomites.

Trentino-Alto Adige. Trento is the most interesting town in this region. The Val di Non and Val Gardena are well known mountain valleys.

Friuli-Venezia Giulia. The 18C city of Trieste is interesting, and Pordenone and Gorizia are agreeable towns. Udine possesses some fine frescoes by Giovanni Battista Tiepolo, and the well preserved little town of Cividale has beautiful Lombard works. Aquileia is an important Roman site, and it also has superb early Christian mosaics. The medieval village of Venzone, carefully reconstructed after earthquake damage, is one of the most remarkable sights in northern Italy.

Emilia Romagna. Bologna, an important large university town with a pleasant atmosphere, is well worth a visit: it has numerous interesting churches and museums. Ravenna has the most important Byzantine mosaics in western Europe, while in Rimini there are Roman monuments and the famous Renaissance Tempio Malatestiano. Parma has a splendid Baptistery and many masterpieces by Correggio. Faenza is famous for its ceramics. Ferrara, home of the Renaissance Este dukes, is a particularly pleasing and well preserved town.

Practical Information

Before Departure

When to Go
The best months for a visit to the greater part of northern Italy are September and October, and May and June, although there is always a risk of rain. The earlier spring months, though often dry and sunny, are sometimes unexpectedly chilly, with strong northerly winds. Everywhere in Italy is crowded with Italian school parties from March until early May. The height of the summer is unpleasantly hot, especially in the Po valley and the larger towns. Winter days in Milan or Venice are sometimes as cold and wet as an English winter. The upper Alpine valleys of Piedmont, Lombardy and the Dolomites are cool in summer, and the winter sports season in the Alpine resorts is extended even to midsummer in the high Alps. Seaside resorts are crowded from mid-June to early September; before and after this season many hotels are closed and the beaches are practically deserted.

Passports
These are necessary for all British and American travellers entering Italy. A stolen or lost passport can be replaced with little trouble by the British or US embassy in Rome.

Information
Italian Tourist Boards. General information can be obtained abroad from the Italian State Tourist Ofice (ENIT; Ente Nazionale Italiano per il Turismo), who distribute free an excellent *Traveller's Handbook* (revised about every year), and provide detailed information on Italy. In London their office is at 1 Princes Street, WIR 8AY (tel. 0171 408 1254); in New York at 499 Park Avenue (tel. 212 8436884); in Chicago at 401 North Michigan Avenue, Suite 3030 (tel. 312 6440996); in Los Angeles at 12400 Wilshire Blvd, Suite 550 (tel. 310 8201898). In Canada the ENIT office is in Montreal, at 1 Place Ville Marie, Suite 1914 (tel. 514 8867667).

Tour operators
Tour operators who sell tickets and book accommodation, and also organise inclusive tours to some parts of northern Italy, include: Prospect Music and Art Tours Ltd, 454/458 Chiswick High Road, London W4 5TT, tel. 0181 995 2151, fax 0181 742 1969; Martin Randall Travel, 10 Barley Mow Passage, Chiswick, London W4 4PH, tel. 0181 742 3355, fax 0181 742 1066; Page and Moy Ltd, 136–140 London Road, Leicester LE2 1EN, tel. 01533 542000, fax 01533 529123; Specialtours, 81a Elizabeth Street, London SW1W 9PG, tel. 0171 73-2297, fax 0171 823 5035; Abercrombie and Kent, Sloane Square House, Holbein Place, London SW1W 8NS, tel. 0171 730 9600, fax 0171 730 9376; Italian Escapades, 227 Shepherds Bush Road, London W6 7AS, tel. 0181 748 2661, fax 0181 748 6381; Italiatour, 205 Holland Park Avenue, London W11

4XB, tel. 0171 371 1114, fax 0171 602 6172; Citalia, Marco Polo House, 3–5 Lansdowne Road, Croydon CR9 1LL, tel. 0181 686 5533, fax 0181 686 0328; Magic of Italy, 227 Shepherds Bush Road, London W6 7AS, tel. 0181 748 7575, fax 0181 748 3731. Chapter Travel, 102 St John's Wood Terrace, NW8 6PL, tel. 0171 722 9560; Ilios Travel Ltd, 18 Market Square, Horsham, West Sussex RH12 1EU, tel. 01403 259788. Vacanze in Italia, Bignor, Pulborough, West Sussex RH20 1QD, tel. 01798 869485 specialise in self-catering accommodation in Italy.

Getting to Northern Italy

By air

Throughout the year there are direct air services between London and Milan, Turin, Genoa, Venice, and Bologna. These are operated by British Airways (tel 0181 897 4000) and Alitalia (tel. 0171 6027111). There are scheduled flights to Rimini in summer, as well as numerous charter flights. Charter flights (often much cheaper) are also now run to most of the main cities in Italy; the fare often includes hotel accommodation. Scheduled services offer special fares which are available according to season. Youth fares can be purchased. Car hire schemes in conjunction with flights can also be arranged.

By rail

The most direct route to Italy is now from London Waterloo by the frequent services through the Eurotunnel via Calais to Paris Nord (in c 4hrs). From Paris Lyon there are two fast trains a day via Chambery and Modane to Milan (in 6hrs 40min) and an overnight train with sleeping compartments (in 10hrs). There are also services (with sleeping compartments) from Paris Lyon via Domodossola to Venice (in c 12hrs), from Paris Lyon to Bologna, and from Paris Lyon via Modane to Turin. Information on the Italian State Railways (and tickets and seat reservations) may be obtained in London from Citalia, Marco Polo House, 3–5 Lansdowne Road, Croydon, Surrey, CR9 1LL (tel. 0181 686 5533) and Wasteels Travel, adjacent to Platform 2, Victoria Station, London SWIV 1JT, who also issue Italian Rail passes.

By bus

A bus service, taking two days, operates between London (Victoria Coach Station) and Rome via Dover, Calais, Paris, Turin, Milan, Bologna, and Florence, daily from June to September, and once or twice a week for the rest of the year. Youth fares are available. Information in London from the National Express office at Victoria Coach Station (tel. 0171 730 0202), from local National Express Agents, and in Italy from SITA offices.

By car

British drivers taking their own cars by any of the routes across France, Belgium, Luxembourg, Switzerland, Germany and Austria need the vehicle registration book, a valid national driving licence (accompanied by a translation, issued free of charge by Wasteels and the Italian State Tourist Office), insurance cover, and a nationality plate attached to the car. If you are not the owner of the vehicle, you must have the owner's written permission for its use abroad.

A Swiss Motorway Pass is needed for Switzerland, and can be obtained from the RAC, the AA or at the Swiss border.

The continental rule of the road is to drive on the right and overtake on the left. The provisions of the respective highway codes in the countries of transit, though similar, have important variations, especially with regard to priority, speed limits, and pedestrian crossings. Membership of the Automobile Association (tel. 01256 20123), or the Royal Automobile Club (membership enquiries and insurance, tel. 01345 3331133; route information, tel. 01345 333222) entitles you to many of the facilities of affiliated societies on the Continent. They are represented at most of the sea and air ports.

Motorway routes to Italy from Europe. The main routes from France, Switzerland, and Austria are summarised below.

A. The direct motorway route from France, bypassing Geneva, enters Italy through the **Mont Blanc Tunnel** (see Chapter 26). The road from Courmayeur to Aosta has not yet been improved. At Aosta the A5 motorway begins; it follows the Valle d'Aosta. Just beyond Ivrea is the junction with the A4/5 motorway; the A5 continues south to Turin, while the A4/5 diverges east. At Santhia the A4 motorway from Turin is joined for Milan via Novara, or the A26/4 can be followed south via Alessandria, reaching the coast at Voltri, just outside Genoa.
B. The most direct approach to Turin from France is through the **Mont Cenis Tunnel** (see Chapter 19) from Modane in France to Bardonecchia, where a motorway (A32) continues via Susa to Turin. From Turin a motorway (A6) descends direct to the coast at Savona, or the motorway (A21, A26) via Asti and Alessandria leads to Genoa. The A4 motorway leads east from Turin to Milan for destinations in the Veneto and Emilia Romagna.
C. The **coastal route from the South of France** follows the A10 motorway through the foothills with frequent long tunnels to enter Italy just before Ventimiglia (see Chapter 31). The motorway continues past Alassio, Albenga, and Savona (where the motorway from Turin comes in), to Voltri (where the A26 motorway from Alessandria comes in) to Genoa (with the junction of the A7 motorway from Milan). The coastal motorway continues through Liguria via Rapallo and La Spezia.
D. The approach to Italy from Switzerland (Lausanne) is usually through the **St Bernard Tunnel** (see Chapter 26)—or by the pass in summer—which only becomes motorway at Aosta (see A. above).
E. Another motorway route from Switzerland is via the St Gotthard Tunnel and Lugano. The motorway (A9) enters Italy at Como (see Chapter 6) and continues to Milan where the 'Autostrada del Sole' (A1) continues south through Lombardy and Emilia Romagna, and other motorways lead to Genoa, or east via Brescia and Verona to Venice.
F. From Germany and Austria (Innsbruck) the direct approach to northern Italy is by the motorway over the **Brenner Pass** (see Chapter 57). The motorway (A22) continues down the Isarco valley to Bolzano and the Adige valley via Trento to Verona. Here motorways diverge west for Brescia and Milan, or east for Vicenza and Venice, or continue south via Mantua to join the A1 motorway just west of Modena for Emilia Romagna.

Car Sleeper Train services operate from Boulogne and Paris, Hamburg. Vienna, and Munich to Milan and Bologna.

Arriving in Northern Italy

There are Regional State Tourist offices in the eight regions of northern Italy: **Lombardy**: Assessorato Regionale al Turismo, 22 Via Fabio Filzi, Milano (tel. 02 67651). **Piedmont:** Assessorato al Turismo, 12 Via Magenta, Torino (tel. 011 43211). **Valle d'Aosta:** Assessorato Regionale del Turismo, 3 Piazza Narbonne, Aosta (tel. 0165 303725). **Liguria:** Assessorato Turismo, 15 Via Fieschi, Genova (tel. 010 54851). **Veneto:** Assessorato Regionale al Turismo, Palazzo Balbi, Dorsoduro 3901,Venezia (tel. 041 792818). **Friuli-Venezia Giulia:** Azienda Regionale per la Promozione Turistica, 6 Via Rossini, Trieste (tel. 040 365152). **Trentino-Alto Adige:** Provincia Autonoma di Trento, Servizio Turismo, 132 Corso 3 Novembre, Trento (tel. 0461 896518) and Alto Adige Promozione Turismo, 11 Piazza Parrocchia, Bolzano (tel. 0471 993808). **Emilia Romagna:** Assessorato al Turismo, 30 Viale Aldo Moro, Bologna (tel. 051 283760).

Each region is divided into sectors (usually following the provincial boundaries), each with a local tourist information office, usually called the Azienda di Promozione Turistica (APT), which provides invaluable help to travellers on arrival; they supply a free list of accommodation (revised annually), including hotels, youth hostels, and camping sites; up-to-date information on museum opening times and annual events; and information about local transport. They also usually distribute, free of charge, illustrated pamphlets about each town and province, sometimes with a good plan, etc. The headquarters are normally open Mon–Sat 8–14, but in the towns of particular interest there is sometimes a separate information office (IAT), which is often also open in the afternoon. All the local information offices have been listed, with their addresses and telephone numbers, in the text.

Travelling around Northern Italy

By rail
The Italian State Railways (FS—Ferrovie dello Stato) run various categories of trains. (1) *EC (Eurocity)*, international express trains (with a special supplement, approximately 30 per cent of the normal single fare) running between the main Italian and European cities; seat reservation is sometimes obligatory. (2) *IC (Intercity)*, express trains running between the main Italian towns, with a special supplement; on some of these seat reservation is obligatory, and some carry first class only. (3) *P (Pendolino; ETR 450)*, an extra fast service (first and second class) which costs considerably more; advance booking is obligatory. *(4) Espressi*, long-distance trains (both classes), not as fast as the *IC* trains. (5) *IR (Interregionali)*, although not stopping at every station, a good deal slower than the *espressi*. All other trains are called *Regionali* or *Diretti*, local trains stopping at all stations, mostly with second-class carriages only.

Buying tickets. Tickets (valid for two months after the day sold) must be bought before the journey, otherwise a fairly large supplement has to be paid to the ticket-collector on the train. The most convenient way of buying rail tickets (and making seat reservations) is from a travel agent who are agents for the Italian State Railways, as there are often long queues at the station ticket offices. Some trains carry first class only; some charge a special supplement; and on some seats must be booked in advance: when buying tickets you therefore have to specify which train you intend to take as well as the destination. Trains in Italy are usually crowded, especially on holidays and in summer, and it is now always advisable to book your seat when buying a ticket. There is a booking fee of Lire 5000 and the service is available from 2 months to 3 hours before departure.

In the main stations the better known credit cards are now generally accepted (but there is a special ticket window which must be used when buying a ticket with a credit card). There are limitations on travelling short distances on some 1st-class *Intercity* trains. Tickets can be purchased up to two months before departure. Tickets for journeys under 70km can now be bought in main cities at newsagents and tobacconists. **In order to validate your ticket it has to be stamped at an automatic machine in the railway station before starting the journey (there is always a machine at the beginning of each platform and sometimes half way up the platform).** If, for some reason, you fail to do this, try to find the ticket conductor on the train before he finds you. Once the ticket has been stamped it is valid for 6 hours for distances up to 200km, and for 24 hours for distances over 200km.

Fares and reductions. In Italy fares are still much lower than in Britain. Children under the age of 4 travel free, and between the ages of 4 and 12 travel half price, and there are certain reductions for families. For travellers over the age of 60 (with Senior Citizen Railcards), the *Carta Res* (valid one year) offers a 30 per cent reduction on international rail fares. The Inter-rail card (valid 1 month) which can be purchased in Britain by young people up to the age of 26, is valid in Italy (and allows a reduction of 40per cent on normal fares). In Italy the *Carta d'Argento* and the *Carta Verde* (which both cost Lire 40,000 and are valid one year) allow a reduction on rail fares for those over 60, and between the ags of 12 and 26. A *tessera di autorizzazione* can be purchased, allowing a reduction of 20per cent on any number of tickets within one month. A *Chilometrico* ticket is valid for two months for 3000km (and can be used by up to five people at the same time) for a maximum of 20 journeys. A *Eurodomino* ticket is valid for one month's travel in a number of European countries (for 3, 5, or 10 days). You can claim reimbursement (on payment of a small penalty) for unused tickets and sleepers not later than 24 hours before the departure of the train. Bicycles are allowed on most trains (a day ticket costs Lire 5000).

A *Carta Blu* is available for the disabled, and certain trains have special facilities for them (information from the main railway stations in Italy).

Timetables. The timetable of the train services changes on about 26 September and 31 May every year. Excellent timetables are published twice a year by the Italian State Railways (*In Treno*; one volume for the whole of Italy) and by Pozzorario in several volumes (*Nord e Centro Italia* covers northern Italy). These can be purchased at news-stands and railway stations.

Left luggage offices are usually open 24 hrs at the main stations; at smaller stations they often close at night, or for a few hours in the middle of the day.

Porters are entitled to a fixed amount (shown on notice boards at all stations) for each piece of baggage, but trollies are now usually available in the larger stations.

Restaurant cars (sometimes self-service) are attached to most international and internal long-distance trains. Also, on most express trains, snacks, hot coffee and drinks are sold throughout the journey from a trolley wheeled down the train. At every large station snacks are on sale from trolleys on the platform and you can buy them from the train window.

Sleeping cars, with couchettes, or first- and second-class cabins, are also carried on certain trains, as well as 'Sleeperette' compartments with reclining seats (first class only).

By bus

Local country buses abound between the main towns in Italy, and offer an excellent alternative to the railways. It is difficult to obtain accurate information about these local bus services outside Italy. Details can be obtained from Citalia, London, or at the local tourist offices (APT) in Italy (some information is given in the text relating to the main towns, and at the beginning of chapters).

Town buses. Now that most towns have been partially closed to private traffic, town bus services are usually fast and efficient. You buy a ticket before boarding (at tobacconists, bars, newspaper kiosks, information offices, etc.) and stamp it on board at automatic machines. In the larger cities, the main bus routes have been indicated in the text. Twenty-four hour tickets are usually available in the larger cities.

By car

Temporary membership of the Automobile Club d'Italia (ACI) can be taken out on the frontier or in Italy. The headquarters of the ACI is at 8 Via Marsala, Rome (branch offices in all the main towns). They provide a breakdown service (Soccorso ACI, tel. 116).

Rules of the road. Italian law requires that you carry a valid driving licence when driving. It is obligatory to keep a red triangle in the car in case of accident or breakdown. This serves as a warning to other traffic when placed on the road at a distance of 50 metres from the stationary car. It can be hired from the ACI for a minimal charge, and returned at the frontier. It is compulsory to wear seat-belts in the front seat of cars . Driving in Italy is generally faster (and often more aggressive) than driving in Britain or America. Road signs are now more or less standardised to the international codes, but certain habits differ radically from those in Britain or America. If the driver of a car coming towards you flashes his headlights, it means he is proceeding and not giving you precedence. In towns, Italian drivers are very lax about changing lanes without much warning. Unless otherwise indicated, cars entering a road from the right are given precedence. Italian drivers tend to ignore pedestrian crossings. In towns beware of motor-bikes, mopeds, and Vespas, the drivers of which seem to consider that they always have the right of way.

Motorways (*autostrade*). Italy probably has the finest motorways in Europe, although in the last 20 years or so too many have been constructed to the detriment of the countryside. Tolls are charged according to the rating of the vehicle and the distance covered. There are service areas on nearly all autostrade (open 24 hours), and, generally speaking, the FINI cafés and restaurants are usually the best. Most autostrade have SOS points every two kilometres. Unlike in France, motorways are indicated by green signs (and normal roads by blue signs). At the entrance to motorways, the two directions are indicated by the name of the most important town (and not by the nearest town) which can be momentarily confusing. There are APT information offices on the motorway approaches to the most important big towns in Italy.

Superstrade are dual carriageway fast roads which do not charge tolls. They do not usually have service stations, SOS points or emergency lanes. They are also usually indicated by green signs.

Petrol stations are open 24 hours on motorways, but otherwise their opening times are: 7–12, 15–20; winter 7.30–12.30, 14.30–19. There are now quite a number of self-service petrol stations open 24hours operated by bank notes (Lire 10,000), usually near the larger towns. Unleaded petrol is available at all petrol stations. Petrol in Italy costs more than in Britain, and a lot more than in America.

Car parking. Almost every town in Italy has taken the wise step of closing its historic centre to traffic except for residents (although access is allowed to hotels, and for the disabled). This makes them much more pleasant to visit on foot. It is always advisable to leave your car well outside the centre (places to park are usually indicated, and have been given in the text below). Some car parks are free, while others charge an hourly tariff. In some towns mini-bus services connect car parks with the centre. With a bit of effort it is almost always possible to find a place to leave your car free of charge, away from the town centre. In the centre of towns car parking is usually extremely difficult (if allowed at all). It is forbidden to park in front of a gate or doorway marked with a '*passo carrabile*' (blue and red) sign. Always lock your car when parked, and never leave anything of value inside it. When leaving a car parked on a street, it should be borne in mind that once a week street cleaning takes place at night and so cars have to be removed (or they may be towed away and a fine charged); ask locally for information.

Car hire is available in most Italian cities. Arrangements for the hire of cars in Italy can be made through Alitalia or British Airways (at especially advantageous rates in conjunction with their flights) or through any of the principal car-hire firms (the best known include Maggiore, Avis and Hertz).

Roads in northern Italy. As in the rest of Italy the north has an excellent network of roads, and you are strongly advised to avoid motorways and *super-strade* and use the secondary roads, which are usually well engineered and provide fine views of the countryside. Buildings of historic interest are often indicated off these roads by yellow signposts (although there are long-term plans to change the colour to brown). White road signs sometimes indicate entry into a municipal area which is (confusingly) often a long way from the town of the same name. Main roads (*strade statale*) are designated in the text by their official number. *Autostrade* (motorways) always carry 'A' before their number.

Maps. Although detailed town plans have been included in this book, it has not been possible, because of the format, to provide an atlas of northern Italy adequate for those travelling by car. The maps at the end of the book are only intended to be used when planning an itinerary. The Italian Touring Club publishes several sets of excellent maps: these are constantly updated and are indispensable to anyone travelling by car in Italy. They include the *Grande Carta stradale d'Italia* on a scale of 1:200,000. This is divided into 15 sheets covering the regions of Italy, of which six (*Piemonte, Valle d'Aosta; Lombardia; Trentino-Alto Adige; Veneto, Friuli-Venezia Giulia; Liguria; Emilia-Romagna*) refer to the area dealt with in this guide. These are also published in a handier form as an atlas (with an index), called the *Atlante stradale d'Italia* in three volumes (*Nord* covers the area in this book). Special maps at 1:50,000 are also available for certain Alpine areas and national parks. All these maps can be purchased from the Italian Touring Club Offices and at many booksellers; in London they are obtainable from Stanford's, 12–14 Long Acre, London WC2E 9LP.

The *Istituto Geografico Militare* of Italy has for long been famous for its map production (much of it done by aerial photography). Its maps are now available in numerous bookshops in the main towns of Italy. It publishes a map of Italy on a scale of 1:100,000 in 277 sheets, and a field survey partly 1:50,000, partly 1:25,000, which are invaluable for the detailed exploration of the country, especially the more mountainous regions; the coverage is, however, still far from complete at the larger scales, and some of the maps are out of date.

By air
The larger towns have airports with internal services: the airports have been indicated in the text.

By bicycle
In the main cities, the municipality now sometimes provide bicycles (available at bicycle stands in several parts of the city) for the temporary use of residents and visitors (availabilty is indicated below in the text). Areas particularly good for cycling in the north include the flat area around the Po delta (see Chapter 36). More and more tour operators are now offering cycling holidays in Italy. Bicycles can be carried on most trains in Italy. Cycle lanes now exist in the big cities, and in some towns in Emilia Romagna, such as Ravenna and Ferrara, the bicycle is the favourite means of transport. A number of cross-country cyling routes are being introduced (information from the local APT offices).

Taxis

Taxis (yellow or white in colour) are provided with taximeters; it is advisable to make sure these are operational before hiring a taxi. Taxis are hired from ranks or by telephone; there are no cruising taxis. When you telephone for a taxi you are given the approximate arrival time and the number of the taxi. A small tip of about a thousand lire can be given to the driver, but is often not expected. A supplement for night service, and for luggage is charged. There is a heavy surplus charge when the destination is outside the town limits (ask roughly how much the fare is likely to be).

Accommodation

Hotels

Hotels in Italy are classified by 'stars' as in the rest of Europe. Since 1985 the official category of *pensione* has been abolished. There are now five official categories of hotels from the luxury 5-star hotels to the cheapest and simplest 1-star hotels.

A small selection of hotels appears in the text for each major town or area. They have been given with their official star rating in order to give an indication of price. In making the selection for inclusion, smaller hotels have been favoured, and those in the centre of towns, or in particularly beautiful positions in the countryside.

Each local tourist board (APT, see above) issues a free list of hotels giving category, price, and facilities. Local tourist offices will try to help you find accommodation on the spot, but it is essential to book well in advance at Easter and in autumn and summer. In the larger cities,when trade fairs are being held it is virtually impossible to find accommodation. To confirm the booking a deposit should be sent (you have the right to claim this back if you cancel the booking at least 72 hours in advance). Hotels equipped to offer hospitality to the disabled are indicated in the APT hotel lists. There are now numerous agencies and hotel representatives in Britain and America who specialise in making hotel reservations (normally for 5-star and 4-star hotels only).

Up-to-date information about hotels and restaurants can be found in numerous specialised guides to Italy. These include the red guide to Italy published by Michelin (*Italia*, revised annually). In Italian, the Touring Club Italiano publish useful information about hotels in *Alberghi e Ristoranti in Italia* (published every year), and in the *Guida Rapida d'Italia* (two volumes cover the area in this book).

Gambero Rosso publish a selection of 3-star hotels (*Alberghi d'Italia*), and another sound publication is the *Charming Small Hotel guide: Italy* (Duncan Petersen). A complete list of hotels in Italy is published by Dossier (*Italy: Hotels*).

In many localities the 3-star and 4-star hotels are not on a par with hotels of the same category in other European countries. The star system in Italy now tends to reflect only the services offered, such as telephone in the room, television, mini-bar, public rooms, etc, and does not necessarily reflect quality. Charges vary according to season and can be considerably lower in winter in resort towns on the coast and on the lakes. 3-star hotels in the big cities such as Milan are bound to be a lot more expensive than hotels of the same category in small towns.

   In all hotels the service charges are included in the rates. The total charge is exhibited on the back of the door of the hotel room. Breakfast (usually disappointing and costly) is by law an optional extra charge, although a lot of hotels try to include it in the price of the room. When booking a room, always specify if you want breakfast or not. If you are staying in a hotel in a town, it is usually well worthwhile going round the corner to the nearest bar for breakfast. Hotels are now obliged by law (for tax purposes) to issue an official receipt to customers: you should not leave the premises without this document.

   A new type of hotel has been introduced into Italy, called a *residence*. They are normally in a building, or group of houses of historic interest, often a castle or monastery. They may have only a few rooms, and sometimes offer self-catering accommodation. They are listed separately in the APT hotel lists, with their prices.

Agriturism and self-catering

Recently developed throughout Italy, this provides accommodation in farmhouses in the countryside. Terms very greatly from bed-and-breakfast, to self-contained flats. These are highly recommended for travellers with their own transport, and for families, as an excellent (and usually cheap) way of visiting the Italian countryside. Some farms require a stay of a minimum number of days. Cultural or recreational activities, such as horse riding, are sometimes also provided. Information about such holidays is supplied by the local APT offices. The main organisations in Italy concerned with Agriturism are: Agriturist (27 Via Isonzo, Milano, tel. 02 58302122); Terranostra (8 Via Marocco, Milano, tel. 02 2613083); and Turismo Verde (19 Via Cornalia, Milano, tel. 02 5591316). Terranostra publish an annual list of Agriturism accommodation under the title *Vacanze Natura.*

Renting accommodation for short periods in Italy has recently become easier and better organised. Villas, farmhouses, etc. can be rented for holidays through specialised agencies (information from ENIT, London, and APT offices in Italy).

Camping

This is now well organised throughout Italy. An international camping carnet is useful. Camping sites are listed in the local APT hotel lists, giving details of all services provided, size of the site, etc. In some sites caravans are allowed. The sites are divided into official categories by stars, from the most expensive 4-star sites, to the simplest and cheapest 1-star sites. Their classification and rates charged must be displayed at the camp site office. Some sites have been indicated in the text, with their star ratings. Full details of the sites in Italy are published annually by the Touring Club Italiano and Federcampeggio in *Campeggi e Villaggi Turistici in Italia*. The Federazione Italiana del Campeggio has an information office and booking service at 11 Via Vittorio Emanuele, Calenzano, 50041 Florence (tel. 055 882391).

Youth Hostels

The Italian Youth Hostels Association (Associazione Italiana Alberghi per la Gioventù, 44 Via Cavour, 00184 Rome (tel. 06 4741256) has 54 hostels situated all over the country. A membership card of the AIG or the International

Youth Hostel Federation is required for access to Italian Youth Hostels. Details from the Youth Hostels Association, Trevelyan House, 8 St Stephen's Hill, St Albans, Herts AL1 2DY, and the American Youth Hostel Inc, National Offices, PO Box 37613, Washington DC 20013-7613.

Students' Hostels exist in many Italian university towns and are available not only to students taking courses, but also to students visiting the country for holiday purposes. Application should be made to the *Casa dello Studente* in Bologna, Ferrara, Genoa, Modena, Milan, Parma, Pavia, Padua (Casa Fusinato, Via Marzolo), and Venice (Foresteria dell'Istituto di Ca' Foscari). Meals may be taken at the University Canteens. The *Guide for Foreign Students* , giving detailed information on students' hostels, students' facilities, etc., can be obtained from the Italian Ministry of Education, Viale Trastevere, Rome. There are also some hostels run by religious organisations (information from the APT).

Eating and Drinking

Restaurants

In Italy restaurants are called *ristoranti* or *trattorie*; there is nowadays no difference between the two. Italian food is usually good and not too expensive. The least pretentious restaurant almost invariably provides the best value. Almost every locality has a simple (often family-run) restaurant which caters for the local residents. The décor is generally very simple and the food excellent value. This type of restaurant does not always offer a menu and the choice is usually limited to three or four first courses, and three or four second courses, with only fruit as a sweet. The more sophisticated restaurants are more attractive and comfortable and often larger and you can sometimes eat at tables in the open air. They display a menu outside, and tend to be considerably more expensive.

Throughout the text a small selection (by no means exhaustive) of restaurants open in northern Italy in 1997 has been given. The restaurants have been divided into three categories to reflect price ranges in 1996: **A:** luxury-class restaurants,where the prices are likely to be over Lire 60,000 a head (and sometimes well over Lire 100,000). These include some of the most famous restaurants in northern Italy and they usually offer international cuisine. **B:** first-class restaurants where the prices range from Lire 40,000 upwards. These are generally comfortable, with good service, but are not cheap. The third category, **C:** comprises trattorie and pizzerie where you can eat for around Lire 25,000–35,000 a head, or even less. Although simple and by no means 'smart', the food in this category, which often includes local specialities, is usually the best value.

Specialised guides to the restaurants (in the A and B categories as described above) in Italy (revised annually) include the red guide published by Michelin (*Italia*), *I Ristoranti di Veronelli*, and *Alberghi e Ristoranti* (Touring Club Italiano). An excellent (annual) guide to cheaper eating is published in Italian by Slow Food: *Osterie d'Italia*. Gambero Rosso also produces sound advice on where to eat in *Ristoranti d'Italia* (published annually).

All prices on the menu include service, unless otherwise stated. Tipping is therefore not necessary, but a few thousand lire left on the table convey appreciation. A cover charge (*coperto*—shown separately on the menu) is still sometimes added to the bill, although it has been officially abolished.

It is acceptable to order a first course only, or skip the first course and have only a second course. Restaurants are now obliged by law (for tax purposes) to issue an official receipt to customers: you should not leave the premises without this document (*ricevuta fiscale*). Note that fish is always the most expensive item on the menu in any restaurant.

Snacks. Pizze (a popular and cheap food throughout Italy) and other excellent snacks are served in a *Pizzeria*, *Rosticceria* and *Tavola Calda*. Some of these have no seating accommodation and sell food to take away or eat on the spot. A *Vinaio* or *Osteria* (mostly now found only in the Veneto) sells wine by the glass and good simple food for very reasonable prices. For **picnics** sandwiches (*panini*) are made up on request (with ham, salami, cheese, anchovies, tuna fish, etc.) at *Pizzicherie* and *Alimentari* (grocery shops) and *Fornai* (bakeries) often sell delicious individual pizzas, bread with oil and salt (*focaccia* or *schiacciata*), cakes, etc. Some of the pleasantest places to picnic in towns or their environs have been indicated in the text below.

Bars (cafés) are open all day. Most customers eat the numerous excellent refreshments they serve standing up. You pay the cashier first, and show the receipt to the barman in order to get served. If you sit at a table the charge is considerably higher (at least double) and you will be given waiter service (and should not pay first). However, some simple bars have a few tables which can be used with no extra charge (it is always best to ask before sitting down). Black coffee (*caffè* or *espresso*) can be ordered diluted (*alto* or *lungo* or *americano*), or with hot milk (*cappuccino*), or with a liqueur (*corretto*). In summer, cold coffee (*caffè freddo*), or cold coffee and milk (*caffè-latte freddo*) are served. Ice creams are always best in a *gelateria* where they are made on the spot: bars usually sell packaged ice cream only.

Italian Food

Characteristic dishes of Italian cuisine, to be found all over the country, are included in the **menu** given below. Many of the best dishes are regional specialities; these are given in a separate section at the end.

Antipasti, Hors d'oeuvre

Prosciutto crudo o cotto, Ham, raw or cooked

Prosciutto e melone, Ham (raw) and melon

Salame, Salami

Salame con funghi e carciofini sott'olio, Salami with mushrooms and artichokes in oil

Salsicce, Dry sausage

Tonno, Tuna fish

Fagioli e cipolle, Beans with onions

Carciofi o finocchio in pinzimonio, Raw artichokes or fennel with a dressing

Antipasto misto, Mixed cold hors d'oeuvre

Antipasto di mare, Seafood hors d'oeuvre

Bresaola, Cured beef

Crostini, Fresh liver paste served on bread (sometimes together with other 'homemade' pâté)

Frittata, Omelette

Minestre e Pasta (Primi Piatti), Soups and pasta (First courses)

Minestre, zuppa, Thick soup

Brodo, Clear soup

Minestrone alla toscana, Tuscan vegetable soup

Spaghetti al sugo or *al ragù*, Spaghetti with a meat sauce

Spaghetti al pomodoro, Spaghetti with a tomato sauce

Tagliatelle, flat spaghetti-like pasta, almost always made with egg

Lasagne, Layers of pasta with meat filling and cheese and tomato sauce

Cannelloni, Rolled pasta 'pancakes' with meat filling and cheese and tomato sauce

Ravioli, Pasta filled with spinach and ricotta cheese, or with minced veal

Tortellini, Small coils of pasta, filled with a rich stuffing served either in broth or with a sauce, or with cream

Agnolotti, Ravioli filled with meat

Fettuccine, Fresh ribbon noodles, often served with a meat sauce or porcini mushrooms

Spaghetti alla carbonara, Spaghetti with bacon, beaten egg, and black pepper sauce

Spaghetti alle vongole, Spaghetti with clams

Pappardelle alla lepre, Pasta with hare sauce

Gnocchi, A heavy pasta, made from potato, flour, and eggs

Risotto, Rice dish

Risotto alla Milanese, Rice with saffron and white wine

Stracciatella, Broth with beaten egg

Taglierini in brodo, Thin pasta in broth

Ribollita, Thick soup made with bread, white beans, cabbage, etc.

Pasta e fagioli, Pasta and beans

Penne all'arrabbiata (or '*Strascicata*'), Short pasta with a rich spicy tomato sauce

Penne all'Amatriciana, Short pasta served with a sauce of salt pork and tomato

Cappelletti, Form of ravioli, often served in broth

Polenta, yellow maize flour, usually served with a meat or tomato sauce

Pappa di pomodoro, a thick tomato 'soup', with bread, seasoned with basil, etc.

Pesce, Fish (always more expensive than meat)

Zuppa di pesce, A variety of fish cooked in a light tomato sauce (or soup)

Fritto misto di mare, A variety of fried fish and crustacea

Fritto di pesce, Fried fish

Pesce arrosto, *Pesce alla griglia*, Roast, grilled fish

Pescespada, Swordfish

Aragosta, Lobster (an expensive delicacy)

Calamari, Squid

Sarde, Sardines

Coda di Rospo, Angler fish (monkfish)

Dentice, Dentex

Orata, Bream

Triglie, Red mullet

Sgombro, Mackerel

Baccalà (alla Livornese), Salt cod (fried and cooked in a tomato sauce)

Anguilla, Eel

Sogliola, Sole

Tonno, Tuna fish

Trota, Trout

Cozze, Mussels

Gamberi, Prawns

Polpi or *Polipi*, Octopus

Seppie, Cuttlefish

Acciughe, Anchovies

Secondi Piatti, Main courses

Bistecca alla fiorentina, T-bone steak (usually cooked over charcoal)

Vitello, Veal

Manzo, Beef

Agnello, Lamb

Maiale (arrosto), Pork (roast)

Pollo (bollito), Chicken (boiled)

Cotolette Milanese, Veal cutlets, fried in breadcrumbs

Cotoletta alla Bolognese, Veal cutlet with ham, covered with melted cheese

Saltimbocca, Rolled veal with ham and sage

Bocconcini, As above, with cheese

Ossobuco, Stewed shin of veal

Spezzatino, Veal stew, usually with red pepper, tomatoes, onions, peas, and wine

Petto di pollo, Chicken breasts

Pollo alla cacciatore, Chicken with herbs and (usually) tomato and pimento sauce

Cotechino e Zampone, Pig's trotter stuffed with pork and sausages

Stracotto, Beef cooked in a sauce, or in red wine

Trippa, Tripe

Fegato, Calf's liver

Tacchino arrosto, Roast turkey

Cervello, Brains (usually served fried)

Bollito, Stew of various boiled meats

Fagiano, Pheasant

Coniglio, Rabbit

Lepre, Hare

Cinghiale, Wild boar

Scaloppine al marsala, Veal escalope cooked in wine

Coda alla vaccinara, Oxtail cooked with herbs and wine

Stufato, Stewed meat served in pieces in a sauce

Polpette, Meat balls (often served in a sauce)

Involtini, Thin rolled slices of meat in a sauce

Fegatini, Chicken livers cooked with sage

Fegatelli , Pork livers

Rosticciana, Grilled spare ribs

Arista, Pork chop

Rognoncini trifolati, Sliced kidneys in a sauce

Animelle, Sweetbreads

Piccione, Pigeon

Porcini, Large wild mushrooms (best grilled), only served in season (Oct–Dec and around Easter)

Contorni, Vegetables

Insalata verde, Green salad

Insalata mista, Mixed salad

Pomodori,Tomatoes

Funghi, Mushrooms

Asparagi, Asparagus

Zucchine, Courgettes

Melanzane alla parmigiana, Aubergines in a cheese sauce

Radicchio rosso, Red chicory (in the Veneto, often served grilled)

Fagioli, Haricot (dried) beans

Peperonata, Stewed red peppers, often with aubergine, onion, tomato, potato, etc.

Spinaci, Spinach

Broccoletti, Tender broccoli

Piselli, Peas

Piselli al prosciutto, Peas cooked with bacon and parsley

Fagiolini, French beans

Carciofi, Artichokes

Peperoni, Red peppers

Finocchi, Fennel

Patatine fritte, Fried potatoes

Dolci, Sweets

Torta, Tart
Monte Bianco, Chestnut flavoured
  pudding
Zuppa inglese, Trifle
Panettone, Milanese sweet cake

Gelato, Ice cream
Sant Honorè, Rich meringue cake
Crostata, Fruit flan
Zabaione, A hot sweet with beaten
  eggs and Marsala wine

Frutta, Fruit

Fragole con panna, Strawberries and
  cream
Fragole al limone, Strawberries with
  lemon
Fragole al vino, Strawberries with wine
Fragoline di bosco, Wild strawberries
Melone, Melon
Cocomero, Popone or *Anguria*, Water
  melon

Mele, Apples
Pere, Pears
Arance, Oranges
Ciliegie, Cherries
Pesche, Peaches
Albicocche, Apricots
Uva, Grapes
Macedonia di frutta, Fruit salad
Fichi, Figs

Regional Dishes include:
Piedmont—*Fonduta*, a hot dip with Fontina cheese, milk, and egg yolks sprinkled with truffles and white pepper
Bagna cauda, a hot spicy sauce with garlic and anchovies used as a dip for raw vegetables
Bolliti misti (*con salsa verde*), various types of meat stewed together (with a green sauce made with herbs)
Lombardy—*Risotto alla Milanese*, Rice cooked in broth with saffron
Zuppa Pavese, Clear soup with poached eggs
Stracotto or *brasato di carne*, meat baked in a sauce, often served with polenta.
Meneghina is a typical cake, sometimes served warm with Grand Marnier.
Veneto—*Fegato alla Veneziana*, Calf's liver, thinly sliced, fried with onions
Baccalà alla vicentina, Salt cod simmered in milk
Polenta, a maize flour cake served with a sauce as a pasta dish, or with sausages, game, fish etc.
Liguria—*Pesto*, a sauce made from fresh basil, garlic, pine nuts and cheese and served with pasta

Excellent **cheeses** to be found in northern Italy include Parmigiano-Reggiano, Gorgonzola, Bitto (in the Valtellina), Fontina (in the Valle d'Aosta), and Taleggio. The cured **hams** of San Daniele in Friuli and of Parma are famous.

Northern Italian Wines

Wines are very regional, and you will usually find the local carafe wine the best value for money. The hilly district of Le Langhe in Piedmont is famous for its excellent wines including *Barolo, Barbera, Barbaresco, Dolcetto, Nebbiolo, Roero, Roero Arneis, Pelaverga* and *Moscato*. A good sparkling red wine is *Bonarda dell'Oltrepò Pavese*. Verona is the centre of the wines of the Veneto, somewhat lighter, among the best of which are *Soave*, *Bardolino*, and *Valpolicella*. *Prosecco*, a sparkling white wine, is served all over the Veneto as an aperitif. The excellent wines of the Friuli region include *Pinot*, *Merlot*, *Tocai*, and *Cabernet*. The white wines of the Alto Adige are less well known but are well worth seeking out (particularly good are those from *Tramin*, *Lake Caldaro*, and *Novacella*). In Emilia, the sparkling red *Lambrusco* and *Sangiovese* are to be recommended and the white *Albana*, as well as the unusual *Fontanina* and *Malvasia di Maiatico*.

More and more farms which produce wine are opening their cellars to the public, and allowing wine tasting. Information from local APT offices.

Musems and Churches

Opening Times of Museums, Sites and Churches

The opening times of **museums and monuments** have been given in the text below, but it is always advisable to consult the local tourist office (APT) on arrival about up-to-date times. The opening times of state-owned museums and monuments are in the process of change: they are usually open 9–14, but in some cases they are now also open in the afternoon. On Monday, for long the standard closing day, many museums are now staying open (so that they remain open seven days a week). However, there is not, as yet, a standard timetable, and great care should be taken to allow enough time for variations in the hours shown in the text when planning a visit to a museum or monument. Some museums etc. are closed on the main public holidays: 1 January, Easter, 1 May, 15 August, and Christmas Day (but there is now a policy to keep at least some of them open on these days in the larger cities; information has to be obtained about these on the spot).

Admission charges vary, but are usually between Lire 4000 and Lire 13,000. British citizens under the age of 18 and over the age of 60 are entitled to free admission to state-owned museums and monuments in Italy (because of reciprocal arrangements in Britain). The 'Settimana per i Beni Culturali e Ambienti' is usually held during the year, when for a week there is free entrance to all state-owned museums and others are specially opened, etc.

Churches, although they usually open very early in the morning (at 7 or 8), are normally closed for a considerable period during the middle of the day. Almost all churches close at 12 and do not reopen until 15, 16, or even 17, although cathedrals and some of the large churches (indicated in the text) may be open without a break during daylight hours. Smaller churches and oratories are often open only in the early morning, but it is sometimes possible to find the key by asking locally. The sacristan will also show closed chapels, crypts, etc., and sometimes expects a tip. Some churches now ask that sightseers do not enter during a service, but normally visitors not in a tour group may do so, provided they are silent and do not approach the altar in use. An entrance fee is becoming customary for admission to treasuries, cloisters, bell-towers, etc. Lights (operated by lire coins) have now been installed in many churches to illuminate frescoes and altarpieces, but a torch and binoculars are always useful. Sometimes you are not allowed to enter important churches wearing shorts or with bare shoulders.

Historic houses and gardens, many of them still in private hands, are now often open to the public on certain days. These are all listed in an annual publication *Dimore e Giardini Storici* (Mondadori), produced in collaboration with the Associazione Dimore Storiche Italiane (ADSI), and the Fondo per l'Ambiente Italiano (FAI). The FAI was founded in 1975 on the model of the British National Trust, and now owns eight properties open to the public in northern Italy. Its office is in Milan (5 Viale Coni Zugna, tel. 02 4815556). On two days in early spring there is a day on which numerous monuments all over Italy are opened specially by the FAI.

General Information

Money
The monetary unit is the Italian lira (plural: lire). There are coins of 50, 100, 200 and 500 lire, and notes of 1000, 2000, 5000, 10,000, 50,000, and 100,000 lire. There are still two sizes of 50 and 100 lire coins. Travellers' cheques and Eurocheques are the safest way of carrying money while travelling, and most credit cards are now generally accepted in shops and restaurants (and at some petrol stations). The commission on cashing travellers' cheques can be quite high. For banking hours, see under 'Working Hours', below. Money can also be changed at exchange offices (*cambio*), in travel agencies, some post offices, and main railway stations. Exchange offices are usually open seven days a week at airports and some main railway stations. Some hotels, restaurants, and shops change money (but usually at a lower rate). There are now automatic machines for changing foreign bank notes outside some banks in the main towns, and Bancomat machines.

Health
British citizens, as members of the EU, have the right to claim health services in Italy if they are in possession of the E111 form (issued by the Department of Health and Social Security). There are also a number of private holiday health insurance policies. First Aid services ('Pronto Soccorso') are available at all hospitals, railway stations, and airports. **Chemist shops** ('Farmacie') are usually open Monday–Friday, 9–13, 15.30–19.30. On Saturdays and Sundays (and holidays) a few are open (listed on the door of every chemist). In every town there is also at least one chemist shop open at night (also shown on the door of every chemist). For emergencies, dial 113.

Assistance
Help is given to British and American travellers in Italy who are in difficulty by the British and American embasssies in Rome. They will replace lost or stolen passports, and will give advice in emergencies. There is a British Consul General in Milan (and honorary British consulates in Trieste and Venice), and a US Consul in Milan. You are strongly advised to carry some means of identity with you at all times while in Italy, since you can be held at a police station if you are stopped and found to be without a document of identity.

Disabled travellers
Italy is at last catching up slowly with the rest of Europe in the provision of facilities for the disabled. All new public buildings are now obliged by law to provide access for the disabled, and specially designed facilities. In the annual list of

hotels published by the local APT office, hotels which are able to give hospitality to the disabled are indicated. Airports and railway stations provide assistance, and certain trains are equipped to transport wheelchairs. Access for cars with disabled people is allowed to the centre of towns (normally closed to traffic), where parking places are reserved for them. For all other information, contact local APT offices.

Working Hours

Government offices usually work six days a week from 8 to 13.30 or 14. Shops (clothes, hardware, hairdressers, etc.) generally open 9–13, 16–19.30, including Saturday, and for most of the year are closed on Monday morning. Food shops usually open 8–13, 17–19.30 or 20, and for most of the year are closed on one afternoon a week. From mid-June to mid-September all shops are closed instead on Saturday afternoon. Banks are usually open Monday–Friday 8.20–13.20, 14.30–15.45. They are closed on Saturday and holidays, and close early (about 11) on days preceding national holidays.

Telephones and Postal Information

Stamps are sold at tobacconists (displaying a blue 'T' sign), and post offices (open 8.10–13.25, Mon–Sat). Central offices in main towns are open 8.10–19.25, and also now on Sundays (8.30–19.30) in the main cities. Correspondence can be addressed c/o the Post Office by adding 'Fermo Posta' to the name of the locality. It is always advisable to post letters at post offices or railway stations; collection from letterboxes may be erratic. There are numerous public telephones all over Italy in bars, restaurants, kiosks, etc. These are operated by coins or telephone cards. Telephone cards (5000 l, 10,000 l, or 15,000 l) can be bought from tobacconists, bars, some newspaper stands, and post offices. Phone numbers in Italy can have from 4 to 8 numbers. Placing a local call costs 200 lire. For directory assistance (in Italian), dial 12.

Public Holidays

The Italian national holidays when offices, shops, and schools are closed are as follows: 1 January (New Year), 25 April (Liberation Day), Easter Monday, 1 May (Labour Day), 15 August (Assumption), 1 November (All Saints' Day), 8 December (Immaculate Conception), Christmas Day and 26 December (St Stephen). Each town keeps its Patron Saint's day as a holiday, e.g. Venice (25 April, St Mark), Genoa and Turin (24 June, St John the Baptist), Bologna (4 October, St Petronius), Milan (7 December, St Ambrose).

Festivals

Annual festivals are celebrated in most towns and villages in commemoration of a local historical or religious event, and are often very spectacular. At these times, the towns become extremely lively, and—apart from the central race or competition—numerous celebrations take place on the side, and local markets are usually held at the same time. The most important traditional local festivals have been mentioned in the text. They are particularly exciting events for children. Information from local APT offices.

Music. The Opera season in Italy usually begins in December and continues until June. The principal opera house in northern Italy is La Scala in Milan.

During the summer operas are performed in the open air in the Arena of Verona. Annual music and drama festivals take place in many towns (mentioned in the text). Details of their programmes are widely published by wall posters in the streets of the town.

Newspapers

The most widely read northern Italian newspapers are the *Repubblica*, *Corriere della Sera* (of Milan), the *Stampa* (of Turin), and *Il Resto del Carlino* (of Bologna). Foreign newspapers are readily obtainable at central street kiosks and railways stations. The *International Herald Tribune* is published daily in Bologna.

Public Toilets

There is a notable shortage of public toilets in Italy. All bars (cafés) should have toilets available to the public (generally speaking the larger the bar, the better the facilities). Nearly all museums now have toilets. There are also toilets at railway stations and bus stations.

Crime

Pickpocketing is a widespread problem in towns all over Italy: it is always advisable not to carry valuables in handbags, and be particularly careful on public transport. Crime should be reported at once to the police, or the local carabinieri office (found in every town and small village). A detailed statement has to be given in order to get an official document confirming loss or damage (essential for insurance claims). Interpreters are usually provided. For all emergencies, dial 113.

Golf

There are now quite a number of golf courses in northern Italy. There are 18-hole courses in Piedmont, Lombardy, the Veneto, Liguria, and Emilia Romagna. Information from ENIT or the Federazione Italiana Golf, 388 Via Flaminia, Rome 00196 (tel. 06 394641).

Lombardy

Lombardy, with Milan—the largest city in northern Italy—as its capital, has plaed an important part in the making of Italy. The region includes areas of remarkable diversity within its boundaries, extending as it does from the summits of the central Alps to the low-lying fertile plain of the Po. Some of the loveliest scenery in the country surrounds the great Italian Lakes (all of which, except Orta, are wholly or partly in Lombardy). The Lombard provinces are Bergamo, Brescia, Como, Cremona, Mantua, Milan, Pavia, Sondrio, Varese and Lodi.

In Roman times the centre of Cisalpine Gaul, Lombardy takes its present name from the Lombards, one of the so-called barbarian tribes that invaded Italy in the 6C. They settled in various parts of the peninsula and founded several states; that which centred roughly round Milan became the most important, and retained the founders' name.

The association of Lombardy with transalpine powers dates from the time of Charlemagne, and Lombardy, though actually under the control of the Bishops of Milan, remained nominally a part of the Germanic Empire until the 12C. At this time the most important Lombard cities, having freed themselves of the temporal power of the bishops, formed the Lombard League, which defeated the Emperor, Frederick Barbarossa, at Legnano in 1176. In the following two centuries local dynasties held despotic power, the richest of which also encouraged the arts within their dominions: these included the Torriani, Visconti and Sforza at Milan, Pavia, Cremona, and Bergamo; the Suardi and Colleoni at Bergamo; the Pallavicini, Torriani, Scaligeri, and Visconti at Brescia; and the Bonacolsi and Gonzaga at Mantua.

After the fall of the powerful Visconti rulers at the beginning of the 15C, the Venetian Republic encroached on the eastern part of the region. In the 16C Lombard territory was invaded by the kings of France, and in 1535 the Duchy of Milan became a dependency of the Spanish Habsburgs, though Ticino and the Valtellina in the north were incorporated into the Swiss Confederation. With the extinction of the Habsburg line in Spain, Lombardy was transferred to the Austrian dominion, and, with the brief intervention of the Napoleonic Cisalpine Republic and the French kingdoms of Lombardy and of Italy (1797–1814), it remained a subject-province of Austria, the Valtellina being detached from Switzerland in 1797. National aspirations were repressed by the Austrian military governors of the 19C until the victory of the allied French and Piedmontese brought Lombardy beneath the Italian flag in 1859.

1 · Milan

Milan, in Italian *Milano*, is famous as the principal commercial and industrial centre of the country, and the second largest town in Italy (1,580,000 inhab.). It has the appearance and characteristics of a busy modern city, with excellent shops (including those of numerous well-known fashion designers). At the same time it is a place of great historical and artistic interest, with magnificent art collections (notably the Brera picture gallery), the beautiful Cenacolo by Leonardo da Vinci, a remarkable Gothic cathedral, and many important churches. It has the most efficient public transport system of any town in Italy, featuring a wide network of trams (as well as underground railway lines and buses). The Scala opera house is still world famous. Many of the large palaces of Milan have handsome courtyards; some of the most interesting are to be found on Via Borgonuovo and Via Brera (most of them are marked with yellow signs). Huge 19C residential blocks with numerous apartments arranged around pretty interior courtyards are characteristic of the city. The northern skyline is punctuated by skyscrapers, and Milan is a good place to study 19C and 20C Italian architecture.

■ **Information offices**. APT, 1 Via Marconi (Piazza Duomo; Pl. II,11), tel. 02 861287, with IAT information office. There is another IAT information office at the central railway station. The APT distribute free a booklet on Milan, a list of hotels, a map, and a pamphlet on current exhibitions and concerts (*Milano mese*). The Comune of Milan run an information office in the Galleria Vittorio Emanuele II (Pl. II,7), tel. 02 878363. 'Informa Giovani', 1 Via Marconi is a special office for students.

■ **Railway stations**. **Centrale** (Pl. I,4), Piazzale Duca d'Aosta, northeast of the centre, for all main services of the FS (tel. 02 675001). Some international expresses stop only at **Lambrate** (beyond Pl. I,4). **Nord** (Pl. II,5) for services of the Nord-Milano railway (for Como, Novara, etc.). **Porta Genova** (Pl. I,13) for Alessandria (connections to Genoa). Subsidiary stations include: **Porta Vittoria** (beyond Pl. I,3). FS Lost Property Office, 108 Via Sammartini (tel. 02 67712667).

■ **Airports** are at **Malpensa**, 45km northwest and at **Linate**, 7km east, both for international and internal flights. For **Linate** bus 73 from Piazza San Babila (Pl. II,8) every 10 minutes (near the underground station of San Babila on line 1), or from the central station (Piazza Luigi di Savoia; Pl. I,4) STAM bus every 20–30 minutes. For **Malpensa** airport bus in connection with all flights from the central station (Piazza Luigi da Savoia; Pl. I,4). Information on both airports, tel. 02 74852200.

■ **Car parking**. The centre of the city (see Pl. 2) is closed to traffic 7.30–18 (except for those with permits), and parking is restricted at all times. If you are travelling to Milan by car, you are strongly advised to park on the outskirts and make use of the excellent public transport system. There are free car parks by the underground stations of Pagano (on line 1) and Lambrate (line 2), and fee-paying car parks at Rogoredo (line 3) and Romolo (line 2). **Car Pound**, Piazza Beccaria (city police station, tel. 02 77271).

■ **Public transport** (three underground lines, buses, and trams), well run by ATM, is very efficient. Information offices (with a map of the system) in the underground station of Piazza Duomo and at the central railway station (tel. 02 89010797). Tickets (which can be used on buses, trams, or the underground) are valid for 1hr 15 minutes (flat rate fare). They are sold at ATM offices, automatic machines at bus stops, and news-stands and tobacconists and must be stamped on board. Tickets valid for 24 or 48 hours can also be purchased at ATM offices or news-stands.

Some of the tram and bus lines most useful to the visitor are the following:
Trams:
1 Central railway station—Piazza Cavour—Piazza Scala—Largo Cairoli (for the Castello Sforzesco)—Milano Nord railway station—Corso Sempione. **4** Piazza Repubblica—Via Manzoni—Piazza Scala—Via Legnano—Via Farini. **24** Via Mazzini—Corso Magenta (Santa Maria delle Grazie, for the Cenacolo). **19** Corso Sempione—Milano Nord railway station—Via Broletto—Via Orefici (for Duomo)—Via Torino.
Buses:
50, **54** Largo Augusto (Duomo)—Corso Magenta—Via Carducci (for Sant'Ambrogio)—Via San Vittore. **61** Corso Matteotti—Piazza Scala—Via Brera—Via Solferino (for San Marco). **65** Central railway station—Via San Gregorio—Corso Buenos Aires—Corso Venezia—Piazza Fontana—Via Larga—Corso Italia—Porta Lodovico.
Underground (metropolitana: M):
Three lines are now open: **Line 1 (red)** from Sesto railway station to Bisceglie and Molino Dorino. The central section runs from Loreto via Lima, Porta Venezia, Palestro, San Babila, Duomo, Cordusio, Cairoli (for Castello Sforzesco) to Cadorna (for Milan Nord station). **Line 2 (green)** from Gessate and Cologno Nord to Famagosta in its central section links the railway stations of Lambrate, Centrale, Garibaldi, Milano Nord (Cadorna) and (via Sant'Ambrogio) Porta Genova. **Line 3 (yellow)** from Sondrio to San Donato links the central station via Repubblica, Turati and Monte Napoleone with the Duomo and continues along Corso di Porta Romana to southern Milan.

A comprehensive network of **country buses** run by the Trasporti Regione Lombardia serve western Milan (and the province of Varese), southern Milan and the province of Pavia, and the Brianza in the north. The 'autostradali' from Piazza Castello run to the main towns in northern Italy.

■ **Taxis**. Various companies run taxi services, and as in the rest of Italy there are no cruising taxis. Tel. 02 5353; 02 6767; 02 8585, etc.

■ **Hotels**. There are some 370 hotels in Milan, including five 5-star, and 74 4-star hotels, but a very small selection is given below. It is difficult to find accommodation when big international trade fairs are in progress (especially in February and March, and from September to November).
5-star: *Grand Hotel et de Milan*, 29 Via Manzoni (Pl. II,7); *Principe di Savoia*, 17 Piazza della Repubblica (Pl. I,4).

4-star: *Sir Edward*, 4 Via Mazzini (Pl. II,11); *Pierre Milano*, 32 Via De Amicis (Pl. II,13); *Carlton Senato*, 5 Via Senato (Pl. II,4); *Manin*, 7 Via Manin (Pl. I,7,8).
3-star: *Adriatico*, 20 Via Conca del Naviglio (Pl. II,13); *Cairoli*, 4 Via Porlezza (Pl. II,6); *Gran Duca di York*, 1/A Via Moneta (Pl. II,10); *Manzoni*, 20 Via Santo Spirito (Pl. II,4).
2-star: *Antica Locanda Solferino*, 2 Via Castelfidardo (Pl. 1: 3); *Vecchia Milano*, 4 Via Borromei (Pl. I,10).

■ **Youth hostel**, 2 Via Salmoiraghi (tel. 02 39267095).

■ **Camping sites**. *Città di Milano*, Via Airaghi, and, north of Milan at Monza, *Camping di Monza* (open April to September).

■ **Restaurants**. Milan is very well supplied with good restaurants of all categories, down to the cheapest self-service restaurants, and only a very small selection is given below. **A:** *Al Porto*, Piazzale Generale Cantore (Pl. I,13,14), specialising in fish; *Bice*, 12 Via Borgospesso, off Via Monte Napoleone (Pl. II,8). **B:** *La Brisa*, 15 Via Brisa (Pl. II,6, 10); *Trattoria Latteria San Marco*, Via San Marco (Pl. I,7); *Trattoria Torre di Pisa*, 21 Via Fiori Chiari, on the corner of Via Mercato (Pl. II,2); *La Libera*, 21 Via Palermo (also for pizza) (Pl. I,6,7); *Alla Collina Pistoiese*, 1 Via Amedei, near Piazza Missori (Pl. II,11). **C:** *Ristorante Ponte Rosso*, 23 Ripa di Porta Ticinese (lunch only) (Pl. I,13,14); Restaurant in the department store of *Rinascente*, Piazza del Duomo (Pl. II,11); *Premiata Pizzeria*, 2 Alzaia Naviglio Grande. Numerous good inexpensive self-service restaurants in Piazza del Duomo, in Via Dogana (Pl. II,11), and in Via San Marco (Pl. I,7).

■ **Cafés and cake shops**. *Ranieri*, Via della Moscova; *Supino*, Via Cesare de Sesto; *Marchesi*, 13 Corso Magenta; *Panarello*, 3 Via Speronari (Corso di Porta Romana); *San Carlo*, 1 Via Bandello (near Santa Maria delle Grazie); *Buonarroti*, 9 Via Buonarroti (for ice creams). **Piano Bars** (with jazz music) *Il Capolinea*, 119 Via Ludovico il Moro and *Il Bolgia Umana*, 7 Via Santa Maria Segreta.

■ **Picnic places** in Parco Sempione, in the Giardini Pubblici off Via Palestro, and in the Giardini della Guastalla, Via Francesco Sforza (near the University). At the central station there is a supermarket open every day and all night.

■ **Theatres**. Information on theatre performances and concerts from the APT in *Milano mese* published free every month. *La Scala*, Piazza della Scala, a famous opera house (the season opens on 7 December). Ballet and concerts in September to November. *Piccolo Teatro*, 2 Via Rovello (Via Dante). *Teatro Manzoni*, 42 Via Manzoni. *Lirico*, Via Larga. *Nuovo*, Piazza San Babila. *Nazionale*, Piazzale Piemonte. *Carcano*, 66 Corso di Porta Romana. Tickets can be purchased at the theatres or at various agencies, including 'La Biglietteria', 81 Corso Garibaldi (tel. 02 6590188).

■ **Shopping in Milan**. Milan is the centre of Italian fashion. The most important Italian fashion designers have shops between Via Montenapoleone, Via Spiga, Via Sant'Andrea, and Via Santo Spirito. These include *Moschino*, 12 Via Sant'Andrea; *Giorgio Armani*, 9 Via Sant'Andrea (for children at 27 Via Durini); *Krizia*, 23 Via della Spiga (for women) and 17 Via A. Manin (for men); *Trussardi*, 5 Via Sant'Andrea; *Valentino*, 3 Via Santo Spirito (women) and 3 Via Montenapoleone (for men), *Gianni Versace*, 2 Via Montenapoleone; *Romeo Gigli*, 11 Corso Venezia and 115 Via Palermo; *Gianfranco Ferré*, 11 and 13 Via della Spiga.

Biffi Boutique, 6 Corso Genova and 45 Via Fabio Filzi stocks clothes by important international fashion designers (as well as shoes and handbags). *Prada*, 11 Galleria Vittorio Emanuele II, 1 Via della Spiga, and 21 Via Sant'Andrea is well known for its handbags and shoes. Other boutiques include *Marisa*, 10A Via Sant'Andrea (avant-garde womens' clothes); *Brigatti*, 15 Corso Venezia and *Bardelli*, 13 Corso Magenta (both specialising in classic clothes for men); *Pupi Solari*, 2 Piazza Tommaseo (classic clothes for women and children including cashmere); *Corso Como 10*, 10 Corso Como (avant-garde design); *Lisa Corti hometextiles*, 6 Via Conchetta (redesigned Indian fabrics).

Well-known elegant shoe shops include: *Henry Beguelyn*, 7 Via Caminadella; *Sergio Rossi*, 6a Via Montenapoleone; *Fausto Santini*, 1 Via Montenapoleone; and *Diego della Valle*, 12 Via XX Settembre.

Fiorucci, 1 Galleria Passarella is a large store with reasonably priced and trendy clothes that are particularly popular with the young. Department stores for good inexpensive but fashionable clothes include *La Rinascente*, Piazza Duomo; *Coin* (the biggest branch is at 1A Piazza V Giornate), and *Standa* (numerous branches including Piazza San Babila).

■ **Markets**. The Fiera di Senigallia, a large 'flea market', is held on Saturday morning in Viale d'Annunzio. Another market is held in Via Lorenzini on Sunday morning. Open-air markets in Viale Papiniano (Tuesday and Saturday), Piazza Mirabello (Monday and Thursday), and Largo Quinto Alpini (Friday).

■ **Annual festivals**. 7 and 8 December, Festival of St Ambrose (patron saint of Milan): 'Oh Bei! Oh Bei!' street fair near Sant'Ambrogio. 'Stramilano' in April, a marathon race in which some 50,000 people take part. In October and April an open-air art exhibition is held in Via Bagutta. On June evenings the 'Festa del Naviglio' takes place around the Naviglio Grande (street fairs, musical events, and restaurants on boats, etc.). For a week in May the Associazione Dimore Storiche Italiane (tel. 02 9547311) organise the opening of some historic courtyards in the city ('Cortili Aperti').

■ **British Consul General**, 7 Via San Paolo (off Corso Vittorio Emanuele). **US Consulate**, 2/10 Via Principe Amadeo. **English Church**, All Saints, 17 Via Solferino. **British Council** (with a library), 38 Via Manzoni.

■ **Medical emergencies**. For ambulance, tel. 7733. Chemist shop open 24 hours a day at the Central Station.

History

Mediolanum was a Celtic settlement which came under Roman control in 222 BC. By the end of the Empire it had a population of nearly 100,000 and rivalled Rome in importance. Constantine the Great officially recognised the Christian religion by the famous Edict of Milan of AD 313. The influence of the great bishop of Milan St Ambrose (340–397) was so profound that the adjective 'ambrosiano' has become synonymous with 'Milanese'. The Emperor Valentinian II died here in 392. Most of the male population was massacred by the Goths in 539.

By the mid-11C it was a typical early Italian city-state, constantly at war with its neighbours (especially Pavia, Como and Lodi). The Emperor Barbarossa sacked Milan in 1158 and 1162, before being beaten at Legnano in 1176 by the Lombard League. Milan was later ruled by a succession of powerful families, including the Torriani who took control of the city around 1260. They were overthrown in 1277 by the Visconti who held power in Milan until 1447, and the city had a period of particular splendour under Gian Galeazzo (1385–1402). After a Republican interlude of three years, Francesco Sforza, famous condottiere and defender of Milan against Venice, who had married Bianca, daughter of the last Visconti, proclaimed himself Duke. He was succeeded by his son Galeazzo Maria, and then by his infant grandson Gian Galeazzo under the regency of his mother Bona di Savoia. His power was usurped by his uncle Lodovico il Moro, who was a great patron of the arts, and under whose rule the city flourished.

A succession of foreign invasions began with the expedition in 1494 of Charles VIII of France. Between 1499 and 1535 the dukedom was contested by the French and the Spanish, and under Charles V Milan became capital of a province of the Holy Roman Empire.

Milan was taken by the Austrians in 1713. In 1796 it was seized by Napoleon, who three years later made it capital of the Cisalpine Republic, and, after a brief occupation by the Austrians and Russians, capital of the Italian Republic (1802) and of the kingdom of Italy (1805). After the fall of Napoleon the Austrians returned, but the Milanese rebelled against their tyranny during the 'Cinque Giornate' (18–22 March 1848). Milan was liberated by Vittorio Emanuele II and Napoleon III after the battle of Magenta in 1859.

With the industrial development of the city at the end of the 19C, Milan expanded to absorb a huge influx of immigrant workers from all over Italy. The city was bombed 15 times in the Second World War; the worst air raids were in August 1943, when a great part of the city centre burned for several days. The years of reconstruction were followed by a period of economic boom when sprawling new suburbs were built. Since 1974 the population has been in decline.

Art

The most important Romanesque churches in the city are Sant'Ambrogio and San Lorenzo. The Cathedral is practically the only Gothic building in Milan, but one of the most splendid in the country. The wealthy and cultured court of the Sforzas attracted many great artists of the Renaissance, including the architects Filarete, Michelozzo, and Bramante,

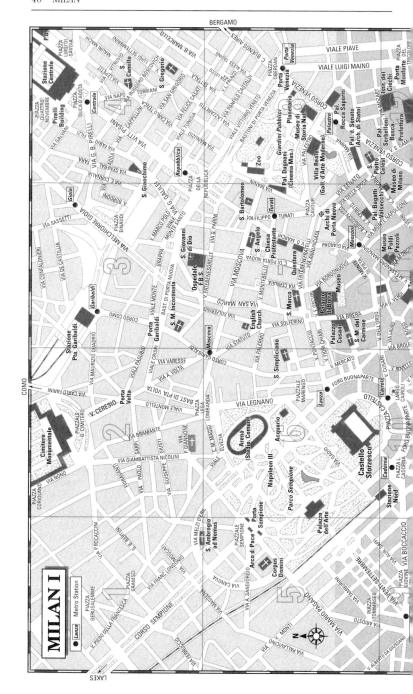

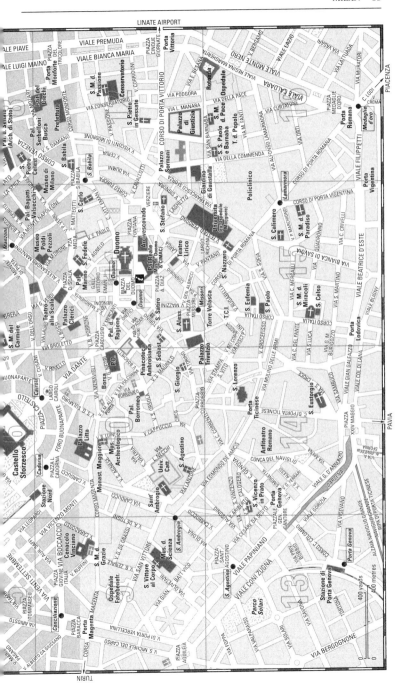

the sculptor Amadeo, and the painters Bergognone and Foppa. Milanese art, however, was completely transformed by the arrival from Tuscany in 1483 of Leonardo da Vinci. This great artist and the city he adopted were the centre of an artistic and humanistic flowering which ended with the fall of Lodovico il Moro in 1499. Leonardo's many pupils and disciples who carried on his tradition of painting in Milan included Boltaffio, Cesare da Sesto, Marco d'Oggiono, Giampietrino, and Andrea Solario. His pupils Luini and Guadenzio Ferrari formed schools of their own. The sculptors Bambaia and Cristoforo Solari also felt his influence.

Towards the end of the 16C Camillo and Giulio Procaccini introduced a new style of painting from Bologna, and Galeazzo Alessi imported ideas from Rome into architecture. The neo-classical buildings of Luigi Cagnola and Luigi Canonica (both born in 1762) represent the Napoleonic period, and a number of districts of the city were built at the turn of the century in a distinctive Art Nouveau style. In the 1920s Giovanni Muzio built a few interesting buildings in the city, and some modern buildings continue the tradition of originality.

Piazza del Duomo

PIAZZA DEL DUOMO (Pl. II; 11) is the centre of the life of Milan. It is closed to traffic (except for the west end) and is dominated by the splendid cathedral. The crowded Portici Settentrionali (1873), along the north side, are characteristic of the bustling atmosphere of the city. The equestrian statue of Vittorio Emanuele II is by Ercole Rosa (1896).

Duomo

The **duomo (Pl. II; 11) is a magnificent late Gothic building, the only one in Italy, and one of the largest churches in the world (second only to Rome's St Peter's in Italy). Its remarkable exterior, with numerous flying buttresses, is decorated with some 2000 sculptures, and the roof has a forest of pinnacles and spires. It has a superb tower over the crossing and a remarkable 16C façade in the Gothic style. It was particularly admired in the Romantic Age.

On the site of Santa Maria Maggiore (revealed through excavations), it was begun in 1386 under Gian Galeazzo Visconti, who presented it with a marble quarry at Candoglia which still belongs to the Chapter. The design is attributed to the Lombard masters Simone da Orsenigo and Giovanni Grassi, who were assisted by French, German, and Flemish craftsmen. In 1400 Filippino degli Organi was appointed master mason, and he was succeeded by Giovanni Solari and his son Guiniforte, and Giovanni Antonio Amadeo. In 1567 St Charles Borromeo appointed Pellegrino Tibaldi as architect, and under him the church was dedicated. The tower over the crossing was completed in 1762 and the statue of the Virgin placed on its summit in 1774. The façade, begun in the 17C, was completed in 1805. The 'Veneranda Fabbrica del Duomo' has looked after the cathedral for centuries, and is responsible for the conservation of its numerous delicate sculptural works. The famous choir school of the cathedral was directed by Franchino Gaffurio from 1484 to 1522.

The *façade was begun by Pellegrino Tibaldi in the 16C on a classical design but was considerably altered by Carlo Buzzi (1645) and Francesco Castelli who adopted a Gothic style. It was completed in 1805 by Carlo Amati using Buzzi's design. The doors date from 1906 (Lodovico Pogliaghi), 1948 (Arrigo Minerbi), 1950, and 1960 (Luciano Minguzzi). The best view of the exterior is from the courtyard of Palazzo Reale. The splendid apse has three huge windows.

The huge cruciform *interior (open all day), with double-aisled nave, single-aisled transepts and a pentagonal apse, has a forest of 52 tall columns, most of which bear circles of figures in canopied niches instead of capitals. The splendid effect is heightened by the stained glass of the windows. The classical pavement is by Tibaldi.

South aisle. Above the plain granite sarcophagus of Archbishop Aribert (died 1045) is a stained-glass window by Cristoforo de' Mottis (1473–77). The red marble sarcophagus on pillars is of Archbishop Ottone Visconti (died 1295). The next three windows have 16C stained glass. The tomb of Marco Carelli is by Filippino degli Organi (1406). Beyond a relief with a design for the façade by Giuseppe Brentano (1886) is the small monument of Canon Giovanni Vimercati (died 1548), with two fine portraits and a damaged Pietà by Bambaia. The stained glass (1470–75) shows the influence of Vincenzo Foppa. The glass above the sixth altar is by Nicolò da Varallo (1480–89).

South transept. *Monument of Gian Giacomo Medici, with bronze statues, by Leone Leoni (1560–63). The stained glass in the two transept windows is by Corrado de' Mocchis (1554–64). In the transept apse is the monumental altar of San Giovanni Bono (1763). On the altar with a marble relief by Bambaia, is a statue (right) of St Catherine, by Cristoforo Lombardo. The statue of St Bartholomew flayed and carrying his skin is by Marco d'Agrate (1562).

On the impressive **tiburio**, or tower over the crossing, are medallions (on the pendentives) with 15C busts of the Doctors of the Church, and some 60 statues (on the arches). The four piers had to be reinforced in 1984 in order to consolidate the structure of the building. The *presbytery (usually open to worshippers only) was designed by Pellegrino Tibaldi (1567). It contains two pulpits (supported by bronze figures by Francesco Brambilla), and a large bronze ciborium also by Tibaldi. High above the altar hangs a paschal candlestick by Lorenzo da Civate (1447).

The **treasury** (closed 12.30–14.30) contains a silver reliquary box of the late 4C; a 13C dove with Limoges enamels; three ivory diptychs (5C–11C); an ivory bucket of 979–80; the pax of Pio IV attributed to Leone Leoni; the evangelistary cover of Archbishop Aribert (11C) decorated with enamels; and church vestments. The **crypt**, decorated with stucco reliefs by Galeazzo Alessi and Tibaldi, contains the richly-robed body of St Charles Borromeo, the leading spirit of the Catholic Counter-Reformation, made Cardinal Archbishop of Milan in 1560 and canonised in 1610.

The **ambulatory** is separated from the choir by a beautiful marble screen designed by Pellegrino Tibaldi (1567). The sacristy doorways date from the late 14C. The sacristy contains a statue of Christ at the column by Cristoforo Solari. Beyond (high up) is a statue of Martin V, the pope who consecrated the high altar in 1418, by Jacopino da Tradate (1424), and the black marble tomb of Cardinal Caracciolo (died 1538), by Bambaia. The large embroidered standard dates from the late 16C.

In the middle of the **north transept** is the Trivulzio *candelabrum, a seven-branched bronze candlestick nearly 5m high, of French or German workmanship (13C or 14C). The stained-glass window above the sculptured altarpiece of the Crucifix (1605) is by Nicolò da Varallo (1479). The altar in the transept apse dates from 1768. The Gothic altar of St Catherine has two statues attributed to Cristoforo Solari.

North aisle. The eighth altarpiece is by Federico Barocci. The next four stained-glass windows date from the 16C. Sixth altar, Crucifix carried by St Charles Borromeo during the plague of 1576; third altar, tomb of three archbishops of the Arcimboldi family, attributed to Galeazzo Alessi; second bay, late 12C marble reliefs of apostles. Opposite is the font, a porphyry urn thought to date from Roman times, covered with a canopy by Tibaldi.

The **excavations** beneath the church are entered from the west end (10–11.45, 15–16.45 exc. Mon). Here can be seen a 4C octagonal baptistery where St Ambrose baptised St Augustine in 387; remains of the basilica of Santa Tecla (begun in the 4C); and Roman baths of the 1C BC.

The entrance (open 9–17.30, winter 9–16.30; also lift, entered from outside the north or south transept) to the **roof** is a small door in the corner of the south transept, near the Medici tomb. The *ascent provides a superb view of the sculptural detail of the exterior and is highly recommended. 158 steps lead up to the roof of the transept from which can be seen numerous pinnacles and flying buttresses. From the walkways across the roof the details of the carving can be seen, and beyond are magnificent views of the city. At the angle facing the Corso is the Carelli spire, the oldest pinnacle. From above the west front it is possible to walk along the spine of the nave roof to the base of the crossing, by Amadeo (1490–1500), who also planned the four turrets but finished only the one at the northeast angle. From the southwest turret stairs lead up to the platform of the crossing. From here another staircase, in the northeast turret, ascends to the topmost gallery at the base of the central spire, surmounted by the Madonnina (108m from the ground), a statue of gilded copper, nearly 4m high. From this height there is a magnificent *view of the city, the Lombard plain, the Alps from Monte Viso to the Ortler (with the prominent peaks of the Matterhorn, Monte Rosa, the two Grigne, and Monte Resegone), and the Apennines.

An interesting series of 52 paintings illustrating the life and miracles of St Charles Borromeo are hung in a double row between the nave and transept pillars from 1 Nov to 6 Jan every year. Known as the '**quadroni di San Carlo**', they were commissioned in 1602 by Cardinal Federico Borromeo to honour the memory of his cousin Charles. Above are hung the scenes from his life (1602–04) and below the scenes of his miracles (1609–10): the best ones are by Il Cerano and Giulio Cesare Procaccini (others are by Morazzone, Carlo Buzzi, Il Duchino, Il Fiammenghino, and Domenico Pellegrini). The last eight were painted in 1660–1740 to complete the series which survives intact.

Museo del Duomo

Opposite the south transept of the cathedral, in a wing of Palazzo Reale (see below), is the entrance to the Museo del Duomo (Pl. II.11; open 9.30–12.30, 15–18 exc. Mon). The collection is well labelled. Beyond the ticket office is **room 2** with statues by Giorgio Solari and Bernardo da Venezia (1392). **Room 3**, an 18C neo-classical vaulted hall by Piermarini, has a fine display of sculpture from the Visconti period from the exterior of the cathedral, and 14C–15C stained glass. Room 5 is entered below a cast of the arms of Gian Galeazzo used as a centrepiece for the apse window. **Room 6** has 15C statues. **Room 7**. Crucifix in beaten copper (c 1040) from Archbishop Aribert's tomb in the Duomo, and a painting attributed to Michelino da Besozzo (1418). **Room 8** contains late 15C sculpture. The St Agnes is attributed to Benedetto Briosco. Works by Cristoforo Solari include a statue of Job.

Room 9 contains sculptures attributed to Giovanni Antonio Amadeo and Andrea Fusina, and a 15C Flemish tapestry of the Passion. **Room 10**. Altar frontal of St Charles Borromeo (1610); drawings by Il Cerano. **Room 11**. Tapestries made in Ferrara c 1540 probably on cartoons by Giulio Romano, and *The Infant Christ among the Doctors*, an early work by Jacopo Tintoretto. **Room 12** displays numerous sculptures from the Duomo from the end of the 16C and beginning of the 17C, including works by Francesco Brambilla.

Room 13 (right). Models by Giuseppe Perego for the Madonnina which crowns the central spire of the Duomo, and the original armature. **Room 14** contains 19C sculptures from the façade (Camillo Pacetti, Pompeo Marchesi, etc.). The **gallery (Room 15)** displays plans illustrating the history of the Duomo. **Room 16** contains a splendid wooden *model of the Duomo constructed by Bernardino Zenale da Treviglio in 1519, and later models. **Room 17** is dedicated to the five 20C doors of the Duomo (bozzetti, etc.). **Rooms 18 and 19** illustrate the remarkable restoration work carried out on the four pillars of the crossing in 1981–84 in order to consolidate the structure of the building (during which much of the stone was replaced). Off Room 12 is **Room 20** with a fine display of church vestments (and statuettes by Francesco Messina).

Palazzo Reale

To the south of the cathedral is the former Palazzo Reale (Pl. II,11), on the site of the 13C town hall. It was rebuilt in neo-classical style in 1772–78 for the Austrian grand-dukes by Giuseppe Piermarini (and altered again in the 19C, and restored after bomb damage in 1943). It now belongs to the municipality, and there are long term plans to restore it and open it to the public. At present important exhibitions are held here.

On the second floor (entered through the main courtyard) is the **CIVICO MUSEO D'ARTE CONTEMPORANEA**, known as **CIMAC** (Pl. II,11), open 9.30–17.30 exc. Mon. This fairly representative collection, in a stark temporary arrangement, is divided into two parts: works up to 1950 in the rooms on the left, later works and the Jucker collection in the right-hand rooms. The rooms on the left (1–23) contain works by Umberto Boccioni, Ardengo Soffici, Amedeo Modigliani, Gino Severini, Giacomo Balla, Picasso, Giorgio De Chirico (*Autumn*, 1935 in Room 7), Virgilio Guidi (*The Visit* c 1925 in Room 8), Pietro Marusig, Carlo Carrà (*Summer*, 1930, and *Fishermen* in Room 9), Mario Sironi, Arturo Martini, Giorgio Morandi, Felice Casorati, Massimo Campigli, Gino Severini, Filippo De Pisis, Aligi Sassù and Arturo Tosi. The rooms on the right of the entrance include the Jucker Collection in Rooms 30–32 with works by Balla, Severini, Sironi, De Pisis, Carrà, Morandi, Braque, Matisse and Picasso.

The **Arengario**, on Via Manzoni, is an interesting building (1939–56) begun by Giovanni Muzio with reliefs by Arturo Martini. It is now the headquarters of the APT tourist office.

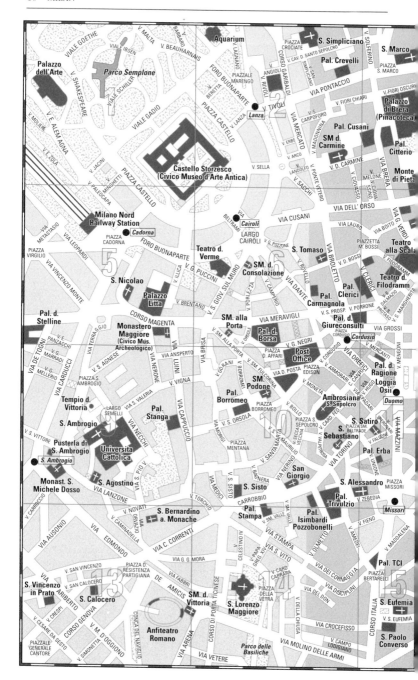

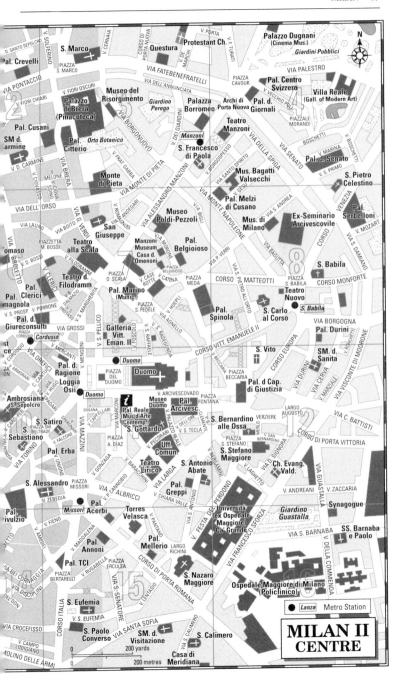

MILAN II CENTRE

Beyond the courtyard of Palazzo Reale (with a view of the campanile of San Gottardo) is the church of **San Gottardo** (Pl. II,11), formerly the palace chapel, entered from Via Pecorari. The exterior and beautiful campanile are attributed to Francesco Pecorari (1330–36), and the neo-classical interior has stuccoes by Giocondo Albertolli. It contains a very damaged 14C fresco of the Crucifixion showing the influence of Giotto, who is known to have been in the city in 1335. The monument to Azzone Visconti is by Giovanni di Balduccio. The **Archbishops' Palace** is mainly the work of Tibaldi (1570 et seq), with a façade by Giuseppe Piermarini (1784–1801) on PIAZZA FONTANA (Pl. II,11). This square is associated with one of the most disquieting episodes in recent Italian history after a terrorist bomb killed 16 people here (and wounded 88) in 1969.

The north side of Piazza del Duomo is connected with Piazza della Scala by the colossal **Galleria Vittorio Emanuele II** (Pl. II,7). This huge glass-roofed shopping arcade, with cafés and restaurants, was designed (1865) by Giuseppe Mengoni, who fell from the top and was killed a few days before the inauguration ceremony in 1878. It was financed by the City of Milan Improvement Company Ltd.

On the west side of Piazza del Duomo Via Mercanti leads past (right) **Palazzo dei Giureconsulti** (1560–64), recently restored and now used for exhibitions. The fine **Palazzo della Ragione** (Pl. II,11; right), erected in 1228–33 has an upper storey added in 1771, and remains of 13C frescoes inside. On its rear wall, in the peaceful PIAZZA MERCANTI, is a remarkable equestrian relief of 1233. In this old square (partly under restoration) is the Gothic **Loggia degli Osii** (1316) and the Baroque **Palazzo delle Scuole Palatine** (1645).

The Scala

PIAZZA DELLA SCALA, reached from Piazza Duomo by the Galleria Vittorio Emanuele, has a monument to Leonardo da Vinci (by Pietro Magni, 1872), surrounded by figures of his pupils, Boltraffio, Salaino, Cesare da Sesto and Marco d'Oggiono. Here is the **TEATRO DELLA SCALA** (Pl. II,7), famous in operatic art. It was begun in 1776 by Giuseppe Piermarini on the site of the church of Santa Maria della Scala, after the destruction by fire of the Regio Ducale Teatro. It opened in 1778 with *Europa Riconosciuta* by Antonio Salieri and Mattia Verazi. Works by Rossini, Donizetti, Bellini, Verdi and Puccini were first acclaimed here. From the beginning of this century its reputation was upheld by the legendary figure of Toscanini (who led the orchestra again in 1946 when the building was reopened after serious war damage).

Under the portico, to the left of the theatre, is the **Museo Teatrale alla Scala** (open 9–12, 14–18 exc. fest.), with a valuable collection relating to theatrical and operatic history. From the museum the theatre can be visited.

Opposite the Scala is ***Palazzo Marino** (Pl. II,7), the town hall, with a fine façade on Piazza San Fedele by Galeazzo Alessi (1553–58), who also designed the splendid Mannerist courtyard. The façade on Piazza Scala was completed by Luca Beltrami (1886–92). Behind is Piazza San Fedele, in which are a statue of Manzoni, and the church of **San Fedele**, begun by Tibaldi (1569) for St Charles Borromeo, and completed by Martino Basi and Francesco Maria Richini, with an elaborate pulpit.

From the Scala the busy and fashionable VIA MANZONI (Pl. II,7) leads northeast towards Piazza Cavour; No. 29, the Grand Hotel et de Milan (founded in 1865), still the most elegant hotel in Milan, was where Giuseppe Verdi died in 1901.

Museo Poldi Pezzoli

At No. 12 is the entrance to the *Museo Poldi Pezzoli (Pl. II,7), once the private residence of Gian Giacomo Poldi Pezzoli. It was bequeathed by him, with his art collection, to the city in 1879, and opened to the public in 1881. It is now a delightful well-run museum, open 9.30–12.30, 14.30–18 exc. Mon (Sat open until 19.30, and Apr–Sep closed on Sun afternoon).

In the entrance hall with the ticket office is a portrait of Poldi Pezzoli by Francesco Hayez. A delightful elliptical staircase, with a Baroque fountain and landscapes by Alessandro Magnasco, ascends to the main picture gallery on the **first floor**. To the left are the three little **Salette dei Lombardi**, with Madonnas by Vincenzo Foppa and Ambrogio Bergognone; a portrait by Vincenzo Foppa; *The Rest on the Flight* (with a charming landscape) by Andrea Solario; a Madonna by Boltraffio; and works by Luini and the Lombard school.

Beyond the vestibule is the **Antechamber** (or **Sala degli Stranieri**) with paintings by Cranach (portraits of Luther and his wife). The **Saletta degli Stucchi** contains porcelain from Meissen, Doccia and Capodimonte. The **Salone Dorato** has the masterpieces of the collection: a *Madonna and Child, and *Portrait of a Man* by Mantegna; a Pietà by Giovanni Bellini; a Pietà and *Madonna by Botticelli; *St Nicholas of Tolentino* by Piero della Francesca; and a famous *portrait of a lady by Antonio Pollaiolo (or his brother Piero).

The three rooms beyond contain the **Emilio Visconti Venosta collection**, including a portrait of Cardinal Ascanio Sforza by the Lombard school (c 1490) and a small Cross painted on both sides attributed to Raphael. Also the Bruno Falck donation of antique clocks and scientific instruments, and a series of portraits, mostly by Vittore Ghislandi of Bergamo (1655–1743).

Beyond the Salone Dorato and the Saletta degli Stucchi (right) is the **Sala Nera**, so called from its decoration (partly preserved) in ivory and ebony. It contains a Florentine table in pietre dure and a statue of Faith by Lorenzo Bartolini. The beautiful painting of *Artemesia is attributed to the 'Maestro di Griselda' (recently also attributed to Luca Signorelli). Also here are works by Bergognone and Sassoferrato, and a 16C Flemish triptych. As well as examples of glass (15C–19C) from Murano, the **Sala dei Vetri Antichi di Murano** contains 17C–19C miniatures. The **Saletta di Dante** is an interesting room decorated at the end of the 19C in the neo-Gothic style. The marble bust of Rosa Poldi Pezzoli is by Lorenzo Bartolini.

From the Sala Nera is the entrance to the **Sala del Palma**, with a portrait of a courtesan by Palma il Vecchio, and a small painting by Giovanni Battista Moroni. Also displayed here is the Portaluppi collection of some 200 sundials of the 16C–19C. Beyond are the two **Sale Trivulzio**. The first has paintings by Bernardo Strozzi, Alessandro Magnasco, and Giuseppe Ribera, as well as Islamic bronzes (14C–16C). The second, the **Sala dei Bronzetti**, has small Renaissance bronzes, and a Hellenistic head of the young Bacchus (2C BC).

Beyond the Sala del Palma is the **Gabinetto degli Ori** which contains a precious collection of ancient jewellery and goldsmiths' work, and medieval religious bronzes and Limoges enamels. The **Sala del Settecento Veneto** has works by Guardi (*Gondolas on the Venetian lagoon), Rosalba Carriera, and Gian Battista Tiepolo. **Sala del Perugino**. Works by Cima da Conegliano, Francesco Morone, Andrea Previtali, Mariotto Albertinelli (a tiny portable *altar), Perugino, Biagio di Antonio di Firenze, and Lorenzo Lotto. The **Saletta dei Trecenteschi** contains 14C works by Jacopo Bellini, Carlo Crivelli, Cosmè Tura, Lazzaro Bastiani, and Bernardo Daddi.

On the **ground floor** is the **Sala dell'affresco** named after its ceiling fresco by Carlo Innocenzo Carloni. Here is displayed a splendid Persian *carpet with hunting scenes, signed and dated 1542–43. Other precious carpets and tapestries are displayed here in rotation. The **Sala dei Tessuti** is being arranged to contain the Bertini collection of textiles, which has 268 examples from the 14C to the 19C. Some of these will be displayed in rotation, and there will be access to the rest of the collection by a computer installed here. On the other side of the Sala dell'affresco is the **lace collection** (displayed in cupboards), which includes examples of Italian and Flemish work from the 16C–19C, and a **library** (which includes books printed in 1495–1515 by Aldo Manuzio). Another room off the entrance hall displays the **armoury**, with 14C–19C arms and armour.

VIA MORONE (Pl. II,7) is a characteristic 19C street. At No. 1 is the **Museo Manzoniano** (open 9.30–12, 14–16 exc. Sat, Mon and fest.) in the house where Alessandro Manzoni (1785–1873), author of *I Promessi Sposi*, lived from 1814 until his death here in 1873. It contains mementoes of Italy's most famous novelist, who met Balzac here in 1837. In Piazza Belgioioso is the huge Palazzo Belgioioso by Giuseppe Piermarini (1772). In Via Omenoni (right), the house of the sculptor Leone Leoni is decorated with caryatids.

Museo Bagatti Valsecchi

Further along Via Manzoni, VIA MONTENAPOLEONE, another interesting 19C street, with fashionable shops, diverges right. At No. 5 Via del Gesù is the entrance to the *Museo Bagatti Valsecchi (Pl. II,4), open 13–17 exc. Mon. The palace was built by the brothers Fausto and Giuseppe Bagatti Valsecchi in 1876–87 in the style of the Lombard Renaissance and furnished by them with 16C works of art or excellent 19C imitations by Lombard craftsmen. It was the family home until 1974 when the Bagatti Valsecchi established a foundation and sold the palace to the Regional government of Lombardy. Its main façade is in Via Santo Spirito (opposite another fine palace in red brick also built by the brothers in 1895 in 15C style). The palace and its contents represent an extremely interesting and well preserved example of the eclectic taste of 19C collectors. It was opened to the public in 1994 as a delightful private museum, carefully looked after by volunteer custodians. All the works are well labelled also in English.

The two brothers lived in separate apartments in the palace on either side of the drawing room, gallery of arms, and dining room which they shared. The rooms are richly decorated with carved ceilings, fireplaces, doorways, floors and wall hangings, and filled with a miscellany of furniture and works of art, some of it Renaissance and some exquisitely made 19C imitations commissioned by the brothers to fit the rooms.

The main **staircase** leads up to a **vestibule**, beyond which a marble portal carved in 1884 in Renaissance style gives access to the **Fresco Room**, with a fresco by Antonio Boselli (1496). The **Bevilacqua Room** takes its name from a painting by Ambrogio Bevilacqua. Beyond the panelled **Library**, with a collection of 17C sundials, is **Fausto's bedroom** with an intricately carved 16C bed and two paintings by Giampietrino. Beyond the dressing room and bathroom, with ingenious plumbing masked by Renaissance carvings, is the **Cupola Gallery**, interesting for its architecture and containing a collection of ceramics.

The three rooms of **Giuseppe's apartment** have a magnificent old stove, a late 15C Venetian painting of the Blessed Lorenzo Giustiniani, a painting attributed to Giovanni Bellini, and an early 17C Sicilian bed. The largest room in the house is the **Drawing Room**, with a 19C fireplace (made up of 16C fragments) and red wall hangings. The long **Arms Gallery** was created to display the collection of 16C and 17C armour. The **Dining Room** has a pair of sideboards, one 16C and one a 19C copy. The walls are covered with 16C tapestries. The cupboards contain 16C Murano glass and Faenza ceramics. Beyond the study a staircase leads down to the Via Santo Spirito entrance.

The Brera Gallery

Via Verdi and Via Brera lead north from the Scala to **Palazzo di Brera** (Pl. II, 3), famous for its picture gallery. The building was begun by Francesco Maria Richini in 1651 on the site of the medieval church of Santa Maria di Brera, the nave of which survives. The main portal is by Giuseppe Piermarini (1780). In the monumental **courtyard**, by Richini, is a heroic statue in bronze of Napoleon I by Antonio Canova (1809; the marble version of the statue is in Apsley House, London). The Brera is a centre of the arts and sciences in Lombardy: in addition to the picture gallery, it contains the Accademia di Belle Arti, the Biblioteca Nazionale, with some 1,000,000 vols, including 2357 incunabula and 2000 MSS, the Astronomical Observatory, and the Institute of Science and Letters.

The ****PINACOTECA DI BRERA** (open 9–17.30 exc. Mon; fest. 9–12.30) is one of the most famous picture galleries in Italy, and contains the finest existing collection of Northern Italian painting. It is extremely well displayed, and the rearrangement of the gallery chronologically and by schools is almost complete (rooms VIII and X–XIII are expected to reopen in 1997). There are long-term plans to open the adjacent Palazzo Citterio in Via Brera as an extension to the gallery to exhibit the 19C and 20C works and the Jesi collection.

The Pinacoteca was founded in the 18C by the Accademia di Belle Arti, and was enlarged through acquisitions and paintings from Lombard and Venetian churches before it was officially inaugurated in 1809. The collection has continued to grow in this century with numerous donations. By no means all the collection is permanently on view. Some rooms are closed when there is a shortage of custodians; scholars can sometimes ask for special permission to see them.

All the rooms are clearly numbered in Roman numerals as on the Plan on p 52, and the pictures are well labelled. The standard of the paintings is exceptionally high, and only some have been mentioned in the description below.

Stairs lead up from the far side of the courtyard to the loggia on the **first floor**, off which is the entrance to the gallery with the ticket office. Beyond a small room with the self-portrait of Francesco Hayez, the long gallery (**Room I**) temporarily displays early 20C works (particularly the Futurists) from the **Jesi collection**, including works by Umberto Boccioni, Mario Sironi, Giacomo

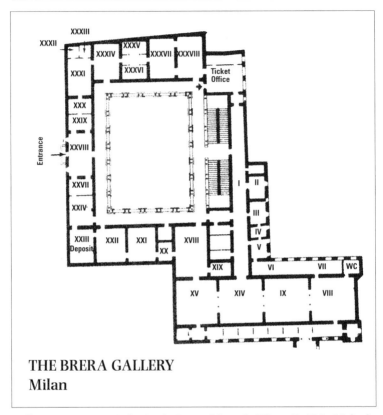

THE BRERA GALLERY
Milan

Balla, Gino Severini, Carlo Carrà, Giorgio Morandi, Filippo De Pisis, Medardo Rosso and Arturo Martini. New acquisitions are also hung here, including a work by Massimo Campigli. In a little room off the gallery, the **Mocchirolo chapel**, frescoed by a close follower of Giovanni da Milano, has been reconstructed.

The chronological display begins in **Rooms II and III** with 13C Italian paintings, including works by Giovanni da Milano, Ambrogio Lorenzetti (*Madonna and Child), and Bernardo Daddi. A fine *polyptych by Gentile da Fabriano is displayed in **Room IV. Rooms V and VI** contain works of the 15C and 16C Venetian school. In Room V is a polyptych by Antonio Vivarini and Giovanni d'Alemagna. Room VI contains works by 15C painters from Padua and the Veneto, including some masterpieces by **Mantegna:** his famous *Dead Christ, with remarkable foreshortening, and a *polyptych representing St Luke the Evangelist with saints (1453). Also three exquisite works by **Giovanni Bellini**: a *Pietà, *Madonna Greca* (one of his most beautiful paintings), and a Madonna and Child in a landscape (1510). **Vittore Carpaccio** is also well represented with scenes from the life of the Virgin, two works from the Scuola degli Albanesi in Venice, and *St Stephen Disputing with the Doctors* (1514). *St Peter Martyr with Saints, and *Madonna and Child Enthroned* are two works by **Cima da Conegliano**, and the St Sebastian here is by Liberale da Verona. **Room VII** displays 16C Venetian portraits by Titian, Lorenzo Lotto, Torbido, and Tintoretto.

Room VIII (to reopen in 1997) will display *St Mark Preaching in Alexandria*, a splendid large painting commissioned from **Gentile** and **Giovanni Bellini** by the Scuola Grande di San Marco in Venice. Also here will be displayed works by Michele da Verona, and Giovanni Battista Martini da Udine.

Room IX (16C Venetian paintings). Works by Jacopo Bassano; **Veronese**, *Agony in the Garden, St Anthony Abbot with Saints, Supper in the House of Simon, *Baptism and Temptation of Christ, Last Supper*; **Tintoretto**, *Deposition, and Saints beneath the Cross*; *Finding of the body of St Mark at Alexandria*; Titian, St Jerome; Lorenzo Lotto, Pietà (1545).

Rooms X–XIII are not expected to reopen until the end of 1997. They will display works by Bonifacio Bembo; *frescoes by Donato Bramante; paintings and frescoes by Bernardino Luini; and frescoes by Bergognone.

Room XIV (16C Venetian school). Works by Palma Vecchio; Paris Bordon (*Baptism of Christ*), Bonifacio Veronese, Giovanni Cariani, Giovanni Battista Moroni and Gerolamo Savoldo. **Room XV** (15C–16C Lombard paintings and frescoes). Works by Marco d'Oggiono and Bergognone. The *Pala Sforzesca (Madonna enthroned with doctors of the Church and the family of Lodovico il Moro) is by an unknown Lombard painter (c 1490–1520), known from this painting as the **'Maestro della Pala Sforzesca'**. Also here are works by Vincenzo Foppa (*polyptych), Bramantino (*Bartolomeo Suardi*), and Gaudenzio Ferrari.

The collection continues in **Room XVIII** (16C Lombard paintings). Works by Callisto Piazza (*Baptism of Christ*), Giulio Campi, Boccaccino, Bernardino Campi, Giovan Paolo Lomazzo and Antonio Campi, and *portrait of Alda Gambara by Altobello Melone. **Room XIX** contains a very fine collection of paintings by followers of Leonardo da Vinci. Portraits by Giovanni Ambrogio de Predis, Andrea Solario, and **Giovanni Antonio Boltraffio** (*Gerolamo Casio*), and works by Bartolomeo Veneto, Giampietrino, Cesare da Sesto, **Bernardino Luini** (*Madonna del Roseto*), and Ambrogio Bergognone.

Room XX (15C Ferrarese and Emilian schools). **Francesco del Cossa**, *St John the Baptist, *St Peter*; works by Lorenzo Costa, Gian Francesco Maineri, Marco Palmezzano, Francesco Zaganelli, and Filippo Mazzola. **Room XXI** displays polyptychs by 15C painters from the Marches, and a delightful group of works by **Carlo Crivelli**: Crucifixion, *Madonna 'della Candeletta*, *Coronation of the Virgin and Pietà (1483), and a *triptych painted for the Duomo of Camerino. **Room XXII** (15C–16C Ferrarese and Emilian schools): Francesco and Bernardo Zaganelli, Nicolò Rondinelli, Ercole de' Roberti, and Giovanni Luteri. **Room XXIII** contains two works by Correggio.

Room XXIV displays the two most famous works in the collection: **Raphael's** *Marriage of the Virgin** (the *Sposalizio*, 1504), the masterpiece of his Umbrian period, with a remarkable circular temple in the background; and **Piero della Francesca's** *Montefeltro altarpiece**, with the Madonna surrounded by angels and saints, in the presence of Federigo, duke of Montefeltro. This is Piero's last known work and has a highly refined architectural setting. Also displayed here is a processional standard, an early work by Luca Signorelli, painted on both sides with the *Flagellation and Madonna and Child, and *Christ at the Column* (from Chiaravalle), the only known panel painting by **Donato Bramante**.

The collection continues in **Room XXVII** (central Italian paintings of the 15C–16C). Works by Gerolamo Genga, Luca Signorelli, Francesco Salviati, Giovanni Antonio Sogliani and Agnolo Bronzino. **Room XXVIII** contains works of the 17C Bolognese school: **Federico Barocci** (*Martyrdom of St Vitale*), Ludovico Carracci, **Annibale Carracci** (*Samaritan at the Well*), Guercino, **Guido Reni** (*Saints Peter and Paul). **Room XXIX** (Caravaggio and his followers). Works by **Caravaggio** (*Supper at Emmaus*), Mattia Preti, Jusepe de Ribera, Giovanni Battista Caracciolo, and Orazio Gentileschi (*Three Martyrs*). **Room XXX** displays works by the 17C Lombard school (Giulio Cesare Procaccini, Daniele Crespi, Giovanni Battista Crespi, Morazzone and Tanzio).

Room XXXI. Flemish and Italian 17C paintings: Pietro da Cortona, Bernardo Strozzi, Evaristo Baschenis, Rubens, Van Dyck. **Room XXXII** displays16C and 17C Flemish and Dutch paintings including works by the 'Maestro di Anversa' (1518), a triptych by Jan de Beer, and *St Francis* by El Greco. **Room XXXIII** contains portraits by Rembrandt (of his sister) and Van Dyck, and works by Brueghel the Elder. **Room XXXIV** has 17C works by Pierre Subleyras, Giuseppe Maria Crespi (*Crucifixion), Sebastiano Ricci, Luca Giordano (*Ecce Homo), and Giovanni Battista Tiepolo.

Rooms XXXV and **XXXVI**, with 18C paintings, are on either side of a corridor in which are displayed portraits by Sir Joshua Reynolds and Anton Raphael Mengs. Room XXXV has Venetian works by Giovanni Battista Tiepolo, Francesco Guardi, Francesco Zugno, Bernardo Bellotto, Canaletto, Giovanni Battista Piazzetta, and Rosalba Carriera. In Room XXXVI are genre scenes by Giacomo Ceruti and portraits by Vittore Ghislandi.

Room XXXVII contains 19C Italian works by Giovanni Fattori, Silvestro Lega (the *Pergolato*), Zandomeneghi, Prud'hon, and portraits by Francesco Hayez, Andrea Appiani and Sir Thomas Lawrence. In **Room XXXVIII** is displayed a version of Giuseppe Pellizza da Volpedo's famous painting entitled the *Quarto Stato*, and Boccioni's self portrait.

In Via Brera, in the little piazza beside the gallery, is a monument to the painter Francesco Hayez, by Francesco Barzaghi (1898). The 18C **Palazzo Citterio** is being restored as an extension of the Brera (see above). The **Botanical Gardens** here were founded in 1783 (admission only with special permission from the Biology Department of the University). On the other side of Via Brera is Palazzo Cusani (No. 15), by Giovanni Ruggeri (1719), now a local military head-quarters. Via del Carmine leads to the 15C church of **Santa Maria del Carmine** (Pl. II,2), with a façade completed in 1879, and a fine Baroque chapel decorated by Camillo Procaccini.

Just behind the Brera is VIA BORGONUOVO with a series of fine palaces with interesting courtyards. At No. 23 is **Palazzo Moriggia**, rebuilt in the 18C by Piermarini, which houses the **Museo del Risorgimento** (Pl. II,3; open 9.30–17.30 exc. Mon). The exhibits, arranged chronologically in 14 rooms, include material dating from the arrival of Napoleon in Lombardy in 1796 up to the taking of Rome in 1870. There is also a good library.

San Marco

The church of San Marco (Pl. II,3), north of the Brera, dates from 1254, but the interior was altered in the Baroque period. On the mock-Gothic façade (1873) the doorway and three statuettes date from the 14C. Verdi's *Requiem* received its first performance here.

In the interior the nave is exceptionally long. **South aisle**. The first chapel has frescoes and an altarpiece by Gian Paolo Lomazzo (1571). At the end of the aisle, Nativity by Legnanino. In the **south transept** is the tomb of the Blessed Lanfranco da Settala (died 1264), ascribed to Giovanni di Balduccio, and mid-14C frescoes. The **presbytery** has a vault and apse frescoed in the early 17C by Il Genovesino (who also painted the two paintings in the choir), and paintings by Camillo Procaccini and Cerano. The altar dates from 1816. In the **north transept** are paintings by Legnanino. In the **north aisle** are altarpieces by Legnanino, Camillo Procaccini, and Giulio Cesare Procaccini. In the third chapel is an interesting grisaille fresco by a painter of the Leonardesque school. A room contains frescoes of the late 13C Lombard school which have been detached from the campanile.

To the north, in Via Mosca, is the 16C church of **Sant'Angelo** (Pl. I,7), with paintings and frescoes by Camillo Procaccini (in poor condition).

The church of **San Simpliciano** (Pl. II,2; being restored), to the west, dedicated to the successor of St Ambrose in the episcopal chair, was probably founded by St Ambrose himself in the 4C and, despite the alterations of the 12C, stands—save for the façade and the apse—largely in its original form. Eighteen huge window embrasures were revealed after 1945. The interior contains, in the restored Romanesque apse, the *Coronation of the Virgin, a fine fresco by Bergognone, masked by the towering altar. At the entrance to the presbytery, beneath the organs, are frescoes of Saints by Aurelio Luini.

Over 1km further north is the **Cimitero Monumentale** (Pl. I,2), designed by Carlo Maciachini in 1863–66. It has a central pantheon, or *famedio*, containing the tombs of Alessandro Manzoni (1785–1873), the novelist and Carlo Cattaneo (1801–69), patriot and scientific writer. Some of the monumental tomb sculpture is to be displayed in a museum here.

The Castello Sforzesco

The castle can be reached easily from Piazza del Duomo on the underground (Line 1) in two stops (Cairoli station), or from Piazza della Scala by tram 1.

The spacious FORO BUONAPARTE, LARGO CAIROLI (with a monument to Garibaldi by Ettore Ximenes, 1895), and PIAZZA CASTELLO, with its trees, were all designed in a huge hemicycle in 1884 in front of the *Castello Sforzesco (Pl. II,1,2). This was the stronghold built for Francesco Sforza in 1451–66 on the site of a 14C castle of the Visconti. After a long period of use as barracks, it was restored by Luca Beltrami (1893–1904). Badly damaged by bombing in 1943, when two-thirds of the archives and many other treasures were lost, it was again carefully restored. It now contains important art collections and cultural institutions, and various projects for the reutilisation and restoration of parts of the castle have been under discussion for years.

The Castello is square in plan; on the façade are three towers, of which the

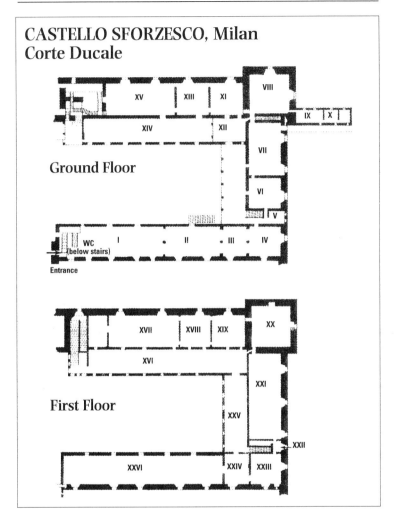

CASTELLO SFORZESCO, Milan
Corte Ducale

Ground Floor

VIII

XV   XIII   XI

IX   X

XIV   XII

VII

VI

V

I   II   III   IV

WC
(below stairs)

Entrance

First Floor

XVII   XVIII   XIX   XX

XVI

XXI

XXV

XXII

XXVI   XXIV   XXIII

central one is the **Filarete Tower**, destroyed by an explosion of powder in 1521 and rebuilt by Beltrami following the supposed design of the original. The entrance to the castle from Largo Cairoli is beneath the tower which gives access to the huge **Piazza d'Armi**, the main courtyard. Almost in the centre of the far side is the 15C **Torre di Bona di Savoia**, beyond which to the left is the **Rocchetta**, with a courtyard, which served as a keep, and on the right is the **Corte Ducale**, the residential part of the castle, with a charming courtyard. Here is the entrance to the *MUSEO D'ARTE ANTICA** and the **PINACOTECA** (open 9.30–17.30 exc. Mon). The large collections of sculpture, paintings, furniture, musical instruments, and decorative arts are beautifully arranged and well labelled (only a few of the works are mentioned below).

Sculpture is displayed on the **ground floor**. **Room I** contains fragments from ancient churches and other Byzantine and Romanesque remains, including a 6C marble portrait head supposedly of the Empress Theodora. **Room II.** Visconti tombs by Bonino da Campione (1363). In **Room III**, beneath a Lombard frescoed ceiling (mid-15C) are remains of the façade of Santa Maria di Brera and statues from the east gate of the city, by Giovanni di Balduccio of Pisa, and a 14C pavement tomb with an effigy thought to be that of Bona di Savoia. **Room IV**, with the arms of Philip II of Spain and Mary Tudor in the vault, contains a *sepulchral monument of the Rusca family by a late 14C Lombard master.

East Wing. Beyond a small chapel (**Room V**) with 14C Venetian sculpture, **Room VI** contains 12C reliefs from the old Porta Romana, showing the triumph of the Milanese over Barbarossa (1171). **Room VII**, with frescoed escutcheons of the Dukes of Milan, is hung with 17C Brussels tapestries. Here is displayed the Gonfalon of Milan designed by Giuseppe Meda (1566) and a statue of Adam by Stoldo Lorenzi.

The ***Sala delle Asse** (**Room VIII**), at the northeast corner of the castle, has remarkable frescoed decoration in the vault designed in 1498 by **Leonardo da Vinci**, but repainted. The ilex branches and leaves are used in a complicated architectural structure in which the form of the octagon recurs. On the far wall are two fascinating *fragments of monchrome tempera decoration by the hand of Leonardo (1498), depicting tree trunks with branches and roots growing out of cracks in stratified rock formations. In the centre of the room the Belgioioso collection of 17C Flemish and Dutch paintings is exhibited, including a monochrome sketch of three female figures and putti by Rubens, a self portrait by Gabriel Metsu, a river scene by Solomon van Ruysdael, and portraits by Joachim Wtewael.

Off the Sala delle Asse are two small rooms over the moat. **Room IX** contains Sforza portraits attributed to Bernardino Luini and reliefs by Bambaia. In **Room X** is an oval low relief carved on both faces by Pierino da Vinci.

In the **north wing**, **Room XI** (the Sala dei Ducali) is decorated with coats of arms showing the ancestry of Galeazzo Maria Sforza. It contains a relief by Agostino di Duccio from the Tempio Malatestiano at Rimini and good 15C sculptures. The former chapel (**Room XII**) has good frescoes (restored) by Bonifacio Bembo and Stefano de' Fedeli and assistants (1466–76). Here is displayed a recently acquired painting of *St Benedict by Antonello da Messina. The seated statue of the Madonna and Child is a Lombard work of the late 15C, and the standing Madonna is by Pietro Solari. Outside can be seen the Renaissance Portico of the Elephant, named after a faded fresco. The Sala delle Colombine (**Room XIII**), on the right, has red and gold fresco decorations with the arms of Bona di Savoia, and sculpture by Amadeo and Cristoforo Mantegazza.

The long Sala Verde (**Room XIV**) is divided by Renaissance doorways salvaged from Milanese palaces: that from the Banco Mediceo (1455) is by Michelozzo. Displayed here are tombs, armorial sculptures, and a fine collection of armour. The Sala degli Scarlioni (**Room XV**) has the ***effigy of Gaston de Foix** and ***reliefs from his tomb** (1525), masterpieces by **Bambaia**. In the second part of the room, on a lower level, uncomfortably placed on a Roman altar, is the **Rondanini Pietà**, the unfinished last work of **Michelangelo**, named from the palace in Rome where it used to be displayed. The sculptor worked at intervals on this moving, but pathetic statue during the last nine years of his life, and up to

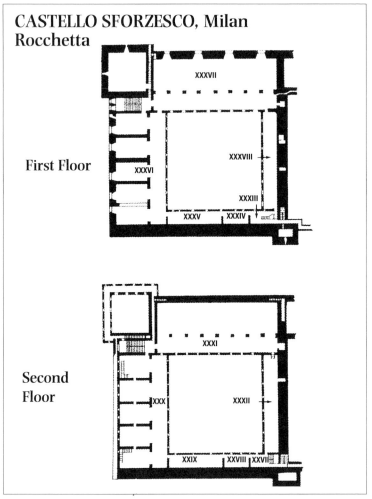

CASTELLO SFORZESCO, Milan
Rocchetta

First Floor

XXXVII

XXXVI

XXXVIII →

XXXIII

XXXV   XXXIV

Second Floor

XXXI

XXX

XXXII →

XXIX   XXVIII   XXVII

six days before his death. According to Vasari, he reused a block of marble in which he had already roughed out a Pietà on a different design and on a smaller scale. A fine bronze head of Michelangelo by Daniele da Volterra (1564) is also displayed here.

From the corner a wooden bridge leads out into the Corte Ducale across a subterranean court with a 16C fountain. On the left stairs lead up to the **first floor** (**Rooms XVI–XIX**) which contains the splendid collection of *furniture arranged to give a progressive chronological impression of Lombard interiors of the 15C–18C.

Steps lead up from Room XIX to the **Pinacoteca** (Rooms XX–XXVI). In the vaulted tower (**Room XX**) are some beautiful paintings: the *Pala Trivulzio, by **Mantegna** (1497); a polyptych signed and dated 1462 by Benedetto Bembo; a superb *Madonna and Child by **Giovanni Bellini**; and a very unusual work (the *Madonna of Humility*) by Filippo Lippi. **Room XXI** contains Lombard Renaissance works by Vincenzo Foppa, Bergognone, and Bramantino; works by followers of Leonardo, including Boltraffio and Cesare da Sesto; and paintings by Sodoma and Correggio. The little **Room XXII** has a small Crucifixion attributed to Marcello Venusti. **Room XXIII** displays Lombard works by Nuvolone, Cerano and Morazzone, and **Room XXIV** late 16C and early 17C northern Italian schools (including Moncalvo).

Room XXV contains a magnificent display of **portraits** by Giovanni Bellini, Correggio, Giovanni Antonio Boltraffio (*Lady in Red*), Baldassarre d'Este, Lorenzo Lotto (*Boy Holding a Book*), Agnolo Allori, Giovanni Battista Moroni, Tintoretto and Titian. At the end of the room on the right wall is a fine portrait of *Henrietta Maria of France by Van Dyck.

The long **Room XXVI** contains 17C and 18C Lombard, Neapolitan, and Venetian works (Daniele Crespi, Cerano, Morazzone, Giacomo Ceruti, Bernardino Strozzi, Giuseppe Ribera, Alessandro Magnasco, Sebastiano Ricci, Giovanni Battista Tiepolo, Francesco Guardi and Canaletto).

It is now necessary to return downstairs to the entrance (Room I, see above). From Room I stairs lead up to the **first floor** of the **Rocchetta** where the *decorative arts** are displayed. **Room XXXVI** contains a splendid large **collection of musical instruments**, with lutes, an outstanding group of wind instruments, a clavichord of 1503, a spinet played on by the 14-year-old Mozart, and a fortepiano by Muzio Clementi. There is also a rich collection of musical MSS and autographs. The Ball Court (**Room XXXVII**), hung with *tapestries of the Months from designs by Bramantino (c 1503), has more musical instruments.

From here return to Room XXXIII and go upstairs to the **second floor**. **Room XXVIII** contains wrought-iron work. **Rooms XXIX and XXX** contain a large collection of *ceramics, both Italian and foreign. Off Room XXX is displayed an interesting collection (formed in 1858) of pre-Columbian works from Peru and Argentina, dating from the 2C BC to the 16C. Stairs lead up to a mezzanine above Room XXX with a collection of costumes from the 1920s and 1930s (including some gorgeous evening gowns). **Room XXXI**, overlooking the ball court (see above) has a good display of European 18C and 19C porcelain. **Room XXXII** contains goldsmiths' work, enamels, *ivories, church silver, and small bronzes. Return to Room XXVII from where stairs descend to the exit.

Archaeological Museum

Three sections of the Archaeological Museum are also displayed in the castle. From the Corte Ducale is the entrance to a basement room with the **epigraphy section**. This includes 101 Roman inscriptions from Milan arranged in four series: those concerning public life; religious inscriptions; community affairs (merchants, artisans and tradesmen); and private family life.

In the arcaded ***courtyard of the Rocchetta**, in the design of which both Filarete and Bramante had a hand, is the entrance to the **Egyptian section**, arranged in the basement, which contains an interesting collection of objects dating from the Old Kingdom to the age of Ptolemy, illustrating the funerary cult of ancient Egypt, with sarcophagi, mummies and books of the Dead (papyri), and household and personal objects, canopic vases, jewellery, funerary masks, stelae, etc.

Also off the courtyard is the entrance to the **Prehistoric section**, which includes a room containing material from Lombardy dating from the late Bronze Age to the Roman period, with the Golasecca culture (9C–5C BC) particularly well represented.

Elsewhere in the castle (admission to scholars) are the Archivio Storico Civico, the Biblioteca Trivulziana (with an oriental art centre), a medal collection, and the Bertarelli collection of prints and maps.

Parco Sempione

On the far side of the castle is the **PARCO SEMPIONE** (Pl. II,1), a large park of 47 hectares laid out by Emilio Alemagna in 1893 on the site of a 15C Ducal park. It contains a fountain by Giorgio De Chirico. The **Palazzo dell'Arte** (Pl. I,6), built in 1931–33 by Giovanni Muzio, has recently been restored as an important exhibition centre. The **Aquarium** (Pl. I,6) in a fine Art Nouveau building of 1906 (open 9.30–17.30 exc. Mon), with delightful 'aquatic' decorations on the exterior, has marine and freshwater fish, and important study collections. The **Stadium** (Pl. I,6) was first built by Luigi Canonica in 1806-07. The high tower (110m), made of aluminium, was erected in 1933 by Giò Ponte and Cesare Chiodi. The fine equestrian monument to Napoleon III is by Francesco Barzaghi (1881). At the far end of the park is the **Arco della Pace** (Pl. I,5), a triumphal arch modelled on the Arch of Severus in Rome, built by Luigi Cagnola in 1807–38. It was begun in honour of Napoleon I, but was dedicated to Peace by Ferdinand I of Austria on its completion. It marks the beginning of the **CORSO SEMPIONE** (Pl. I,1), part of the 182km-long historic Simplon Road, constructed by order of Napoleon from Geneva to Sesto Calende across the Simplon Pass (1800–05).

Sant'Ambrogio

Sant'Ambrogio and the Museum of Science and Technology can be reached from Piazza Duomo (Via Mazzini) by Bus 54.

The basilica of *Sant'Ambrogio (Pl. II,9; closed 12–14.30), the most interesting church in Milan, was the prototype of the Lombard basilica. Founded by St Ambrose, Bishop of Milan, it was built in 379–86 beside a Christian cemetery, and enlarged in the 9C and again after 1080. The present building is the result of numerous careful restorations, and the dating of the various parts of the building is still uncertain. After a radical restoration in the 19C, it had to be repaired again after serious war damage in 1943.

Exterior. The splendid **atrium** in front of the church, on an early Christian plan, was probably built in 1088–99, but was reconstructed in 1150. The austere **façade** consists of a five-bayed narthex below, with five arches above, graduated to fit the gable with decorative arcading. The south or monks' campanile dates from the 9C, the higher canons' campanile on the north is a fine Lombard tower of 1128–44, crowned with a loggia of 1889. The great **doorway** has wood imposts made up of fragments from the 8C and 10C (heavily restored in the 18C); the bronze doors date from the 11C–12C.

The beautiful **interior** has a low rib-vaulted nave divided from the side aisles by wide arcades supported by massive pillars beneath a matroneum. There are no transepts, and beyond the tower over the crossing, with its magnificent ciborium, are three deep apses, the centre one raised above the crypt.

On the right is a statue of Pius IX (1880). On the left, beyond a column with a bronze serpent of the 10C, is the *pulpit, reconstituted from fragments of the 11C and early 12C saved after the vault collapsed in 1196 and one of the most remarkable Romanesque monuments known. Beneath it is a Roman palaeochristian *sarcophagus (4C).

In the **south aisle**, the first chapel has a fresco attributed to Gaudenzio Ferrari and Giovanni Battista Della Cerva. The second chapel has an altarpiece by Gaudenzio Ferrari, and two detached frescoes by Giovanni Battista Tiepolo. In the sixth chapel, *Legend of St George*, by Bernardino Lanino. The last chapel in this aisle dates from the 18C, with an altarpiece by Andrea Lanzani. To the left, beyond a fine 18C wrought-iron screen is another 18C chapel with frescoes by Ferdinando Porta. At the end is the **Sacello di San Vittore in Ciel d'oro** (coin-operated light), a sepulchral chapel built in a Christian cemetery in the 4C and altered later. Its name refers to the splendid 5C *mosaics, with a golden dome and six panels representing saints (including St Ambrose) on the walls. At the end of the south aisle is a 6C sarcophagus.

In the **north aisle** (first chapel) is a fresco of the Redeemer (with very unusual iconography) by Bergognone, and (third chapel), a tondo attributed to Bernardino Luini.

In the **sanctuary** (light in north aisle; fee), under the dome (which was rebuilt in the 13C and restored in the 19C), is the great *ciborium, thought to date from the 9C. The shafts of the columns, however, are probably of the time of St Ambrose. The four sides of the baldacchino are decorated with reliefs in coloured stucco in the Byzantine style (mid-10C). The *altar has a magnificent and justly celebrated casing presented in 835 by Archbishop Angilberto II, made of gold and silver plates sculptured in relief, with enamel and gems, the work of Volvinius, and representing scenes from the Lives of Christ and St Ambrose. In the apse are mosaics of the 4C or 8C reset in the 18C and restored after the Second World War, and the 9C marble Bishop's throne.

The **crypt** contains the bodies of Saints Ambrose, Gervase, and Protasius in a shrine of 1897. From the east end of the north aisle a door admits to the Portico della Canonica, with columns carved in imitation of tree trunks, which was left unfinished by Bramante in 1499 (and reconstructed after the war). A second side was added in 1955. The upper part houses the **Museo di Sant'Ambrogio** (open 10–12, 15–17; fest. & Sat 15–17; closed Tue and in Aug). This contains textiles including the 'Dalmatic of St Ambrose' (protected by a curtain); early Christian mosaic fragments; wood fragments (4C and 9C) from the old doors of the basilica; medieval capitals; a triptych by Bernardino Zenale; frescoes by Bergognone and Bernardino Luini; a 15C embroidered altar frontal; and two 17C Flemish tapestries. The illuminated MSS (10C–18C; removed), include a missal of Gian Galeazzo Visconti (1395). The church treasury includes a 12C Cross and the Reliquary of the Innocents (early 15C). Most of the frescoes of the 15C Oratorio della Passione by the school of Bernardino Luini were detached in 1869 and sold to the Victoria and Albert Museum in London.

To the north of the church is a war memorial erected in 1928 by Giovanni Muzio. In the piazza is the **Università Cattolica**, founded in 1921 and of extremely high academic standing. It is housed in the ex-monastery of Sant'Ambrogio, which includes two fine cloisters designed by Bramante: the Ionic cloister was finished by Cristoforo Solari in 1513, and the Doric cloister in 1620–30. During work to enlarge the buildings, Roman remains have come to light here.

At the beginning of Via San Vittore the Pusterla di Sant'Ambrogio, a gate in the medieval city walls, was reconstructed in 1939. Nearby in Via Carducci is a castellated palace built in 1910 by Adolfo Coppedè. Further on is **San Vittore al Corpo** (Pl. I,9), in part by Galeazzo Alessi. The dark interior contains important early 17C works including frescoes and paintings by Camillo Procaccini and Ambrogio Figino. The cupola is frescoed by Moncalvo and Daniele Crespi, and the beautifully carved choir stalls date from around 1583. In the north aisle are frescoes and paintings by Daniele Crespi, an altarpiece by Pompeo Batoni, and paintings by Pierre Subleyras.

Museum of Science and Technology 'Leonardo da Vinci'

The old Olivetan convent (1507), which still contains a collection of frescoes by Bernardino Luini, was rebuilt in 1949–53 after war damage to house the huge *MUSEUM OF SCIENCE AND TECHNOLOGY 'LEONARDO DA VINCI' (Pl. I,9). Open daily, exc. Mon, 9.30–16.50. The museum is much enjoyed by children. The vestibule contains frescoes of the 15C Lombard school. To the right in the **first cloister** are displayed ancient carriages and velocipedes. To the left is the library, with the cinema beyond.

Staircases take you up to the **first floor**. On the right is the Sala della Bifora (kept locked) with the Mauro collection of **goldsmiths' work and precious stones**. The gallery is devoted to **cinematography**. Rooms to the right demonstrate the evolution of the **graphic arts** (printing, typewriters, etc.). At the end of the gallery, to the right, is the long **Leonardo Gallery**, which extends the entire length of the first and second cloisters. Here are exhibited *models of machines and apparatus invented by Leonardo da Vinci*, of the greatest interest.

The rooms (right) which border the first cloister are devoted to **time measurement and sound**, including musical instruments and the reproduction of a lute-maker's shop. In the middle of the Leonardo Gallery are detached frescoes, and (right), the Sala delle Colonne, formerly the conventual library, used for exhibitions. Three galleries round the **second cloister** illustrate the science of **physics**, including electricity, acoustics, and nuclear reaction. Beyond the **astronomy** gallery are rooms devoted to **optics** and **radio and telecommunications** (with mementoes of Marconi).

At the end of the Leonardo Gallery stairs (right) lead down to the **lower floor** devoted to **metallurgy**, **petrochemical industries**, **and transport**, with a fine gallery of early motor cars. An **external pavilion**, in the form of a 19C railway station, contains **railway locomotives** (from *Bayard*, one of Stephenson's engines supplied from Newcastle for the Naples–Portici line in 1843) and rolling stock. Another huge **external pavilion** illustrates **air and sea transport**, with a splendid display of aeroplanes, along with relics of aeronautical history, and ships, including a naval training ship.

On the **ground floor** is the **Civico Museo Navale Didattico**, founded in 1922, with navigational instruments and models of ships.

Santa Maria delle Grazie and the Cenacolo

The Cenacolo (Santa Maria delle Grazie) can be reached by Tram 19 from near Piazza Duomo (Via Torino) as far as Via Monti.

From Via San Vittore, Via Zenale (right) leads to **SANTA MARIA DELLE GRAZIE** (Pl. I,9; closed 12–15), a church of brick and terracotta, with a very beautiful *exterior. It was erected in 1466–90 to the design of Guiniforte Solari. In 1492 Ludovico il Moro ordered the striking new choir and unusual domed crossing, and this has for long been attributed to Bramante, although it is now uncertain how much he was directly involved. The fine west portal is also usually attributed to Bramante.

Interior (closed 12–15). The nave vault and aisles have fine frescoed decoration of c 1482–85 (restored in 1937). In the aisles, between the chapels are good frescoes of Dominican saints attributed to Bernardo Butinone. In the **south aisle**, the first chapel has a fine tomb of the Della Torre family; in the third chapel are lunette frescoes attributed to Aurelio and Gian Piero Luini. The fourth chapel has frescoes by Gaudenzio Ferrari (1542), and in the fifth are stucco bas-reliefs (late 16C) of angels. The seventh has an altarpiece by Marco d'Oggiono.

The lovely light *tribuna, or domed crossing, designed by Bramante, has very unusual bright graffiti decoration. The choir also has graffiti decoration and fine stalls of carved and inlaid wood. A door leads out to the *chiostrino, also traditionally attributed to Bramante, with a delightful little garden. Off it is the **old sacristy** (only open for concerts), which marked a significant step in the development of Renaissance architecture.

At the end of the **north aisle** is the elaborate entrance (with 17C stuccoes and a lunette painting by Cerano) to the **Chapel of the Madonna delle Grazie**, containing a highly venerated 15C painting of the Madonna beneath a vault with restored 15C frescoes. The sixth chapel has a small Holy Family by Paris Bordon, and the second chapel (being restored) has a funerary monument with sculptures attributed to Bambaia. The first chapel has frescoes by Giovanni Donato Montorfano.

In the **refectory** of the adjoining Dominican convent (entrance on the left of the façade; 8–13.45 exc. Mon) is the world-famous ****CENACOLO** or **LAST SUPPER BY LEONARDO DA VINCI**, painted in 1494–97. In order to protect the painting from dust and lessen the effects of pollution, visitors (only 15 or 20 at a time) go through a series of glass 'cubicles', installed with air filtering systems, from which there is a good view of the main cloister and exterior of Santa Maria delle Grazie. The vault and right wall of the refectory were rebuilt after they were destroyed by a bomb in 1943.

The Last Supper is painted with a technique peculiar to Leonardo, in tempera with the addition of later oil varnishes, on a prepared surface in two layers on the plastered wall. It is therefore not a fresco, and errors in the preparation of the plaster, together with the dampness of the wall, has caused great damage to the painted surface, which had already considerably deteriorated by the beginning of the 16C. Since that time it has been restored repeatedly, and was twice repainted (in oils) in the 18C. Careful work (begun in 1978 and expected to be completed by around 1997) is now being carried out to eliminate the false restorations of the past, and to expose as far as possible the original work of Leonardo. Results so far (on the right-hand figures) have been spectacular. Work is now in progress on the central figure of Christ and the left-hand figures.

This extraordinary painting, which was to have a lasting effect on generations of painters, depicts the moment when Christ announces Judas's betrayal at the Last Supper. The monumental classical figures of the Apostles are shown in a stark room in perfect perspective, an extension of the refectory itself. The light enters through the real windows on the left and the painted windows in the background which look out over a landscape, and the wonderful colours culminate in the blue and red robe of Christ. On the side walls Leonardo painted tapestries decorated with bunches of flowers. Fascinating details of the objects on the table have recently been revealed including the colour of the Apostles' robes reflected in the pewter plates and the transparent glass carafes. Above are lunettes with garlands of fruit and flowers around the coats of arms of the Sforza family. There is no evidence that Leonardo made use of a cartoon while working on this masterpiece.

The fresco decoration on the long wall is attributed to Bernardino de' Rossi. On the wall opposite the Cenacolo is a large Crucifixion by Donato Montorfano (1495), the fine preservation of which is a vindication of the lasting quality of true fresco-painting. At the bottom of the fresco, at either side, are the kneeling figures, now nearly effaced, of Ludovico il Moro and his wife Beatrice d'Este and their two children, added by Leonardo (before 1498).

Corso Magenta (Pl. I,9) leads back towards the centre of the city. At No. 24, Palazzo Litta, built by Francesco Maria Ricchino (1648), has a Rococo façade added in 1752–63. Opposite is the **ex Monastero Maggiore** to which belonged the church of **SAN MAURIZIO** (Pl. II,5; open Wed 9.30–12, 15.30–18.30) begun in 1503, perhaps by Gian Giacomo Dolcebuono, with a façade of 1574–81.

The harmonious *interior is divided by a wall into two parts. The western portion, originally for lay worshippers, has small chapels below and a graceful loggia above and contains numerous *frescoes by Bernardino Luini and his sons Aurelio and Giovan Pietro (1522–29), and other members of his school. A long and careful restoration project has been in progress here since 1980. In the loggia are frescoed medallions by Giovanni Antonio Boltraffio (1505–10).

The cloisters of the Monastero Maggiore now form the entrance to the **CIVICO MUSEO ARCHAEOLOGICO** (Pl. II,5; No. 5 Corso Magenta; 9.30–17.30 exc. Mon), with Greek, Etruscan and Roman material relating to the history of Milan. In the cloisters are displayed Roman sculpture, and a large incised stone from Valle Camonica dating from the Late Bronze Age.

On the **ground floor** is displayed the famous *Coppa Trivulzio** dating from the early 4C AD, a double coloured glass drinking cup of intricate workmanship with the inscription 'Drink and live many years!'. It was found in a sarcophagus near Novara in 1675 and was acquired by Abbot Carlo Trivulzio in 1777 (and published by the German scholar Winckelmann in 1779). Also displayed here is the silver *Parabiago patera** with Attis and Cybele and other fine figures in relief, a Roman work of the late 4C AD. There is also a good display of antique vases; **Roman sculpture** (including a colossal torso of Hercules); mosaics found in the city; and portrait busts (1C BC–4C AD). Also displayed here are finds from Caesarea in the Holy Land and 6C–7C jewellery from Nocera Umbra and Milan.

In the **basement** is (left) **Etruscan material** (bucchero vases, etc.) and (right) Indian Gandhara sculpture (2C–3C AD). The hall beyond has a fine display (chronological and topographical) of **Greek ceramics** (including Attic red- and black-figure vases). At the end of the room can be seen the base of a stretch of Roman wall, part of the city walls.

In the garden is the **Torre di Ansperto**, an octagonal tower of Roman origin (being restored), with interesting traces of 13C frescoes, and a Roman sarcophagus of the 3C AD.

Via Santa Maria alla Porta, on the right further on, and Via Borromei (right) lead to **Palazzo Borromeo** (Pl. II,10), a reconstructed 15C building. In an office (adm. on request), off the second courtyard, are interesting frescoes depicting card games, etc. by a painter of the early 15C, in the International Gothic style.

The Pinacoteca Ambrosiana (see below) is a short way to the east.

The Pinacoteca Ambrosiana

The **Palazzo dell'Ambrosiana** (Pl. II,10) contains the famous library and pinacoteca founded by Cardinal Federico Borromeo at the beginning of the 17C. The palace was begun for the Cardinal by Lelio Buzzi in 1603–09 and later enlarged. The *Pinacoteca Ambrosiana, entered from the left side of the courtyard contains a superb collection of paintings. It has been closed since 1990 for restoration and rearrangement, but is expected to reopen in 1997. During work on the foundations remains of Roman paving have come to light.

It contains works by: Botticelli (*tondo of the Madonna and Child), Ghirlandaio, Pinturicchio, Bartolomeo Vivarini, Timoteo Viti, Bergognone (*Madonna Enthroned), Marco Basaiti, Bernardino Zenale, Baldassarre Estense, Bambaia (*fragments of the tomb of Gaston de Foix), Bernart van Orley, Hans Muhlich, Jan Soreau, Jan Brueghel the Younger, Hendrik Averkamp, Giorgione (attributed), Antonio Solario, Bramantino, Bernardino Luini (*Holy Family with St Anne and the young St John, from a cartoon by Leonardo, and portraits of the confraternity of Santa Corona, 1521), Giampietrino, Antonio Salaino, Leonardo da Vinci, (*Portrait of a musician, thought to be Franchino Gaffurio, c 1485), Ambrogio De Predis (*Profile of a young lady, often identified as Beatrice d'Este), Marco d'Oggiono, Sodoma, and Bachiacca. Venetian painters represented include Giovanni Battista Moroni, Bonifacio Veronese and Jacopo Bassano (*Rest on the Flight into Egypt). Paintings by Titian include: Deposition, Sacred Conversation, *Adoration of the Magi (painted, with assistants, for Henri II and Diane de Poitiers in 1560, and still in its original frame), and a portrait of an old man in armour.

A fine 17C chamber provides a fit setting for Raphael's *cartoon for the School of Athens, the only remaining cartoon of the fresco cycle in the Vatican, purchased by Cardinal Borromeo in 1626. The copy of Leonardo's Cenacolo was made in 1612–16 by order of Cardinal Borromeo by Andrea Bianchi (Il Vespino).

There are also later works by Giulio Romano, Pellegrino Tibaldi, Barocci, Caravaggio (*Basket of Fruit), Gian Domenico Tiepolo, Thorvaldsen, Canova, and Andrea Appiani.

The **Library** contains about 750,000 volumes, including 3000 incunabula, and 35,000 MSS. Among the most precious works are Arabic and Syriac MSS; a *Divine Comedy* (1353); Petrarch's Virgil illuminated by Simone Martini; the *Codice Atlantico*, a collection of Leonardo's drawings on scientific and artistic subjects; a printed Virgil (Venice, 1470); and a Boccaccio (1471).

To the north, centering on PIAZZA EDISON (Pl. II,10) and Piazza degli Affari is the main business district of Milan with the stock exchange and a number of banks, most of them built at the beginning of the century. PIAZZA CORDUSIO (Pl. II,6) was laid out in 1889–1901 as the financial centre of the city. Beyond Piazza Cordusio is **Palazzo Clerici** (Pl: II: 6,7), in the hall of which is a magnificent ceiling painting by Gian Battista Tiepolo (1740).

San Satiro
From the Ambrosiana, Via Spadari (with luxury food shops) leads to the busy Via Torino, across which is the church of *San Satiro (Pl. II,10). The beautiful exterior, with a campanile of the mid-11C and the Cappella della Pietà, can be seen from Via Falcone. The church was rebuilt by Bramante from 1478, with the exception of the façade, which though begun by Giovanni Antonio Amadeo in 1486 to Bramante's design was finished by Giuseppe Vandoni (1871). The T-shaped interior, by a clever perspective device and the skilful use of stucco, is given the appearance of a Greek-cross; the rear wall is actually almost flat. On the high altar is a 13C votive fresco. The **Cappella della Pietà**, dating from the time of Archbishop Ansperto (868–81), was altered during the Renaissance with an attractive plan and large capitals. The terracotta Pietà is by Agostino De Fondutis. The eight-sided baptistery is a beautiful Renaissance work, with terracottas by Fondutis (on a design by Bramante).

Off Via Torino, at 5 Via Unione, is the fine 16C **Palazzo Erba Odescalchi** (Pl. II,11), now a police headquarters, with a good courtyard and a remarkable elliptical spiral staircase, which is attributed by some scholars to Bramante.
   Via Unione ends in Piazza Missori, with **Sant'Alessandro** (Pl. II,10), the best Baroque church in the city. It contains elaborate marquetry and inlaid confessionals, as well as a striking Rococo high altar of pietre dure, inlaid gems, and gilt bronze. **Palazzo Trivulzio** (1707–13) is attributed to Giovanni Ruggeri, and contains in its courtyard a doorway from a destroyed house attributed to Bramante.
   Via Torino continues towards the Carrobbio past the round church of San Sebastiano (Pl. II,10), dating from 1577, and **San Giorgio al Palazzo**, a church with a chapel decorated by Bernardino Luini.

Southern Milan
Southeast of the Duomo is the ex-church of **Santo Stefano Maggiore** (Pl. II,12), a Baroque building (1584–95) with a later campanile, outside the predecessor of which Galeazzo Maria Sforza was murdered in 1476. In the same piazza is the church of **San Bernardino alle Osse**, with an ossuary chapel frescoed by Sebastiano Ricci.
   Fronting Via Festa del Perdono is the huge building of the former *OSPEDALE MAGGIORE** or **CA'GRANDE** (Pl. II,16), which has been the

headquarters of the **University** since 1958. The hospital was founded by Francesco Sforza in 1456. The remarkable building, one of the largest in the city, was designed by Filarete with two matching wings, one for men and one for women, each laid out around four courtyards which were separated by central courtyards off which was the church. Filarete only completed the right wing (towards the church of San Nazaro) by 1465, and the work was continued by Guiniforte Solari, and (in the 17C) by Francesco Maria Ricchino and others. The hospital was moved in 1939, and the buildings were badly damaged in the war. Careful restoration and renovation has been in progress since 1953.

The long **façade** on Via Festa del Perdono preserves the 15C wing at the right-hand end, with terracotta decorations thought to have been designed by Guiniforte Solari. The left-hand end, in neo-classical style, dates from 1797–1804. Beyond the central 17C portal is the huge main *courtyard designed by Francesco Maria Ricchino, following the design of Filarete. The other courtyards can usually be visited on request. The huge collection of paintings which belonged to the hospital includes portraits of benefactors from 1602 onwards by the best known artists of the day. There are long-term plans to move it to the Abbazia di Mirasole (see page 74). The natural science schools of the University (founded in 1924) and other important educational institutions are in the Città degli Studi laid out in 1927, about 2km east of Porta Venezia (Pl. I,8).

Opposite the Ospedale can be seen the 12C campanile of **Sant'Antonio Abate** (Pl. II,11,12), a church of 1582 with good 17C stalls. Adjoining (No. 5 Via Sant'Antonio) is a charming cloister of the early 16C.

San Nazaro Maggiore

In Largo Richini, at the southwest end of the Ospedale façade, is a colossal bust of Dr Andrea Verga (died 1895) by Giulia Branca. Just beyond is San Nazaro Maggiore (Pl. II,15), a basilica consecrated in 386, one of the four churches founded by St Ambrose outside the walls. It was reconstructed after a fire of 1075, altered c 1578 (and restored in this century after war damage). The entrance on Corso di Porta Romana is preceded by the hexagonal **Trivulzio Chapel**, begun in 1512 by Bramantino and continued by Cristoforo Lombardo. It has an elegant plain interior with uniform family tombs in niches high up on the walls. The **interior** of the church is interesting for its architecture since it preserves in part the plan of the early Christian church (and some of its masonry). In the **nave** are paintings by Camillo Procaccini and Daniele Crespi. The architecture of the crossing is particularly fine. In the **south transept** is a Last Supper by Bernardino Lanino. In the **sanctuary** is the reconstructed dedication stone (with two original fragments), and off the south side the little 10C **Chapel of St Lino** (restored in 1948). In the **north transept** is a 16C carved wood Gothic *tabernacle of the Nativity (light on right), very well preserved; a reconstructed funerary epitaph (435); and a painting by Bernardino Luini. The **Chapel of St Catherine** has good frescoes by Bernardino Luini.

Off the busy Corso di Porta Romana (Pl. II,15) rises the **Torre Velasca**, built in 1956–58 and one of the most important modern buildings of its time in the city. Via Lentasio and Via Sant'Eufemia connect Corso di Porta Romana with Corso Italia. Here are the churches of **Sant'Eufemia**, rebuilt in a Lombard Gothic style in 1870, and **San Paolo Converso** (Pl. II,15), an attractive building of 1549–80 (now used by a cultural society), containing frescoes by Giulio and Antonio Campi. At No. 10 in Corso Italia is the headquarters of the **Touring Club Italiano**, famous for the production of excellent maps and guides, with a statue of its founder Luigi Vittorio Bertarelli (1927).

Further south in Corso Italia stands ***Santa Maria dei Miracoli** or **Santa Maria presso San Celso** (Pl. I,15), next to a pretty little garden in front of San Celso (with a façade reconstructed in 1851–54 and a graceful campanile). Santa Maria was begun by Gian Giacomo Dolcebuono in 1490 with a façade by Galeazzo Alessi and Martino Bassi (1572). The fine atrium is by Cesare Cesariano.

In the dark **interior** the pictures are difficult to see. At the end of the south aisle is a *Holy Family, by Paris Bordon; on the dome-piers are statues by Annibale Fontana and Stoldo Lorenzi. The inlaid choir stalls are by Galeazzo Alessi. In the ambulatory are altarpieces by Gaudenzio Ferrari and Moretto. In the north aisle is an altarpiece by Bergognone. The Romanesque church of **San Celso** (normally kept closed), entered from the south aisle, dates from the 10C. It has a well-restored interior with fine capitals and a 14C fresco.

Sant'Eustorgio

To the west is the church of *Sant'Eustorgio (Pl. I,14). Of ancient foundation, the 11C church was rebuilt except for the apse in the 12C–13C, and the façade reconstructed in 1863–65. The three 15C chapels on the south side, the apse, the slender campanile (1297–1309), and the graceful Portinari chapel are well seen from the outside. To the left of the façade is a 16C open-air pulpit.

The long and low **interior**, with aisles and apse, is typical of the Lombard basilicas, but an important series of chapels was added on the **south side** from the 13C to 16C. The first *chapel (light on right) dates from 1484, and has good sculptural detail. It contains the tomb of Giovanni Brivio, by Tommaso Cazzaniga and Benedetto Briosco (1486), and an *altarpiece by Bergognone. In the second chapel is the tomb of Pietro Torelli (died 1412), and in the fourth chapel, the tomb of Stefano Visconti (died 1327), probably by Giovanni di Balduccio, and a 14C painted Crucifix. In the sixth chapel is the tomb of Uberto Visconti (14C). In the **south transept** is the **Chapel of the Magi**, where the relics of the Magi were preserved until their transfer to Cologne in 1164 (some were returned to Milan in 1903). It contains a huge Roman sarcophagus that held the relics, and on the altar are reliefs of 1347. On the **high altar** is a finely carved 14C dossal.

Entered from the confessio, with nine slender monolithic columns (above early Christian foundations), beneath the raised apse is the ***Cappella Portinari** (1462–68) which is closed to visitors during a lengthy and complicated restoration. It is a beautiful Renaissance chapel, built for Pigello Portinari and dedicated to St Peter Martyr. In the drum of the dome is a graceful choir of angels with festoons, in coloured stucco. The frescoed scenes of the life of St Peter Martyr, by Vincenzo Foppa (1466–68), represent the most important Renaissance fresco cycle in the city (but they are in very poor condition). In the centre is the *tomb, borne by eight Virtues, of St Peter Martyr (Pietro da Verona, the inquisitor, murdered in 1252), by Giovanni di Balduccio (1339).

On request to the sacristan the early Christian **cemetery** beneath the nave can be visited, with tombs dating from the 1C–4C AD and some inscriptions, and the **old sacristy** where the church treasury and vestments are carefully preserved in 16C cupboards.

Just to the south is the huge PIAZZA XXIV MAGGIO (Pl. I,14), with the handsome neo-classical **Porta Ticinese**, an Ionic gateway by Luigi Cagnola (1801–14), in the centre. To the west is the **Darsena**, once the port of Milan, connected to an extensive system of rivers and canals, particularly busy in the 19C and beginning of the 20C. Into it runs the **Naviglio Grande** (Pl. I,13,14), the most important of Milan's canals, which connected the river Ticino (50km away) to the Darsena. It was begun in the 12C and was navigable as far as Milan by the 13C. It used to carry commodities to and from Milan, and there was a regular passenger navigation service along it from the beginning of the 19C. The nearby **Naviglio Pavese** was begun as an irrigation canal from Milan to Pavia by Gian Galeazzo Visconti in the 14C. In this area, known as the **NAVIGLI**, once a neglected part of the city, many of the characteristic houses and courtyards have recently been restored, and it now has numerous architects' and designers' studios and restaurants. It is particularly lively at night, with restaurants, cafés, snack bars, nightclubs, etc. open till late and frequented by the young—and there is a festival here in June, when restaurants are opened on boats, etc.

From Sant'Eustorgio (see above) the attractive Corso di Porta Ticinese leads north and, across Via Mulino delle Armi, passes through the arches of the medieval Porta Ticinese (c 1330; with a tabernacle by the workshop of Balduccio). Beyond are 16 Corinthian *columns, the remains of a Roman portico erected in the 4C, restored in the Middle Ages and again in 1954–55.

On the right is *SAN LORENZO MAGGIORE (Pl. I,14), a church founded in the 4C. It was rebuilt after the collapse of the vault in 1103 and again in 1574–88 by Martino Bassi (who preserved the original octagonal form and much of the original masonry) and has four heavy square towers. The façade dates from 1894. The spacious domed *interior, built of grey stone, is of great architectural interest; it is surrounded by an ambulatory beneath a gallery.

The *Chapel of Sant'Aquilino was built in the 4C, probably as an Imperial mausoleum. In the vestibule (light on right) are fragments of 5C mosaics, and early 14C frescoes. The door jambs (1C–3C AD) were brought from a Roman building. The octagonal hall (light on right), a remarkable Roman room, contains an early Christian sarcophagus and two lunettes with 5C *mosaics. Beyond is a 17C silver urn which contains the relics of St Aquilino, beneath a little vault frescoed by Carlo Urbini. Behind it steps (light on the stairs) lead down to an undercroft with Roman masonry of the Imprerial period, probably once part of an amphitheatre.

Corso di Porta Ticinese ends at the **Carrobbio** (Pl. II,10,14), a busy crossroads, which was the Roman and early medieval centre of Milan. In the ex-church of San Sisto at No. 4 Via San Sisto is a **Museum of the works of Francesco Messina**, open 9.30–17.30 exc. Mon, with many sculptures and drawings by this sculptor (1900–95).

The Giardini Pubblici and districts to the east

At the end of Via Manzoni are the **Archi di Porta Nuova** (Pl. II,14), a gate reconstructed in 1171, with sculptures by a follower of Giovanni di Balduccio

(14C). From Piazza Cavour, outside the gate, with a monument to Cavour by Odoardo Tabacchi (1865) and **Palazzo dei Giornali** by Giovanni Muzio (1937–42) with external reliefs by Mario Sironi (and a mosaic by him inside), is the entrance to the **Giardini Pubblici** (Pl. II,4), notable for their fine trees. The gardens contain monuments to distinguished citizens, and on Via Manin, **Palazzo Dugnani** (Pl. I,7,8; owned by the Comune), with *frescoes by Giovanni Battista Tiepolo (1731) in the salone. The palace contains a **Cinema Museum** (open 15–18 exc. Sat, Sun & Mon).

On the farther side of the gardens is the neo-classical building by Piero Portalupi of the **Planetarium** (entered from Corso Venezia, No. 57). Nearby, facing Corso Venezia, is the **Natural History Museum** (Pl. I,8; open 9.30–17.30 exc. Mon) founded in 1838 and the most important collection of its kind in Italy. The museum building was erected in 1893, but was badly damaged in the war. Only the ground floor is at present open. The mineral collection includes the largest sulphur crystal in the world, and a topaz weighing 40 kilogrammes. The extensive zoological section contains reptiles, giant dinosaurs, etc. There is also a good library, and study collections.

Gallery of Modern Art

On the other side of Via Palestro which borders the southern side of the park, is Villa Belgioioso or **VILLA REALE** (Pl. II,4), built by Leopold Pollack in 1790. Once occupied by the regent Eugène Beauharnais and by Marshal Radetzky, who died here in 1858, it is in urgent need of restoration. Its attractive garden '*all'inglese*' was laid out in 1790 (open as a public park). It now contains the Gallery of Modern Art (open 9.30–17.30 exc. Mon). On the **first floor**, in the state rooms overlooking the garden, are 19C Lombard paintings including the large painting called the 'Quarto Stato', a well-known work by Giuseppe Pellizza da Volpeda. Other artists represented include Andrea Appiani, Antonio Canova, and Francesco Hayez (good portraits).

Stairs lead up to the **second floor**, where the large Carlo Grassi bequest of 19C French and Italian works is displayed (Corot, Millet, Zandomeneghi, Domenico Morelli, Giovanni Fattori, Silvestro Lega, Telemaco Signorini, Giovanni Boldini, and especially good works by Giuseppe De Nittis).

The section dedicated to the French Impressionists is represented by Eugène Boudin, Alfred Sisley, Gauguin, Manet, and Van Gogh. There are also graphic works by Corot and Toulouse-Lautrec. In the last group of rooms are Italian paintings of the late 19C and early 20C by Armando Spadini, Giovanni Segantini, Antonio Mancini, Umberto Boccioni, Giacomo Balla, Giorgio Morandi, Renato Guttuso, and Filippo De Pisis. The last gallery has a display of carpets from Anatolia.

On the first floor (on the other side of the stairs) is a section dedicated to Marino Marini, with drawings and sculptures. Next door a **Pavilion**, known as PAC, which was built in 1955 to display contemporary works and as an exhibition hall, is being restored after it was destroyed by a bomb explosion in 1993.

From Piazza Cavour, Via Filippo Turati and Via Vittor Pisani lead towards the station. In Via Turati the **Palazzi della Montecatini**, office buildings built in 1926–36 by Giò Ponti and others, face the houses known as **Ca' Brutta** (1923) by Giovanni Muzio. The huge PIAZZA DELLA REPUBBLICA (Pl. I,3,7) has skyscrapers, including the first to be built in the city (1936, by Mario Baciocchi) at No. 27, and more houses (Nos 7–9) by Giovanni Muzio. The regularly built Via Pisani leads up to the monumental **Railway Station** (Pl. I,4), the largest in Italy, designed by Ulisse Stacchini and built in 1925–31. In the piazza is the **Pirelli Building**, built in reinforced concrete in 1955–59 by Giò Ponti and others (127m high), one of the best modern buildings in the city. On the site of the first Pirelli factory, it is now the seat of the Lombard Regional government. The area to the west around Via Galvani, known as the **Centro Direzionale**, has numerous skyscrapers built in the 1960s.

From the Giardini (see above), Via Marina leads southwest to Palazzo del Senato, now the **State Archives** (Pl. II,4), a fine Baroque building by Fabio Mangone and Francesco Maria Ricchino. To the south, at No. 12 Via Mozart (Pl. II,8), is the **Collezione Alighiero de' Micheli**, left to the FAI in 1995 (adm. by appointment on the first Sat of the month, exc. Jul & Aug, 10.30–17, tel. 02 4815556). It contains 18C furniture and works of art.

Via Sant'Andrea, opposite the State Archives, leads back towards the centre. At No. 6 in this street the 18C Palazzo Morando (Pl. II,8) houses, on the upper floor, the **Museo di Milano** (open 9.30–17.30, exc. Mon), with an interesting collection of paintings, drawings, prints, etc., depicting the changing face of Milan from the mid-16C onwards. On the ground floor is the **Museo di Storia Contemporanea** (adm. as above), with material related to the two World Wars.

Via Sant'Andrea ends in Via Montenapoleone, with its fashionable shops, which leads (right) to Via Manzoni.

From behind the Duomo, CORSO VITTORIO EMANUELE (Pl. II,8), a pedestrian street with numerous shops and shopping arcades as well as theatres and hotels, leads through a modern area. On the left is the classic portico of the round church of **San Carlo** (1839–47), modelled on the Pantheon, and on the right, at the beginning of CORSO VENEZIA (Pl.II; 8), is **San Babila** (Pl. II,8), a 12C church over-restored at the end of the 19C. The 17C column outside bears the Lion of St Mark. At No. 11 Corso Venezia is the monumental gateway of the former Seminary (1564), with huge caryatids; opposite is **Casa Fontana**, now Silvestri (No. 10), with interesting terracotta work of c 1475. The Corso, with fine mansions of the 18C–19C, including the neo-classical Palazzo Serbelloni (No. 16) by Simone Cantoni (1793), Palazzo Castiglioni (No. 47; 1900–04), a famous Art Nouveau palace, and Palazzo Saporiti (No. 40), built in 1812, goes on to the Giardini Pubblici, Piazzale Oberdan, and the modern area east of the station.

Santa Maria della Passione

From San Babila (see above), Corso Monforte continues east to the Prefettura, and **Palazzo Isimbardi**, seat of the provincial administration, which has a fresco by Giovanni Battista Tiepolo. Via Conservatorio leads right to reach the huge church of Santa Maria della Passione (Pl. 12), founded c 1485, with an octagonal dome by Cristoforo Lombardi (1530–50), and a **façade** by Giuseppe Rusnati (1692).

Interior. In the nave are hung a fine series of portraits of popes and monks (in matching frames), some of them by Daniele Crespi. The vault is frescoed by

Martino Bassi. The chapels in the **south aisle** have Lombard frescoes and altar-pieces of the 16C–17C. In the **crossing**, beneath the fine dome, is another good series of paintings (in their original frames) of the Passion, one by Daniele Crespi. The organ on the right by Antegnati (1558) has doors painted by Carlo Urbini, and the one on the left (1613) has doors painted by Daniele Crespi. Beneath the organ on the right is the funerary monument of the founder of the church, Archbishop Daniele Birago, by Andrea Fusina (1495). The beautiful choir stalls are attributed to Cristoforo Solari.

In the south and north transepts are altarpieces by Bernardino Luini, Gaudenzio Ferrari and Giulio Campi. The chapels in the **north aisle** have more 16C–17C works, including one by Daniele Crespi.

Various rooms of the ex-**Convent** and the **Museum** can usually be visited on request. Beyond the old sacristy is the **Chapter House* decorated c 1510 by Bergognone, including nine paintings of Christ and the apostles opposite frescoes of saints and doctors of the church. Beyond is a gallery with 17C Lombard paintings, and a room with the church treasury in 17C cupboards, vestments, and a large painting, *Daniel in the Lions' Den* by Giuseppe Vermiglio.

Entered from Via Chiossetto, a turning off Via Corridoni, further south, is **SAN PIETRO IN GESSATE** (Pl. I,12), a Gothic church built c 1475. In the last chapel in the south aisle is a very damaged detached fresco of the funeral of St Martin, by Bergognone. The **Cappella Grifo** has interesting remains of frescoes depicting the Life of St Ambrose, by Bernardino Butinone and Bernardino Zenale (1490–93), the best preserved part of which is the vault with delightful angels. The tomb effigy of Ambrogio Grifo (with two portrait medallions) was carved by Benedetto Briosco c 1490. In the south transept is an unusual painting of the Madonna and Child by the Leonardesque school. In chapels in the north aisle are works by Giovanni Donato Montorfano. Opposite San Pietro, in the Corso di Porta Vittoria, is the huge **Palazzo di Giustizia** (1932–40, by Marcello Piacentini). At the east end of the Corso is a monument by Giuseppe Grandi (1883–91) commemorating those who died during the 'Cinque Giornate' (five days) of March 1848, and a little to the south of that is the **Rotonda** (Pl. I,16), the old mortuary of the Ospedale Maggiore locally known as 'Foppone', now a children's garden and exhibition centre. The church was built by Attilio Arrigoni in 1713, and the portico by Francesco Raffagno.

2 · The province of Milan and the Lodigiano

The most important place in the province of Milan is the large industrial town of Monza, with an interesting cathedral and the grand Villa Reale. On the outskirts of Milan are the three abbeys of Chiaravalle, Mirasole and Viboldone. There are a few other places of interest, widely scattered in the province. The Lodigiano now forms part of the new province of Lodi.

15.5km northeast of Milan, **MONZA** is the most important town in its province, and the third largest town in Lombardy. It is an industrial city (114,300 inhab.), internationally known to motor-racing enthusiasts. It was important under the

Lombard Queen Theodolinda in the 7C, and has a cathedral of great interest.

■ **Information office.** IAT, Palazzo Comunale (tel. 039 323222).

■ **Hotels.** 4-star: *De La Ville*, 15 Viale Regina Margherita; 3-star: *Della Regione*, 4 Via Elvezia.

■ **Camping site**: Parco Reale (open April to September).

■ **Transport. Bus** from Milan (Via Jacini) near Nord station or Piazza 4 Novembre beside the central station in 20 minutes. Frequent **train** service from Milan (Porta Garibaldi station) in 10–15 minutes. Inaugurated in 1840, this was the second line to be opened in Italy.

The **Cathedral** is a 13C–14C building on the site of a church founded by Theodolinda, Queen of Lombardy, c 595. The fine parti-coloured marble *façade by Matteo da Campione (1370–96; restored) is flanked by a brick campanile of 1606 by Pellegrino Tibaldi. The interior contains more work by Matteo da Campione, including the organ gallery in the nave and the relief of an imperial coronation. The **Chapel of Queen Theodolinda** contains the tomb of Theodolinda and is decorated with frescoes (being restored) by the Zavattari family (1444). Enclosed in the altar is the famous *__iron crown of Lombardy__ (shown with the contents of the treasury, see below) used at the coronation of the Holy Roman Emperors since 1311, and containing a strip of iron said to have been hammered from one of the nails used at the Crucifixion. The last emperors crowned with it were Charles V (at Bologna), Napoleon and Ferdinand I (at Milan). The Rococo chapel of the Corpus Domini has frescoes by Mattia Bortoloni (1742).

The *__Cathedral Museum__ (open 9–11.30, 15–17.30 exc. Mon) houses the rich **treasury**. Here are the personal relics of Theodolinda, including her silver-gilt *__hen and chickens__, supposed to represent Lombardy and its seven provinces (possibly dating from the 4C and 7C), her votive cross and crown, and a book-cover with a dedicatory inscription. Also here are three ivory diptychs (4C–9C). Sixteen phials from Palestine, illustrated with biblical scenes, are rare works dating from the 6C. The silk embroideries date from the 6C–7C. The processional cross was given to Theodolinda by St Gregory (altered in the 15C and 17C). There is also a collection of 26 glass phials from Rome (5C–6C), and 16C tapestries made in Milan.

In Piazza Roma is the **Arengario**, the brick town hall of 1293, with a tall battlemented tower and a balcony for public announcements.

Just to the north of the old city is the huge decaying **Villa Reale,** a neo-classical masterpiece by Giuseppe Piermarini (1777–80), built as a residence for the Archduke Ferdinand of Austria, son of the Empress Maria Teresa, and presented by the king to the State in 1919. This remarkable palace is in urgent need of restoration, and the state rooms and royal apartments are all closed indefinitely (although Umberto I's apartment has been restored). The ownership of the palace has been contested for years between the State and the Comune of Monza and Milan.The Pinacoteca Civica, with a collection of 19C paintings, has been closed since 1983. There are long-term plans to open a neo-classical museum in the villa. In the garden is a rotonda with delightful frescoes by Andrea Appiani (1789). Its huge **park** (7 sq. km), traversed by the Lambro river, with fine trees, was created in 1805–10 by Luigi Canonica and Luigi Villoresi. It now contains the famous **autodromo** (adm. 8–19), a motor-racing circuit built in 1922 (plans to extend it have so far been suppressed) and an 18-hole golf course. From behind the villa an avenue leads to the expiatory chapel, by Giuseppe Sacconi, erected by Vittorio Emanuele III on the spot where his father Umberto I was assassinated on 29 July 1900 by the anarchist Gaetano Bresci.

North of Monza is **Agliate**, with a remarkable 10C–11C *church and baptistery traditionally thought to have been founded in 881 by Ansperto, Bishop of Milan. Restored by Luca Beltrami in 1895, they contain remains of 10C frescoes.

Southeast of Monza is **Gorgonzola**, which gave its name to an excellent creamy veined cheese which is produced in the district (as well as Bel Paese cheese).

To the south of Milan, within a few kilometres of each other, are the three abbeys of Chiaravalle, Viboldone, and Mirasole. The **abbey of Chiaravalle** is in an unattractive position (near the Rogoredo station of underground line 3). This Cistercian abbey was founded by St Bernard in 1135 and named after his own abbey of Clairvaux. The brick church, consecrated in 1221, has an imposing tower (the upper tiers were added in the 14C). The interior was extensively altered in the 17C, but preserves inside the lantern some 13C–14C frescoes; the other frescoes are the work of the Fiamminghini (1614), except that at the top of the night-stairs (south transept), which is by Bernardino Luini (1512). The carved stalls are by Carlo Garavaglia (1645). The sacristan shows the cemetery, which contains tombs of the 13C; the remains of the chapter house, with interesting graffiti; and two walks of the 13C cloister. In the Chapel of St Bernard are interesting fragments of frescoes, attributed by some scholars to Hieronymus Bosch (c 1499). There is a festival at the abbey in October.

The **abbey of Viboldone** was founded in the 13C, and the church contains a Madonna enthroned by a Florentine master (1349), and a 14C Last Judgement by Giusto de' Menabuoi.

The **abbey of Mirasole** was founded in the 13C, and has been in restoration for many years. It has been the property of the Ospedale Maggiore of Milan since 1797, and will one day house its collection of paintings.

To the west, near the intersection of the Genoa motorway and the ring-road, is **Milanofiori**, a commercial district begun in 1976 with a World Trade Centre by Renzo Piano.

On the road to Lodi, southeast of Milan is **Melegnano**. In the church of San Giovanni Battista is a Baptism of Christ by Bergognone. The 14C castle was built for Bernarbò Visconti.

On the western border of the province, near the Ticino, is the **abbey of Morimondo**, founded in 1134 by Cistercian monks from Marimond in France, with a fine church (good choir of 1522), cloister and chapter house. In the big agricultural town of **Abbiategrasso** (26,000 inhab.), the church of Santa Maria Nuova is preceded by a pronaos of 1497 by Bramante. The Visconti castle was built in 1382. The town is on the **Naviglio Grande** (see page 69) which extends north for some 30km and continues east into Milan. It was cut in the 12C, and in the 17C and 18C was lined with the country villas of the Milanese nobility. Places of interest on the canal north of Abbiategrasso include **Cassinetta di Lugagnano** and **Robecco sul Naviglio**, both with fine villas (some of them recently restored).

On the stretch of the Naviglio Grande which runs towards Milan is a secondary canal cut by Filippo Maria Visconti north to **Cusago**, with a castle in the main piazza, the 14C country residence of Bernabò Visconti. The woods of Cusago are a bird sanctuary.

North of Abbiategrasso is **Magenta**, famous for the victory of the French and Italians over the Austrians in 1859, which is commemorated by an ossuary and a monument to Marshal MacMahon.

Northwest of Milan is **Legnano** (48,000 inhab.), remembered for the battle in which Barbarossa was defeated by the Lombard League in 1176 (monument). The battle is also celebrated in a traditional festival in the town in May (the 'Sagra del Carroccio', with a *palio*). The church of San Magno (1504) houses a polyptych and frescoes by Bernardino Lanino. There is a local archaeological museum here.

On the outskirts of Milan, to the west, on Via Monte Rosa (underground line 1 to Piazzale Lotto) is the sports area of **San Siro**. Here is the football stadium (1926; enlarged 1950), the hippodrome, and the Palasport, a stadium opened in 1976 and capable of holding 14,500 spectators. Also in this district is the **British Military Cemetery** for the dead of the Second World War.

Just off the Varese road, is **Arese** with a museum dedicated to the history of the firm of Alfa Romeo, who put their first car on the road in 1910.

Lodi

Lodi, 31km southeast of Milan, is an important centre (42,000 inhab.) for dairy produce on the right bank of the Adda, in the fertile and well irrigated district of Lodigiano. It was founded in 1158 by Frederick Barbarossa, and became the capital of a new province in 1995. The Piazza family of painters were born here in the 16C, and good works by Callisto are preserved in churches in the town and province. It was known for its ceramics in the 17C and 18C (and several small ceramics factories still operate here, including Franchi in Via Sant'Angelo). At the famous Battle of Lodi in 1796, on the bridge over the river, Napoleon defeated the Austrians.

■ **Information office.** APT, 4 Piazza Broletto.

■ **Restaurants. A**: *Isola Caprera*, 14 Via Isola Caprera; *La Quinta*, Piazza Vittoria; *Tre Gigli all'Incoronata*, Piazza Vittoria. **B**: *Sobacchi*, Via Feriolo. Near **Lodi Vecchio**: *Trattoria del Cacciatore* (**B**); near **Abbadia Cerreto**: *L'Antica Osteria Lungo l'Adda* (**B**). **Cake shop**: *La Lombarda*, 16 Via Garibaldi. **Cafés** in Piazza Vittoria.

■ **Transport.** There are good **train services** to Milan.

■ **Car parking** in Viale Dalmazio.

■ **Annual festivals.** San Bassiano (the patron saint), 19 Jan; 'Palio dei Rioni' on 1 Oct; fair and market around 13 Dec (Santa Lucia).

History
The town was founded on this higher site after the destruction of Lodi Vecchio by the Milanese in 1158. Mary Hadfield Cosway (1759–1838), the painter and educationalist, founded a college for girls (the 'Collegio delle Dame Inglese') here in 1812 which flourished up until 1948 (and was attended by Alessandro Manzoni's daughter). Mary was the wife of the court miniaturist Richard Cosway, and the supposed lover of Thomas Jefferson. The college was at No. 6 Via Paolo Gorini, next to the church of Santa Maria delle Grazie where Mary is buried (plaque on the wall).

In the centre of the town is the large arcaded PIAZZA DELLA VITTORIA. Here is the 18C façade of the **Broletto,** and the **Duomo**, with a 12C façade including a fine portal (in need of restoration) bearing the carved figures of Adam and Eve on the door jambs, attributed to sculptors from Piacenza. The interior was well restored in the 1960s in the Romanesque style. In the first south chapel (lights) is a triptych of the Coronation of the Virgin by Alberto Piazza, and a polyptych with the Massacre of the Innocents by Callisto Piazza, both in their original frames. The tomb of Andrea Fusina dates from 1510. In the nave is a 13C gilt statue of San Bassiano. In the choir are intarsia *panels set into modern stalls, exquisite works by Fra Giovanni da Verona (1523). By the entrance to the crypt is a Romanesque relief of the Last Supper above fresco fragments. In the crypt, where the body of St Bassiano is preserved is a well preserved wooden Deposition group by a local 16C sculptor. The Diocesan Museum (usually closed) contains vestments and church silver.

On the north side of the Duomo is PIAZZA BROLETTO with remains of the 13C part of the Broletto and the Romanesque font from the cathedral used as a fountain. From here a passageway leads into Piazza Mercato (markets on Tue, Thu, Sat and Sun).

From Piazza Vittoria, Via dell'Incoronata leads to the inconspicuous entrance to the church of the *Incoronata, built in 1488–94 by Giovanni Battagio and Gian Giacomo Dolcebuono. The octagonal interior is totally covered with 16C paintings, frescoes, and gilded decoration, on a design by Callisto Piazza. In the first chapel on the right, the altarpiece of the Conversion of St Paul, a late work (1580) by Callisto, is flanked by four exquisite *panels by Bergognone. The chapels on either side of the main altar also have altarpieces by Callisto, with the intervention of his son Fulvio, and his brother Scipione. In the last chapel is a polyptych of 1519 by Alberto Piazza in its original frame, and four small paintings by Scipione. The original 16C organ survives. Over the west door is an Adoration of the Magi, the only signed and dated work by Scipione Piazza (1562). The charming frescoed decoration on the pilasters, etc. is also by the Piazza. Behind the high altar is a gonfalon painted on silk by Alberto Piazza, and Rococo carved stalls. The 18C sacristy preserves its cupboards and pretty vault. A small museum with 15C–16C church silver, and vestments is usually kept closed.

Corso Umberto leads out of Piazza Vittoria to the **Museo Civico** with a fine collection of local ceramics on the ground floor, including works with floral decorations in the 'Vecchia Lodi' style produced by the Ferretti family in the late 18C. There is also an archaeological section, a collection of paintings, and a Risorgimento museum.

From the other side of Piazza della Vittoria, Via Marsala leads to **Sant'Agnese** (left), a 15C church with terracotta decoration on the façade, and a polyptych by Alberto Piazza. From here Via XX Settembre, with the fine 15C **Palazzo Mozzanica** (No. 51; now Varesi), with a good portal and terracotta friezes, leads east to **San Francesco** (1289), a church with an unusual façade. The interior has numerous 14C–15C frescoes, the most interesting on the nave pillars, and on the south side and transept. In the hospital in the piazza there is a charming little 15C cloister with a double loggia decorated with terracotta.

The Lodigiano

The Lodigiano was an unhealthy marshy area before the local monastic communities constructed canals, many of which still survive. In the well irrigated countyside there are numerous dairy farms which produce *mascarpone* and a cheese known locally as *raspadura*, a type of unmatured Parmesan, which is served as an hors d'oeuvre which you eat with your fingers. Near the river Adda which borders the eastern side of the province are itineraries recommended for cyclists (for information and guide, enquire at the APT in Lodi; there are also various places where bicycles can be hired).

Lodi Vecchio is 5km west of Lodi. The Roman *Laus Pompeia* was a constant rival of Milan until its total destruction in 1158. Only the church of **San Bassiano** was left standing, and it is now in an isolated position outside the village of Lodi Vecchio. Of ancient foundation, it was rebuilt in Gothic style in the early 14C, with a fine exterior. High up on the façade is a ceramic statue of the 4C bishop, St Bassiano. The interior is interesting for its delightful early 14C frescoed *decoration (restored in the early 1960s) in the nave vaults and apse, with colourful geometric designs and flowers, and including one bay with very unusual rustic scenes of four carts drawn by oxen (the frescoes were financed by a local farming corporation in 1323), and Christ Pantocrator in the apse. Votive frescoes include the scene of St Eligius blessing a horse. At the end of the north aisle (high up) is a relief with bulls and a man on a horse dated 1323. The 11C capitals are also interesting, and in the south aisle is a series of 17C paintings.

The site of the Roman city was identified in 1987 by aerial photography and excavations are in progress near the village.

At **Sant'Angelo Lodigiano** to the southwest (on the Pavia road) the restored 14C Visconti castle may be visited. It has 17C–18C furniture, a fine armoury, etc.

Codogno (4-star hotel, *Albergo del Sole*, at Maleo, with restaurant), south of Lodi, is an agricultural centre (14,900 inhab.). In the 16C church of San Biagio are an Assumption by Callisto Piazza, *Madonna and Child between St Francis and Charles Borromeo* by Daniele Crespi, and 16C works by Cesare Magni.

At **Ospedaletto Lodigiano**, west of Codogno, is an abbey founded in 1433, with a 16C church containing paintings (formerly part of a triptych) by Giampietrino. Part of the 16C cloister survives. At **Borghetto Lodigiano** the town hall occupies Palazzo Rho (c 1490).

East of Lodi is **Abbadia Cerreto** where there is a Cistercian Lombard church, built in the 12C, with a fine exterior and an altarpiece by Callisto Piazza.

3 · Pavia and its province

Pavia

Pavia is an old provincial capital (86,000 inhab.) of Roman origin on the Ticino, with one of the most ancient universities in Europe, still very much at the centre of the life of the town. Although virtually nothing remains of the Roman city, Pavia has a number of fine medieval churches and palaces in its cobbled streets, and interesting well arranged art collections in the Castello Visconteo. Its development in this century as an important industrial and agricultural centre led to indiscriminate new building outside the limits of the historical centre. On 24 February 1525 the famous Battle of Pavia was fought here, in which the French king Francis I was defeated and taken prisoner by the Emperor Charles V, representing a decisive moment in European history. The beautiful 15C–16C Certosa di Pavia is a few kilometres north of the town.

■ **Information office.** IAT, 2 Via Fabio Filzi (tel. 0382 22156).

■ **Car parking.** Piazza Petrarca and Piazzale Libertà. Pay car parks on Viale Matteotti, Viale II Febbraio and Piazzale Cairoli.

■ **Hotels**. 4-star: *Ariston*; 10 Via Scopoli; 3-star: *Rosengarten*, Piazzale Policlinico.

■ **Camping site.** *Ticino*, 2.5km outside the town.

■ **Restaurants. A**: *Vecchia Pavia*, 2 Via Riboldi. **B**: *Del Previ*, 65 Via Milazzo; *Ca' Bella*, 2 Via Ca' Bella; *Della Madonna*, Via dei Liguri. **C**: *Regisole*, 4 Piazza Duomo; *Piedigrotta*, 38 Via Teodolinda; *Marechiaro*, 9 Piazza della Vittoria.

■ **Picnic places** in the public gardens around the Castello Visconteo.

■ **Transport. Bus** No. 3 from the railway station to the centre of the town along Corso Cavour and Corso Mazzini. **Bus Station** in Via Trieste for buses to places in the province.

■ **Theatre.** *Fraschini*, Strada Nuova (music and theatre season).

History

The Roman *Ticinum* wa s founded on this site about 220 BC, and the town became capital of the Lombards in the 6C, and appears under the name *Papia* in the 7C. In the church of San Michele were crowned Charlemagne (774), Berengar, the first king of Italy (888), Berengar II (950) and Frederick Barbarossa (1155). The commune took the Ghibelline side against Milan and Lodi, and afterwards passed to the Counts of Monferrato and, from 1359 onwards, to the Visconti. After the failure of the French to win control of Pavia from the Spaniards in the decisive Battle of Pavia here in 1525 Francis I wrote to his mother: 'Madame, tout est perdu fors l'honneur' ('all is lost save honour'). The ramparts which

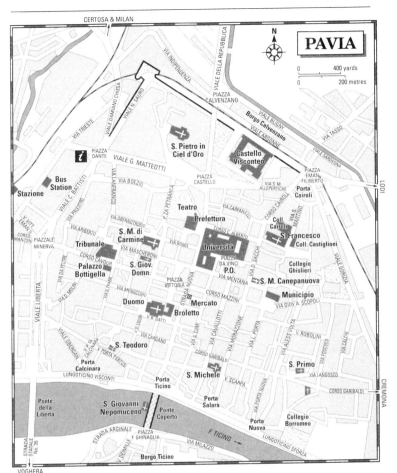

still surround part of the city were built by the Spanish in the 17C. Pavia was the birthplace of Lanfranc (1005–89), first archbishop of Canterbury. The name of the Piazza Petrarca recalls Petrarch's visits to his son-in-law here.

The two straight main streets of the town, the Strada Nuova and Corso Cavour-Corso Mazzini intersect in the centre of the town in true Roman style near the huge arcaded PIAZZA VITTORIA, its market now relegated below ground. At the end rises the **Broletto** (12C; restored in the 19C), with a double loggia of 1563. Next to it is the **Duomo**, begun in 1488 from designs by Cristoforo Rocchi and Giovanni Antonio Amadeo, and afterwards modified by Bramante (with, possibly, also the intervention of Leonardo da Vinci). The immense cupola, the third largest in Italy, was not added until 1884–85 and the façade was completed in 1933. The rest of the exterior remains unfinished. The impressive, centrally planned interior has a very pronounced cornice above the capitals. On the west wall are paintings by Cerano, Daniele Crespi and Moncalvo. In the transepts are altarpieces by Carlo Sacchi and Bernardino Gatti, and the 17C *Madonna di Piazza Grande*.

In are several palaces with porticoes, including the handsome Palazzo Vescovile (1577). The equestrian statue, by Francesco Messina (1937), recalls the gilded bronze Roman statue which stood here from the 11C until its destruction in 1796. Next to the Duomo are the neglected ruins of the **Torre Civica**, the campanile of two demolished Romanesque churches, with a bell-chamber by Pellegrino Tibaldi (1583), which collapsed without warning in 1989, killing four people, and wounding 15. Discussions continue about whether it should be reconstructed.

Via dei Liguri leads downhill out of the piazza and Via Maffì continues right to the 12C church of **San Teodoro** with its octagonal cupola-tower and 16C lantern. Inside, the remarkable 15C–16C frescoes include a view of Pavia with its numerous towers (west wall) in 1522, by Bernardino Lanzani, and the *Life of St Theodore* (sanctuary) attributed to Lanzani. The crypt runs crossways beneath the sanctuary and extends beyond the walls.

From here Via Porta Pertusi continues to the picturesque **Ponte Coperto**, a covered bridge across the Ticino, still used by cars. The original bridge built in 1351–54 on Roman foundations and roofed in 1583, collapsed in 1947 after bomb-damage. The present one, a few metres further east, is to a different design, as is the chapel replacing the 18C bridge-chapel. In the suburb across the bridge is the 12C church of **Santa Maria in Betlem**, which has a façade decorated with faience plaques, and a plain Romanesque interior.

The Strada Nuova leads uphill from the bridge back towards the centre of the town. Via Capsoni leads right to *SAN MICHELE, the finest church in Pavia, consecrated in 1155, with an octagonal cupola. The elaborately ornamented front has profusely decorated triple portals and sculptured friezes, but the sandstone in which they are carved has been almost totally worn away, despite restoration in 1967. The portals of the transept and the galleried apse also have interesting carving. The campanile, decorated with terracotta tiles, dates from c 1000. The interior is similar to that of San Pietro in Ciel d'Oro (see below), while the gallery above the nave recalls that of Sant'Ambrogio in Milan. There is fine sculptural detail in many parts of the interior, particularly on the *capitals. In the crypt is the tomb of Martino Salimbeni (died 1463), by the school of Amadeo. Opposite the church, behind a railing and surrounded by a garden, is **Palazzo Corti (Arnaboldi)**, an 18C building altered in 1875 by Ercole Balossi (being restored).

Via Cavalotti leads uphill to the north. Across Corso Mazzini, Via Galliano continues past the post office to PIAZZA LEONARDO DA VINCI, where three ancient **tower-houses** survive, built by the noble families of Pavia (the town was once called the 'city of a hundred towers', and some 80 of them survived up to the last century). Under cover are remains of the 12C **Crypt of Sant'Eusebio** (adm. by appointment at the Castello Visconteo), with restored early 13C frescoes.

Here is the **UNIVERSITY**—one of the oldest in Europe—the successor of a famous school of law, the ancient *Studio* where Lanfranc is said to have studied. The school was made a university in 1361 by Galeazzo II Visconti, and is now particularly renowned for its faculties of law and medicine. The buildings of 1533 were extended by Giuseppe Piermarini in 1771–79, and by Leopoldo Pollack in 1783–95. The Aula Magna was begun in 1827. Off Corso Carlo Alberto and the Strada Nuova are numerous attractive courtyards, all of which are open to the public. Off the one with a statue of Alessandro Volta is the entrance to the **Museo per la Storia dell'Università di Pavia** (Mon 15.30–17, & Fri 9.30–12), with interesting collections relating to the history of medicine and physics in an old-fashioned arrangement (the showcases survive from the 18C), with mementoes of the most distinguished alumni including Volta himself. The Teatro Fisico and the anatomical theatre (named after Antonio Scarpa) were both designed by Leopoldo Pollack (1787). The adjoining courts of the former **Ospedale di San Matteo** (1499), to the east, are also part of the university.

Via Roma leads left from the Strada Nuova to the large red brick church of **Santa Maria del Carmine**, begun in 1373, which has an attractive façade adorned with terracotta statues and an elaborate rose-window. On some of the nave pillars are frescoes by local 15C painters. The charming lavabo in the sacristy (south transept) is by Giovanni Antonio Amadeo. In Piazza Petrarca, reached by Via XX Settembre, is the **Biblioteca Civica** in **Palazzo Malaspina**, built for the Malaspina collection (now displayed in the Castello Visconteo),which was opened to the public here in 1838 by Luigi Malaspina as a museum for the town and as a study-collection. To the west, in Via Orfanotrofio, is **San Felice**, with an interesting Lombard crypt (9C; being restored), and a Renaissance cloister.

The Strada Nuova continues north past the **Teatro Fraschini**, built in 1771–73 by Antonio Galli, to the **CASTELLO VISCONTEO**, surrounded by public gardens. The great fortress was built by Galeazzo II Visconti in 1360–65, and here he housed his important collections of literature and art. A huge park (with a perimeter wall of some 22km) extended north from the ducal residence as far as the Certosa di Pavia. It was in this park that the famous Battle of Pavia took place in 1525, and two years later, in revenge for their defeat in battle, the French destroyed the northern wing of the castle and two of its corner turrets. The restored interior (entrance on the west side; open 9–13.30 exc. Mon; in spring and autumn also sometimes open 15–17.30 at weekends), with a splendid *courtyard, houses the collections of the **MUSEO CIVICO**.

On the ground floor (**Rooms I–VI**) is the **archaeological collection**, which includes Roman finds with good glass and sculpture, and exhibits from the **Lombard period**, when Pavia was capital of the Lombard court (sculptures and inscriptions from the royal tombs, 572–774), but the Lombard jewellery is not yet on display.

On the other side of one of the castle's entrance gates is the **Romanesque collection** (**Rooms VII–X**) with architectural fragments, capitals, friezes, portals from the Romanesque cathedrals (8C–12C). In **Room X** are the best Romanesque sculptures from San Giovanni in Borgo, with finely carved capitals. In the last wing (**Room XI**) are mosaic pavements.

The **Renaissance collection** is displayed in **Rooms XII–XIV**, and includes sculpture and a 16C fresco (being restored), detached in 1895 and in 1945 sold to the Philadelphia Museum of Art, who in 1994 decided to give it to this museum. There is more sculpture arranged beneath the **portico**.

First Floor. The entrance to the **Pinacoteca Malaspina** is at the end of the east loggia. The collection was formed by Luigi Malaspina di Sannazzaro (1754–1835) and is interesting as an example of a private collection of this time. It is arranged in fine rooms with 16C vault frescoes. **Room 1.** *Madonna and Saints by Vincenzo Foppa, 1478 (the *Pala Bottigella* from the monastery of San Tommaso); *Portrait of a Condottiere by Antonello da Messina (being restored); and early works by Hugo van der Goes and Giovanni Bellini. The painting of *Christ Carrying the Cross* by Bergognone shows a procession of Carthusian monks in front of the Certosa di Pavia (with the façade still under construction, c 1494).

Room 2. Local ceramics; carved wood dossals (1470); gilded wood relief of the Nativity (late 15C; from the Certosa); paintings by Correggio, Bartolomeo Montagna, Boltraffio (*Portrait of a lady) and Giampietrino; and a fresco by Bernardino Luini.

In the corner room is a remarkable wooden *model of the Duomo, a masterpiece by Gian Pietro Fugazza (1493–1502). Beyond is a huge hall with 17C and 18C paintings, including works by Camillo Procaccini, Nuvolone, Daniele Crespi, Orsola Maddalena Caccia (the daughter of Moncalvo), Carlone, Alessandro Magnasco and Gian Domenico Tiepolo; and 18C ceramics.

On the **second floor** is a **Gipsoteca** (gallery of plaster casts—opened on request). The **Museo del Risorgimento**, with relics of the Pavese Cairoli brothers, is to be reopened here.

From Piazza Castello Via Griziotti leads northwest to the quiet square in front of the Lombard church of ***SAN PIETRO IN CIEL D'ORO** (closed 12–15), consecrated in 1132. The church's name comes from its former gilded vault, mentioned by Dante in his *Paradiso* (X, 128; quoted on the façade). The single portal in the handsome façade is asymmetrically placed, and the buttress on the right is made broader than that on the left in order to contain a stairway. The fine Romanesque interior, restored in 1875–99, has good 'bestiary' capitals. The altarpiece is the ***Arca di Sant'Agostino**, a masterpiece of Italian sculpture, executed c 1362 by Campionese masters (from Campione d'Italia on Lago di Lugano) influenced by the Pisan Giovanni di Balduccio, with a galaxy of statuettes, and bas-reliefs illustrating the story of the saint (the details are difficult to see from a distance). It is supposed to contain the relics of St Augustine (died 430), removed from Carthage during the Arian persecutions. The large crypt contains the remains of the Roman poet and statesman Boëthius (476–524), executed by Theodoric on a charge of treason.

Other churches of interest in the eastern part of the city include **San Francesco d'Assisi**, a late Romanesque church (1238–98) with a restored Gothic façade. Also on Corso Cairoli is a Renaissance building readapted to its original purpose when the **Collegio Cairoli** was founded in 1948. Further east in Via San Martino (No. 18) is the **Collegio Castiglione-Brugnatelli** (for women), which occupies a 15C college building. The college chapel (shown on request) has restored 15C frescoes by the school of Bonifacio Bembo. A bronze statue of Pope Pius V, by Francesco Nuvolone (1692), faces the **Collegio Ghislieri**, his foundation (1567). The square is closed by the façade of **San Francesco di Paola**, by Giovanni Antonio Veneroni, beyond which are the **Botanical Gardens** with roses, aquatic plants, conifers, etc.

Via Scopoli returns towards the centre of the town past **Santa Maria delle Cacce**, rebuilt in 1629, with frescoes of the life of St Theodoric (being restored) and an 8C crypt, and (right) **Palazzo Mezzabarba**, a Baroque building by Giovanni Veneroni (1730), now the Municipio. The church of **Santa Maria Canepanova**, at the corner of Via Sacchi and Via Mentana, is a graceful octagonal building begun by Giovanni Antonio Amadeo in 1507, probably on a design by Bramante; it has a pretty little cloister.

In the southern part of the town, near Corso Garibaldi, is the much altered Lombard church of **San Primo**. Further south, reached by Via San Giovanni, is the **Collegio Borromeo**, founded by St Charles Borromeo in 1561 and built in 1564–92 largely by Pellegrino Tibaldi; the river façade was added in 1808–20, to a design by Leopoldo Pollack.

In the western part of the town, off Corso Cavour is the little Lombard (11C) campanile of **San Giovanni Domnarum**. In Corso Cavour is a 15C tower (at No. 17) and the Bramantesque **Palazzo Bottigella** (No.30), with fine brick decorations. Corso Manzoni prolongs Corso Cavour to the railway, beyond which is (5 minutes) the church of **San Salvatore**, reconstructed in 1467–1511, with good frescoes by Bernardino Lanzani. A further 10 minutes' walk brings you to **San Lanfranco**, a 13C building containing the fine cenotaph (by Amadeo; 1498) of the beatified Lanfranc—actually buried at Canterbury—and traces of 13C frescoes on the right wall of the nave, including one showing the murder of St Thomas Becket at Canterbury. One of the cloisters retains some terracotta decoration also by Amadeo.

The province of Pavia

■ **Information offices.** At the entrance to the **Certosa di Pavia** (closed in winter); at **Vigevano** (29 Corso Vittorio Emanuele, tel. 0381 299282).

■ **Hotels.** At **Certosa di Pavia**: 3-star *Hotel Certosa*. 3-star hotels at **Mortara**. Hotels of all categories at **Salice Terme**. At **Vigevano** 4-star *Europa* and 2-star *Internazionale*. At Cervesina, 6km outside **Voghera**, 4-star *Castello di San Gaudenzio. Youth Hostel*, 25 Viale Repubblica, Voghera.

■ **Restaurants.** At **Certosa di Pavia**: *Vecchio Mulino* (**A**); *Chalet della Certosa* and *La Bruschetta* (both **B**). At **Bereguardo**: *Del Fagiano* (**B**). Near **Voghera**, at Cervesina: *Castello di San Gaudenzio* (**A**). At **Montesegale**: *Al Gallo d'Oro* (**B**). At **Rivanazzano**: *Bona* (**B**). At **San Martino Siccomario**: *Giannino* (**B**)

Certosa di Pavia

The most important building in the province of Pavia is the Certosa di Pavia, 8km north of Pavia. It is difficult to reach by public transport: buses (SGEA) run every 30 minutes from the bus station in Pavia, but from the bus stop it is an unpleasant walk of at least 20 minutes along a busy road; from the train station, on the other side of the Certosa, the walk is even longer. The Milan road from Pavia is skirted by the Naviglio di Pavia, an irrigation canal begun by Galeazzo Visconti; there are a number of abandoned locks and lock-houses.

The *CERTOSA DI PAVIA is one of the most famous buildings in Italy. The Carthusian monastery was founded by Gian Galeazzo Visconti in 1396 as a family mausoleum. The building was entrusted to the Lombard masons of Milan cathedral and the builders of the castle of Pavia. The monastery proper was finished in 1452, the church in 1472, under the Sforzas, with the exception of the façade which was completed in the 16C. The Certosa, now occupied by ten Cistercian monks, is open 9–11.30 & 14.30–16.30, 17 or 18 (closed Mon & major national holidays); the east end of the church is unlocked by a monk and visitors are conducted in parties (but if you are on your own you can usually visit the monastery in your own time).

From the **entrance**, facing west, a **vestibule**, with frescoed saints by Bernardino Luini, leads through to the great **garden-court** in front of the church. On the left are the old pharmacy and food and wine stores; on the right the prior's quarters and the so-called **Palazzo Ducale**, rebuilt by Francesco Maria Richini (1620–25) to house distinguished visitors (now containing a museum, described below).

The sculptural and polychrome marble decoration of the *west front of the church, of almost superabundant richness, marks the height of the artistic achievement of the Quattrocento in Lombardy; it was begun in 1473 and worked on up to 1499 by Cristoforo and Antonio Mantegazza and Giovanni Antonio Amadeo. In the 16C Cristoforo Lombardo continued the upper part in simplified form, but it was never completed. The attribution of the various parts is still under discussion. On the lowest order of the façade are medallions of Roman emperors; above, statues and reliefs of prophets, apostles, and saints by the Mantegazza; and scenes from the Life of Christ by Amadeo. The *great portal was probably designed by Gian Cristoforo Romano (also attributed to Gian Giacomo Dolcebuono and Amadeo) and executed by Benedetto Briosco, the sculptor also of the bas-reliefs representing the Life of the Virgin and of four large reliefs: the Foundation of the Carthusian Order, 1084; Laying the First Stone of the Certosa, 27 August 1396; Translation to the Certosa of the body of Gian Galeazzo, 1 March 1474; Consecration of the Church, 3 May 1497. On each side are two very rich *windows, by Amadeo. The upper part, by Cristoforo Lombardo (1540–60), is decorated with 70 statues of the 16C by Lombard masters. The rest of the exterior is best seen from the northeast.

The *interior is purely Gothic in plan, but Renaissance decorative motives were introduced towards the east end; the chapels opening off the aisle were expensively redecorated and provided with handsome Baroque grilles in the 17C–18C, and only traces remain of their original frescoes and glass. Since the grilles are kept locked, the works of art in the chapels are extremely difficult to see.

South aisle. The first chapel is a good Baroque work by Camillo Procaccini with a lavabo by the Mantegazza. The altarpiece of the second chapel incorporates panels by Macrino d'Alba and Bergognone. In the fourth chapel is a Crucifixion by Bergognone, and in the fifth chapel an altarpiece of *St Syrus, first bishop of Pavia by Bergognone, and unrestored ceiling frescoes by Jacopo de' Mottis (1491). Over the door from the transept, Madonna by Bergognone.

North aisle. The first chapel has a lavabo by the Mantegazza (c 1470). The altarpiece in the second chapel is made up from a painting representing God the Father by Perugino, flanked by Doctors of the Church by Bergognone, and—below—17C copies of panels by Perugino (1499), now in the National Gallery,

London. In the fourth chapel, the Massacre of the Innocents by Dionigi Bussola is the best of the Baroque altar reliefs. The altarpiece in the sixth chapel, of *St Ambrose and saints, is by Bergognone (1492).

The gate leading into the transepts and east end of the church is unlocked by a monk (who shows the rest of the monastery on a conducted tour).

North transept. In the centre, *tomb statues of Lodovico il Moro and Beatrice d'Este, by Cristoforo Solari (1497), brought from Santa Maria delle Grazie in Milan in 1564. The frescoes include Ecce Homo (over the small west door) and Coronation of the Virgin, with the kneeling figures of Francesco Sforza and Lodovico il Moro (north apse), both by Bergognone. The two *angels on either side of the window above are attributed to Bramante. The two *candelabra are by Annibale Fontana.

South transept: *Tomb of Gian Galeazzo Visconti, by Gian Cristoforo Romano (1493–97; the Madonna is by Benedetto Briosco, the sarcophagus by Galeazzo Alessi, the figures of Fame and Victory by Bernardino da Novate). The lunette fresco in the south apse by Bergognone depicts Gian Galeazzo, with his children, presenting a model of the church to the Virgin; higher up are two angels attributed to Bramante. Over the altar is the Madonna enthroned with St Charles and St Bruno, by Cerano.

Off the south transept, a pretty *door by Amadeo, with medallion-portraits of the Duchesses of Milan, leads into the **lavatorium**, which contains a finely-carved lavabo by Alberto Maffiolo of Carrara, and, on the left, a charming fresco of the *Madonna by Bernardino Luini. A matching doorway by Amadeo, with medallions of the Dukes of Milan, in the north transept, leads into the **old sacristy**, with a good vault. It contains fine 17C presses. The remarkable ivory *altarpiece, with nearly 100 statuettes, attributed to Baldassarre degli Embriachi, was made in the early 15C.

The **choir** contains carved and inlaid *stalls (1498), frescoes by Daniele Crespi (1629), and a sumptuous late 16C altar.

From the south transept a pretty doorway by the Mantegazza leads into the *small cloister*, with a garden embellished by terracotta decorations in the Cremonese style by Rinaldo De Stauris (1465), and a terracotta lavabo. The beautiful little *doorway into the church, with a Madonna, is by Amadeo (1466). There is a good view of the southern flank of the church. Off this cloister is the **new sacristy** (only open for services), with an altarpiece of the Assumption by Andrea Solari (completed by Bernardino Campi) and 16C illuminated choirbooks. The **refectory** has ceiling frescoes by Ambrogio and Bernardo Bergognone, a reader's pulpit, and a little fresco of the Madonna by the Zavattari or Bergognone (1450).

A passage leads from the small cloister into the *great cloister*, with 122 arches and more terracotta decoration by De Stauris (1478). Above the porticoes on three sides can be seen 24 identical monks' cells, each with its chimney. Entered by a decorative doorway, they have two rooms, with a little garden below, and a bedroom and loggia above.

The **Chapter House** (no admission), entered through a charming little court, perhaps the work of Bramante, has reliefs by the Mantegazza and in the style of Amadeo.

The **Museum** in the Palazzo Ducale on the garden-court in front of the church is to be reopened after years of closure. It is displayed in two frescoed rooms by Fiamenghino and Giovanni Battista Pozzo (attributed). The paintings include works by Bartolomeo Montagna, Bergognone, Bernardino Luini, Giuseppe Vermiglio, and Vincenzo and Bernardino Campi. The portrait of Pope Paul V is a copy by Gerolamo Ciocca of a work by Caravaggio. There are also sculptures by Bambaia, Mantegazza, and Cristoforo Solari. A gipsoteca will occupy the ground floor, where the arms from the tomb of Gian Galeazzo Visconti are also preserved. The 15C and 16C illuminated choirbooks are displayed in the library.

Northeast of the Certosa, near Landriano, is the **Oasis of Sant'Alessio** (open mid-Mar–Oct, Sat & fest. 10.30–18.30), a bird sanctuary founded in 1973, used as a breeding ground for storks, ibis, flamingo, heron, etc.

East of Pavia is **Belgioioso**, with the well-preserved medieval castle (open Apr–Sep, 14–sunset), where Francis I was imprisoned immediately after the battle of Pavia.

The Lomellina

The western part of the province of Pavia is known as the Lomellina, a cultivated plain between the Ticino, Sesia and Po rivers, which has been provided with irrigation canals since the 14C and where rice has been grown since the 16C. A number of castles survive in the area. The ancient capital of the region is **Lomello**, 32km west of Pavia, interesting for its medieval monuments, including Santa Maria Maggiore (11C) and its baptistery (5C; upper part rebuilt in the 8C), but the chief town is now **Mortara** (14,000 inhab.). Here the church of Santa Croce contains paintings by Bernardino Lanino, and the church of San Lorenzo (Romanesque and Gothic) has paintings by Bernardino Lanino and Giulio Cesare Procaccini. A local speciality is salami made from goose meat. Nearby is **Cilavegna** known for its asparagus.

Northeast of Mortara near the Ticino is **VIGEVANO**, an ancient town which grew to prominence in the 14C under the Visconti. Lodovico il Moro and Francesco il Sforza were born here. It has been famous for the manufacture of shoes since the end of the 19C and the modern city expanded rapidly in the 1950s. In 1492–94 buildings were demolished to create space for the *PIAZZA DUCALE (138m x 48m), a beautiful rectangular Renaissance square, built by order of Lodovico il Moro. It is surrounded on three sides by uniform graceful arcades and its classical design may have been projected with the help of Bramante (or even Leonardo da Vinci). The other end was closed in 1680 when the unusual curved façade of the **Duomo** was added to give the cathedral prominence. The interior (1532–1612) is interesting for its paintings by the 16C Lombard school. A **Museum** (open fest. 15–18 exc. Aug & mid-Dec–mid-Jan) houses the cathedral's rich treasury, which includes Flemish and local tapestries, illuminated codexes, and goldsmiths' work.

A tall Lombard **tower** (probably redesigned by Bramante; open on request) belongs to the huge **Castle** (open 8.30–13.30; Sat & fest. guided visits at 14.30 and 18.30; closed Mon and mid-Dec–mid-Jan), begun by Lucchino Visconti in the mid-14C. On a raised site, this was connected to the piazza by a monumental entrance (destroyed) beneath the tower. The castle was transformed by Lodovico il Moro (with the help of Bramante) into a very grand ducal palace. It has remarkable stables and a beautiful loggia. The raised covered way built by Lucchino Visconti to connect the castle with the Rocca Vecchia survives.

In Palazzo Crespi, in Corso Cavour on the outskirts of the old town, there is a **Museum** illustrating the history of footwear, including a collection of shoes (some dating from the 15C), and the **Museo Civico** (not at present open), with an archaeological collection and picture gallery.

Southeast of Vigevano is the large **Sforzesca**, a model farm designed by Guglielmo da Camino for Lodovico il Moro in 1486.

Vigevano is in the centre of the large **Parco Regionale della Valle del Ticino** instituted in 1974 as a protected area on either side of the Ticino river from Sesto Calende to Pavia (90,000 hectares). Where cars are banned, the paths can be followed on foot or by bicycle to see the wildlife in an interesting landscape. Information from the park office in Magenta (tel. 02 9794401).

The Oltrepò Pavese

The southern part of the province of Pavia, beyond the Po, is known as the Oltrepò Pavese, and it is well known for its wines (particularly *pinot nero*). **Voghera** is an important industrial centre (43,100 inhab.) and railway junction. It has the 12C church of Santi Flavio e Giorgio (a cavalry memorial chapel), a Visconti castle, and a museum of fossils.

A road ascends the **Staffora valley** to the southeast passing **Salice Terme**, a little spa with iodine-impregnated waters (season May–October). Just beyond Ponte Nizza, a byroad (left) leads to the **Abbazia di Sant'Alberto di Butrio**, founded in the 11C. Three Romanesque churches here have 15C frescoes. The road continues through **Varzi**, noted for its salami and up over the **Passo del Penice** (1149m; with skiing facilities). Here is the **Giardino Alpino di Pietra Corva** (950m), open May–Sep, 9–12, 15–19 exc. Mon, a little botanical garden planted in 1967.

East of Voghera is **Montebello della Battaglia**, where a monument marks the site of two important battles: the victory of the French over the Austrians in 1800; and the Franco-Italian success of 1859, the first battle of the second War of Independence. Nearby is **Casteggio,** where the 18C Palazzo della Certosa contains the Museo Storico archeologico dell'Oltrepò Pavese, with material from the Roman *Clastidium* (222 BC).

East of Casteggio is **Stradella**, where another museum contains fossils found near the Po, and archaeological material.

4 · Lago Maggiore

Lago Maggiore is the second largest lake (212 sq. km) in Italy (after the Lago di Garda). Its west bank has belonged to Piedmont since 1743 while its east bank lies in Lombardy. The north end (about one-fifth of its area), including Locarno, is in Swiss territory. Surrounded by picturesque snow-capped mountains, Lake Maggiore became well known at the beginning of the 19C as a European resort, visited for its romantic scenery and good climate. The end of the Simplon highway constructed by Napoleon in 1800–05 from Geneva to Italy skirts its southwest shore. A mild climate and high rainfall account for the luxuriant vegetation on its banks. Among its famous gardens, open from spring to autumn, are those on the Isola Madre and the Isola Bella, and at the Villa Taranto. The central part of the lake around Stresa and the Borromean islands is particularly interesting, and the northern reach has the best scenery. Since the 15C the Italian family of Borromeo have held important possessions on the lake, notably the Borromean islands and the castle of Angera. There is a road around the shore of the lake and public boat services (inaugurated in the last century) linking all the main towns on its shores. The lake is often called Verbano, from the Latin *Lacus Verbanus*, a name derived from the vervain (verbena) which grows abundantly on its shores.

■ **Information offices**. For the west (Piedmontese) side of the lake: APT Lago Maggiore, 70 Via Principe Tomaso, Stresa (tel. 0323 30150). IAT information offices at Arona, Baveno and Verbania. For the east (Lombard) side of the lake: APT del Varesotto, 9 Viale Ippodromo, Varese (tel. 0332 284624) with IAT information offices at Laveno and Luino.

■ **Boat services**. Information from Navigazione Lago Maggiore, Arona (tel. 0322 46651). There are frequent services between Stresa and Intra, calling at Isola Bella, Isola dei Pescatori, Baveno, Isola Madre, Pallanza and Villa Taranto. There is also a frequent service between Arona, Angera and Belgirate. In summer the route from Arona to Locarno, calling at the main ports, is served once a day by a hydrofoil (in 2hrs) and a boat (in 3hrs 30 mins). There are also services linking Cannero, Luino and Cannobio. There is a car ferry every 20 minutes between Intra and Laveno (10 mins). The timetable changes for each of the four seasons.

■ **Hotels**. There are numerous hotels of all categories in all the main resorts, many of them open only from Easter to October. **Stresa:** 5-star: *Des Iles Borromées*; 4-star: *Regina Palace*; 3-star: *Du parc*; 2-star: *Ariston*. **Isola Pescatori (Stresa)**: 3-star: *Verbano*. **Belgirate**: 4-star: *Villa Carlotta, Villa Treves*. **Baveno**: 4-star: *Lido Palace Hotel Baveno*. **Cannobio**: 3-star: *Pironi*; 2-star: *Antica Stallera*. **Verbania**: 4- star: *Majestic*; 3-star: *Belvedere* and *San Gottardo*; 2-star: *Villa Azalea*. **Angera**: 3-star: *Dei Tigli*, 2-star: *Lido*. **Ispra** 3-star: *Europa*. **Laveno Mombello**: 3-star: *Bellevue* and *Moderno*. **Leggiuno-Arolo**: 2-star: *Campagna* and *Sasso Moro*. **Luino**: 4-star: *Camin*. **Sesto Calende**: 3-star: *David* and *Tre Re*.

■ **Camping sites** (1-star and 2-star), mostly open Apr–Oct, on the lakeside at Baveno, Cannero, Cannobio, Verbania, etc.

■ **Restaurants** of all categories in all the resorts on the shores. At Laveno: *Osteria del Vecchio Porto* (**A**); at Angera *La Rocca* (**B**).

■ **Public transport.** The southwest bank from Baveno to Arona is served by the **railway** line through the Simplon tunnel via Domodossola to Milan, opened in 1906. The stations of Baveno, Stresa, Belgirate, Lesa, Meina, and Arona built by Luigi Boffi date from that time.The east bank is followed by the line from St Gotthard and Bellinzona in Switzerland (Luino was the frontier station). Laveno has a second station serving the Nord Milano railway for Varese and Milan. There are also local **bus services** between the main towns.

■ **Hiking** in the hills and mountains above the west side of the lake, especially on Monte Mottarone and in the Parco Nazionale della Val Grande. Information and map from APT Lago Maggiore and the Parco Nazionale della Val Grande (tel. 0323 557960).

■ **Sport**. Water-skiing and sailing on the lake. Skiing on Monte Mottarone. 18-hole golf course at Motta Rossa above Stresa and two 9-hole courses at Vezzo and Pian di Sole (Premano).

Geography
The total length of the lake, from Magadino to Sesto Calende, is 64.3km, and its greatest breadth 4.8km between Baveno and Laveno; its greatest depth, off Ghiffa, is 372m. The chief affluent is the Ticino, which flows in at Madagino and out at Sesto Calende. Other important feeders are the Maggia, which enters the lake at Locarno; the Toce or Tosa, which flows into the gulf of Pallanza, and is joined just before its inflow by the Strona, fed by the waters of the Lake of Orta; and on the east side the Tresa, which drains the Lake of Lugano and enters Lago Maggiore at Luino.

The west side of the lake (in Piedmont)
STRESA (4800 inhab.) is the most important place on the west shore of the lake. It became fashionable as a European resort in the mid-19C, but is now somewhat in decline and little visited in winter. On the lake front, with pleasant gardens, is the orange and grey **Villa Ducale**, built in 1770, which later belonged to the philosopher Antonio Rosmini (1797–1855). It is now a study centre devoted to Rosmini, who founded an order of charity in 1852 (the Rosminian college is above the town). Beyond the Regina Palace hotel opened in 1908, at the bend of the road, is the huge monumental **Hotel des Iles Borromées** which has had many famous guests since it opened in 1863. Frederick Henry in Hemingway's *Farewell to Arms* also stayed here. South of the pier is the **Villa Pallavicino**, built in 1855 with a small formal garden at the front of the house. It is surrounded by a fine wooded park (open mid-Mar–mid-Oct, 9–18) planted with palms, magnolias, and cedars, with a zoological garden.

The *ISOLE BORROMEE are a group of beautiful little islands in the lake close to Stresa, named after the Italian Borromeo family who still own the Isola Madre, Isola Bella and Isola San Giovanni. There are regular daily boat services (see above) for Isola Bella, Isola dei Pescatori and Isola Madre from Stresa, Baveno, Pallanza, and Intra.

The most famous of the islands is the *ISOLA BELLA, which was a barren rock with a small church and a few cottages before it was almost totally occupied by a huge palace with terraced gardens built in 1631–71 by Angelo Crivelli for Count Carlo III Borromeo, in honour of his wife, from whom it takes its name. The island measures just 320 by 180 metres, and there is a tiny hamlet

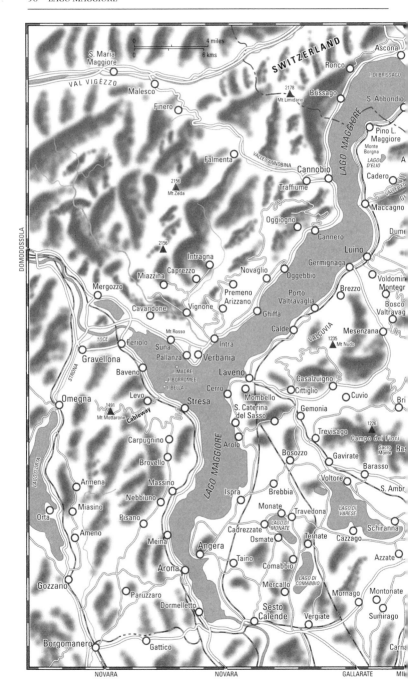

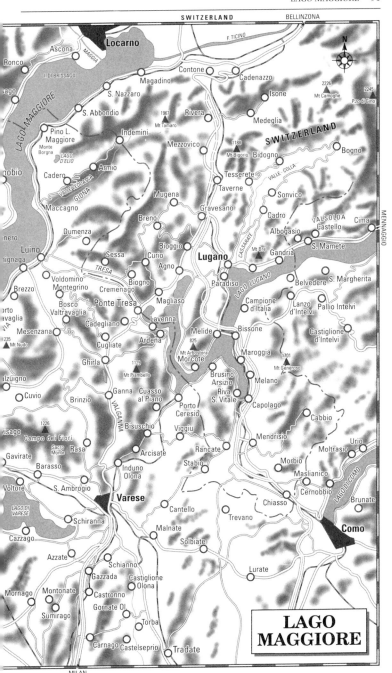

LAGO MAGGIORE

(about 20 inhab.) by the pier outside the garden gates, with tourist shops and a few restaurants and cafés. The palace and gardens (combined ticket) are open only from the end of March to the end of October (daily, 9–12, 13.30–18).

To the left of the pier is the vast grey **Palace** entered from an open courtyard behind four palm trees. On the right of the courtyard (seen through a grille) is the **chapel** which contains three family *tombs with elaborate carvings by Giovanni Antonio Amadeo and Bambaia, brought from demolished churches in Milan. On the left of the courtyard is the entrance to the palace. Twenty-five rooms on the *piano nobile*, decorated with Murano chandeliers and Venetian mosaic floors, can be visited (the three floors above are the private apartments of the Borromeo family). Edward Gibbon stayed here as a guest of the Borromeo in 1764.

The octagonal blue and white **Sala dei Concerti** was built in 1948–51 in Baroque style following the original plans. There is a view of the Isola dei Pescatori and (right) the Isola Madre. The **Sala di Musica** has musical instruments, two Florentine cabinets in ebony and pietre dure (17C–18C), and paintings by Jacopo Bassano and Tempesta. In 1935 a conference took place here between Mussolini and the French and British governments in an attempt to guarantee the peace of Europe. Napoleon stayed in the next room in 1797. The **library** preserves, besides its books, some paintings by Carnevalis. Another room has paintings by Luca Giordano, and beyond a room with views of the Borromeo properties by Zuccarelli is the ballroom.

Stairs leads down to the **grottoes** built on the lake in the 18C. Beyond a room with 18C–20C puppets once used in puppet shows held in the 'amphitheatre' in the garden, are six grottoes encrusted with shells, pebbles, marbles, etc. Displayed here are statues by Gaetano Matteo Monti, remains of an ancient boat found in the lake off Angera, archaeological material (Golasecca period), and bridles. A spiral staircase in an old tower which pre-dates the palace leads up to a short corridor of mirrors and thence to the **anticamera**, with a ceiling tondo attributed to Giovanni Battista Tiepolo and two paintings by Daniele Crespi. Beyond the chapel of St Charles Borromeo is the **gallery of tapestries** with a splendid collection of 16C Flemish *tapestries commissioned by St Charles Borromeo. The painting of St Jerome is by Moretto.

A door leads out to the famous ***gardens** inhabited by white peacocks. The terraces are built out into the lake, and soil for the plants had to be brought from the mainland. A double staircase leads up onto a terrace with a huge camphor tree, camellias, bamboos, breadfruit, sugar cane, tapioca and tea and coffee plants, etc. Beyond is the 'amphitheatre', an elaborate Baroque construction with statues, niches, pinnacles and stairs, crowned by a unicorn (the family crest). The terrace at the top looks straight to Stresa, and below is the Italianate garden with box hedges and yew, and ten terraces planted with roses, oleanders, and pomegranates descending to the lake. Other parts of the garden are laid out in the 'English style' with beds of tulips and forget-me-nots in spring and geraniums in summer. Below the terraces are rhododendrons and orange trees (protected in winter). The azaleas are at their best in April and May. The second exit leads out of the gardens through the delightful old-fashioned greenhouse.

Near Isola Bella are a tiny islet inhabited by cormorants in winter and the **Isola dei Pescatori** or **Isola Superiore**, not owned by the Borromeo. It is occupied by a pretty little fishing village, and has a hotel and restaurant.

The ***ISOLA MADRE** (330m x 220 m) is nearer to Pallanza than Stresa. It is entirely occupied by a Borromeo villa and botanical garden (open 27 March to end of October), and inhabited only by a custodian. It has one restaurant (otherwise you can bring a sandwich). The landscaped gardens, at their best in April, are laid out in the 'English style', and were replanted in the 1950s by Henry Cocker. The particularly mild climate allows a great number of exotic and tropical plants to flourish here (most of the plants are labelled), and white peacocks and white pheasants inhabit the gardens. **Viale Africa**, with the warmest exposure, is lined with a variety of plants including citrus fruits. The **Camellia terrace** has numerous species or camellia, and mimosa. Beyond a wisteria-covered arboured walk is the **Mediterranean garden** with rosemary, lavender, etc. and a rock garden. The cylindrical tower was once used as an ice house; beyond it are ferns. From the little port with its boat house (and an 18C boat suspended from the roof) is a view of Pallanza. Nearby is the oldest camellia on the island (thought to be some 150 years old). On a lawn is a group of taxodium trees, with their roots sticking up out of the ground (an odd sight), and beyond are banks of azaleas, rhododendrons, camphor trees, and ancient magnolias. Beside steps up to the villa, by a remarkable Kashmir cypress—said to be 200 years old—is an aviary with parrots that nest in the cedar of Lebanon here. Near the villa are ornamental banana trees and the Art Nouveau family chapel. The terrace near the villa is planted with tall palm trees including a majestic Chilean palm, planted in 1858, which bears miniature edible coconuts. The steps nearby are covered with a trellis of kiwi fruit.

The 18C **villa** is also open to the public. It contains 17C and 18C furnishings from Borromeo properties, and servants' livery, as well as a collection of porcelain, puppets and dolls (19C French and German), and paintings by Pitocchetto. The little theatre dates from 1778.

The **Isola San Giovanni** is not open to the public. The villa on the island was once the summer home of Toscanini.

Above Stresa is **Monte Mottarone** (1491m) reached by a cableway (which replaces a funicular inaugurated in 1911), or by road. The road (20km) passes a 9-hole golf course at **Vezzo**. The local industry of umbrella-making at **Gignese** is recorded in the Umbrella Museum here, founded in 1939, which has a collection of umbrellas and parasols dating from 1840 to 1940. At **Alpino** is the **Giardino Alpinia** (605m), a botanical garden founded in 1933, with some 544 species of Alpine plants. It is open April–mid-Oct exc. Mon, 9–18. Here a private tollroad, owned by the Borromeo since 1623 (9km; always open), continues through the meadows and woods of the **Parco del Mottarone** on the slopes of Monte Mottarone, with a view of the whole chain of the Alps from Monte Viso in the west to the Ortler and Adamello in the east, and the Monte Rosa group especially conspicuous to the northwest. Below seven lakes are visible and the wide Po valley. The mountain has been visited by skiers since the beginning of the century, and there are spectacular walks in the area.

BAVENO (4400 inhab.), northwest of Stresa, is in a fine position on the south shore of the gulf of Pallanza opposite the Borromean Islands. Quieter than Stresa, it preserves a pleasant little square with a Renaissance baptistery (frescoes) and a church with an early façade and bell-tower. The landing stage is a pretty art Nouveau building, and the delightful shore road to Stresa, with a good view of the Borromean Islands, is flanked by villas and hotels built in the 19C when the town was well known as a resort, among which is the Castello Branca (formerly Villa Clara), built in 1844, where Queen Victoria spent the spring of 1879. To the northwest of Baveno rises Monte Camoscio (890m), with quarries of pink granite for which Baveno is famous.

Across the lake from Baveno is **VERBANIA** (34,700 inhab.) which includes the towns of Pallanza and Intra on either side of the promontory of the Punta della Castagnola. In a charming position in full view of the Borromean Islands and below Monte Rossa (618m), it has a mild climate which makes the flora particularly luxuriant; the lake front is planted with magnolias. The Hotel Majestic was opened here in 1870. Near the pier is the mausoleum, by Marcello Piacentini, of Marshal Cadorna (1850–1928), a native of Pallanza; and just inland is the market-place, with the town hall and the church of **San Leonardo** (16C; modernised in the 19C), the tall tower of which was completed by Pellegrino Tibaldi in 1589. In the Baroque Palazzo Dugnani is a small local **museum** (9–12, 15–18 exc. Mon), founded in 1914 and containing 19C landscapes of the lake, and sculptures by Paolo Troubetzkoy and Arturo Martini. The Villa Kursaal (1882), surrounded by gardens, is open to the public.

The narrow Via Cavour leads north from the market-place, and some way beyond is the fine domed church of the **Madonna di Campagna**, which was begun in 1519 and contains contemporary decorations including works attributed to Carlo Urbini, Aurelio Luini and Gerolamo Lanino.

On the **PUNTA DELLA CASTAGNOLA**, a promontory on the lake, is the **Villa San Remigio** built in 1903 (now the seat of the administrative offices of the Regional government; adm. only by previous appointment, tel. 0323 504401). The formal gardens, when they were laid out in 1905 by Sophie Browne, an Irish painter, and Silvio della Valle di Casanova, were among the best in northern Italy, with topiary terraces, fountains, and statues by Orazio Marinali. The plants include yellow and white banksia roses, wisteria, camellias, myrtle, conifers and palm trees. Next to Villa San Remigio on the slopes of the Punta della Castagnola is the 19C **VILLA TARANTO**, with famous botanical *gardens (open Apr–Oct, 8.30–19.30) much visited by tourists—the villa has a landing stage served by regular boat services. The huge estate was bought by Captain Neil McEacharn (1884–1964) in 1930, and he created (together with Henry Cocker) a garden with an outstanding collection of exotic plants from all over the world, later donated by him to the Italian State. The plants include magnolias (at their best at the beginning of April), superb camellias (which flower in April), rhododendrons (which flower in May and June), azaleas and paulownias (best in May). The herbaceous borders and dahlias (over 300 varieties) are at their best in July and August. Birches, maples and conifers distinguish the woodlands. The statues include a bronze fisher-boy by Vincenzo Gemito.

Above Verbania is the Parco Nazionale della Val Grande, a protected mountainous area with fine walks.

Intra is the most important commercial centre on the lake with a car ferry (every 20 minutes) across the lake to Laveno on the opposite shore. To the north, close to the lake, are the beautiful private gardens of the Villa Poss and Villa Ada. Roads lead up to **Miazzina** (719m), at the foot of Monte Zeda (2188m), and **Premeno** (802m), a winter and summer resort, above which is **Pian di Sole** (949m), with a 9-hole golf course.

From Intra to Cannobio

The road skirts the lake to **Ghiffa**, a scattered village, with the castle of Frino. The little 13C church of Novaglio, above the road, is built in a mixture of Lombard and Gothic styles. Above **Oggebbio**, in chestnut groves, is the little oratory of Cadessino, with 15C–16C frescoes. Ahead, across the lake, Luino comes into view, as, beneath **Oggiogno** high up on its rock, the road passes the villa of the statesman Massimo d'Azeglio (1798–1866), where he wrote most of his memoirs.

Cannero Riviera is a resort lying in a sheltered and sunny position at the foot of Monte Carza (1118m). Off the coast are two rocky islets on which stood the castles of Malpaga, demolished by the Visconti in 1414. One island is now occupied by the picturesque ruins of a castle built by Ludovico Borromeo in 1519–21. On the hill above the town is the church (14C–15C) of Carmine Superiore built on the summit of a precipice, and containing some good ceiling paintings and a triptych of the 14C Lombard school. The road rounds Punta d'Amore opposite Maccagno.

Cannobio (5200 inhab.) has ancient origins and preserves some medieval buildings. Near the pier is the **Santuario della Pietà** (reconstructed in 1583–1601), with a fine altarpiece by Gaudenzio Ferrari. The town hall, called Il Parrasio, is a 13C building with 17C alterations. Inland, in the **Val Cannobina** is the **Orrido di Sant'Anna**, a romantic gorge with a waterfall.

Just beyond Cannobio is the frontier with Switzerland (see *Blue Guide Switzerland*), beyond which is Locarno at the northern end of the lake.

From Stresa to Arona

The road follows the last stretch of the Simplon highway built by Napoleon in 1800–05. **Belgirate** is a pretty hamlet with a good view of the lake and some old houses surviving in its highest part. At **Lesa**, the novelist Alessandro Manzoni often stayed at Palazzo Stampa. **ARONA** is an ancient town (15,000 inhab.) looking across the lake to Angera. The Palazzo Podestà dates from the 15C. In the upper town, the church of **Santa Maria** contains an *altarpiece by Gaudenzio Ferrari (1511) in its Borromeo chapel. The lunette over the main door has a charming 15C relief of the Holy Family. The nearby church of the **Santi Martiri** has an altarpiece by Bergognone. The church of the Madonna di Piazza (1592) is attributed to Pellegrino Tibaldi. To the north, above the road, stands **San Carlone**, a colossal copper statue of St Charles Borromeo (1538–84), archbishop of Milan and an important figure of the Counter-Reformation. He was born in the castle that now lies in ruins above the town. The statue, 23m high, standing on a pedestal 12m high, was commissioned by a relative of the saint from Giovanni Battista Crespi (Il Cerano) and finished in 1697. It can be climbed by steps and an internal stair.

The east side of the lake (in Lombardy)

LUINO is the most important tourist centre on the Lombard side of the lake. A small industrial town (15,400 inhab.), it lies a little north of the junction of the Tresa and Margorabbia, which unite to flow into the lake at Germignaga. Near the landing stage is a statue of Garibaldi, commemorating his attempt, on 14 Aug 1848, to renew the struggle against Austria with only 1500 men, after the armistice which followed the defeat of Custozza. The Town Hall occupies an 18C palazzo by Felice Soave. An Adoration of the Magi attributed to Bernardino Luini, who was probably born here, decorates the cemetery church of **San Pietro**, and the **Madonna del Carmine** has frescoes by his pupils (1540). A market has been held in the town on Wednesday since 1541. On the landward side of the town is the railway station where the Swiss line from Bellinzona meets the Italian line from Novara and Milan. This was an important frontier station (with custom-house) on the St Gotthard line. A short distance to the north, at Zenna, the road enters Switzerland (see *Blue Guide Switzerland*).

LAVENO, south of Luino, now part of the municipality of Mombello, is in a fine position on the lake (with good views of the Punta della Castagnola and the Isola Madre in the distance). Its small port serves the car ferry to Intra. The old-fashioned railway station of the Milano–Nord line for Varese and Milan (one of two stations in Laveno) adjoins the ferry station. The town was once noted for its ceramics, and there is a Ceramics Museum (open 14.30–17.30; Fri, Sat & Sun also 10–12) in the locality of Cerro. A monument in the piazza by the waterside commemorates the Garibaldini who fell in an attempt to capture the town from the Austrians in 1859 (the Austrian fort was on the Punta di San Michele).

A cableway (closed on Mon and in bad weather) mounts to **Poggio Sant'Elsa** with a view north to Monte Rosa, the Mischabel group and the Fletschhorn group. From the cableway station here it is 30 minutes on foot to the **Sasso del Ferro** (1062m), the beautiful hill to the east. The panorama is still better from Monte Nudo (1235m).

From Laveno to Sesto Calende

The road follows the shore of the lake past the ceramics museum at Cerro (see above) and **Leggiuno**, where the Oratory of Santi Primo e Feliciano (9C) has Roman foundations. The solitary convent of **Santa Caterina del Sasso** (reached in 10 minutes by a steep path which descends from the main road, or by boat from Laveno or Stresa in summer) was founded in the 13C, and rein-habited by Dominicans in 1986. Open daily 9.30–12 & 14 or 15–17 or18, it is built into a sheer rock face directly above the lake (there is an 18m drop to the water). The picturesque Romanesque buildings (particularly attractive when seen from the water) were restored in 1624 and have a good view of the gulf of Pallanza and the Borromean Islands. They contain 15C and 16C frescoes and a 17C Last Supper.

Ispra is the seat of Euratom, the first centre in Italy for nuclear studies. **ANGERA** has a pleasant spacious waterfront planted with horse chestnuts. A road (signposted) leads up to the *Rocca (open Apr–Oct, 9.30–12.30 & 14 or 15–17 or 19). Formerly a castle of the Visconti, it passed to the Borromeo in 1449, and is still owned by them. It was extensively restored in the 16C–17C. The fine gateway leads into a charming courtyard with a pergola open to the south end of the lake. Off the second courtyard is a wine press dating from

1745. The Sala di Giustizia has interesting 14C Gothic frescoes commissioned by Giovanni Visconti, Bishop of Milan, with signs of the zodiac and episodes from the battles of Archbishop Ottone Visconti. In other rooms are displayed paintings, Roman altars, and detached frescoes from Palazzo Borromeo in Milan. It also has a Doll Museum, and the 13C Torre Castellana can be climbed.

In Via Mazzini there is a grappa distillery dating from 1850.

North of Angera at **Ranco** is an interesting Transport Museum (free admission daily exc. Mon 10–12, 15–17), mostly displayed in the open air. It illustrates the history of transport from horse-drawn carriages to steam engines, electric tramways, funicular railways, etc. As well as many original vehicles, various stations have been reconstructed.

SESTO CALENDE is the southernmost town on the east bank of the lake. It is said to derive its name from its market day in Roman times—the sixth day before the Calends. A small **Museo Civico** houses archaeological finds from tombs of the local Golasecca culture (800–450 BC).

5 · Varese and its province

The town of Varese has only a few monuments worth visiting, but there are various places of interest nearby, notably Castiglione Olona (where there are no hotels) with its Renaissance works of art and frescoes by Masolino. The province is situated between Lago Maggiore and the Lago di Lugano and has numerous minor lakes, but the countryside has been ruined in many places by new building in this century. The Sacro Monte above Varese has beautiful 17C chapels, and Castelseprio, south of the town, is one of the most important Lombard sites in Italy. Villas in the province with particularly beautiful gardens open to the public include the Villa Porta Bozzolo at Casalzuigno, Villa Cicogna Mozzoni at Bisuschio, and the Palazzo Estense in Varese.

Varese
Varese is a flourishing industrial town of 95,000 inhabitants, one of the richest in Italy, and has a typically Lombard character. The rapid increase in its population in this century resulted in much indiscriminate new building and sprawling suburbs, but a few attractive streets of old houses with fine courtyards have survived in the centre. After the opening of the State and Nord Milano railway lines to Milan (only 50km away) in 1865 and 1886, many Milanese built their summer homes in the environs, and some Art Nouveau villas survive.

■ **Information office.** APT del Varesotto, 9 Viale Ippodromo (tel. 0332 284624). IAT information office, 1 Via Carrobbio (tel. 0332 283604).

■ **Hotels.** 4-star: *Crystal Hotel*, 10 Via Speroni; *Palace Hotel*; 11 Via Manara, Colle Campigli. 3-star: *Bologna*, 7 Via Broggi; *Europa*, 1 Piazza Beccaria.

■ **Restaurants.** A:*Teatro*, 3 Via Croce; *Lago Maggiore*, 19 Via Carrobbio.

■ **Public transport.** The two **railway** stations (one for the State railways and one for the Nord Milano line) are only a few metres apart. **Buses**: Bus C every 15 minutes to Sacro Monte and Campo dei Fiori; Bus A to Biumo Superiore. Country buses to towns in the province, Lago Maggiore, Lago di Lugano, Como, etc.

■ **Market day** on Saturday between the two railway stations.

■ **Annual festival** on 17 January (Sagra di Sant'Antonio).

The attractive, arcaded CORSO MATTEOTTI leads to Piazza del Podestà, separated from the church square by a War Memorial arcade. **San Vittore** was built in 1580–1625 probably on designs by Pellegrino Pellegrini, with a neoclassical façade by Leopold Pollack (1788–91). The detached campanile is by the local architect Giuseppe Bernasconi (1617). In the interior are paintings by Il Cerano, Morazzone and Pietro Antonio Magatti. The **Baptistery** behind (unlocked on request by the sacristan) dates from the 12C. It has an interesting plan and good 14C Lombard frescoes on the right wall. The unfinished 13C font has been raised to reveal the earlier 8C font.

At the southern end of Corso Matteotti is Piazza Monte Grappa laid out in 1927–35, and typical of the Fascist period of architecture. Via Marcobi and Via Sacco lead to the huge monumental **Palazzo Estense** (now the town hall), built by Francesco III d'Este, Duke of Modena, in 1766–72 as the seat of his imperial court. Called by Stendhal the Versailles of Milan, it is one of the most interesting palaces of its period in Italy. The attractive garden façade overlooks the spacious **gardens** (open daily), laid out by Giuseppe Bianchi in imitation of the Imperial gardens of Schönbrunn in Vienna. Paths lead up past a grotto to terraces with a good view of the Alps, and a little children's playground in a wood.

On the hill is the eccentric 18C–19C **Villa Mirabello** with a tall tower, surrounded by a garden in the English style. There is a café on the pleasant south side. The villa houses the **Musei Civici** (open Tue–Sat, 9.30–13, 14.30–17.30; fest. 14.30–18). The **Pinacoteca** contains works by Jacopo Bassano, Innocenza da Imola, Carlo Francesco Nuvolone, Camillo Procaccini and Giacomo Ceruti (Il Pitocchetto), as well as a wood model of the campanile of San Vittore (c 1677). The 19C works include paintings by Carlo Bossoli, Mosè Bianchi, Giuseppe Pellizza da Volpedo and Giacomo Balla, and busts by Vincenzo Vela and Lorenzo Bartolini. Upstairs is the **archaeological collection** with prehistoric finds from Lombardy, as well as Roman and medieval material, and the mummy of a boy dating from 1645. Another room has a display of butterflies and birds.

North of the centre of Varese, on a low hill, is the residential district of **Biumo Superiore**. Here is the 18C Villa Litta which was donated to the FAI in 1996 by Giuseppe Panza, together with 133 works from his collection of 20C American art (most of which was sold, and partially donated, to the Museum of Contemporary Art in Los Angeles and the Guggenheim Museum of New York). The villa (which will be opened to the public) also contains furniture and African and pre-Columbian sculpture, and is surrounded by a park. Also in this district is the Villa Andrea Ponti, a vast 19C pile by Giuseppe Balzaretto, with a park, adjoining another 19C Villa Ponti.

On the northern outskirts of the town rises the **SACRO MONTE**, one of the most important of the numerous shrines known as Sacri Monti erected during the Counter-Reformation in the 17C in Piedmont and Lombardy in honour of the Madonna, consisting of a series of chapels illustrating the Mysteries of the Rosary. The 14 pretty chapels lining a broad winding path some 2km long up the steep hillside, were designed to be seen by pilgrims on their way up the hill (a walk of about an hour). The first chapel can be reached from the centre of Varese by car or bus along Via Veratti and Viale Aguggiari. The road climbs up through the residential district of Sant'Ambrogio with numerous Art Nouveau villas and their gardens, to end at an archway near the first chapel.

A less strenuous way of visiting the chapels is to continue up a byroad from the first chapel under the old stone arches of a funicular railway (no longer in operation) with a view of the hill of Campo dei Fiore. At the top of the Sacro Monte is a small village (880m) with a few Art Nouveau houses huddled around the sanctuary church of Santa Maria del Monte. The view (on a clear day) takes in Como with the mountains beyond and the plain towards Milan, and in the opposite direction the Lago di Varese. The bronze monument to Paul VI dates from 1984.

The **church** dates mostly from 1472. On the high altar of 1662 is the venerated 14C image of the Madonna. Outside the west door is a terrace with a view of five lakes: Lago di Varese in the foreground, Comabbio and Biandronno on the left, and Monate beyond. On the right can just be seen the tip of Lago Maggiore. The hill of Campo dei Fiore is prominent on the right with a huge abandoned Art Nouveau hotel.

From the terrace a cobbled passageway leads down to the broad cobbled path which descends past a statue of Moses and the **Museo Pogliaghi** (open Apr–Sep), surrounded by a garden, in the villa which belonged to the sculptor Lodovico Pogliaghi (1857–1950). It contains his eclectic collection of works of art, archaeological material, and some of his own sculptures including the model for the bronze doors of the Duomo of Milan.

The path leads downhill to the 14th (last) chapel. The monumental *chapels, all of them of different design, are excellent works by the local architect Giuseppe Bernasconi (Il Mancino) from 1604 onwards. They are all kept locked but you can see the interiors (push-button lights) through the windows. They contain life-size terracotta groups representing the Mysteries of the Rosary by Francesco Silva, Cristoforo Prestinari and Dionigi Bussola. The frescoes are by Carlo Francesco Nuvolone, Giovanni Battista and Giovan Paolo Recchi, and Morazzone. Outside the chapel of the Nativity is a good 20C fresco by Renato Guttuso depicting the Flight into Egypt. From the hillside there are views of Como to the left and of Lago di Varese on the right.

A road continues up from Monte Sacro to **Monte delle Tre Croci** (1033m), which has a wonderful view (and an observatory). The road deteriorates into a track to cross the **Campo dei Fiori** (1227m), a protected area with an even wider panorama. Here in 1908–12 Giuseppe Sommaruga built a huge hotel, restaurant and funicular station, all fine Art Nouveau buildings which have been abandoned since 1953.

In the western outskirts of Varese is the **Castello di Masnago** (Sat 14–18; fest. 10–12, 14–18) owned by the municipality, a 15C building which incorporates a 12C tower. It contains frescoes of court life dating from 1450, and the park is open to the public daily.

In the southern outskirts of the town, in the locality of **Bizzozero**, is a Romanesque cemetery church on 7–8C foundations, containing interesting frescoes (14C–16C), including some by Galdino da Varese (1498), and an 11C frescoed altar.

Castiglione Olona

The most interesting place to visit near Varese is Castiglione Olona, off the road to Saronno (poorly signposted), which was practically rebuilt by Cardinal Branda Castiglione (1350–1443) when he returned from a stay in Florence, bringing with him Masolino da Panicale. The works of art he commissioned to adorn the little town take their inspiration from the Florentine Renaissance. There are now a number of antiquarian bookshops in the little town, and an antiques and bric-a-brac fair is held in the streets on the first Sunday of the month. **Restaurants**. *Il Cardinale, La Corte del Ragno*, and *L'Oasi* (all **B/C**).

*Palazzo Branda Castiglione**, open 9–12, 14.30–17.30 exc Mon; fest. 15–18 (also10.30–12.30 in summer) is where the cardinal was born and died. The little **courtyard** has an interesting exterior, and the **chapel** has good frescoes attributed to Vecchietta. Stairs lead up to a **loggia** (enclosed in the 19C) with a wooden coffered ceiling and traces of frescoes. Low down on the wall is a frescoed still life with jars, attributed to Paolo Schiavo. The **main hall** has a Renaissance fireplace and family portraits, and Baroque stucco decoration on the upper part of the walls. The **bedroom** has very unusual allegorical frescoes; dated 1423 and thought to be by Michelino da Besozzo, they show ten trees and white putti. In the **study** are frescoes attributed to Masolino of the Hungarian city of Veszprem, where Castiglione served as bishop in 1412–24, with strange rocky landscapes.

Opposite the palace, preceded by a courtyard, is the *Chiesa di Villa**, with an unusual dome, built and decorated in 1431–44 by local masons and sculptors in the style of Brunelleschi. It has a handsome exterior, and flanking the fine portal are two colossal carved saints. In the lovely, simple interior, with a dome and apse, are six good stone and terracotta statues (including a polychrome Annunciatory Angel and Madonna which have been attributed to Vecchietta) high up on corbels. In the apse is a small fresco of the Resurrection of Christ, and a delightful red and white frescoed frieze of flowers below. Beneath the altar is a 15C stone statue of the Dead Christ.

The road continues uphill past the 19C **town hall**, which incorporates a school building founded by the Cardinal in 1423 to teach grammar and music. Above the door is a bust of the Cardinal dating from 1503 and on the left is a fresco from the early 15C. The courtyard dates from the 18C. A cobbled lane leads up to the top of the hill where the **Collegiata** was built in 1422–25, replacing the Castiglione family's feudal castle. Above the portal is a bright lunette of the Madonna with Saints and the Cardinal, dating from 1428. The church is entered through a side door off the garden (ring for adm. on the left of the church, daily exc. Mon 10–12, 14.30–17; 1 Apr–30 Sep 10–12, 15–19). The well proportioned and luminous interior has neo-Gothic decoration in the side aisles. In the sanctuary is the funerary monument (1443) of the Cardinal with his effigy supported by four statues of the Virtues. On the vault are six frescoed *scenes from the Life of the Virgin signed by Masolino. In the lunettes below and above the windows are scenes from the lives of Saints Stephen and Lawrence by Paolo Schiavo and Vecchietta. In the apse is a painting of the Crucifixion attributed to Neri di Bicci.

Across the garden, in a former tower of the castle, is the entrance to the family chapel, later used as a baptistery and museum. The ***Baptistery** is a beautiful and well proportioned little building dating from 1435. The *frescoes of the Life of St John the Baptist are Masolino's masterpiece, executed on his return to the town in 1435. On the right wall is the Banquet of Herod with a long loggia, and in the sanctuary, the Baptism of Christ with a splendid group of nude figures on the right and the river disappearing into the distance. In the vault are the symbols of the Evangelists, and in the vault of the sanctuary, God the Father with angels and Doctors of the Church on the arch. The other frescoes (including a view of Rome on the entrance wall) are very damaged. The font is a good 15C Venetian work.

Opposite the baptistery a small room serves as a **museum** with a miscellany of objects which have survived from the rich treasury (pillaged over the centuries) which the Cardinal donated to the church. They include reliquaries, and a small painting of the Annunciation by Paolo Schiavo.

Castelseprio, south of Castiglione, on a plateau in a wood above the Olona valley, is an extensive archaeological area (open 9–18, fest. 9–16.45; closed Mon), beautifully kept and owned by the State since 1950 when excavations were begun here. On the site of a Late Bronze Age settlement, it includes the ruins of the late Roman *castrum* of *Sibrium* occupied throughout the Lombard period (AD 568–771). A fortified *borgo* grew up around the camp, but this was destroyed by Milan in 1287. The site is well labelled and includes the remains of two churches, an octagonal baptistery, defensive walls, towers, medieval houses, and cisterns and wells. A custodian accompanies you to unlock the most important church, **Santa Maria Foris Portas**, a short distance away from the *castrum*, which has a remarkable plan with lateral apses and windows in the corners of the nave. The building dates from somewhere between the 7C and 9C; it was restored and partly reconstructed in the 1940s when the frescoes were discovered, and remains of its black and white marble floor survive. In the apse are extraordinary *mural paintings with scenes from the Apocrypha illustrating the Infancy of Christ, including the Nativity with the reclining figure of the Madonna, and the Journey to Bethlehem (with a graceful donkey). They are in an Oriental (Alexandrian) style and are thought to date from the 8C.

Part of the camp of *Sibrium* extended across the Olona to the site later occupied by the **Monastero di Torba** (open daily except Mon 10–13, 14–17; Feb–Sep 10–18), which is reached by a path down through woods (c 200 metres, but temporarily impassable) or—much longer—by a (signposted road) from Gornate Olona. There is a restaurant here (*Il Refettorio*, **B**); booking preferable, tel. 0331 820301. Part of the ruined defensive walls have been exposed and the massive corner tower survives, both dating from the 5C. A Benedictine nunnery was established here in the late Lombard period (8C), and the monastic buildings were occupied up until 1480. In a pretty position at the foot of a wooded hill, they were donated to the FAI in 1976 and have been beautifully maintained since their restoration in 1986. The early medieval church has an 8C crypt and a 13C apse. Opposite is a 15C farmhouse built above the ancient defensive walls, which incorporates the refectory, a splendid old room with a fireplace. The corner tower, on 5C–6C foundations, was also occupied by the nuns in the 8C. Steps lead up past an oven, which may date from the 12C, to the first floor and a room used as a burial place (with an 8C fresco of a nun named Aliberga). The room above functioned as an oratory, and it contains fascinating Carolingian (late 8C) frescoes of female saints and nuns (uncovered in this century).

The province of Varese

■ **Hotels. Lago di Varese**: 4-star: *Continental*. **Arcumeggia** 1-star: *del Pittore*. **Cunardo** 4-star *Delle Arti* . For the hotels on the east bank of Lago Maggiore, see page 88.

■ **Restaurants. Lago di Varese**: *Il Cacciatore* (**B**). **Arcumeggia**: *del Pittore* (**C**).

West of Varese is the **Lago di Varese**, 8.5km long, a lake once admired for its scenery by Edward Lear. It used to have an abundance of fish, but is now polluted. **Voltorre** on the shore of the lake has an old monastery with an interesting Romanesque brick cloister where concerts are held in June. From **Biandronno** (yellow signposts), boats can be hired for the little **Isola Virginia**, an island on which is the Museo Preistorico di Villa Ponti (open Jun–Sep) which contains objects found in prehistoric lake dwellings here (Neolithic to Bronze Age). In May–Oct guided visits to the island are organised by the Musei Civici of Varese (tel. 0331 281590). At **Gavirate**, at the north end of the lake, is a Pipe Museum (adm. on request), with some 20,000 pipes from all over the world and of all periods.

A road leads north from Varese through the **Valganna**, the narrow valley of the Olona. At the beginning of the valley, near Induno Olona, is the Poretti beer distillery, in a remarkable Art Nouveau factory building. The road passes the little Laghetto di Ganna, and the **Abbey of San Gemolo**, founded in 1095 and Benedictine until 1556. It has a 12C church and a five-sided cloister. The **Lago di Ghirla** (used for swimming in summer) has a nice Art Nouveau tram station. At Ghirla the Lugano road branches right and descends to **Ponte Tresa** on the frontier with Switzerland. This consists of an Italian and a Swiss village separated by the river Tresa, which here marks the frontier, entering a little land-locked bay of the Lago di Lugano. Beyond Ghirla is **Cunardo**, known since Roman times for the production of ceramics. The interesting old 18C pottery of Ibis, with its conspicuous chimneys, is still in use and family run, and produces traditional 18C blue-and-white ware (visitors are welcome).

From Cunardo a road leads west into the **Valcuvia**, with hills of chestnut woods and an open landscape extending towards Lago Maggiore. Here is **Casalzuigno** a hamlet with the splendid *****Villa Porta-Bozzolo**, formerly Ca' Porta (the garden and villa are open Oct–Dec 10–13, 14–17; Feb–Sep 10–13, 14–18; closed Mon & in Jan). It was left to the FAI in 1989 and is beautifully maintained. The villa dates from the 16C when it was in the centre of a huge estate purchased by the Porta family, and silkworms were bred in the farm buildings. Additions were made to the house in the 17C, and the splendid *****garden** was laid out in the French style on the hillside at the beginning of the 18C by

Gian Angelo III Porta. Beyond the parterre are four stone terraces with balustrades and statues on either side of steps up to a green lawn surrounded by cypresses and in front of a fountain. A cypress avenue climbs the wooded hillside behind. There is another little garden to the right of the parterre, on a line with the façade of the villa, approached by a gate with statues of the Four Seasons, and with an avenue of oak trees leading to a little Rococo frescoed garden house. The **villa** preserves elaborate frescoes by Pietro Antonio Magatti (1687–1768).

Above the villa a narrow road winds up to **Arcumeggia**, a tiny hamlet in the hills. Since 1956 the exterior of many of the houses have been frescoed by contemporary artists, including Aligi Sassù.

A road (N344) leads northeast from Varese to Porto Ceresio on the Lago di Lugano. It passes **Bisuschio**, where the 16C *Villa Cicogna Mozzoni, frescoed by the school of the Campi brothers and with 17C and 18C furnishings, stands surrounded by a classical Renaissance garden and fine park. The greenhouses protect a good collection of orchids. The villa and gardens are open Apr–Oct on Sun & fest. 9–12, 15–19.

Porto Ceresio is situated at the foot of Monte Pravello on a wide bend in the **LAGO DI LUGANO** (270m; 52 sq km), a little more than half of which belongs to Switzerland; only the northeast arm, the southwest shore between Ponte Tresa and Porto Ceresio, and the enclave of Campione, nearly opposite Lugano, belong to Italy. The scenery of the shores, except for the bay of Lugano, is far wilder than on the greater lakes. There are regular boat services between all the main places along the shore. For a full description of the lake, see *Blue Guide Switzerland*.

Lugano, the main place on the lake, and the largest town of the Swiss Canton Ticino, is Italian in character. In the centre of the lake is the small Italian enclave of **Campione d'Italia**, in the province of Como, which uses Swiss money and postal services. It has long been noted for its sculptors and architects; the chapel of St Peter (1327) is a good example of their work. In the parish church are some 15C reliefs, and here is kept the key to the cemetery chapel of **Santa Maria dei Ghirli**, with frescoes outside (Last Judgement, 1400) and in the interior (14C). The village is famous for its Casinò.

At the head of the northeast arm of the lake, also in the province of Como, is **Porlezza**, where the church of San Vittorio contains good 18C stuccowork. In the **Valsolda**, above the northern shore of the lake, is the picturesque village of **San Mamette**, with a 12C campanile. On the road which descends to Lake Como is the attractive Lago del Piano (279m).

A road traverses the southwest corner of the province from Sesto Calende on Lago Maggiore (described on page 97) to Milan, passing **Somma Lombardo** with its Visconti castle (privately owned). Nearby at **Arsago Seprio** is the ancient basilica of San Vittore and its baptistery (12C), and an archaeological museum. Another road leads from Somma Lombardo to **Golasecca** with its Iron Age necropolis. **Gallarate** is the first of three large industrial towns (the others are Busto Arsizio and Legnano) near the Olona river (now polluted) northwest of Milan, noted in the 19C for their cotton-spinning works. They are now important manufacturing towns inhabited mainly by immigrant workers from the south. In the centre of Gallarate (46,000 inhab.) is the 12C church of San Pietro. At **Busto Arsizio** (78,700 inhab.) is the church of Santa Maria di

Piazza (1517–27; restored in 1992) with a polyptych by Gaudenzio Ferrari (1541). The octagonal cupola is frescoed by Giovan Pietro Crespi (1531). Legnano is in the province of Milan, see page 75.

East of Busto Arsizio is **Saronno**, an industrial town (32,600 inhab.) noted for its macaroons. The sanctuary of the **Madonna dei Miracoli** here was begun in 1498 perhaps by Giovanni Antonio Amadeo, who designed the cupola in 1505. It was enlarged after 1556 by Vincenzo Seregni. The façade is by Pellegrino Tibaldi (1596). It contains beautiful, brightly coloured *frescoes by Bernardino Luini (1525 and 1531), including the Presentation in the Temple and Adoration of the Magi, admired by Stendhal in his diary. They were well restored in 1992. The large fresco in the cupola of the Virgin in Paradise, with a concert of angels, was painted after Luini's death by Gaudenzio Ferrari, and is usually considered his masterpiece. The remarkable group of life-size polychrome wood figures representing the *Last Supper by Andrea da Milano (c 1548–52) have recently been restored. They are apparently a copy of Leonardo's famous Cenacolo in Milan.

6 · Como and the Lago di Como

The **LAGO DI COMO** is a beautiful large lake, some 50km long, surrounded by wooded hills below the Alpine foothills. Many of the small towns on its shores, originally fishing villages, became resorts in the 19C. The lake was visited by the English Romantic poets, including Shelley and Byron, and Wordsworth lived here in 1790. Numerous villas surrounded by lovely gardens were built on its steep banks in the 18C and 19C, but in more recent times its shores have been disfigured in places by unattractive holiday houses, many of them built by the Milanese. There is an efficient regular service of boats, hydrofoils and car ferries throughout the year between all the main towns, used by residents as well as visitors. Como, at its southern end, is the most important town on the lake: Roman in origin, it has an interesting plan and a splendid cathedral. The most beautiful part of the lake is in the centre, at Bellagio. Spectacular natural scenery can be seen at the Villa Serbelloni, the Villa del Balbianello and the Isola Comacina. Villas with famous gardens open to the public include Villa Carlotta at Tremezzo, Villa Melzi at Bellagio, and Villa Olmo at Como. The most pleasant resorts, with good old-established hotels, include Bellagio, Menaggio, Varenna, Cernobbio and Tremezzo.

■ **Information offices.** APT di Como, 17 Piazza Cavour (tel. 031 269712); APT di Lecco, 6 Via N. Sauro (tel. 0341 362360). IAT information offices at Bellagio, Cernobbio, Lanzo Intelvi, Menaggio and Barzio.

■ **Boat and hydrofoil services.** An efficient service of boats and hydrofoils is maintained throughout the year between Como and Colico, calling at numerous places of interest on the way. It is run by the Navigazione Lago di Como, 18 Via per Cernobbio, Como (tel. 031 579211). Tickets valid for 24hrs or several days can be purchased. The timetable changes according to season. Most of the boats run between Como and Bellano (boats in c 2hrs 30mins, hydrofoils in c 1hr), while most of the hydrofoils continue to Colico (Como to

Colico in c 1hr 30mins). There is a less frequent service between Bellagio and Lecco in summer (only on holidays for the rest of the year). In the central part of the lake a service runs between Bellano (or Varenna) and Lenno. A car ferry runs frequently between Bellagio and Varenna (in 15mins), Bellagio and Cadenabbia (in 10mins), and Cadenabbia and Varenna (in 30mins). Fewer services in winter.

■ **Hotels.** See relevant sections of chapter.

■ **Camping sites** at Domaso, Castiglione Intelvi, Menaggio, Porlezza, Sorico, Abbadia Lariana, Colico (*Green Village*), Oliveto Lario and Taceno.

■ **Restaurants**. See relevant sections of chapter.

■ **Transport.** Como and Lecco are easily reached by frequent **train** services from Milan. There is a railway line which skirts the eastern shore of the lake from Lecco to Colico. There are also **bus** services between all the main centres around the lake, run by Trasporti Regione Lombardia (information offices in Lecco: tel. 0341 367244; Como: tel. 031 247111).

Geography
The lake is 199m above sea level. Virgil called it *Lacus Larius*, and it is still often known as Lario. The lake is formed of three long, narrow arms which meet at Bellagio, one stretching southwest to Como, another southeast to Lecco, the third north to Colico. Its total length is 50km from Como to Gera, its greatest breadth 4·4km just north of Bellagio, its greatest depth 410m off Argegno, and its area 145 sq. km. The chief feeder is the Adda, which flows in at Colico and out at Lecco. The lake is subject to frequent floods (last in 1980 when Como was inundated), and is swept regularly by two winds, the *tivano* (north to south), and the *breva* (south to north) in the afternoon.

Como
The town of Como, in a fine position on the southern shore of Lake Como, has preserved to a marked degree its Roman plan within high walls, the southern and western stretches of which have survived. It has a particularly attractive old centre with long, straight, narrow streets, many of their houses with pretty courtyards. The cathedral is a splendid Gothic building with remarkable sculptures inside and out. A delightful path, shaded by huge old trees, skirts the lake as far as the public gardens of Villa Olmo, passing charming villas with gardens and boathouses on the waterfront. The traditional local industry of silk weaving survives here in several large factories (and silk products can be purchased at low prices all over the town). As a provincial capital and manufacturing town with 98,000 inhabitants, Como's economy has developed rapidly in this century together with unattractive suburbs.

■ **Information offices.** See beginning of chapter.

■ **Hotels.** 4-star: *Barchetta Excelsior* and *Metropole e Suisse*, both in Piazza Cavour, *Villa Flori*, just outside Como on the road to Cernobbio. 3-star: *Tre Re*, 20 Via

Boldoni; 2-star: *Posta*, 2 Via Garibaldi. About 12km north of Como, above the lake on the road to Bellagio, at **Faggeto Lario**, is the 1-star *San Giorgio*.

■ **Restaurants. A**: *Da Angela*, 16 Via Foscolo and *Sant Anna 1907*, 1 Via Turati. **B**: *Imbarcadero*, 20 Piazza Cavour.

■ **Car parks** (with an hourly tariff or time limit) in Piazza Roma, Piazza Volta, Lungo Lario Trento, Via Recchi, Viale Varese, etc.

■ **Railway stations.** San Giovanni for the State Railway line to Milan, Lecco, and to Lugano and the rest of Switzerland. Como-Lago (on the lakeside; the most convenient station for visitors) and Como-Borghi for trains on the Nord–Milano line to Milan via Saronno.

■ **Buses** from Piazza Matteotti for towns on the lake, and in the province.

■ **Boat and hydrofoil services** on the lake, see above. Boats for hire (Ditta Tasell) at Piazza Cavour.

■ **Theatre.** Teatro Sociale with a music season from September to November.

■ **Sport. Swimming** in summer (depending on pollution levels) at Villa Geno, on the eastern shore, beyond the funicular station. **Golf course** (18 holes) at Montofrano, 4km southeast (Villa d'Este).

■ **Annual festivals.** Fiera di Pasqua, with a flea market by the walls from Maundy Thursday to Easter Monday.

History

Originally a town of the Insubrian Gauls, Como was captured and colonised by the Romans in the 2C BC. The town was a republic by the 11C, but in 1127 it was destroyed by the Milanese. Frederick Barbarossa rebuilt it in 1155, and Como secured its future independence by the Peace of Constance (1183). In the struggles between the Torriani and the Visconti, Como fell to the latter in 1335 and became a fief of Milan. From then on it followed the vicissitudes of the Lombard capital. In March 1848 a popular rising compelled the surrender of the Austrian garrison, and the city was finally liberated by Garibaldi on 27 May 1859.

Among the most famous natives (*Comaschi*) are the Elder and the Younger Pliny (AD 23–79 and AD 62–120), uncle and nephew. The Younger Pliny often mentions Como and its surroundings in his *Letters*, and he endowed a library and school here. Alessandro Volta (see below) was also born here. Walter Savage Landor lived in Como in 1815–18, where he was unjustly suspected of spying on Queen Caroline who was staying at Cernobbio.

The centre of the life of Como is PIAZZA CAVOUR, open to the lake and adjoining the quay. It was created in 1887 by filling in the old harbour. The piazza has a splendid view with the Tempio Voltiano on the left and beyond it the large Villa Olmo; straight ahead in trees is the Villa Flori, and in the distance the town of Cernobbio climbing the hillside above the lake. On the right bank can be seen Villa Geno and the line of the funicular up to Brunate. An avenue of lime trees skirts the lake to the **public gardens** with the **Tempio Voltiano** (open 10–12 & 14 or 15–16 or 18), erected in 1927 as a memorial to the physicist Alessandro Volta (1745–1827). The neo-classical rotunda contains his scientific instruments, charmingly displayed in old-fashioned show cases. The conspicuous **war memorial** was designed by Antonio Sant'Elia, a native of Como, himself killed in 1916.

Beyond the stadium, Via Puecher leads past a naval club and a hangar for sea planes, beyond which a very pleasant LAKESIDE PATH continues past a number of lovely private villas with their gardens and boathouses and decorative gazebos. Beyond **Villa Pallavicino**, with statues on the façade and stuccoes inside by Piermarini and Giocondo Albertolli, is the **Villa Resta Pallavicini** (called La Rotonda) with a semicircular neo-classical rotunda in the centre of its façade. The path ends at **VILLA OLMO**, built for the Odescalchi by Simone Cantoni (1782–95; altered in 1883). It is preceded by an attractive formal garden (open daily as public gardens) with topiary, statues and a charming fountain, and behind are remains of its large park. The villa is used for exhibitions.

From Piazza Cavour (see above) the short Via Plinio leads away from the lake to Piazza del Duomo, with the **BROLETTO** (1215; the old town hall), built in alternate courses of black and white marble, with a few red patches, and the **Torre del Comune** of the same period, used as a campanile since the addition of the top storey in 1435 (partly rebuilt in 1927).

The Cathedral

The *Cathedral (Santa Maria Maggiore), built entirely of marble, dates mainly from the late 14C, when it replaced an 11C basilica. The union of Renaissance with Gothic architecture has here produced a remarkably homogeneous style. The rebuilding, financed mainly by public subscription, was entrusted first to Lorenzo degli Spazzi who, like his many successors, worked under the patronage of the Milanese court. Many of the works of art were restored in 1988–92.

The **west front** (1460–90), designed by Fiorino da Bontà and executed by Luchino Scarabota of Milan, is in a Gothic style with a fine rose window, though the three doorways are unexpectedly round-arched. The 20 15C statues framing the two large windows between the central doorway and the rose window are still Gothic in conception, whereas the numerous other reliefs and statues from the workshop of Tommaso and Jacopo Rodari (local sculptors from Maroggia), dating from c 1500, show a new Renaissance style. The delightful seated figures of the two Plinys on either side of the main doorway are probably by Amuzio da Lurago. The two lateral doorways, also decorated by the Rodari, are wonderful examples of detailed carving. The work of rebuilding continued through the 16C (choir) and 17C (transepts), and ended with completion of the dome in 1770 by Filippo Juvarra.

Interior. The aisled **nave** of five bays is covered with a groined vault and hung with tapestries (1598). On the **west wall** are good brightly coloured stained-glass windows by Giuseppe Bertini (1850). The two stoups supported by lions are survivals from the ancient basilica. A graceful little rotunda (1590) serves as baptistery. In the **south aisle** the first altar has a wood ancona dating from 1482. Beyond a neo-classical funerary monument by Agliati is another *ancona by

Tommaso Rodari (1492), and more good stained-glass windows. Past the south door (also well carved) is the tomb of Bishop Bonifacio da Modena (1347). The Altar of Sant'Abbondio (coin-operated light) is finely decorated with gilded wood-carving (1514), and three marble panels below. The *Virgin and Child with four Saints and the Donor, Canon Raimondi and a beautiful angel-musician in front, is a masterpiece of Bernardino Luini. The two paintings above are attributed to Francesco del Cairo and Simone Peterzano. Opposite, beneath the organ, is a standard attributed to Giovanni Pietro Malacrida (c 1515).

South transept. The Baroque altar is a good work designed by Francesco Richino (begun c 1641). In the **sanctuary** are five good stained-glass windows (1861–78) and an altar (1674) with a Crucifix of the late 15C and 16C polychrome wooden statues. The Gothic high altar dates from 1317.

North aisle. On the fourth altar is a carved Deposition group by Tommaso Rodari (1498) and opposite, hanging in the nave, a painted and embroidered *standard of the Confraternity of Sant'Abbondio by Morazzone (1608–10). On either side of the third neo-classical altar are paintings by Bernardino Luini and Gaudenzio Ferrari. By the side door is the sarcophagus of Giovanni degli Avogadri (died 1293), with primitive carvings. On the second altar, between busts of Innocent XI and Bishop Rovelli, is a lovely carved ancona by Tommaso Rodari, and on the first altar, a painting by Andrea Passeri di Tomo (1502).

In Piazza Grimoldi are the yellow Bishop's Palace and **San Giacomo** (closed) with an unusual yellow and red façade. The church has Romanesque elements (columns, brickwork in aisles, apse and dome). Behind the fine east end of the Duomo is the ruined Palazzo Pantera, the **Teatro Sociale** built in 1811 by Giuseppe Cusi with a neo-classical façade, and—across the Nord–Milano railway line—the white **Casa del Fascio** built in 1932–36, by Giuseppe Terragni and an important example of architecture of this period.

Via Vittorio Emanuele leads south from the cathedral to the 17C Municipio, opposite which is the five-sided apse of the church of **SAN FEDELE** (12C), which at one time served as cathedral. The angular northeast doorway, with remarkable bas-reliefs, shows Byzantine influences. The church is entered from the delightful piazza behind. The interior, partly under restoration, has an unusual plan. It contains a fresco signed by G. A. Magistris (1504), and a little painted and stuccoed 17C vault.

In the piazza and on Via Natta are several old houses with wooden eaves and brickwork. Further along Via Vittorio Emanuele two good palaces house the **MUSEO CIVICO** (open 9–12, 15–17 exc. Mon; fest. 9–12). The old-fashioned arrangement is in the course of renovation. The interesting material includes Neolithic, Bronze Age and Iron Age finds, a stele of the 5C BC, Roman finds, and medieval fragments. There are also 19C American artefacts, a natural history section, an Egyptian collection, and a good Risorgimento museum (and material relating to the First and Second World Wars) There are wooden models of the Duomo and casts of the Pliny statues on the façade. A small organ dates from 1795, and there is a local ethnographical collection with 18C costumes.

Nearby, at 84 Via Diaz, the **PINACOTECA** has been arranged in the modernised Palazzo Volpi (1610–30), which is also used for exhibitions. On the ground floor, beyond an 11C arch salvaged from a monastery in the town, are sculptural fragments, including capitals, from the Carolingian and

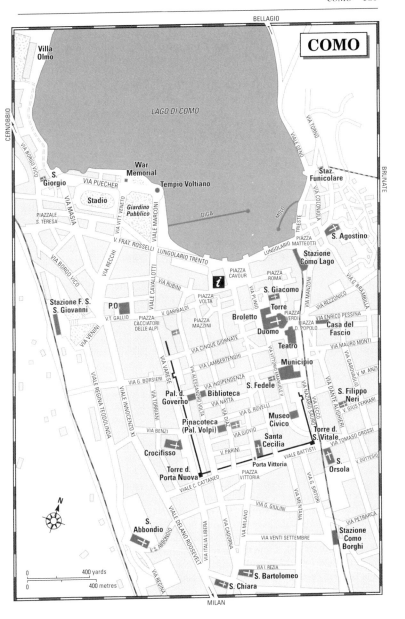

Romanesque periods, and frescoes (including charming scenes from the lives of Saints Liberata and Faustina). Upstairs are 16C–17C paintings (a Madonna Annunciate attributed to Antonello da Messina is not at present on show).

The second turning on the left off Via Giovio leads to the church of **Santa Cecilia**, the front of which incorporates some Roman columns. It has a good Baroque interior. Next door was the school where Volta once taught; there is a fragment of the Roman wall in the courtyard. The **Porta Vittoria** is surmounted by a tower of 1192 with many windows. It is named in memory of the surrender of the Austrian garrison (1848) in the barracks immediately opposite. The Garibaldi monument by Vincenzo Vela, in Piazza Vittoria, was erected in 1889.

Outside the gate, beyond a busy road in an unattractive area (see the Plan), is the fine Romanesque basilica of *SANT'ABBONDIO (open 8–12, 14–18), isolated amid industrial buildings near the railway. On the site of an early Christian building, the present church dates from the 11C and is dedicated to St Abondius, bishop of Como. The exterior has two graceful campanili and a finely decorated **apse**.

The **interior** has five tall aisles, despite its comparatively small size, and a deep presbytery. The apse is entirely frescoed with scenes from the Life of Christ by mid-14C Lombard artists. The statue of St Abondius is attributed to Cristoforo Solari (1490).

On Viale Varese, which skirts the walls and gardens, is the sanctuary of the **Crocifisso**, a huge 16C building with a façade of 1864 by Luigi Fontana, and good Baroque decorations inside. In Via Alessandro Volta, inside the walls, is the house where the scientist lived and died (plaque).

On the outskirts of the town, beyond Como Borghi station, at 3 Via Valleggio there is a **Silk Museum** (open by appointment, tel. 031 303180).

Environs of Como

From Piazza Cavour (see above), Lungo Lario Trieste leads past several large hotels, the old-fashioned station of the Nord–Milano line, and a small port, to the funicular station for **BRUNATE** (services every 15 mins, taking 7 mins). Brunate (713m) can also be reached from Via Grossi by road or by path. In a fine position overlooking the lake, it became a resort at the end of the last century. The **funicular** climbs steeply up the hillside through a tunnel and then traverses woods and the gardens of some fine villas. From the upper station a 10-minute walk (signposted 'panoramic view') leads gently uphill past huge, elaborate 19C and 20C villas and their gardens, beneath an archway to emerge high above the lake and the Breggia river. The fine view takes in the boatyard of the Villa Lariana on the left, and to the right is Cernobbio with the huge Villa d'Este on the lakeside.

Near the funicular station (the mechanism of which can be seen in the engine room) is the church of **Sant'Andrea** at the highest point of the village, with 19C and 20C frescoes and a charming 15C fresco of a certain St Guglielma, thought to have been an English princess who married king Theodoric of Hungary in the 8C (her cult has been known in Brunate since before the 15C and her feast day is celebrated here on the fourth Sunday in April). Steps lead down the other side of the hill away from the lake to the centre of the village (pedestrians only). At **San Maurizio** (871m), 2km higher, is the Faro Voltiano, a monument to Alessandro Volta (1927).

South of Como above the suburb of Camerlata, is the 11–12C church of **San Carpoforo** with the supposed tomb of St Felix in its crypt. Monte Baradello above the church, with a good view of the lake, is crowned by the conspicuous tower of the **Castello Baradello** (open Thu, Sat & fest.10–12, 14.30–17), the solitary remnant of a stronghold reconstructed by Barbarossa c 1158 and destroyed by Charles V's Spaniards in 1527. In 1277 Napo Torriani and other members of his family were exposed here in cages after their defeat by the Visconti.

The road goes on to **Cantù**, a pleasant town (32,400 inhab.) with lace and furniture industries. The parish church has a remarkably slender Romanesque campanile, and San Teodoro has a fine apse in the same style. At **Galliano**, to the east, are the 10–11C basilica and baptistery of San Vincenzo. The church has a *fresco cycle of 1007. The fertile **Brianza** region here used to have many imposing country houses built by the Milanese. At **Inverigo** is the fine Villa La Rotonda built by Luigi Cagnola (1813–33), now a children's home (adm. by appointment). At **Alzate Brianza** the 17C Villa Odescalchi is now a hotel. **Erba**, on the road which links Como with Lecco, is a scattered community with an open-air theatre (the Licinium) built in 1926. There is an archaeological museum at Crevenna.

From Como to Colico by water

Frequent services of boats and hydrofoils (see page 105) connect Como with Colico all year round, and a road follows the west shore.

■ **Hotels. Cernobbio:** 5-star: *Grand Hotel Villa d Este*; 3-star: *Miralago*. **Argegno**: 2-star: *Argegno* and *Lago Belvedere*. **Lenno**: 3-star: *San Giorgio*. **Tremezzo**: 4-star: *Grand Hotel Tremezzo*. **Bellagio**: 5-star: *Grand Hotel Villa Serbelloni*; 3-star: *Metropole*. **Menaggio**: 4-star: *Grand Hotel*. **Gravedona**: 2-star: *Lauro* .

■ **Restaurants. Lenno**: **C**: *Santo Stefano*, 3 Piazza XI Febbraio. **Bellagio**: **B**: *La Busciona*, 161 Via Valassina. *Silvio*, 12 Via Cercano, Loppia.

After leaving Como the boats soon cross to the west shore and the red Villa Lariana surrounded by poplars on the delightful Breggia river. Beyond is a modern congress centre in the gardens of the Villa Erba. **CERNOBBIO** is a resort at the foot of Monte Bisbino (1325m). It has a pleasant waterfront with boats pulled up on the quay and an attractive landing stage. Beyond is the huge white **Villa d'Este** hotel which occupies a villa built in 1568 by the beneficent Cardinal Tolomeo Gallio (1527–1607), a native of Cernobbio. In 1816–17 it was the home of the future Queen Caroline of England, who had the park landscaped in the English style. On the headland in trees is the Villa Pizzo with cypresses in its park and a garden gazebo, and low down on the waterfront is the yellow Villa Fontanella.

Moltrasio, with a Romanesque church, is less pretty. Here at the Villa Salterio in 1831 Bellini composed the opera *Norma*. On the bay on the east bank beyond Torno is the **Villa Pliniana** (1570; adm. by previous appointment only May–Oct). In the garden is the famous intermittent spring described in detail by the Younger Pliny in his *Letters*, and also studied by Leonardo da Vinci. The abundant flow of water is channelled from a grotto down the cliff into the lake. Ugo Foscolo, Percy Bysshe Shelley, Stendhal and Rossini (who composed *Tancredi* here in 1813) were among the illustrious visitors to the villa in the 19C. The 18C Villa Passalacqua was built by Felice Soave and has an Italianate garden. Bellini composed *La Sonnambula* here.

On the west bank beyond Moltrasio are the yellow Villa Angelina behind cypresses and a garden, and the twin villages of **Carate Urio**; Urio has a tall Lombard campanile, but a lot of unattractive new building spoils Carate. **Laglio**, beyond, has another tall church tower. A mountain torrent enters the lake in a waterfall between two hills near the green and white Villa Annetta. At the narrowest reach of the lake is **Torriggia**, with the small Villa Pia and its garden on the point. Beyond the churches of Sant'Anna and Brienno is **Argegno**, where the high mountain ranges northeast of the lake come into view.

Argegno lies at the foot of the fertile **Val d'Intelvi**, reached by a road to Lanzo d'Intelvi above Lago di Lugano. At **Castiglione d'Intelvi** the medieval Casa del Capitano has a room with 14C frescoes. At San Fedele a scenic road branches right, climbing through Laino and Ponna before descending to Porlezza on Lago di Lugano. The Lanzo d'Intelvi road continues to Pellio and Scaria, which has a Diocesan Museum with works by Ercole Ferrata and other local sculptors, before reaching the resort of **Lanzo d'Intelvi** (907m). **Campione d'Italia**, beyond on Lago di Lugano, is described on page 103.

On the Lago di Como, opposite Sala Comacina, is the **ISOLA COMACINA**, a pretty little wooded island. The regular boat services call here and a ferry service operates from Sala Comacina; it has a trattoria open from March to October but no permanent residents. The island was used as a hiding place by political refugees during the disturbed medieval history of Lombardy, and it was captured and raided by the men of Como in 1169. In 1917 it passed by inheritance to Albert, King of the Belgians, but was later given to the Accademia delle Belle Arti of Milan, who built three houses here as artists' retreats. Paths lead along the shore of the lake and over the top of the island through wild vegetation past the ruins of its six medieval churches.

The boats skirt the wooded headland called the **Punta del Balbianello** with an excellent view of the ***Villa del Balbianello**, the garden and loggia of which can be visited Apr–Oct, Tue, Thu, Sat & Sun 10–12.30, 15.30–18.30. It can only be reached by water (regular boat service every 30 minutes from Sala Comacina to coincide with the opening hours) or on foot (only Apr–Oct, on the last Sun of the month) by a signposted path (c 800 metres) which starts from the church square in Lenno. The villa is surrounded by plane trees, magnolias, ilexes and cypresses. Silvio Pellico, author of *Le Mie Prigioni*, stayed here in 1819. It was left to the FAI in 1988 by the explorer Guido Monzino, who was the first Italian to climb Everest (in 1973), and who reached the North Pole in 1971.

From the dock a steep flight of steps lead up to the villa, built by Cardinal Angelo Maria Durini in 1787, incorporating the scant remains of a Franciscan convent (the façade of the church and its twin campanili survive). In the small formal garden above the villa, with laurel and box hedges and planted with

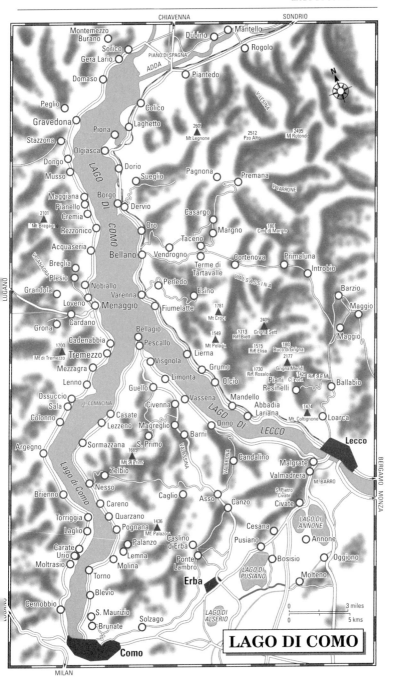

LAGO DI COMO

wisteria, azaleas, and rhododendrons, is a delightful garden loggia with fine views. It incorporates a library and map room with Monzino's collections relating to the polar regions and mountaineering. The villa (not at present open to the public) contains more of Monzino's collections from his explorations, and 18C and 19C English and French furniture.

At **Lenno** the shore is flatter at the mouth of the Acquafredda, at the south end of the Tremezzina (see below). The parish church has an 11–12C crypt and an 11C octagonal baptistery adjoining. Here on the shore was the site of Pliny's villa 'Comedia' (his other villa, called 'Tragedia', was at Bellagio). Near here, in the locality of Giulino, Mussolini was shot by partisans in 1945. Beyond Lenno the boats follow the attractive Tremezzina, the fertile green shore dotted with villas and gardens, which extends along the foot of Monte di Tremezzo as far as La Maiolica, north of Cadenabbia.

TREMEZZO and **CADENABBIA** are both elegant resorts with numerous hotels and some fine villas. On the busy road between them is the prominent ***VILLA CARLOTTA** (open Apr–Sep, 9–18; Mar–Oct, 9.30–12.30, 14–16.30), built at the beginning of the 18C by the marchese Giorgio Clerici. The interior was altered after 1795 by the marchese Giambattista Sommariva, and the opening scenes of *La Chartreuse de Parme* (1839) recall Stendhal's stay here as Sommariva's guest in 1818. The villa was bought in 1843 by Princess Albrecht of Prussia who gave it to her daughter Carlotta on her marriage to the crown-prince of Saxe-Meiningen. The magnificent wooded park was laid out by Princess Carlotta in the Romantic style. It has always been much admired by the English, and has beautiful camellias, rhododendrons, and azaleas in spring.

Beside the ticket office is the neo-classical funerary chapel of the Sommariva. The **villa** is interesting for its early 19C decorations including neo-classical works and Empire-style French furniture, and for its lovely painted ceilings dating from the 18C. In the main room is Thorvaldsen's frieze of the Triumphal Entry of Alexander into Babylon, cast in plaster for Napoleon in 1811–12 and intended for the throne-room at the Quirinal. Also here are works by Canova (Cupid and Psyche, the Repentant Magdalen, and Palamedes) and Mars and Venus by Luigi Acquisti. In other rooms on the ground floor are three Gobelins tapestries (1767–73), fine frescoes by Andrea Appiani, paintings by Francesco Hayez and Giovanni Battista Wicar, and plaster models by Canova and Acquisti.

The upper floor has good views of the gardens, fine painted wood 18C ceilings and Empire-style French furniture. The view from the terrace extends across the lake to San Giovanni with its church, just to the left of which is Villa Melzi and further left on the hill the Villa Serbelloni with Bellagio and its church below. Beyond Bellagio the Lecco arm of the lake can just be seen.

In front of the house is a formal Italianate garden reached by a theatrical flight of steps which descend to the entrance gate on the lake. The **park** is of great botanical interest (all the plants are labelled), and is very well cared for. A path leads past rhododendrons and tropical plants to a hillside planted with azaleas. Beyond a rock garden is a plantation of palms and cacti. A valley watered by a stream has a splendid variety of tree ferns. Beyond, a straight path leads past banks of azaleas, and higher up the hillside are conifers, camphor trees, and beech trees. Behind the villa is a hedge of azaleas, and a bridge leads across a stream to a smaller garden on the other side of the villa, with tropical plants, plane trees, monkey-puzzle trees, Japanese maples, and palms.

It was at the Villa Margherita on the shore just north of Cadenabbia, while staying with his publisher Ricordi, that Verdi composed Act II of *La Traviata* in 1853.

The **centro lago**, where the Como and Lecco arms meet, is the most beautiful part of the lake. In a lovely quiet position on a headland at the division of the lake is the famous resort of **BELLAGIO**, which retains much of the picturesque aspect of an old Lombard town. It has local industries of silk-weaving and olive-wood carving.

To the left of the car ferry station is an attractive arcaded **piazza** with the boat and hydrofoil pier. Stepped streets lead up to the church of **San Giacomo**, with a 12C apse. It contains a reconstructed primitive pulpit with symbols of the Evangelists, a good painted triptych by the late 15C Lombard school, a 19C copy of a Deposition by Perugino, and a 16C wooden Dead Christ (a Spanish work). In the apse is a gilded tabernacle (16C and 18C).

In the old tower opposite is the Tourist Information Office and, on the floor above, the ticket office for the *VILLA SERBELLONI (the park is shown at 10 and 16 to a maximum of 30 people on a guided tour of about 1hr 30mins in Mar–Oct exc. Mon and when raining). The entrance gate is behind San Giacomo. The villa and grounds were left to the Rockefeller Foundation of New York in 1959 by Ella Walker Della Torre Tasso to be used as a study centre for students (who come here on scholarships for one month) from all over the world. The younger Pliny's villa 'Tragedia' is thought to have occupied this site. Stendhal stayed here in 1825.

The magnificent **park** on the spectacular high promontory overlooking the lake was laid out at the end of the 18C by Alessandro Serbelloni. A gravel road leads up past a delightful little pavilion used as a student's study and just before the villa there is a good view of Cadenabbio. In front of the villa, which incorporates a Romanesque tower, is a formal garden with topiary and olives, cypresses and fruit trees. From here there is a view of the Lecco branch of the lake, with the little fishing village of Pescallo and a 17C monastery. On the hill in front is the Villa Belmonte, below which can be seen a neo-Gothic building which was once the English church and is now a private villa. A path continues through the park past artificial grottoes created in the 19C up to the highest point on the promontory with remains of a ruined castle and 11C chapel. The splendid view takes in Varenna with the Villa Cipressi and the Villa Monastero (separated by a prominent square boathouse), and to the north are the high mountains beyond Colico. Another path returns to the villa from which steps continue down to the exit in the little town of Bellagio.

From the car ferry station it is a 5–10 minute walk along the road to Loppia to **VILLA MELZI** (the grounds are open Mar–Oct 9–18), standing in a fine park with an interesting garden.The villa, chapel and greenhouse were built in 1808–10 by Giocondo Albertolli as a summer residence for Francesco Melzi d'Eril. Franz Liszt, the composer and pianist, stayed here (his daughter Cosima was born at the Casa Lillia in Bellagio in 1837). From the entrance a path leads past a little Japanese garden and a circular pavilion on the lake to an avenue of plane trees which leads to the villa. On the left is the former orangery which contains a small museum. The two statues in front of the villa of Meleager and Apollo are 16C works by Guglielmo della Porta. The park contains beautiful trees and shrubs including rhododendrons and azaleas. Beyond the villa at the end of the gardens is the chapel with particularly good neo-classical family tombs.

The road continues to **Loppia** with a half-ruined church in a romantic site beside a great grove of cypresses. At San Giovanni the church contains an altarpiece by Gaudenzio Ferrari. Further on is Villa Trotti with fine gardens (no adm.).

A road leads south from Bellagio to Asso via Civenna, with a fine panorama of the lake. Beyond Guello a road on the right ascends to the park of **Monte San Primo** (1686m). At the edge of the town of **Civenna** by the cemetery is a small park with spectacular views of the lake from Gravedona in the north to Lecco in the south. From the small church of Madonna del Ghisallo (754m; with votive offerings from champion cyclists), the highest point of the road, there is a *view of the lake (left) with the two Grigne beyond, and of Bellagio behind. The road descends the steep **Vallassina** to **Asso** with remains of a medieval castle. Here the graceful 17C church of San Giovanni Battista has an elaborate gilded wood Baroque altar and an Annunciation by Giulio Cesare Campi. Almost continuous with Asso is **Canzo**, the most important place in the valley.

Another road from Bellagio, with magnificent views, goes along the west bank of the Lecco arm of the lake, via Limonta, Vassena and Onno, and ascends the Valbrona to Asso.

The next place of importance on the west bank of the lake is **MENAGGIO**, a pleasant little town. Beyond the pier and the Grand Hotel the busy main road can be followed on foot for a few minutes to the pretty piazza on the waterfront. Roads lead uphill behind the church to the narrow cobbled lanes which traverse the area of the Castello with some fine large villas and a 17C wall fountain.

Beyond the Sangra river is **Loveno**; near its church is Villa Vigoni (now owned by the German State; adm. on application), with a garden pavilion containing sculptures by Thorvaldsen. The Villa Calabi was the home of Massimo d'Azeglio (1798–1865), patriot and writer. There are several fine walks in the area beneath the beautiful Monte Bregagno (2107m).

Acquaseria lies at the foot of the Cima la Grona, while to the south rises the Sasso Rancio. Further north is **Rezzonico**, with a castle, the home of the powerful family which bore its name and numbered Clement XIII among its famous members. The old church of **San Vito** has a fine Madonna and Angels attributed to Bergognone. The locality of **Pianello del Lario** has a 12C church and marble quarries. At **Calozzo**, on the lake, is a museum with a collection of boats used on the lake (adm. fest. Easter–Nov; guided tours 14.30–17.30).

Musso is overlooked by the almost impregnable Rocca di Musso, the stronghold in 1525–32 of the piratical Gian Giacomo Medici who levied tribute from the traders of the lake and the neighbouring valleys. **DONGO**, with Gravedona and Sorico, formed the independent Republic of the Three Parishes (Tre Pievi), that survived until the Spanish occupation of Lombardy. Mussolini was captured by partisans at Dongo in the spring of 1945 and was executed at Giulino di Mezzegra above Lenno (see above). The 12C church of Santa Maria in the adjacent hamlet of Martinico preserves an interesting doorway.

GRAVEDONA is the principal village of the upper lake. The great square **Villa Gallio** with four turrets and surrounded by a garden (where there is a giant rhododendron), at the north end of the village, was built c 1586 by Pellegrino

Tibaldi for Cardinal Tolomeo Gallio. It is now used for exhibitions. Nearer the boat station are the very scant remains of the ivy-covered castle with its clock tower. Beyond several piazze with hotels and restaurants the main road can be followed on foot for 5 minutes to two churches, side by side, on the lake in a less attractive part of the town. ***Santa Maria del Tiglio** is a little 12C building with an eccentric west tower, square in its lower storeys and octagonal higher up, and a very unusual plan with one eastern and two transverse apses. It contains good columns and capitals, as well as frescoes and a fragment of mosaic pavement. The fine wooden Crucifix dates from the 12C. Beside it is the large church of **San Vincenzo**, with a very ancient crypt which can be visited by descending steps outside Santa Maria. There are a number of other churches of interest in and around Gravedona.

Beyond **Domaso**, at the mouth of the Livo, at the extreme north end of the lake where the Mera flows in, are the villages of Gera and Sorico. Colico and the eastern shore of the lake are described below from Lecco.

Lecco and its province

■ **Hotels**. Although Lecco has three 3-star hotels, **Malgrate**, just across the lake, is a much pleasanter place to stay: 4-star: Il Griso; 3-star: Promessi Sposi. Just outside Malgrate at **Parè di Valmadrera**, in the 18C Villa Giulia, is the 3-star Al Terrazzo. Also on the outskirts of Lecco, on the Lago di Garlate, is **Pescate** with the 3-star Parco Belvedere. Above Lecco at **Piani d Erna** (1300 m) is the 1-star Marchett. **Varenna**: 4-star: Royal Victoria and Du Lac; 3-star: Villa Cipressi. **Bellano**: 3-star: Meridiana.

■ **Restaurants. Lecco**: **B**: *Da Giovannino* in the *Promessi Sposi* hotel in Malgrate; **C**: *Trattoria Pontile*, by the ferry station, and *Brambilla*, Via Cavour. At **Acquate:** *Antica Osteria Casa di Lucia* (**C**). **Varenna**: **A**: *Vecchia Varenna* (on the port), *Royal Victoria*. **Lierna**: **B**: *La Punta* and *La Breva*. **Brivio**: **B**: *La Sosta*. **Villa d'Adda**: **B**: *Osteria il Boschetto*.

Lecco

Lecco is an unattractive town (45,000 inhab.), with a diminishing population, which became the capital of a new province in 1991. Its old metalworks have been demolished and numerous ugly new buildings have taken their place. The town suffers from traffic congestion, which will be relieved when a tunnel is completed to connect the road from Milan with the new *superstrada* to Colico. Lecco is, however, in a fine position at the southeast end of the Lago di Como at the outflow of the Adda and beneath high mountains (the Grigna group to the north with San Martino on the lake, and the Resegone to the south). The town is well known in Italy for its associations with the novelist Alessandro Manzoni (1785–1873) who lived here as a boy and whose famous novel *I Promessi Sposi* is set in and around Lecco. The most important buildings in the town are by the local architect Giuseppe Bovara (1781–1873).

The Lungolago leads to the large arcaded PIAZZA XX SETTEMBRE, just off the lakefront, where a market is held on Wednesday and Saturday. At one corner is the 14C Torre Viscontea. Steps lead up to the basilica of **San Nicolò**, a neo-classical building by Bovara with an eccentric and unusually tall campanile (96m) built in 1904 on a medieval base. Via Mascari crosses Via Bovara in which (uphill to the left) is the Palazzo del Governatore Spagnolo and a short stretch of 16C walls. Beyond Via Bovara is the little church of Santa Marta with an 18C façade in the Baroque style. Via Mascari crosses VIA CAVOUR (the main street of the town) and leads right to PIAZZA GARIBALDI with a statue of the hero by Francesco Confalonieri and the theatre by Bovara (1840). Via Roma leads into Piazza Manzoni with a bronze seated statue of the novelist also by Confalonieri.

Beyond the railway is **Villa Manzoni** (open 9.30–14 exc. Mon), a gloomy austere house bought by Manzoni's ancestors before 1621 where Manzoni lived as a boy. It contains a small museum of memorabilia, and a collection of local paintings. To the north (800 metres) is **Palazzo Belgioioso**, an 18C palace surrounded by public gardens containing a natural history museum, with minerals and fossils found locally.

The river Adda is crossed by four bridges including **Ponte Vecchio**, built by Azzone Visconti in 1336–38 (later altered and enlarged), the only road bridge before 1956. Nearby is the little (privately owned) Isola Viscontea.

Environs of Lecco

In the southern suburbs, beyond the rail bridge, is the locality of **Pescarenico**, a fishermen's hamlet also associated with Manzoni, with narrow streets and an attractive little piazza on the waterfront (paved in the 17C). Here can sometimes be seen the flat-bottomed covered *lucie*, charateristic fishing boats once used all over the lake (and named after Lucia in I Promessi Sposi). Across the main road is the church, interesting for its eccentric triangular campanile of 1472 and a 16C ancona with little polychrome scenes in papier mâché and wax. In front of the church is a tabernacle with friars' skulls, a reminder of the plague.

On the opposite shore of the lake, reached by the Ponte Nuovo, is **Malgrate**, a quiet pleasant little lakeside resort with good views of Lecco backed by mountains. The huge old red silk mill on the waterfront has been restored as a conference centre.

To the south of Lecco the Adda expands to form the **Lago di Garlate** beneath Monte Barro. **Garlate** has a Romanesque church and a silk museum in the old Abegg factory. The **Monte di Brianza** (or **San Genesio**; 800m), interesting for its vegetation, is traversed by a number of marked paths. Further south at **Brivio** on the Adda is another old silk mill (restored and used for exhibitions). In the environs is an unusual sanctuary with an 18C outside staircase. From Brivio a pretty path follows the river all the way downstream to Trezzo sull'Adda. At **Imbersago** a car ferry still runs across the Adda river to Villa d'Adda—a barge operated by hand using the river current and an overhead cable (a design taken from Leonardo da Vinci).

From the end of the road to Malnago a cableway leads part way up the saw-shaped **Monte Resegone** (1875m) which dominates Lecco from the east.

The **Valsassina**, the valley of the Pioverna, northeast of Lecco has skiing facilities. Its principal village **Introbio** is known for its cheeses. A road leads northeast from Lecco through **Ballabio**, a rock-climbing centre, past a byroad for the ski resort of **Piani Resinelli** (1276m) with the wooded Parco Valentino (marked paths and a museum dedicated to the Grigne group) overlooking the lake. At the Colle di Balisio the road divides: the right-hand branch leads to the resorts of **Moggio** and **Barzio** (with skiing facilities), and the left-hand branch traverses the Valsassina.

To the west of Lecco is the **Lago d'Annone**. From **Civate** a footpath leads in 1–1½hrs up to the sanctuary of *San Pietro al Monte** with the partly ruined church of San Pietro dating from the 10C; it has lateral apses, 11C–12C mural paintings, and a remarkable baldacchino above the main altar. The triapsidal oratory of San Benedetto was also built in the 10C. On the other side of the lake are **Annone** where the church has a magnificent carved wooden altarpiece of the 16C (removed), and **Oggiono** which has a polyptych by Marco d'Oggiono in its church, and a Romanesque baptistery. Further east is the Lago di Pusiano with its poplar-grown islet.

The Lecco reach of the Lago di Como

The old road skirts the lake with good views, while the new *superstrada* (N 36) traverses numerous tunnels beneath the mountains a short distance inland (with exits only at Bellano and Fuentes). The first six kilometres are dual carriageway and then the old road diverges left onto the lakeside. The old *Strada dei Viandanti*, an ancient bridlepath which links the villages on the east bank of the lake from San Martino to the Madonna di Val Pozzo, has recently been cleared (information from Lecco APT). The route starts just over 6km north of Lecco at the church of San Martino (Abbadia Lariana) and is c 36km long, following paved bridlepaths and estimated to take some 17 hours on foot. It used to serve as an important link between Milan and the Valtellina.

At **Fiumelatte** the road crosses a torrent, in flood usually only from March to October. It gushes into the lake from a spring just 250m away (there is a path up to the source). Although it has been studied by numerous experts (including Leonardo da Vinci) it is still not known why the water is intermittent.

VARENNA is a delightful little town (800 inhab.) whose port can only be reached on foot by narrow stepped streets. It has a good view across the lake of the promontory of Bellagio with the park of Villa Serbelloni. On the main road is the piazza with plane trees, the Royal Victoria hotel and four churches. **San Giorgio** has a 14C fresco on its façade. It contains a pavement and altar made of the local black marble, and a 15C polyptych by the local artist Pietro Brentani. The 11C church of **San Giovanni** has a fine apse and remains of frescoes. The spring of Fiumelatte (described above) can be reached from the piazza by a pretty path (c 1km; recently cleared by local volunteers) via the cemetery.

Just out of the piazza, on the main road to Lecco is the entrance to **VILLA CIPRESSI** (garden open daily Apr–Oct), an annexe of the Royal Victoria hotel, with a 19C–20C interior. The villa takes its name from its numerous cypresses, 60 of which had to be felled after a tornado in 1967. The well maintained garden, with a venerable wisteria, descends in steep terraces down to the lakeside. It has a good view of Villa Monastero, which it adjoins, beyond an attractive little boathouse and private dock.

A few metres further along the main road towards Lecco is the entrance to the **VILLA MONASTERO** (adm. to the garden only as for Villa Cipressi). The monastery here founded in 1208 was closed down in the 16C by St Charles Borromeo, and the villa is now owned by a science research centre (CNR) and administered by the province as a centre for scientific conventions. The garden is laid out on a long narrow terrace on the lakeside with 19C statuary, fine cypresses, palms, roses, and cineraria, and one huge old magnolia tree. The enormous greenhouse protects orange and lime trees. The gloomy villa, with elaborately carved furniture, yellow and black marble, and Art Nouveau decorations, is in urgent need of repair.

The old stepped streets of Varenna lead down from the piazza (see above) to the picturesque little **PORT**, with an arcaded street on the waterfront where the workers who prepared the black marble and green lumachella, or shell-marble, from the neighbouring quarries for shipping used to have their workshops. A walkway built in 1982 continues above the lake (with wonderful sunsets across the water in October) round to the car ferry pier. There is an **ornithological museum** in the upper town.

From Varenna a road inland follows the right bank of the Esino through Perledo, with the medieval Vezio castle, to **Esino** (907m, with a fine view), with the Museo della Grigna (ask at the town hall for the key). The road ends at Cainallo (1245m) beneath **Monte Grigna Settentrionale** (2410m), a dolomitic peak.

Back on the lake shore, **BELLANO** is a town (3700 inhab.) with silk and cotton mills, at the mouth of the Pioverna. The deep **Pioverna gorge** can be viewed from stairs and walkways (Easter–Sep 9.30–12.30, 13.30–17.30 exc. Wed). The restored church of **Santi Nazaro e Celso** is a good example of the 14C Lombard style. From Bellano a road runs to **Premana** (with a local ethnographical museum).

Dervio has a ruined castle and an old campanile at the foot of Monte Legnone (2601m). Just beyond Dorio a cobbled road (signposted for Piona) diverges left and traverses woods for c 2km to end at the Benedictine **Abbey of Piona** in a peaceful spot on the lake. The simple church has two large stoups borne by Romanesque lions, and behind it is the ruined apse of an earlier church. The irregular cloister has a variety of 12C capitals. There is a ferry station here open in summer.

The main road continues to **Colico**, an uninteresting town on a plain near the mouth of the Adda at the junction of the routes over the Splügen and Stelvio passes.

7 · The Valtellina and Valchiavenna in the province of Sondrio

This chapter covers the province of Sondrio, a mountainous area in the northernmost part of Lombardy on the borders with Switzerland. The Valtellina, the upper valley of the Adda, is famous for its numerous ski resorts, including Bormio. It also produces good wines (Grumello, Sassella, etc.) from vines trained to grow on frames on the steep hillsides. The valley has had a chequered history, but has a high cultural tradition. In the 14C it came under the control of Milan, but in 1512 it was united to the Grisons in Switzerland. The Reformation took a firm hold here, and on 19 July 1620, at the instigation of the Spanish governor of Milan, the Catholic inhabitants of the valley ruthlessly massacred the Protestants (the 'Sacro Macello'). Twenty years of warfare followed, but in 1639 the valley was regained by the Grisons, who held it until Napoleon's partition of 1797. The area has for long been subject to disastrous landslides and flooding, particularly in the 1980s as a result of uncontrolled new building, deforestation, and changes in the traditional methods of cultivation. In some places, notably in the area around Sant'Antonio Morignone south of Bormio, landslides have interrupted the course of the Adda and changed the geological formation of the valley.

■ **Information office.** APT Valtellina, 12 Via Cesare Battisti, Sondrio (tel. 0342 512500), with offices in Chiavenna, Aprica, Bormio, etc. Comunità Montana Valtellina di Sondrio, 33 Via Nazario Sauro (tel. 0342 210331).

■ Numerous **hotels** of all categories at the winter and summer resorts of Bormio, Valfurva (Santa Caterina), Val Malenco, Aprica, Valdidentro and Valdisotto, and Teglio. Chiavenna and Madesimo are also well served with hotels.

The Valtellina

SONDRIO (23,000 inhab.) is a provincial capital in the centre of the Valtellina, with a museum of the valley (archaeological collections, 18C paintings by the Ligari family, furniture, etc). To the north is the **Val Malenco**—frequented for winter sports—beneath the central massif of the Bernina, rising to 4068m, which marks the frontier with Switzerland.

A few kilometres east of Sondrio, above Montagna in Valtellina, are the ruins of **Castel Grumello**, donated to the FAI in 1987 (open 10–15, 17–24 exc. Mon & Sun afternoon). Situated on a rocky ridge, it consists of two fortresses built in the late 13C to early 14C by Corrado de Piro, one used for defensive purposes, and the other as a residence. It was destroyed in 1526. The castle commands a splendid view towards the Adamello mountain range, and is surrounded by terraced vineyards.

At **Ponte in Valtellina**, east of Sondrio, the 14C–16C church has a fresco by Bernardino Luini and a bronze ciborium of 1578. A monument commemorates the astronomer Giuseppe Piazzi (1746–1826), a native of the town, who discovered the first asteroid.

West of Sondrio is the industrial town of **Morbegno**, at the end of the Bitto valley, with skiing facilities. The church of San Lorenzo (the Santuario dell'Assunta), east of the town, was begun in 1418. There is also a small natural history museum here. Palazzo Malacrida, with an interesting garden, was finished in 1762 by Pietro Solari. At the head of the western arm of the valley rises the Pizzo dei Tre Signori (2554m), so called from its position on the boundaries of the old lordships of Milan, Venice and the Grisons. On the other side of the Adda is the **Val Masino**, with a number of climbing centres and, at the head of the valley, the spa town of **Bagni di Masino** (1171m), whose curative waters have been known since ancient times.

TIRANO, with 8500 inhab., is another important town in the Valtellina. It has an old district on the left bank of the Adda, with the historic mansions of the Visconti, Pallavicini and Salis families.The late 16C Palazzo Salis (still owned by the family), with a garden, is open from April to November (10–12, 14–16).

Many of the Protestant inhabitants of the town were massacred in 1620 (see above). The Bernina and Valtellina railways terminate here. To the north is the pilgrimage church of the **Madonna di Tirano**, begun in 1505, in the style of Bramante, with a fine doorway by Alessandro della Scala. The richly stuccoed interior has a large organ of 1617; outside is a painted fountain of 1780. The convent buildings house a local ethnographical museum.

North of Tirano is the Swiss border: the road continues over the Bernina pass to St Moritz (see *Blue Guide Switzerland*).

South of Tirano at **Tresenda**, a road ascends steeply over the Passo dell'Aprica (1181m), where **Aprica** is a scattered summer and winter resort. On the other side of the Adda is **Teglio** (776m), once the principal place in the valley to which it gave its name (Vallis Tellina). Here Palazzo Besta, rebuilt in the 16C, is open to the public (daily exc. Mon 9–12; summer also 14.30–17.30). It has a good 16C frescoed courtyard, and a museum of local prehistory. The late 15C church of Santa Eufemia is also of interest. The chapel of San Pietro has an 11C campanile.

North of Tirano on the Adda is **Mazzo di Valtellina** where the church of Santo Stefano has a portal carved by Bernardino Torigi (1508), and the Casa Lavizzari contains frescoes by Cipriano Valorsa (see below). Nearby is **Grosotto**, with its 15C houses, and the Santuario della Madonna, erected in the 17C as a thank-offering for the defeat of the Swiss Protestants in 1620, with a good choir.

The most important place on the main road between Tirano and Bormio is **GROSIO**, a large village (4600 inhab.) with 15C–16C houses, including a mansion owned by the Venosta (restored as the seat of the Museo Civico). It was the birthplace of Cipriano Valorsa (1514/17–1604), 'the Raphael of the Valtellina', whose paintings adorn nearly every church in the valley. In the chestnut woods above the road are the ruins of two Venosta castles, one dating from the 12C with the Romanesque campanile of the church of Santi Faustino e Giovita, and the other from the 14C, with fine battlements. Here in 1966 were discovered thousands of rock carvings (including human figures) dating from the Neolithic period to the Iron Age, the most interesting of which are on the Rupe Magna. The park is open Apr–Oct, 10–18, otherwise on request at the Municipal Library. Yellow signs indicate the paths through the park from near the huge electric power station (1917–22) beside the main road.

BORMIO (920m), backed by a magnificent circle of mountain peaks, is an ancient town (3900 inhab.) whose many ruined towers and picturesque old houses with carved doorways and painted façades recall its once prosperous transit trade between Venice and the Grisons. It is now well equipped for a long season of winter sports: in 1985 much new building took place when the world ski championships were held here, and new ski slopes were created, to the detriment of the natural beauty of the area. Valdisotto and Valdidentro are also now ski resorts.

The most interesting church is the **Crocifisso**, on the south side of the Frodolfo, which is decorated with 15C and 16C frescoes. The painting of the Crucifixion by Agostino Ferrari dates from 1376. The **Castello de Simoni** (now the town hall), reconstructed in the 17C, contains a small museum. Bormio is the administrative centre of the Stelvio National Park, described in Chapter 55.

Above Bormio on the Stelvio road are the **Bagni di Bormio**, a well-known spa with warm springs. Some remains of the Roman baths are visible, but the 19C baths were demolished in 1977.

To the east of Bormio is the **Valfurva**, with the ski resort of **Santa Caterina** (1718m).

A remarkable road ascends the **Valdidentro**, west of Bormio, to the Italian frontier station at Passo di Foscagno (2291m) beyond which lies the duty-free zone of the **Valle di Livigno**, watered by the Spöl (good trout fishing) and one of the few parts of Italian territory north of the Alpine watershed. It has recently been developed as a winter sports centre. **Livigno** is a long straggling village (1816m), with characteristic wooden houses built at a set distance one from the other to lessen the risk of fire. The church contains good 18C wood carving. It is connected by road with the Bernina pass in Switzerland (see *Blue Guide Switzerland*). East of Livigno is the source of the Adda on the Alpisella pass (2285m).

A road leads north from Bormio past Rovinaccio, where the botanical garden of **Rezia** has c 1000 species of flora from the Stelvio National Park (open in summer, and particularly beautiful in July and August). The Adda valley comes in from the left and the road ascends steeply up the Val Braulio, rarely altogether free from snow, to the **Stelvio Pass** (2758m), the second highest road pass in the Alps (generally open only from June to October), see Chapter 55.

The Valchiavenna

CHIAVENNA, the Roman *Clavenna*, perhaps so named because it was the key (*clavis*) of the Splügen, Septimber and Julier passes, is a small town (7100 inhab.) in a charming position in the fertile valley of the Mera. Above the turreted 15C Palazzo Balbiani rises the **Paradiso** (view), a rock with, on its slopes, botanic gardens and an archaeological collection. The church of **San Lorenzo** dates from the 16C, and has a massive detached campanile. The octagonal baptistery contains a font with reliefs of 1156, and in the treasury is a gold *pax by a 12C German artist.

In the wide valley to the south of Chiavenna is **Samolaco** which indicates by its name ('*summus lacus*') the point to which Lake Como extended in Roman times. The Lago di Mezzola is separated from the Lake of Como by the silt brought down by the Adda.

The **Val Bregaglia** is the fertile upper valley of the Mera, which has traces of a Roman road. The road soon enters Switzerland and continues across the Maloja pass to St Moritz (see *Blue Guide Switzerland*).

North of Chiavenna are the resorts of **Campodolcino** (1103m), beneath the snowfields of Motta (1725m), and, in the sunless valley of Pianazzo, **Madesimo** (1533m), an old-established climbing centre beneath the frontier peaks of Pizzo d'Emet (3211m) and Pizzo Spadolazzo (2948m). The Val di Lei is the only part of Italy where the waters flow into the Rhine.

The **Splügen Pass** (2118m) lies on the narrow frontier-ridge with Switzerland, between the Pizzo Tambò (3274m) and the Surettahorn. The pass was known to the Romans, and the route from *Clavenna* (Chiavenna) to *Curia* (Coire) is mentioned in the Antonine itinerary. In 1800, between 26 November and 6 December, Marshal Macdonald, despite stormy weather and bad snow conditions, succeeded in conveying an army of infantry, cavalry, and artillery from Splügen to Chiavenna to guard the left flank of Napoleon's Army of Italy, losing 100 men and over 100 horses in the snow. The pass is usually closed from November to May. The road descends steeply to Splügen, see *Blue Guide Switzerland*.

8 · Bergamo

A beautiful and interesting city (115,600 inhab.), Bergamo is divided into two sharply distinguished parts: the pleasant **Città Bassa**, laid out on a spacious plan at the end of the 19C and the beginning of the 20C with numerous squares between wide streets, which has the station and nearly all the hotels and the principal shops; and the **Città Alta** (366m), the lovely old town. With its varied and attractive skyline crowning a steep hill and its peaceful narrow streets, the latter is still no less important than the lower town. The Città Bassa and Città Alta have been connected since 1887 by an efficient funicular railway. Bergamo is one of the richest towns in Italy, with a booming economy (clothes manufacturies, metalworks, etc.), and much new building has taken place on the outskirts in recent years. The town has its own newspaper and symphony orchestra. The hotels are often full in the spring and autumn. Bergamo stands just below the first foothills of the Alps, between the valleys of the Brembo and the Serio.

■ **Information offices.** In the lower town: APT, 106 Viale Papa Giovanni (tel. 035 242226); in the upper town (Mar–Oct), 2 Vicolo Aquila Nera (just off Piazza Vecchia).

■ **Funicular railway** from the end of Viale Vittorio Emanuele II to the upper town every 10–15 minutes (in connection with Bus No. 1 to and from the railway station: same ticket), used by residents as well as visitors.

■ **Railway station**: Piazza Marconi in the lower town.

■ **Buses.** No 1: from the station along Viale Papa Giovanni through Piazza Matteotti (the centre of the lower town), Viale Roma, and Viale Vittorio Emanuele II to the funicular station for the upper town (same ticket). No. 3: through the lower town to the funicular station and through the upper town to Colle Aperto.
   Long distance buses depart from the bus station in front of the railway station for the Valli Bergamaschi and places in the province (SAB) and for Milan (Piazza Castello Sforzesco) along the motorway every half hour taking one hour ('Autostradali').

■ **Car parking.** In the upper town (except on Sunday afternoon when the upper town is totally closed to cars): in front of Sant'Agostino, along the walls, and at Colle Aperto; pay car park in Piazza Mercato del Fieno. In the lower town: Piazzale della Malpensata, otherwise numerous pay car parks.

■ **Hotels.** In the lower town: 4-star: *Excelsior San Marco* , 6 Piazzale Repubblica; 3-star: *Arli*, 12 Largo Porta Nuova and *Piemontese*, 11 Piazzale Marconi. In the centre of the upper town there are only two very simple hotels (2-star): *Sole*, 1 Via Colleoni and *Agnello d Oro*, 22 Via Gombito. Outside the upper gate in quiet positions on the hill of San Vigilio are two 3-star hotels: *Il Gourmet*, 1 Via San Vigilio and *San Vigilio* 15 Via San Vigilio. **Youth Hostel** in the district of Monterosso (Bus 14 from Largo Porta Nuova).

■ **Restaurants.** In the upper town: **A**: *Taverna del Colleoni*, Piazza Vecchia; *La*

Marianna, 2 Colle Aperto. **B**: *Trattoria del Teatro*, 3 Piazza Mascheroni. **C**: *Da Ornella* , 15 Via Gombito; *La Colombina*, 12 Via Borgo Canale; and numerous pizzerie. In the lower town: **A**: *Da Vittorio*, 21 Viale Papa Giovanni; *dell'Angelo*, 55 Via Borgo Santa Caterina; *Lio Pellegrini*, 47 Via San Tomaso (near the Accademia Carrara). **B**: *La Valtellinese*, 57 Via Tiraboschi; *La Bruschetta*, 1 Via G. D'Alzano.

■ **Cafés.** In the upper town: *Cavour*, Via Colleoni; *Caffè del Tasso*, 3 Piazza Vecchia; and *La Marianna*, Colle Aperto. In the lower town (in front of the Teatro Donizetti): *Balzer*.

■ **Picnic places.** In the upper town in the public gardens on Colle Aperto, near Sant'Agostino, and around the Rocca.

■ **Theatre.** *Donizetti* in the lower town, with an opera season in Sep–Oct and important musical events throughout the year, including concerts given by the Bergamo symphony orchestra. A Donizetti festival is held every two years. International Piano festival held jointly with Brescia in April and June. Concerts are also often held in the basilica of Santa Maria Maggiore (season of Baroque music in October).

■ **Annual festivals.** Festival in the middle of Lent with a bonfire, etc. Music festivals, see above.

■ In summer (Jun–Sep) **guided visits** are organised to the lesser known parts of the city. **Summer courses** in the Italian language for foreigners at the university.

History

Bergamo emerged as a free commune in the 12C. In the 14C the Visconti and the Torriani disputed possession of the city and in 1408–19 Pandolfo Malatesta was its overlord. Another period of Visconti rule ended in 1428, when Venice took the town. Bergamo remained a Venetian possession until the fall of the Republic in 1797, then until 1859 it was part of the Austrian dominion. The Bergamasques played a prominent part in the Risorgimento and contributed the largest contingent to Garibaldi's 'Thousand'. Its most famous citizens were Bartolomeo Colleoni, the 15C condottiere, and Gaetano Donizetti (1797–1848), the composer. The painters Giovanni Battista Moroni (c 1525–78) and Palma Vecchio (c 1480–1528) were born in the neighbourhood. Another native, the explorer Costantino Beltrami (1779–1855), found the source of the Mississippi in 1823.

Città Bassa

The Città Bassa was laid out at the foot of the hill on which the old city was built, in the area between the old *borghi* or suburbs. The broad avenues and pleasant squares which were planned by Marcello Piacentini in the first decades of the 20C give it a remarkable air of spaciousness. The principal thoroughfare consists of Viale Papa Giovanni XXIII and its continuation, Viale Vittorio Emanuele. Beyond **Porta Nuova** with its two little Doric 'temples', opened in 1837 as the monumental entrance to the new city, Viale Papa Giovanni XXIII crosses the huge PIAZZA MATTEOTTI, with **Palazzo del Comune** to the left, begun in 1836 by

Rodolfo Vantini. In front is a monument to the Calvi brothers (1933) with bas-reliefs by Giacomo Manzù, and a monument to Cavour by Leonardo Bistolfi (1913). Next to the town hall is a bank in a building of 1909 decorated by Luca Beltrami. Adjoining Piazza Matteotti to the north is the arcaded PIAZZA VITTORIO VENETO, designed by Piacentini (1929), with the Torre dei Caduti (1924) as a war memorial. The monument to Partisans is by Giacomo Manzù.

The wide promenade known as the 'SENTIERONE', opened in 1762, leads (right) past the **Teatro Donizetti** with a façade of 1897 by Pietro Via and a late 18C interior, to Piazza Cavour, with gardens surrounding a monument to Donizetti by Francesco Jerace (1897). Opposite is the church of **San Bartolomeo**, with a large but poorly lit *altarpiece by Lorenzo Lotto (1516) and fine intarsia choir stalls.

Via Torquato Tasso continues past the Palazzo della Prefettura e Provincia (1870) to the church of **Santo Spirito** with a good interior of 1521. It contains paintings by Lorenzo Lotto, Andrea Pevitali and Bergognone, and in the sacristy is a monument to Bishop Luigi Tasso (1524).

VIA PIGNOLO, which leads left through Borgo Pignolo, is the street with the greatest number of noble houses in Bergamo, dating from the 16C–19C. No. 80 once belonged to Tasso's family, and the 17C Palazzo Agliardi (No. 86) has a *salone* frescoed by Carlo Carloni. On the corner of Via San Giovanni is the church of **San Bernardino** (if closed ring at the door on the left of the façade) which contains a particularly beautiful *altarpiece by Lorenzo Lotto, painted in 1521 (and restored in 1993). Further on is **Sant'Alessandro della Croce** (being restored) with small paintings in the sacristy by Lorenzo Lotto, Lorenzo Costa and Andrea Previtali. Via San Tommaso continues uphill to the Accademia Carrara (described below at the end of the description of the upper town).

Beyond Borgo Pignolo is the old Borgo Santa Caterina and, across the railway, the huge **cemetery** with a monumental entrance by Ernesto Pirovano (1900–13) and sculptures by Ernesto Bazzaro.

To the west of Piazza Matteotti, reached by Via XX Settembre, a shopping street, is the old district of **Borgo Sant'Alessandro** (or Borgo San Leonardo). Here Piazza Pontida is still the commercial centre of the city. The interesting old VIA SANT'A-LESSANDRO runs north from the piazza past the church of **Sant'Alessandro in Colonna**. Outside is a column erected in 1618 made up from Roman fragments. The paintings in the interior include works by Leandro Bassano, Lorenzo Lotto and Francesco Zucco. Via Sant'Alessandro winds northwards around an old fort before entering the upper town by a stone bridge built in 1780 through **Porta San Giacomo**, a splendid 16C gateway in the Venetian walls.

Città Alta

Higher up Viale Vittorio Emanuele (see above) is the lower station of the **funic-ular**, which tunnels through the Venetian walls to the Città Alta. By far the quickest and most convenient way of reaching the upper town, it has been in operation since 1887 (and was last restored in 1987). The well-preserved Città Alta, or upper town, is no less prosperous than the lower town, and contains the most important monuments. Its quiet narrow streets, attractively paved in a herringbone pattern, have many large mansions, handsome shop fronts, and some old-fashioned cafés. The university of Bergamo was founded here in 1970.

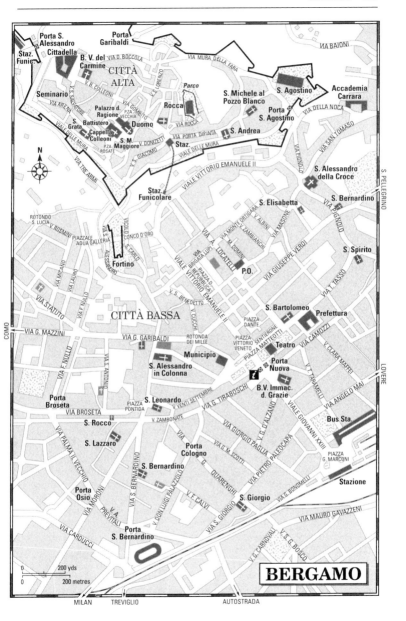

BERGAMO

Porta S. Alessandro
Staz. Funic.
Cittadella
B. V. del Carmine
VIA D. BOCCOLA
Porta Garibaldi
VIA MURA DELLA FARA
VIA BAIONI
CITTÀ ALTA
V. B. COLLEONI
S. LORENZO
Parco
S. Michele al Pozzo Bianco
S. Agostino
Accademia Carrara
Seminario
V. S. SALVATORE
VIA ARENA
Palazzo d. Ragione
VIA GOMBITO
P.ZA VECCHIA
Rocca
VIA DELLA NOCA
S. Grata
Battistero
Duomo
P.ZA DUOMO
Cappella Colleoni
S. M. Maggiore
P.ZA ROSATE
V. DONIZETTI
V. PORTA DIPINTA
Porta S. Agostino
S. Andrea
VIA SAN TOMASO
VIALE DELLE MURA
VIA TRE ARMI
VIA ROCCA
Staz.
V. S. GIACOMO
VIALE DELLE MURA
VIA PIGNOLO
S. Alessandro della Croce
S. PELLEGRINO
VIALE VITTORIO EMANUELE II
Staz. Funicolare
S. Elisabetta
S. Bernardino
VIA PIGNOLO
ROTONDO S. LUCIA
V. ROSMINI
PIAZZALE ADUA
GALLERIA
CONCO D'ORO
V. S. CARLO
VICOLO
VIA MONTE ORTIGARA
V. ALBINI
VIA MASONE
VIA BRIGATA LUPI
VIA A. LOCATELLI
V. M. DOMINI
VIA GIUSEPPE VERDI
S. Spirito
COMO
VIA G. MAZZINI
Fortino
VIA ALESSANDRO
PIAZZA D. REPUBBLICA
VIALE VITTORIO EMANUELE II
P.O.
VIA T. TASSO
VIA MICANO
VIA LAURO
VIA F. NULLO
VIA STATUTO
VIA S. BENEDETTO
V. S. BENEDETTO
V. CUCCHI
CITTÀ BASSA
S. Bartolomeo
Prefettura
PIAZZA DANTE
VIA G. GARIBALDI
ROTONDA DEI MILLE
PIAZZA VITTORIO VENETO
SENTIERONE
PIAZZA MATTEOTTI
Teatro
VIA CAMOZZI
VIA F. NULLO
VIA S. ANTONINO
Municipio
Porta Nuova
V. T. TARAMELLI
V. CLARA MAFFEI
LOVERE
S. Alessandro in Colonna
B.V. Immac. d. Grazie
VIA ANGELO MAI
Porta Broseta
VIA BROSETA
S. Leonardo
PIAZZA PONTIDA
V. VENTI SETTEMBRE
VIA G. TIRABOSCHI
V. ZAMBONATE
VIA GIORGIO PAGLIA
V. G. D'ALZANO
Bus Sta.
S. Rocco
VIA
VIALE GIOVANNI XXIII
S. Lazzaro
VIA PALMA IL VECCHIO
VIA S. BERNARDINO
Porta Cologno
VIA G. M. SCOTTI
VIA PIETRO PALEOCAPA
PIAZZA G. MARCONI
Porta Osio
VIA MORONI
S. Bernardino
V. F. CALVI
QUARENGHI
VIA G. BONOMELLI
Stazione
VIA CARDUCCI
VIA A. PREVITALI
V. DON LUIGI PALAZZOLO
S. Giorgio
VIA S. GIORGIO
VIA MAURO GAVAZZENI
Porta S. Bernardino
V. S. CARNOVALI
V. S. G. BOSCO

0   200 yds
0   200 metres

MILAN   TREVIGLIO   AUTOSTRADA

N

The upper station of the funicular is on PIAZZA MERCATO DELLE SCARPE, paved with small cubes of porphyry, where seven roads meet. The fountain covers a cistern built in 1486. The narrow old VIA GOMBITO, with pretty old-style shop fronts, climbs up past a little piazza with a 16C fountain and the church of **San Pancrazio**, its Gothic portal decorated with 14C statues and a 15C fresco. Beyond the 12C **Torre di Gombito** (52m high) the road ends in the spacious PIAZZA VECCHIA, the centre of the old town, with a pretty fountain (1780). On the right is **Palazzo Nuovo** (designed by Vincenzo Scamozzi in 1611, but unfinished until the 20C), opposite which rises **Palazzo della Ragione**, rebuilt in 1538–43, bearing a modern Lion of St Mark and with a meridian of 1789 beneath the portico. The massive 12C **Torre Civica**, over 52m high (open 10–12, 14–16 or 18; in winter at weekends only) can be climbed (the lift is at present out of action). From the top, beside the three bells, the view north takes in the green fields within the walls with an old ammunition store, the hill of San Vigilio and, nearer at hand, the Colleoni chapel, Santa Maria Maggiore and the Cathedral. Beyond Piazza Vecchia rises the square medieval Torre di Gombito and the Rocca on its hill.

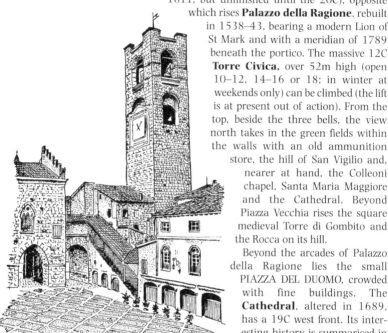

Piazza Vecchia

Beyond the arcades of Palazzo della Ragione lies the small PIAZZA DEL DUOMO, crowded with fine buildings. The **Cathedral**, altered in 1689, has a 19C west front. Its interesting history is summarised in an inscription on the southwest pier of the crossing. The St Benedict altarpiece on the first south altar is by Andrea Previtali (1524). In the south transept is an altar by Filippo Juvarra and a painting by Sebastiano Ricci. Opposite is a painting by Giovanni Battista Cignaroli. The 18C paintings in the apse include one by Giovanni Battista Tiepolo. The carved panels in the north transept are by Andrea Fantoni. On the second north altar is a statue of St Charles Borromeo by Giacomo Manzù. The altarpiece on the first north altar is by Giovanni Battista Moroni.

The charming little **Baptistery**, opposite, by Giovanni da Campione (1340), originally stood inside Santa Maria Maggiore. Between the cathedral and the baptistery rises the church of Santa Maria Maggiore (described below), against the south wall of which—behind a railing of 1912—is the colourful *COLLEONI CHAPEL. The famous condottiere Bartolomeo Colleoni, having ordered the demolition of the sacristy, commissioned Giovanni Antonio Amadeo in 1472 to erect his funerary chapel on this site. It is one of the most important High Renaissance works in Lombardy, although the over-lavish decorations are unconnected with the architectural forms. The elaborate carving celebrates the brilliant captain-general (who served both the Visconti and the Venetian Republic) by means of complicated allegories combining classical and biblical allusions. The charming exterior details include copies of cannon shafts (which Colleoni used for the first time in pitched battle) in the eccentric windows. The 12 statues are to be replaced by copies.

The **interior** (open 9–12, 14–17.30 or 18.30), under restoration, contains the tomb of Colleoni (died 1476) and the *tomb of his young daughter Medea (died 1470), both by Giovanni Antonio Amadeo. The equestrian statue in gilded wood is by Leon and Sisto Siry (c 1493). The tomb of Medea was transferred in 1842 from the country church of Basella, on the Crema road. The three altar statues are by Pietro Lombardo (1490). The remaining decoration of the chapel is 18C work, including some excellent marquetry seats, ceiling-frescoes by Giovanni Battista Tiepolo, and a Holy Family by Angelica Kauffmann.

*SANTA MARIA MAGGIORE, a Romanesque church begun by a certain Maestro Fredo in 1137, has a beautiful exterior. Next to the Colleoni Chapel is the *north porch of 1353 by Giovanni da Campione. Above the delightful arch, borne by two red marble lions, is a tabernacle with three statues of Saints, including an equestrian statue of St Alexander. Above is another tabernacle with the Madonna and Child and Saints sculpted by Andreolo de' Bianchi (1398). The door itself is surrounded by more good carving. To the left can be seen the exterior of the apses, the Gothic sacristy door (northeast), also Campionese, and the exterior of the polygonal new sacristy (1485–91). Steps lead up beside the fine apse and campanile (1436) and a lane goes round to the **south porch**, also by Giovanni da Campione (1360) above which is a little tabernacle with statues by Hans von Fernach (1401).

The centrally planned **interior** is decorated with splendid 16C stuccoes, and late 16C and 17C frescoes and paintings in the vault. At the west, north and south ends are three large paintings in elaborate frames, and on the walls are hung fine tapestries, most of them Florentine works dating from 1583–86 to designs by Alessandro Allori. At the **west end** the well-preserved Flemish tapestry of the Crucifixion dates from 1696–98. Above it is a painting by Luca Giordano. The monument to Donizetti is by Vincenzo Vela. The elaborate confessional was carved by Andrea Fantoni in 1705, and the funerary monument of Cardinal Longhi is attributed to Ugo da Campione (1330).

In the **south transept** is a fresco of the Tree of Life dating from 1347, a large painting of the Flood by Pietro Liberi, and an altarpiece of the Last Supper by Francesco Bassano, and in the **north transept** are interesting 14C frescoes (including a scene in a smithy, and the Last Supper). The two cantorie are decorated with paintings by the local painters Il Talpino and Gian Paolo Cavagna (1595 and 1593). In the chapel to the right of the choir are four more tapestries and an altarpiece by Antonio Boselli (1514).

At the entrance to the **sanctuary** are six 16C bronze candelabra, and two 16C pulpits with fine bronze railings. Above hangs a wooden Crucifix. The choir screen has four splendid large intarsia *panels (kept covered except on holidays, but shown on request by the custodian) designed by Lorenzo Lotto, showing the Crossing of the Red Sea, the Flood, Judith and Holofernes, and David and Goliath. There are also beautiful intarsia choir stalls in the sanctuary and in the **apse** is a large curving painting of the Assumption by Camillo Procaccini.

Just behind the cathedral and Santa Maria Maggiore is a building dating from 1769, which was adapted in the early 19C as the seat of an academy known as the **Ateneo** (it is now in very poor repair).

Between the Colleoni Chapel and the Baptistery, steps lead up to a passageway through the ground floor of the **Curia Vescovile**. It has a fine arch and frescoes of the 13–14C. Beyond is the centrally planned **Tempietto di Santa Croce** (probably dating from the 11C, but altered in the 16C). Steps lead down to the south porch of Santa Maria Maggiore. On the right is the pretty, cobbled Via Arena which leads uphill past the interesting monastery wall of Santa Grata (with traces of frescoes) and an eccentric portal opposite the **Istituto Musicale Donizetti** (No.9). Here is a **Donizetti Museum** (open 9–12, 15–18 exc. Sat & Sun; ring for the custodian), founded in 1903. In a large room, decorated at the beginning of the 19C, are MSS, documents, wind instruments, portraits, mementoes, etc. Also here is the piano at which the composer worked. Via Arena ends at the huge Seminary building (1965); Via Salvecchio leads right to Via Salvatore (left), which continues downhill past high walls and gardens into Piazza della Cittadella (see below).

From Piazza Vecchia (see above) VIA COLLEONI, with attractive shops and cafés, is a continuation of Via Gombito. It passes (left) the **Teatro Sociale** designed by Leopoldo Pollack (1803–07) and (right; No. 9) the **Luogo Pio Colleoni** (open Tue & Fri 9.30–11.30), beside a little garden bequeathed by the condottiere to a charitable institution founded by him in 1466. On the ground floor are 15C detached frescoes (two of them depicting Colleoni), and a pretty vault dating from the late 15C. Upstairs a room contains a few mementoes and a portrait of Colleoni by Giovanni Battista Moroni.

Via Colleoni next passes the church of the **Carmine**, rebuilt in the 15C and again in 1730. It contains a painting by Andrea Previtali, and a finely carved 15C Venetian wooden ancona. The road ends in Piazza della Cittadella with a good 14C portico and two museums. The **Natural History Museum** (open 9–12, 14.30–17.30 exc. Mon) contains a well arranged collection, including a section devoted to the explorer Costantino Beltrami (see above). The **Archaeological Museum** (adm. as above), which originated in a collection formed by the town council in 1561, is also well arranged and has locally found material from prehistoric times to the early Christian and Lombard era. The Roman section includes epigraphs, funerary monuments, statues, mosaics, and frescoes from a house in Via Arena.

Beyond the courtyard is the Torre di Adalberto, a tower probably dating from the 12C, beside a little walled public garden. Outside the gateway is COLLE APERTO, usually busy with cars and buses, with an esplanade overlooking fields which stretch to the northwest corner of the walled city (the powder store was built in the 16C by the Venetians). Here is the well preserved **Porta Sant'Alessandro.**

Just outside the gate is the station of the **funicular railway** (open 10–20, every 15 mins taking 3 mins; longer hours in summer) to **San Vigilio** (461m). Opened in 1912, closed in 1976, but rebuilt in 1991, it runs along the walls of the Forte di San Marco. San Vigilio is a quiet little resort with several restaurants and a hotel. On the right of the upper station a cobbled lane (with a view of the Città Alta) leads up towards the Castello: by an Art Nouveau house, steps continue up left to a little public garden on the site of the **Castello** (511m) with remains of a 16C–17C Venetian fortress on a mound with views on every side. A number of pleasant walks can be taken in the surrounding hills (Monte Bastia and San Sebastiano); or the Città Alta can be reached on foot by descending, from the church of San Vigilio, the stepped Via dello Scorlazzone and (left) Via Sudorno.

Also outside Porta Sant'Alessandro, on the hillside at 14 Via Borgo Canale, is **Donizetti's birthplace** (adm. by appointment only, tel. 035 399230).

From Colle Aperto, Via Costantino Beltrami continues uphill to a traffic light: on the left is a signpost for the Botanical Garden. Beyond a powder store with a conical roof, built by the Venetians in 1582, steps continue up to the little **Botanical Garden** (open Mar–Oct 9–12, 14–17 or 18) opened in 1972, from which there is a good view of the two towns below. The plants (600 species) in an area of only 1357 square metres are well labelled.

From Piazza Mercato delle Scarpe (see above) a road is signposted uphill for the **Rocca** (open spring–autumn), the remains of a castle built by the Visconti in 1331 and reinforced by the Venetians in the 15C (restored in 1925). It contains a Risorgimento museum (closed indefinitely), and incorporates the little church of Sant'Eufemia, documented from 1006. Outside the walls is a public park, with conifers, cypresses and a few palm trees, laid out as a war memorial with cannon used in the First World War, tanks, etc. There is a path right round the castle and the fine view takes in Santa Caterina and the lower town and a hillside with the orchard and terraced gardens of Palazzo Moroni, while to the west there is a splendid panorama of the upper city, with its towers and domes.

Via Donizetti leads steeply uphill out of Piazza Mercato delle Scarpe past (No. 3) the **Casa dell'Arciprete**, a Renaissance mansion of c1520 attributed to the local architect Pietro Isabello, with an elegant marble façade and delicate windows. It contains a small Diocesan Museum (adm. by appointment only).

From Via Gombito, just out of Piazza Mercato delle Scarpe, Via Solata leads to Piazza Mercato del Fieno, with two medieval towers and the former **Convent of San Francesco**, dating from the end of the 13C, with two fine cloisters and 14C frescoes.

VIA PORTA DIPINTA (for centuries the main approach to the town) descends from Piazza Mercato delle Scarpe. At No. 12 is the 17C **Palazzo Moroni** (still owned by the family but usually opened at weekends from mid-April to mid-July: enquire at the APT) with good windows and a handsome portal and a grotto in the courtyard. It has a very large garden behind, which covers about a twelfth of the entire area of the Città Alta. The interior has 17C frescoes by Gian Giacomo Barbelli on the staircase and on the ceilings of the *piano nobile*. The furnished rooms have 15C–19C paintings including three by Giovanni Battista Moroni, and works by Previtali, Fra Galgario and Hayez. Opposite the palace is a little garden with a view of the lower town. The neo-classical church of **Sant'Andrea** (only open on Sunday morning) has a Madonna enthroned by Moretto. Further on is **San Michele al Pozzo Bianco** (open 8.30–16.30) with a fine interior having 12–14C frescoes in the nave and, in the chapel on the left of the sanctuary, a good fresco cycle of the Life of the Virgin by Lorenzo Lotto.

The road now skirts the Prato della Fara, a pleasant green with an attractive row of houses. At the end is the former church of **Sant'Agostino** (which has been undergoing restoration for years), with a good Gothic façade. It has a green and red vault dating from the 15C and numerous interesting fresco fragments.

From the church, Viale della Fara leads above the northern stretch of walls overlooking open country in which defence banks can be seen. Via San Lorenzo leads away from the walls to the church of San Lorenzo, next to which is the **Fontana del Lantro** (opened by a group of volunteers who restored it in 1992; enquire at APT). This 16C cistern fed by two springs was built at the same time as the city walls. The water source was already known by 928, and the name is thought to come from *atrium* or from *later*, referring to the milky colour of the water as it gushes out of the spring. There is a walkway with a view of the cistern with its 16C vault pierced by holes through which buckets were drawn up. A second cistern dates from the 17C.

Beside the church of Sant'Agostino is the **Porta Sant'Agostino** (being restored) near a little public garden. There is a good view of the Venetian **walls** (begun 1561–88) which still encircle the upper town. Off Via Vittorio Emanuele is the entrance to the **Cannoniera di San Michele** (open usually at weekends; for information, tel. 035 262566). One of about 27 such defences in the walls, this protected Porta Sant'Agostino. A tunnel leads down to a hall used by the soldiers which still contains cannon balls. The two holes (now blocked) used for positioning the cannon can be seen, as can a passageway—high enough for a horse—which leads outside the walls. The limestone has formed into stalactites.

Galleria dell'Accademia Carrara

From outside Porta Sant'Agostino (see above), Via della Noca (left; pedestrians only) leads downhill; it is the most pleasant (and easiest) way of reaching the Galleria dell'Accademia Carrara from the upper town.

The *GALLERIA DELL'ACCADEMIA CARRARA (open 9.30–12.30, 14.30–17.30 exc. Tue) was founded, together with the academy, in 1780 by Count Giacomo Carrara, and the splendid collection of paintings has since been augmented (notably with the Guglielmo Lochis and Giovanni Morelli collections). The Venetian school is particularly well represented. There are long-term plans to re-hang the works by collections rather than chronologically. In the courtyard is a sculpture by Giacomo Manzù. The building was purchased by Carrara for his gallery and academy, and was enlarged in 1807–10 by Simone Elia.

The main collection is exhibited on the **second floor**. **Room 1**. Works by Bonifacio Bembo, Antonio Vivarini and Jacopo Bellini (*Madonna and Child).

Room 2. Works by Alesso Baldovinetti (*Self-portrait in fresco), Sandro Botticelli (including a *portrait of Giuliano de' Medici, one of several versions of this subject), Donatello (a relief), Francesco Botticini, Francesco Pesellino, Benedetto da Maiano, Fra' Angelico (and his school), Pisanello (*Portrait of Lionello d'Este) and Lorenzo Monaco.

Room 3. Works by Jacobello di Antonello (a copy of 1480 of a lost painting by the father of Antonello da Messina), Bartolomeo Vivarini, Pietro de Saliba, Giovanni Bellini (Pietà, and *Madonna Lochis, *Madonna di Alzano, Portrait of a young man), Marco Basaiti, Andrea Mantegna (*Madonna and Child), Vincenzo Catena, Lorenzo Lotto, Carlo Crivelli (*Madonna and Child), and small works by Gentile Bellini and Lazzaro Bastiani.

Room 4. Lorenzo Costa, Gian Francesco Bembo, and Bergognone.

Room 5. Andrea Previtali and Marco Basaiti. **Room 6**. Lorenzo Lotto

(*Mystic Marriage of St Catherine*, *Holy Family with St Catherine*, 1533), Giovanni Cariani (*Portrait of Giovanni Benedetto Caravaggi), Palma Vecchio and Titian. **Room 7**. El Greco (attributed), Jacopo Bassano, and Gaudenzio Ferrari. **Room 8**. Portraits by the Florentine school, Marco Basaiti and Pier Francesco Foschi. **Room 9** contains a fine series of portraits by Giovanni Battista Moroni, including an *Old man with a book. **Room 10.** Dürer, 'Master of the St Ursula Legend', Jean Clouet (*Portrait of Louis of Clèves).

From the top of the stairs outside Room I is the entrance to **Room 11**, with portraits by the local painter Carlo Ceresa, and works by Guercino and Sassoferrato. In **Room 12** are portraits by the local painter Fra' Galgario, and beyond are three small rooms with 19C works by Il Piccio, Giuseppe Pelliza da Volpedo (allegorical *Portrait of a woman) and Francesco Hayez. **Room 13.** Flemish and Dutch paintings, inlcuding one by Rubens, and a portrait by Velasquez. **Room 14.** Francesco Zuccarelli, Piero Longhi and Piazzetta. **Room 15.** The Venetian school including Francesco Guardi, Giovanni Battista Tiepolo and Canaletto.

The fine collection of **prints and drawings**, especially important for the Lombard and Venetian schools, is open to scholars by special request.

The seven rooms on the **first floor** (usually closed, but opened with special permission) contain more 15C–17C paintings (Lombard and Veneto masters).

Across the road, a 14C monastery which was transformed into the Camozzi barracks has been partially restored by Vittorio Gregotti as an exhibition centre. Another part of the building is to be used to display the permanent collection of 20C works.

The centre of the lower town is reached from the Accademia by descending Via San Tomaso, Via Pignolo and Via Torquato Tasso (all described above).

9 · The Bergamasco

The Bergamasco (province of Bergamo) consists of two main valleys, the Val Brembana and the Valle Seriana, in the mountains north of Bergamo. The lower reaches of the valleys are now industrial with unattractive buildings, but the higher regions are prettier with small ski resorts. The interesting churches in these two valleys and the castle of Malpaga on the plain south of Bergamo, are best reached in a day from Bergamo (preferably by car since they are not well served by bus).

The Val Brembana

The lower valley runs through part of the Parco Regionale dei Colli di Bergamo, an area of some 8500 hectares protected since 1977. **Ponteranica** has a fine parish church containing a polyptych by Lorenzo Lotto.

In the hills of the **Valle Imagna**, Valcalepio wine (red and white) is produced. **ALMENNO SAN BARTOLOMEO** and **ALMENNO SAN SALVATORE** are two neighbouring municipalities. In the latter is the **Pieve di San Salvatore** (or the **Madonna del Castello**), marked by its tall campanile, above the river Brembo in which can be seen a few remains of a large Roman bridge destroyed in a flood.

This is the oldest church in Almenno and is thought to have been founded c 755. The interior (key at the priest's house next door), altered in the 12C, has a fine 12C pulpit in sandstone with the symbols of the Evangelists. The sanctuary has good Ionic capitals and frescoes (c 1150). The ancient columns in the crypt date from before the 11C. The church adjoins the 16C Santuario della Madonna del Castello which has a delightful early 16C ciborium over the high altar, with paintings of sibyls attributed to Andrea Previtali, and an altarpiece by Gian Paolo Cavagna.

Close by (5 minutes' walk) is the large 12C **Basilica di San Giorgio**, with a good exterior. The whale bone hanging in the nave, dating from the Pliocene era, was found nearby. The most interesting frescoes are those high up—and difficult to see—on the inside of the nave arches (on the right): they date from the late 13C or early 14C.

Also outside Almenno San Salvatore is the church of **San Nicola** (or **Santa Maria della Consolazione**), next to the ex-convent of the Agostiniani founded in 1486. It has an attractive interior, with stone vaulting supporting a painted wood roof, and side chapels beneath a matroneum. It contains 16C frescoes by Antonio Boselli, and an altarpiece of the Trinity by Andrea Previtali.

Outside Almenno San Bartolomeo is the little circular church of *****SAN TOMÉ**, one of the most interesting Romanesque buildings in Lombardy. It is usually open at weekends from spring to October; otherwise the key is kept at a house nearby (No. 21). Excavations in the area have revealed remains of tombs dating from the 1C and the 9C, but the date of the church is still under discussion. It is now generally thought to be an 11C building, although the apse and presbytery may have been added later. The nun's door connected the church to a fortified convent. It was restored in 1892. The beautiful interior has an ambulatory and above it a matroneum (which can be reached by stairs) beneath a delightful cupola and lantern lit by four windows. The good capitals are decorated with sirens, eagles, etc.

In Almenno San Bartolomeo is the Museo del Falegname, a private museum dedicated to the work of carpenters, with a collection of tools (from the 17C), reconstructed artisans' workshops, bicycles and puppets.

A road leads west to **Pontida** with a Benedictine abbey, the upper cloister of which is a fine work probably by Pietro Isabello (c 1510). On the other side of Monte Canto, **Sotto il Monte Giovanni XXIII** has taken the papal name of Angelo Roncalli, born here in 1881, and pope 1958–63.

Zogno is the chief place in the lower Val Brembana and it has a local museum. **Serina** (visited for cross-country skiing) was the birthplace of Palma il Vecchio (polyptych in the sacristy of the church).

SAN PELLEGRINO TERME has famous mineral water springs. The elegant spa town was laid out at the beginning of this century: the grand Art Nouveau buildings include the Palazzo della Fonte and the former Casinò Municipale. The Val Taleggio is noted for its cheese. In the main valley is the remarkable medieval village of **Cornello**, which was the 14C home of the Tasso family, who are supposed to have run a European postal service from here. **Piazza Brembana** is a summer resort and a base for climbs in the mountains.

Above Piazza the valley divides, both branches giving access to numerous little climbing and winter-sports resorts, the most important of which is **Foppolo** (1545m).

The Valle Seriana

This is the principal valley in the Bergamesque Alps, and is mainly industrial, with many silk and cotton mills and cement works, but the upper reaches are unspoilt. The churches have some fine works by the Fantoni family of sculptors and carvers, who lived and worked in the valley in the 15C–19C.

ALZANO LOMBARDO is noted for its wool workers. The **Basilica of San Martino** was rebuilt in 1670 and has a splendid interior designed by Girolomo Quadrio, with coupled marble columns and stuccoes by Angelo Sala. It has a pulpit by Andrea Fantoni, and a painting by Andrea Appiani. The three *sacristies have superb carvings and intarsia work, beautifully restored in 1992. The first sacristy has Baroque walnut cupboards carved by Grazioso Fantoni (1679–80), while the second sacristy (1691–93) has even better carving in walnut and box wood by his son Andrea Fantoni and his three brothers. Above are statuettes showing the martyrdom of saints and apostles, and in the ovals the story of Moses and scenes from the New Testament. The seated statues represent the Virtues; the prie-dieu has a Deposition, also by Fantoni; and the stuccoes are by Girolamo Sala. The intarsia in the third sacristy is partly by Giovanni Battista Caniana (1700–17); the barrel vault has more stuccoes by Sala.

At **Olera** the parish church contains a polyptych by Cima da Conegliano. **Albino**, an industrial village, has a Crucifixion by Giovanni Battista Moroni (born nearby at Bondo Petello) in the church of San Giuliano.

GANDINO, an ancient little town noted for its carpets, was the birthplace of the sculptor Bartolomeo Bon the elder. The *Basilica of Santa Maria Assunta** was rebuilt in 1623–30 and has a very fine interior on an interesting central plan. The dome was finished in 1640 and the trompe l'oeil fresco added in 1680. The bronze balustrade dates from 1590. Giacomo Ceruti painted the spandrels above the arches and the organ was built by Adeodato Bossi in 1868 (in an earlier case by Andrea Fantoni). Outside the church a little baptistery was erected in 1967, and beside it is the **Museo della Basilica**, first opened in 1928. It contains two series of Flemish tapestries (1580), a silver altar (begun in 1609 and finished in the 19C), and an organ made by Perolini in 1755. On the first floor are vestments, church silver, a 16C German sculpture of Christ on the Cross (with movable arms), and ancient textiles.

Vertova has a prominent 17C parish church surrounded by a portico. On the wooded hillside above can be seen the sanctuary of **San Patrizio**, a 16C building with an earlier crypt. The valley now becomes prettier.

CLUSONE is a small resort in the Valle Seriana. The medieval **town hall** has a remarkable astronomical clock made by Pietro Fanzago in 1583, and numerous remains of frescoes. Above is the grand basilica of **Santa Maria Assunta**, built in 1688–1716 by Giovanni Battista Quadrio, preceded by an impressive terrace with statues added at the end of the 19C. The high altar has sculptures by Andrea Fantoni (who also designed the pulpit) and an Assumption by Sebastiano Ricci. The altarpieces are by Domenico Carpinoni, Gaspare Diziani, Giambettino Cignaroli and Gian Paolo Cavagna. Above the west door is a large painting by the local painter Lattanzio Querena.

To the left is the **Oratorio dei Disciplini** with a remarkable *fresco on the exterior depicting the Dance and Triumph of Death (1485), fascinating for its iconography. Inside (unlocked by the sacristan of the church) are well preserved frescoes showing small colourful scenes of the Passion dating from 1480. Over the choir arch is a fresco of the Crucifixion (1471). The life-size polychrome wood group of the Deposition is attributed to the school of Fantoni.

Further downhill are the grand Palazzo Fogaccia built in the early 18C by Giovanni Battista Quadrio, with a garden, and the church of Sant'Anna with 15C and 16C frescoes inside and out, and a fine altarpiece by Domenico Carpinoni, in a lovely frame.

Just outside Clusone is **Rovetta**, where the house and workshop of the Fantoni family of sculptors, who were born here, is now a little museum, and the church has an early altarpiece by Giovanni Battista Tiepolo. The **Passo della Presolana** (1286m) is a ski resort, and there are more resorts in the upper Valle Seriana.

East of Bergamo is **Trescore Balneario**, a small spa with sulphur and mud baths. A chapel (shown on request) in the park of the Suardi villa at Novale contains frescoes by Lorenzo Lotto (1524). At **Credaro** the church of San Giorgio has another chapel with more frescoes carried out a year later by Lotto.

South of Bergamo between the rivers Adda and Oglio

The **Castle of Malpaga* (open for guided tours on fest. 14.30–dusk; otherwise by appointment; tel. 035 840003; restaurant *Osteria del Castello*, **C**) is approached by a road bordered on either side by narrow canals regulated by locks connected to the Serio river. It is set in the centre of an agricultural estate, surrounded by farm buildings with double loggias. The 14C castle, on the extreme western limit of the land owned by the Venetian Republic, was bought as a residence by Bartolomeo Colleoni in 1456, the year after he became Captain of the Venetian army. He heightened the castle in order to protect it against firearms (the castellations of the first castle can be seen in the walls) and built the pretty loggias, and it also used to be defended by two moats.

The castle is particularly interesting for its frescoes carried out at the time of Colleoni and in the following century. The main entrance has 16C frescoes of courtiers, and the courtyard has frescoes commissioned by Colleoni's grandchildren in the early 16C to illustrate his achievements in battle: the siege of Bergamo in 1437 includes a good view of the Città Alta, and under the loggia is a scene of the great soldier's last battle in 1497 (Colleoni is shown in a red hat). The Sala Banchetti contains more good 16C frescoes, here showing the visit of King Christian I of Denmark to the castle in 1474 on his way to Rome (the soldiers in white-and-red uniform are those of Colleoni). The reception room upstairs retains its original 15C frescoes (in poor condition), with courtly scenes in the International Gothic style. Colleoni died, at the age of 80, in the bedroom which has a 15C Madonna and Child with saints in a niche.

At **Treviglio**, an agricultural and industrial centre (25,000 inhab.), the

Gothic church of San Martino contains a beautiful polyptych by Bernardino Zenale and Bernardino Butinone (1485). Santa Maria delle Lacrime is a Renaissance building with another triptych by Butinone. Here in 1915, while in hospital with jaundice, Mussolini was married (probably bigamously) to Donna Rachele. **Caravaggio** was the probable birthplace of the painter Michelangelo Merisi, known as Caravaggio (1571–1610). An avenue leads to a large sanctuary dedicated to the Madonna who is said to have appeared to a peasant woman here in 1432 on the site of a miraculous spring. The domed church was enlarged by Pellegrino Tibaldi in 1575, and is visited by thousands of pilgrims every year (festival on 26 May).

On the other side of the Serio river is **Romano di Lombardia**, with an interesting urban plan. The medieval Palazzo della Comunità was altered in later centuries. The church of Santa Maria Assunta, reconstructed in the 18C by Giovanni Battista Caniana, contains a Last Supper by Giovanni Battista Moroni, and intarsia by Caniana. Above the neo-classical Palazzo Rubini is the 13C Visconti castle.

10 · Brescia

Brescia (210,000 inhab.) is the second most important industrial town in Lombardy after Milan and has a flourishing economy based on the service industries and the manufacture of iron and steel (it has long been known for its production of arms, cutlery, etc.). Situated at the mouth of the Val Trompia it has always enjoyed an abundance of water and still has numerous fountains. It has interesting Roman remains (including a reconstructed temple and an exceptionally fine bronze statue), important Lombard relics in the huge, once powerful monastery of Santa Giulia founded by the Lombard king Desiderius in 753, a beautiful Renaissance building known as the Loggia, and numerous churches with good paintings by the early 16C local artist Moretto. However, it is not usually visited for its artistic treasures (except by tour groups on day trips from the Lago di Garda) and is poorly provided with hotels in the centre of the city.

■ **Information office.** APT, 34–38 Corso Zanardelli (tel. 030 45053).

■ **Hotels.** There is only one hotel in the historic centre of the city: 5-star, *Vittoria*, 20 Via X Giornate. The hotels in the unattractive modern parts of the city cater for businessmen, groups attending conventions, etc. with their own transport.

■ **Restaurants. A**: *La Sosta*, Via San Martino della Battaglia. **B**: *Raffa*, 15 Corso Magenta; *Trattoria al Frate*, 25 Via Musei; *Circolo delle Arti*, 3 Via Trieste (Piazza Paolo VI); *I Templari*, 19 Corso Matteotti. **C**: *Hosteria Porta Bruciata*, 11 Via Beccaria; *Trattoria Bianchi*, Via Gasparo da Salò; *Le Due Colonne*, Contrada Mangano; *Trattoria Mezzeria*, 66 Via Trieste.

■ **Cafés.** *Pasticceria San Carlo* on the corner of Corso Zanardelli and Via 10

Giornate; *Bar Impero*, Piazza Vittoria; *Capuzzi*, Via Pia Marta.

■ **Car parking** for cars with foreign number plates in Piazza Duomo and on the Castle hill.

■ **Buses.** Bus D runs from the station to Corso Zanardelli. There is a comprehensive network of buses in the province, with services also to Bergamo, Milan, the Lago di Como, Cremona and Mantua (information, tel. 065 387547; departures from the bus station or the railway station).

■ **Theatres.** *Teatro Grande*: opera season September–November; concerts October–March. Theatre season Nov–Apr. International Piano Festival held jointly with Bergamo in April and June. *Teatro di Santa Chiara*: performances of plays.

■ **Annual festivals.** Organ concerts from mid-September to mid-October in various churches in the city. Choral music is performed in various churches from April to June. In summer, music is performed in the gardens of palaces, etc (information from the APT). The *Mille Miglia* is a veteran car race held in May (the three-day course of 1000 miles—1600km—runs from Brescia via Ferrara to Rome and back to Brescia).

History

The Roman colony of *Brixia* re-emerges into prominence under the 8C Lombard king Desiderius, who was born in the neighbourhood. The city was a member of the Lombard League, but in 1258 it was captured by the tyrant Ezzelino da Romano. The town was then contested by the Lombard Torriani and Visconti, the Veronese Scaligeri, and Pandolfo Malatesta, but from 1426 to 1797 it prospered under Venetian suzerainty. Between 1509 and 1516 it was twice captured by the French under Gaston de Foix. In March 1849 the town held out for ten days against the Austrian general, Haynau (nicknamed the 'hyena of Brescia'), and it was heavily bombed in the Second World War.

The wide arcaded CORSO ZANARDELLI, together with the adjoining Corso Palestro and Via delle X Giornate, can be regarded as the centre of the town. Here is the **Teatro Grande** (entered from Via Paganora), founded in 1709 and rebuilt in 1863, but with a façade of 1782. The arcades continue north along Via delle X Giornate.

Just to the west is PIAZZA DELLA VITTORIA, by Marcello Piacentini (finished in 1932), built in grey marble and white stone, an interesting example of Fascist architecture. The red marble Arengario, a rostrum for public speaking has bas-reliefs by Antonio Maraini. At the north end is the striped post office, near which (hidden by a war memorial) is the church of **Sant'Agata**, built c 1438–72. In the attractive interior is an apse fresco of the Crucifixion (1475; attributed to Andrea Bembo). The nave frescoes (1683) are by Pietro Antonio Sorisene and Pompeo Ghitti. In the 18C Chapel of the Sacrament (right) are two oval paintings by Giovanni Antonio Pellegrini.

An archway under the **Monte di Pietà** (with a loggia of 1484, and an addition of 1597), behind the post office, leads to the harmonious PIAZZA DELLA LOGGIA. On the left rises the *LOGGIA, or Palazzo Pubblico, a beautiful Renaissance building with exquisite sculptural detail. The ground floor was built between 1492 and 1508, the upper storey between 1554 and 1574; the architect is unknown, although Lodovico Beretta, Jacopo Sansovino, Galeazzo Alessi and Andrea Palladio are all thought to have been involved. It was restored in 1914. On the right of the Loggia is a fine 16C portal.

Above the northeast of the square rises the **Porta Bruciata**, a fragment of the oldest city wall. The arcade at the east end was the scene in 1974 of one of the most brutal political murders in modern Italian history when a bomb exploded; eight people lost their lives and over 100 were injured (memorial by Carlo Scarpa).

Beneath the **Torre dell'Orologio** (c 1547) a passageway leads to PIAZZA PAOLO VI (right; formerly Piazza del Duomo), with a delightful row of buildings lining its east side. The local inhabitants gravitate here in summer when it is the coolest place in the town; for the rest of the year it remains comparatively deserted.

The **DUOMO NUOVO**, begun in 1604 by the local architect Giovanni Battista Lantana on the site of the old 'summer cathedral' of San Pietro de Dom, was only completed in 1914 (the cupola built in 1825 is 82m high). The bust of Cardinal Querini over the main entrance is by Antonio Calegari. The elaborate white marble **interior** contains a wooden 15C Crucifix, and the fine tomb (1504) of the bishop saint Apollonius with beautiful carving attributed to Maffeo Olivieri. The Mannerist Zorzi Chapel has an altarpiece by Palma il Giovane, and above a monument to Pope Paul VI are four panels by Gerolamo Romanino.

Rotonda

The Romanesque *ROTONDA or **DUOMO VECCHIO** (sometimes closed in winter; apply at the Duomo Nuovo) is an extremely interesting circular building of the 11C or early 12C with a central rotunda supported on eight pillars. At the east end, the transepts and choir are a 15C addition. The church was built above a 6C basilica of Santa Maria Maggiore, remains of which have survived. Inside, in front of the entrance, is the red marble *sarcophagus of Bishop Berardo Maggi (died 1308) by a Lombard sculptor. In the **ambulatory** (right) is a chapel with a fine marble altar and an altarpiece of the Guardian Angel by Bernardino Gandino. Beside it (above) is the wall monument of Bishop Balduino Lambertini by Bonino da Campione. Two stairways lead down to the Romanesque **crypt** of San Filastrio, which preserves columns of various periods (Roman–11C) and traces of frescoes. Stairs lead up to the east end.

In the **south transept** is an elaborate painting by Francesco Maffei, the Translation of the Patron Saints from the castle to the cathedral. Above the altar opposite is a curious 15C fresco of the Flagellation. Glass panels in the pavement show remains of the presbytery of the earlier church and walls and mosaic pavement thought to belong to Roman baths of the Republican era excavated in 1975. The vault of the ancient presbytery of Santa Maria Maggiore preserves some fresco fragments including, on the entrance arch, a tondo with the Virgin between angels and the sun and the moon. The organ, in a 16C case, was built by Giangiacomo Antegnati in 1536 (restored by Serassi in 1826).

In the **presbytery** are two paintings by Moretto and over the high altar is an *Assumption, also by him. In the **north transept** are three more works by Moretto. The contents of the **treasury** here are displayed only on the last Friday in March and on 14 September. They include a Byzantine cross-reliquary (with a base by Bernardino delle Croci, 1487) and the 'Croce del Campo', dating from the 12C. Protected by glass in the pavement is a mosaic fragment of the apse of the 8C basilica di San Filastrio, burned down in 1097 with the exception of the crypt. Other fragments of the mosaic pavement can be seen beneath the floor on the west side of the rotunda. In the **ambulatory** of the rotunda is the tomb of Bishop De Dominicis (died 1478). The ancient stairs which led up to the bell-tower (destroyed in 1708) survive.

At 3 Via Mazzini, behind the new cathedral, is the **Biblioteca Queriniana**, founded by Cardinal Querini in 1750. Among its treasures are a 6C evangelistary with silver letters on purple vellum, and a Concordance of the Gospels by Eusebius (11C).

On the left of the Duomo Nuovo is the **Broletto**, a fine Lombard town hall of 1187–1230, now serving as the Prefettura. The exterior preserves its original appearance; in the courtyard one loggia is a Baroque addition. Frescoes attributed to Gentile da Fabriano were found in the Cappella Ducale here in 1986. Beyond the sturdy battlemented **Torre del Popolo** (11C), the north part of the Broletto incorporates the little church of **Sant'Agostino**, the west front of which has early 15C terracotta ornamentation, with two lion gargoyles.

At the top of Vicolo Sant'Agostino is the little secluded PIAZZA TITO SPERI, with a public garden. Steps (signposted) lead steeply uphill from here in 15 minutes to the castle hill (described below, from Via Piamarta). Via dei Musei leads east from the piazza to the imposing *CAPITOLIUM, a Roman temple erected by Vespasian (AD 73) which stands on a high stylobate approached by steps, 15 of which are original, and has a hexastyle pronaos of Corinthian columns with, behind, a colonnade of three columns on each side. The three cellae were probably dedicated to the Capitoline Trinity (Jupiter, Juno and Minerva). The temple was excavated in 1823–26 and reconstructed in brick in 1939–50. Beneath it is a Republican **sanctuary** (adm. only with special permission), dating from after 89 BC, with mosaics of small uncoloured tesserae.

The temple stood at the north end of the **Roman Forum**, of which remains of porticoes can be seen in the piazza, beside a stretch of the paved Decumanus Maximus. On the right of the temple are the neglected remains of a Roman **amphitheatre**.

The **Museo Romano** (open 9–12.30, 15–17; summer 10–12.30, 15–18; closed Mon), founded in 1826, is arranged in the cellae of the temple and in a building behind it. In the cellae are inscriptions and mosaics. Stairs lead up to **Room 1** with a Greek amphora (c 510 BC), Gaulish silver horse-trappings (3C BC), an Italic bronze helmet and a marble head of an athlete (5C BC). **Room 2** has Roman terracottas and glass, and in **Room 3** are Lombard arms and bronzes. **Room 4** displays the remarkable *Winged Victory, a splendid bronze statue nearly 2m high, probably the chief figure of a chariot group from the roof

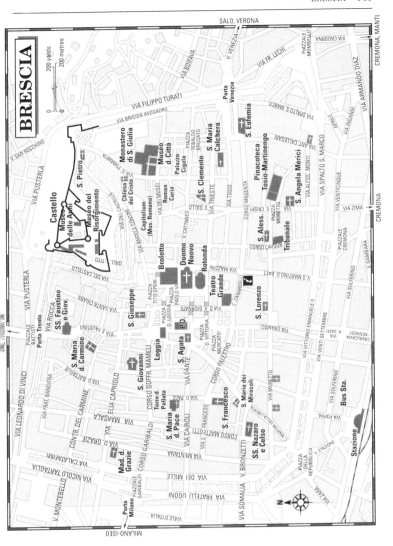

of the Capitol. It appears to be a Venus of the Augustan age (of the Venus of Capua type) remodelled as a Victory under Vespasian. Also displayed here is a gilded bronze statuette of a captive (2C AD?) and six bronze heads, all from the same group, discovered at the same time as the statue in 1826.

Monastero di Santa Giulia

Further on, on the corner of Via dei Musei (No. 81) and Via Piamarta, is the **MONASTERO DI SANTA GIULIA**, a huge group of buildings with three Renaissance cloisters and several churches which have been under restoration for some 20 years as the seat of the **Museo della Città**. This will cover all periods of the city's history. Meanwhile only some of the buildings are open and exhibitions are held frequently in the church of Santa Giulia, in rooms near the entrance to the monastery, and in the lower part of Santa Maria in Solario. The monastery of Santa Giulia (formerly San Salvatore) was founded by the Lombard king Desiderius in AD 753 on the site of a Roman edifice. Ermengarde, daughter of Lothair I, and many other royal and noble ladies were sisters in the original Benedictine nunnery which survived here until it was suppressed in 1798.

The entrance is at 4 Via Piamarta (adm. 9–12.30, 15–17; summer 10–12.30, 15–18, c every half-hour with a guide; closed Mon). The first area visited is a **Roman house** (seen from a walkway) with remains of rooms round a peristyle with black-and-white mosaic floors and traces of wall paintings. Beyond is the **atrium of the church of San Salvatore**, where Lombard sculptural fragments (8C) are displayed. A walkway continues (above excavations of various periods from the Roman era to the 9C) to the church of **San Salvatore**, founded c 753, with 13 Roman columns in the nave with good capitals (some of them Roman and some 8C). It has chapels frescoed in the 15C and traces of Carolingian frescoes above the nave arches. The southwest chapel has frescoes by Gerolamo Romanino. Below is the **crypt** dating from 760–63 (enlarged in the 12C) with 42 columns of varying origins and capitals by the school of Antelami.

The square undercroft below Santa Maria in Solario, with a cippus for a central column, is used for exhibitions. The building beyond is to exhibit the Renaissance collections. The upper church of **Santa Maria in Solario**, built in the 12C, is covered with good early 16C frescoes by Floriano Ferramola and his bottega. Three showcases here contain the rich treasury of San Salvatore. The so-called *Cross of Desiderius (late 8C–early 9C) is made of wood overlaid with silvergilt and set with over 200 gems (dating from the Roman period to the 9C) and incorporating cameos, miniatures (9C–15C), a 16C crucifix and, on the lower arm, a remarkable triple portrait painted on gilded glass in the 4C. Another case has early *ivories, including the Querini Diptych (5C), with Paris and Helen (?) on each leaf; the consular Diptych of Manlius Boethius (5C), and a leaf of the Diptych of the Lampadii, with circus scenes (late 5C). The last case displays an exquisite *ivory coffer with scriptural scenes in relief dating from the 4C.

The former church of **Santa Giulia** (1599), which has good 16C frescoes by Floriano Ferramola, is only open for exhibitions.

Other items in the collection which are not at present on display include Lombard gold jewellery; 13C–14C ivories; Renaissance medals; Murano glass; Limoges enamels; majolica; and works by Maffeo Olivieri, Alessandro Vittoria, Antonio Canova, Francesco Hayez, Telemaco Signorini and Silvestro Lega.

Via Piamarta, a deserted old cobbled street between high walls, ascends towards the castle: on the left is the **Chiesa del Cristo**, with good terracotta decoration (15C). Paths lead through pleasant public gardens on the side of the hill up to the main gateway into the **CASTLE**, a huge edifice on the Cydnean hill (mentioned by Catullus, and now pierced by a road-tunnel), which was rebuilt by the Visconti in the 14C. Its extensive walls now enclose gardens and various museums and an observatory. At the highest point of the hill is the **Museo delle**

Armi 'Luigi Marzoli' (adm. 9–12.30, 15–17; summer 10–12.30, 15–18; closed Mon). Beyond a drawbridge, a path leads up through a fort to the cylindrical Torre della Mirabella on a lawn with wide views. The museum was opened in 1988 in a fine 14C building with traces of painted decoration inside, and the collection of 15C–18C arms and armour is excellently displayed on two floors. Many of the arms and firearms were made in Brescia, which was renowned for its production of arms. In one room there are remains of the steps of a Roman temple.

Downhill to the right is the **Museo del Risorgimento** (adm. as for the Museo delle Armi, see above) founded in 1887 and arranged on two floors of a large 16C grain store. The interesting collection illustrates 19C Italian history from the last years of the 18C up to Unification, with prints, arms, uniforms, mementoes, etc.

The best way of reaching the centre of the town from the castle hill is by descending the steps below the public gardens to Piazza Speri, just north of the Duomo.

From the Capitolium (see above), Via Gallo leads south past the site (No. 3 Piazza Labus) of the Roman **Curia**, fragments of which can be seen below ground level and on the façade of the house. Further on, Vicolo San Clemente (left) leads to the church of **San Clemente** containing paintings by Romanino, Moretto (who is buried here) and Callisto Piazza.

Pinacoteca Tosio-Martinengo

Via Crispi leads across Corso Magenta to Piazza Moretto. On the left is the Pinacoteca Tosio-Martinengo (open 9–12.30, 15–17.30; summer: 10–12.30, 15–18; closed Mon), a large collection of paintings and frescoes in which the local schools are well represented. It was opened to the public in 1908 to display the two collections of Paolo Tosio (1844) and Francesco Leopardo Martinengo (1884), and more works have since been added. Stairs lead up to the first floor. In **Room 1** are portraits of Tosio and Martinengo, the two principal benefactors of the museum. **Room 2** contains the treasures of the Tosio collection: portraits by the circle of François Clouet, and Romanino; Moretto, *Salome*; Raphael, *Angel, and Risen Christ* (two fragments); a copy of a Raphael Madonna by an early 16C painter; and works by Andrea Appiani and Cavalier d'Arpino. **Rooms 3 & 4** contain 13C–14C frescoes, and a charming painting of *St George and the dragon by a Lombard master (c 1460–70).

Rooms 5, 6 & 7. Vincenzo Foppa, Vincenzo Civerchio and Moretto; early 16C works by Marco Palmezzano and Floriano Ferramola; *Christ and the Adulterer* by a painter close to Titian.

Room 9 contains a beautiful *painting of the Nativity by Lorenzo Lotto, and another painting of the same subject by Savoldo. **Room 10** displays 16C portraits by Giovanni Battista Moroni, Sofonisba Anguissola, Moretto and Savoldo (*Boy with a Flute*).

Room 11 contains large Renaissance paintings and frescoes by Moretto, Romanino and others, and a lectern with intarsia by Raffaello da Marone (1520). **Room 12.** Detached *frescoes by Moretto from Palazzo Ugoni (c 1525). **Room 13** has late 16C works by Giulio and Antonio Campi and **Room 14** works by Luca Mombello. **Room 15** has works by 17C artists including Lo

Spadarino, and **Room 16** paintings by Giacomo Ceruti and Antonio Cifrondi. **Room 17** has preserved its original decoration from the late 18C and beginning of the 19C.

Rooms 18–23 contain 17C and 18C paintings. **Room 24**, the 'galleria', has works by Sassoferrato, Luca Giordano and Francesco Albani. **Room 25** has 17C works.

Outstanding in the fine collection of drawings (shown only with special permission) is a *Deposition by Giovanni Bellini. On the ground floor is an exhibition of 15C illuminated MSS from San Francesco and the Duomo (also shown only with special permission) and the Print Room with works by Jacopo Filippo d'Argento and others.

Sant'Angela Merici (formerly Sant'Afra), just to the south, rebuilt since the war, has a Transfiguration by Jacopo Tintoretto in the apse, and works by Francesco Bassano and Giulio Cesare Procaccini among others.

From the Pinacoteca, Via Moretto leads back towards the centre of the town passing (right) the church of **Sant'Alessandro**, with a pleasant fountain outside. It contains a beautiful painting of the *Annunciation by Jacopo Bellini, and works by Vincenzo Civerchio and Lattanzio Gambara.

On the left is the 17C Palazzo Martinengo-Colleoni. Via San Martino della Battaglia leads right to Corso Zanardelli (described above) and Via Palestro continues west to the church of **San Francesco**, built in 1254–65, with a good façade. The interior has many interesting frescoes. The south aisle contains an altarpiece by Moretto; a Giottesque *fresco of the Entombment (with a scene of monks above, dating from the mid-14C); and 14C frescoes including a charming frieze of angels. The high altarpiece is by Romanino, in a frame of rich workmanship by Stefano Lamberti (1502). In the north aisle are an elaborately decorated chapel (15C–18C), a 14C Cross, and an altarpiece by Francesco Prato. The fine cloister dates from 1394.

Just to the south, in Corso Martiri, is **Santa Maria dei Miracoli**, rebuilt since the war but preserving intact an elaborately carved Renaissance façade of 1488–1560. It contains *St Nicholas of Bari with his Pupils, taken to be a copy of a work by Moretto (now in the Pinacoteca). The paintings (1590–94) in the presbytery are by the local artists Tommaso Bona, Pietro Bagnadore, Grazio Cossali and Pietro Marone.

In Via Fratelli Bronzetti, on the right, is the 16C side doorway of the church of **Santi Nazaro e Celso** (if closed, ask for admission at Santa Maria dei Miracoli), an 18C building, with the *Polyptych Averoldi—a superb early work by Titian (1522)—and paintings by Moretto (including the *Coronation of the Virgin), Giovanni Battista Pittoni and Antonio Zanchi, and monuments by Maffeo Olivieri.

From San Francesco, Via della Pace leads north to the massive 13C Torre della Pallata. Nearby is **San Giovanni Evangelista** which contains good paintings (1521) by Moretto and Romanino in the Corpus Domini chapel, as well as an altarpiece of the *Madonna and Saints by Moretto. Also works by Bernardino Zenale and Francesco Francia (*Holy Trinity).

Further north **Santa Maria del Carmine**, a 15C building with a fine façade and portal, contains paintings by Vincenzo Foppa. At the west end of Via Capriolo is the **Madonna delle Grazie** by Lodovico Barcella (1522). The delightful Rococo *interior (1617) has an exuberance of stucco reliefs and frescoes. A 16C courtyard gives access to a venerated sanctuary, rebuilt in the 19C and covered with charming ex-votos.

From Via Turati the Strada Panoramica (see the plan) leads up to **Monte Maddalena** (875m), a noted viewpoint.

11 · The province of Brescia, with the Valle Camonica

The province of Brescia is exceptionally large and includes the Valle Camonica in the north, famous for its prehistoric rock carvings, the Lago d'Iseo, the smaller Lago d'Idro, and several mountain valleys with ski resorts. The western side of the Lago di Garda, also within the province, is described in Chapter 12.

■ **Information offices. Lago d'Iseo**: 2 Lungolago Marconi, Iseo (tel. 030 980209). **Valle Camonica**: in Edolo, 2 Piazza Martiri della Libertà, (tel. 0364 71065); in Darfo-Boario Terme, 2 Piazza Einaudi; and in Ponte di Legno, 41 Corso Milano. Comunità Montana di Valle Camonica, Via Aldo Moro, Breno. **Lago d'Idro**: Località Pieve, Idro (tel. 0365 83224). **Valle Trompia**: Piazza Zanardelli, Collio Val Trompia (tel. 030 927330).

■ **Hotels. Franciacorta**: 4-star: *L'Albereta Locanda in Franciacorta* (with a renowned restaurant) near Erbusco. **Lago d'Iseo**: 3-star and 2-star hotels at Iseo, Sale Marasino, Monte Isola, Pisogne and Lovere; 1-star hotels at Zone. **Valle Camonica**: numerous hotels of all categories at Darfo-Boario Terme; many hotels also at Borno, Breno and Ponte di Legno. A few simple hotels on the **Lago d'Idro.**

■ **Camping sites** of all categories on the Lago d'Iseo (especially at Clusone, Iseo and Sale Marasino), on the Lago d'Idro, and in Valle Camonica.

■ **Transport. Bus services** (information, tel. 085 387547) run from Brescia to all the places of interest in the province.

There is a **railway** run by the Ferrovie Nord Milano from Brescia to Iseo, following the east bank of the Lago d'Iseo to Pisogne and then on a very scenic route through the Valle Camonica as far as Edolo.

The fertile foothills south of the Lago d'Iseo, with numerous vineyards, are known as the **FRANCIACORTA**, a pretty region with a number of villas built by the noble families of Brescia in the 18C. It has long been known for its excellent red and white wines (and since the 1960s for the spumante *Franciacorta*, produced with Chardonnay, Pinot Bianco and Pinot Nero grapes). Numerous cellars in the area welcome visitors, and at the Villa Evelina at Capriolo there is a private agricultural museum. At **Rodengo** is the Abbazia di San Nicola, a Cluniac foundation, inhabited by Olivetan monks since 1446. It contains three cloisters, frescoes by Romanino and Lattanzio Gambara, a painting by Moretto, and fine intarsia stalls by Cristoforo Rocchi (1480). Outside **Passirano** is an interesting castle, and at **Provaglio d'Iseo** the Romanesque church of San Pietro in Lamosa.

Lago d'Iseo

The pretty Lago d'Iseo, an expansion of the Oglio river, surrounded by mountains, has a perimeter of 60km and an average width of 2.4km; its maximum depth is 251m. It was the *Lacus Sebinus* of the Romans. In the centre is the island of Monte Isola, the largest island of any European lake. Lovere, Iseo and Pisogne are holiday resorts on its banks, which have suffered less from modern development than those of the more famous lakes. It is much visited for sailing.

Boat services run from Iseo to Monte Isola, Lovere and Pisogne. There are frequent services for Monte Isola from Sulzano (to Peschiera Maraglio) and from Sale Marasino (to Carzano).

Iseo is a pleasant resort on the south bank of the lake which bears its name. The church tower was built by Count Giacomo Oldofredi (1325), whose tomb is built into the façade alongside. Inside is a painting of St Michael by Francesco Hayez. On the southern edge of the lake is a marshy area known as the **Torbiere d'Iseo**, a large peatbog surrounded by reeds, of great interest to naturalists. Water lilies grow here in abundance and it is a sanctuary for aquatic birds. Traces of Bronze Age pile-dwellings were found here.

On the east bank are **Sulzano**, a sailing centre and port for Monte Isola, and **Sale Marasino**, another port for the island, with a conspicuous church by Giovanni Battista Caniana (1737–54), and the 16C Villa Martinengo. The wooded island of **Monte Isola**, 3.2km long, where all the boats call, is also well served by ferries from the eastern shore (see above). It is closed to private cars (although there is a bus service from the fishing village of Peschiera Maraglio) and it can be visited on foot in c 3hrs. The hill in the centre is covered with chestnut woods and broom. There is a large tourist development on the west side of the island, north of Menzino.

Marone is a large village beneath Monte Guglielmo (1949m), the highest point of the mountain range between the lake and the Valle Trompia. A road winds up to **Zone** in chestnut woods, of geological interest for its erosion pyramids surmounted by granite boulders, caused by the erosion of the moraine deposits.

At the northeast end of the lake is the little town of **Pisogne**. The church of Santa Maria della Neve contains splendid *frescoes of the Passion of Christ by Romanino (1532–34).

On the Bergamo side of the lake is **Lovere**, the principal tourist resort on its shores. To the north of the town is the church of Santa Maria in Valvendra (1473–83) which contains organ-shutters decorated outside by Ferramola and inside by Moretto (1518). To the south, on the shore of the lake, is the **Galleria dell'Accademia Tadini** (adm. May–Oct, 15–18; fest. 10–12, 15–18), founded in this neo-classical building in 1828 by Luigi Tadini. It contains a collection of paintings including works by Jacopo Bellini, Magnasco and Vincenzo Civerchio, as well as porcelain, arms and bronzes. In the garden, the cenotaph of Faustino Tadini (died 1799) is by Antonio Canova. There is a path above the town to the Altipiano di Lovere (990m), with some attractive country villas, and to Bossico, among meadows and pine woods.

A road follows the west side of the lake through **Riva di Solto** whose quarries provided the black marble for the columns of the basilica of San Marco in Venice, with two little bays displaying unusual rock strata. On the western side of the lake, beneath the barren slopes of Monte Brenzone (1333m), is **Sarnico**, at the outflow of the Oglio, wellknown to motor-boat racing enthusiasts. It has a number of Art Nouveau villas built at the beginning of the century by Giuseppe Sommaruga.

The Valle Camonica

To the north of Pisogne and the Lago d'Iseo is the lovely, fertile Valle Camonica, the upper course of the Oglio. It is famous for the remarkable prehistoric rock carvings of the Camuni which can be seen throughout the valley, especially in the two parks at Capo di Ponte and Darfo-Boario Terme, and at Cimbergo, Ossimo and Sellero. The chestnut woods were once an important source of wealth, since both nuts and timber were exported. The inhabitants of the valley (and especially of Boario) are excellent woodcarvers. Ironworks were established here in the Middle Ages, and the valley now has generating stations for hydro-electric power. The cheeses and salt meats locally produced are of excellent quality. The extreme upper end, below the Tonale Pass, was the scene of many dramatic battles in the First World War.

The first village of importance is **Darfo** where the parish church has an Entombment attributed to Palma Giovane. At **Montecchio** the little church of the Oratorio contains 15C frescoes. **Boario Terme** is the main town (13,000 inhab.) in the valley and an important mineral spa. It is noted for its cabinet-makers. Over 10,000 rock carvings may be seen here in the **Parco delle Luine** (open 9–12, 14–18 exc. Mon). Most of them date from 2200–1800 BC, but some are even earlier—the oldest so far found in the valley. The rock known as Corni Freschi, with its rock carvings, can be seen on a country road just outside the town near the *superstrada* for Edolo.

A road ascends the **Val di Scalve** past **Gorzone**, dominated by a castle of the Federici first built in the 12C (privately owned), through **Angolo Terme**, a small spa with a very fine view of the triple-peaked Pizzo della Presolana. Further on the road enters the gorge of the Dezzo, a narrow chasm with overhanging cliffs (the torrent and its falls have almost been dried up by hydroelectric works).

Just north of Boario is **Erbanno**, unusual for its plan consisting of parallel straight streets along the hillside and a piazza on two levels. The main road continues to **Esine**, with the church of Santa Maria Assunta containing fres-coes by Giovan Pietro da Cemmo (1491–93). **Cividate Camuno** is the site of *Civitas Camunnorum*, the ancient Roman capital of the valley. It preserves a few ancient remains and a much more conspicuous medieval tower. Roman finds are displayed in an archaeological museum

A winding road ascends west via **Ossimo** (where prehistoric statue-stele have been found dating from 3200–2000 BC) to **Borno**, a resort among pine woods in the Trobiolo valley, beneath the Corna di San Fermo (2326m). The Santuario dell'Annunciata, with a fine view of the valley, has two 15C cloisters.

Breno, an important town in the valley (5200 inhab.), is dominated by the ruins of its medieval castle (9C and later). The parish church has a granite campanile and frescoes by Giovan Pietro da Cemmo and Girolamo Romanino. The Museo Camuno merits a visit.

A mountain road leads east towards the Lago d'Idro via **Bienno**, a medieval village with 17C and 18C palaces, one of the most interesting places in the valley. Several old forges are still operating here, worked by channelled water. The church of Santa Maria degli Orti has frescoes by Girolamo Romanino.

Above Breno the dolomitic peaks of the Concarena (2549m) rise on the left and the Pizzo Badile (2435m) on the right. The villages are mostly high up on the slopes of the foothills on either side, and include **Cerveno** with a remarkable 18C Via Crucis which has nearly 200 life-size statues.

Capo di Ponte came to prominence with the discovery in the Permian sandstone of tens of thousands of rock engravings dating from Neolithic to Roman times (16 BC), a span of some 8000 years. These are the feature of the ****Parco Nazionale delle Incisioni Rupestri di Naquane** (open 9–17 or 19 exc. Mon), one of the most important prehistoric sites in the world. It can be visited on foot in c 2hrs. So far some 180,000 engravings made by the Camuni, a remarkable Alpine civilisation, depicting hunting scenes, everyday life, religious symbols, etc., have been catalogued here on the wooded hill of Naquane. The largest rock has 900 figures carved in the Iron Age. Other prehistoric carvings have been found in the localities of **Ceto**, **Cimbergo** and **Paspardo**, on a secondary road to the south, and above **Sellero** to the north. There is a research centre (the Centro Camuno di Studi Preistorici) at Capo di Ponte.

Just outside Capo di Ponte, in woods to the north, is **San Salvatore**, a Lombard church of the early 12C. Across the river in Cemmo is the church of ****San Siro**, dating from the 11C probably on the site of a Lombard church. The road continues to **Pescarzo**, a pretty little village with interesting peasant houses.

Cedegolo, with a church entirely frescoed by Antonio Cappello (17C), stands at the foot of the lovely Val Saviore, below Monte Adamello (3555m). **Edolo**, surrounded by beautiful scenery, is the main place (4200 inhab.) in the upper Valle Camonica, and the terminus of the railway. It stands on the road from Switzerland and Tirano in the Valtellina via the Aprica pass to Tonale and the Tyrol. The Oglio is on the edge of two large protected areas, the Parco Nazionale dello Stelvio and the Parco dell'Adamello. **Ponte di Legno** (1260m) is the main resort of the region in a wide open mountain basin, beneath the Adamello and Presanella mountains. To the north a road, one of the highest in Europe, ascends the Val di Pezzo and crosses the Passo Gavia (2652m) to Bormio.

The **Tonale Pass** (1884m), in the Presanella foothills, is on the former Austro-Italian frontier, separating Lombardy from the Trentino. There are ski slopes on Presena and Monte Tonale.

The **LAGO D'IDRO**, the Roman *Lacus Eridius*, 9.5km long and 2km wide, is surrounded by steep and rugged mountains. Its waters are utilised for hydroelectric power, and it is renowned for its trout. It is frequented by sailors and windsurfers. On the west bank are **Anfo** with an old castle, founded by the Venetians in 1486 but largely rebuilt, and **Sant'Antonio**, where the church has a 15C fresco cycle. **Bagolino** is a mountain village in a good position on the Caffaro (visited by skiers, and famous for its carnival). **Ponte Caffaro**, beyond the head of the lake, marks the old international frontier.

To the south of Brescia is **Montirone**, where the beautiful Palazzo Lechi

(1738–46), by Antonio Turbino, is very well preserved and has magnificent *stables of c 1754. It contains paintings by Carlo Carloni (his best work), and was visited by Mozart in 1773 and Napoleon in 1805. At **Verolanuova** the church contains two large paintings by Giovanni Battista Tiepolo, in excellent condition. **Gottolengo** was the main residence, in 1746–56, of Lady Mary Wortley Montagu who often visited the Lago d'Iseo.

The road from Brescia to Crema passes the suburban church of **Chiesanuova**, with a charming *Nativity by Foppa, and crosses the plain to **Orzinuovi**, with imposing remains of the Venetian ramparts designed by Michele Sanmicheli.

On the road to Milan is **Chiari**, with a small Pinacoteca founded in 1854 by Pietro Repossi, and a library founded by Antonio Morcelli in 1817.

12 · Lago di Garda

The *Lago di Garda is the largest and perhaps the most beautiful of the northern Italian lakes. The west bank is in Lombardy (the province of Brescia), the east bank in the Veneto (the province of Verona), and the northern tip in the Trentino region. Its mild climate permits the cultivation of olives and lemon trees and the vegetation of its shores is characterised by numerous cypresses in thick woods. Before the lake was developed as a resort at the beginning of this century, the local economy was based on the production of olive oil (particularly on the east bank) and the cultivation of lemons (the lake was the northernmost locality in the world where citrus fruits could be grown commercially).

Sirmione, in a spectacular position on a narrow peninsula on the south shore, has been known since Roman times as a resort on *Lacus Benacus* (from the Celtic, meaning 'horned'). The little resorts of Salò, Desenzano and Gardone on the west shore were first developed as such in the 1920s and 1930s, although some grand hotels had already been built at the end of the 19C for Austrian and German clients who came to the mild western shore, many of them to cure respiratory disorders. In 1931 the road was continued north from Gargnano to Limone (previously accessible only by boat) by cutting tunnels through the sheer rock face which drops straight into the lake and provides some of its most dramatic scenery. The east side, beneath the conspicuous Monte Baldo (notable for its unique vegetation) has only been developed as a holiday area since the Second World War.

Goethe visited the lake at the start of his Italian journey in 1786, and here saw his first olive trees. He sailed down the lake from Torbole past Limone where he admired the lemon gardens, and was forced to land for a night at Malcesine because of unfavourable winds. While sketching the castle there he was almost arrested as an Austrian spy. The next day he docked at Bardolino where he mounted a mule to cross into the Adige valley for Verona. Byron stayed at Desenzano in 1816, and Tennyson visited the lake in 1880. D.H. Lawrence lived on its shores in 1912 and 1913, and he describes the lemon gardens in *Twilight in Italy*. Winston Churchill wintered at the Grand Hotel in Gardone Riviera in 1949.

Citrus cultivation around the lake dates from at least the 16C and reached a height in commercial production in the early 19C. A few of the characteristic monumental pavilions with tall stone pilasters and covered with wooden slats and glass in winter, where lemons and citrons were cultivated in the last century, still survive at Gargnano and Torri del Benaco. These shelters, unique to Garda, were designed for maximum protection from the cold. Duck and swans abound all over the lake and fishing is still practised in a few localities (the *salmo carpio*, a kind of large trout, is found only in Garda; other fish include pike, trout and eel).

Remains of two of the most important Roman villas in northern Italy are to be found on the shores of Garda at Sirmione and Desenzano. There are fine Scaliger castles open to the public at Sirmione, Malcesine and Torri del Bernaco. The most curious sight on the lake is the famous 'Vittoriale', the last home of the eccentric poet Gabriele d'Annunzio.

The best time to visit the lake is in May and June: in August it is very crowded and can be extremely hot. Garda is now visited mostly by German tourists. The breezier upper part of the lake, where the water is deepest, is much used for sailing and windsurfing (boats can be hired), and there are sailing regattas in summer. A purifying plant near Peschiera has successfully cleaned the waters of the lake, which is now considered the cleanest of the big Italian lakes, and swimming is permitted (the best places include the peninsula of Sirmione, the Isola dei Conigli off Moniga, the Baia del Vento between Salò and Desenzano, and the Isola San Biagio).

There are boat and hydrofoil services, as well as two paddle-steamers, to many places on the lake (except in winter). The finest trip (4.5 hours) is from Riva via Malcesine, Gargnano, Gardone, Salò and Sirmione to Desenzano.

A scenic road (143km) follows the shore of the lake. This remarkable engineering feat entailed the blasting of a passage for the roadway through many kilometres of solid rock, and the construction of some 80 tunnels.

■ **Information offices. Desenzano del Garda**: 34 Via Porto Vecchio (tel. 030 9141510). **Sirmione**: 2 Viale Guglielmo Marconi (tel. 030 916114). **Salò**: Palazzo Municipale, Lungolago Zanardelli (tel. 0365 21423). **Gardone**: 35 Corso Repubblica (tel. 0365 20347). **Toscolano Maderno**: Lungolago Zanardelli (tel. 0365 641330). **Limone**: 15 Via Comboni (tel. 0365 954070)**. Malcesine**: Palazzo dei Capitani, 6 Via Capitanato (tel. 045 7400044). **Garda**: 3 Lungolago Regina Adelaide (tel. 045 7255194).

■ **Hotels. *Province of Brescia***

Desenzano del Garda: Numerous 4-star and 3-star hotels. 2-star: *Al Cacciatore, Alessi, Flora, Primavera*, and *Touring*.

Sirmione: Among the 90 or so hotels are: 5-star: *Grand Hotel Terme* and *Villa Cortine Palace Hotel;* numerous 4-star; 3-star: *Catullo*, etc.; 2-star: *Grifone, Villa Paradiso*, etc. **Salò:** 4-star: *Hotel Laurin;* 3-star: *Bellerive;* 2-star *Lepanto*. **Gardone**: 4-star: *Fasano Grand Hotel Villa del Sogno, Villa Principe;* 3-star: *Monte Baldo, Bellevue, Montefiori;* 2-star *Agli Angeli;* 1-star *Hohl*. Above the town on the hill of San Michele: 2-star *Colomber* and 1-star *Miramonti*. **Toscolano Maderno**: 3-star: *Maderno, Milano;* 2-star: *Splendid, Vienna, Vittoria, Bel Soggiorno, Garden, San Marco*. **Gargnano**: 3-star *Giulia*. **Limone**: 5-star: *Park Hotel Imperial* 4-star: *Le Palme;* 3-star: *Lido, Coste;* 2-star: *Villa Margherita;* 1-star: *Augusta, SE*.

Province of Verona
Malcesine: 3-star: *Du Lac, Vega*. In Val di Sogno: 3-star: *Maximilian*. At Campogrande 3-star: *Alpi*. **Torri del Benaco**: 3-star: *Hotel Gardesana*. **San Vigilio:** 4-star: *Locanda San Vigilio*. **Garda**: numerous hotels of all categories, including 2-star: *Conca d Oro* and *San Marco*. **Bardolino**: 3-star: *Cristina, Kriss Internazionale*, 2-star: *Bologna, Maria Pia*; 1-star *Bardolino*. **Lazise** and **Peschiera del Garda** also have numerous hotels.

■ **Youth hostel**: *Villa Pariani*, località Val di Sogno, Malcesine.

■ **Camping sites** of all categories in the Province of Brescia at Moniga, Manerba, San Felice del Benaco, Limone, etc. In the Province of Verona sites of all categories at Bardolino, Lazise, Peschiera del Garda, and 1-star sites at Malcesine and Torri del Benaco.

■ **Restaurants. Desenzano del Garda**: **A**: *Cavallino*, 29 Via Murachette; *Esplanade*, 10 Via Lario; *La Lepre*, 33 Via Bagatta; *La Villetta*, 4 Via Colli Sorici. **B**: *Il Molino*, 16 Piazza Matteotti; *L'Arava e L'Afava*, 71 Via del Molin; *Mayer*, 40 Piazza Matteotti; *Toscana*, 10 Via Benedetto. **C**: *Massadrinoì*, 1 Via Massadrino; *Da Renato e Serenella*, 61 Via Gramsci; *La Goccia*, Via Montonale; *La Rossa*, Via Montelungo. **Sirmione**: **A**: *La Rucola, Al Cantuccio, Vecchia Lugana*; **B**: *Risorgimento, Grifone, Antica Contrada, Pozzo*; **C**: *Osteria del Pescatore, Progresso, Il Porticciolo*. **Gardone**: **A**: *Fiordaliso* and *Lido 84*; **B**: *Casinò, La Stalla, Ristoro, Gli Olivi, Agli Angeli*. **C**: *Riolet, Barchetta, Cacciatore*, and *Taverna di Via Repubblica*. **Toscolano Maderno**: **C**: *Oasi* and *Vecchia Padella*. Above the town on Via Cecina, *La Sosta* and *La Macina*. **Limone**: **B**: *Torcol, Le Palme*. **C**: *Monte Baldo, Gemma, All' Azzurro, Bellavista, Tovo*. **Bardolino**: **C**: *Cantina Guerrieri Rizzanti* and *Osteria Solferino*.

■ **Bus services** run several times daily by the roads on the west and east banks from Peschiera and Desenzano to Riva. Frequent service from Verona via Lazise and Garda to Riva, and from Brescia to Desenzano, Sirmione, Peschiera and Verona, and between Salò and Desenzano, and Desenzano, Salò and Riva.

■ **Boat services** (including two modernised paddle-steamers built in 1902 and 1903) run by Navigazione sul Lago di Garda, Piazza Matteotti, Desenzano (tel. 030 9141321) from around mid-March to the beginning of November (the timetable changes three times a year). A daily boat service runs between Desenzano and Riva in 4.5 hrs, calling at ports on the west bank and Malcesine. Hydrofoils run twice daily in 2hrs (with fewer stops). More frequent boats between Desenzano and Maderno (in 1hr 50 mins). Services also between Peschiera, Lazise, Bardolino and Garda, and between Malcesine, Limone, Torbole and Riva. A boat or hydrofoil runs c every hour between Desenzano and Sirmione. All year round a car ferry operates between Maderno and Torri di Benaco in 30 minutes (every 30 minutes, but less frequently in winter). Tickets are available allowing free circulation on the lake services for a day. Tours of the lake in the afternoons in summer are also organised.

■ **Walks** along marked paths can be taken on Monte Baldo on the eastern bank, and in the Parco Alto Garda Bresciano (in the territory of Valvestino, Tremosine and Tignale) above Salò, Toscolano Maderno and Limone on the western bank . Information and maps from the Comunità Montana del Baldo (tel. 045 7241600) and the Comunità Montana Parco Alto Garda Bresciano (tel. 0365 71449), and the local APT offices.

■ **Golf courses** at Marciaga, Costermano, Sommacampagna (18-holes), Soiano and Toscolano Maderno (9-holes).

■ **Swimming**, see introductory section, above.

Geography
The lake is 51km long and 369 sq km in area; its maximum depth is 346m. The only important stream flowing into it is the Sarca, descending from the Trentino; the outlet is the Mincio. The predominant winds (which can swell into violent storms) are the *sover*, from the north, in the morning, and the *ora*, from the south, in the afternoon.

Desenzano, Sirmione, and the west bank

DESENZANO DEL GARDA, is a pleasant little resort (17,900 inhab.), well equipped with hotels. From the quay a bridge crosses a tiny picturesque inlet used as a harbour for small boats. Behind is the main **piazza**, with pretty arcades, and a monument to St Angela Merici (1474–1540), foundress of the Ursuline order, who was born here. Just out of the piazza is the **parish church** with a *Last Supper by Giovanni Battista Tiepolo.

Nearby is the entrance to the excavations of a **Roman villa** (open 9–dusk exc. Monday), mostly dating from the 4C AD but on the site of an earlier edifice of the 1C AD; the various building stages are still unclear. It is the most important large late Roman villa in northern Italy, of great interest for its polychrome 4C mosaics. The grandiose design of the reception rooms of the main villa includes an octagonal hall, a peristyle, an atrium with two apses, and a triclinium with three apses, all with good mosaics. Other, less grand rooms to the south may have been baths. An antiquarium (beneath which a Roman edifice of the 1C AD, with an underfloor heating system was discovered) has finds from the site, including remains of wall paintings. Separate excavations to the north have revealed a residential area, with part of an apsidal hall and, to the east, baths. The villa was discovered in 1921, and excavations have continued even though the site is in the centre of the town.

The road along the shore of the lake leads east to **SIRMIONE**, a narrow promontory in the centre of the southern shore of the lake, 3.5km long and in places only 119m wide. It was a Roman station on the Via Gallica, half-way between Brescia and Verona. Now it is a famous resort with some 90 hotels and is usually crowded with tourists in the season (though deserted in winter). There are a number of enjoyable walks on the peninsula, and you can swim in the lake on the east side. In September there is a festival dedicated to Catullus.

At the entrance to the little town is the picturesque 13C ***Rocca Scaligera** (open daily 9–13; summer 9–18), where Dante is said to have stayed. Completely surrounded by water, it was a stronghold of the Scaliger family, lords of Verona.

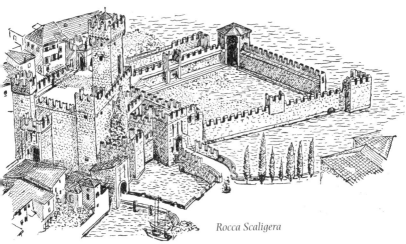

Rocca Scaligera

The massive central tower, 29m high, has a good view. Via Vittorio Emanuele (closed to cars) leads north from the castle through the scenic little town towards the Grotte di Catullo at the end of the peninsula. On the right a road leads to the 15C church of **Santa Maria Maggiore** which preserves some antique columns. At the end of Via Vittorio Emanuele is a spa with a hotel which uses warm sulphur springs rising in the lake. Via Catullo continues, passing close to **San Pietro in Mavino**, a Romanesque church of 8C foundation with early frescoes.

At the end of the road is the entrance to the so-called ***GROTTE DI CATULLO** (open 9–dusk, exc. Mon), really the romantic ruins of a large Roman villa, the most important of its date in northern Italy, set amid olive groves on the end of the headland, with splendid views out over the lake and of the rocks beneath the clear shallow water. The most beautiful spot on the lake, the site is very well maintained and planted with trees. The vast ruins belong to a notable Roman villa of the 1C AD (abandoned by the 4C) which may have belonged to the family of Valerii Catulli. Many wealthy Romans came to Sirmione for the summer, and Catullus—who is known to have had a villa here—speaks of '*Paene peninsularum, Sirmio, insularumque ocelle*' ('Sirmione, gem of all peninsulas and islands'). Though the ruins have been known for many centuries as the 'Grotte di Catullo', excavations took place here only in the 19C and the beginning of the 20C. Near the entrance is a small **antiquarium**, with exquisite fragments of frescoes dating from the 1C BC.

The most conspicuous ruins are the vast substructures and vaults built to sustain the main buildings of the villa, which occupied an area over 150 metres long and 100 metres wide on the top of the hill: virtually nothing is left of the villa itself since it was used as a quarry for building stones over the centuries, and its site is now covered by an olive grove. An earlier edifice of the 1C BC has been discovered here. A number of huge cisterns can be seen, as well as thermal buildings and a long colonnaded terrace with a covered walkway below.

From Rivoltella, half-way between Sirmione and Desenzano a byroad leads away from the lake up to the tower (74m high) of **San Martino della Battaglia**, which commemorates Vittorio Emanuele II's victory over the Austrian right wing on 24 June 1859. The interior contains sculptures and paintings relating to the campaign. At Solferino (in the province of Mantua, see page 186), Napoleon III, in alliance with Vittorio Emanuele, defeated the rest of the Austrian army on the same day.

The low moraine-hills south of the lake, formed by the ancient glacier of the Adige, have been the theatre of many battles: during Prince Eugène's campaign in the War of the Spanish Succession (1701–06), during Napoleon's enterprises (1796–1814), and during the Wars of Italian Independence (1848–49, 1859 and 1866).

The road along the west shore of the lake continues north from Desenzano. **Lonato** has a 15C castle built by the Visconti, which was the scene of French victories over the Austrians in 1509, 1706, and 1796, the last an early success of Napoleon's. The castle (open Easter–Sep, 9–20) was reconstructed in its 15C form by Antonio Tagliaferri at the beginning of the 20C and houses a small museum and a fine library (50,000 vols, with 411 incunabula). Nearby, at **Fornace dei Gorghi**, excavations in 1988 revealed a number of Roman brick ovens of the 1C–2C AD, near the largest of which is a small antiquarium.

The road leaves the lake, with many camping sites, and crosses the hilly district of **Valtenesi**, noted for its olive oil and wine. A byroad leads to the **Rocca di Manerba**, a headland once crowned by a castle. The Pieve of Santa Maria (or San Rocco) dates from the 11C–12C, with remains of frescoes, and is one of a number of Romanesque country churches in the Valtenesi. Further north there is a narrow channel between the romantic headland of Punta San Fermo and the **Isola di Garda** on which is the Villa Borghese Cavazza, built c 1900 in the Venetian-Gothic style on the ruins of a Franciscan convent. The lovely gardens are open by previous appointment in Apr–Jun, and Sep and Oct.

SALÒ (10,200 inhab.), the Roman *Salodium*, is perhaps the most appealing town on the western shore, with a slightly old-fashioned atmosphere. It has two gates, one surmounted by a lion, the other by a clock. It was the birthplace of Gaspare Bertolotti, or da Salò (1540–1609), generally considered to be the first maker of violins, and gave its name to Mussolini's short-lived puppet republic (the Repubblica Sociale Italiana). A few months after Mussolini's release from prison by order of Hitler in 1943 four days after the Armistice, and his escape to Germany, he returned here, under the protection of Hitler, in a last attempt to re-establish the Fascist government of Italy. Salò was an ideal place since the borders of the Reich had reached Limone, only 20km north, with the annexa-tion of Trentino Alto Adige, and the many huge hotels and villas by the lake were easily adapted as ministries, etc. The Republic of Salò ended with the Liberation in 1945, and Mussolini's execution a few days later. A music festival is held here in July.

Near the waterfront is the **Cathedral**, a fine building in the late Gothic style built at the end of the 15C, with a good Renaissance portal (1509). It contains paintings by Zenon Veronese and Romanino, and a carved 15C tabernacle. **Palazzo Fantoni** is the seat of the Biblioteca Ateneo, which has its origins in the Accademia degli Unanimi founded by Giovanni Maione in 1560. The library has over 25,000 volumes many of great historical interest. There is also a small

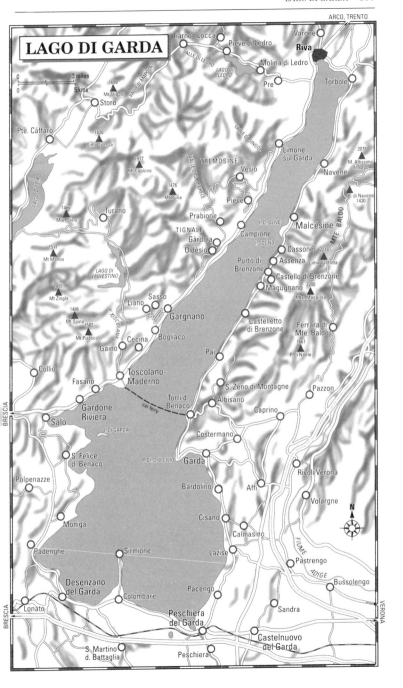

LAGO DI GARDA

ARCO, TRENTO

0 — 3 miles
0 — 5 kms

BRESCIA

VERONA

N

museum relating to the Republic of Salò. **Villa Laurin** (now a hotel), built in 1905, has a fresco by Angelo Landi.

The road continues through **Barbarano** with the huge Palazzo Martinengo (no adm.) on the right, connected by a bridge across the road with its garden, which has numerous fountains. The palace was built in 1577 by the Marchese Sforza Pallavicino, the Venetian general.

GARDONE RIVIERA was once famous as a winter resort since it has a sheltered position and used to enjoy a particularly mild winter climate—its parks and gardens are planted with rare trees. On the left of the road is the **VITTO-RIALE DEGLI ITALIANI** (adm. 9–12.30 & 14 or 14.30–18 or 18.30; villa closed on Mon), the famous residence of Gabriele d'Annunzio (1863–1938), designed for him in the last years of his life by Gian Carlo Maroni. It takes its name from the Italian victory over Austria in 1918. D'Annunzio donated the Vittoriale to the Italian State 15 years before his death here in 1938, and it is a remarkable monument to the eccentric martial poet who had a great influence on Italian poetry in this century.

From the gate a path leads up past the amphitheatre (used for theatre and music performances in summer), built by Maroni, to the 18C **Villa** (shown in a 30-minute tour to a maximum of 6–10 people by appointment at the ticket office). With its elaborate and gloomy décor, it has been preserved as a museum. Off the dark hallway is a reception room with an inscription that D'Annunzio made Mussolini read on his visit here: 'Remember that you are made of glass and I of steel.' Other rooms are crammed full of eclectic items: Art Nouveau objets d'art, chinoiserie, mementoes, sacred objects, Indian works of art, even an organ. The Art Deco dining room was designed by Maroni.

The private **garden** in front of the villa harbours such items as odd statuary and columns surmounted by projectiles. A path leads down through the pretty woods of the Acquapazza valley towards the main road. Behind the villa, Viale di Aligi leads up past a building which houses d'Annunzio's motor boat to his grand mausoleum at the top of the hill, where he and his architect are buried. Another path leads through woods to the prow of the ship *Puglia*, reconstructed here as a monument. His private aeroplane is also exhibited. The Fondazione del Vittoriale promotes the study of d'Annunzio's works.

Downhill, on the other side of the road, are the small privately owned **Botanical Gardens** (open Mar–Oct, 9–dusk), laid out by Arturo Hruska in 1940–71, with narrow paths through luxuriant vegetation. Nearer the lake is the conspicuous neo-classical **Villa Alba**, now a conference centre with a fine large public park. Claretta Petacci, Mussolini's mistress, lived in Villa Fiordaliso (now a restaurant) during the Republic of Salò.

TOSCOLANO-MADERNO is another resort, with a little port. In Maderno the 12C church of **Sant'Andrea** on the waterfront shows remains of Roman and Byzantine architecture, especially in the decoration of the pillar capitals, doors and windows; an older church seems to have been incorporated in the building. Across the Toscolano river, in Toscolano, is the church of **Santi Pietro e Paolo** (unlocked on request at the house on the right). It has paintings by Celesti and early 20C stained glass. Behind it, on the lake, is the **Santuario della Madonna di Benaco** with a barrel vault and numerous 15C frescoes (recently restored). In front of the church are four Roman columns. Nearby, opposite a large paper mill, is an enclosure with scant remains (under a roof) of a Roman villa of the 1C–2C AD with mosaics. Toscolano, called *Benacum*, was the chief Roman settlement on the west shore of the lake.

A pretty road ascends from Toscolano (just after the bridge) to **Gaino** in a valley which was a centre of paper-making from the 15C to the early 20C. Another road (just before the bridge) leads up to Monte Maderno and Monte Pizzocolo, with fine walks (marked paths). There is a 9-hole golf course here.

Beyond Toscolano the landscape becomes prettier with green hills and few buildings. At **Bogliaco**, on the right of the road, is the huge 18C Villa Bettoni (no adm.) with a collection of 17C–18C works of art; its lovely garden is on the left of the road. This was the seat of the 'Prime Minister' of Mussolini's Republic of Salò.

Gargnano is a very attractive little port. Conspicuous to the left of the road, in terraces climbing the hillside, are several large stone pavilions where lemon trees were once cultivated (see page 149). San Francesco is a 13C church with a cloister. An inland road from Gargnano to Limone has spectacular views: it passes the hill sanctuary of **Madonna di Monte Castello**, which has the finest view of the whole lake. Mussolini lived at Villa Feltrinelli (1892) here during the puppet Republic of Salò, from 1943 until three days before his death.

The main road (built in 1931) continues along the shore through numerous 'Gothic' tunnels cutting through the sheer rock face which here drops straight into the lake. The scenery, with lots of cypresses, is spectacular as the lake becomes narrower. **Campione** stands on the delta of a torrent and has a large cotton mill. A very fine road ascends, with many tunnels, viaducts and sharp curves, to **Pieve di Tremosine**, a village on a steep cliff descending into the lake, with a good view. This is in the **Parco Regionale Alto Garda Bresciano**, a protected area with marked walks.

LIMONE SUL GARDA takes its name from its lemon plantations, said to be the first in Europe. Up until the beginning of this century it was surrounded by terraced lemon and citron gardens, but now only two pavilions survive; one of them, in Via Orti, was bought by the town council in 1995 in order to preserve it. Limone was only accessible by boat before the road along the shore from Gargnano was built in 1931, and its unattractive buildings and numerous hotels date from its development as a resort in the 1950s and '60s. There are some nice walks in the district.

Beyond the next point the road enters the region of Trentino and there is a good view of the north end of the lake with the isolated Monte Brione.

RIVA, the Roman *Ripa*, an agreeable, lively little town (12,100 inhab.) and the most important place on the lake, is sheltered by Monte Rochetta to the west. It became a fashionable winter resort at the turn of the century, and remained in Austrian territory until 1918. The centre of the old town is Piazza 3 Novembre overlooking the little port. Here are the 13C **Torre Apponale**, **Palazzo Pretorio** (1370), **Palazzo Comunale** (1475) and some medieval porticoes. The **Rocca**, a 14C castle encircled by water, has been heavily restored over the centuries. The **Museo Civico** here has an archaeological section including finds from the lake dwellings of the Lago di Ledro; there is also a collection of armour, and locally printed works, including a Talmud of 1558. On the road to Arco is the church of the **Inviolata**, begun in 1603 by an unknown Portuguese architect and with a graceful Baroque interior.

In the valley of the Sarca is the little health resort of **ARCO** (10,800 inhab.), particularly fashionable before the First World War. The **Collegiata** is a handsome 17C church by Giovanni Maria Filippi. The former palace of the Counts, to the left, is a good 16C building. In the **Giardino Pubblico** is a monument by Bistolfi to the painter Giovanni Segantini (1858–99) who was born here. To the west is the **Parco Arciducale** with remains of the villa of Archduke Albert of Austria. Near Via dei Capitelli are a number of large 19C buildings including the former **Casino** (now a public library). The **Castle** of the counts of Arco, on a rocky eminence, provides a fine view of the valley of the Sarca and the lake.

Beyond the waterfall known as *Cascata del Varone** is the turquoise-blue **Lago di Tenno**.

At the mouth of the **Vale di Ledro**, a valley of great botanical interest, is the **LAGO DI LEDRO**, nearly 3km long, with the little resort of **Pieve di Ledro**. On the east side of the lake near **Molina**, when the water is low, you can see some of the c 15,000 wooden stakes from lake dwellings of the early Bronze Age discovered in 1929. There is a small museum (9–12, 13–18) and a Bronze Age hut has been reconstructed on the lakeside.

Riva to Peschiera along the east bank

Torbole, a summer resort near the mouth of the Sarca, played a part in the war of 1439 between the Visconti and the Venetians, when fleets of warships were dragged overland by teams of oxen and launched into the lake here. Goethe stayed at Torbole in 1786, before embarking on a boat down the lake on his way to Verona.

The east side of Lake Garda is bounded by the cliff of Monte Altissimo di Nago (2079m), the northern peak of **Monte Baldo**, which lines the shore as far as Torri del Benaco. A region of great interest for its flora and fauna, part of it is a protected area. It was once known as *Hortus europae* from its remarkable vegetation, which varies from lemon trees and olives on its lower slopes to beech woods and Alpine flowers on the summit. The highest peaks are Cima Valdritta (2218m) and Punta Telegrafo (2290m). There are numerous marked hiking trails on the slopes of Monte Baldo, some of them starting from Navene and Malcesine (information and excellent guide from the Comunità Montana del Baldo, tel. 045 7241600). There is a botanical garden at Novezzina.

MALCESINE (3500 inhab.) is a likeable resort (much visited by Germans) with a little port. It was the seat of the Veronese Captains of the Lake in the 16C–17C, and their old palace is now used as the **town hall**. The little garden on the lake is open to the public. Narrow roads lead up to the 13C–14C **castle** of the Scaligers, restored by Venice in the 17C. Very well maintained and open daily, it has various small museums in separate buildings, including one dedicated to Goethe who, while making a sketch beneath its walls, was taken to be an Austrian spy and nearly arrested, and another with finds from a Venetian galley salvaged from the lake off Lazise since 1990; it was probably used in the battle of 1439 against the Visconti (see Torbole, above). The tower, with a fine view, can be climbed. Concerts are often held in the castle.

A cableway mounts to ski-slopes on Monte Baldo (1748m), and there are pleasant walks in the area.

A little island (privately owned) can be seen just offshore from Malcesine. The road continues south and the coast soon becomes less wild. At **Cassone** a river (only 175m long) enters the lake, and at **Brenzone** there is another small island offshore. Further on the road passes a cemetery and the early 12C church of **San Zeno**, and at Pai there is a magnificent view of the opposite shore of the lake.

The coast here is known as the **Riviera degli Olivi**, from its many olive trees. **TORRI DEL BENACO**, the Roman *Castrum Turrium* and the chief town of the Gardesana after the 13C, has a pretty **port** (with a duck house). The fine **castle** of the Scaligers dates from 1383 and is open daily. It contains a small local museum which illustrates the history of fishing on the lake and the production of olive oil. There is a also a section dedicated to the rock carvings found in the district, the oldest dating from 1500 BC. A splendid pavilion of 1760, which protects a plantation of huge old lemon trees—as well as citrons, mandarins and oranges—against its south wall, can also be visited; this is one of very few such structures to survive on the lake where once lemons were cultivated in abundance (particularly on the western shore, but also here at Torri). On the other side of the castle is a tiny botanical garden illustrating the main plants which grow on the shores of the lake. There are 15C frescoes in the church. Benaco is locally famous for its red and yellow marble. A car ferry crosses from here to Maderno.

The headland of **PUNTA DI SAN VIGILIO** (car park on the main road) is the most romantic and secluded place on the lake. A cypress avenue ends at Villa Guarienti (1540), possibly by Sanmicheli, and a path continues downhill on the left, past a walled lemon garden, to a hotel in a lovely old building next to the church of San Vigilio among cypresses. A stone gate leads out to a picturesque miniature port, with reeds and a few old fig trees.

The resort of **GARDA** was developed after the Second World War, at the head of a deep bay. It was famous in the Roman and Lombard periods, and was later a fortified town; it still retains some interesting old houses.

The hills become lower and the landscape duller as the broad basin at the foot of the lake opens out. **Bardolino**, another ancient place retaining some commercial importance, is well known for its wine; there is a private wine museum in the Cantina Guerrieri Rizzanti. A tower and two gates remain from an old **castle** of the Scaligers. On the left of the main road, in a little courtyard, is the tiny Carolingian church of **San Zeno**, which retains its 9C form with a tower above the crossing and ancient paving stones. It has four old capitals and fragments of frescoes. Also on the road is the 12C church of **San Severo** with contemporary frescoes.

Lazise retains part of its medieval wall, and a castle of the Scaligers, with Venetian additions. The 16C Venetian customs house on the lake front attests to its former importance. San Nicolò is a 12C church with 16C additions and 14C frescoes.

PESCHIERA DEL GARDA, an ancient fortress and one of the four corners of the Austrian 'quadrilateral', stands at the outflow of the Mincio from the Lake of Garda. The impressive fortifications, begun by the Venetians in 1553, were strengthened by Napoleon and again by the Austrians. **Gardaland**, the most famous children's theme park in Italy, is nearby (free bus service from the station; open daily Apr–Sep, and weekends in Mar and Oct). With reconstructions of a pirates' ship, a town in the American Wild West and a castle, as well as a funfair, cinemas and other entertainments, it is especially attractive to children under ten.

13 · Cremona and its province

Cremona

Cremona, a busy and cheerful city (82,000 inhab.) has a world-wide reputation for its stringed instrument makers and restorers. It was the home in the 16C–18C of the most famous violin-makers of all time, including Andrea and Nicolò Amati, Giuseppe Guarneri and Antonio Stradivari (some of whose most precious instruments are preserved here). Cremona's many ancient brick buildings are survivals of the age of the Lombard city-states, and it has a beautiful Romanesque cathedral. Its churches are particularly noteworthy for their 16C frescoes, many of them by the Campi brothers, a gifted Cremonese family of painters, some of whose best work can be seen in San Sigismondo. Cremona is an important agricultural market for the province.

■ **Information office.** APT, 5 Piazza del Comune (tel. 0372 23233).

■ **Hotels.** 4-star: *Impero*, 23 Piazza Pace; 3-star: *Astoria*.

■ **Camping site** (3-star): *Parco al Po*, Via Lungo Po Europa (open May–Nov).

■ **Restaurants. A**: *Aquila Nera*, 3 Via Sicardo; *Ceresole*, 4 Via Ceresole; **B**: *Cigno*, 7 Vicolo del Cigno; *La Locanda*, 4 Via Pallavicino; *La Sosta*, 9 Via Sicardo; *Mellini*, 105 Via Bissolati; *Osteria Porta Mosa*, 11 Via S. Maria in Betlem; *Taverna La Botte*, 5 Via Porta Marzia. **C**: *Alba*, 40 Via Persico; *Cerri*, 3 Piazza Giovanni XXIII; *Il Ceppo*, 222 Via Casalmaggiore; *Osteria Settecento*, 1 Piazza Gallina.

■ **Cafés and cake shops**. *Lanfranchi*, 30 Via Solferino; *Al Duomo*, 6 Piazza Duomo; *Ebli*, 5 Via Cavallotti.
Snack Bars. *Lo Snack Italia '68*, 4 Via Anguissola; *Rio Bar*, 2 Piazza Pace; *Paninoteca No. 1*, 21 Via Cavallotti.

■ **Car parking.** Viale Trento e Trieste and Via Cadore. Pay car park in Piazza Marconi (except Wed and Sat). Garage in Via Massarotti and Via Villaglori.

■ **Transport. Bus** No. 3 from the station to the centre of the town. Buses from Via Dante next to the railway station for places in the province. Brescia, Bergamo and Milan are best reached by **train**.

■ **Theatre.** *Ponchielli*, Corso Vittorio Emanuele, with a theatre season in October and November, and concerts in April and May.

■ A **festival** of stringed instruments is held in October every 3 years (next in 1997).

■ A **market** is held on Wednesday and Saturday in Piazza Marconi.

History

Founded by the Romans as a colony in 218 BC, Cremona became an important fortress and road junction on the Via Postumia. Its decline after a siege and sacking in AD 69 ended in destruction by the Lombards in 603. Cremona re-emerged as a free commune in 1098, at war with its neighbours, Milan, Brescia and Piacenza. In 1334 it was taken by Azzone Visconti of Milan, and from then on remained under Milanese domination. It enjoyed a century of patronage and prosperity after it was given in dowry to Bianca Maria Visconti on her marriage to Francesco Sforza in 1441.

The Campi family of painters were born here and many of their works can be seen in the town. Cremona is also celebrated for its terracotta sculpture work. Andrea Amati was the founder here in the 16C of a school of stringed instrument makers which is still renowned. His grandson Nicolò Amati (1596–1684) was his most famous follower. Two later famous Cremonese families of instrument-makers were headed by Antonio Stradivari (Stradivarius, 1644–1737) and Giuseppe Guarneri (c 1660–1740), and his son Giuseppe Guarneri del Gesù (1698–1744). The composer Claudio Monteverdi (1567–1643) is another famous native.

The beautifully paved *PIAZZA DEL COMUNE is the centre of the life of Cremona and has its most important buildings. The Romanesque ***TORRAZZO** (open Apr–Nov, 10.30–12, 15–18) is one of the highest medieval towers in Europe (112m). It was completed in 1250–67 and crowned with a Gothic lantern in 1287–1300, probably by the local sculptor Francesco Pecorari. 502 steps lead up past a room with an astronomical clock, made in 1583 by the Divizioli, still with its original mechanism (it is wound by hand every day).

A double loggia, known as the Bertazzola, stretches across the front of the cathedral. It was built in 1497–1525 and beneath its arcades are the sarcophagus of Folchino Schizzi (died 1357), by Bonino da Campione, and that of Andrea Ala (1513), by Giovanni Gaspare Pedoni.

Duomo

The *Duomo is a splendid Romanesque basilica of 1107, consecrated in 1190 and finished considerably later. It has a particularly fine **exterior.** The **west front** (1274–1606) has a rose window of 1274 and a tabernacle above the **main door** with three large statues of the Madonna and Child and the patron saints, Imerio and Omobono. These unusual works, influenced by the French Gothic style, are now thought to be by Marco Romano (c 1310). The

Cremona

lions date from 1285 and the marble frieze of the Months from 1220–30. The later **transepts**, which altered the basilican plan of the church to a Latin-cross, have splendid brick façades: the north transept dates from 1288, with a fine porch (the Annunciation is attributed to Wiligelmus, and Christ and the Apostles date from the 12C), and the south transept from 1342. The beautiful **apse** faces the piazza behind.

The **interior** is remarkable especially for the *frescoes (1514–29; extremely difficult to see without strong light; being restored) on the walls of the nave and apse, by Boccaccino, Gian Francesco Bembo, Altobello Melone, Gerolamo Romanino, Pordenone and Bernardino Gatti. On the west wall is a *Deposition, beneath a Crucifixion, both by Pordenone. In the **south aisle**, the first altarpiece is by Pordenone, the second by Alessandro Arrighi (1650), and the third by Luca Cattapane. In the **south transept** (high up, looking back towards the nave) is a huge painting by Giulio Campi. The Sagrestia dei Canonici has a ceiling painted by Antonio Bibiena and an Assumption by Giulio Campi. The unusual funerary monument of Cardinal Sfondrati is by Giovanni Battista Cambi. Outside the 17C Cappella del Sacramento stairs lead down to the **crypt** with the beautifully carved tomb of Saints Peter and Marcellius (1506). On a nave pillar by the crypt steps is a marble triptych of 1495, and (protected by glass) a high *relief by Amadeo (1482) showing the Charity of St Imerio.

The **Cappella della Madonna del Popolo** is beautifully decorated with stuccoes by Carlo Natali (1654) and paintings by Bernardino and Giulio Campi. In the **north transept** is an altarpiece by Giulio Campi, and a splendid silver *Cross, nearly two metres high, with numerous tabernacles and statuettes. The work of Ambrogio Pozzi and Agostino Sacchi, it was completed in 1478 (the base was added in 1774). Also here are a Deposition by Antonio Campi, four marble reliefs by Giovanni Antonio Amadeo, and high up, looking back towards the nave, a large painting by Sante Legnani (1815). Twelve Brussels tapestries which illustrate the story of Samson (1629, by Jas Raes) are not at present on view.

The octagonal *Baptistery, a plain Lombard building dating from 1167 and partially faced with marble, has been closed for many years for restoration.

The **Loggia dei Militi** is a fine Gothic Lombard building of 1292 (with good three-light windows), restored as a war memorial. *PALAZZO DEL COMUNE (open 8.30–18 exc. Mon; fest. 9.30–12.30, 15–18) was built in 1206–45 but has an older tower. It was enlarged in 1245, and altered in the 16C and 19C. On the first floor landing is a 16C doorway designed by Francesco Dattaro. The grand rooms of the palace contain paintings by Francesco Boccaccino, Luca Cattapane and il Genovesino, and a marble chimney piece by Giovan Gaspare Pedoni (1502).

The 19C Room of the Violins contains five famous *violins made in Cremona. The one by Andrea Amati is thought to have been commissioned by Charles IX of France in 1566, the *Hammerle* of 1658 is by Nicolò Amati, Andrea's grandson. The others are a violin made by Giuseppe Guarneri in 1689, the *Cremonese* made in 1715 by Antonio Stradivari, and the *Guarneri del Gesù* by Giuseppe Guarneri del Gesù (1734). A recording of the instruments is provided, but it is also possible, by appointment, to hear them being played by a violinist who comes here regularly to keep them in tune.

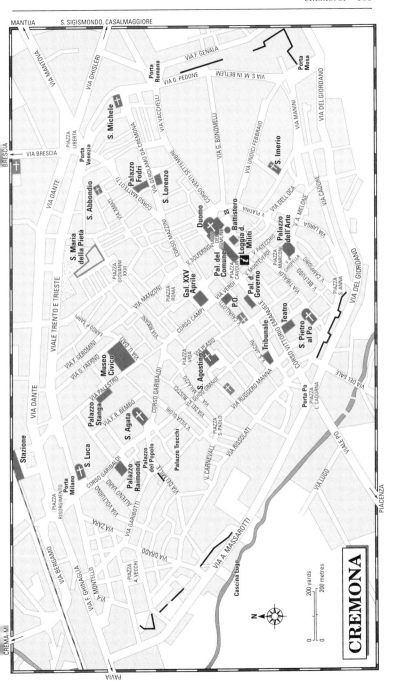

Via Solferino leads out of the piazza and Corso Mazzini continues right. It leads into CORSO MATTEOTTI with many fine old mansions, notably **Palazzo Fodri** (No. 17) dating from c 1500, decorated with a terracotta frieze and with a lovely courtyard. A road on the other side of the Corso leads to the church of **Sant'Abbondio**, with an interesting 16C interior. The vault frescoes are by Orazio Sammacchini. In the sanctuary are paintings by Malosso and Giulio Campi. The Loreto chapel dates from 1624, and there is a Renaissance cloister.

On the other side of the Corso, narrow roads lead to Via Gerolamo da Cremona which continues east to the church of **San Michele**, near remains of the walls. Lombard in origin (7C), it is the oldest church in Cremona. It was reconstructed in the 11C and 12C (the exterior of the apse dates from this time), and contains 12C columns in the nave with fine leafy capitals as well as noteworthy fresco fragments, including one by Benedetto Bembo. The paintings include works by Bernardino Campi, Alessandro Pampurino and Antonio della Corna (attributed).

Museo Civico

Corso Mazzini (see above) leads back towards the centre of the town and PIAZZA ROMA, a public garden. Here is a statue of the native composer Amilcare Ponchielli (1834–86), and the tombstone of Stradivarius salvaged from the church of San Domenico on this site (demolished in 1878). Just off the square, there is a monumental arcade beneath a building of 1935 leading into Corso Campi, which continues right to the Museo Civico (open 8.30–17.45; fest. 9.30–12, 15–18; closed Mon), housed in the huge Palazzo Affaitati built in 1561 by Francesco Dattaro, with a good staircase by Antonio Arrighi (1769). The collection of Count Sigismondo Ala Ponzone, left to the city in 1842, was transferred here in 1928. The arrangement is provisional.

Pinacoteca. In the first room are 15C paintings by Benedetto and Bonifacio Bembo, and works by Boccaccio Boccaccino. The central hall contains ten wooden high *reliefs by Giacomo Bertesi (1643–1710), and works by Bernardino Campi, Bernardino Gatti and Camillo Boccaccino. Beyond are paintings by Antonio Campi, Giuseppe Arcimboldo (*Scherzo con ortaggi*; a well-known Surrealist portrait), L'Ortolano, Panfilo Nuvolone, Il Genovesino, and Caravaggio (*St Francis in Meditation*). On the right is a large room with 16C–17C works by the Cremonese school.

Stairs lead up to a display of small icons. The section dedicated to the **decorative arts** contains 16C Limoges enamels, ivories, wrought-iron work, etc. The collection of **18C–19C porcelain** includes Viennese, Wedgwood, Meissen and Ginori (Doccia) ware. There is also Italian majolica and 16C–18C Cremonese ceramics.

From the central hall another flight of stairs leads up to a room with **15C–17C Flemish paintings**, including a Madonna by Jan Provost. Beyond are three rooms with **19C paintings** including portraits by Il Piccio, and works by Luigi Sabatelli and Giuseppe Dotti.

Off the courtyard is the extensive **archaeological collection**, with exhibits from the prehistoric era (including a sword of the 9C BC), Attic craters, and a good Roman section: helmets, fine geometric mosaic pavements (1C–3C AD), coins, epigraphs, portrait heads, and the front of a legionary's strongbox. The cache of at least 650 amphorae was found in the centre of Cremona in 1993, in an area once probably part of the Roman port on the Po. The medieval finds include wrought-iron work and sculpture.

At No. 17 Via Palestro is the **Stradivarius Museum** (open as for the Museo Civico), founded in 1893 and including the Salabue bequest of 1920. In the well arranged gallery are models made by Stradivarius in wood and paper, his tools, drawings, etc., as well as a fine collection of stringed instruments (17C–20C). **Palazzo Stanga**, at No. 36 Via Palestro, has a Rococo front rebuilt in the 19C and a handsome courtyard, probably by Pietro da Rho.

In Corso Garibaldi, which branches off from Corso Campi, is the conspicuous neo-classical façade of **Sant'Agata**, built in 1848 by Luigi Voghera. The campanile is Romanesque. Inside, on the right, is the Trecchi tomb by Giovanni Cristoforo Romano (1502–05), with beautifully carved bas-reliefs. The painting of the life of St Agatha (painted on both sides) is by a northern Italian master of the 13C. The good frescoes on the sanctuary walls are by Giulio Campi (1536).

Across the Corso is **Palazzo del Popolo** or **Cittanova** (1256), with a ground floor portico, the headquarters of the popular—or Guelf—party in the days of the free commune of Cremona; it is adjoined by **Palazzo Trecchi** with a neo-Gothic façade of 1843–44. Nearby, in Via Grandi, is the little church of **Santa Margherita** (1547), in an extremely ruinous state. The frescoes inside (now almost invisible) are the best work of Giulio Campi. Not far off, at 16 Via Milazzo, is a remarkable Art Nouveau house façade with floral motifs and leaves.

On the left of Corso Garibaldi (No. 178) is the fine **Palazzo Raimondi** (1496; by Bernardino de Lera) with damaged frescoes on its curved cornice. It is the seat of the international **Scuola di Liuteria**, and the centre of musical activity in Cremona. This school for violin-makers continues a tradition for which the city has been famous since the 16C. Beyond on the right is the church of **San Luca** with a 15C façade in poor repair adorned with the terracotta ornament typical of Cremona; adjoining is the little octagonal Renaissance chapel of Cristo Risorto (1503), attributed to Bernardino de Lera.

From Sant'Agata (see above), Via Trecchi and Via Guido Grandi lead south to *Sant'Agostino, a 14C church with a good tower and terracotta ornamentation on the façade. In the interior are frescoes by Bonifacio Bembo, a stoup with reliefs by Bonino da Campione (1357), an Annunciation by Antonio Campi, and a *Madonna and Saints by Perugino (removed for restoration).

Via Plasio leads south to the church of **Santi Marcellino e Pietro**, with elaborate marble and stucco decorations in the interior (1602–20; being restored). Further south is Corso Vittorio Emanuele with (right) the **Teatro Ponchielli** by Luigi Canonica (1808). Behind the theatre is the monastic church of **San Pietro al Po**, sumptuously decorated with 16C paintings and stuccoes by Malosso, Antonio Campi, Gian Francesco Bembo, Bernardino Gatti and others. The cloister at No. 14 Via Cesari is by Cristoforo Solari (1509).

On the outskirts of the town (on the Casalmaggiore road; bus No. 2 for the hospital) is the important church of *SAN SIGISMONDO (open 8.30–12, 15–18), where Francesco Sforza was married to Bianca Visconti in 1441. The present building was started in 1463 in celebration of the event; it is a fine Lombard Renaissance work. The interior contains splendid painted decoration carried out between 1535 and 1570, much of it by the local artists Camillo Boccaccino, Bernardino

Gatti and the Campi family. The **nave vault** was decorated by Bernardino and Giulio Campi, and Bernardino Gatti. In the **south aisle**, the first chapel contains a niche in which two glass carafes are preserved; these were found in 1963 on a brick dated 1492 at the base of the façade (they were filled with oil and wine to commemorate the beginning of its construction). The fifth chapel has a vault exquisitely decorated by Bernardino Campi and an altarpiece by Giulio Campi, and the sixth chapel has an altarpiece by Bernardino Campi.

The **transept vaults** were painted by Giulio Campi; the choir stalls by Domenico and Gabriele Capra (1590–1603) are partially in restoration; and the Menarini organ has recently been restored. The dome bears a fresco of Paradise by Bernardino Campi. The **presbytery** and apse have fine *frescoes by Camillo Boccaccino, and the high altarpiece, in a beautiful contemporary wooden frame, is by Giulio Campi (1540). Behind the high altar is the foundation stone of the church. In the **north aisle,** the fifth *chapel is entirely decorated with paintings, frescoes and stuccoes by Antonio Campi, and the third chapel has fine works by Bernardino Campi. Off the **cloister**, a Renaissance work finished in 1505, there is a carved door by Paolo and Giuseppe Sacca (1536), and the refectory with a Last Supper by Tomaso Aleni (1508).

The province of Cremona

■ **Hotels.** At **Crema**: 4-star, including *Il Ponte di Rialto*. At **Casalmaggiore**: 3-star accommodation.

The small province of Cremona is bordered to the south by the Adda and Po rivers, on the north by the Oglio, and at Crema it is crossed by the Serio. The most important town after Cremona is **CREMA** (33,000 inhab.) on the west bank of the Serio. It was under Venetian rule from 1454 to 1797 and was the birthplace of the composer Francesco Cavalli (1600–76). The **Cathedral**, in the Campionese style (1284–1341), has a fine tower, and contains one of the last works of Guido Reni. The piazza in front of it is surrounded by Renaissance buildings, including the 16C **Palazzo Pretorio** with an archway leading to the main street. The ex-convent of **Sant'Agostino** houses the library and **Museo Civico** (open 14.30–18.30; Sat & fest. 10–12, 15–19), which has burial armour from Lombard tombs. The refectory, restored as a concert hall, has frescoes attributed to Giovanni Pietro da Cemmo (1498–1505). **Santa Maria della Croce**, north of the town, is a handsome centrally planned church (1490–1500) in the style of Bramante, by Giovanni Battagio. It contains altarpieces by Benedetto Diana and the Campi brothers.

Pandino has an impressive castle (open 9–12.30, 13–18.30) begun by the Visconti in 1379. At **Palazzo Pignano** excavations beneath the 12C Pieve di San Martino revealed remains of an early Christian basilica. The church contains 15C frescoes and a 15C terracotta Pietà. Behind the church remains of a late-Roman villa have been found. **Rivolta d'Adda** has a good basilica of 1088–99, with interesting carvings. A park here (open 9–dusk exc. Dec–Feb) displays life-size models of prehistoric animals.

East of Crema is **SONCINO** where the *castle (open 10–12; Sat & fest. 10–12.30, 14.30–8), rebuilt by Galeazzo Maria Sforza, is among the best preserved in Lombardy (restored in 1886 by Luca Beltrami). Ezzelino da Romano died here after his defeat in the battle of Cassano d'Adda. The splendid town *walls (13C–15C) are nearly 2km in circumference. Five watermills survive in or near the town, one of which is still in operation, and the town preserves a 13C drainage system. The wide main street descends from the site of the south gate past the 15C **Palazzo Azzanelli**, with terracotta decoration, to the main square with the 11C **Torre Civico** and the church of **San Giacomo**, which has a curious seven-sided tower (1350) and a cloister. It contains two stained-glass windows by Ambrogio da Tormoli (1490), and a late 15C terra-cotta Pietà. Nearby is the **Casa dei Stampatori** (open as for the castle), a medieval tower house which may be on the site of the first printing works founded in the town in 1480 by the Jewish family Nathan,who were allowed by the Sforza (in return for cash loans) to take up residence here having been forced to leave Germany. They adopted the name of the town for their press and in the decade in which they lived and worked here, they printed their first book in 1483, and the first complete Hebrew bible in 1488. There is a little museum, and a reproduction press is still in operation. The **Pieve di Santa Maria Assunta** was reconstructed in the 17C–19C on the site of a much older church. On the outskirts of the little town is the church of **Santa Maria delle Grazie** (ring for admission at the convent 10–12, 15–18) begun in 1492 and conse-crated in 1528, splendidly decorated with terracotta friezes and *frescoes, many of them by Giulio Campi (including the triumphal arch and sanctuary vault).

South of Soncino is **Soresina**, where the church of San Siro contains altar-pieces by Malosso and il Genovesino, and the church of San Francesco a wooden Crucifix by Giacomo Bertesi. The delightful theatre (restored in 1991) was built to a design by Carlo Visioli in 1840. A large market is held in the town on Monday.

West of Soresina is **Castelleone**, where the Museo Civico (open 16–19) displays local archaeological finds (prehistoric and Lombard), and the church of Santa Maria di Bressanoro built in 1460–65 has terracotta decorations and interesting frescoes.

Pizzighettone, west of Cremona, is an old town divided in two by the Adda. Significant remains of its fortifications are preserved, including the circuit of *walls (last strengthened in 1585), the passageways and battlements of which can be visited, and the Torrione, where Francis I was imprisoned after the battle of Pavia (1525). The church of San Bassiano dates from the 12C, but has been greatly altered. Inside is a frescoed Crucifixion by Bernardino Campi, and three carved 14C panels.

In the southeast corner of the province is the town of **Piadena**. A small archae-ological museum (open Wed, Thu & Sat 9.30–12.30) includes finds from the supposed site of *Bedriacum*, scene of a battle in AD 69 in which the generals of Vitellius defeated Otho. West of the town is **Torre de' Picenardi**, with the 18C Villa Sommi-Picenardi surrounded by a moat in the centre of a park.

At **San Giovanni in Croce**, the Villa Medici del Vascello is a castle of 1407 remodelled with a graceful loggia in the 16C, and surrounded by a romantic park. **Casalmaggiore** has impressive embankments along the Po, which is crossed on a long bridge. It has a theatre dating from 1783.

14 · Mantua

Mantua, in Italian *Mantova*, is a charming old town (58,000 inhab.) famous for its associations with the Gonzaga, under whose rule it flourished as a brilliant centre of art and civilisation in the 15C and 16C, when Mantegna, Leon Battista Alberti and Giulio Romano created some of their most important works here. It is in the extreme southeastern corner of Lombardy—and has much in common with neighbouring towns in Emilia Romagna and the Veneto. Mantua's feeling of isolation is emphasised by the practical difficulties of reaching it by public transport. In the centre of the town, with its quiet old cobbled streets and piazzas, is the huge Palazzo Ducale of the Gonzaga, celebrated for its 'Camera degli Sposi', frescoed by Mantegna. The Dukes' summer villa, the suburban Palazzo Te, is the masterpiece of Giulio Romano.

- **Information office.** APT, 6 Piazza Mantegna (tel. 0376 328253).

- **Hotels.** 4-star: *San Lorenzo*, 14 Piazza Concordia. 3-star: *Broletto*, 1 Via Accademia; *Dante*, 54 Via Corrado; *Mantegna*, 10 Via Filzi. **Youth Hostel**: Via Legnago, 1km outside the town (open Apr–Oct).

- **Restaurants. A**: *San Gervasio*, 15 Via San Gervasio; *Trattoria dei Martini (Cigno)*, 1 Piazza d Arco; *Aquila Nigra*, 4 Vicolo Bonacolsi; *Osteria Vecchia Mantova*, 26 Piazza Sordello. **B**: *Ai Garibaldini*, 7 Via San Longino; *Al Portichetto*, 14 Via Portichetto; *Cento Rampini*, 11 Piazza Erbe; *Il Grifone Bianco*, 6 Piazza Erbe. **C**: *Antica Osteria ai Ranari*, 11 Via Trieste; *Due Cavallini*, 5 Vicolo Salnitro; *Leoncino Rosso*, 33 Via Giustiziati; *Quattrotette*, 4 Vicolo Nazione; *Al Quadrato*, 49 Piazza Virgiliana.

- **Café.** *Caravatti*, Piazza delle Erbe.

- **Picnic places** around Palazzo Te, in Piazza Lega Lombarda, and Piazza Virgiliana.

- **Bus station**, Piazzale Mondadori. A limited service is run by APAM to Sabbioneta, San Benedetto Po, Brescia, etc.

- **Market day.** Thursday (in Piazza delle Erbe).

- **Car parking.** Lungolago dei Gonzaga (near Palazzo Ducale) and around Palazzo Te.

History

Virgil was born on Mantuan territory about 70 BC, and some of the town's earliest recorded history is due to the poet's interest in his birthplace. Mantua became a free commune about 1126, and was afterwards dominated by the Bonacolsi and Gonzaga families. Under Gonzaga rule from 1328 the town was a famous centre of art and learning, especially in the reigns of Ludovico II (1444–78), Francesco II (1484–1519), husband of

Isabella d'Este, the greatest patron of her time (who died in Mantua in 1539), and their son Federico II (1519–40).

The city was sacked by Imperial troops in 1630, and many of the best Gonzaga paintings were sold to Charles I of England. The duchy was extinguished in 1708 by the Austrians who fortified the town as the southwest corner of their 'quadrilateral'. It held out against Napoleon for eight months in 1796–97, and was retaken by the French in 1799. The town was again under Austrian rule in 1814–66. It was damaged by bombs in 1944.

Art

Among the artists who flourished at the court of the Gonzagas were Leon Battista Alberti, Luca Fancelli and Pisanello. Andrea Mantegna was court artist from 1460 until his death in 1506. Giulio Romano, architect and painter, was called to Mantua in 1524 by Federico II, and worked there under the duke's patronage until his death in 1546, leaving numerous monuments in the city. Titian often visited the city and it was here he first saw the works of Giulio Romano. Alari Bonacolsi, nicknamed 'L'Antico', was born in Mantua, and he was commissioned by the Gonzaga to make bronze copies of classical statues. Rubens worked at the court from 1600 to 1606. The success of Monteverdi's *Orfeo* at court in 1607 was the first landmark in the history of opera. The popularity of Verdi's *Rigoletto* has endowed several Mantuan localities with spurious associations.

Palazzo Ducale

The whole of the upper side of the large, cobbled PIAZZA SORDELLO is occupied by the famous **Palazzo Ducale, a huge fortress-palace which remains a fitting emblem of the hospitality of the Gonzaga princes, who were especially famous as patrons of the arts (see above). The vast rambling palace is divided into three main parts, all connected by corridors and courtyards: the original 14C Bonacolsi palace known as the Corte Vecchia, on Piazza Sordello, which was adapted by the Gonzaga rulers; the castle added by the Gonzaga in the 15C to defend the approach to the city from the lake (and once connected to the palace by drawbridges only); and the Corte Nuova wing mainly planned by Giulio Romano in the 16C. Architects who worked on the palace included Luca Fancelli in the 15C and, in the 16C and early 17C, Giulio Romano, Giovanni Battista Bertani and Antonio Maria Viani. The palace is now chiefly remarkable for its decorations, including the famous Camera degli Sposi in the castle, since most of the great Gonzaga art collections begun by Isabella d'Este, wife of Francesco II, and enriched in the 16C, have been dispersed; Charles I acquired a large part of them in 1627–30. Many of the rooms of the palace contain excellent classical sculpture.

■ **Admission.** 9–13, 14.30–18; Mon 9–13. From 15 March to 15 May the palace opens at 8.30. Visitors are conducted in parties of about 30 (there is usually no more than 15 mins' wait at the ticket office for a group to form), although a small part of the palace is at present also open to visitors not on the guided tour. The most crowded periods of the year are Mar–May and Sep–Oct.

History

The Corte Vecchia, or Ducal Palace proper, overlooking Piazza Sordello, consists of the low 'Domus Magna' founded by Guido Bonacolsi c 1290, and the higher Palazzo del Capitano, built a few years later by the Bonacolsi, at the expense of the Comune. The Austrians altered the windows of the façade in the Gothic style, and it was restored to its original 15C appearance at the beginning of this century by the Samuel Kress Foundation. After the sack of Mantua in 1630 a large part of the fabric of the palace deteriorated. The restoration of the palace, begun in 1902, was completed in 1934.

The palace consists of some 700 rooms and 15 courtyards. Some of these are never open to the public, while other parts are sometimes closed. The description below covers all the areas normally accessible: scholars may be given special permission to see any parts not shown on the tour. Since the order of the visit sometimes changes, the room numbers given below refer to the plan on page 172–173.

The **entrance** to the palace is through the door on the left-hand side of the façade. The 17C **Scalone delle Duchesse** (1) by Antonio Maria Viani ascends to the **first floor**. Here has been placed an interesting *painting of Piazza Sordello by Domenico Morone, illustrating the expulsion of the Bonacolsi in 1328. It shows the front of Palazzo Ducale (a detail of which was useful during restoration work on the building in this century) and the Gothic façade of the Duomo (pulled down in 1761). On the right are two rooms (2 and 3) with a ruined fresco of the Crucifixion (14C). On the left is the entrance to the **Palazzo del Capitano**, with a collection of medieval and Renaissance sculpture in rooms 4–9. The long **Corridoio del Passerino** or **Corridoio del Palazzo del Capitano** (4) has interesting late-Gothic mural decorations and numerous coats of arms. The seated figure of *Virgil dates from c 1220, and the stemma of the *podestà* Ginori (1494) is by the Della Robbia workshop. The mantelpiece is attributed to Luca Fancelli.

Off the corridor is the **Appartamento Guastalla** (5–10). These rooms contain a lapidary collection; a group of five teracotta statues attributed to the school of Mantegna; a terracotta bust of Francesco II Gonzaga by Gian Cristoforo Romano; the tomb effigy of Margherita Malatesta (wife of Francesco I) by Pier Paolo dalle Masegne; a classical relief of Philoctetes attributed to Tullio Lombardo; a 16C sleeping cupid with two serpents; and a large ruined fresco of the Crucifixion attributed to the 14C–15C Bolognese school. In the last room (10) are displayed detached frescoes (1303) and a Byzantine Madonna.

The **Sala del Pisanello** or **Sala dei Principi** (11) contains a splendid fragment of a mural *painting discovered in the 1960s showing a battle tournament. The unfinished but vivacious composition is one of the masterpieces of Pisanello. Forming a border along the top of the painting is a beautiful frieze incorporating the Lancastrian SS collar entwined with marigold flowers, the emblem of the Gonzaga—it was Henry VI who granted the Gonzaga the concession to use the heraldic crest of the House of Lancaster. On the other wall are *sinopie* of Arthurian scenes by Pisanello. The adjoining room (12) displays the *sinopia* of the battle tournament.

The **Salette dell'Alcova** (13 and 14) are not always open. At present they contain 18C works including St Thomas with Angels by Giuseppe Bazzani. The

Galleria Nuova (15; at present closed) displays 17C paintings including works by Carlo Bononi and Giuseppe Maria Crespi.

The next four rooms form the **Appartamento degli Arazzi** (16–19), overlooking the Cortile d'Onore, with neo-classical decoration by Paolo Pozzo (1779). The Brussels *tapestries here, designed after Raphael's cartoons of the Acts of the Apostles (now in the Victoria and Albert Museum, London), are the most important replica of the Vatican series. They were acquired by Ercole Gonzaga. Some of the other rooms have false painted 'tapestries'. The ceiling of the **Sala dello Zodiaco** (20) has delightful frescoes by Lorenzo Costa the Younger (1580).

To the left is the **Sala dei Fiumi** (21), decorated in 1775 by Giorgio Anselmi, with a 16C table of pietre dure made in Florence. It overlooks the **giardino pensile**, a hanging garden off which is a 'Kaffeehaus' with ceilings decorated in the 18C by Antonio Bibiena. Three rooms near here (22–24), known as the **Appartamento dell'Imperatrice,** with Empire-style furniture dating from the early 19C, are usually closed.

Beyond the Sala dello Zodiaco (see above) is the **Sala dei Falconi** (25), named after a ceiling painting of hawks, attributed to Ippolito Andreasi. The **Saletta dei Mori** (26) has a fine gilded wood ceiling and 16C and 17C paintings. Beyond the **Loggetta dei Mori** (27) is the narrow **Corridoio dei Mori** (28; with a view of the handsome 16C campanile of the Palatine Basilica of Santa Barbara), decorated in the early 17C. It leads to the 18C neo-classical **Galleria degli Specchi** (29) with a 17C frescoed ceiling.

The **Salone degli Arcieri** (30) has an unusual frescoed frieze of horses behind curtains. Here are hung some of the most important paintings in the palace. *The Gonzaga Family in Adoration of the Trinity* by Rubens was cut into pieces during the French occupation; two other fragments of the same painting are exhibited here. Three works by Domenico Fetti include a monochrome lunette showing Viani presenting a model of the church of Sant'Orsola to Margherita Gonzaga d'Este, and a lunette with the Miracle of the Loaves and Fishes. There are also two paintings by Anton Maria Viani.

The **Appartamento Ducale** (31–38) was arranged by Vincenzo I shortly after 1600. The **Sala di Giuditta** (31) has paintings of the Apostles and Saints by Domenico Fetti. The **Sala del Labirinto** (32), named after the labyrinth carved in the wood ceiling, was rearranged in 1995 with sculptures and paintings from the Palazzo Ducale of the Pico at Mirandola. The episodes from the story of Psyche are by Sante Peranda, and the two marble busts by Lorenzo Ottoni are portraits of Beatrice d'Este Pico (with lace) and Maria Cybo Pico (with a veil), both duchesses of Mirandola. High up on the walls are paintings by Sante Peranda and Palma Giovane. The ceiling of Room 33 has the gold crucible motif, Vincenzo's emblem, and more Pico portraits, including Alfonso and Giulia d'Este by Sante Peranda. Beyond are small neo-classical rooms (34–38).

In the Domus Nova (closed) are the **Appartamento di Eleonora Medici Gonzaga** (39–42), wife of Vincenzo II, designed by Viani, and the **Scala del Paradiso** (43). On a mezzanine floor, the so-called **Appartamento dei Nani** (also closed), once thought to have been for the Court dwarfs, is in fact a miniature reproduction of the Scala Santa in Rome made by Viani for Ferdinando Gonzaga c 1620, and used for religious functions.

The **Appartamento delle Metamorfosi** (44–47), with ceilings by Viani and

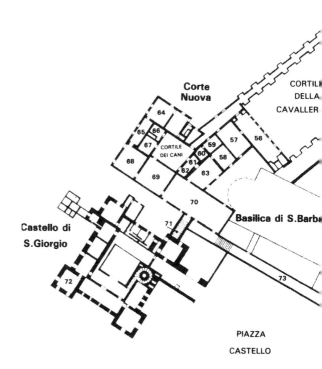

Palazzo Ducale

52
54 51
53 50
48—54
48 49

Giardino Padiglione

N

47
46
45
44

39—42
42
41
40
39

43 PIAZZETTA PARADISO
37 38
35 36 31—38

PIAZZA
S.BARBARA

34 33 32 31
30
29

28

CORTILE D'ONORE 15 **Palazzo di Corte Vecchia**

PIAZZA LEGA
27
26 14 LOMBARDA
25 13

20 19 18 17 16 12

nging
1 11
21
rden
2
22 10 9 8 7 6 5
23 24 3
4

22—24

Palazzo del Capitano

his school, and Roman busts and reliefs, looks out onto the ***Giardino del Padiglione**, with a view of the Domus Nova by Luca Fancelli. The **Appartamento Estivale** (48-54), redecorated by Bertani and Viani, is closed.

The ***Galleria della Mostra** (55), with a magnificent ceiling, was built by Viani for the display of the most important part of the ducal collection: it now contains original busts of Roman emperors. There is a view of the splendid **Cortile della Cavallerizza** by Giulio Romano and Bertani, and the lake beyond.

Beyond the **Galleria dei Mesi** (56), built as a loggia by Giulio Romano, is the **Sala di Troia** (57), with frescoes designed by Giulio Romano and executed by his pupils. Beyond is the pretty **Sala di Giove** or **delle Teste** (58).

The next series of small rooms (59–62) are closed. These include the Stanza dei Cesari (59), the Camerino di Ganimede (60), and the Loggetta dei Cani (61) which opens on to the Giardino dei Cani. The Camerino degli Uccelli (62) has a pretty ceiling and contains a statuette of Aphrodite, a Roman copy of a 3C BC original.

Next to the Sala di Giove is the **Sala dei Cavalli** (63) which takes its name from paintings of horses by Giulio Romano which formerly hung here. It has a fine wooden coffered ceiling. The classical sculpture includes two circular altars.

The rooms (64–69) on the opposite side of the Giardino dei Cani are closed. They include the Sala dei Duchi (64), and the Appartamento del Tasso (65 and 66), where the Gonzaga are supposed to have received Torquato Tasso on his flight from Ferrara, which contains more classical sculpture.

The **Stanza di Apollo** (67) has beautiful decoration traditionally attributed to Francesco Primaticcio (from a previous building). The **Sala dei Marchesi** (68) has fine allegorical figures and busts in stucco by Francesco Segala. The beautiful Greek sculpture here includes the stele of a male figure and child (4C BC), and an Attic lute player. The **Sala dei Capitani** (69) has a fine Hellenistic *torso of Aphrodite. The handsome **Salone di Manto** (70) contains more good classical sculpture including a *caryatid of the 5C BC and the 'Mantua Apollo'.

The Camera degli Sposi

The **Scalone di Enea** (71) leads into the **Castello di San Giorgio**, a keep built in 1395–1406 with an interesting exterior (formerly covered with frescoes). The design of the loggia of the courtyard built by Luca Fancelli is attributed to Mantegna. A spiral ramp leads up to a series of rooms beyond which is the famous *Camera degli Sposi (72), formerly known as the Camera Picta, one of the most celebrated works of the Renaissance. The magnificent paintings by Mantegna were commissioned by Ludovico, the second Marquis of Mantova, and carried out in 1465–74. Beautifully restored in 1984–86, they illustrate the life of Lodovico and his wife Barbara of Brandenburg. The painted decoration of the room, with a remarkable use of light, was immediately recognised as a masterpiece and was of fundamental importance to later Renaissance artists. It is now known that only part of the work was executed as a true fresco. The room appears to have been used by Ludovico as a bedroom, as well as an office and as a place for receiving visiting dignitaries.

On the **north wall**, above the fireplace, the Marquis and his wife are shown seated, surrounded by their family, courtiers and messengers. Between the husband and wife is their son Gianfrancesco with his hands on the shoulders of a younger son Lodovico, and a daughter Paola, shown holding an apple. Rodolfo stands behind his mother, and to the right is his pretty sister Barbara (with her nurse behind and a dwarf in front). Beneath Lodovico's chair is his old dog Rubino, who died in 1467. On the right is a group of courtiers dressed in the Gonzaga livery.

On the **west wall** are three scenes presumed to represent the meeting in 1462 at Bozzolo between the Marquis, on his way to Milan, and his son Francesco, the first member of the Gonzaga family to be nominated cardinal, travelling back from Milan. On the left are servants in the Gonzaga livery with hounds and a horse—the Gonzaga were famous as horse breeders and dog lovers. Above the door is a dedicatory inscription, supported by winged putti, signed, and dated 1474, by Mantegna. In the right-hand section is the scene of the meeting: the first full figure in profile is the Marquis, dressed in grey with a sword at his side, talking to Francesco, in cardinal's robes; the children are also members of the Gonzaga family. The group to the right is thought to include the Holy Roman Emperor Frederick III (in profile) and, dressed in red in the background, Christian I of Denmark. The landscape in the background of all three scenes is particularly beautiful and includes classical monuments (derived from buildings in Rome and Verona) and an imaginary city. In the frieze on the pilaster to the right of the door is Mantegna's self-portrait.

The vaulted **ceiling**, also by Mantegna, has a trompe l'oeil oculus in the centre, one of the first examples of aerial perspective in painting. The curious, inventive scene shows a circular stone balustrade on which winged putti are playing; and peering over the top of it are five courtly female figures, a peacock and more putti, and balanced on the edge is a plant in a tub. The vault, with a background of painted mosaic, is divided by trompe l'oeil ribs into eight sections with medallions containing the portraits of the first Roman emperors and, below, (damaged) mythological scenes.

The last two walls were decorated with painted gold damask (now very damaged), and the lower part of the walls has painted marble intarsia.

The exit from the palace is usually along the long **Corridoio Bertani** (73), with modern copies of the stucco portraits of the Gonzaga in the Palazzo Ducale of Sabbioneta, and down to the Cortile d'Onore. The ***Appartamento di Isabella d'Este**, off the Cortile d'Onore, is sometimes opened on request. Her **studiolo**, for which she commissioned paintings from Mantegna, Perugino, Lorenzo Costa and Correggio (all of them now in the Louvre) has a door by Gian Cristoforo Romano. Her **grotto** contains intarsie by the Della Mola brothers. Both rooms have fine gilded wood ceilings.

The palatine **Basilica di Santa Barbara** (closed) was built for Duke Guglielmo by Giovanni Battista Bertani in 1562–65.

On the opposite side of Piazza Sordello are two grim battlemented **Bonacolsi palaces**, belonging to the family who ruled Mantua before the Gonzaga. Above the first rises the Torre della Gabbia from which (seen from Via Cavour) protrudes an iron cage where condemned prisoners were exposed. The second, Palazzo Castiglioni, dates from the 13C. Beyond is the Rococo Palazzo Bianchi, now the **Bishop's Palace**.

At the end of the piazza is the **DUOMO**. The late Gothic building burned down in 1545 (although part of the south side of this church survives), and the unsuccessful façade was built in 1756 next to the broad brick campanile. The light ***interior** was designed by Giulio Romano (after 1545) in imitation of an early Christian basilica. It is covered with exquisite stucco decoration. In the south aisle is a 6C Christian sarophagus, and the baptistery with remains of 14C and 15C frescoes. The ***Cappella dell'Incoronata**, a charming work in the style of Alberti, is reached by a corridor off the north aisle. The octagonal **Cappella del Sacramento** at the end of the north aisle has two altarpieces by Domenico Brusasorci and Paolo Farinati.

At the opposite end of the piazza an archway leads into PIAZZA DEL BROLETTO, where a small daily market is held. On the **Broletto** (1227), with its four corner towers, is a quaint figure of Virgil sculpted in the 13C, showing the poet at a rostrum wearing his doctor's hat. At No. 9 is the entrance to the small **Tazio Nuvolari Museum** (open 10–13, 15.30–18.30 exc. Mon & Thu), dedicated to Nuvolari (1892–953), the famous motor-racing champion, who was born in Mantua. Connected to the Broletto by an archway is the **Arengario**, a little 13C building with a loggia. A restaurant beneath the archway occupies a Gonzaga office with an early 14C fresco of the city, and the arms of Gianfrancesco, the first Marquis. **Palazzo Andreasi**, with a portico, has an interesting first floor, now used by a shop (entered from 79 Via Cavour), with good wood ceilings.

On the other side of the Broletto is PIAZZA DELLE ERBE, a charming square with a delightful row of houses at the far end. A long portico faces **Palazzo della Ragione**, dating partly from the early 13C but with 14C–15C additions, including a conspicuous clock-tower (1473) by Luca Fancelli with an astrological clock by Bartolomeo Manfredi (1473), in perfect working order since its restoration in 1990. Next to it is the **Rotonda di San Lorenzo**, a small round church founded in 1082 and restored in 1908. The domed interior has two orders of columns and a matroneum. There is a small daily market in the square, and a large general market is held here on Thursday.

Sant'Andrea

In the adjoining Piazza Mantegna is the basilica of *Sant'Andrea, a very important Renaissance building commissioned from Leon Battista Alberti by Lodovico II Gonzaga in 1470 as a fit setting to display the precious relic of the Holy Blood. Although it was not built until after Alberti's death by Luca Fancelli (1472–94), then enlarged in 1530 under the direction of Giulio Romano, and the dome added by Filippo Juvarra in 1732, it remains the most complete architectural work by Alberti. The brick campanile of 1413 is a survival from the 11C monastery on this site. The remarkable **façade,** with giant pilasters, is classical in inspiration. In the barrel-vaulted vestibule, a beautiful marble frieze with animals and birds surrounds the **west door**.

The huge ***interior** (open 8–12, 15–19), on a longitudinal plan, has a spacious barrel-vaulted nave without columns or aisles. The rectangular side chapels, also with barrel vaults, are preceded by giant paired pilasters raised on pedestals. Between them are small, lower domed chapels. The transepts, with the same proportions, are also rectangular. The nave chapels were decorated in the 16C, partly by pupils of Giulio Romano, and the rest of the church in the 18C. **South side**. Alberti's architecture can be appreciated in the first little chapel (the baptistery), since its walls are bare. Detached frescoes by Correggio have been placed here. In the next chapel are 16C frescoes attributed to Benedetto Pagni, and the pretty little third chapel is frescoed by Rinaldo Mantovano

(1534). In the fourth chapel is a 16C wood ancona. The sixth chapel has a fine altarpiece, a 16C copy of the original by Giulio Romano (now in the Louvre); the frescoes designed by Giulio Romano were executed by Rinaldo Mantovano. **South transept**. In the chapel to the right are 16C funerary monuments, including that of Cantelmi (1534) with a painting attributed to Francesco Borgani. On the end wall of the transept is the fine Andreasi tomb by Prospero Clementi (1549), possibly on a design by Giulio Romano. The chapel of the Holy Sacrament has two paintings by Felice Campi.

The **dome** and **apse** are frescoed by Giorgio Anselmi (1782). On the left of the high altar is a statue of Guglielmo Gonzaga in prayer (1572). Beneath the dome is an octagonal balustrade marking the crypt which contains the precious reliquary of the Holy Blood. Inside the balustrade is a black marble plaque by Giovanni Bellavite and marble tondi by Gaetano Muttoni. The **crypt** is opened on request.

In the **north transept** is a door which leads out to a piazza from where the exterior of the church can be seen, and a walk of the Gothic cloister of the monastery which stood on this site. The transept chapel contains 16C and 17C funerary monuments including that of Pietro Strozzi, an ingenious work of 1529 with four caryatids, designed by Giulio Romano. On the **north side**, the sixth chapel has an altarpiece of the Crucifix by Fermo Ghisoni, a pupil of Giulio Romano. The third chapel has an early 17C wooden ancona, and in the second chapel there is a beautiful altarpiece by Lorenzo Costa (1525).

The first little chapel, the *Cappella del Mantegna** (unlocked on request by the sacristan), was chosen by Mantegna in 1504 as his funerary chapel. It contains his tomb with his *bust in bronze, possibly his self-portrait. The charming *panel of the Holy Family and the family of St John the Baptist is almost certainly by Mantegna. Above is his coat of arms. The terracotta decoration and frescoes on the walls and dome, including the symbols of the Evangelists, were designed by Mantegna and probably executed by his son Francesco. The painting of the Baptism of Christ, probably on a design by Mantegna, is also the work of Francesco.

Palazzo Te

On the southern edge of the old town (see Plan), about 1.5km from Piazza Sordello, surrounded by a public garden is *Palazzo Te (open 9–18 exc. Mon), one of the most important Mannerist villas in Italy. This delightful suburban villa, on the site of the Gonzaga stables, was used in the summer by Federico II Gonzaga. Begun in 1525 and built of brick and stucco with bold rustication and numerous classical elements, it is Giulio Romano's most famous work, inspired by the great villas of Rome. The low building is spaciously laid out around a courtyard with symmetrical loggias, and has a large walled garden beyond two fishponds. Here Federico held splendid entertainments and, in 1530, received Charles V, on which occasion he was granted the Dukedom of Mantua by the emperor. The name is probably derived from 'teieto', the name of the locality.

The architect and painter Giulio Romano was called 'that rare Italian master' by Shakespeare in *The Winter's Tale*. In the decorative design of Palazzo Te he was helped by his pupils, including Primaticcio who executed some of the stucco-work. The rooms of the palace, bare of furniture, are of interest for their painted and stuccoed decoration: they are beautifully maintained after a careful restoration in 1979–89.

The entrance is through the west loggia, beyond which can be seen the beautiful **Cortile d'Onore**. The **Camera di Ovidio** has a red Verona marble fireplace and landscapes by Anselmo Guazzi and Agostino di Mozzanega. The **Camera del Sole** has a fine ceiling with stuccoes by Primaticcio and a painting of the Sun and Moon by Giulio Romano. On the walls are casts of ancient reliefs put here in the neo-classical era. Across the **Loggia delle Muse** is the *Sala dei Cavalli**, with frescoed portraits of horses from the Gonzaga stables by Rinaldo Mantovano (on a design by Giulio Romano) and a carved ceiling by Gasparo Amigoni (1528). The **Sala di Psyche** has splendid *frescoes by Giulio Romano illustrating the story of Psyche as told by Apuleius. The next room, the **Sala dei Venti**, was the studio of Federico II. It has a ceiling with signs of the zodiac, and tondi illustrating horoscopes, together with a fine stucco frieze and fireplace. The **Camera di Fetonte** or **Camera delle Aquile** has a fresco of the Fall of Phaëthon in the centre, and stuccoes including four eagles. The fine **Loggia di Davide (**or **d'Onore**), with biblical frescoes, opens onto two fishponds and the gardens beyond. The **Sala degli Stucchi** was the last work executed by Primaticcio before his departure for France. The two classical friezes, in imitation of a Roman triumphal column, are thought to have been executed in honour of Charles V's visit. The **Sala dei Cesari** has a trompe l'oeil frieze of putti and Roman historical scenes in the vault.

The famous **Sala dei Giganti**, in which painting and architecture are united in a theatrical trompe l'oeil, is the work of Rinaldo Mantovano, Fermo da Caravaggio and Luca da Faenza (1532–34), on designs by Giulio Romano. It represents the fall of the giants, crushed by the thunderbolts of Jupiter hurled from Mount Olympus. The pavement was originally concave and was made up of large stones in imitation of a river bed. The room has strange acoustical properties.

The three **Camerini a grottesche** were painted with grotesques in 1533–34 by Luca da Faenza and Gerolamo da Pontremoli. Beyond are three more rooms, the **Camere dell'ala meridionale**, with coffered ceilings and friezes of 1527–28, and neo-classical stuccoes on the lower part of the walls.

The **Garden**, beyond the fishponds, is closed at the end by an exedra, added c 1651 probably by Nicolò Sebregondi. The huge **Frutteria** to the right is now used for important exhibitions. On the left is the little **Casino della Grotta**, a secret apartment with more charming stuccoes by Giulio Romano and Primaticcio. There are long-term plans to reconstruct the gardens to the north of the villa.

The upper floor of Palazzo Te contains collections from the **Museo Civico.** These include the Egyptian collection of Giuseppe Acerbi; the Gonzaga collection of weights and measures; a numismatic collection; and a gallery of modern art including works by Federico Zandomeneghi and Armando Spadini.

Viale Te leads back towards the centre of the town: across Piazzale Vittorio Veneto and the Porta Pusterla, Largo XXIV Maggio leads to the ducal church of **San Sebastiano** (1460), designed by Alberti on a Greek-cross plan. This unusual building with a beautiful raised vestibule, a side portico and a ground level crypt, has been brutally altered over the centuries. The interior (for adm. apply at Palazzo Te) now contains the sarcophagus of the 'Martyrs of Belfiore'

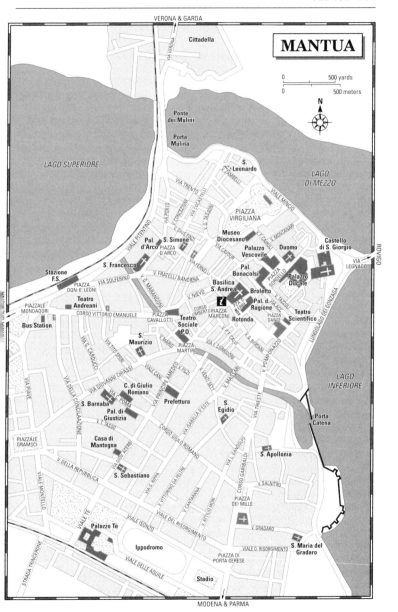

(Italian patriots shot by the Austrians in 1851–52), and the crypt serves as a war memorial.

Opposite is the plain brick **House of Mantegna** (open 10–12.30, 15–18, exc. fest.). It was built to Mantegna's design in 1466–74 as a studio and private museum, and has a remarkable circular courtyard. The artist lived here until 1502 when he donated it to Francesco II Gonzaga. A painting by Titian of Mantegna (or Giulio Romano) is exhibited here.

Via Giovanni Acerbi continues north to Via Carlo Poma in which is the **Palazzo Guerrieri**, now **Palazzo di Giustizia** (No. 7) with bizarre monster caryatids attributed to Viani. On the other side of the road (No. 18) is **Giulio Romano's house** (no adm.), which he purchased in 1538 when it was on the outskirts of the town. He transformed it in the 1540s, and it was enlarged in the 19C. The huge domed church of **San Barnaba** contains works by Lorenzo Costa the Younger (16C) and Giuseppe Bazzani (18C), and a fine high altar in pietre dure.

The Museo Diocesano and Palazzo d'Arco

From Piazza Sordello (see page 175), Via Fratelli Cairoli leads west to the spacious PIAZZA VIRGILIANA, laid out in the Napoleonic period at the beginning of the 19C, with fine trees and a grandiose monument to Virgil. At No. 55 is the **MUSEO DIOCESANO FRANCESCO GONZAGA** (open 9.30–12, 14.30–17 exc. Mon; in winter open only on fest, and Jul and Aug only on Thu, Sat and Sun), which contains a large miscellany of works of art in a provisional arrangement. It is entered through a pleasant courtyard with four large lime trees.

In the corridor is a Greek marble female head dating from the 1C AD (from the campanile of the Duomo). In the large hall are paintings including a tondo of the Ascension attributed to Mantegna (with its sinopia). The church silver includes processional crosses of the 14C and 15C. Also here are paintings by Francesco Borgani, Girolamo Mazzola Bedoli, Giuseppe Bazzani and Domenico Fetti. The second part of the room displays a bronze crucifix by Pietro Tacca; more paintings by Bazzani; a *collection of Limoges enamels (mostly 16C–19C); a 17C oval relief in silver; and the missal of Barbara of Brandenburg illuminated by Belbello da Pavia, Girolamo da Cremona and others.

At the end is a small room which displays ivories, a German jewel pendant which belonged to Duke Guglielmo Gonzaga, and a large *reliquary chest made of rock crystal (Venetian, c 1600).

Another section of the museum displays the splendid suits of *armour (some of them 15C) found on the life-size ex-voto statues in the sanctuary of Santa Maria delle Grazie. Also displayed here is a marble statue by the Dalle Masegne family (1401).

Beyond the other side of the piazza, reached by Via Zambelli, is the church of **San Leonardo**, with a high altarpiece attributed to Francesco Francia, and a fresco attributed to Lorenzo Costa the Elder.

From the south end of the piazza, Via Virgilio, Via Cavour (right) and Via Finzi lead to Piazza Carlo d'Arco with the neo-classical **PALAZZO D'ARCO** (open Mar–Oct daily exc. Mon 9–12, Thu, Sat, & fest. also 15–17; in winter fest. only 9–12, 14.30–16). Built by Antonio Colonna in 1784 and decorated and furnished by the d'Arco Counts, it was recently left to a foundation by Giovanna d'Arco. A large number of rooms in the palace are on show, with their 18C and 19C furniture. A room dedicated to Andreas Hofer, the Tyrolese patriot who was tried by a Napoleonic court here in 1810 before being shot outside the walls, is decorated with wallpaper of 1823, painted with grisaille views of Italy. Other rooms contain a collection of musical instruments, including a spinet, and many paintings, including works by Lorenzo Lotto (attrib.), Giuseppe Bazzani, Pietro Muttoni, Sante Peranda, Fra Semplice da Verona and Alessandro Magnasco. The library and kitchen, with a good collection of pewter, are not usually shown.

In the garden are the remains of a 15C palace, where the ***Sala dello Zodiaco** has remarkable painted decoration attributed to Giovanni Maria Falconetto (c 1520). The frieze around the top of the walls, decorated with gilded wax, illustrates classical myths. Below are 12 lunettes with the signs of the zodiac over elaborate representations of classical myths against landscapes with Roman or Byzantine buildings (derived from monuments in Rome, Ravenna and Verona). Below each scene is a panel in grisaille.

Nearby is the Gothic church of **San Francesco** (1304; rebuilt in 1954), which contains a chapel where the first Gonzaga were buried with their wives, with frescoes (very worn) by Tommaso da Modena.

From Piazza d'Arco Via Fernelli leads back towards the centre past **Piazza Canossa** with the large **Palazzo Canossa** (with an interesting long façade and a good staircase), a little 18C chapel (two paintings by Bazzani have been removed from the interior), a fountain and a cast-iron kiosk. In Via Fratelli Bandiera there is an interesting palace (No. 17) with remains of frescoed decoration and a good doorway.

Via Verdi continues back to the church of Sant'Andrea (described above), to the south of which Corso Umberto I, with its dark and heavy porticoes, widens out as it reaches Piazza Cavallotti, with the handsome **Teatro Sociale** (1822, designed by Luigi Canonica). Corso della Libertà leads east to Piazza Martiri di Belfiore, beside which, below a little park on the river is a **Fish Market,** with a rusticated portico, built by Giulio Romano in 1546.

Just north of Piazza Broletto, Via Accademia leads to Piazza Dante with the **Accademia Virgiliana**, built by Piermarini in 1767, which contains the ***Teatro Accademico Bibiena** by Antonio Bibiena (open daily except fest. 9–12.30, 15-17.30), where Mozart gave the inaugural concert in 1770 at the age of thirteen, during his first visit to Italy. It is still sometimes used for concerts. In Via Pomponazzo are several palaces with handsome courtyards (nos. 31, 27, and 23).

In a remote part of the town to the southeast (see the Plan) is the restored Romanesque church of **Santa Maria di Gradaro**, with a good Gothic portal of 1295 and Gothic frescoes in the presbytery.

Mantua is surrounded on three sides by the **River Mincio** which widens out to form a lake of three reaches, Lago Superiore, Lago di Mezzo and Lago Inferiore. In recent years naturalists have taken an interest in the birdlife and flora of the marshlands surrounding the lakes, where lotus flowers introduced from China in 1921 grow in abundance. The valley of the Mincio is now a protected area. Boat excursions can be arranged by appointment (information from the APT).

15 · Sabbioneta and the province of Mantua

Sabbioneta

Sabbioneta, southwest of Mantua, towards Cremona, was planned in 1556 by Vespasiano Gonzaga (1531–91) as an ideal fortified city, with regular streets within hexagonal walls and some beautiful buildings, including two palaces, a gallery and a theatre, all of which reflect his admiration for the classical world of Rome. Now a quiet little town (400 inhab.), it is extremely well preserved, with fields reaching up to its walls and no ugly buildings on the outskirts. Vespasiano, who received the Dukedom of Sabbioneta from the Emperor in 1577, was a cultivated man, as well as a condottiere, and he spent many years at the court of Philip II of Spain. Besides its splendid 16C monuments, many of them recently restored, the town—which probably had a population of some 2000 at its height—preserves pretty streets of simple houses with a number of walled gardens.

- **Information office.** Associazione Pro Loco, Via Vespasiano Gonzaga (tel. 0375 52039). The office is open Oct–Mar 9–12, 14.30–17 or 18 exc. Mon; Apr–Sep daily 9–12, 13.30 or 14.30–18 or 19. It is necessary to book here (and purchase a ticket) for a guided tour of the monuments of the town (the theatre, the Palazzo Ducale, the church of the Incoronata, Palazzo del Giardino and the Galleria); otherwise they can only be seen from the outside. A separate ticket has to be purchased here for the tour of the Synagogue.

- **Hotels.** 2-star: *Al Duca*, 18 Via della Stamperia; *Ca' d'Amici*, 2 Via d'Aragona. 1-star: *Giulia Gonzaga*, 65 Via Vespasiano Gonzaga.

- **Restaurants. C**: *Al Duca* and *Ca'd'Amici* (see above).

- **Picnic places** near the walls.

- **Buses** (infrequent service), run by APAM, from Mantua in 45 mins (with a stop on the main road, N420 outside the town).

- **Concerts** are held in May–Jun in the Theatre; organ recitals take place in Sep in the Incoronata.

History
Roman remains have been found in the area, and there was a *castrum* here in the Lombard period. There was already a castle here when Vespasiano Gonzaga chose the site for his new town in 1556. Many of the most important buildings were erected from 1578 to 1591, the date of Vespasiano's death, after which the town declined in importance. Because of its low position, it has often been subject to flooding from the river Po (especially in 1595, 1705 and 1951).

At the entrance to the town is the huge PIAZZA D'ARMI, on the site of a 14C castle (only the foundations of two towers remain) which occupied this part of the town until it was demolished at the end of the 18C. The Corinthian **Roman Column** which supports a Roman statue of Athena was set up here by Duke Vespasiano. Also here are the Palazzo del Giardino and the Galleria (both described below), and a monumental school building erected in 1930, as well as the tourist office.

Just off Via Vespasiano Gonzaga is the *TEATRO ALL'ANTICA, by Vincenzo Scamozzi, the last building erected for the Duke (1588–90). This is the first example of a theatre built as an independent structure (not within a larger building), and provided with a foyer, separate entrances for the public and artists, changing rooms, etc. It has a handsome exterior with an inscription dedicated to Rome, and a charming interior (which can hold 200). The peristyle has stucco statues and busts of the Greek gods, and monochrome painted figures of Roman emperors. Above is a frescoed loggia with painted spectactors and musicians, by a Venetian artist. On the two side walls are large frescoes of the Campidoglio and Hadrian's Mausoleum in Rome. The fixed scena, which represented a piazza and streets, was destroyed in the 18C (although there are plans to reconstruct it). The ceiling, which is lower than the original ship's keel roof, also dates from the 18C.

The **Porta Vittoria** (1567) was the main gate of the town. From outside there is a good view of the walls. The **Convent of the Servi di Maria** incorporates the octagonal church of the **Incoronata**, built in 1586–88, and modelled on the Incoronata of Lodi. It was beautifully decorated with frescoes in the 18C. The late 17C mechanical organ has its original pipes (concerts are given here in Sep). The monument to Vespasiano, with numerous rare marbles, was erected by Giovanni Battista della Porta in 1592, and incorporates his bronze statue by Leone Leoni (1588). He is buried in the crypt below.

In the delightful Piazza Ducale is **PALAZZO DUCALE**, the first important building built by the Duke, and his official residence. On the **first floor** the **Salone delle Aquile** has frescoes with festoons of fruit, and four wooden equestrian *statues representing Vespasiano, two of his ancestors, and a captain. They were made in 1589 by a Venetian sculptor and were part of a group of ten (the others six perished in a fire in the early 19C, except for the five busts exhibited here). The **Sala degli Imperatori** has a panelled oak ceiling, and a frieze of fruit and vegetables including peppers and maize (which Vespasiano must have seen in Spain since they were not grown in Italy in the 16C). The **Galleria degli Antenati**, probably used as a studio, has *reliefs in stucco of Vespasiano's ancestors by Alberto Cavalli, and a barrel-vaulted ceiling with stuccoes and paintings. Other rooms on this floor have a painted frieze of elephants, a ceiling of carved cedar, and frescoes with views of Constantinople and Genoa.

On the **ground floor** are rooms with *grotteschi*, gilded wood ceilings, and a monumental fireplace.

Also in the Piazza is the church of **Santa Maria Assunta** (only open for services on fest.), built in 1582. The chapel of the Holy Sacrament was added by Antono Bibiena in 1768 and has a delightful double perforated dome in stucco and wood and two marble reliquary 'cupboards'. The **Museo d'Arte Sacra** (open 10–12, 15–18 exc. Mon and on Fri morning; closed Nov–Mar and in Aug) has two paintings by Bernardino Campi. The *'teson d'oro' ('Golden Fleece') was the gold medal presented to Vespasiano in 1585 by Philip II of Spain when he was made a knight of the Order; it was found in his tomb in the Incoronata. Also exhibited here are a portable 16C organ, 17C–18C vestments, and church silver.

In Piazza d'Armi is the ***PALAZZO DEL GIARDINO**, which was Vespasiano's summer villa built in 1578–88, with an oak cornice on the exterior. The atrium on the **ground floor** has a pretty vault, while the adjoining room has another charming vault with birds attributed to Bernardino Campi, and a lovely fireplace. From here can be seen the remains of the walled garden with three nymphaeums. The **first floor** has a delightful series of *rooms with stuccoes and frescoes by Campi and his pupils. They depict the Circus Maximus and Circus of Flaminius in Rome; myths from Ovid; Gonzaga personal devices (*imprese*); scenes from the *Aeneid*; and exotic animals (some of them probably seen by Vespasiano on his travels in Africa). The original polychrome marble floors are preserved. Another room (once decorated with Venetian mirrors) has painted landscapes.

Beyond a little room with grotesques is the entrance to the ***GALLERIA**, built in 1583–84. This remarkable gallery, 96m long, was built to display the Duke's superb collection of classical busts, statues and bas-reliefs (most of them taken to Palazzo Ducale in Mantua in 1774). Decorated with frescoes and trompe l'oeil perspectives at the two ends, it has a handsome brick exterior and an open, well ventilated loggia below.

The **Synagogue** (for admission, enquire at the tourist office) is on the top floor of a house in Via Barnardino Campi. It has a fine interior by Carlo Vizioli (1824). There was a Jewish community in the town from 1436.

Outside Sabbioneta is the church of **Villa Pasquali** (if closed, ring at No. 1), built in 1765 by Antonio Bibiena. The second tower on the handsome brick façade was never completed. The interior is especially remarkable for the beautiful perforated double ceiling of the dome and three apses in terracotta. The various treasures of the church are carefully preserved.

The province of Mantua

Southeast of Mantua is **Pietole**, a village usually regarded as the birthplace of Virgil. At **Bagnolo San Vito** is the first Etruscan site (5C BC) discovered north of the Po and the most ancient site in Lombardy. The road crosses the Po and there is a good view from the bridge of the pretty landscape on its banks.

On the right bank is **San Benedetto Po** which grew up round the important Benedictine abbey of **SAN BENEDETTO POLIRONE**, founded in 1007 and protected by Countess Matilda of Canossa (1046–1115), who was buried here. It was united to the abbey of Cluny until the 13C, and was suppressed by Napoleon in 1797. The church and extensive abbey buildings, mostly dating from the 15C, are in the large central piazza of the little town.

The fine ***Church** was rebuilt by Giulio Romano in 1540–44, and is one of his most interesting works. It contains 33 terracotta statues in various parts of the church by Antonio Begarelli and his school, including St Benedict in the ambulatory. On the north side are altarpieces by Francesco Bonsignori and Fermo

Ghisoni. The church also has good 18C wrought-iron work, 16C stalls, a neo-classical altarpiece by Giovanni Battista Bottani, and an 18C organ.

Off the ambulatory is the Romanesque church of **Santa Maria**, with a pretty interior. The fine mosaic pavement of 1151, with figures of animals, the Cardinal Virtues, etc. is well preserved at the east end (and there is another fragment in the nave). The altarpiece is by Fermo Ghisoni. In the **sacristy**, with frescoes by the school of Giulio Romano, and fine wooden cupboards, is an equestrian portrait of Matilda of Canossa by Orazio Farinati: her empty tomb is just outside (her remains were sold by the abbot to Pope Urban VIII in the 1633 when Bernini was commissioned to provide a monument in St Peter's).

To the right of the church is the entrance to a cloister off which a Baroque staircase by Giovanni Battista Barberini (1674) leads up to the **Museo della Cultura Popolare Padana** (open 9–12.30, 14–17.30 exc. Mon; by appointment in winter), a large and interesting local ethnographical museum related to the region along the banks of the Po, arranged around the upper floor of the cloister of San Simeone, in the grand abbot's apartments and the simpler monks cells, and in the late 18C library, a neo-classical work by Giovanni Battista Marconi. The lower walk of the 15C **cloister of San Simeone** has 16C frescoes and a garden which has been replanted following its 16C design.

Across the piazza, on the other side of the church, is the former **refectory** (open at weekends, or by appointment) built in 1478, with a museum of sculptural fragments and ceramics, and a Madonna by Begarelli. The huge *fresco, discovered in 1984, and attributed as an early work (1514) to Correggio, provided the architectural setting for a Cenacolo by Girolamo Bonsignori (now in the Museo Civico of Badia Polesine, and replaced here by a photograph). Two sides of the 15C cloister of St Benedict survive in the piazza, and the huge 16C infirmary behind the refectory is to be restored.

Southwest of San Benedetto Po is **Gonzaga**, a pretty little town which was the ancestral home of the famous Ducal family.

On the Po, further downstream, is **Ostiglia** where the marshes have been declared a bird sanctuary. A short distance further down the river is the **Isola Boschina**, its woods a rare survival of the vegetation which was once typical of the Po landscape. There are plans to make the island into a nature reserve. On the south bank of the river is **Revere** where there is a palace of Lodovico Gonzaga with a charming courtyard and portal by Luca Fancelli, and an 18C parish church with paintings by Giuseppe Bazzani. Here the Museo del Po has archaeological and historical material relating to the river. The Romanesque pieve of **Coriano** was founded c 1085.

South of Mantua is **Borgoforte**, with an 18C castle and a parish church containing works by Giuseppe Bazzani. On the south bank of the Po at **Motteggiana** is the Ghirardina, a 15C fortified villa attributed to Luca Fancelli.

West of Mantua on the Cremona road is the unusual church of *****Santa Maria delle Grazie**, founded by Francesco Gonzaga in 1399. The nave has two tiers of life-size statues in various materials set up as ex-votos—an astonishing sight. Some of the figures were clad in the armour now exhibited in the Museo Diocesano in Mantua. Also here is the tomb of Baldassarre Castiglione (died

1529), probably by Giulio Romano. From **Rivalta**, to the north, boat excursions can be taken on the Mincio.

Canneto sull'Oglio, west of Mantua, preserves a massive tower belonging to its former castle. The Museo Civico (open at weekends except in Aug), is dedicated to life on the Oglio river, and also has a collection of dolls which have been manufactured in the town since 1870. Nearby are **Asola**, which preserves its old walls, and **Bozzolo**, with its 14C tower and a palace of the Gonzaga.

In the northern part of the province is **Castiglione di Stiviere**, which was once a fief of the Gonzaga. The Museo Storico Aloisiano in the Collegio delle Nobili Vergini (open 9–11, 15–17 or 18) has mementoes of St Luigi Gonzaga born here in 1568, and paintings by Francesco Bassano, Federico Barocci, Giulio Carpioni and Giambettino Cignaroli, as well as collections of glass, ironwork and furniture. The Museo Internazionale della Croce Rossa (open 9–12, 14 or 15–17.30 or 19) commemorates the Red Cross, which was founded after the famous battle which took place at **Solferino** to the southeast, in which Napoleon III—in alliance with Vittorio Emanuele—defeated the Austrians in 1859. There is a memorial here to Jean Henri Dunant who, horrified by the sufferings of the wounded in this battle, took the first steps to found the Red Cross. The tower of Solferino was erected on a hill probably by the Scaligers in 1022; it contains a Risorgimento museum. At the foot of the hill is Piazza Castello, a remarkably well preserved rectangular piazza on the site of the 11C–16C castle, whose domed watchtower survives. The attractive houses surround the 17C church.

Piedmont

The ancient principality of **Piedmont**, the cradle of the Italian nation, is divided into the provinces of Turin, Cuneo, Alessandria, Asti, Vercelli, Biella, Novara and Verbania. Physically the region occupies the upper basin of the Po and, as its name implies, lies mainly 'at the foot of the mountains' which encircle it: the Pennine, Graian, Cottian, and Maritime Alps. The cultural relations of Piedmont with France have always been very close, and the French language was used at the Court and Parliament of Turin down to the days of Cavour—its influence survives in the Piedmontese dialects.

Historically Piedmont combines the territories of the old marquisates of Ivrea and Monferrato and the county of Turin; the name Piedmont does not occur until the 13C. In 1045 the territory of Turin came into the hands of the House of Savoy by the marriage of Adelaide of Susa with Otho (Oddone), son of Humbert, Count of Savoy. In the 14C, under the guidance of Amedeo VI and VII, the princely house gained so much power that Amedeo VIII was made Duke of Savoy by the Emperor in 1391.

In the 16C and 18C Saluzzo and Monferrato were added to Piedmont. In 1720 Vittorio Amedeo II, appointed King of Sicily in 1713, was awarded the Kingdom of Sardinia in exchange for Sicily. The Piedmontese kingdom, like all other Italian states, was obliterated by the Napoleonic conquests, but the Treaty of Vienna reinstated the Savoy kings at Turin and gave them suzerainty over Liguria in addition.

Vittorio Emanuele II who, thanks to the astuteness of his minister Cavour, had taken part in the Crimean War and so won the goodwill of France and England, found a powerful though expensive ally in Napoleon III when the second War of Italian Independence, against Austria, broke out in 1859. The Austrian army was crushed in a succession of defeats, and Lombardy was annexed to Piedmont after the final victory of Solferino. The Piedmontese dominions west of the Alps (Savoy and Nice) were handed over to France, and the remaining Italian provinces were added one by one to Vittorio Emanuele's kingdom. In 1865 he transferred his capital from Turin to Florence, and the history of Piedmont became merged in the history of Italy.

16 · Turin

Turin, in Italian *Torino*, the main town (900,000 inhab.) of Piedmont and the capital of the former kingdom of Sardinia, is one of the most important industrial centres of Italy, famous since 1899 as the site of the Fiat car factory. It is regularly built on a Roman plan consciously developed in the 17C–18C, and this gives it the air of a European rather than Italian town. Carlo Alberto, who succeeded to the Savoy throne in 1831, had a profound influence on the appearance of the city, and most of its important art collections date from his time. The centre of the city, with some splendid palaces and churches built in the late 17C and early 18C by Guarini and Juvarra, presents a remarkably homogeneous

19th-century aspect, while trams still traverse the long straight streets, and there are numerous elegant old-fashioned cafés. Although one of the least visited large towns in Italy, Turin has very fine artistic and archaeological collections (many of which are in the process of rearrangement). The city stands on the River Po, on a plain at the foot of the Alps, and there are a number of large parks and grand Savoy residences in the immediate environs.

■ **Information offices.** APT Torino, 226 Via Roma (tel. 011 535181), with an information office at Porta Nuova station. 'Informagiovani' is an information centre for young people (2 Via Assarotti, tel. 011 57654976).

■ **Railway stations.** Porta Nuova (Pl. 9) is the main station, for all services. Porta Susa (Pl. 1) is a secondary station on the Milan, Domodossola and Aosta lines, at which all trains stop; also for the line to Pont Canavese.

■ **Airport.** Caselle (tel. 011 5676361), 16km north, with flights to Europe. **Air terminal** (Pl. 1), Corso Inghilterra (corner of Via Cavalli). Buses to the airport run c every hour.

■ **Car parking** near the centre of the city is difficult. Underground car park in Via Roma. Limited car parking available in Corso Galileo Ferraris (Pl. 5), Piazza Solferino (Pl.6) and near the main railway station (Piazza Carlo Felice; Pl. 9, 10).

■ **Public transport** (run by Consorzio Trasporti Torinesi, tel. 011 167019152). **Trams**: **4**. Via XX Settembre (near the main railway station) to the Duomo. **1**. Stazione Porta Nuova—Corso Vittorio Emanuele II—Stazione Porta Susa. **15**. Station (Corso Vittorio Emanuele)—Via XX Settembre—Piazza Castello—Via Po—Piazza Vittorio Veneto—Via Napione—Corso Regina Margherita—Corso Belgio—Corso Casale—Sassi (for the Superga cogtramway). **13**. Stazione Porta Susa—Via Cernaia—Via Micca—Piazza Castello—Via Po—Piazza Vittorio Veneto—Piazza Gran Madre di Dio (at the foot of Monte de Cappuccini). **16**. Piazza Repubblica—Corso Regina Margherita—Via Rossini—Corso San Maurizio—Via Bava—Piazza Vittorio Veneto—Corso Cairoli—Corso Vittorio Emanuele II—Corso Massimo d'Azeglio (Parco del Valentino).

Buses: **67**. Largo Marconi—Corso Marconi—Corso Massimo d'Azeglio—Piazza Zara—Corso Moncalieri—Moncalieri. **35**. Stazione Porta Nuova—Lingotto.

Suburban buses: **41**. Corso Vittorio—Stupinigi. **36**. Corso Francia—Rivoli.

Country buses depart from the bus station, 3 Corso Inghilterra (Pl. 1) to Sestriere, Milan, Valle d'Aosta, etc., and from Corso Marconi (corner of Via Nizza; Pl. 9) to Cuneo, Saluzzo, Alba, etc.

■ **Hotels.** Turin has numerous hotels all over the city of all categories. **4-star**: *Turin Palace*, 8 Via Sacchi, and *Grand Hotel Sitea*, 35 Via Carlo Alberto. **3-star**: *Piemontese*, 21 Via Berthollet, *Victoria*, 4 Via Nino Costa, and *Venezia*, 70 Via XX Settembre.

■ **Youth hostel**. 1 Via Alby.

■ **Restaurants. A**: *Cambio*, 2 Piazza Carignano; *Al Gatto Nero*, 14 Corso Turati; *Vecchia Lanterna*, 21 Corso Re Umberto; *Monferrato*, 6 Via Monferrato; *Porticciolo*, 58 Via Barletta (specialising in fish); *Tiffany*, 16 Piazza Solferino; *Trait d Union*, 4 Via Stampatori; *Villa Somis*, 138 Strada Val Pattonera (on the outskirts). **B**: *Antiche Sere*, 9 Via Cenischia; *Bocciofila trattoria Unione Famigliare di Reaglie*, 124 Corso Chieri; *Ij Brandè*, 5 Via Massena; *Dai Saletta*, 37 Via Belfiore; *Tre Galline*, 37 Via Bellezia.

■ **Cafés**. *San Carlo*, *Avvignano*, *Torino* and *Stratta*, all in Piazza San Carlo. *Mulassano* and *Baratti*, both in Piazza Castello. *Al Bicerin*, Piazza della Consolata; *Fiorio*, 8 Via Po; and *Platti*, 72 Corso Vittorio Emanuele II.

■ **Theatres**. *Regio* (Pl. 7), Piazza Castello, the opera-house; *Stabile di Torino*, 215 Piazza Castello; *Carignano*, Piazza Carignano; *Alfieri*, Piazza Solferino; *Nuovo*, Palazzo Torino Esposizioni. **Concerts**. *Auditorium della RAI* (Pl. 7), 15 Via Rossini; *Conservatorio Giuseppe Verdi*, 11 Via Mazzini.

History

The marriage of Countess Adelaide (died 1090), heiress of a line of French counts of Savoy, to Oddone (Otho), son of Humbert 'the White-Handed', united the Cisalpine and Transalpine possessions of the House of Savoy, and Turin became their capital. After a period of semi-independence in the 12–13C, the city consistently followed the fortunes of the princely house of Savoy. In 1506–62 it was occupied by the French, but it was awarded to Duke Emanuele Filiberto 'the Iron-Headed' by the Treaty of Cateau-Cambrésis (1559). It was besieged in 1639–40, and again in 1706 when it was saved from the French by the heroic action of Pietro Micca (see page 199).

From 1720 Turin was capital of the kingdom of Sardinia, and after the Napoleonic occupation (1798–1814) it became a centre of Italian nationalism and the headquarters of Camillo Cavour (1810–61), a native of the town and the prime mover of Italian liberty. The writer Silvio Pellico lived here from 1838 until his death in 1854. In 1861–65 it was the capital of Vittorio Emanuele II (1820–78) as king of Italy. During the Second World War, Allied air raids caused heavy damage. After the war ugly new suburbs grew up around the city to accommodate the huge number of immigrants from the south of Italy who came here to find work.

Among famous natives of Turin were the writer Primo Levi (1919–87) and writer and artist Carlo Levi (1902–75).

The centre of the civic life of Turin is included in the large quadrangular area lying between Corso Vittorio Emanuele, Corso Galileo Ferraris, Corso Regina Margherita, Corso San Maurizio, and the Po. Roughly bisecting this area is the fashionable VIA ROMA (Pl. 6), lined with wide arcades, which connects the main station with Piazza Castello; on either side of it and parallel with it are streets laid out at right angles.

Piazza San Carlo

The main railway station, **Stazione di Porta Nuova** (Pl. 9) was built in 1868 and has a monumental façade in the form of an arch which was designed to close the vista from Via Roma. It faces Piazza Carlo Felice (1823–55), with a garden. Half-way along Via Roma is the arcaded PIAZZA SAN CARLO (Pl. 6) a handsome monumental square begun in 1640. Here are the twin churches of **San Carlo** and **Santa Cristina**, the latter with a façade by Filippo Juvarra (1715–18) and 18C stucco decoration in the interior. The **monument to **Duke Emanuele Filiberto** (1838), whose equestrian figure ('El caval d'brôns') is shown sheathing his sword after the victory of St Quentin (1557), is considered the masterpiece of the local sculptor Carlo Marochetti. The two long yellow and grey palazzi have wide porticoes, beneath which are several cafés, including, on the corner of Via San Teresa, the well-known Caffè San Carlo. On the opposite side of the piazza, **Palazzo Solaro del Borgo** (No. 183), partly reconstructed by Benedetto Alfieri in 1753, is the seat of the Accademia Filarmonica and the Circolo del Whist, an exclusive club with delightful 18C premises.

At the end of the piazza (right; entrance on Via Accademia delle Scienze) is the **Palazzo dell'Accademia delle Scienze** (Pl. 6), with a fine exterior, built for the Jesuits by Guarino Guarini (1678). The Accademia delle Scienze, founded in 1757, has had its seat here since 1783. The building also houses the Egyptian Museum and the Galleria Sabauda.

Egyptian Museum

The famous *Egyptian Museum (open 9–19; fest. 9–14; closed Mon) has the third most important collection of Egyptian antiquities in existence, after Cairo and London. It is at present undergoing radical restoration and reorganisation. The real founder of this remarkable museum was Carlo Felice, who in 1824 bought the collections of Bernardo Drovetti, the trusted counsellor of Mohammed Ali. Later important acquisitions came from the expeditions of Schiaparelli (1903–20) and Farina (1930–37), notably in the Theban region, at Ghebelein (Aphroditopolis), Qau el-Kebir (Antaepolis, near Assiut) and Heliopolis. The museum played a leading part in the rescue digs in Nubia before the completion of the Aswan high dam, and was rewarded with the rock temple of Ellessya, which was transported by sea in sections via Genoa in 1967 and then reconstructed.

The large sculptures are on the **ground floor**. **Room I**. Black diorite *statue of Rameses II (1299–33 BC), statues of Amenhotep II and Thothmes I; Horemheb and his wife; figures of Sekhmet and Ptah.

Room II. Seated *figure of Thothmes III (1496–1422 BC) and statue of Tutankhamen, with the god Amen-ra. Another room contains the reconstructed **rock temple of Ellessya** (15C BC), with its bas-relief frieze showing Thothmes III.

In an underground room (where parts of the Roman wall of Turin are visible) are finds from the excavations of Schiaparelli, including a fragment of painted linen (c 3500 BC).

First floor. In **Room I** (right) are the most important discoveries from Heliopolis, Qau el-Kebir (limestone heads), Ghebelein, and Deir el Medina (tomb-gateway and wooden statuettes). **Room II** contains mummies and mummy-cases, scarabs, amulets, Canopic vases, ushabti figures, etc.

Room III. Archaeological material arranged chronologically, from the Predynastic to the Coptic periods, giving an excellent idea of the evolution of Egypt over the centuries. The reconstructed tomb of Khaiè, director of the works at the Necropolis of Thebes, and his wife Meriè (XVIII Dynasty) preserves intact its furniture, food, cooking utensils, etc. The small **Room IV** contains textiles.

Room V contains administrative and literary papyri with architectural plans and plans of gold mines; a love poem; the Royal Papyrus, with a list of the Kings of Egypt from the Sun to the XVII Dynasty; the Papyrus of the Palace Conspiracy (XX Dyn.); writing materials, rolls of papyrus, etc. **Room VI**. Objects showing the daily life of the Egyptians: clothes, furniture, toilet articles and some interesting jewels. **Room VII**. Statuettes of animal deities. **Room VIII** contains mural paintings from the tomb of Iti at Ghebelein (c 2100 BC).

Galleria Sabauda

The *Galleria Sabauda (open 9–14, exc. Mon), on the second and third floors, had as a nucleus the collections of paintings made by the princes of the House of Savoy, from the 16C onwards, and was first opened to the public in 1832 by Carlo Alberto. Remarkably rich in Flemish and Dutch works acquired in 1741 through Eugenio of Savoy, it is interesting also for its paintings by Venetian and Piedmontese masters, some of them hardly represented elsewhere. Recent acquisitions include works by Rubens, Defendente Ferrari and David Teniers. The works are arranged in two distinct groupings: the Savoy family collections,and the acquisitions made after 1832. Rearrangement has been in progress since 1987.

Second floor. The first section illustrates the birth of the collection with works acquired c 1550–1630. Works by Roger van der Weyden, Gaudenzio Ferrari, **Mantegna** (*Madonna), Veronese, court painters (including Moncalvo), Orazio Gentileschi (*Annunciation, painted in 1623 for Carlo Emanuele I), Guercino, Morazzone, Giulio Cesare Procaccini, Cerano and Rubens.

The second section, displayed in one large gallery, illustrates the history of the collection from the time of Vittorio Amedeo I to Vittorio Amedeo II (1630–1730).

Here are displayed works by Francesco Duquesnoy, Francesco Albani, Francesco Cairo (1598–1674), and Guercino. The *Children of Charles I (1635) by **Van Dyck** was presented by Henrietta Maria, Charles' queen, to her sister Cristina of Savoy.

The third section has works reflecting the artistic taste of the Savoy court from 1730 to 1830. These include: two *views of Turin commissioned by Carlo Emanuele III in 1745 from **Bernardo Bellotto**, and works by Carlo Andrea Van Loo, Sebastiano Conca, Pompeo Batoni, Anton Raphael Mengs and Elisabeth Vigée-Lebrun. The copies on porcelain of famous works owned by the Tuscan grand-dukes and acquired by Carlo Alberto in 1826 are by Abraham Constantin.

The fourth section is dedicated to the works collected by Prince Eugenio in 1737–41, including some by Nicolas Poussin, Carlo Cignani, Francesco Albani and Guido Reni (*St John the Baptist*). The superb **Flemish and Dutch collection** includes works by: Cornelis Engelbrechtsz, Jan van Eyck, Petrus Christus, Rembrandt (*Old Man Asleep, perhaps the artist's father), Willem van de Velde the Younger, Jacob van Ruisdael, Hans Memling (*_Passion of Christ_), Bernart van Orley, Paulus Potter, David Teniers the Younger, Jan van Huysum, Jan Brueghel, Phillipe Wouwerman, Paul Mignard, Jan de Heem, Gerard Dou, Holbein the Younger and Van Dyck (*Madonna and Child). The *Portrait of a young boy was formerly attributed to Van Dyck.

The rest of the collection, which contains the works acquired by the gallery from 1832 onwards, is still in the course of rearrangement. The **Piedmontese school** is represented by Macrino d'Alba, Gaudenzio Ferrari, Bernardino Lanino, Girolamo Giovenone, Defendente Ferrari and Giovanni Martino Spanzotti. Among the works of the **Tuscan school** are a *Madonna (c 1433) by Fra Angelico, *_Tobias and the Archangel Raphael_ by Piero and Antonio Pollaiolo, *_Tobias, and the Three Archangels_ by Filippino Lippi, and a *Madonna and Saints by Sodoma. Also here are works by the **Lombard school** (Bergognone, Moretto, Savoldo, Giampietrino and Cesare da Sesto) and **Venetian school** (Giovanni Bellini, Veronese, Tintoretto and Francesco Bassano).

The **Gualino collection**, donated to the museum in 1928, contains good Italian paintings (including a Madonna attributed to Duccio di Buoninsegna, and works by Taddeo di Bartolo, Veronese, and Jacopo Sansovino); German paintings; ancient sculpture; Byzantine, Roman and medieval ivories; gold-smiths' work; Chinese works (good 6C head); medieval furniture; and lace.

The **modern collection**, with works by Italian painters between the two world wars, is not at present on view.

Opposite the palace, on the corner of Via Accademia delle Scienze, is the large church of **San Filippo Neri** (Pl. 6), rebuilt by Filippo Juvarra (c 1714), with a Corinthian pronaos by Giuseppe Talucchi (1823). The fine Baroque interior (with, unexpectedly, a parquet floor) has a high altar by Antonio Bertola (1697) with an altarpiece by Carlo Maratta, and a painting by Francesco Trevisani.

Palazzo Carignano

Just beyond Palazzo dell'Accademia delle Scienze, on Piazza Carignano, is Palazzo Carignano (Pl. 6), the residence of the princes of Savoy until 1831 (being restored). It has an interesting Baroque front, faced with brick, by Guarino Guarini (1679), and an oval vestibule with a pretty double staircase. The east façade on Piazza Carlo Alberto dates from 1864–71.

The palace was the birthplace (1798) of Carlo Alberto and (1820) of Vittorio Emanuele II, and it was used for the meetings of the lower house of the Subalpine Parliament (1848–59) and of the first Italian Parliament (1861–64). On the piano nobile is the **Museo Nazionale del Risorgimento** (open 9–18.30; fest. 9–12.30; closed Mon), founded in 1878 and one of the most important of its kind. The fine hall of the Subalpine Parliament is also shown.

Piazza Carlo Alberto has a bronze equestrian statue of Carlo Alberto by Marochetti (1861). Here is the **Biblioteca Nazionale**, with over 850,000 volumes and some 5000 MSS, mainly from religious institutions in Piedmont. At No. 9 Via Bogino is the 17C Palazzo Graneri della Roccia, seat of the Circolo degli Artisti, founded in 1855 and closed to women until 1987.

In Piazza Carignano, with a monument by Giovanni Albertoni (1859) to the philosopher Vincenzo Gioberti (1801–52), is the **Teatro Carignano**, recon-structed in 1787 by Giovanni Battista Feroggio. Here Vittorio Alfieri's tragedy

Cleopatra was given its first performance in 1775. In the square is the celebrated Ristorante del Cambio, famous as a meeting place during the Risorgimento.

Piazza Castello

Via Roma ends in the huge rectangular PIAZZA CASTELLO (Pl. 6; 7), the centre of the city, laid out by Ascanio Vittozzi in 1584 around the castle, now called Palazzo Madama. It is surrounded by uniform monumental buildings with porticoes, and near Via Roma is a skyscraper of 1934. Several trams traverse the piazza which is lit by attractive street lamps. Beneath the porticoes, on the corner nearest Via Accademia delle Scienze are two elegant cafés (*Mulassano* and *Baratti*, with elaborate decorations by Edoardo Rubino) on either side of the **Galleria dell'Industria Subalpina** (Pl. 6), a delightful shopping arcade built in 1873–74 by Pietro Carrera. In the centre of the square, beside Palazzo Madama, is a monument to the Duke of Aosta (died 1931) by Eugenio Baroni (1937), and war memorials by Vincenzo Vela (1859) and Pietro Canonica (1923).

Palazzo Madama

Palazzo Madama (Pl. 6; 7), the most imposing of the old buildings of Turin, is a four-square castle of the 15C, one side of which has been replaced by a characteristic wing and façade of 1718–21, by Filippo Juvarra.

A castle was begun here after 1276 by William VII of Monferrato on the site of the Roman Porta Praetoria, the east gate of the Roman city. The palace takes its present name from the two regents, Maria Cristina, widow of Vittorio Amedeo I, and Giovanna Battista, widow of Carlo Emanuele II; both were entitled 'Madama Reale', and both resided here and 'improved' the old castle. The palazzo was the seat in 1848–60 of the Subalpine Senate and in 1861–65 of the Italian Senate.

Since 1935 the palace has housed the *MUSEO CIVICO DI ARTE ANTICA, which has been closed since 1988 for restoration. It is hoped that it will be partially reopened in 1998. The contents include Romanesque, Gothic and Renaissance sculpture, including works by Tino da Camaino and Bambaia (reliefs from the tomb of Gaston de Foix). The precious collection of codexes includes the illuminated 14C statutes of the city of Turin and the celebrated *Book of Hours of the Duc de Berry (*Les Très Riches Heures de Milan*, c 1450), illustrated by Jan van Eyck. The paintings include a *Portrait of a man by Antonello da Messina, signed and dated 1476, one of his best and last works. There is also a very fine collection of decorative arts.

On the **first floor**, beyond the Salone Centrale (the seat of the Senate—see above) are the **Royal Apartments**. Some of the furniture here dates from the time of Carlo Emanuele II (died 1675), but the fittings are mainly in early 18C style, with paintings by Vittorio Amedeo Cignaroli and sculptures by Simon Troger. One room was frescoed by Domenico Guidobono (1714), with 18C tapestries of local weave, after Cignaroli.

In the northeast corner of the square, beneath the arcades, is the **Teatro Regio** (Pl. 7), rebuilt in 1973, with a disappointing interior. Remnants of the old theatre, burnt down in 1936, survive behind the modern buildings. Further on, beneath the portico, is the Prefettura (No. 201).

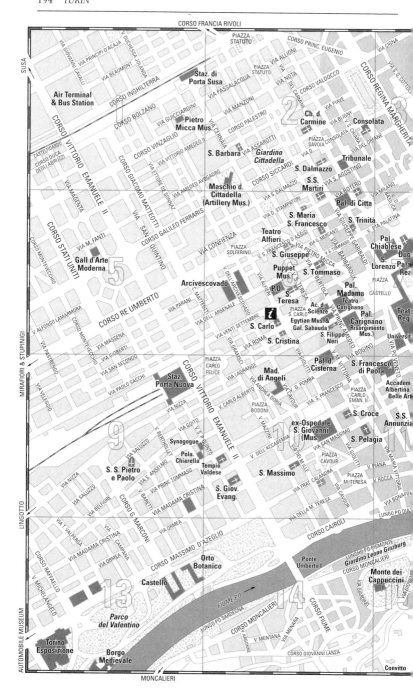

LANZO

CHIVASSO

Istit. Salesiano

Cottolengo

V. CIGNA

VIA CIRIE

CORSO VERONA

CORSO GIULIO CESARE

VIA NOVARA

EUGENIO

VALDOCCO

CORSO REGINA MARGHERITA

VIA S. E. COTTOLENGO

PIAZZA BORGO DORA

Staz. Cirie-Lanzo Torinese

VIA VITTORIO ANDREIS

Ponte C. Mosca

CORSO GIULIO CESARE

CORSO BEMILIA

VIA AOSTA

CORSO PALERMO

VIA COMO V. R. LEONCAVALLO

VIA PIAVE

VIA BLIGNY

Consolata

VIA DEL ORFANE

VIA CHIARA

ZZA OIA

Tribunale

S. AGOSTINO

CORSO GIULIO CESARE

PIAZZA DELLA REPUBBLICA

VIA ALESSANDRIA

VIA BOLOGNA

VIA PADOVA

CORSO NOVARA

VIA BOTERO

Pal. di Citta

S. Trinità

VIA MILANO

PIAZZA MILANO

S. Maurizio e Lazzaro

Porta Palatina

VIA C. UNDICI FEBBRAIO

LUNGO DORA FIRENZE

CORSO PALERMO

VIA PERUGIA

CORSO BRESCIA

VIA VERONA

VIA GIUSEPPE GARIBALDI

V. PTA PALATINA

Teatro Romano

VIA PISA

VIA PARMA

VIA MODENA

CORSO VERONA

CANTI

STOMMASE BARBAROUX

Pal. Chiablese

Duomo

Palazzo Reale

TOCCHETTO

CORSO REGIO PARCO

S. Lorenzo

Ponte Regio Parco

VIA MESSINA

VIA REGGIO

Pal. Madama

PIAZZA CASTELLO

Armeria Reale

Giardino Reale

V. PRIMO MAGGIO

V. DEI PARTIGIANI

Teatro Carignano

Pal. Carignano (Risorgimento Mus.)

Teatro Regio

Accademia Militare

Auditorium RAI

Ponte Rossini

CORSO VERONA

VIA C. M. BUSCALIONI

Cimitero

Filippo Neri

VIA MATTITORIA

Università

VIA ROSSINI

LUNGO DORA FIRENZE

DORA RIPARIA

LUNGO DORA SIENNA

Ponte Carlo Emanuele I

S. Francesco di Paola

VIA PO

VIA BOGINO

VIA MONTEBELLO

VIA SANTA GIULIA

CORSO REGINA MARGHERITA

RICASOLI

LUNGO DORA VOGHERA

S. FRANCESCO

PIAZZA CARLO EMAN. II

Accademia Albertina di Belle Arti

Mole Antonelliana

VIA GIUSEPPE VERDI

VIA TARINO

VIA SANT OTTAVIO

ola ng.

S. Croce

S.S. Annunziata

VIA AMEDEO AVOGADRO

VIA GUASTALLA

VIA BUNIVA

BAROLO

CORSO C. L. FARINI

CORSO NOVARA

VIA MANIN

S. Pelagia

VIA SAN MASSIMO

VIA DIRITTI

CORSO SAN MAURIZIO

VIA GIULIA

VIA DEGLI ARTISTI

CORSO

FONTANESI

ZZA OUR

V. PIANA

VIA MARIA VITTORIA

N. ROCCA

PIAZZA VITTORIO VENETO

VIA VANCHIGLIA

VIA DI

VIA

BELGIO

VIA CAVOUR

PIAZZA M TERESA

VIA BONAFOUS

VIA BAVA

VIA NAPIONE

CORSO TORTONA

CORSO MONGRANDO

VIA ANDORNO

LUNGO PO CADORNA

VIA MACHIAVELLI

RSO CAIROLI

LUNGO PO DIAZ

Ponte Vitt. Emanuele I

FIUME PO

Parco Ignazio Michelotti

Ponte Regina Margherita

LUNGO PO ANTONELLI

PIAZZA GRAN MADRE DI DIO

PIAZZA BORROMINI

LUNGHO PO PIEMONTE

Giardino Leone Ginzburg

CORSO MONCALIERI

V. MONFERRATO

VIA COSMO

Gran Madre di Dio

CORSO CASALE

Monte dei Cappuccini

VIA V. GIOVANNINI

VIA V. MANCINI

VIA MARTIRI

VIA CARO MAURIZIO

VIA ROMANI

VIA D. LIBERTA

VIA MONCALVO

VIA BRICCA

VIA ASTI

CORSO GABETTI

CORSO GIOVANNI LANZA

VIA G. LANZA

VIA VILLA DELLA REGINA

CORSO SELLA

SASSI, BASILICA OF SUPERGA

0   300 yards

0   300 metres

PIAZZALE V. D. REGINA

RSO

Convitto

Il Fortino

C. ALBERTO PICCO

TURIN

VILLA D. REGINA

Armeria Reale

At No. 191 is the entrance to the *Armeria Reale (Pl. 7; visitors are admitted every 45 minutes; Tue & Thu 14.30–19.30; Wed, Fri & Sat 9–14; closed Sun & Mon), housed in a wing of the Palazzo Reale (see below). The Royal Armoury is one of the most important in Europe, and includes some remarkable pieces by the great Bavarian and Austrian armourers and gunsmiths. It was transferred here by Carlo Alberto and opened to the public in 1837. The monumental stair-case, designed by Filippo Juvarra and built by Benedetto Alfieri, leads up to the three 18C–19C galleries which provide a magnificent setting for the collection. The so-called **Rotonda** (from 'rondò') was decorated in 1841–45 by Pelagio Pelagi. Here are displayed the collections of the last princes of the House of Savoy, and arms and ensigns of the Risorgimento period. The splendid **Galleria Beaumont**, designed by Filippo Juvarra in 1733, is named after Claudio Francesco Beaumont who painted the vault in 1738–64, and contains a superb display of about 30 complete suits of armour (12 equestrian), some of which were made for the Martinengo family of Brescia. In the **Medagliere** are displayed oriental arms.

The **Biblioteca Reale** has 150,000 volumes, 5000 MSS, and many minia-tures and drawings collected by Carlo Alberto, including a self-portrait of Leonardo da Vinci, and works by Dürer, Rembrandt and Raphael.

Palazzo Reale

The PIAZZETTA REALE, with railings by Pelagio Pelagi of 1842 surmounted by statues of the Dioscuri by Abbondio Sangiorgio, precedes Palazzo Reale (Pl. 7; open 9–19, exc. Mon), the former royal residence, built for Madama Reale Cristina of France, with a façade on the piazzetta by Amedeo di Castellamonte (1646–60). The Chapel of the Sacra Sindone was built in 1694 to contain the Holy Shroud in the west wing of the palace, adjoining the apse of the cathedral (described below); its delightful spiral dome by Guarino Guarini is well seen from here.

The **state apartments** on the first floor (shown on conducted tours) were lavishly decorated from the mid-17C to the mid-19C, with some good ceilings and floors; they contain furniture (some by Pietro Piffetti), porcelain and tapes-tries. The Gabinetto Cinese is a delightful work by Filippo Juvarra. The Galleria del Daniele was begun in 1684 by Daniel Seyter. The charming neo-classical dancing figures in the Sala da Ballo were painted by Carlo Bellosio and Francesco Gonin (1842). The *Scala degli Forbici is an ingenious staircase by Filippo Juvarra (1720).

The **Giardino Reale**, approached through the palace, is normally open from May–Oct, daily 9–dusk. The garden was enlarged by André Le Nôtre in 1697 for Carlo Emanuele II but has since been altered. In the centre is a fountain by Simone Martinez (c 1750).

San Lorenzo and the Duomo

In Piazza Castello is the church of San Lorenzo (Pl. 7), formerly the chapel royal, a superb Baroque work by Guarino Guarini, with a delightful cupola and lantern. The beautifully lit *interior (1667) has a complex plan.

The duomo (Pl. 7) was built in 1491–98 for Archbishop Domenico della Rovere by Meo del Caprino and other Tuscans, after three churches had been demolished to make way for it. It has a Renaissance façade, and a campanile (1468–70) completed by Juvarra in 1720. Behind can be seen the delightful Baroque cupola of the chapel of the Sacra Sindone (see above).

The **interior** contains 15C tombs and a *polyptych, in a fine Gothic frame, attributed to Giovanni Martino Spanzotti, with delightful little pictures of the life of Saints Crispin and Crispinian including scenes of mercantile life.

Behind the apse is the **Chapel of the Holy Shroud** (Cappella della Sacra Sindone; severly damaged by fire in 1997) by Guarino Guarini (1668–94). It has black marble walls, and family monuments erected in 1842 by Carlo Alberto. On the altar is the urn containing the Holy Shroud in which the body of Christ was traditionally believed to have been wrapped after his descent from the Cross. This greatly revered sacred relic was said to have been taken from Jerusalem to Cyprus, and from there to France in the 15C, and to have been brought to Turin by Emanuele Filiberto in 1578. On the linen shroud (4·36 x 1·10m) is the negative image of a crucified man. In 1988 the Archbishop of Turin announced that scientific research using carbon 14 dating had proved that this icon must have been made between 1260 and 1390, but discussion still continues about its origins. It is kept in a silver casket inside an iron box enclosed in a marble case. The shroud will next be shown in 1998.

Beside the campanile are the pretty railings in front of a wing of Palazzo Reale (see above), built in 1900. Here are the ruins of a **Roman Theatre** (1C AD). On the left, in an unattractive setting, is a stretch of Roman and medieval wall beside the conspicuous ***Porta Palatina** (Pl. 7), an exceptionally well preserved two-arched Roman gate flanked by two 16-sided towers. This was the Porta Principalis Sinistra in the wall of the Roman colony *Augusta Taurinorum*.

In a garden house of Palazzo Reale (entrance at No. 105 Corso Regina Margherita) is the **Museo di Antichità** (open 9–19 exc. Mon), still in the course of arrangement. The archaeological material includes objects discovered mainly in Piedmont and Liguria from the Stone Age up to the Barbarian invasions. Roman finds include the Marengo treasure discovered in 1928, with a silver bust of Emperor Lucius Verus (reigned 161–69).

Via Garibaldi

At Piazza Castello begins the handsome VIA GARIBALDI (Pl. 6, 2), a pedestrianised street about 1km long, lined with some characteristic 18C balconied palaces. On the right at this end is the church of the **Trinità** (1590–1606), by Ascanio Vittozzi, with a marble interior by Filippo Juvarra (1718). It contains fine carved confessionals. In Via Porta Palatina on the right is the church of **Corpus Domini** (1607–71), also by Vittozzi, with a lavishly decorated interior by Benedetto Alfieri. In this church, in 1728, Jean Jacques Rousseau abjured the Protestant faith.

From here Via Porta Palatina leads into PIAZZA DI PALAZZO DI CITTÀ, laid out in 1756 by Benedetto Alfieri, with a bronze monument to the 'Green Count' Amadeus VI (died 1383), the conqueror of the Turks, by Pelagio Pelagi (1853). Here is **Palazzo di Città** (Pl. 6), the town hall, begun in 1659 by Francesco Lanfranchi and modified a century later by Benedetto Alfieri. The nearby church of **San Domenico** (Pl. 2) dates from 1354, and its belfry from 1451. It contains a painting by Guercino and a chapel with 14C frescoes.

Via Milano, a less elegant street, leads from San Domenico past the huge elliptical domed church of **Santi Maurizio e Lazzaro**, begun in 1679 by Carlo Emanuele Lanfranchi, with a neo-classical façade by Carlo Bernardo Mosca. Beyond lies the large PIAZZA DELLA REPUBBLICA (Pl. 3), known locally as Porta Palazzo, the scene of a popular general market (and, on Saturdays and the second Sunday of the month, of the 'Balôn' antiques market). In Via Cottolengo, to the north, are two noted charitable institutions of Piedmontese origin: the **Cottolengo**, founded for the aged infirm in 1828 by St Joseph Benedict Cottolengo (1786–1842), and the **Istituto Salesiano**, established in 1846 by St John Bosco (1815–88) for the education of poor boys, with the basilica of **Maria Santissima Ausiliatrice** by Antonio Spezia (1865–68).

Further on in Via Garibaldi (left) is the church of the **Santi Martiri** (Pl. 6), begun in 1577 probably by Pellegrino Tibaldi, with an 18C cupola by Bernardino Quadri and a good Baroque interior. The frescoed ceiling is by Luigi Vacca (1836) and the high altar by Filippo Juvarra.

Next door is the **Cappella dei Banchieri e Mercanti** (No. 25; Pl. 2, 6; open Sat afternoon, or by appointment, tel. 011 5627226), a delightful Baroque chapel dating from the late 17C, with paintings by Andrea Pozzo, Stefano Maria Legnani, Carlo Innocenzo Carlone and others, in huge black frames decorated in gold. The painted wood statues are by Carlo Giuseppe Plura, and the vault is frescoed by Legnano. The high altar is by Filippo Juvarra. The benches and lanterns survive intact, and there is a good organ of 1748–50. In the sacristy is an ingenious mechanical calendar constructed by Antonio Plana in 1831.

Further on in Via Garibaldi, Via della Consolata diverges right through Piazza Savoia, with an obelisk, to the church of the **Consolata** (Pl. 2), a popular place of worship made up from the union of two churches by Guarino Guarini (1679), one oval, the other hexagonal.

In Via Piave, which also diverges right from Via Garibaldi, is the 18C church of the **Sudario** (being restored), next to a museum dedicated to the Holy Shroud.

Via Garibaldi ends in Piazza dello Statuto, laid out in 1864, with a monument (1879) to the engineers of the Mont Cenis railway tunnel.

The western districts

From Piazza San Carlo, Via Santa Teresa leads to **Santa Teresa** (Pl. 6), a Baroque church probably by Andrea Costaguta (1642–74), hemmed in between two modern buildings. It contains an altarpiece by Sebastiano Conca. Next to the church is the **Teatro Gianduja**, the puppet theatre of the Lupi family (performances on fest. at 16), with a delightful *Puppet Museum** (Pl. 6; open 9–13; Sun 15–18; closed Sat), with puppets, backcloths, etc. collected by the family since the 18C.

Via Santa Teresa continues to the large Piazza Solferino. Here VIA PIETRO MICCA (Pl. 6), an elegant street with a portico on one side, leads towards Piazza Castello. Laid out in 1894 on a diagonal line, it has a conspicuous neo-Gothic palace by Carlo Ceppi.

Via Cernaia continues the line of Via Santa Teresa west to the **Mastio** (Pl. 2), or keep, of the old citadel (1564–68), the rest of which was demolished in 1857. It contains the **Museo Nazionale di Artiglieria** (Pl. 2; closed for restoration), founded by Carlo Emanuele III in 1731 and on this site since 1899. It is one of the most important artillery museums in Italy.

Further on, on the corner of Via Guicciardini, is the RAI (Italian radio and television company) skyscraper (1965–68). At No. 7 in Via Guicciardini is the **Museo Pietro Micca** (Pl. 1; open Tue, Wed, Fri & Sat 9–19; Thu. 9–13, 15–21; fest. 9–13, 14–19; closed Mon), with material relating to the French siege of 1706. Part of the remarkable underground defence works (which extend for several kilometres beneath the city) can be visited. Pietro Micca was a Piedmontese sapper who exploded a mine here and saved the city from the French at the cost of his own life.

From the Mastio (see above), Corso Galileo Ferraris leads south for nearly 1km across Corso Vittorio Emanuele II to Via Magenta, in which (right) is the entrance to a building of 1956 which houses the **Galleria Civica d'Arte Moderna e Contemporanea** (Pl. 5; open Tue, Wed., Fri & Sat 9–19; Thu 9–13, 15–21; fest. 9–13, 14–19. Founded in 1863 and reopened in 1993, this is one of the most important collections of 19C and 20C painting in Italy.

On the **second floor** are 19C works by Francesco Hayez, Antonio Canova, Massimo d'Azeglio, Vincenzo Vela, Antonio Fontanesi, Giuseppe Pellizza da Volpedo, Giacomo Favretto, Mosè Bianchi, Vincenzo Gemito, the Macchiaioli (Telemaco Signorini, Silvestro Lega, Giovanni Fattori), and works by French artists (Renoir, Courbet).

First floor. Early 20C artists represented include Leonardo Bistolfi, Umberto Boccioni, Giacomo Balla, Giorgio De Chirico, Armando Spadini, Felice Carena, Gino Severini, Felice Casorati, Giorgio Morandi, Carlo Carrà, Antonio Donghi, Alberto Savinio and Filippo De Pisis. There are also works by the artists (including Carlo Levi) known as the 'Gruppo dei Sei', influential in Turin from about 1928 until 1935. Another wing has an extensive collection of works from the 1950s and 1960s. Contemporary works are displayed on the **ground floor**.

Nearby, at No. 8 Via Bricherasio, in a palace built in 1898, is the **Museo Civico di Numismatica Etnografia e Arte Orientale** (open as for the Galleria d'Arte Moderna). It contains Greek, Roman and Byzantine coins; ethnographical material collected from 1864 onwards; and a section on oriental art.

Via Po and the Mole Antonelliana

From Piazza Castello the arcaded VIA PO (Pl. 7, 11), the main street of the east district of Turin, leads towards the river. On the left at No. 17 is the **University** (Pl. 7), with a brick façade facing Via Verdi. The college, which has a chequered history dating back to the early 15C, has occupied its present site since 1720. Erasmus took a degree here in theology in 1506. On the right is the church of **San Francesco di Paola**, containing 17C sculptures by Tommaso Carlone. Beyond, in Via dell'Accademia Albertina (right) is the **Accademia Albertina di Belle Arti** (Pl. 11), an academy of fine arts founded in 1678, with the **Pinacoteca dell'Accademia Albertina**, a picture gallery (adm. usually on request 10–12), principally of interest for its 60 drawings by Gaudenzio Ferrari and his bottega, as well as paintings by Filippo Lippi, Bernardino Lanino, and Piedmontese masters.

Via Accademia dell'Albertina leads through Piazza Carlo Emanuele II, with a monument to Cavour by Giovanni Dupré (1873), to the former **Ospedale di San Giovanni** (Pl. 10), where the university museums of zoology, anatomy, mineralogy and geology are being arranged.

Off the other side of Via Po, in Via Montebello, rises the ***MOLE ANTONELLIANA** (Pl. 11), which has become the symbol of Turin. Begun in 1863 as a synagogue, it is the most famous work of the Piedmontese architect Alessandro Antonelli and, with its extraordinary shape and enormous height, is an amazing feat of engineering skill. It was finished by the municipality in 1897 and became a monument of Italian Unity, when the Risorgimento museum (now in Palazzo Carignano, see above) was first opened here. The building was much admired by Nietzsche. The terrace (86m; view) is reached by a lift (Tue–Fri, 10–16; Sat & fest. 9–19; closed Mon); the granite spire, 167m high, was rebuilt in aluminium after it lost its upper 47m in a gale in 1953.

In Via Po the Palazzo degli Stemmi is being restored to house the **Cinema Museum**, which has an absorbing collection founded in the 1950s. It illustrates the history of photography and cinema in Italy and abroad, and incorporates an important film library.

Via Po ends in the spacious Piazza Vittorio Veneto (Pl. 11), laid out in 1825–30, beyond which Ponte Vittorio Emanuele I leads across the Po.

The right bank of the Po

At the end of Ponte Vittorio Emanuele I is the church of the **Gran Madre di Dio** (Pl. 15), built by Bonsignore in 1818–31, in imitation of the Pantheon at Rome, to celebrate the return from exile of Vittorio Emanuele I (1814). The king's monument, by Giuseppe Gaggini, stands in front of the church. On the banks of the river here are pleasant public gardens.

From Piazza di Gran Madre di Dio, Via Villa della Regina leads straight to the Baroque **Villa della Regina** (Pl. 15), built for Cardinal Maurizio of Savoy on a design probably by Ascanio Vittozzi, executed by Amedeo di Castellamonte in 1620. It was altered in the 18C by Filippo Juvarra. The villa is named after Marie-Anne d'Orléans, queen of Vittorio Amedeo II, who resided here. It has a beautiful park and garden laid out in terraces on the hillside in the style of a Roman villa. After years of neglect it is being restored and may be opened to the public.

From Corso Moncalieri (right) Via Giardino ascends to the wooded **Monte dei Cappuccini** (283m; Pl. 15), on whose summit are a Capuchin church by Ascanio Vittozzi (1596), and convent, and the **Museo Nazionale della Montagna 'Duca degli Abruzzi'** (open Sat, Sun & Mon 9–12.30, 14.30–19; Tue–Fri 8.30–19). Founded by the Club Alpino Italiano in 1863, it illustrates the history of mountaineering, with mementoes of the most famous ascents in Italy. A section with relief maps and models is dedicated to the geology of the mountains and their vegetation. There is also an observatory with a panorama of the western Alps, including Monte Rosa.

The Parco del Valentino

The beautiful Parco del Valentino (Pl. 14, 13), laid out on the left bank of the Po, was opened in 1856. It contains a fine Botanic Garden (open by appointment only, tel. 011 6699884), founded in 1729, with a museum and library, containing the remarkable Iconographia Taurinensis made up of 7500 botanical drawings dated 1752–1868. The Castello del Valentino (under restoration), was built in 1630–60 by Maria Cristina in the style of a French château.

The reproductions of a medieval Piedmontese village (open 8–20) and

castle in the Valle d'Aosta (open 9.30–17 exc. Mon; fest. 10.30–17) were erected for the Turin exhibition of 1884. In the park, nearby, is the fine equestrian monument of Prince Amedeo, the masterpiece of Davide Calandra (1902).

At the southwest end of the park is an exhibition ground with various buildings erected between 1938 and 1950, some of them by Pier Luigi Nervi. **Palazzo Torino-Esposizioni**, was built in 1948 for the first Motor Show (now held at the Lingotto, see below).

Beyond the park the Corso Massimo d'Azeglio is prolonged as Corso Unità d'Italia, where (No. 40; 2km further) is the splendid ***MUSEO DELL'AUTOMO-BILE Carlo Biscaretti di Ruffia** (open 10–18.30 exc. Mon), founded in 1933. The building, designed by Amedeo Albertini, contains an international collection of vehicles, admirably displayed and technically documented.

Further on still, overlooking the river, is the huge **Palazzo del Lavoro**, designed by Pier Luigi Nervi for the 1961 exhibition.

In Via Nizza (see Pl. 9), parallel to Corso Unità to the west, beside the railway, is the huge **Lingotto Fiat factory**, which started production in 1923 and closed down in 1983. The interesting building, which has played an important part in the history of the industrialisation of the city, has a test circuit on the roof. In 1991 part of it was demolished and part converted by Renzo Piano into an exhibition and congress centre (also used for concerts). The Turin Motor Show is now appropriately held here (biennially in April–May). The **Mirafiori Fiat factory**, built in 1935–38 and extended 1958–70, where the Fiat motorworks now operate, is to the west, across Corso Unione Sovietica and Corso Giovanni Agnelli.

17 · The environs of Turin

The environs of Turin are notable for their 18C royal Savoy palaces, some of them surrounded by large parks, the most famous of which is the royal hunting lodge at Stupinigi, built by Filippo Juvarra (it is, however, under restoration). On the outskirts of the city is the Basilica of Superga, Juvarra's masterpiece (also being restored). The other important Savoy residences on which Juvarra worked include the castles of Rivoli, Venaria Reale and Mandria. For transport from Turin, see Chapter 16.

The **Basilica of Superga** (open 8–12.30; 14.30–18.30) is on a wooded hilltop on the right bank of the Po (beyond Pl.16), in a protected park which commands a splendid *view. It was built in 1717–31 by Vittorio Amedeo II in fulfilment of a thanksgiving vow for the deliverance of Turin from the French in 1706. The church is considered Filippo Juvarra's finest work, and has an impressive exterior, with a columned portico, a dome, and two campanili. It has been undergoing restoration since 1988. In the crypt are the tombs of the Kings of Sardinia from Vittorio Amedeo II (died 1732) to Carlo Alberto (died 1849).

Moncalieri, 8.5km from the centre of Turin, also on the right bank of the Po (beyond Pl. 13), is an industrial town (56,100 inhab.) with a **Castle** (open Thu, Sat & Sun 9–13, 15–18), reconstructed in the 15C and much enlarged in the

17–18C, which was the favourite residence of Vittorio Emanuele II; Vittorio Amedeo II (1732) and Vittorio Emanuele I (1824) died here. The apartment of the Savoy princess Letizia Bonaparte, and the 19C royal apartments can be visited.

At **Stupinigi**, 10km from the centre (beyond Pl. 9) is the magnificent **Palazzina di Caccia**, a royal hunting lodge built for Vittorio Amedeo II in 1729–30 by Filippo Juvarra on an ingenious and complex plan. Surrounded by a fine park, it is now the property of the Mauritian Order. The palace has been undergoing restoration since 1988, but it is open 9–12.30, 14–17 exc. Mon, and contains a **Museum of Furniture**, arranged in some 40 rooms. The Appartamento della Regina has ceiling paintings by Carle Van Loo and Giovanni Battista Crosato, and a splendid central Salone is frescoed by Giuseppe and Domenico Valeriani (1732). The apartments of Carlo Felice and Carlo Alberto are also shown. The original 18C bronze stag by Francesco Ladatte, which used to crown the roof of the elliptical central hall, is now displayed inside the palace. A stable block is used for exhibitions.

Rivoli, 13km from the city centre, was once a favourite residence of the Counts of Savoy. The so-called Casa del Conte Verde is a typical early 15C patrician house. The huge **Castello di Rivoli** was left unfinished by Filippo Juvarra in 1715. It was restored and modernised in 1984 to house a **Museo d'Arte contemporanea**, an international collection of contemporary art, and for use as an exhibition centre (open 10–17; weekends 10–19; closed Mon).

Near Piazza Rivoli is **Villa La Tesoriera**, built in 1714 by Jacopo Maggi. The garden is open to the public.

The **Castello della Venaria Reale**, 9km north of the centre, is a royal hunting lodge built for Carlo Emanuele II in 1660 by Amedeo di Castellamonte, and destroyed by French troops in 1693. It was reconstructed by Juvarra in 1714–28. The Galleria di Diana (1718) has been restored and is open on request; the rest of the building (now owned by the Region) is being restored and may be used as a museum. It contains an apartment used by Vittorio Emanuele II, as well as eight carriages. A long avenue of plane trees leads to the **Castello della Mandria**, built for Vittorio Amedeo II in 1713 by Filippo Juvarra, in a large park (open daily), once a hunting reserve.

In the outer environs, south of Turin near the Po, is **Carignano**, an ancient lordship long associated with the royal house of Savoy. The cathedral (1757–67) is the masterpiece of Benedetto Alfieri. The banks of the Po in this area are protected and of interest for their vegetation and birdlife.

To the east of Turin is the pleasant little industrial town (30,500 inhab.) of **CHIERI**. The *Cathedral, built in 1405–36, has a 13C baptistery with a 15C fresco cycle and a small 9C–10C crypt incorporating Roman work. The 14C church of **San Domenico** and remains of the **Commandery of the Templars** are also worth seeing.

18 · The province of Turin, with Ivrea

Pinerolo and the Valle del Pellice and Valle del Chisone

■ **Information office**. APT Pinerolese, 7/9 Viale Giolitti, Pinerolo (tel. 0121 795589).

PINEROLO (37,800 inhab.), the historic capital of the Princes of Acaia, ancestors of the House of Savoy, is in a beautiful position at the foot of the hills where the Chisone and Lemina valleys merge into the Piedmontese plain. The fortress of Pignerol was under French control from 1630 to1706 and, because of its remoteness from Paris, was used as a state prison.

The centre of the town is the large Piazza Vittorio Veneto which adjoins Piazza Cavour, beyond which are the public gardens and the **Waldensian Church** (1860). In the military school, founded in 1849 and closed down in 1943, is a museum dedicated to the history of Italian cavalry regiments.

In the centre of the old town is the restored Gothic **Cathedral**. Via Trento and Via Principi d'Acaia (right), with ancient houses, ascends to the early 14C **Palace of the Princes of Acaia**, and the church of **San Maurizio**, reconstructed in 1470, with a campanile of 1336. It is the burial place of eight princes of Acaia (1334–1490).

South of Pinerolo is **Cavour**, ancestral home of the great statesman's family. Giovanni Giolitti, five times prime minister of Italy, died here in 1928.

In the **VALLE DEL PELLICE** is **Torre Pellice**, the main centre of the Waldensians, and a pleasant little town (4700 inhab.) with some good 19C buildings, including a Waldensian church and college, and a museum illustrating their history.

This valley and the Valle del Chisone, also known as the **Valli Valdesi**, have been inhabited for centuries by the Protestant Waldensians or Vaudois. This religious community originated in the south of France about 1170, under the inspiration of Peter Waldo, a Lyons merchant who sold his goods and started preaching the gospel. His adherents were formally condemned by the Lateran Council in 1184 and persecution drove them to take refuge in these remote valleys. About 1532 the Vaudois became absorbed in the Swiss Reformation. When renewed persecution broke out in 1655 under Carlo Emanuele II, assisted by the troops of Louis XIV, a strong protest was raised by Cromwell in England, and Milton wrote his famous sonnet, beginning: 'Avenge O Lord thy slaughter'd saints, whose bones/Lie scatter'd on the Alpine mountains cold.' Still further persecution followed the Revocation of the Edict of Nantes (1685), but the remnant of the Vaudois, about 2600 in number, were allowed to retreat to Geneva. In 1698 Henri Arnaud led a band of 800 to the reconquest of their valleys, and a rupture between Louis XIV and Vittorio Amedeo of Savoy was followed by their recognition as subjects of Savoy, in a spirit of religious tolerance. At the beginning of the 19C much interest was taken in Protestant countries on their behalf, and an Englishman, General Charles Beckwith, helped them personally and built their church in Turin (1849). Since 1848 they have been allowed complete religious liberty. Towards the close of the 19C large colonies emigrated to Sicily, Uruguay, and the Argentine Republic.

In the **VALLE DEL CHISONE** are remarkable *fortifications built in 1727 by Vittorio Amedeo II and his son Carlo Emanuele III to defend **Fenestrelle** (1154m), now a summer resort surrounded by forests between the peaks of the Orsiera (2878m) and the Albergian (3043m). The fortifications climb up the hillside from the Chisone to Pra Catinat, with numerous forts, barracks, bridges, a five-storeyed palace used also as a prison, and a church, connected by a splendid covered ramp with 4000 steps, about 1km long. The buildings are now abandoned, but have been partly restored and can be visited by appointment (tel. 0121 83600).
    Pragelato is noted for its Alpine flowers and for the honey they produce. Beyond is the famous ski resort of Sestriere, described in Chapter 19.

The Valli di Lanzo

■ **Information office.** APT delle Valli di Lanzo, 9 Via Umberto I, Lanzo Torinese (tel. 0123 28080).

The **VALLI DI LANZO** are three scenic Alpine valleys (the **Valle di Viù**, **Valle di Ala** and **Val Grande**) northwest of Turin, extending to the French frontier. They are the heart of the **Graian Alps**, which lie between the valleys of the Dora Riparia and Dora Baltea, and are visited by climbers and skiers.
    The valleys are approached by the Stura valley in which is **Lanzo Torinese**, with a 14C tower and bridge.

Ivrea and the Canavese

■ **Information office.** APT Canavese, 1 Corso Vercelli, Ivrea (tel. 0125 618131).

■ **Hotels. Ivrea**: 4-star: *La Serra*, 30 Corso Botta. 3-star: *Sirio*, on the Lago Sirio (with restaurant). **Quincinetto**: 2-star: *Mini Hotel Praiale*, 15 Via Umberto.

■ **Restaurants. Ivrea**: B: *La Trattoria*, 47 Via Aosta. **Cake Shop**: *Pasticceria Balla*, 2 Via Gozzano. **Quincinetto**: B: *Da Marino*, località Montellina. **San Giorgio Canavese**: C: *Della Luna*, 12 Piazza Ippolito San Giorgio.

■ **Annual festival.** Carnival celebrations have been held at **Ivrea** for some 200 years. The most important events take place from the Thursday before Ash Wednesday (with a famous battle of oranges).

Ivrea, a pleasant old town (25,000 inhab.), was the Roman *Eporedia*, a bulwark in the 1C BC against the Salassian Gauls of the Upper Dora. In the Middle Ages its marquises rose to power, and Arduino of Ivrea was crowned King of Italy in

1002. Since the Olivetti typewriter factories were founded here in 1908, the town has expanded as an industrial centre.

The **Ponte Vecchio** was built across the Dora Baltea in 1716 on older foundations. In the upper part of the town, approached by steep lanes, is the **Cathedral**, of which two apsidal towers and the crypt date from the 11C. In the raised ambulatory is a row of columns taken from older buildings. The sacristy contains two paintings by Defendente Ferrari.

The *Castle was built by Aymon de Challant (1358) for Amedeo VI, with four tall angle towers, one of which was partially destroyed by an explosion in 1676. It was used as a prison from 1700 to 1970, and has since been restored. The **Bishop's Palace** has Roman and medieval fragments in its loggia. The **Diocescan Museum** is in San Nicola da Tolentino. In Piazza Ottinetti (neo-classical, 1843), the **Museo Civico** has oriental and archaeological collections.

In the public park by the river, below the Dora bridges, is the Romanesque campanile (1041) of **Santo Stefano**. Beyond the railway station are the extensive **Olivetti** works built between 1898 and 1971. They incorporate the late Gothic convent of **San Bernardino** with an interesting fresco cycle by Giovanni Martino Spanzotti (late 15C).

The Canavese

The Canavese is a subalpine district extending from the level moraine ridge of the Serra d'Ivrea, to the east, up to the foot of the Gran Paradiso. It has a number of interesting castles, some of them recently opened to the public.

To the south of Ivrea, on an isolated wooded hill, surrounded by a borgo, is the *Castello di Masino**, one of the best preserved castles in Piedmont. It was purchased, with its contents, in 1988 by the FAI, and has been beautifully restored by them (open Feb–Sep 10–13, 14–18; Oct–Dec. 10–13, 14–17, exc. Mon & Jan; guided visits every hr). On the site of an 11C castle, it was rebuilt in the following centuries, and its present appearance dates largely from the 18C, when it was the residence of Carlo Francesco II, viceroy of Sardinia, and his brother Tommaso Valperga, abbot of Caluso. At this time the double ramp was constructed up to the entrance, and many of the rooms were furnished. These include the print room, with French etchings, the library, the Spanish ambassador's bedroom, and a gallery lined with family portraits. Tommaso Valperga, friend of the poet Vittorio Alfieri, designed the decoration in the poets' gallery.

The medieval northeast tower was adapted in 1730 as a ballroom, and the rectangular keep has a lower room frescoed in the 1690s with coats of arms, and an upper hall with numerous 18C portraits of the royal house of Savoy. In the little family chapel are preserved the remains (brought here in the 18C from the castle of Agliè) of King Arduino. The stable block has a collection of carriages (open at weekends). The castle is surrounded by an attractive formal garden (a flower show is held on the first weekend in May), the design of which survives in part from the 17C and 18C, and a large park (open 10–17 or 18, exc. Mon & Jan), laid out in 1840.

A short way south is **Borgomasino**, with another castle (open by appointment, tel. 0125 770181), on the site of an 11C building, which was also once the property of the Masino. It was largely rebuilt in the 19C.

Further south, across the Dora Baltea, is **Mazzè**, with two castles in a park, first built in the 12C but reconstructed in the late 19C. The interior of one of them (open Mar–Sep on Sun afternoon) is furnished in the Gothic style.

Across the Dora Baltea from Ivrea is the **Castello di Pavone Canavese**, first built in the 11C, reconstructed in the 16C, and well restored in 1885; it is now a restaurant and congress centre. On a hill to the west is the **Castello di Parella**, a 17C building (on medieval foundations), surrounded by a park. It has pretty courtyards, and rooms with fine ceilings and frescoes. Privately owned, it can sometimes be visited by appointment (tel. 0125 76288).

The **VALLE DELL'ORCO** is the chief valley of the Canavese. At **Chivasso** (25,000 inhab.), an important railway junction, the 15C church contains a painting by Defendente Ferrari (1470–1535), born in the town. **San Benigno** has remains of the abbey of **Fruttuaria**, where King Arduino of Ivrea died, a monk, in 1013. At **Rivarolo** is the **Castello Malgrà** dating from the 14C–15C, heavily restored in 1884–1926. To the west is the medieval **Castello di Rivara**, with a villa in the Baroque style.

At **Agliè** is the 12C **Castello Ducale** (open to the public, tel. 0124 330102). It was rebuilt as a ducal palace in 1646, and reconstructed by the Savoy rulers in 1763—when the park was laid out—and again by Carlo Felice in 1825. The interior has 19C decorations, and Roman sculptures. To the southeast is the **Castello di San Giorgio**, a 14C castle rebuilt c 1726 with contemporary decorations, surrounded by a park.

Cuorgnè is an ancient little town on the Orco. Nearby **Valperga** has a restored castle, near which is a charming little 15C church (frescoes). Above rises the **Santuario di Belmonte**, founded by Arduino, but rebuilt in the 14C.

19 · The Valle di Susa

The Valle di Susa in the western corner of Piedmont, some 50km west of Turin, has been traversed by travellers and armies on their way across the Alps for many centuries. It belonged to Dauphiny until it was transferred to Turin in 1713 (the carved symbol of the dolphin can still be seen in some places in the valley). Three roads across the Alps from France now converge here, the busiest of which is via the Mont Cenis Tunnel. The main ski resorts in the valley are Sestriere, Sauze d'Oulx, and Bardonecchia.

■ **Information office.** APT della Valsusa, 5 Piazza Garambois, Oulx (tel. 0122 831596).

■ **Hotels** of all categories in the ski resorts. At **Susa**: 3-star: *Napoleon*, 44 Via Mazzini.

SUSA, on the Dora Riparia, is on the main roads from France through the Mont Cenis tunnel and over the passes of Mont Cenis and Montgenèvre. It preserves some interesting buildings of Roman *Segusium*, the seat of the Gaulish chief Cottius who received the dignity of prefect from Augustus and gave his name to the surrounding Cottian Alps (Alpi Cozie). The town was burned in 1173 by Barbarossa in revenge for its rebellion against him in 1168.

San Giusto, a cathedral since 1772, is an interesting 11C church, with a massive tower. It has 14C stalls, an incomplete polyptych attributed to Bergognone, and the *triptych of Rocciamelone, a Flemish brass of 1358 (shown on 5 August).

From the 4C **Porta Savoia**, Via Archi ascends past the Parco d'Augusto to the *Arco di Augusto**, an arch erected in 8 BC by Cottius in honour of Augustus, decorated with processional reliefs. Higher up is a double Roman arch, with remains of an aqueduct and Roman baths. Below a tower of the **Castle** of Countess Adelaide (11C; small archaeological museum) is Piazza della Torre, with the best of the medieval mansions of the town (13C). Southwest of the town is the 13C church of **San Francesco**, with ruined 15C frescoes near a small Roman **amphitheatre** (2C AD).

North of Susa is the **MONT CENIS PASS** (Colle del Moncenisio; 2083m), one of the historic passes over the Alps, crossed by Pepin the Short (755), Charlemagne (774) and Charles the Bald (877), and many other sovereigns with their armies. **Novalesa** has remains of a Benedictine abbey founded in 726, a famous centre of learning in the Middle Ages (Charlemagne stayed here in 773). It was suppressed under Napoleon, but the Benedictines returned here in 1973, and now run a restoration centre for books. The main church was rebuilt in 1712, but several 11C chapels survive, one of them dedicated to St Heldrad (died 842), abbot here for 30 years. In the parish church of Novalesa are some paintings donated by Napoleon in 1805 to the abbot of the hospice of Mont Cenis, including a good copy of the *Crucifixion of St Peter* by Caravaggio.

Before the carriage road was constructed by Napoleon in 1803–13 the old road to Italy terminated here, and travellers continued on mule-back or were carried over the pass in a wicker chair. Edward Gibbon, on his way from Lausanne to Rome in 1764, chose the latter means of transport and praised the 'dexterous and intrepid Chairmen of the Alps'. Beyond the French frontier is the huge lake of Moncenisio (1974m), used for hydroelectricity, which submerged the hospice of Mont Cenis built here by Louis I of France c 815 at the request of St Heldrad. The road winds down to Lanslebourg (see *Blue Guide France*).

In the Valle di Susa is the fort of **Exilles** (strengthened by Vauban in 1799), on the site of many previous impregnable fortifications which defended the frontier here with Dauphiny. **Salbertrand** was the site of a famous defeat of the French by the Waldensians in 1689. It has a fine parish church (1506–36). The lovely woods on the left bank of the Dora Riparia are now in a protected area. **Sauze d'Oulx** (1510m) is a well known ski resort.

Bardonecchia is another ski resort (1312m) in a wide basin at the junction of several valleys. It is at the end of the **Mont Cenis road tunnel** (Traforo del Fréjus), the second longest road tunnel in Europe (12.8km). It was begun by France and Italy in 1974–75 and opened to traffic in 1980. The motorway through the tunnel (toll) descends from 1296m to 1228m at the French exit at Modane (see *Blue Guide France*). The **railway tunnel** across the frontier was begun in 1857 and finished in 1871 on the plans of the engineers Sommeiller, Grandis, and Grattoni. The first great Transalpine tunnel, it reaches a summit level of 1295m. It had an immediate effect on world communications, speeding the transmission of mail from the East to northern Europe by several days, with

Brindisi replacing Marseilles as the transit port. Originally 12.2km long, the tunnel was realigned in 1881 and again after the Second World War and is now 12.8km long. Cars were carried by train through the tunnel from 1935 until the opening of the road tunnel.

Southwest of Oulx is **Cesana Torinese** where the painter Paul Cézanne spent much time in his family home. **Claviere** is another ski resort (1765m) on the French frontier. The **Col du Montgenèvre** (1860m), the frontier before 1947, is one of the oldest, as well as one of the lowest passes over the main chain of the Alps. It was crossed by the armies of Marius, Augustus, Theodosius and Charlemagne, and again in 1494 by Charles VIII of France and his army, dragging with them 600 cannon. The present road was constructed by Napoleon in 1802–07. French armies entered Italy by it in 1818 and 1859; and in 1917–18 French reinforcements were sent to the Italian armies over this pass. The road descends to Briançon (see *Blue Guide France*).

A little to the south, and almost from a common source, rise the Dora, which flows through the Po into the Adriatic, and the Durance, flowing through the Rhône into the Mediterranean.

SESTRIERE (2030m) is the most fashionable ski resort in Piedmont, which has become one of the best known in Europe since it was first developed in 1928–32. In 1997 the Winter Olympics were held here.

In the lower Valle di Susa is **Avigliana**, an ancient little town with many fine 15C mansions, dominated by a ruined castle of the Counts of Savoy. The church of San Giovanni contains two paintings by Defendente Ferrari. Above the valley, with a fine view of the Alps, is the **Sacra di San Michele** (open 9–12.30, 15–17 or 18), an important abbey founded c 1000, enlarged in the 12C, and suppressed in 1622.

The abbey church of ***Sant'Antonio di Ranverso** is one of the most interesting buildings in Piedmont. Founded in 1188, it was extended in the 13C–14C, and the apse and the unusual façade were added in the 15C. The interior (ring for the custodian exc. Fri & Mon) has 15C frescoes and a polyptych of the Nativity by Defendente Ferrari (1531) on the high altar. The presbytery and sacristy contain good frescoes by Giacomo Jaquerio. The tower and the little cloister are Romanesque.

20 · The province of Cuneo with Le Langhe

The province of Cuneo lies in the southwest corner of Piedmont, between the Alps, the source of the river Po and its plain, and the low hills of the Langhe. The main towns are Saluzzo, below the splendid mountain peak of Monviso and at the head of the Po valley, Cuneo with its Alpine valleys, Alba and Bra in the Langhe and Roero districts, and Mondovì. The province is famous for its wines (including Barolo and Barbaresco), and has numerous small ski resorts. The area around Cuneo and Alba was badly hit by floods in 1994.

■ **Information offices.** APT Saluzzese, 6 Via Griselda, Saluzzo (tel. 0175 46710); APT Valli di Cuneo, 17 Corso Nizza, Cuneo (tel. 0171 693258); APT del Monregalese, 17 Viale Vittorio Veneto, Mondovì (tel. 0174 40389); APT delle Langhe e Roero, Piazza Medford, Alba (tel. 0173 35833).

■ **Hotels**. **Saluzzo**: 3-star: *Astor* and *Griselda*. **Bra**: 3-star: *Elizabeth* and *Giardini*. **Alba**: 3-star: *Savona*. **Mondovì**: 3-star: *Park*. **Cuneo**: 4-star: *Principe*. 3- star: *Royal Superga*. Also at **Limone Piemonte** (all categories).

■ **Restaurants. Saluzzo**: C: *Osteria dei Mondagli* and *La Gargotta del Pellico*. **Bra**: C: *Boccondivino*. Cafè *Converso*. **Alba**: B: *Osteria dell'Arco*. C: *Osteria Italia;* Café *Umberto*. **Cuneo**: B: *Osteria della Chiocciola*. **Mondovì**: B: *Croce d'Oro*, in the environs at Sant'Anna Avagnina.

Cuneo

Cuneo, approached by a monumental viaduct over the Stura, is a regularly built provincial capital (54,500 inhab.) deriving its name from the 'wedge' of land at the confluence of the Gesso and the Stura. The huge arcaded piazza, the cathedral, and the public buildings were mostly rebuilt after a destructive but unsuccessful siege in 1744. A large market is held in the main square on Tuesdays. Via Roma, with heavy arcades, is the main street of the old town. **San Francesco**, a secularised church of 1227, with a good portal (1481), houses a Museo Civico. Magnificent boulevards have replaced the former ramparts.

The spectacular railway line between Cuneo and Ventimiglia through the mountains is a remarkable feat of engineering skill, with numerous tunnels and viaducts. Inaugurated in 1928 it was finally reopened in 1979, having been put out of action in the Second World War. Between Limone Piemonte and Ventimiglia it traverses 46km of French territory.

Cuneo is the gateway to the southern Cottian Alps, approached by the **Val Maira** and the Val Varaita.

In the valley of the Gesso are the **Terme di Valdieri** (975m)—rebuilt in 1952–53—with hot sulphur springs. Monte Matto (3088m) and Cima di Argentera (3297m), the highest peak of the Maritime Alps, lie within the **Argentera Park**, once part of the royal hunting reserve of Valdieri-Entracque, and declared a protected area in 1980. The **Col du Clapier** is now thought by some scholars to have been Hannibal's route across the Alps.

At the head of the wooded **Valle Stura**, with hot sulphur springs at **Terme di Vinadio** (1274m), is the **Colle della Maddalena** (1991m), an easy pass with meadows noted for their varied flowers, and free from snow between mid-May and mid-October. Francis I passed this way on his invasion of Italy in 1515, and Napoleon decreed that 'the imperial road from Spain to Italy' should be carried over the pass. The descent leads to Barcelonnette (see *Blue Guide France*).

The **Palanfrè park** in the upper Val Vermenagna has remarkable beech-woods and interesting wildlife. **Limone Piemonte** (998m) is a large village among open pastures, one of the oldest ski resorts in Italy, with a 12C–14C church. The French frontier is on the **Colle di Tenda** (1909m).

The districts of Tende and La Brigue, although parts of the County of Nice, were given to Italy in the Franco-Italian treaty of 1860, by courtesy of Napoleon III, because a great part of the territory was a favourite hunting-ground of Vittorio Emanuele II. In 1947 they were rejoined to the rest of the county by treaty, an act which was confirmed a month later by a local plebiscite resulting in a large majority in favour of France.

Mondovì and the Monregalese

Mondovì (21,600 inhab.) grew up in the Middle Ages and by the 16C it probably had more inhabitants than any other city in Piedmont. The architect Francesco Gallo (1672–1750), a native, designed numerous buildings in the town. It was the birthplace of Giovanni Giolitti(1842–1928), who was five times prime minister from 1892 to 1921, and introduced universal suffrage into Italy.

In the upper town of **Mondovì Piazza**, with an attractive large piazza, is the elaborate Chiesa della Missione (1678), with a trompe-l'oeil vault-painting by Andrea Pozzo. The Cathedral was built by Gallo in 1743–63. From the garden of the Belvedere there is a fine view.

Southwest of Mondovì is **Lurisia**, a spa with radioactive springs, developed since 1928. **Frabosa Soprana** is a summer and winter resort near **Artesina** and **Prato Nevoso**, ski resorts in the eastern group of the Maritime Alps.

Bossea in the Val Corsaglia has stalacite *caves, among the most interesting in Italy (guided tours 10–12, 14–18). A skeleton of the gigantic extinct cave bear (*Ursus spelaeus*), found here, is on display.

To the east of Mondovì is **Vicoforte** with a huge domed pilgrimage church, begun in 1596 by Ascanio Vitozzi, continued after 1728 by Francesco Gallo, and completed in 1890. The Castello di Casotto (1090m), on the site of an 11C Carthusian monastery, was built in 1835 by Carlo Alberto and used as a summer residence by Vittorio Emanuele II. **Ormea** is another pleasant hill-resort, with a ruined castle and Gothic frescoes of 1397 in the parish church.

The Langhe and Roero districts

The Langhe and Roero, in the northeast corner of the province of Cuneo, are traversed by the Tanaro river. The rolling low hills are famous for their vineyards which produce excellent wines including Barolo, Dolceto, Nebbiolo, Barbera, Barbaresco, Roero, Roero Arneis, Pelaverga and Moscato. Many of the estates with vineyards welcome visitors. The territory includes numerous chestnut, pine and oak woods, particularly beautiful in the autumn. The main towns are Alba and Bra, and there are good restaurants in the area, many of them special-ising in truffles (found locally).

BRA is a town of 24,000 inhabitants. The archaeological museum in the 15C Palazzo Traversa contains finds from the Roman *Pollentia* (now Pollenzo). The Rococo church of Santa Chiara was built by Bernardo Antonio Vittone in 1742. Nearby is a natural history museum founded in 1843.

South of Bra are **Pollenzo**, where the church contains fine 15C stalls brought from Staffarda, and **Cherasco**, of Roman origins. The latter has a Visconti castle of 1348, a 13C church, 17C palaces, and the Museo Adriani (good coins and medals).

At **ALBA** (30,000 inhab.) the historic centre has preserved its polygonal plan from Roman days, and some tall medieval brick tower-houses and decorated house fronts survive. The **Duomo**, over-restored in the 19C, contains fine carved and inlaid stalls by Bernardino da Fossato (1512). In **Palazzo Comunale** is a painting of the Madonna and Child, one of the best works by the 16C artist Macrino d'Alba, and a *Concert* attributed to Mattia Preti (17C). The deconsecrated church of the **Maddalena** (rebuilt in 1749) contains the **Museo Federico Eusebio**, with local neolithic finds, Roman material, and natural history and ethnographic sections. **San Giovanni** contains a Madonna by Barnaba da Modena (1377) and two more paintings by Macrino. **San Domenico** contains 14C and 15C frescoes.

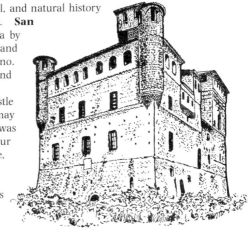

South west of Alba is the castle of **Grinzane Cavour**, which may date from the 13C (although it was enlarged in the 17C). Cavour spent part of his childhood here, and it now houses a wine cellar open to the public.

At **Santo Stefano Belbo** is the birthplace (open at weekends) of the writer Cesare Pavese (1908–50), and there is also a study centre (badly damaged in the 1994 flood) devoted to him.

The Castle of Grinzane Cavour

Saluzzo

Saluzzo (16,000 inhab.) is the historic seat of a line of marquises famous in the 15C and 16C; the upper town is particularly attractive. The large **Cathedral** was built in 1481–1511. The ancient streets of the upper town lead up to the **Castle** (turned into a prison in 1821). Just below it is the church of ***San Giovanni** erected in 1330, with a choir extension of 1480 containing good stalls and the tomb of Marquess Lodovico II (died 1503) by Benedetto Briosco. On the north side are the cloister and chapter house, the latter with a monument to Galeazzo Cavassa of 1528.

Further along Via San Giovanni, is the charming 15C–16C **Casa Cavassa** (open Wed–Sun 9–12, 15–18), once the residence of Galeazzo. Restored in 1883, it is of interest for its architecture and furniture; the marble portal was added in the early 16C by Matteo Sanmicheli. Since 1891 it has housed the Museo Civico, illustrating the history of the Marquisate. There is also a section devoted to Silvio Pellico (1789–1854), the patriot author who was born in the town.

To the south is the **Castello della Manta** (open 10–13, 14–17 or 18 exc. Mon and Jan), donated to the FAI in 1984. This medieval castle was rebuilt by the Saluzzo della Manta family at the beginning of the 15C, later modified (and 'reconstructed' in 1860). The church contains early 15C frescoes, and the late

16C funerary chapel of Michelantonio di Saluzzo. In the Palazzo di Michelantonio, with a Mannerist staircase, one of the rooms (1563) has a ceiling decorated with painted grotesques and stuccoes. In the Castello di Valerano are remarkable *frescoes (c 1420; restored in 1989) in the International Gothic style (attributed to the 'Maestro della Manta') with 18 historical heroes and heroines in contemporary costume, and allegorical scenes of the Fountain of Eternal Youth. They form one of the most interesting secular fresco cycles of this period to have survived. The **park** is open 10–18 (exc. Mon and in Jan).

Southwest of Saluzzo is **Castellar** where the 14C castle (reconstructed in the 19C and after the last war) contains the Museo Aliberti (open 14–18) devoted to the uniforms of the Italian army from the Unification to the Second World War.

West of Saluzzo is **Revello** where, next to the town hall, the Cappella Marchionale, with 15C-16C frescoes, is all that remains of the summer palace built by Marquess Lodovico II.

Savigliano, east of Saluzzo, is the birthplace of the astronomer Giovanni Schiaparelli (1835–1910). Near the central Piazza Santarosa are the Museo Civico and a Gipsoteca with works by the sculptor Davide Calandra (1856–1915), the church of San Pietro with a polyptych by Gandolfino di Roveto (1510), and the Teatro Civico (1834–36).

The castle at Racconigi

At **Racconigi**, north of Savigliano, is a castle (open 9–13, 14–17 or 19 exc. Mon), built 1676–1842 by the kings of the house of Savoy and owned by the state since 1980 (still being restored). The main façade is by Giovanni Battista Borra (1755) and the front overlooking the park is by Guarino Guarini (1676). Umberto of Savoy was born here in 1904 (the ex-king died in exile in 1983). The large park can be visited in summer on Sun 14–19 or by appointment.

South of Savigliano is **Fossano** with a castle of the Acaia family (1324–32), now the seat of the municipal library (adm. on request on weekdays), and 17C and 18C palaces and churches, including Santa Trinità by Francesco Gallo (1730).

North of Saluzzo near the Po is **Staffarda** with a fine Cistercian *abbey, founded in 1135 and well restored. Since 1750 the abbey has been owned by the Order of Santi Maurizio e Lazzaro. It contains a polyptych by Oddone Pascale (1531) and an altar by Agostino Nigra (1525).

The source of the Po is at **Pian del Re** (2050m) in the upper **Valle Po**, in an area interesting for its flora. The banks of the Po, the largest river in Italy, are now protected as a park by the Region of Piedmont for its first 235km.

The splendid mountain of **Monviso** (3841m) was climbed by Quintino Sella in 1863 (after which he founded the Club Alpino Italiano). Beneath the **Colle**

delle Traversette (2950m) is a tunnel built by Marquis Lodovico II in 1480 for the use of merchants trading with Dauphiny. It leads into the French valley of the Guil and Abriès (see *Blue Guide France*). This pass is thought by some scholars to have been Hannibal's route over the Alps (but see page 209).

In the **Valle Varaita** (skiing), on the southern slopes of Monviso, is **Casteldelfino** (1295m), a village named from a castle founded in 1336, once the centre of the Dauphins' Cisalpine territory. The **Col Agnel** (2699m) on the French frontier was often used by invading armies: it was crossed by the French hero Bayard in 1515 and by Philip, Duke of Parma in 1743.

21 · Asti and Alessandria

The two provinces of Asti and Alessandria were severely damaged in a disastrous flood in 1994 when 70 people lost their lives, and some 4000 became homeless. The banks of the Tanaro overflowed after several days of torrential rain, also causing much damage to agriculture and industry in the area. Reconstruction is in progress. The most interesting town in the area is Asti, and the region of the Monferrato is well known for its excellent wines.

■ **Information offices.** APT di Asti, 34 Piazza Alfieri, Asti (tel. 0141 530357). APT di Alessandria, 26 Via Savona, Alessandria (tel. 0131 251021). APT di Acqui Terme e dell'Ovadese, 8 Corso Bagni, Acqui Terme (tel. 0144 322142). APT del Casalese, 2 Via Marchino, Casale Monferrato (tel. 0142 70243).

■ **Hotels**. **Asti**: 4-star: *Reale*, 6 Piazza Alfieri; *Aleramo*, 13 Via Emanule Filiberto. 3-star: *Rainero*, 85 Via Cavour. **Alessandria**: 4-star: *Alli Due Buoi Rossi* (with restaurant), 32 Via Cavour; *Domus*, 12 Via Castellani. 3-star: *Europa*, 1 Via Palestro. **Casale Monferrato**: 3-star: *Business*, 4 Strada Valenza. Also hotels of all categories at the spa town of **Acqui Terme**.

■ **Restaurants**. **Asti**: **A**: *Gener Neuv*, 4 Lungotanaro; *L'Angolo del Beato*, 12 Via Gattuari; *Il Convivio Vini e Cucina*, 4 Via Giuliani. **B**: *Barolo & Co*, 14 Via Cesare Battisti. **Cake Shop**: *Pasticceria Giordanino*, 254 Corso Alfieri. **Alessandria**: **A**: *Il Grappolo*, 28 Via Casale; *Fermata*, 3 Via Casale. **Casale Monferrato**: **A**: *La Torre*, 3 Via Garoglio.

■ **Annual festivals.** The ancient Palio of Asti, a pageant and horse race similar to that of Siena, takes place in early September when there is also a wine fair.

Asti and its province

ASTI, an old Piedmontese city (76,100 inhab.) and provincial capital, is of Roman origins. It was particularly important in the 13C, and became a possession of the house of Savoy from 1532. The town was badly hit by the 1994 flood.

The main street is the long CORSO VITTORIO ALFIERI, extending the whole length of the town. The **Torre San Secondo**, a Romanesque tower on a Roman base, serves as campanile for the church of **Santa Caterina** (1773). The early

18C **Palazzo Alfieri**, birthplace of the poet Vittorio Alfieri (1749–1803), has collections devoted to his work. Beneath the adjoining school is the 8C crypt of the destroyed church of **Sant'Anastasio**, with fine capitals and an interesting lapidary collection.

The **Cathedral** is a Gothic building of 1309–54, with a campanile of 1266 and a florid south porch of c 1470; the east end was extended in 1764–69. It contains stoups and a font with Roman elements, 18C stalls, and frescoes by Carlo Carlone and Francesco Fabbrica. Near the cloister is the small church of **San Giovanni**, covering a 7C or 8C crypt, perhaps the original baptistery.

The 18C **Palazzo Mazzetti** houses the small **Pinacoteca Civica** (works by Valerio Castello) and **Museo del Risorgimento**. In Piazza Medici is the ***Torre Troyana**, the finest medieval tower in the city. The large Gothic church of **San Secondo** contains a fine polyptych by Gaudenzio Ferrari. At the extreme east end of the Corso is the church and cloister of **San Pietro in Consavia** (1467), which now contains a small local geological and archaeological collection. It is adjoined by a circular 10C ***Baptistery**.

There are fine Romanesque churches at **Viatosto**, **Montechiaro** and **Cortazzone** northwest of Asti. On the western border of the province is the hill-village of **Castelnuovo Don Bosco**, the home of St John Bosco. He was born at **Becchi** where a large Salesian pilgrimage church has been erected. Further north is **Albugnano** with the Benedictine ***Abbey of Vezzolano** (1095–1189), the finest group of Romanesque buildings in Piedmont, with remarkable sculptures, especially on the façade and the unusual rood-screen.

North of Asti is **Moncalvo**, with a good Gothic church of the 14C (with paintings by the local artist, Guglielmo Caccia, called Moncalvo). The local wines are renowned.

In the southern corner of the province is **Roccaverano**, a typical cheese-making townlet of the Langhe, with a church (1509–16) in a Bramantesque style and the tall round tower (1204) of its ruined castle.

Alessandria and its province

Alessandria, a cheerful town (102,000 inhab.) and capital of an interesting province, is important for its position almost equidistant from Turin, Milan and Genoa. It was founded by seven castellans of the Monferrato who rebelled against Frederick Barbarossa in 1168 and named their new city after Pope Alexander III. Most of its buildings date from the 18C–19C. The town was damaged in the flood of 1994.

Palazzo della Prefettura (1733), by Benedetto Alfieri, in the central Piazza della Libertà, is the best of the city's mansions. The 14C–15C church of **Santa Maria di Castello** incorporates remains of an earlier 6C church.

To the south of Alessandria is the battlefield of **Marengo**, where Napoleon defeated the Austrians on 14 June 1800, in a battle which he regarded as the most brilliant of his career. There is a small museum in the villa. At **Bosco Marengo** is the remarkable church of Santa Croce erected in 1567 by Pius V (died 1572), a native of the village, as his mausoleum. His splendid tomb remains empty, however, as he is buried in Rome. The paintings include works by Giorgio Vasari.

Near **Serravalle Scrivia** are the remains of the Roman town of *Libarna*, with remains of its decumanus maximus, amphitheatre and theatre. At **Arquata Scrivia** the communal cemetery contains 94 Second World War graves of British soldiers.

Nearby **Gavi** is an ancient little town with a good 13C church. Above it towers a huge castle (open May–Oct exc. Mon) reconstructed by the Genoese in 1626, surrounded by imposing bastions. **Voltaggio** is a summer resort in the upper Lemme valley, with a pinacoteca and local ethnographical museum. In the southern corner of Piedmont is the **Capanne di Marcarolo nature reserve**.

To the east of Alessandria, across the Scriva is the industrial town of **Tortona** (29,800 inhab.). The church of **Santa Maria Canale** may date from the 9C or 10C (it was altered in the 13C–14C). The **Museo Civico** in the 15C Palazzo Guidobono contains relics of ancient *Dertona*, including the sarcophagus of Elio Sabino (3C AD), medieval works of art, and a 16C terracotta Pietà.

Southwest of Alessandria is **ACQUI TERME**, the Roman *Aquae Statiellae*, well known for its sulphurous waters and mud baths. In the middle of the town (21,800 inhab.) the thermal waters (75°C) bubble up beneath a little pavilion, known as **La Bollente** (1870; by Giovanni Ceruti).

The Romanesque **Cathedral** has a fine portal beneath a 17C loggia, and still has its triple apse of the 11C, a campanile completed in the 13C, and a 15C Catalan triptych. In the public gardens are remains of the **Castle** of the Paleologi (see below) with an archaeological museum (open 16–19 exc. Mon; fest. 10–12). The church of **San Pietro** has a fine 11C apse and octagonal campanile. On the other side of the Bormida river are four arches of a **Roman aqueduct**.

Ovada was the birthplace of St Paul of the Cross (Paolo Danei; 1694–1775), founder of the Passionist Order.

To the north of Alessandria is **CASALE MONFERRATO** (43,600 inhab.), on the south bank of the Po, the chief town of the old duchy of Monferrato, whose princes of the Paleologi family held a famous court here from 1319 to 1533. In 1873 the first Italian Portland cement was made here, and the town was noted for its production of cement and artificial stone up to the Second World War. Excellent wines are produced in the vineyards of the Monferrato including the red Barbera and Grignolino.

The **Duomo**, consecrated in 1107, was over-restored in the 19C, but it preserves a remarkable narthex. Inside is a Romanesque sculpted Crucifix. **San Domenico** is a late Gothic church with a fine Renaissance portal of 1505. Via Mameli has a number of fine buildings including **Palazzo Treville** by Giovanni Battista Scapitta (1725; fine Rococo atrium and courtyard), the 18C **Palazzo Sannazzaro**, **Palazzo Gozani di San Giorgio** (now the town hall) built in 1775 and still with its late 18C furnishings, and the church of **San Paolo** (1586). In Via Cavour the cloister of Santa Croce houses the **Museo Civico** with sculptures by Leonardo Bistolfi (1859–1933) and late 16C paintings by Matteo da Verona, Moncalvo, etc. The **Synagogue** (1595) contains an important **Jewish Museum** (open fest. 10–12, 15–17, otherwise by appointment, tel. 0142 71807). The huge Piazza Castello to the west, on the Po, surrounds the 14C **Castle** (transformed in the 19C); the church of **Santa Caterina** here is by

Scapitta (c 1725). The **Teatro Municipale** is a very fine building (recently restored) dating from 1791.

To the west of Monferrato, in a protected park, is the **Santuario di Crea**, founded in 1590 on the site of the refuge of St Eusebius, Bishop of Vercelli (340–70). In the church (13C, altered 1608–12) are frescoes by Macrino d' Alba (1503), and a triptych of 1474. The 23 chapels of the **Sacro Monte** contain late 15C sculptures by Tabacchetti and paintings by Moncalvo. The highest chapel, restored in 1995, contains frescoes attributed to Giorgio Albertini, and remarkable terracotta statues by Tabacchetti hanging from the ceiling. It has a good view over the Monferrato.

To the north, on the Po, surrounded by a fine park, is the picturesque **Castello di Camino** (privately owned), the finest of a number of castles in the Monferrato. First built in the 11C, and enlarged in the 15C, it was restored at the end of the 19C.

22 · Vercelli and Biella

■ **Information offices.** APT Vercelli, 90 Viale Garibaldi (tel. 0161 64631). APT Biella, 3 Piazza Vittorio Veneto (tel. 015 351128).

■ **Hotels. Vercelli**: 3-star: *Il Giardinetto*, 3 Via Sereno (with restaurant). **Biella**: 4-star: *Astoria*, 9 Viale Roma, *Augustus*, 54 Via Italia, *Michelangelo*, 5 Piazza Adua. 3-star: *Coggiola*, 5 Via Cottolengo. There are 3-star and 2-star hotels near the **Lago di Viverone**.

■ **Restaurants. Vercelli**: **A**: *Il Giardinetto*, 3 Via Sereno. **Biella**: **A**: *Prinz Grill*, 14 Via Torino, *Orso Poeta*, 7 Via Orfanotrofio. **B**: *Baracca*, 36 Via Torino. **C**: *Stazione*, 13km outside Biella at the Sanctuary of Oropa. **Café**: *Ferrua*, 1 Via San Filippo.

Vercelli

Vercelli (50,000 inhab.) was a Roman *municipium* founded in 49 BC. It was noted in the 16C for its school of painters, including Giovanni Martino Spanzotti, Sodoma, Gaudenzio Ferrari and Bernardino Lanino. It is now the largest rice-producing centre in Europe. Both the town and its environs suffered damage in the 1994 flood.

PIAZZA CAVOUR is the old market square with attractive arcades, and the battlemented Torre dell'Angelo rising above the roofs. In Via Gioberti is the tall square **Torre di Città**, dating from the 13C. Corso Libertà is the main street of the old town. At No. 204 is **Palazzo Centoris** with a delightful interior *courtyard with frescoes and arcades in three tiers (1496). In Via Cagna is **San Cristoforo** with crowded scenes frescoed by Gaudenzio Ferrari (1529–34), and the *Madonna of the Pomegranate* (1529), considered his masterpiece. The church of **San Paolo** (begun c 1260) has a Madonna by Bernardino Lanino.

Civico Museo Borgogna

The *Civico Museo Borgona (open 14.30–17 or 15–17.30; Sat & Sun 9.30–12.30; closed Mon) is the most important collection of paintings in Piedmont after the Galleria Sabauda in Turin. Founded by Antonio Borgogna (1822–1906), it was donated to the city by him together with the handsome neo-classical palace, and first opened to the public in 1907. It is especially representative of the Piedmontese and Vercelli schools.

Rooms V & VI display part of the original Borgogna collection, including works by Antonio da Viterbo, Francesco Francia, Marco Palmezzano, Bergognone and Bernardino Luini. **Room VI** displays a *Deposition, a replica by Titian of his painting in the Louvre, a portrait of Doge Grimani attributed to Titian, and works by Francesco Santacroce. **Room VII** has good works by Gian Martino Spanzotti, Defendente Ferrari, Girolamo Giovenone, Gaudenzio Ferrari, Sodoma and Bernardino Lanino. **Room VIII** has early 16C *altarpieces by Defendente Ferrari and Lanino.

Room XII displays works by Ludovico Carracci, Pietro Liberi, Sassoferrato and Carlo Maratta. **Rooms XIII–XVI** have works by Lanino and Boniforte degli Oldoni.

On the **first floor** are 18C and 19C works by Andrea Appiani, Angelica Kauffmann, Girolamo Induno, Filippo Palizzi, Stefano Ussi and others. Flemish works are displayed in **Room XXIII** and **XXIV** including a 16C *Madonna and Child by Hans Baldung Grien, and works by Jan Brueghel the Elder. The **third floor** has a Holy Family attributed to Andrea del Sarto, and a collection of porcelain (Meissen, Doccia, Ginori).

Nearby is **San Francesco**, a restored church of 1292 containing a good St Ambrose, by Girolamo Giovenone (1535).

The **Museo Leone** (open Tue & Thu, 15–17.30; fest. 10–12; closed in Jan & Feb) is an unusual museum housing the collection of Camillo Leone (1830–1907), first opened to the public in 1910 (and rearranged in 1934). The entrance is through the lovely courtyard of the 15C **Casa degli Alciati**, which has early 16C frescoes and wood ceilings.

Rooms built in 1939 to connect the house with the Baroque Palazzo Langosco have a didactic display illustrating the history of Vercelli, interesting for its arrangement dating from the Fascist period. The 18C **Palazzo Langosco**, once the residence of Leone, retains part of its original decorations. The Risorgimento period is illustrated in **Room XII**.

In front of the station is the basilica of ***Sant'Andrea** (1219–27), Romanesque but showing Cistercian Gothic elements at a very early date for Italy. It was founded by Cardinal Guala Bicchieri with the revenues of the Abbey of St Andrew at Chesterton (Cambridgeshire) bestowed on him by his young ward, Henry III of England. The fine façade is flanked by two tall towers connected by a double arcade, and the cupola is topped by a third tower. In the two lunettes are sculptures by the school of Antelami. The detached campanile dates from 1407.

The interior has pointed arcades carried on slender clustered piers, with shafts carried up unbroken to the springing of the vaults. The crossing and cupola are particularly fine. At the east end are intarsia stalls of 1514. The remains of the Cistercian abbey include a fine cloister and chapterhouse.

Via Bicheri leads to the huge **Cathedral**, begun in 1572 to a design of Pellegrino Tibaldi, but preserving the Romanesque campanile of an older church. The octagonal chapel—built in 1698 and decorated in 1759—of the Blessed Amedeo IX of Savoy (died in the castle 1472) contains his tomb and that of his successor Charles I (died 1490). The **Chapter Library** includes the 4C Evangelistary of St Eusebius (in a 12C binding); some Anglo-Saxon poems (11C); the Laws of the Lombards (8C); and other early MSS, perhaps relics of the Studium, or early university which flourished here from 1228 for about a century.

To the south of Vercelli is **Trino**, which has been noted for its printers and binders since the 15C. Roman remains have been excavated here, and northeast of the town is the ancient Basilica di San Michele in Insula.

Varallo and the Valsesia

The **Valsesia** is famous for its lace. **Valduggia** was the birthplace of Gaudenzio Ferrari (1471–1546); in the church of San Giorgio are a Nativity by him, and a Madonna by Bernardino Luini.

Varallo, the capital of the upper Valsesia, is famous for its *SACRO MONTE, the ascent to which begins at the church of **Madonna delle Grazie**, with *frescoed scenes of the Life of Christ by Gaudenzio Ferrari (1513). The sanctuary (608m; reached on foot in 20 minutes or by cable railway or road), was founded c 1486 by the Blessed Bernardino Caimi, a Friar Minor. The 45 chapels, completed in the late 17C, recall various holy sites in Jerusalem, and are decorated by local artists (Gaudenzio Ferrari, Giovanni Tabacchetti, Giovanni D'Errico, Morazzone). Tabacchetti's best chapels are the Temptation (No. 38; with a Crucifixion by Ferrari) and Adam and Eve (No. 1); D'Errico's is the Vision of St Joseph (No. 5). The **Basilica dell'Assunta** dates from 1641–49, with a façade of 1896. The hillside was damaged in the 1994 flood.

North of Varallo, in the picturesque **Val Mastallone**, **Rimella** (1180m) retains many traces in its dialect of the German-speaking colony from the Valais that migrated here in the 14C.

Above Varallo the Valsesia is known as **Valgrande**. **Alagna Valsesia** (1183m) is a fashionable summer and winter resort. In a characteristic wooden house here (1628) is the Museo Walser. The Funivia di Monte Rosa, a cableway in three stages, rises to Punta Indren (3260m), another resort. The Regina Margherita CAI Refuge observatory (4559m), on the site of a hut built here in 1893 and inaugurated by Queen Margherita, is the highest refuge in Europe.

The province of Biella

Biella, on the Cervo, is capital (54,000 inhab.) of a new small province. A funicular railway connects the lower town, where there is a 10C *baptistery and the Renaissance church of San Sebastiano, with the upper town and its 15–16C mansions. The **Villa Sella** was the home of the photographer, alpinist, and explorer Vittorio Sella (1859–1943). The **Istituto Nazionale di fotografia alpina Vittorio Sella** here conserves his remarkable collection of negatives made during mountain expeditions in Europe, Asia, Africa and Alaska, as well as his photographic equipment.

Northwest of Biella is **Pollone** with the **Parco della Burcina** (open daily), created in 1849 by Giovanni Piacenza. It has fine trees and flowers, and is noted especially for its rhododendrons, in flower from May to June. Beyond is the **Sanctuary of Oropa** (1181m), the most popular pilgrimage resort in Piedmont, and one of the most famous in Italy. Said to have been founded by St Eusebius in 369, it consists of a large hospice of three quadrangles, which can house hundreds of visitors, a modest church by Filippo Juvarra, and a grander church, with a large dome, begun in 1885 to a design by Ignazio Galletti (1774) and completed in 1960.

South of Biella is **Gaglianico**, which has a splendid castle, mainly 16C, with a well decorated courtyard. **Candelo** has a remarkable Ricetto, or communal fortress and storehouse, built in the 14C as a refuge for the townsfolk.

In the northern part of the province a panoramic road, built by Count Ermenegildo Zegna in 1939, leads west from **Trivero** through **Caulera** (1080m), with lovely woods of rhododendrons, and fine views north to Monte Rosa.

23 · Novara

NOVARA, one of the oldest towns in Piedmont, is an extremely pleasant and well kept provincial capital (102,000 inhab.). Its streets are paved in granite and porphyry, quarried locally, and it has particularly good 19C architecture.

■ **Information office.** APT di Novara, 4 Via Dominioni (tel. 0321 623398).

■ **Hotels.** 4-star: *Italia*, 10 Via Solaroli; *La Rotonda*, 4 Baluardo d'Azeglio. 3-star: *Croce di Malta*, 2 Via Biglieri; *Parmigiano*, 4 Via Dei Cattaneo. 2-star: *Garden*, 25 Corso Garibaldi**.**

■ **Camping site** (2-star) at Galliate.

■ **Restaurants**. **A**: *Monte Ariolo*, 2 Vicolo Monte Ariolo; *La Famiglia*, 10 Via Solaroli; *Il Duca*, 4 Via Ferrari (specialising in fish). **B**: *Caglieri*, 12 Via Tadini. **C**: *Moroni*, 6 Via Solaroli; *Garden*, 25 Corso Garibaldi.

■ **Car parking**. All car parks in the centre of the town have an hourly tariff. Free car parking at Allea di San Luca.

■ **Railway stations.** FS, 5 Piazza Garibaldi for services to Milan, Turin, etc. Ferrovia Nord Milano, 15 Corso della Vittoria, for services via Saronno to Milan.

■ **Bus services** from the railway station (FS) run by ANI and other companies to towns in the province.

■ **Theatre.** *Teatro Coccia*, with a theatre and music season.

■ **Annual festival.** San Gaudenzio, 22 January.

History

A Roman town, Novara was occupied in 569 by the Lombards and became a free Commune in 1116. Important battles were fought here throughout the town's history, after one of which, in 1500, Lodovico il Moro was taken prisoner by the French. The last famous battle was in 1849 which resulted in the defeat of the Piedmontese by Radetzky's Austrians. In the town that same evening Carlo Alberto abdicated in favour of his son, Vittorio Emanuele II, which marked the beginning of the Risorgimento movement in Italy.

In the arcaded VIA FRATELLI ROSSELLI is the **DUOMO**, rebuilt by Alessandro Antonelli in 1865–69 with a neo-classical colonnade. In the gloomy interior, with huge orange stucco columns, are hung six Brussels tapestries (1565) by Jan de Buck. On the **south side** are a 14C carved wooden crucifix, an altarpiece by Gaudenzio Ferrari (c 1525–30), and works by Bernardino Lanino.

The **Cappella di San Siro**, which survives from the earlier church, contains damaged late 12C frescoes; the Crucifixion dates from the 14C. The adjoining 18C room contains frescoes by Bernardino Lanino (1546–53) from the old cathedral, and paintings by Gaudenzio Ferrari and Callisto Piazza da Lodi.

In the **sanctuary** are remarkable black-and-white mosaic panels from the old cathedral dating from the 12C, with symbols of the Evangelists, Adam and Eve, etc. The neo-classical high altar is by Antonelli and Thorvaldsen. On the **north side** are a reliquary bust of St Bernardo of Aosta (1424), and an altarpiece by Giuseppe Nuvolone.

The 16C cloister of the **canonica** has an interesting lapidary collection founded in 1813.

The **BAPTISTERY** is a centrally planned octagonal building of the late 4C, with classical columns of the 1C AD, and an 11C cupola. High up above the windows are very worn frescoes (11C) of the Apocalypse, one of them covered with a 15C Last Judgement. The funerary monument (1C AD) of Umbrena Polla was once used as a font.

Opposite the Duomo is the entrance to the finely paved courtyard of the **Broletto**, a medley of buildings dating from the 13C and 15C with terracotta windows and remains of frescoes above Gothic arches. The third side dates from the 18C. Here is the entrance to the **Museo Civico** (open 9–12. 15–18 exc. Mon; Sun 15–18), founded in 1874–90. Inside are terracotta statuettes, 17C–18C paintings, and an **archaeological collection** including finds dating from the Golasecca culture (9–8C BC) and the Roman period, and medieval ceramics and sculpture.

Via Fratelli Rosselli, with porticoes, leads east to the arcaded Piazza delle Erbe, the old centre of the town. In the other direction, classical colonnades continue past a statue of Carlo Emanuele III (by Pompeo Marchesi, 1837) to PIAZZA MARTIRI DELLA LIBERTÀ with the equestrian statue of Vittorio Emanuele II by Ambrogio Borghi (1881). Here are the handsome neo-classical buildings of the huge **Teatro Coccia** (1888) and **Palazzo del Mercato** (1817–44). On the south side of the piazza are remains of the Sforza castle. In Via Dominioni is the yellow building of the former **Collegio Gallarini** (restored as a music conservatory), with remarkable late 19C terracotta decoration and a coloured roof. Also here, in a little park, are stretches of Roman walls. There is a good view of the elaborate exterior of the Duomo from here.

From the courtyard of the Broletto there is access to Corso Italia from which (left) Via San Gaudenzio continues north to the church of **SAN GAUDENZIO**, built 1577–1690 on a design by Pellegrino Tibaldi, with a fine brick exterior. The *cupola, crowned by an elaborate *spire 121m high, is by Alessandro Antonelli (1844–80). The campanile (92m) is another exceptionally original work by Benedetto Alfieri (1753–86). In the **interior**, on the south side are works by Morazzone, Fiammenghino and Gaudenzio Ferrari. Off the south transept is the Baroque chapel of San Gaudenzio. On the north side are works by Gaudenzio Ferrari (a polyptych of 1514 in a beautiful frame), Paolo Camillo Landriani, Tanzio da Varallo and Giacinto Brandi.

Nearby in Via Ferrari, **Palazzo Faraggiana** is being restored as the seat of the natural history, ethnographical and music museums. In Via Negroni is the church of **San Marco** (1607), with good woodwork and a painting by Daniele Crespi (1626).

Via Fratelli Rosselli (see above) is continued east by Via Canobio in which are **Palazzo Natta-Isola**, attributed to Pellegrino Tibaldi, and **Casa dei Medici** by Seregni.

To the west of the town, on the Sesia river, is the abbey of **San Nazzaro Sesia**, with remains of a fortified Benedictine abbey, including a 15C church and cloister.

To the north of Novara is **Oleggio**, where the Romanesque church of San Michele has frescoes of the 11C and 13C. Further north is **Agrate Conturbia**, with a nature reserve and an interesting baptistery in front of the church.

24 · The Lago d'Orta

The Lago d'Orta is a beautiful little lake (12.8km long and about 1.2km wide), surrounded by mountains, at the northern end of the province of Novara, and just west of the much more famous Lago Maggiore. The most attractive place on the lake is **Orta San Giulio**, with the little **Isola San Giulio** just offshore. Sailing regattas are held here in the summer. The lake, also called Cusio (from the Roman *Cusius)*, has been admired by numerous travellers over the centuries, including Honoré de Balzac and Friedrich Nietzsche. Its only outlet is the little river Nigoglia which flows northwards from Omegna (all the other subalpine Italian lakes have southern outflows). The waters of the lake were polluted in the first half of this century by acid effluents from a few factories, but they were cleaned in 1989–90 when the lake surface was spread with a finely powdered natural limestone (a technique known as liming).

*ORTA SAN GIULIO** is a charming lakeside town (600 inhab.) with elegant buildings, and is well equipped with pleasant hotels and restaurants. It has a remarkably peaceful atmosphere, with picturesque narrow old streets, its cobbled lanes leading down to the lake and a splendid view of the Isola San Giulio. It has numerous attractive houses, most of them built from the 16C to 18C, and on the outskirts are some grand villas.

- **Information office**. APT del Lago di Orta, 9 11 Via Olina (tel. 0322 911937). In summer there is another information office open on the approach road (Via Panoramica).

- **Hotels**. 4-star: *San Rocco* (with swimming pool), 11 Via Gippini; *Villa Crespi*, 8 Via Fava. 3-star: *Orta* and *Leon d'Oro*, 1 and 43 Piazza Motta. 2-star: *Olina*, 40 Via Olina. 1-star: *Taverna Antico Agnello*, 18 Via Olina.

- **Camping sites** (2-star) here and at Pettenasco.

- **Restaurants**. **A**: *Villa Crespi*, 8 Via Fava. **C**: *Olina*, 40 Via Olina. On the **Isola San Giulio**, *Ristorante San Giulio* (**B**). **Sandwich bar**: *L'Edera*, 11 Via Bersani. There are also a café and restaurant on the hill of Sacro Monte. Good places to **picnic** include the Passeggiata del Movero (on the lakeside, beyond Villa Motta) and on the Sacro Monte.

- **Car parks** at the entrance to the town, off the Via Panoramica ('Diania' and 'Prarondo'); only cars with special permission are allowed into the centre .

- **Railway station** at Miasino (with some buses to the lakeside) on the line from Novara to Domodossola, opened in 1884. The APT office has up-to-date information on all local transport.

- **Boat services** run from Easter to Oct to the Isola San Giulio (5 minutes) and Pella (20 minutes). A less frequent service runs from Orta, via the Isola San Giulio and Pettenasco to Omegna (in 1 hr 15 mins). Information from Navigazione Lago d'Orta, tel. 0322 844862. There is also a regular cheap motorboat service (c every 20 minutes) throughout the year from Piazza Motta to the Isola San Giulio.

- **Market day** on Wednesday in the Piazza.

- **Annual festival** of early music in June on the Isola San Giulio. The steps up to the parish church in Orta San Giulio are covered with flowers in April and May.

In Piazza Motta, which opens onto the lake, is the attractive little **Palazzo della Comunità**, the former town hall built in 1582. Nearby, a wide thoroughfare with steps, known as LA MOTTA, leads up past a number of handsome palaces, including the neo-classical Palazzo Fortis Penotti opposite the 16C frescoed Palazzo Gemelli, to the **parish church**, with a decorative façade (1941) and an 11C doorway. In the Baroque interior are interesting frescoes, and works by Carlo Beretta, Giulio Cesare Procaccini, Morazzone and Fermo Stella.

To the right of the church, a lane (Via Gemelli) continues uphill for 20 minutes past the cemetery (with an 18C wrought-iron gate) to an avenue (left) which ends at the monumental gateway of the ***Sacro Monte** (it can also be reached by car from the Via Panoramica). On this low wooded hill (396m), now a protected park with some rare plants (including palm trees), are 20 pretty little chapels, dedicated to St Francis of Assisi. Most of them were built between 1592 and 1670, and they contain remarkable groups of life-size terracotta figures illustrating scenes from the life of the saint, as well as frescoes.

Beyond the gateway a path continues straight uphill, with good views over the lake, and then leads through the woods past each chapel (usually kept unlocked 9.30–16; otherwise enquire at the Capuchin monastery at the top of the hill). Most of them were designed by Padre Cleto (1556–1619), and each has a different ground plan, usually with a pretty loggia or porch. There are notices in each chapel describing the works of art. Carved wooden or wrought-iron screens protect the sculptures from the spectator; the best are the earliest (1607–17) by Cristoforo Prestinari (chapels I–VI, XI and XV). The other sculptures are by Giovanni and Melchiorre d'Enrico (1624–34), Dionigi Bussola, Bernardo Falcone, Giuseppe Rusnati (all late 17C), and Carlo Beretta (mid 18C). The 17C frescoes are by Giacomo Filippo Monti, the della Rovere brothers, Antonio Maria Crespi, Il Rocca, Carlo Francesco and Giuseppe Nuvolone, Morazzone, Giacomo Filippo Monti, Giovanni Battista and Girolamo Grandi, Federico Bianchi, Federico Ferrari, Stefano Maria Legnani, and Antonio Busca.

At the northern end of the town, beyond the Hotel San Rocco, a gravel lane leads past a few villas and ends at the wrought-iron gate in front of the pink **Villa Motta**, built in the late 19C in Venetian style and surrounded by a pretty garden (which can be visited by appointment Mar–Dec, tel. 02 48009161). First laid out in 1880, it has camellias, rhododendrons and azaleas, and some fine trees. A delightful path called the **Passeggiata del Movero**, continues to the left round the headland, following the water's edge past more villas with their boathouses (including an eccentric Art Nouveau villa) and lawns.

Outside the town, on the Via Panoramica is **Villa Crespi** (now a hotel), a remarkable building in the Arab style.

Just offshore is the **ISOLA SAN GIULIO** (for boats, see above), a picturesque little island which is especially beautiful from a distance (the best view, which changes constantly according to the light, is from Orta San Giulio). With a perimeter of just 650m, it has no cars, and hardly any shops, and there is only one lane which circles round the island, past a few villas. The huge former Seminary building, with an overgrown garden, is now a Benedictine convent. The 30

Isola San Giulio

nuns (closed order) run a restoration centre here, and offer hospitality for retreats.

The boats dock in front of the **Basilica di San Giulio** (open 9.30–12.30, 14–18 or 19; Mon 11–12.30, 14–18 or 19), traditionally thought to have been founded by St Julius who is supposed to have purged the island of serpents and other dangerous beasts in 390. However, the first written document testifying to the cult of the saint dates from 590 (Paolo Diacono). The **interior** of the church is Baroque, but there are 14C–16C frescoes. The *pulpit** or ambone in dark Oira marble, dates from the 11C–12C and the sombre carvings show German influence.The white marble sarcophagus with Roman carvings now serves as an alms-box. Some of the chapels are decorated with 15C Lombard frescoes, one of which is attributed to Gaudenzio Ferrari.

In 962 the island was defended by Willa, wife of Berengar II of Lombardy, against the incursions of the Emperor Otho the Great: in the **sacristy** the charter of Otho giving thanks for his eventual capture of the island is preserved. The whale's vertebra here is supposed to be a bone of one of the serpents destroyed by St Julius. In a room off the **crypt** (which preserves the body of St Julius) are fragments of exquisite marble intarsia panels (4–5C) from the cenotaph of the saint, formerly in the apse (destroyed in 1697). Also here is displayed a Greek marble panel incised with the palm, peacock and Cross (6–7C).

On the other side of the lake is **Pella** with a little port, above which, on the terraced hills, are some small villages and the sanctuary of the **Madonna del Sasso**, built in 1748 on a granite spur, overlooking the lake (panoramic view).

Between Orta San Giulio and Gozzano to the south is **Vacciago** where, in the former home of the painter Antonio Calderara (1903–78), a large collection of modern art is open mid-May–mid Oct, 10–12, 15–18, exc. Mon. The 17C villa was built in the Renaissance style. At the southern end of the lake is a hill crowned by the **Torre di Buccione**, a Lombard tower (24m), in need of restoration.

Omegna, a small manufacturing town (16,300 inhab.) at the north end of the lake retains a few old houses, a medieval bridge, and the ancient town gate. It is at the foot of the **Valstrona**, a narrow winding glen which descends from the **Laghetto di Capezzone** (2104m), a lovely tarn beneath the Cima di Capezzone (2420m).

Another road leads from Omegna to **Quarna Sotto** where wind instruments have been made since the early 19C. The Forni manufactory was succeeded here by the Rampone company at the end of the century. A museum (open Jul and Aug, 16–19) illustrates the history of the craft of making woodwind and brass instruments (and preserves a collection of clarinets, oboes, saxophones, flutes and brasses). Another section is devoted to the peasant life of the valley.

25 · The Val d'Ossola

In the northernmost corner of Piedmont, this Alpine region is bordered on three sides by Switzerland. Formerly in the province of Novara, it has recently become part of the new province of Verbania. The main town is Domodossola at the entrance to Italy from the Simplon pass and railway tunnel, and it has seven beautiful Alpine valleys, including the Valle Anzasca beneath Monte Rosa. Many of these have scenic paths, and are also visited by skiiers and climbers.

■ **Information offices.** APT dell'Ossola, 49 Corso Ferraris (tel. 0324 481308). Parco Naturale Alpe Veglia, 2 Piazza Castelli, Varzo (tel. 0324 72572).

■ **Hotels. Domodossola**: 3-star: *Corona*. 2-star: *Sempione*. **Bognanco**: 3-star: *Villa Elda*. 2-star: *Regina*. **Macugnaga**: 3-star: *Alpi* and *Girasole*. 2-star: *Chez Felice*. Baceno, Crodo, Druogno, Formazza, Santa Maria Maggiore and other small resorts also have hotels.

■ **Restaurant.** In **Domodossola**: *Piemonte da Sciolla* (**B**).

DOMODOSSOLA (19,700 inhab.) became important as a halting place for travellers after the opening of the road over the Simplon pass by Napoleon in 1805 and the construction of the railway tunnel through the Alps in 1906. It is still an important rail junction and preserves its grand station built in 1906. Of Roman origin, it is the main town in the Val d'Ossola, and has expanded in a disorderly way around its tiny old centre. The inhabitants played an important part in the Resistance movement in 1944.

Corso Ferraris leads from the station to the old part of the town. **Palazzo San Francesco** houses the 19C **Museo Galletti** (at present closed) which includes a room illustrating the construction of the Simplon tunnel; material relating to the flight of Georges Chavez, the Peruvian airman who was killed in his fall near Domodossola after having made the first flight over the Alps (29 September 1910); a small pinacoteca; and a natural history collection. Beyond Piazza 5 Vie is the pretty arcaded PIAZZA MERCATO, with 15C–16C houses, some with balconies and loggias. A market is held here on Saturday. Just off the piazza is the handsome grey-and-white **Teatro Municipale Galletti**.

Via Paletta leads from Piazza Mercato to Piazza della Chiesa with **Santi Gervaso e Protasio**, which has a façade rebuilt in 1953 but retains an old porch with 15C frescoes. **Palazzo Silva** is a handsome building, begun in 1519 and enlarged in 1640, with a frieze and pretty windows, and a spiral staircase. In the courtyard are sculptural fragments and inside is a small museum (closed for restoration). **Via Carina** is an attractive old street with wooden balconies, and water chanelled beneath the paving stones. To the north, on Via Monte Grappa, is an old medieval tower.

To the west of the town, in a protected park, is an interesting **Via Crucis** (with a view from the top). The 14 chapels, built from the 17C to the 19C, each on a different design, contain life-size sculptures of the Passion of Christ by Dionisio Bussola, Giuseppe Rusnati and others, as well as frescoes.

The **Val Divedro**, northwest of Domodossola, leads to the Simplon Pass. The **Parco Naturale di Alpe Veglia** (1753m) below Monte Leone (3552m) has beautiful scenery, with meadows and larch woods, and lovely walks can be taken in the area. Excavations here in 1990 uncovered a mesolithic site.

The **Simplon railway tunnel** is the longest rail tunnel in the world (19·8km), the first gallery of which was constructed in 1898–1905. It is the lowest of the great Alpine tunnels, with a maximum elevation of only 705m; but there are 2134m of mountain overhead where the main ridge is pierced.

The **Simplon Pass** (2009m; *Passo del Sempione*) is wholly on Swiss soil (see *Blue Guide Switzerland*). It became important when Napoleon chose it (after the battle of Marengo) as the route for the **Simplon road** connecting the Rhône valley with the northern Italian plain (182km from Geneva to Sesto Calende). It was begun on the Italian side in 1800, on the Swiss side a year later, and was completed in 1805. About 1km below the summit on the south side is the **Simplon Hospice** (2001m), built by Napoleon as barracks in 1811 and acquired by the monks of St Bernard in 1825.

The **Val d'Ossola**, with spectacular scenery, vineyards, fig trees, and chestnut woods, extends north to Switzerland. The **Alpe Devero** (1640m) is in the centre of a park (created in 1990) with fine scenery and Alpine lakes. The beautiful **Val Formazza** is an interesting region colonised in the Middle Ages by German-speaking families from the Valais. The *****Cascata della Frua** falls (1675m), are among the grandest waterfalls in the Alps (viewable on Sun in Jun–Sep). The road ends at the **Passo di San Giacomo** (2315m).

The **Val Vigezzo**, followed by a spectacular railway line to Locarno opened in 1923, has been much visited by artists since the 19C. **Santa Maria Maggiore** has a little museum illustrating the work of chimneysweeps.

In the **Valle d'Antrona** is the beautiful little *****Lago d'Antrona** (1083m), formed in 1642 by a landslip from the Cima di Pozzoli (2546m) to the north.

The **Valle Anzasca** also has spectacular mountain scenery, beneath **Monte Rosa** (*Dufourspitze*, 4638m); **Macugnaga** (1326m) is its most important resort.

Valle d'Aosta

The **Valle d'Aosta** extends from Piedmont to the border with France and Switzerland at the Italian end of the Mont Blanc and Great St Bernard tunnels, two of the most important entrances to Italy across the Alps. The Dora Baltea river runs the length of the valley, the head of which is surrounded by the high mountains (all of them over 4000m) of Mont Blanc, the Matterhorn and Monte Rosa, and the region has numerous ski resorts including Courmayeur and Breuil-Cervinia. Just south of Aosta rises the Gran Paradiso mountain (4061m) in the centre of the Parco Nazionale del Gran Paradiso, the first national park to be created in Italy (in 1922). The Roman road from Milan to Gaul over the St Bernard pass traversed the valley over some 17 bridges: three of these survive, as well as a stretch of the road itself. The ancient town of Aosta has particularly impressive Roman remains. The river valley above the Dora Baltea was once defended by numerous castles, the most important of which were built by the powerful Challant family in the 14C and 15C and are now owned by the Regione (five of them can be visited). The side valleys have resorts, visited both in summer and for winter sports.

The valley has always been a place of transit for both travellers and armies entering Italy. One of the earliest visitors to the valley was Sir Roger Newdigate in 1774, but the valley was 'discovered' in the early 19C by British alpinists and excursionists who came here to admire the mountain scenery. Murray's guide of 1838 was the first guide to the region in any language. Well-known alpinists who made ascents in the mountains, many of whom published descriptions of their travels illustrated with engravings, included the Rev. Henry Budden, John Ball and Douglas William Freschfield.

The area was developed for skiing in the 1970s. The guides of Valtournenche and Courmayeur are world-famous and many have accomplished first ascents not only in Switzerland, but also in America and Africa and among the Himalayas. The valley is now visited also for cross-country skiing, and besides the famous resorts of Courmayeur and Cervinia, numerous other resorts have hotels and winter sports facilities (including Pila, La Thuile, Cogne, Champoluc and Gressoney-la-Trinité), which are also visited by mountaineers, rock climbers and walkers.

Under the Italian Constitution of 1945 the valley was granted a statute of administrative and cultural autonomy, with a Regional Council of 35 members, sitting in Aosta. The region also sends one deputy and one senator to the Italian parliament. Although never for long under French dominion, the valley has had a long tradition of bilingualism under the Savoy rulers: most of the 118,000 inhabitants of the valley can speak both French and Italian, even though the French language was severely prohibited during the Fascist regime. Italian and French are now both official languages of the Region; all the signs are written up in both languages and French is obligatory in schools, even though Italian is the common language heard all over the valley. In the villages 'patois', a French Italian dialect is spoken. An interesting relic of the colonisation of the valley from the Swiss Valais remains in the German dialect which survives at Gressoney.

The most important industry in the valley from the Second World War up to the 1960s was the Cogne steelworks outside Aosta, now in decline (the magnetite mines in the mountains above Cogne were closed down in 1974). Agriculture is subsidised by the Regional government, and the dark red-and-white cows (with loud bells) are still taken up to pasture in the high alps from May to the end of September. The valley is noted for its *Fontina* cheese. There are still some old farm buildings raised on stone bases and wooden stilts, with slate roofs. The slopes of the valley are covered with trellised vineyards, and good wines are produced here including red at Aymavilles (Torrette) and Donnas, and white at Chambave, Nus and Morgex (which has vineyards at a height of 1200m).

Economic growth since the 1960s has led to ugly new building throughout the valley, and the motorway (still being completed) detracts from its beauty. The valley is also now visited for its casino at St Vincent, the second most important in Europe after Monte Carlo.

■ **Information offices**. **Regional Tourist Office**, 3 Piazza Narbonne, Aosta (tel. 0165 272725). There are APT offices in the following localities: Aosta (3 Piazza Chanoux, tel. 0165 33352), Saint-Vincent, Gressoney-St-Jean, Champoluc, Breuil-Cervinia, Etroubles, Courmayeur and Cogne. For the **Gran Paradiso National Park**, Comunità Montana Gran Paradis, Villeneuve (tel. 0165 95055).
    Club Alpino Italiano, 8 Piazza Chanoux, Aosta (tel. 0165 40194).

■ **Hotels**. For **Aosta**, see below. There are numerous hotels of all categories at the ski resorts of Courmayeur, Breuil-Cervinia, Cogne, Pila, Gressoney and La Thuile. Saint-Vincent also has hotels of all categories. There are also many hotels in smaller localities throughout the valley. Accommodation can also be found in numerous **Alpine refuges** and mountain huts.
    There are **camping sites** at Arvier, Châtillon, Lillaz, Valnontey, Courmayeur, Gressoney-Saint-Jean, La Salle, Sarre and Valsavarenche.

■ **Restaurants**. For **Aosta**, see below. On the outskirts of **Aosta**: *Le Foyer*, 146 Corso Ivrea (**A**); *Agip*, 138 Corso Ivrea (**B**); *Casale*, località Condemine, near Saint-Christophe (**A**); *Da Manuel*, località Grand Chemin, near Saint-Christophe (**C**). **Arnad**: *Lo Convento* (**B**). **Cogne**: *Lou Ressignon* (**A**); *La Brasserie du Bon Bec* and *Les Trompeurs*, both **B**. **Lillaz**: *Lou Tchappe* (**B**). **Donnas**: *Les Caves de Donnas* (**B**). **Fénis**: *La Châtelaine* (just below the castle; **C**). **Nus**: *Maison Rosset* (**B**). **Pont-Saint-Martin**: *Le Rocher Fleuri*, open in summer (**C**). **Quart**: *Le Bourricot Fleury*, in Villair (**A**). **Verrès**: *Chez Pierre* (**A**).
    There are **picnic places** (with tables and grills) in many wooded areas in the side valleys.

■ **Transport**. A **motorway** (A5) runs from Turin along the floor of the valley via Aosta to Morgex: work is in progress to complete it up to the mouth of the Mont Blanc tunnel.
    The single-track **railway** opened in 1886 (with infrequent local services)

up the valley from Chivasso (on the line between Milan and Turin) via Ivrea to Aosta is operated in part by soldiers. A pretty line, built between the two wars, continues from Aosta to Pré-St-Didier, a few kilometres south of Courmayeur.

There are good **bus** services throughout the valley (for the side valleys a change is usually necessary at the town at the beginning of the valley).

■ **Walking.** There are numerous **marked paths** all over the region for walkers and hikers. The most spectacular mountaineering routes for experienced hikers are the two 'Alte Vie' which cover 282 kilometres at altitudes ranging from 1200 to 3296 metres (best undertaken from the end of June to the beginning of October). They lead from Gressoney-St-Jean via Valtournenche and St Rhémy to Courmayeur (No. 1) and from Courmayeur via La Thuile, Valgrisenche and the Gran Paradiso National Park to Champorcher (No. 2); information from the APT and CAI offices.

■ **Annual festivals.** At Cogne, the *Veillà*, a local artisans' fair, is held on a Sat in mid-Jul and in mid-Aug. The *Battaglia delle Regine*, a contest between horned cattle, is held in various heats throughout the valley (the finals in late Oct usually take place in a field outside the castle of Fénis). Carnival is celebrated with a traditional festa on Shrove Tues at Pont-Saint-Martin when the devil is 'hung' from the Roman bridge, followed by a party in the castle of Verrès. From Fontainemore there is a procession every 3 or 4 years in summer across the mountains to the sanctuary of Oropa in Piedmont. At Perloz in Oct there is a contest between mountain goats. At Gressoney-St-Jean a procession in local costume is held on 24 June and 15 Aug. On 30 and 31 Jan the Fair of St Orso is held in Aosta, with local artisans' products exhibited in the streets. On the last Sun of May there is a music festival in the park of the castle of Aymavilles.

■ **Shopping.** Local artisans' products are sold in IVAT shops in Aosta, Cogne, Courmayeur, Valtournenche, and Gressoney-St-Jean.

26 · Aosta and the Valle d'Aosta

Aosta (579m) is a pleasant small town (36,000 inhab.) of ancient foundation, surrounded by snow-capped mountains. The old centre, less than two kilometres square, is still enclosed by well preserved Roman walls and contains many Roman monuments including the main gate, a cryptoporticus of the forum, and a theatre. A suburban villa and Roman baths are in the process of excavation. St Orso and the cathedral are both interesting medieval buildings with remarkable 11C paintings, and the cathedral museum has numerous works of art. The outskirts now have unattractive buildings, and the huge steelworks, once important to the economy of the whole valley, are now partly abandoned.

■ **Information office.** Assessorato del Turismo, 3 Piazza Narbonne; information office at 8 Piazza Chanoux (tel. 0165 236627).

■ **Hotels.** 4-star: *Europe*, 8 Piazza Narbonne. 3-star: *Bus*, 18 Via Malherbes. 2-star: *Sweet Rock Café*, 18 Via Porta San Bernardo. 1-star: *La Belle Epoque*, 18 Via D'Alvise.

■ **Restaurants. A**: *Vecchio Ristoro*, 4 Via Tourneuve; *Vecchio Aosta*, 4 Piazza Porta Pretorio; *Le Foyer*, 146 Corso Ivrea. **B**: *Borgo Antico*, 143 Via Sant'Anselmo; *Moderno*, 21 Via E. Aubert; *Piemonte*, 13 Via Porta Pretorio. **C**: *Taverna Nando*, 41 Via de Tillier; *Da Manuel*, 33 Via Antica Zecca; *Ulisse*, 58 Via E. Aubert.

■ **Cafés.** *Nazionale*, Piazza Chanoux. **Cake shop**: *Pasticceria Boch*, Piazza Chanoux.

■ **Picnic places** in the small gardens outside the southern stretch of walls, in the gardens in front of the station, and in the small garden off Via Hotel des Monnais (behind St Orso).

■ **Car parking** (free) in Piazza Plouves.

■ **Buses** from the bus station in front of the railway station for places all over the Valle d'Aosta.

■ **Theatre.** *Giocoso*, with a theatre and music season Nov–Mar.

■ **Market.** Tue in Piazza Cavalieri di Vittorio Veneto.

History

Once the chief town of the Gallic Salassi, Aosta was captured by Terentius Varro in 24 BC and renamed *Augusta Praetoria*; its centre still retains a Roman plan almost intact. The character of the later city, however, is southern French rather than Italian, the architecture is essentially Burgundian, and the people speak a French dialect. Throughout the later Middle Ages, town and valley owed allegiance to the great house of Challant, viscounts of Aosta, and later the dukedom was a prized apanage of the house of Savoy. The most famous native of Aosta is St Anselm (1033–1109), Archbishop of Canterbury from 1093.

PIAZZA EMILE CHANOUX is the centre of the town, site of the **Hôtel de Ville**, the grand town hall of 1837, with a war monument (1924) by Pietro Canonica outside. There is an attractive old-fashioned café here. VIA PORTA PRETORIA leads east. Under an archway on the left, an alley leads to a terrace overlooking the Roman theatre (see below) near recently excavated houses with pebble pavements on a Roman road once lined with a portico. At No. 41 is the house of Philippe-Maurice de Challant (1724–1804), the last descendant of the important family who built numerous castles in the valley. Opposite, No. 46 is one of the few old houses to survive in the town.

At the end of the street is the ***PORTA PRAETORIA**, a massive, well preserved double Roman gateway of three arches, which was the main gate of the city. The two fortified gates, built in pudding-stone, are separated by a small square defended by two towers. The side facing away from the city was originally faced in marble. The side arches were used by pedestrians and the central one for carriages. The level of the Roman road was 2·60 metres below the present pavement. Up to the 18C the gate was incorporated in a medieval fortress, and the main arches and those on the right were blocked up; this explains why the axis of Via Porta Pretoria is not aligned with the gate.

Beside it is the entrance to the *ROMAN THEATRE (open 9.30–12, 14–16.30 or 18.30) comparable with that of Orange in Provence. The most conspicuous part of the monument is the tall façade,

The Porta Praetoria

22m high, decorated with arched windows; it is, however, in very poor condition and is covered for restoration. Behind it are remains of the seats in the cavea and the foundations of the scena.

On the east side of the theatre is a long stretch of the **Roman walls**. A road leads north outside the walls past several medieval buildings, including the **Tour Fromage** (now used for exhibitions), and the **Torre del Baillage**, a 12C addition at the northeast angle of the walls. Nearby, in the **convent of St Catherine** (ring for adm.), are eight arches of the Roman **amphitheatre**, a building once capable of holding about 20,000 spectators. Some of the arches have been built into the wall of the convent; the others traverse the orchard.

From the Porta Praetoria (see above) Via Sant'Anselmo continues east. On the left Via Sant'Orso leads to the priory and collegiate church of **SANT'ORSO**, or *St-Ours*, founded by St Anselm, with a campanile finished in 1131 and an outré Gothic façade. It contains 16C stalls, and the 11C crypt has 12 plain Roman columns. In the roof vaulting are remarkable **Ottonian *frescoes**, dating from 1030 or 1040, shown by a custodian (10–16.45; in summer 9.30–12, 14–17.30; exc. Mon). By means of platforms and walkways in the roof they can be seen at close range: two of the scenes show the miracles on Lake Gennesaret and at the Marriage at Cana—they were damaged in the 15C by the construction of the nave vault) The frescoes represent (together with those found recently beneath the cathedral roof, see below) extremely interesting examples of mural paintings of this date, hardly any of which have survived elsewhere in Italy.

To the right of the church façade is the *cloister (adm. as for the frescoes in the church) with fascinating Romanesque capitals carved in white marble (covered at a later date with a dark patina), at the top of unusually low columns, dating from c 1132. They illustrate biblical scenes (including the story of Jacob, the Childhood of Christ, the Raising of Lazarus, Noli me Tangere, and the Stoning of St Stephen); two episodes relating to the priory; fantastic and stylised animals; a fable of Aesop (the wolf and the stork); and prophets. This, together with the cloister of Monreale in Sicily, is the only surviving example in Italy of a large Romanesque cloister with representations of historical and legendary scenes. The carvings are suffering from pollution.

The **priory** (1494–1506), with an octagonal tower, has fine terracotta decoration. Opposite Sant'Orso is the church of **San Lorenzo** (closed; deconsecrated); to the left a passage leads round the east end of the church to the excavations (adm. as for the frescoes in Sant'Orso) of an unusual early Christian church of the 5C beneath San Lorenzo. It has a Latin-cross plan with four apses at the end of each arm, and was the burial place of the first bishops of Aosta (the sarcophagus of Bishop Agnello, who died in 528, is preserved here). The church was destroyed in the Carolingian era.

Via Sant'Anselmo continues to the *ARCH OF AUGUSTUS, a triumphal arch erected in 24 BC to commemorate the defeat of the Salassi. This is decorated with ten Corinthian columns, and is fairly well preserved though rather disfigured by a roof of 1716. The arch was drawn and engraved numerous times in the 19C, and before that by Sir Roger Newdigate in 1774 (he gave his drawing to Piranesi on reaching Rome). Further on, beyond the modern bridge over the Buthier, is a remarkable single-arched **Roman Bridge**, still in use, over a dried-up channel.

Cathedral

From Piazza Chanoux (see above), Via Hotel des Etats leads to Via Monsignor De Sales in which remains of **Roman baths** dating from the 1C AD are being excavated. To the left is the Cathedral, an ancient foundation preserving Romanesque campanili at the east end, rebuilt in the Gothic style, and given a sculptured west portal in 1526 (covered for restoration), now framed by a neo-classical façade of 1848. In the **interior** can be seen remains of the baptistery of the early Christian church on this site, and traces of a 3C and 4C edifice. The stained glass dates from the late 14C to early 15C. In the south aisle are 16C frescoes, a large 16C painted lunette illustrating the legend of St Grato, and a stone effigy of the Blessed Bonifacio (late 13C).

The *Museo del Tesoro** is beautifully displayed in the deambulatory (open 10–12, 15–17; winter & fest. 15–17.45). It contains precious treasures belonging to the cathedral and from churches in the valley. The oldest pieces are an agate cameo dating from the 1C (in a gold setting of the 13C), and an ivory diptych dated 406. Cases display 13C church silver including beautiful processional crosses (13C–15C). The 15C tombs include those of Count François de Challant (c 1430), and Bishop Oger Moriset, both by Etienne Mossettaz. The bishop's missal, illuminated c 1420 by Giacomo Jaquerio, is also displayed. In the deambulatory is the tomb of St Grato in wood and silver, exquisitely decorated between 1415 and 1458. Nearby is a crucifix of 1499, removed from below the Arch of Augustus. A beautiful illuminated codex and cope both belonged to Bishop François de Prez. Above can be seen the tomb of Thomas II of Savoy (c 1425–35), attributed to Mossettaz. The chapel of the reliquaries contains the reliquary of San Giocondo (1615).

In the **choir** are interesting mosaic pavements (12C and 14C), one with the Labours of the Months, the other depicting lively animals and the Tigris and Euphrates. Here also are good stalls (c 1469) and a crucifix dating from 1397.

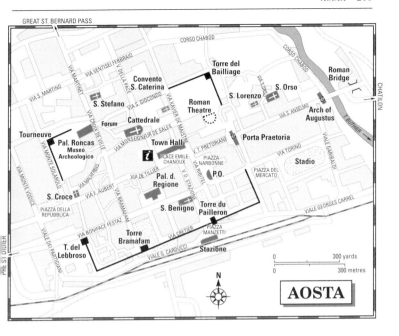

The **crypt** has a miscellany of Roman and medieval columns. Ottonian *frescoes in the **roof vault** were discovered in 1979 and will be on view after restoration. They are the upper band of a fresco cycle illustrating the story of St Eustachio and biblical scenes (with a frieze of animals, some of them symbolic) which once decorated the nave and were covered when the 15C vault of the church was constructed. Thought to be by the same hand as those in Sant'Orso (see above), dating from 1030 or 1040, they are rare survivals in Italy of mural paintings of this date.

The **cloister** on the north side of the church dates from 1460. It is reached by way of Via Conte Tomaso and Via San Bernardo, and can be seen through a locked gate (some of the pillars have inscriptions instead of carvings).

In a sunken garden beside the cathedral façade are some remains of the **Roman Forum**, with the base of a temple now part of the foundations of a house. From here there is access (daily 9–12, 14–17; if closed ask at the Archaeological Museum) to a splendid underground ***ROMAN CRYPTOPORTICUS**. The double north walk, over 92m long, is particularly remarkable.

Via Forum and Via St Bernard lead northwest to Piazza Roncas where a 17C palace houses the **Museo Archeologico Regionale** (open 9–12, 14–18.30). The first two rooms illustrate the history of the city from the 4C BC onwards by means of diagrams, models, and objects found in excavations in the city, including an exquisite bronze of the 2C AD, once part of a horse's bridle, showing a battle scene between Romans and barbarians. Stairs lead down to the excavations of one of the four Roman gates of the city and part of the walls.

Across the courtyard is a room (unlocked on request) with the remarkable *numismatic collection of Andrea Pautasso (1911–85), particularly notable for its Celtic coins found in northern Italy (many of them, in gold, silver and bronze, in imitation of Greek coins). There are also examples from the Roman, Byzantine and medieval periods, as well as the 19C.

On the left side of the palace is a little public fountain, on a canal where the water is regulated by a sluice gate.

Via Martinet leads to the church of **St Etienne** (or Santo Stefano) which has an elaborate high altar and a little museum of 15C–18C liturgical objects. The remarkable colossal wood statue of St Christopher was carved in the 15C.

Via Croix de Ville, on the line of the *cardo maximus* of the Roman town, leads south to the medieval market place and a cross set up in 1541 to commemorate the expulsion of the Calvinists from the town. Via Tillier leads back to Piazza Chanoux past the 15C chapel of **San Grato**, with frescoes.

The **ROMAN WALLS*, forming a rectangle 724m long and 572m broad, are best preserved on the southern and western sides. Standing across the west wall is the medieval **Torre del Lebbroso**. Recently restored, it is now used for exhibitions. Near the **Torre Bramafan**, a relic (11C) of the lords of Challant, remains of the Porta Principalis Dextera have been unearthed, while the **Torre del Pailleron**, with Roman masonry, stands in a garden near the station.

On the northern outskirts of the town, the **Villa della Consolata** is a Roman villa which has been excavated and may be opened to the public.

A cable car from behind the railway station up to the modern ski resort of **Pila** (1800m) operates frequently, taking 20 minutes.

Valle d'Aosta — Pont-St-Martin to Mont Blanc

Pont-St-Martin is on the southernmost border of the region of Valle d'Aosta. It has a very well preserved Roman *bridge (1C BC), with a single arch over the Lys, which can be crossed on foot (the bridge downstream was built in 1876). Above are the ruins of a 12C castle. Just beyond **Donnas** can be seen the best surviving stretch in the valley of the **Roman road to Gaul** above the modern road on the right. It was built just above the level of the river to avoid flooding, and ran mostly along the left bank which enjoys most sun, helping to melt the snow in winter. A conspicuous arch cut into the rock by the Romans survives here—a demonstration of the skill required by the stoneworkers, who in places had to construct the road out of the sheer rock face. A round column serves as a milestone (35 miles from Aosta). The road was in use up to the last century (the ruts were made by cartwheels).

The interesting **CASTLE OF BARD**, an 11C foundation, was largely reconstructed in the 19C. At present only the courtyard can be visited, but there are plans to open the castle in 1998. In 1800 Napoleon's progress was halted here for a week by the defenders of the castle, but in the end he managed to pass unnoticed with his army during the night; they went through the narrow gorge in silence, having protected the wheels of the gun carriages with straw. As an over-Liberal young officer, Cavour was despatched to this remote garrison by Carlo Felice of Savoy, King of Sardinia and Piedmont, in 1830–31.

The church of **Arnad** is one of the oldest in the valley, founded in the 11C and restored in the early 15C. The exterior frescoes in late Gothic style date from the latter time. The **CASTLE OF VERRÈS** (open 9–19; winter 10–17) commands the mouth of the Val d'Ayas. A road leads up to the car park (or a path ascends in 15 minutes from Piazza Chanoux in Verrès village), from where a steep path continues up the hill, taking you to the entrance in 5–10 minutes. This four-square castle, with sheer walls 30m high, was founded by the Challant family in 1390 and strengthened by them in 1536 (it was acquired by the state in 1894). It was never a residence but used purely for defensive purposes, and its bare interior has huge fireplaces, the old kitchen built into the rock, and an imposing staircase. Just below the castle is the **abbey of St Gilles**, founded c 1050 (now a school).

On the other side of the river is the *CASTLE OF ISSOGNE, rebuilt by Georges de Challant in 1497–98, a splendid example of a late medieval residence (open as for the Castle of Verrès), which retains some of its original furnishings and lovely Gothic double doors carved in wood. It was donated to the state in 1907. In the courtyard, beneath the loggia are 16C frescoed lunettes with scenes of everyday life, including a guardhouse with a game of backgammon in progress, and various shops. The unusual fountain in wrought iron in the form of a pomegranate tree was made in the 16C. The little walled garden has box hedges. Next to the dining room is the kitchen with three fireplaces. The chapel has a lovely late 16C altarpiece and an unusual lunette fresco of the death of the Virgin. Stairs continue up to the loggia on the top floor. Off the main staircase is the bedroom of Georges de Challant which has a pretty wood ceiling and a little oratory with a Crucifixion and the kneeling figure of Challant. Another room has views of the two castles of Verrès and and Arnad. A small room used as a schoolroom has sums scratched on the walls. The Sala Baroniale has delightful painted walls depicting the Judgement of Paris, and lovely landscapes with birds behind painted crystal columns.

Near **Champdepraz** is the **Parco Naturale di Mont Avic**, a protected area since 1991, surrounding the pointed mountain of Avic (3006m) with Alpine lakes, pine and larch woods and interesting vegetation, which can be seen from marked paths.

ST VINCENT is the second most important place in the valley (after Aosta), famous for its casino and with numerous hotels. The approach road passes remains of a Roman bridge (which collapsed in the 19C). Beside the Art Nouveau Hotel Billia (1910), and a congress hall built in 1983, is the **Casinò** which was opened in the 1950s (and renovated in the 1970s). The Region has a majority holding in the casino which is closed to residents of the Valle d'Aosta. It is the most important gambling house in Italy (and considered the second in Europe after Monte Carlo). It is frequented mostly by Italians, and there are direct train and bus services from Turin to Saint Vincent in the afternoon (it is open 15–2, although chemin-de-fer is usually played throughout the night).

The old **church**, built on a prehistoric and Roman site, has a 14C fresco in a niche outside the apse. The interior with Romanesque columns has 15C and 16C frescoes and a little museum. The frescoes in the window jambs are attributed to the school of Jaquerio.

Saint Vincent has been known since 1770 as a health resort, and the spa (open May–Oct) is reached by a funicular railway from the centre of the town in 3 minutes. **Palazzo delle Fonti** was built in 1960 above the source of the mineral spring (*fons salutis*).

Châtillon is built on the Marmore torrent, with 19C foundries, mills and forges on its banks. The castle of **Ussel** (1351) is being restored.

Chambave, beneath the ruined castle of Cly, is noted for its wine (moscato). The **CASTLE OF FÉNIS** (open 10–17; summer 10–19; visitors admitted every 30 minutes; recorded guide available) is the most famous castle in the Valle d'Aosta, seat of the Challant family. With numerous towers, it is enclosed by double walls (the outer circuit were reconstructed in 1936). It was rebuilt c 1340 by Aimone de Challant and heavily restored at the end of the 19C. The charming courtyard with wooden balconies and a lovely semicircular staircase has remarkable *frescoes in the refined International Gothic style by Giacomo Jacquerio (1425–30) and his school, including St George and the Dragon (1414) and a frieze of philosophers and prophets holding scrolls with proverbs in Old French. The first floor, with a chapel also frescoed by Jaquerio, has been closed since 1981. The rooms of the castle have interesting local furniture, although not all of it is authentic. The furnished guardroom contains a model of the castle.

The 13C **Castle of Sarre**, rebuilt in 1710, is closed for restoration. It is notable for its hall decorated with thousands of hunting trophies, including numerous ibex shot by Vittorio Emanuele II in the Gran Paradiso park. The **CASTLE OF ST-PIERRE** was first built in the 12C but transformed in the 19C when the four cylindrical towers and castellations were added. In a splendid position on an isolated rock, above the church and campanile of St Pierre, it has a good view of the snow-capped mountain of La Grivola. It is owned by the Comune of St Pierre and houses the Museo Regionale di Scienze Naturali (open mid-Mar–Oct, 9–19), founded in 1850 and opened here in 1985. In the stable block is a display of minerals mostly from Mont Blanc. Other rooms have exhibits illustrating the geology and flora and fauna of the area, including 290 ibex antlers. Above St Pierre is the little summer resort of **St Nicolas** (1126m), in a good position.

Low down on the river is the **Castle of Sarriod de la Tour**, dating in part from the 14C, which may one day be used as an exhibition centre.

Morgex is the principal village in the Valdigne, the upper valley of the Dora. The church, founded in the 6C, has an unusual onion-shaped campanile, and contains early 16C frescoes.

COURMAYEUR (1228m) is a famous ski resort in a deep vale at the southern foot of the Mont Blanc range. It has a much milder climate than Chamonix on the other side of the mountains in Savoy. A museum illustrates the history of Alpinism in the area. La Palud is the starting point of the *cable railway to Chamonix** which traverses the Mont Blanc massif in c 1hr 30 mins. It runs every hour (weather permitting) and provides a magnificent panorama of the Graian Alps, and the south side of the Pennine Alps. It crosses the French frontier at a height of 3462m. **Mont Blanc** (4807m) is the highest mountain in western Europe (the summit is in France and it is fully described in *Blue Guide France*). It was first climbed from Chamonix in 1786. The Col de la Seigne (2512m), on the French frontier, is the watershed between the basins of the Po and the Rhône.

The **Mont Blanc Tunnel**, built through the mountains in 1958–65, is 11.6km long and the road descends over 100 metres from the Italian to the French side.

The side valleys in the Valle d'Aosta

The **VAL DI GRESSONEY**, which leads towards Monte Rosa, is ascended by road from **Pont-St-Martin.** It contains the largest and oldest of the German-speaking colonies which crossed over from Valais in the Middle Ages. The people of this valley, known as the Walsers, are mentioned as early as 1218. They were subjects of the Bishop of Sion, and have kept their language and customs even more distinct from their Italian neighbours than have the people of Alagna or Macugnaga. The attractive chalets (*rascards*) in the lower valley, and the farm-houses (*stadel)* in the upper valley, and the costume of the women, which is brightly coloured in red and black with a remarkable headdress adorned with hand-made gold lace, all suggest a northern origin.

Fontainemore has a lovely medieval single-arched bridge across the Lys. **Issime** (939m) has an interesting German Walser dialect, known as *titsch*, and the signs here are given in all three languages. The church, rebuilt after 1567 has a fresco of the Last Judgement on the façade, opposite which is a pretty 'loggia' with niches, painted in 1752. Inside is a little museum. The elaborate high altar in gold and turquoise is decorated with numerous statues (1690–1710). At the west end is an interesting judge's chair, with a chain collar for those found guilty: it was used up to 1770 in the piazza.

Gaby, where the poet Giosuè Carducci used to stay at the end of the 19C, is a French-speaking village (1032m), but the German dialect is used again at **GRESSONEY-ST-JEAN** (1385m), the principal village in the valley, and a summer and winter resort. On the outskirts can still be seen some old houses (*stadel)* built on stilts above a stone base. From here there is a fine view of snow-covered Monte Rosa (4637m) at the head of the valley. The town hall occupies Villa Margherita, a remarkable Art Nouveau building built for Queen Margherita at the end of the 19C. Across the river in fir and larch woods is the turreted neo-Gothic **Castle of Gressoney** (or **Castel Savoia**; open 9–12, 15–8 exc. Thu; guided visits every 30 minutes). The castle was built in 1899–1904 by Emilio Stramucci for Queen Margherita (widow of Umberto I), who spent every summer here up to 1925. This period piece—the decoration of the wooden stairs is particularly successful—contains a bronze bust of a woman wearing the local headdress by Pietro Canonica. From the veranda is a splendid view of Monte Rosa (the mountain was frequently visited by the queen). The kitchen was in a separate building, connected to the castle by a miniature railway.

In the pretty little village, German in atmosphere, beside the churchyard is the **church**, with a bust of Queen Margherita on the façade. The Baroque interior has charming wooden altars and a small museum. In the adjoining piazza is a statue of Umberto I.

The sister village of **Gressoney-la-Trinité** (1628m), is a ski resort for Monte Rosa, with a view of the grand line of snow peaks from Monte Rosa to the Gran Paradiso.

The **VAL D'AYAS** leaves the main valley at Verrès and follows the Evançon river. The ruined 13C **castle of Graines** stands on a prehistoric site in an attractive landscape with cherry trees. The valley has pine forests and massive wooden chalets. **Antagnod** (1710m) has a fine church. **CHAMPOLUC** (1570m), surrounded by splendid forests, is an important ski resort for Monte Rosa.

The **VALTOURNENCHE**, extending from Châtillon to the base of the Matterhorn along the Marmore valley, has numerous resorts, including **Valtournenche** (1528m). **BREUIL-CERVINIA** (2004m) has become one of the most popular ski resorts in Italy, with numerous cableways ascending the main ridge of the Alps, dominated by the Matterhorn and Breithorn (4171m) on either side of the Theodule pass on the Swiss frontier. Most of the earliest attempts to scale the **Matterhorn** (4478m: *Monte Cervino*) were started from Breuil, but the summit was not reached from this side by a direct route until 1867.

The Great and Little St Bernard Passes

The **GREAT ST BERNARD VALLEY** extends north from Aosta to the Swiss frontier on the Great St Bernard pass. The **Great St Bernard tunnel** (approached by a stretch of motorway) was built in 1958–64 (toll). It is 5·8km long and rises slightly from the Italian side (1875m) to the Swiss (1918m).

The road over the **Great St Bernard Pass** is usually closed Nov–Jun. Known and used by Celts and Romans, its ancient name was *Mons Jovis* (Mont Joux), from a temple of Jupiter Paeninus which once stood on the Plan de Jupiter, and it was only in the 12C that it acquired its present name.

> The pass was much used by pilgrims and clerics bound to or from Rome, and between 774 and 1414 it was crossed 20 times by medieval emperors, including Frederick Barbarossa in 1162. Coaches which entered Italy here in the 18C had to be dismantled and carried piece by piece over the pass on the backs of local mountaineers. In the campaigns of 1798–1800 many French and Austrian soldiers crossed the pass. The most famous passage was made by Napoleon, who on 14–20 May 1800 led 40,000 troops by this route into Italy and a month later defeated the Austrians at the battle of Marengo. After this event and throughout the 19C numerous engravings were made of the pass. It was only in 1905 that a proper road was constructed.

Just beyond the Swiss frontier is the **Great St Bernard Hospice** (2469m), one of the highest inhabited places in Europe. It was supposedly founded in the 11C by St Bernard of Menthon; by 1215 it was inhabited by Austin canons. In their rescue of snow-bound travellers the canons are assisted by the famous St Bernard dogs, a breed said to be a cross between the Pyrenean sheepdog and the Newfoundland, although modern conditions have made their services much less important.

The **Little St Bernard Pass** (2188m) is just over the French frontier, on the watershed between the Dora Baltea and the Isère. Nearby is the **Colonne de Joux**, probably a Roman monument of cipollino marble, with a statue of St Bernard added in 1886, and a little below it is an Iron Age stone circle just over 73m in diameter, in which Gaulish and Roman coins have been discovered. The path across the pass was only transformed into a road for carriages in 1871. The ruined **Hospice du Petit-St-Bernard** (2152m), founded c 1000, used to offer free hospitality to poor travellers. The Botanical Garden established here in 1897 by Abbot Pierre Chanoux is being reconstituted and is open to the public.

The Gran Paradiso National Park

The whole of the **Gran Paradiso** (4061m) massif to the south of Aosta, above the valleys of Cogne, Valnontey, Valsavarenche and Val di Rhêmes, lies within the Gran Paradiso National Park, an area of some 70,000 hectares and the oldest national park in Italy (founded in 1922). The natural beauty of the park has been threatened by attempts to open up part of the Valsavarenche as a resort for skiers. The park was created as a hunting reserve for Vittorio Emanuele II in 1856, and presented to the state by Vittorio Emanuele III in 1919. Many of the bridlepaths made by Vittorio Emanuele II are still in use. This is the only part of the Alps in which the ibex (*stambecco*) has survived in its natural state (some 5000 live here), and the chamois and Alpine marmot are common. The flowers are at their best May–Jun. For information about climbs and walks, etc., contact Comunità Montana Gran Paradiso, località Champagne 18, Villeneuve (tel. 0165 95055), and the APT office in Cogne. There are three entrances from the Valle d'Aosta: at Valnontey, Valsavarenche and Val di Rhêmes (the rest of the park lies within Piedmont, see Chapter 18).

The most direct road from Aosta follows the delightful **VAL DI COGNE**, the upper reaches of which border the national park. The road passes the unusual **Castle of Aymavilles**, altered in the 18C when the turrets were added and it was surrounded by a park. Just off the road, a byroad (signposted) descends right to the tiny isolated hamlet of **PONDEL**, with a remarkable *Roman bridge** which once also served as an aqueduct. As the inscription states, it was built privately by two Paduans in the 3C BC; 50m long and 50m high, it crosses the ravine made by the Grand'Eyvia torrent. Beneath the aqueduct channel is a splendid covered passageway still practicable. It is extremely well preserved, and is one of the most interesting sites in the Valle d'Aosta. The valley on the other side of the bridge is well known for its butterflies (lovely walks can be taken in the area along marked paths). There is a good view from here of the peak of the Grivola mountain (3969m) at the top of the valley. Above the main road is the pretty little resort of **Ozein** (1300m), with a few hotels and a fine view of the peak of the Grivola.

The valley opens out into a wide basin at **COGNE** (1533m), just outside the limits of the national park. It has a large common (where ibex can often be seen in May) across which can be seen the snow-capped Gran Paradiso. After the magnetite mines, once some of the most productive in the country, were closed down in 1974, Cogne was developed as a resort. Remains of the mines, at an altitude of some 2000m, can be seen on the hillside (the miners were transported by lift), and there is a museum in the mining village of Boutillère (open May–Sep). Next to the church is a small museum illustrating the craft of lace-making for which the locality is famous, and the modest hunting lodge of Vittorio Emanuele III.

A byroad ends at **Lillaz** (also reached by a path along the river from Cogne) where most of the houses preserve their typical slate roofs. A path leads past a number of waterfalls. The other road from Cogne enters the park along the Valnontey, which runs due south to the Gran Paradiso and ends at **Valnontey**, an attractive group of houses with a few simple hotels, the starting point of numerous nice walks in the park. The 'Paradisia' alpine garden (1700m), founded in 1955, is open Jul–Sep.

Liguria

The region of **Liguria** comprises the narrow strip of land lying between the Mediterranean and the summits of the Maritime Alps and the Apennines from the frontier of France to the borders of Tuscany. It is made up of the provinces of Genoa, Imperia, La Spezia and Savona. Liguria includes two of the most fertile stretches of the Italian coastline, the Riviera di Ponente and the Riviera di Levante, west and east of Genoa, where the mild winter climate encourages a luxuriant growth of vegetation, including palms, oranges and lemons, and the cultivation of flowers in early spring is important.

The Ligurian people, occupying a territory that has always been easier of access by sea than by land, are noted seafarers, and they have been influenced by immigrations from overseas rather than by landward invasions. Traces of Punic and Greek connections are evident, and Genoa became an important Roman seaport. Liguria was exposed to the attacks of Saracenic pirates in the later Middle Ages. The aristocratic republic of Genoa, at the height of its power after its defeat of Pisa in 1290, ruled the destinies of the whole seaboard from the 13C to the days of Napoleon. The Napoleonic campaigns of 1796 and 1799 resulted first in the creation of a 'Ligurian Republic' and then the absorption of the province into the French Empire; but in 1815 Liguria was attached to the kingdom of Piedmont. Genoa played an important part in the history of the Risorgimento, and Ligurian vessels provided transport for Garibaldi's attack on Sicily in 1860. In the Second World War the coastal area, especially Genoa, suffered severely from air attack.

27 · Genoa

Genoa, in Italian *Genova* (650,000 inhab.), is one of the main cities of Italy and still one of the most important ports on the Mediterranean for container traffic. It is built on an unusually awkward site, the irregular seaward slopes of an amphitheatre of hills, and preserves many relics of an ancient and honourable history, including the numerous palaces and magnificent art collections of its great maritime families (many still in private hands). In the 14C Genoa acquired a powerful maritime empire, and even though rivalry with Venice led to the defeat of the Genoese at Chioggia in 1380, the maritime importance of Genoa lasted well into the 17C. The town is famous as the birthplace of Christopher Columbus.

The old city, clustered round the old port, is still a most interesting district, with its tall houses in steep and narrow alleys or *carugi*, some less than three metres wide. There are long-term plans to restore some of these dark streets, with their quaint old-fashioned shops, which have suffered damage from numerous floods as well as from Allied air and sea bombardment in the last war, and which have greatly deteriorated in the past few decades. Over half the inhabitants of this area are now immigrants.

The city has expanded rapidly since the Second World War, and the raised motorway running between the old town and the port symbolises the chaotic town planning to which Genoa was subjected in the 1960s. Some important restorations, including that of Palazzo Ducale and Palazzo di San Giorgio, and new buildings (the Carlo Felice opera theatre, and the Aquarium) were completed for the controversial celebrations in 1992 which marked the 500th anniversary of the discovery of America by Columbus. An attempt to revitalise the area of the old port by Renzo Piano has been only partially successful, and the city is now having to face the consequences of industrial decline. The hinterland is covered with tower blocks which sprawl across the hills behind and the city limits now extend along the coast in both directions for some 30km between Nervi and Voltri.

■ **Tourist offices.** APT 11\3 Via Roma (Pl. 11), tel. 010 541541; information offices at Principe station, the airport, and in Palazzina Santa Maria, near the aquarium (Pl. 10).

■ **Railway stations.** Principe (Pl. 1) is the most central station, but nearly all trains stop also at Brignole.

■ **Airport.** Cristoforo Colombo, at Sestri Ponente (6km west). Flights to Europe as well as domestic services. Airport bus ('Volabus') regularly from Brignole Station, with stops in Piazza de' Ferrari (Pl. 11) and at Principe Station (Piazza Acquaverde).

■ **Car parking.** There is parking space in the area of the old port, near the aquarium (Pl. 9,10). Multistorey car parks in Piazza Piccapietra (Pl. 12) and Piazza Dante (Pl. 11/12).

■ **Maritime services.** The main quay for passenger and car ferries is Ponte Colombo next to the Stazione Marittima at Ponte Andrea Doria and Ponte dei Mille (Pl. 5). Regular car ferries to Sardinia, Sicily, and Tunis.

■ **Hotels.** 4-star: *City*, 6 Via San Sebastiano; *Bristol Palace*, 35 Via XX Settembre. 3-star: *Metropoli*, 8 Vico Migliorini (Piazza Fontane Marose); *Agnello d'Oro*, 6 Vico Monachette, and numerous others.

■ **Youth hostel.** *Ostello della Gioventù*, 120 Via Costanzi (bus 35 from Principe station; and 40 from Brignole station).

■ **Restaurants. A**: *Saint Cyr*, 8 Piazza Marsala; *Zeffirino*, 2 Via degli Archi; *I Professionisti*, 5 Piazza Matteotti. **B**: *Per Bacco*, 9 Piazza del Cavalletto; *Nabil*, 21 Vico Falamonica; *Pintori*, 68 Via San Bernardo. **C**: *Gaia*, 13 Vico dell'Argento (off Via Cairoli); *Da Maria*, 14 Vico Testadoro (off Via XXV Aprile).

Farinotti are small **snack bars** which sell *farinate*, a type of pizza made with chick-peas, a speciality of Genova. These include *Sa Pesta*, 16 Via dei Giustiniani; *Sciamadda*, 19 Via Ravecca; and *Spano*, 35 Via Santa Zita. Other snack bars can be found in the Portici di Sottoripa, near Palazzo di San Giorgio.

■ **City transport** is run by AMT (tel. 010 5997414). A ticket valid for one day on any line can be purchased at the AMT office at 8 Via d'Annunzio. The following **buses** serve the outskirts of the city:
1 Piazza Caricamento—Sampierdarena—Pegli—Voltri.
15 Piazza Caricamento—Piazza Tommaseo—Sturla—Quarto—Quinto—Nervi.
33 Piazza Acquaverde—Circonvallazione a Monte—Piazza Manin—Piazza Corvetto—Piazza De Ferrari—Stazione Brignole.
34 Piazzale San Benigno—Piazza Principe—Piazza Nunziata—Piazza Corvetto—Piazza Manin—Cimitero di Staglieno.

■ **Funicular railways. F** Largo della Zecca (Pl. 6) to Righi via San Nicolò . **H** Piazza Portello (Pl. 7) to Corso Magenta.
Rack Railway (**G**) from Via del Lagaccio, near Piazza Principe (Pl. 1) to Granarolo.
Lifts. L Via XX Settembre to Corso Podestà (Ponte Monumentale; Pl. 12). **M** Corso Magenta to Via Crocco. **N** Piazza Portello to the Spianata di Castelletto.

■ **Tours of the port**. Organised trips round the harbour by motor boat (c 1hr) depart from the Stazione Marittima (Ponte dei Mille, Calata Zingari; Pl. 1). Information from Cooperativa Battellieri (tel. 010 265712), and Alimar (tel. 010 255975).

■ **Country buses** depart from the bus station in Piazza della Vittoria; frequent service along the coast in both directions.

■ **Theatres.** *Carlo Felice*, Piazza De Ferrari (opera season). For prose: *Sala Duse*, 6 Via Bacigalupo (Piazza Corvetto), *Politeama Genovese*, 2 Via Bacigalupo; *Teatro della Corte*, Corte Lambruschini (Via Duca d'Aosta).

■ **International exhibitions** are held at the Fiera Internazionale, Piazzale Kennedy (beyond Pl. 14). A boat show (the *Salone Nautico)* is held annually in October, and *Euroflora*, a flower show is held in spring every five years (next in 2001).

Associazione Italo-Britannico, Piazza della Vittoria. The Wolfsonian Foundation, 28 Via Garbarino (and Castello Mackenzie).

History

The position of Genoa at the northernmost point of the Tyrrhenian sea and protected by mountains, has given it a lasting maritime importance. The original Ligurian inhabitants of the site established early contact with the first known navigators of the Mediterranean, the Phoenicians and Greeks, and objects excavated have proved the existence of a trading-post here in the 6C BC. In the 3C BC Genoa took up alliance with Rome against the Carthaginians, and when the town was destroyed by the Carthaginians in 205 BC, it was quickly rebuilt under the Roman praetor Cassius.

Roman connections were not entirely severed until the arrival of the Lombards in 641. In the succeeding centuries the sailors of Genoa withstood the attacks of Saracen pirates, and captured their strongholds of Corsica and Sardinia. Sardinia was taken with the help of Pisa, and its occupation led to two centuries of war, which ended in the final defeat of the Pisans at Meloria (1284). With this success began the acquisition of Genoa's great colonial empire, which extended as far as the Crimea, Syria and North Africa. Important Genoese colonies were established in the Morea (Peloponnese). These advances, and the large profits made during the Crusades, led to a collision with the ambitions of Venice; the subsequent war ended in the defeat of the Genoese at Chioggia (1380).

After the fall of the consuls in 1191, power passed to the podestà (mayors) and the 'Capitani del Popolo' (1258–1340), with intervals of submission to the Emperor Henry VII (1311–13) and to Robert of Anjou, King of Naples (1318–35). In 1340 came the election of the first Doge, Simone Boccanegra. Petrarch, on a visit in 1358, described the city as 'la superba', a name used by numerous subsequent travellers to Genoa. Chaucer was sent to Genoa in 1372–73 by Edward II to arrange a commercial treaty with the maritime Republic. The continual strife between the great families (Doria, Spinola and Fieschi) made Genoa an easy victim to the rising military powers and it had a succession of foreign rulers in the 15C. In 1528 Andrea Doria (1466–1560), the greatest of the Genoese naval leaders, formulated a constitution for Genoa which freed the city from foreign rule, though it established despotic government at home and was followed (1547–48) by the insurrections of Fieschi and Cibo.

The conquests of the Turks in their oriental empire, the transfer of overseas trade with America to Atlantic ports, and the domination of Spain, brought about the rapid decline of Genoa in the 17C, and in 1684 Louis XIV entered the town after a bombardment. The Austrian occupation of 50 years later was ended by a popular insurrection in 1746, which was started by the action of a boy, Giovanni Battista Perasso (known as Balilla). In 1768 the Genoese sold to France their rights to their last remaining colony, Corsica. In 1796 Napoleon entered Genoa, and four years later the city was attacked by the Austrians on land and the English at sea. The Ligurian Republic, formed in 1802, soon became a French province, but in 1815 Genoa was joined to Piedmont by the treaty of Vienna, and became a stronghold of the Risorgimento, with Giuseppe Mazzini (born in Genoa) as the leading spirit. He was abetted by Garibaldi (who planned his expedition with the 'Thousand' from here in 1860), the soldier patriot Nino Bixio (1821–73), and Goffredo Mameli (1827–49) the warrior poet. Charles Dickens and his family spent much time in Genoa in 1844, and came 'to have an attachment for the very stones in the streets of Genoa, and to look back upon the city with affection as connected with many hours of happiness and quiet!' He left an interesting description of his stay in *Pictures from Italy*. The poet Eugenio Montale (1896–1981) was born in Genoa.

Art

The architecture of medieval Genoa is characterised by the black-and-white striped façades of the older churches, and the earliest sculpture came from the workshops of the Pisano family and the Comacini. Galeazzo Alessi, the Perugian architect, worked here during the Renaissance, and in the

16C–17C the Gaggini family of sculptors were active. Through its close commercial links with the Netherlands, the city acquired many Dutch and Flemish paintings. In 1607 Rubens visited Genoa, and in 1621 Van Dyck arrived and stayed in the city for six years on and off. The most productive period of Genoese painting is the 17C, with Bernardo Strozzi, Bernardo and Valerio Castello, Giovanni Battista Castiglione, Domenico Fiasella and the Piola brothers.

The centre of the city

PIAZZA DE FERRARI (Pl. 11), where numerous main roads converge, is at the centre of the city. It has a large fountain and the **Teatro Carlo Felice**, rebuilt on a huge scale by Aldo Rossi in 1987–91. The first theatre, designed by Carlo Barabino in 1828, was gutted by fire in 1944, although its neo-classical pronaos survives. The new building includes a massive rectangular tower. Behind Augusto Rivalta's Garibaldi monument (1893), is the neo-classical **Accademia Ligustica di Belle Arti** (1827–31), also by Carlo Barabino. A pinacoteca (open 9–13 exc. fest.) here contains paintings by Ligurian artists (14C–19C). Between Via XX Settembre and Via Dante which lead to the newer districts of the city is the elaborate curved façade of the Borsa (1907–12).

Opposite is the side of Palazzo Ducale, recently repainted, and on the last side of the square is a palace built as offices in 1923 by Cesare Gamba. Behind this, in PIAZZA MATTEOTTI (Pl. 11), is the Baroque church of the **Gesù** (Pl. 11), built 1589–1606 by Giuseppe Valeriani. In the sumptuous polychrome interior are frescoes by Giovanni Carlone and altarpieces by Guido Reni and Rubens.

Surrounding Piazza Matteotti is **PALAZZO DUCALE** (Pl. 11), a huge building of various periods which was restored in 1975–92 as a cultural centre. The left wing, Palazzo di Alberto Fieschi, was the seat of the 'Capitano del Popolo' in 1272 and from 1294 Palazzo del Comune. It became the residence of the doges from 1340 onwards, and Andrea Vannone carried out radical modifications in c 1591–1620, adding the attractive spacious *vestibule with a light courtyard at either end. The palace was reconstructed by Simone Cantoni in 1778–83 and given a neo-classical façade. On the upper floors (closed Mon) are the Salone del Maggior Consiglio, and the doges' chapel frescoed by Giovanni Battista Carlone. Exhibitions are held here, and there are two restaurants.

The Cathedral

In Via San Lorenzo is the flank of the *Cathedral (San Lorenzo; Pl. 11), a Romanesque-Gothic building consecrated (unfinished) in 1118 and modified in the 13C–14C and during the Renaissance. On the south side are Hellenistic sarcophagi, a 15C Grimaldi tomb, and the Romanesque **portal of San Gottardo**. The **façade** (restored in the 20C) has doorways in the French Gothic style. The **campanile** was completed in 1522. On the north side is the 12C **portal of San Giovanni**.

In the **interior** are dark Corinthian columns. The proportions were altered when the nave roof was raised in 1550 and the cupola, by Galeazzo Alessi, added in 1567. The pulpit dates from 1526. The lunette over the west door has early 14C frescoes.

In the **south aisle**, beside a British naval shell that damaged the chapel without exploding in 1941, is a marble relief of the Crucifixion of 1443. In the chapel to the right of the high altar is a painting by Federico Barocci. The stalls in the apse date from 1514–64. In the chapel to the left of the high altar are wall and ceiling paintings by Luca Cambiaso and Giovanni Battista Castello.

The great *Chapel of St John the Baptist** was designed by Domenico and Elia Gagini (1451-65), with a richly decorated front. It contains statues by Matteo Civitali, and Andrea Sansovino (1504), a baldacchino of 1532, and a 13C French sarcophagus. In the adjoining chapel is the tomb of Giorgio Fieschi (died 1461) by Giovanni Gagini.

The *Treasury** (reopened in 1996), in vaults designed in 1956 by Franco Albini, contains Roman glass, copes, the Byzantine *Zaccaria Cross, and precious reliquaries.

From Palazzo Ducale the Salita Pollaioli descends into the **old town** with its narrow dark streets, or *carugi*, with tall houses. Some charming portals survive in this district, in white marble or black stone, often bearing reliefs of St George, patron of the city. There are also numerous Baroque tabernacles with religious images on the streets. VIA CANNETO IL LUNGO is a typical long street of the old town, with food shops and some good doorways.

The church of **San Donato** (Pl. 11), probably founded in the early 12C, has a splendid polygonal campanile and a good doorway. In the beautiful basilican interior is a late 14C painting by Nicolò da Voltri, and a triptych of the *Adoration of the Magi by Joos van Cleve.

Sant'Agostino

The Stradone Sant'Agostino leads up past the new building of the faculty of architecture of the University to PIAZZA DI SARZANO, once a centre of the old city, but partly derelict since the war. Here is the pink building (1977–84) of the **MUSEO DI SANT'AGOSTINO** (Pl. 15; open 9–19; fest. 9–12.30; exc. Mon), housing the city's collection of architectural fragments, sculptures and detached frescoes. The Gothic **church of Sant'Agostino**, begun in 1260, its fine campanile with graceful windows and spire, has been restored for use as an auditorium. The interior of the museum is built in a pretentious modern style with much of the structure in black. The **ground floor** has late medieval sculpture (good 10C–11C capitals). A long stair ramp leads up to the **first floor**, with 13C frescoes, fragments of the funerary *monument of Margherita di Brabante (died 1311), by Giovanni Pisano, and a painted *crucifix by Barnaba da Modena. Another long stair ramp leads up to the **second floor** with 15C black stone *architraves with reliefs of St John the Baptist and St George, carved masques by Taddeo Carlone; detached frescoes by Luca Cambiaso; 16C sculptures (Gian Giacomo Della Porta, Silvio Cosini); paintings by Domenico Piola; and sculptures by Filippo Parodi, Pierre Puget and Antonio Canova.

Santa Maria di Castello

From below Piazza San Donato, Via San Bernardo leads left. Some way along on the left, Vico dei Giustiniani leads left to Piazza Embriaci (Pl. 11), where steps lead up to the Doric portal (by Giovanni Battista Orsolino) of the **Casa Brignole Sale** (No. 5), restored in 1538. On the right, the steep stepped Salita, passing the 12C **Torre degli Embriaci**, restored and completed in 1923, ascends to *Santa

GENOA

| 0 | 200 yards |
| 0 | 200 metres |

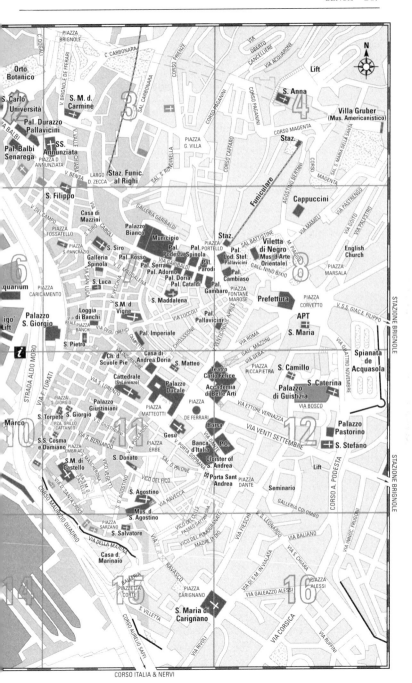

Maria di Castello (Pl. 10), a Romanesque church with 15C Gothic additions. It occupies the site of the Roman castrum and preserves some Roman columns.

Interior (closed 12–15.30). On the west wall is a fresco (c 1498) by Lorenzo Fasolo; in the **south aisle**, altarpieces by Aurelio Lomi, Pier Francesco Sacchi and Bernardo Castello; in the **sanctuary**, a marble group of the Assumption of the Virgin by Antonio Domenico Parodi; and in the chapel to the left of the sanctuary, St Rosa of Lima by Domenico Piola. The **baptistery** contains a 15C polyptych, some ruined 15C frescoes and a Roman sarcophagus.

The **sacristy** has a beautifully carved portal (inner face) by Giovanni Gagini and Leonardo Riccomanno (1452). In the **Dominican convent** (1445–1513) are pretty frescoes in the **loggia of the second cloister**, possibly by 'Iustus de Alemania', the Flemish painter who signed and dated (1451) the *Annunciation on the wall. In the **upper loggia** (view of the port), with Roman and medieval capitals, is a *tabernacle of the Trinity by Domenico Gagini, and a detached *fresco in monochrome of St Dominic, attributed to Braccesco. The **old library** has a wooden crucifix (c 1100), and a polyptych of the Annunciation by Giovanni Mazone (1470; one of only two works known by this local artist). The **museum** (opened on request) contains the *Coronation of the Virgin, a painting showing Flemish influence, signed and dated 1513 by Ludovico Brea.

Via San Bernardo continues past several fine doorways to Piazza Grillo Cattaneo, where a portal by Tamagnino survives at No. 6 surrounded by dilapidated buildings. Vico dietro il Coro di San Cosimo leads past the east end of the 11C church of **Santi Cosma e Damiano** (Pl. 10). Piazza San Giorgio (Pl. 10), an important market square in the Middle Ages, has two attractive, domed and centrally planned churches: **San Giorgio**, documented as early as 964 and reconstructed in 1695, and **San Torpete**, rebuilt with an elliptical cupola after 1730, on a design by Giovanni Antonio Ricca. In Via dei Giustiniani busts and reliefs decorate the portico of the 17C **Palazzo Giustiniani** (No. 6).

From Piazza San Giorgio, Via Canneto il Curto, another typical street of the old town, leads back up to Via San Lorenzo and the cathedral.

Piazza San Matteo

Between Palazzo Ducale and the Cathedral is Via Reggio which skirts the left wing of Palazzo Ducale (see above) and the **Torre del Popolo** (1307), known as the 'Grimaldina'. At No. 12 is the cloister of San Lorenzo (c 1180).

PIAZZA SAN MATTEO was created in the 12C when it was surrounded by the mansions and church of the Doria family with striped black-and-white façades. *San Matteo** (Pl. 11), founded in 1125 but rebuilt by the Doria in 1278, has a striped black-and-white Gothic façade with inscriptions recounting the glorious deeds of the Dorias. The **interior** was transformed in 1543–47 for Andrea Doria by Giovanni Angelo Montorsoli and Giovanni Battista Castello. The sanctuary is an interesting sculptural work by Montorsoli (with the help of Silvio Cosini). The nave was decorated with stuccoes and frescoes by Bergamasco and Luca Cambiaso. The wood group of the Deposition is by Anton Maria Maragliano. The *crypt** and staircase, decorated with marbles and stuccoes, were designed by Montorsoli for the tomb of Andrea Doria. An archway on the left of the church leads to the cloister (1308–10) by Magister Marcus Venetus.

Opposite the church is the **Casa di Lamba Doria** (No. 15), built in the 13C with a portico. The **Casa di Andrea Doria** (No. 17) was built for Lazzaro Doria in 1468 and presented to the famous admiral by his native city in 1528. No. 14 is the **Casa di Branca Doria** (No.14), with a charming relief over the portal.

Off Via Chiossone, in which No. 1 is another Doria house with a blackened portal by Pace Gaggini, the ancient Vico della Casana, a busy lane, leads to the left. The animated Via Luccoli (left again), with many good shops and attractive street lighting, crosses Piazza Soziglia (with a café founded in 1828) to reach the Campetto (Pl. 7). **Palazzo Imperiale** (1560; No. 8) is a sumptuous building by Giovanni Battista Castello. The upper part of the curved façade is decorated with paintings and stuccoes by Ottavio Semino.

On the other side of Via degli Orefici, a short road leads to **Santa Maria delle Vigne** (Pl. 7), a church redesigned in 1640 by Daniele Casella (good Baroque interior), with a façade of 1842. Parts of its Romanesque predecessors (10C and 12C) can be seen from the lane on the left side, together with an interesting 14C tomb incorporating the front of a 2C sarcophagus. Inside is the tomb slab of the goldsmiths' corporation, with a fine relief of St Eligius (1459).

From the piazza in front, Vico dei Greci leads west to Vico Mele with some interesting houses.

In the crooked and busy Via degli Orefici (see above) are more carved reliefs. At the end of the street is PIAZZA BANCHI which, until the end of the 18C, was the commercial centre of the city where the money-changers had their *banchi*. Here is the **Loggia dei Mercanti**, designed in 1589–95 by Vannone and restored in the 19C, when it became an exchange, the first of its kind in Italy (now used for exhibitions). The restored, centrally planned church of **San Pietro in Banchi** was designed by Bernardino Cantone, and built by Giovanni Ponzello and Vannone (1581). Via Ponte Reale leads down to the quays, past the house where Daniel O'Connell—'the Liberator'—died in 1847 (plaque). The arcaded Portici di Sottoripa, with numerous snack bars, are characteristic of the old port area.

Palazzo di San Giorgio

Here is PIAZZA CARICAMENTO (Pl. 6; being redesigned), and the Gothic Palazzo di San Giorgio (Pl. 6; restored in 1992), begun c 1260 and extended towards the sea in 1570. The façade facing the port was frescoed by Lazzaro Tavarone in 1606–08. Once the palace of the Capitani del Popolo, it became in 1408 the seat of the famous Banco di San Giorgio, which was largely responsible for the prosperity of the city from the mid-15C onwards. Here citizens could lend money for compound interest, and the idea of cheques was introduced. It is now occupied by the Harbour Board (adm. usually on weekdays).

Across the road and under the *sopraelevata* (or Strada Aldo Moro), an ugly raised motorway (1965) which has isolated the old town from the harbour, and which distributes the motorway traffic from the western suburbs to the city, is the **OLD PORT** (Pl. 9). The Molo Vecchio was begun in 1257 by the Cistercian friars Oliverio and Filippo, and the imposing **Porta Siberia**, designed by Galeazzo Alessi, dates from 1553. The area was redesigned by Renzo Piano in 1992: he converted the old cotton warehouses into a congress centre (which can hold 1600 people), and created an open-air space on the quay for spectacles and fairs, next to the '**bigo**', an unusual metal structure which serves as a 'crane' for a lift from which there is a panoramic view.

The Aquarium

The Aquarium (Pl. 6; open Tue, Wed, & Fri 9.30–19; Thu, Sat & Sun 9.30–20.30; closed Mon), also designed by Piano in 1992, is the largest in Europe (much visited by school parties), with 50 huge tanks which can be viewed both from an underwater level and from above. The natural habitat of the Red Sea and the Caribbean coral reef have been reconstructed. The aquarium contains some 20,000 creatures, including dolphins, seals and sharks, and tropical fish in smaller tanks. The redesigning of the rest of the area has still to be completed.

From Piazza Banchi VIA SAN LUCA (Pl. 7) leads north. It was the main street of the city in the Middle Ages, and as the principal place of residence of the great Genoese families, it was important up to the 18C. It is now a commercial street, full of shops and offices. The little church of **San Luca**, to the right, rebuilt in 1626, is a fine example of Genoese Baroque, with an interior entirely frescoed by Domenico Piola. It contains sculptures by Filippo Parodi, and an altarpiece by Grechetto.

Palazzo Spinola

Beyond, Vico Pellicceria leads right to Piazza Pellicceria with palaces of the Spinola. No. 1 is now the **GALLERIA NAZIONALE DI PALAZZO SPINOLA** (Pl. 7; open Tue–Sat 9–19; Mon 9–13; fest. 14–19). This 16C mansion became the property of the Spinola in the early 18C when the collection of paintings was formed. It was left by the family, with the contents, to the Italian state in 1958, and is a particularly interesting example of a patrician Genoese residence which preserves more or less intact its 17C–18C decorations, as well as its furniture and paintings. The first two floors have been restored as far as possible to their original state under the Spinola, while the third floor is occupied by the Galleria Nazionale della Liguria, with restored works from churches, and an important porcelain collection.

First floor. The **Salone** has a vault frescoed by Lazzaro Tavarone c 1615, and bronzes by Ferdinando Tacca. The **Primo Salotto** contains works by Stefano Magnasco, Baciccio, and Giovanni Battista Carlone. The **Secondo Salotto** contains a portrait of Ansaldo Pallavicino by Van Dyck, and a portrait of a lady by Bernardo Strozzi.

The **second floor** was decorated for Maddalena Doria (wife of Nicolò Spinola) in 1734. The **Salone**, with another ceiling fresco by Tavarone, was decorated by Giovanni Battista Natali as a setting for the paintings by Domenico Piola, Gregorio De Ferrari, Luca Giordano and Bernardo Strozzi. The **Primo Salotto** still has its 18C decorations and furniture. The **Secondo Salotto** displays paintings by Guido Reni, Luca Cambiaso, Valerio Castello, Luca Giordano and Bernardo Strozzi. The Four Evangelists are by Van Dyck. The **Terzo Salotto** has works by Carlo Maratta, Bernardo Castello, Giulio Cesare Procaccini, Francesco Vanni and Filippo Parodi. The two small female portraits by Mignard are in exquisite 17C frames (one by Filippo Parodi), and the Virgin in Prayer is by Joos van Cleve, who stayed in Genoa in 1515–20 and again in 1525–28. The charming **Galleria degli Specchi** (1736) was probably designed by Lorenzo de Ferrari, who painted the vault fresco. The **Quinto Salotto** has paintings by Marcantonio Franceschini, a portrait of Paolo Spinola by Angelica Kauffmann, and 18C furniture.

The **mezzanine floor** has a collection of Spinola engravings and 19C silver. On the stairs is a statue by Filippo Parodi.

On the **third floor** is exhibited the **Galleria Nazionale della Liguria** which includes an *Ecce Homo by Antonello da Messina, an equestrian *portrait of Gio Carlo Doria by Rubens, a portrait of a lady with a child by Van Dyck, and a statue of Justice, part of the funerary monument of Margherita di Brabante by Giovanni Pisano.

On the **top floor** is a fine display of European and oriental porcelain which belonged to the Spinola. A spiral staircase leads up from here to a little terrace with a delightful view of the city.

Vico della Scienza leads east from Piazza Pellicceria into Via della Posta Vecchia, with many good portals. Via San Luca (see above) continues to **San Siro** (Pl. 7), a large church rebuilt by Andrea Ceresola and Daniele Casella (1586–1613), with a façade of 1821. Its predecessor was the cathedral of Genoa before the 9C. It contains frescoes by Giovanni Battista Carlone and a painting by Pomerancio.

From Via San Luca, the pretty Via della Maddalena (Pl. 7) leads east past a palace (No. 29) which belonged to Simone Boccanegra, elected first doge of Genoa in 1340 (with a delightful courtyard), to the church of **Santa Maria Maddalena** (Pl. 7), rebuilt in 1588 by Andrea Ceresola. The richly decorated interior contains paintings and frescoes by Bernardo Castello and Giovanni Battista Parodi, and five beautiful *statuettes of the Virtues, attributed to Giovanni Pisano. From here numerous alleyways lead up to Via Garibaldi.

Via Garibaldi

*VIA GARIBALDI (Pl. 7), formerly known as the Strada Nuova, was laid out in 1558 by Bernardino Cantone, pupil of Galeazzo Alessi. In the following decade the leading Genoese patrician families built their magnificent mansions here, making it one of the most handsome streets in Europe. Narrow lanes lead down from the street into the old city.

Palazzo Bianco

*Palazzo Bianco (No. 11; open Tue, Thu, Fri, & Sun, 9–13; Wed & Sat 9–19; closed Mon) was built for the Grimaldi c 1565 and enlarged after 1711 by Giacomo Viano for Maria Durazzo, widow of Giovanni Francesco Brignole Sale. It was presented to the municipality in 1884 by Maria Brignole Sale, the Duchess of Galliera. The palace contains part of her collection of paintings, together with later acquisitions, with some particularly beautiful Flemish and Dutch paintings. The gallery was excellently rearranged and modernised in 1950 by Franco Albini. Only the outstanding pieces are on view.

Room 1 (beyond Room 2). 13C Byzantine works; *Madonna of the Goldfinch by Barnaba da Modena; and works by the Brea family (late 15–16C). **Room 2**. Luca Cambiaso.

Second floor. **Room 3** (South Loggia). Filippino Lippi and Giorgio Vasari. **Room 4** contains the masterpieces of the collection: Master of St John the Evangelist (Flemish, late 15C), four *scenes from the Life of the Saint; Hans

Memling (*Christ Blessing*); *Madonnas by Joos van Cleve and Gerard David; Jan Provost (*St Peter, *Annunciation, *St Elizabeth). **Room 5**. Jan Matsys and Jan van Scorel. **Room 6**. Cornelis De Wael and Jan Wildens.

Room 7. Van Dyck, Jan Roos and Rubens. **Room 8**. Flemish and Dutch 17C genre paintings by David Teniers the younger, Jan Steen, Jacob Ruysdael and Aelbert Cuyp. **Room 9** displays Italian paintings from the 16C to early 17C (Veronese and Palma il Giovane; Procaccini, Cerano, Morazzone, Paggi and Salimbeni). **Room 10** (North Loggia). Caravaggio (Ecce Homo), Simon Vouet, and Matthias Stomer. **Room 11**. Works of the Spanish school, including Murillo and Francesco Zurbaran.

Rooms 12–15 contain interesting paintings of the 17C–18C Genoese school: Bernardo Strozzi; Anton Maria Vassallo, Antonio Travi, Giovanni Battista Carlone and Sinibaldo Scorza; Domenico Fiasella, Giovanni Andrea Ansaldo and Giovanni Andrea De Ferrari; Gioacchino Assereto and Silvestro Chiesa. The local collection is continued on the **ground floor** (across the courtyard) in **Rooms 16–20** (Domenico Piola, Gregorio De Ferrari, Bartolomeo Guidobono, Il Baciccio, Valerio Castello, Giovanni Benedetto Castiglione and Alessandro Magnasco).

Palazzo Rosso

Almost opposite Palazzo Bianco is *Palazzo Rosso (Pl. 7; adm. as for Palazzo Bianco), a magnificent building of 1671–77 erected for Ridolfo and Gio Francesco Brignole Sale by Pier Antonio Corradi, and decorated in 1687–89 by Gregorio De Ferrari, Domenico Piola, and others. Like Palazzo Bianco it was bequeathed to the city (in 1874) by the Duchess of Galliera, together with her magnificent art collection, which includes fine portraits of the Brignole family by Van Dyck. It was likewise well restored after damage in the war, in 1953–61 by Franco Albini.

First floor. **Room 2**. Works by Giambono, Veronese, Dürer, and Palma Vecchio. **Room 3**. Portraits by Paris Bordone. **Room 4**. Works by Giulio Cesare Procaccini and Ludovico Carracci. **Room 5**. Guido Reni and Guercino. **Room 6**. Mattia Preti and Ribera. **Rooms 7–10**. Bernardo Strozzi, Giovanni Benedetto Castiglione and Bartolomeo Guidobono.

Second Floor. **Room 12**, the Salone, has frescoes by Antonio and Enrico Haffner. Rooms 13 and 14 have vault frescoes by Gregorio de' Ferrari. **Rooms 13 & 14**. Portraits by Van Dyck: Geronima Sale Brignole with her daughter Aurelia; Frederick, Prince of Orange; a Genoese patrician; *Pucci the goldsmith, and his son; Anton Giulio Brignole Sale and his wife Paolina. Rooms 15–16 have vaults decorated by Domenico Piola. **Room 15**. Brignole portraits by Yacinthe Rigaud. The **loggia** has a good view of the striped campanile of the Duomo, the campanile of Santa Maria delle Vigne, and the Torre degli Embriaci. **Rooms 18 and 19** are frescoed by Giovanni Andrea Carlone. **Room 22** has frescoes by Parodi and Guidobono.

Immediately beyond Palazzo Rosso, on the left, is ***PALAZZO DORIO TURSI** (the town hall), flanked by raised gardens. It was begun in 1568 for Nicolò Grimaldi by the Ponzello brothers, and the loggias were added in 1597 around the magnificent courtyard. It is open Mon–Thu 9–12, 13–16.30, Fri 9–12, 13–15, and contains the Guarneri violin (1742) which belonged to Genoa-born

Nicolò Paganini (1784–1840), the violinist and composer, and three letters from Columbus.

Most of the other mansions in this street can be admired only from the outside, though the courtyards are usually accessible. No. 12 is the late 16C **Palazzo Serra**. **Palazzo Podestà** (No. 7) was begun by Giovanni Battista Castello and Bernardino Cantone in 1563, and has a good stuccoed vestibule and a Rococo grotto and fountain in the courtyard. **Palazzo Spinola** (No. 5) has frescoes in the atrium and vestibule (the fine courtyard has been enclosed for use as a banking hall). **Palazzo Doria** (No. 6) of 1563 was remodelled in 1684, with a charming little courtyard. **Palazzo Carrega Cataldi** (No. 4) is by Giovanni Battista Castello and Bernardino Cantone (1558–60). **Palazzo Lercari Parodi** (No. 3), attributed to Galeazzo Alessi (1571–78), has a portal with two atlantes by Taddeo Carlone (1581). **Palazzo Gambaro** (No.2) is by Bernardo Spazio (1558–64), and **Palazzo Cambiaso** (No. 1) is by Bernardino Cantone (1558–60).

In the irregular Piazza Fontane Marose (Pl. 7) are **Palazzo Pallavicini** (No. 2), begun 1565; **Palazzo Negrone** (No. 4), altered c 1750; and the 15C **Palazzo Spinola dei Marmi** (No. 6), with a particoloured marble façade and statues of the family.

Beyond the western end of Via Garibaldi is Via Cairoli (Pl. 7), in which at the end on the left is **Palazzo Balbi** (No. 18), with an ingenious staircase by Gregorio Petondi (1780). In Largo della Zecca is the entrance to the Galleria Garibaldi, a road-tunnel of 1927.

Via Bensa continues to Piazza della Nunziata dominated by the19C neo-classical pronaos of **Santissima Annunziata** (Pl. 2), a church rebuilt 1591–1620. The elaborate 17C interior has frescoes in the nave vault by Giovanni Battista and Giovanni Carlone, and in the dome by Andrea Ansaldo and Gregorio De Ferrari. The fine altarpieces by the 17C Genoese school, include numerous works by Giovanni Battista Carlone.

Via Balbi

From here the narrow VIA BALBI (Pl. 2) continues uphill towards Principe railway station past many dignified old mansions. On the right is **Palazzo Durazzo-Pallavicini** (No. 1; now Giustiniani Adorno), by Bartolomeo Bianco, with a later double loggia. It contains a remarkable private collection (no adm.) including the best works by Van Dyck in the city. **Palazzo Balbi-Senarega**, opposite (No. 4; used by the University), is also by Bianco. Since 1803 the **University** has occupied the palace at No. 5, built in 1634–36 as a Jesuit college by Bartolomeo Bianco. It has an imposing court, and statues and reliefs by Giambologna (1579) in the Aula Magna. The Botanical Garden (Pl. 2) was founded in 1803.

Opposite (No. 10) is the former **PALAZZO REALE** (or Palazzo Balbi-Durazzo; Pl. 2), designed c 1650 for the Balbi family by Michele Moncino and Pier Francesco Cantone and remodelled in 1705 for the Durazzo by Carlo Fontana. From 1842 to 1922 it was the royal seat in Genoa and it contains several suites of sumptuously decorated 18C rooms (open daily 9–14; in Jul–Sep, Tue–Sat 9–19); a Crucifixion by Van Dyck; and works by Luca Giordano, Domenico Parodi, Bartolomeo Guidobono and Bernardo Strozzi.

San Giovanni di Prè

Via Balbi ends in Piazza Acquaverde, with a monument (1862) to Columbus in front of **Principe railway station**, an impressive building of 1854. Downhill to the left is the church of San Giovanni di Prè (Pl. 1), founded in 1180, with a severe interior (often restored) with an apse at each end. There is an upper and lower church which adjoin the **Commenda** (Pl. 1), the Commandery of the Knights of St John, built at the same time as a convent and hospice for crusaders. On Piazza Commenda is the fine five-spired campanile and flank of the church (with Gothic arches), next to the beautiful triple loggia of the Commenda, altered in the Renaissance (restored in 1992 and used for exhibitions).

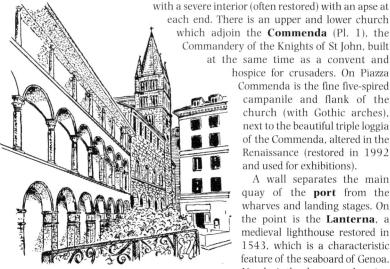

San Giovanni di Prè

A wall separates the main quay of the **port** from the wharves and landing stages. On the point is the **Lanterna**, a medieval lighthouse restored in 1543, which is a characteristic feature of the seaboard of Genoa. Nearby is the skyscraper housing the World Trade Center. Near the maritime station, at 2 Via San Benedetto, is **Palazzo del Principe** (Pl. 1), owned by the Doria Pamphilij family, which has recently been opened to the public (Sat 15–18; Sun 10–13; closed in Aug). Two buildings here were acquired by Andrea Doria in 1521, and were made into one by Domenico Caranca (1529); Montorsoli may have added the loggia (1543–47), facing the garden. Charles V and Napoleon were entertained here in 1533 and 1805, as was the composer Verdi after 1877. It contains frescoes by Perin del Vaga and stuccoes by Luzio Romano and Guglielmo della Porta in the vestibule and on the stairs, as well as portraits of Andrea Doria (by Sebastiano del Piombo) and Giannettino Doria (attributed to Bronzino).

From San Giovanni di Prè (see above), the long and dilapidated Via di Prè (Pl. 2) leads back towards the centre parallel to the sea. It passes the circular neo-classical church of **San Sisto** (1827), behind Palazzo Reale, and ends at **Porta dei Vacca**, a Gothic arch dating from 1155. Beyond the arch is Via del Campo (Pl. 6) which has some good portals, and ends at Piazza Fossatello. From here Via Lomellini leads left to the church of **San Filippo Neri**, with a fine 18C interior decorated by Antonio Maria Haffner, and a polychrome Deposition group by Anton Maria Maragliano. The **Oratory** next door (No. 10; if closed ask at the Casa Mazzini) has an *interior of 1749 (used for concerts), with a statue of the Immacolata by Pierre Puget. The **Casa Mazzini**, at No. 11 Via Lomellini (open 9–13 exc. Mon & Wed), where Giuseppe Mazzini (1805–72) was born, contains an excellent **Museum of the Risorgimento**. Narrow roads lead back up to Via Cairoli (see above).

The modern town

From Piazza De Ferrari, Via Roma leads to Piazza Corvetto (Pl. 8). The Vittorio Emanuele II monument here is by Francesco Barzaghi (1886). Behind the Mazzini monument (by Pietro Costa, 1882) is the hillside garden of the **Villetta di Negro** (Pl. 8). A fine building (1971, by Mario Labò) houses the ***Museo d'Arte Orientale Edoardo Chiossone** (open 9–13 exc. Mon & Wed). This splendid collection of Japanese, Chinese and Thai art was left to the municipality of Genoa by the painter Edoardo Chiossone (1832–98), and has been augmented during this century. It is especially notable for its Japanese works, including large sculptures (10C–18C) and arms and armour.

From Piazza Corvetto the long straight Via Assarotti leads northeast to Piazza Manin passing the sumptuous church of the **Immacolata** (1864–73). On the hill opposite is the beautiful **Villa Pallavicino delle Peschiere** (by Galeazzo Alessi), where Dickens stayed in 1845.

From Piazza Manin are reached the **Mura Nuove**, the 17C walls which extend as far as Forte Sperone. On Via Cesare Cabella is the **Castello Mackenzie**. Derived from Tuscan Gothic buildings, it was commissioned at the end of the last century from Gino Coppedè by a Scottish insurance broker, Evan Mackenzie. Partly restored by the Wolfsonian Foundation as a museum of Italian decorative arts from the period 1885–1945, it was donated to the city in 1996.

At Piazza Manin begin the avenues known as the ***Circonvallazione a Monte** (Pl. 2, 3, 7, & 8), over 4km long, which provide an interesting view of the city. They are traversed by bus 33, and lifts and funicular railways serve as intermediate approaches. The most important monuments are mentioned below. The 17C **Villa Gruber** (Pl. 7/8) is the seat of the **Museo Americanistico Federico Lunardi** (open Tue–Sat 9.30–12, 15–17.30; fest. 15–17.30; closed Mon), with archaeological and ethnographical material from North and South America. The neo-Gothic **Castello Bruzzo** is by Gino Coppedè. The church of **San Nicola da Tolentino** has an interior of 1597 with statues by Taddeo Carlone. Nearby is a station on the funicular which mounts to **Righi** where there are good views of the city and its fortifications. The huge **Albergo dei Poveri** was founded by the Brignole in 1656 as one of the first poorhouses of its kind, and built to a functional design by Stefano Scaniglia and Giovanni Battista Ghiso. The magnificent **Castello D'Albertis** is a reconstruction of 1886 of a medieval Ligurian castle on the old bastion of Monte Galletto. The interior, with an Ethnographical Museum (pre-Columbian art), is closed for restoration.

From Piazza De Ferrari (see above), the wide arcaded Via XX Settembre leads southeast past the church of **Santo Stefano** (Pl. 11), with a particoloured front of the 13C–14C and a 10C crypt. The choir-gallery of 1499 is the work of Donato Benti and Benedetto da Rovezzano. On the south wall is a painting by Giulio Romano. A lift ascends to the **Ponte Monumentale** (Pl. 11) which crosses Via XX Settembre. Above are the **Acquasola Gardens**, with fine trees, and **Santa Caterina**, a church largely rebuilt from 1556, with a portal of 1521 by Pier Antonio Piuma, and containing good 16C Genoese paintings, including works by Giovanni Battista Castello.

Via XX Settembre continues past the church of **Santa Maria della**

Consolazione, by Pier Antonio Corradi (1684–1706), with a dome by Simone Cantone (1769) and a front of 1864. The street ends at the gardens of Piazza Verdi in front of Brignole station, and Piazza della Vittoria (Pl. 16), with a triumphal arch erected as a war memorial by Marcello Piacentini in 1931. In Via Brigata Liguria, in a building of 1905–12, is the **Natural History Museum** (open 9–12, 15–17.30 exc. Mon & Fri), founded in 1867 with the zoological collections of Giacomo Doria.

In Corso Buenos Aires are the glass skyscrapers of **Corte Lambruschini** (which incorporate the Teatro della Corte), built in the 1980s by Piero Gambacciani. In Piazza Tommaseo is a monument to General Manuel Belgrano (1770–1820), liberator of the Argentine Republic, by Arnaldo Zocchi (1927). The interesting 19C district of **Foce** extends to the south as far as the seafront.

From Piazza De Ferrari the short and broad Via Dante runs southeast. On the right, beside a little house reconstructed in the 18C and called the **House of Columbus**, is a garden with the reconstructed 12C **Cloister of Sant'Andrea**. Above rises **Porta Soprana** (Pl. 11), a tall gateway of 1155.

Across **Piazza Dante**, with skyscrapers built in the 1930s, is Via Fieschi, which ascends to the classical church of **Santa Maria Assunta di Carignano** (Pl. 15), one of the best works of Galeazzo Alessi (begun in 1552). The sculptures on the façade are by Claude David, and inside on the dome-piers are statues (1662–90) by Pierre Puget, Filippo Parodi and Claude David. Via Nino Bixio and Via Ruffini lead southeast) to **Villa Croce**, with a **contemporary art museum** (open 9–19; fest 9–12.30; closed Mon), and a library. Nearby, on the seafront are the buildings of the **Fiera Internazionale**, where big international exhibitions are held.

The outskirts of the city

The *Staglieno Cemetery (open daily 8–17) was laid out, with extensive gardens, in 1844–51 and has intriguing 19C funerary sculpture. The conspicuous colossal statue of Faith is by Santo Varni, and near the upper gallery, in a clump of trees, is the simple tomb of Mazzini, surrounded by memorials to members of Garibaldi's 'Thousand'. To the left of the Pantheon and the main enclosure—on the third terrace, planted with oak trees—is the **Protestant temple and cemetery**: Constance Mary Lloyd, the wife of Oscar Wilde, is buried here. From the Viale a long staircase ascends to the **English cemetery** designed by Gino Coppedè in 1902. This includes the British military cemetery from both World Wars.

A single track railway line (29km) built in 1929 winds up the Val Bisagno, the Valpolcevera and the Valle Scrivi from Piazza Manin, to end at **Casella**. It has splendid views.

West of Principe station and the harbour is the port of **Sampierdarena**, known for its old-established engineering and metallurgical works. It was at the Ansaldo works here in 1854 that the first Italian locomotive was built. At **Sestri Ponente** is the **airport of Genoa**, built out into the sea on reclaimed land (modernised in 1986).

PEGLI, now at the western limit of the city, was once a popular weekend resort of the Genoese, and still has a few fine villas backed by pine woods. The **Villa Doria**, a pleasant public park with a 16C mansion (containing frescoes by Lazzaro Tavarone), houses the **Naval and Maritime Museum** (open Tue–Thu 9–13, Fri & Sat 9–19; 1st & 3rd Sun of the month 9–13; closed Mon). This illustrates the history of the great Genoese maritime republic and includes a portrait of Columbus attributed to Ridolfo Ghirlandaio. The splendid luxuriant garden of *Villa Durazzo-Pallavicini (open 10–17; Apr–Sep 9–19; closed Mon), created in the 1840s, includes a partly underground lake and a 'Chinese' temple. The villa of 1837 houses the **Museo di Archeologia Ligure** (open 9–19; Fri & Sat 9–13; 2nd & 4th Sun of the month 9–13; closed Mon), notable for prehistoric finds from Ligurian cave-dwellings, and pre-Roman necropolis finds from the city of Genoa.

The eastern districts of the city include **ALBARO**, which has numerous villas. From Piazza Vittoria (Pl. 16), Corso Buenos Aires leads east to Piazza Tommaseo where steps mount to Via Pozzo, rising below the **Villa Saluzzo Bombrini**, known as Villa Paradiso, with its beautiful garden. Built by Andrea Vannone in the 16C, it is one of the best preserved of the villas in the district of Albaro. Via Pozzo ends at Via Albaro, with **Villa Saluzzo Mongiordino** (No. 1), where Byron lived in 1822. Further on to the left, the Faculty of Engineering of the University occupies the splendid **Villa Giustiniani Cambiaso** (1548, on a design by Galeazzo Alessi), with another garden. The little church of **San Giuliano d'Albaro**, built in 1240, was enlarged in the 15C. In Via San Nazaro, the **Villa Bagnerello** (plaque), was where Dickens lived in 1844 before moving into Genoa (see above): 'I was set down in a rank, dull, weedy courtyard, attached to a kind of pink jail; and was told I lived there.'

A short way east is the tiny old fishing port of **Boccadasse**, well preserved, still with its old gas lamp-standards. It has good fish restaurants and a popular ice-cream shop. Above it is a mock medieval castle by Gino Coppedè.

Further east is **Quarto**, where a monument marks the starting-point of Garibaldi and the 'Thousand' ('I Mille') on their expedition to Sicily (5 May 1860), which ended in the liberation of Italy. In Villa Spinola, where Garibaldi stayed while planning the expedition with his friend Candido Augusto Vecchi, is a small Garibaldi Museum (open 9–12, 14.30–18 exc. Wed).

NERVI, 11km east of the centre of Genoa, is now included in its municipal limits. It became the earliest winter resort of the Riviera di Levante in 1863. The **Passeggiata Anita Garibaldi** extends for nearly 2km between the railway and the rock-bound shore. The **Parco Municipale** incorporates the gardens of **Villa Gropallo**, Villa Serra, and Villa Grimaldi. In **Villa Serra** is a Galleria d'Arte Moderna (not at present open). In **Villa Grimaldi** is exhibited the Frugone collection of 19C and 20C art (open Tue–Sat 9–19; fest. 9–13; closed Mon). Further east is the charming park of the **Villa Luxoro** (open 9–13 exc. fest. & Mon), with a small museum of furniture, lace, paintings, etc.

28 · Portofino and the Riviera di Levante

The coastal strip east of Genoa known as the **Riviera di Levante** (within the province of Genoa) has numerous resorts including Rapallo and Santa Margherita Ligure on the gulf of Tigullio. The beauty of the landscape, with olive groves and luxuriant gardens, has been threatened by indiscriminate new building. The best preserved part is the lovely peninsula of Portofino.

■ **Information office.** APT del Tigullio (Camogli, Portofino, Rapallo, Santa Margherita Ligure), 4 Via XXV Aprile, Santa Margherita Ligure (tel. 0185 287486), with IAT offices at Chiavari and Rapallo.

■ **Hotels. Portofino**: 4-star: *Nazionale*, 8 Via Roma; *Piccolo*, 31 Via Provinciale; *Splendido*, 13 Viale Baratta. 2-star: *Eden*, 18 Vico Dritto. **Camogli**: 4-star: *Cenobio dei Dogi*, 34 Via Cuneo. 2-star: *La Camogliese*, 55 Via Garibaldi. **Santa Margherita Ligure**: 10 4-star hotels, most of them in fine palaces surrounded by parks, including *Continental*, 8 Via Pagana, *Grand Hotel Miramare*, 30 Via Milite Ignoto and *Imperiale Palace*, 19 Via Pagana. 3-star: *Conte Verde*, 1 Via Zara; *Minerva*, 34 Via Maragliano. 2-star: *Europa*, 5 Via Trento; *Fasce*, 3 Via Bozzo. **Rapallo**: Numerous hotels of all categories, including: 4-star: *Astoria*, 4 Via Gramsci; *Rosabianca*, 42 Lungomare Vittorio Veneto. 3-star: *Riviera*, 2 Piazza IV Novembre; *Stella*, 10 Via Aurelia Ponente. **Chiavari**: 3-star: *Mignon*, 7 Via Salietti; *Monterosa*, 6 Via Marinetti. 3-star hotels also at Lavagna and Cavi. **Sestri Levante**: 4-star: *Grand Hotel dei Castelli*, 26 Via Penisola; *Miramare*, 9 Via Cappellini; *Villa Balbi*, 1 Viale Rimembranza; *Vis a vis*, 28 Via della Chiusa. 3-star: *Due Mari*, 18 Vico Coro; *Sereno*, 96 Via Val di Canepa.

■ **Restaurants. Portofino**: **A**: *Puny*, 7 Piazza Martiri Olivetta. **Camogli**: **A**: *Rosa*, 11 Via Ruffini, *Nonna Nina*, 126 Via Molfino, località San Rocco. **Recco**: **A**: *Manuelina*; **B**: *La Focacceria*. **Santa Margherita Ligure**: **B**: *Il Frantoio*, 23 Via del Giuncheto; *Trattoria degli Amici*, 2 Via Torre San Gioacchino, San Lorenzo della Costa. **C**: *Pezzi*, 21 Via Cavour. **Rapallo**: **A**: *Roccabruna*, 6 Via Sotto la Croce, Savagna; **C**: *Bansin*, 49 Via Venezia. **Chiavari**: **C**: *Luchin*, near Palazzo Rocca; *Gran Caffè Defilla*, 4 Corso Garibaldi (wine bar); *Da Franco*, Via Veneto. **Lavagna**: **B**: *A' cantinn-a*, 8 Via Torrente Barassi, località Cavi; *Belvedere*, località Santa Giulia. **Sestri Levante**: **A**: *Angiolina*, 49 Viale Rimembranza; *Polpo Mario*, 163 Via XXV Aprile; *Fiammenghilla dei Fieschi*, 6 Via Pestella, località Riva Trigoso. **C**: *Bottega del Vino*, 530 Via Nazionale (wine bar, only open in the evening).

■ **Boat services** in summer from Rapallo and Santa Margherita Ligure every half hour for Portofino and San Fruttuoso. In winter, 3 or 4 services daily. Information from Servizio Marittimo del Tigullio (tel. 0185 284670). Regular services also from Camogli every hour in summer to San Fruttuoso.

■ **Annual festivals.** At Camogli the Blessing of the Fish (second Sun in May) and the 'Stella Maris' procession of boats to the Punta della Chiappa (first Sun in Aug). Procession at Montallegro, above Rapallo, on 1–3 July.

To the east of Genoa is the delightful **PENINSULA OF PORTOFINO**, of great botanic interest for its characteristic Mediterranean *macchia* mixed with thick vegetation more typical of central Europe. A road leads across the base of the peninsula, and two other roads run to Camogli and Portofino Vetta.

A very fine scenic road skirts the east side of the penin-sula and ends at **PORTOFINO**, a romantic fishing village with pretty houses, now an exclusive resort in a beautiful posi-tion, partly on a small wooded headland, and partly in a little bay which has offered a safe anchorage to boats since Roman times. It was much visited by the English in

Portofino

the 19C. Up to the 1970s important sailing regattas were organised here by the Yacht Club Italiano, and it is now the haunt of rich yachtsmen and Italian VIPs, many of whom own grand villas here. High above the village, towards the Punta del Capo, is the little church of **San Giorgio**, which is reputed to contain the relics of St George, brought by Crusaders from the Holy Land. In front of the church is the 16C **Castello Brown** (reconstructed in the 18C; adm. 10–19 exc. Mon and in Jan).

Delightful walks can be taken in the area, including one over the hill of San Giorgio to the *Punta del Capo, with a lighthouse. A bridlepath leads via Case del Prato to San Fruttuoso, and another to Portofino Vetta. Boat trips (see above) take 20 minutes to San Fruttuoso. On the Santa Margherita road is the tiny sandy bay of **Paraggi**, at the mouth of its wooded glen.

Portofino Vetta (at the end of a road from Camogli) is in a large park beneath *Monte di Portofino** (610m). This has been a protected area since 1935 because of its natural beauty, although long-term plans to designate the area a national park have still not been settled. From the summit there is a wonderful view, and there are beautiful walks in the area.

*San Fruttuoso di Capodimonte** is a picturesque little hamlet on the sea in a rocky inlet of a lovely bay surrounded by wooded hills. It can only be reached by boat (from Camogli, Portofino, Santa Margherita Ligure and Rapallo) or on foot from Portofino or Portofino Vetta (both walks take about 90 mins). San Fruttuoso is owned by the FAI, and visitors are admitted daily exc. Mon, 10–16;

May–Sep 10–18; Dec–Feb weekends only 10–16; closed Nov. An abbey was founded here beside an abundant spring before the 10C, and was of great importance in the 11C and 12C. It was reconstructed by the Doria in the 13C, but deserted by the Benedictines in 1467. It survived under Doria patronage until 1885, after which the buildings were taken over by fishermen, and severely damaged by the sea in 1915. They were donated by the Doria Pamphilij family to the FAI in 1983, and restoration work began in 1989.

The abbey and church are supported on large vaulted arches. The upper cloister was built in the 12C and restored in the 16C (it includes Roman and medieval capitals). In the 13C part of the abbey are exhibited 13C and 14C ceramics found during excavations. The lower cloister and church, with an unusual dome, date in part from the 10C. The 13C crypt contains Doria tombs in white marble and grey stone. The grey square Torre Doria was erected on the point in 1561 as a defence against pirates. A bronze statue of Christ, by Guido Galletti (1954), stands offshore, eight fathoms down, as protector of all those who work beneath the sea.

CAMOGLI is a picturesque little fishing port (6000 inhab.) descending steeply to a rocky shore, which was famous for its merchant ships in the days of sail, its fleet having played a prominent part in the naval wars of Napoleon, of Louis-Philippe, and in the Crimea. It is interesting for its architecture, with unusually tall houses lining the seafront. The Dragonara castle has an aquarium (open 10–12, 15–19; winter Fri, Sat & Sun only). The Museo Marinaro (open Mon, Thu & Fri 9–11.40; Wed, Sat & Sun also 15–17.40) has models of ships, ex-votos, navigational instruments, etc. There is also a local archaeological museum here.

A pretty walk leads south from Camogli to San Rocco, the Romanesque church of San Nicolò, and (75 mins) **Punta Chiappa**, a fishing hamlet, where the view is remarkable for its ever-changing colours of the sea. A rough-hewn altar on the point reproduces in mosaic a graffito found at San Nicolò.

West of Camogli is **Recco**, a little port noted for its hardy seamen in the Middle Ages and for clockmaking today. Its church (1960) contains 17C Genoese paintings.

On the east side of the peninsula, on the Tigullio gulf, is **SANTA MARGHERITA LIGURE** (11,000 inhab.), a fishing village which became a seaside resort at the turn of the century. It is still one of the most popular resorts of the Riviera, with numerous hotels. The lovely park of the 16C **Villa Durazzo** is open daily in summer. In the church of the **Cappuccini** is a fine 13C statue of the Madonna enthroned.

On the road south to Portofino is the former 14C monastery of **La Cervara**, where Francis I of France was held prisoner after the Battle of Pavia (1525), and where Gregory XI rested on the return of the papacy from Avignon to Rome (1377).

The pretty road from Santa Margherita to Rapallo passes **San Michele di Pagana**, where the church contains a fine Crucifixion by Van Dyck. Nearby, in a large garden, is the Villa Spinola, where the Italo-Yugoslav Treaty of Rapallo was signed in 1920. The church of **San Lorenzo della Costa** has a triptych by Quentin Matsys (1499).

RAPALLO (26,700 inhab.), in a sheltered position at the head of its gulf, was much visited by the English in the 19C and 20C. It is the best known holiday resort on the Riviera di Levante, and is popular both in summer and winter. There is an 18-hole golf course at Sant'Anna, north of the town.

The lovely surroundings, which used to be the main attraction of Rapallo, were spoilt by new buildings in the 1960s and 1970s, and the mole of the new port for private boats has blocked the view out to sea. In the town are the **Collegiate Church** (1606), and the restored **Castle** in the harbour (open for exhibitions). In the 19C **Villa Tigullio**, surrounded by a public park, is a museum illustrating the local handicraft of lace-making. The **Villino Chiaro**, on the coast road, was the home of writer Max Beerbohm (1872–1956) from 1910. Ezra Pound also spent much time in Rapallo after 1959.

A winding road (the *funivia* is out of action) ascends inland through woods to the sanctuary of **Montallegro**, where the 16C church contains frescoes by Nicolò Barabino, and a Byzantine painting.

CHIAVARI is a shipbuilding town (30,800 inhab.) with an arcaded old main street, and a sandy beach and port for small boats at the mouth of the Entella. Here Garibaldi, on his arrival in exile from the south, was arrested on 6 Sept 1849 'in the most polite and friendly manner possible', since his forebears came from the town. It was also the family home of Nino Bixio and Giuseppe Mazzini. A large necropolis dating from the 8C–7C BC has been excavated here; the interesting finds are exhibited in the **Civico Museo Archeologico** in the 17C–18C Palazzo Rocca. On the second floor of the palace are 16C–17C paintings, representative of the Genoese school, including the Torreglia collection.

Inland on Monte Caucaso, is **Monteghirfo**, an isolated hamlet amid chestnut woods with a local ethnographical museum.

In the **Sturla valley** is **Terrarossa**, popularly thought to be the home of Columbus' grandparents. In a side valley (reached from Borzonasca) is the lovely **Abbey of Borzone**, with a church of c 1244.

Lavagna, a resort separated from Chiavari by the Entella bridge, has a long sandy beach, and is famous for its slate quarries. A pretty road leads up the valley to the early Gothic **Basilica dei Fieschi**, founded by Innocent IV (Sinibaldo Fieschi, died 1254), who was born in Lavagna.

SESTRI LEVANTE (20,000 inhab.), in a delightful position at the base of the peninsula of Isola (once an island), is a summer resort, spoilt since the 1950s by new buildings. From Piazza Matteotti, with the 17C parish church, a street ascends past the restored Romanesque church of **San Nicolò** to the **Grand Hotel dei Castelli**, rebuilt with antique materials (1925) on Genoese foundations, with a magnificent park, at the end of the peninsula. From the Torretta here Marconi carried out his first experiments in short wave transmission. The **Galleria Rizzi** is open May–Sep (Thu, Sat & fest. 16–18).

29 · The Gulf of La Spezia and the Cinque Terre

■ **Information office.** APT, 47 Viale Mazzini, La Spezia (tel. 0187 770900). IAT offices at Lerici (tel. 0187 967346), Monterosso al Mare (open Jun–Sep, tel. 0187 817204), and Portovenere (tel. 0187 790691).

■ **Hotels. La Spezia**: 3-star: *Firenze*, 7 Via Paleocapa; *Genova*, 84 Via Fratelli Rosselli. **Portovenere**: Two 4-star hotels and the 3-star *Paradiso*. **Island of Palmaria**: 1-star: *Lorena*. **Lerici**: 3-star: *Byron*, 19 Via Biaggini; *Europa*, Via Carpanini, località Maralunga; *Il Nido* and *Villa Maria Grazia*, 75 & 7 Via Fiascherino. **2-star**: *Miranda* (with restaurant), 92 Via Fiascherino. **Ameglia**: 3-star: *Garden*, 162 Via Fabbricotti; *Paracucchi Locanda dell'Angelo* (with restaurant), 60 Viale XXV Aprile, at Fiumaretta. **Deiva Marina**: 3-star: *Caravella*, 1 Lungomare Colombo; *Clelia*, 23 Corso Italia.

In the **Cinque Terre**: **Riomaggiore**: 3-star: *Due Gemelli*, località Campi. **Manarola**: 3-star: *Ca' d'Andrean* and *Marina Piccola*. **Vernazza**: 1-star: *Barbara*, and *Sorriso*. **Monterosso al Mare**: 4-star: *Palme*, 18 Via IV Novembre; *Porto Roca*, località Corone. 3-star: *Degli Amici*, 36 Via Buranco; 2-star: *Souvenir*, 24 Via Gioberti.

■ **Camping sites** (2-star) at Deiva Marina, Framura and Lerici and (3-star) at Tellaro).

■ **Restaurants. La Spezia**: **A**: *Parodi Peyton Place*, 212 Viale Amendola. **B**: *Antica Osteria da Caran*, 1 Via Genova. **C**: *Autedo*, Viale Fieschi, Marola; *Il Moccia*, 30 Via Chiesa, Pegazzano. **Lerici**: **A**: *La Vecchia Lerici*, 10 Piazza Mottini. **B**: *Il Maestrale*, località Zanego. **Montemarcello**: **B**: *Dai Pironcelli*. **Sarzana**: **C**: *Il Cantinone*, 59 Via Fiasella. **Castelnuovo Magra**: **A**: *Da Armanda*, 6 Piazza Garibaldi. **B**: *Al Castello da Marco*, 247 Via Provinciale; *Vallecchia Bianchi Livia*, località Vallecchia. **Corniglia**: **B**: *Osteria a Cantina De Manan*.

■ **Maritime services** from La Spezia and Lerici in the gulf of La Spezia, and (Jun–Sep) from Monterosso al Mare for the Cinque Terre.

■ **Train services** between La Spezia and Sestri Levante (1hr journey) stop at Monterosso al Mare, Vernazza, Corniglia, Manarola and Riomaggiore. Mostly local trains, with a roughly hourly service.

■ **Annual festivals**. 'Festa del Mare' on 1st Sun in Aug at La Spezia. Festival of St Venerio on the Isola del Tino in Sept. Antiques market in Sarzana in early Aug.

LA SPEZIA, at the head of its fine gulf, has been one of the chief naval ports of Italy since a naval arsenal was built here in 1861. A provincial capital (101,400 inhab.), the town—which was laid out in the late 19C—forms a rectilinear L round a prominent hill.

The main Corso Cavour passes the **Museo Civico** (9–19 exc. Mon) with an archaeological section which contains interesting Ligurian statue-stelae of the

Lunigiana cult found on the bed of the river Magra (Bronze and Iron Age), and Roman remains from Luni. **Santa Maria Assunta**, the cathedral until 1975, was founded in 1271 but later rebuilt. It contains a large polychrome terracotta by Andrea della Robbia. At the seaward end of Corso Cavour are fine **public gardens.** The **Naval Arsenal**, the most important in Italy, was built by Domenico Chiodo in 1861–69. Next door is the *Naval Museum** (open Tue, Wed, Thu & Sat 9–12, 14–18; Mon & Fri 14–18), where models and relics collected since 1571 illustrate the marine history of Savoy and Italy. The 13C **Castello di San Giorgio** is undergoing restoration. The **Museo Amedeo Lia**, opened in 1996, contains an important collection (made since the 1940s) fo 13C–15C paintings (Coppo di Marcovaldo, Pietro Lorenzetti, Bernardo Daddi, Sassetta, Giovanni Bellini, as well as later works, decorative arts, illuminated manuscripts, small bronzes, etc.

The Gulf of La Spezia

A byroad leads along the southern arm of the gulf skirting the bay of **Le Grazie** (now spoilt by holiday houses) with the ex-Lazzaretto, an isolation hospital begun by the Genoese in 1724. Excavations are in progress of a Roman villa. The road zigzags through olive groves around little capes and bays.

PORTOVENERE, the ancient *Portus Veneris*, a dependency of Genoa since 1113, is a charming fortified village built on the sloping shore of the Bocchette, the narrow strait (114m wide) separating the Isola Palmaria from the mainland. On a rocky promontory at the southern end of the village, the restored 6C and 13C church of **San Pietro** commands a splendid view of Palmaria and the lofty cliffs of the Cinque Terre. The Grotto Arpaia, formerly beneath it, collapsed in 1932. It was known as 'Byron's Cave' since it was from here that the poet started his swim across the gulf to San Terenzo to visit Shelley at the Casa Magni at Lerici in 1822 (see below).

In the upper part of the village is the beautiful 12C church of **San Lorenzo**, above which (steep climb) towers the 16C **Castello** (open 10–12, 14–18; winter 15–17). Below the church, steps descend to the characteristic '**Calata Doria**', where tall houses rise from the sea.

The rugged island of **Palmaria**, with numerous caves, can be visited by boat (daily service) from Portovenere. The island has been purchased by a company and is in danger of being turned into a tourist resort. On the northern point is the old **Torre della Scuola**, built by the Genoese in 1606 and blown up by the English fleet in 1800. The island is noted for the gold-veined black 'portoro' marble. The **Isola del Tino** has remains of the 8C monastery of Santa Venerio.

On the opposite (northern) shore of the gulf is the **Bay of Lerici**, with the fishing village of **San Terenzo**. On a small cape is the **Casa Magni**, the 'white house with arches', the last home of Shelley (1822).

> Mary Shelley wrote: 'I am convinced that the few months we passed there were the happiest he had ever known. He was never better than when I last saw him, full of spirits and joy, embark for Leghorn, that he might there welcome Leigh Hunt to Italy.' On that fatal voyage to Livorno, on 8 July 1822, Shelley and his friend Lieutenant Williams were drowned when their little schooner sank. Their bodies were recovered on the beach near

Viareggio, where they were cremated in the presence of Shelley's friends Trelawney, Byron and Leigh Hunt. Byron probably visited Shelley at Casa Magni on his boat *Bolivar* while he was staying at Montenero near Livorno. The Casa Magni Shelley Museum was created here in 1972, but when the house was sold in 1979 the contents were moved back to Boscombe Manor in England.

Lerici is a resort (14,600 inhab.) with a splendid 13C–16C **Castle** (opened by appointment with the custodian, tel. 0187 965108). Before the modern Via Aurelia existed, Tuscan coaches were embarked here by felucca for Genoa.

A coast road goes on above the charming little bay of **Fiascherino**, where D.H. Lawrence lived in 1913–14, to **Tellaro**, a medieval village which rises sheer from the sea—and which has suffered damage due to the instability of the rocks here. A higher byroad from Lerici continues around the wooded peninsula up to **Montemarcello**, a pretty village of red and pink houses surrounded by olives, with fine views of Tellaro and of the Gulf of Spezia. A path leads to **Punta Corno** with a bird's eye view of the coast. The road descends through lovely woods to Ameglia (see below).

The Cinque Terre

The *Cinque Terre are five delightful little medieval villages, **Riomaggiore**, **Manarola**, **Corniglia**, **Vernazza** and **Monterosso al Mare**, on a beautiful unspoilt stretch of rocky coast. These were remote fishing hamlets accessible only by sea before the advent in 1874 of the railway, which tunnels through the high cliffs between the railway stations (frequent local services, see above). The Cinque Terre are now famous, having remained relatively isolated and been largely preserved from new building since no coastal road has ever been built here (although one is planned); by car they can only be reached along winding and steep inland roads. They are best visited along the network of steep *footpaths on the edge of the cliffs (map published by CAI) which link Portovenere to Levanto (the walk can be combined with a short train journey between any of the villages). Each walk between the villages takes several hours, while the train (through tunnels) takes only a few minutes. In summer the villages are also connected by boat services. They are noted for their white wine: the vines are trained on wires across gorges and up the cliffs. The terrain is subject to landslides and while methods are being studied to prevent these, the villages are suffering from depopulation. Some of the footpaths between the villages have also been damaged by landslides.

Riomaggiore (2051 inhab.), connected to La Spezia by road, has an interesting layout on the steep cliffside. The fishermen have to pull their boats up on shore (and further up into the streets in rough weather).The village came under the control of the Genoese Republic in 1276. The 14C parish church contains a 15C triptych and a painting by Domenico Fiasella. The painter Telemaco Signorini often stayed here.

Manarola has an even more spectacular position with splendid views. **Corniglia**, the highest of the five villages, lies above the sea, surrounded by orchards and vineyards (it has been known for its excellent wine since Roman times). It has a Gothic church. **Vernazza** is a charming port, interesting for its architecture. It also has a Gothic church (on two levels) on the harbour.

Monterosso al Mare, the largest centre of the Cinque Terre, has a good church of 1300 and, higher up, the church of San Francesco with a Crucifixion attributed to Van Dyck. The poet Eugenio Montale spent much of his youth at Monterosso. It now has some incongruous new buildings, and the sandy beach is crowded in summer.

A winding and steep inland road leads from here to **Levanto**, on the coast to the north, once a secluded bathing resort in a little bay, but now developed for tourism. It has lovely gardens, and a good sandy beach, and preserves remains of its old walls along with a 13C–15C church. **Bonassola** is a village in beautiful surroundings. A sea grotto here has been turned into a marine study centre.

A new coastal road (N370) is under construction from Levanto to Sestri Levante, much discussed in relation to the new building which is taking place in its train which threatens the beauty of the coast.

Sestri Levante and the coast as far as Genoa are described in Chapter 28.

In the **Val di Vara**, inland from Sestri Levante and La Spezia, is **Varese Ligure** with a a 15C castle of the Fieschi (well restored). A steep road leads up from here to the spectacular **Passo di Cento Croci** (1053m) on the border with Emilia.

Sarzana and the Lunigiana

SARZANA is an ancient fortified town (18,700 inhab.), once of great strategic importance. It was the southeastern outpost of the Genoese Republic. The **Cittadella**, a rectangular fort with six circular bastions, was rebuilt for Lorenzo il Magnifico in 1487 by Francesco di Giovanni (Il Francione). For years used as a prison, it is now empty and awaiting restoration. On the main Via Mazzini is the **Cathedral** (the see of the Bishop of Luni was transferred here in 1204). It contains a panel painting of the *Crucifixion, signed and dated 1138 by a certain Guglielmus, and 15C marble reliefs by Leonardo Riccomanni of Pietrasanta. Some of the paintings are by Domenico Fiasella, who was born here in 1589. Nearby is **Sant'Andrea**, the oldest monument in the town probably dating from the 11C. The 16C portal has pagan caryatids. The church of **San Francesco**, north of the town, contains the tomb by Giovanni di Balduccio of Guarnerio degli Antelminelli, son of Castruccio Castracani, who died as a child in 1322. A market is held on Thursdays in Piazza Matteotti.

On a hill to the east is the **Fortezza di Sarzanello** (for adm. tel. 0187 623025), known as the Fortezza of Castruccio Castracani, restored by the Florentines in 1493 (Il Francione and Luca Caprina).

Across the wide river Magra is **Ameglia**, dominated by a 10C castle, with picturesque houses and fishing boats. The old port of Luni and a necropolis have been excavated here.

A road leads back across the river to the site of the important Roman colony of **LUNI**. It was founded in 177 BC beside the sea on the site of a prehistoric settlement famous for its statue-stelae, displayed in La Spezia (see above), and in the museum of Pontremoli (see *Blue Guide Tuscany*). Of great commercial and strategic importance in the 2C AD, Luni was well known for its marble. A bishopric by the 5C and still thriving in the Middle Ages, it was important enough to lend its name to the whole district, the **Lunigiana**. Its fame was recorded by Dante (*Il Paradiso*, xvi, 73–78). By the 13C, partly because of the flooding of the river Magra, and malaria, the town had disappeared. Excavations are still in progress. The walled city has a typical Roman plan, with remains of the forum and capitolium (150 BC) dedicated to Jove, Juno and Minerva, as well as two houses, and another large temple. The **Museo Archeologico Nazionale** (open every day 9–19), in the centre of the excavated area, contains interesting finds from here and the surrounding territory (Ortonovo, Ameglia, etc.), including marble sculptures, bronzes and mosaics. An honorific inscription is dedicated to M. Acilius Glabrio, who defeated Antiochus III at Thermopylae in 191 BC. To the east, outside the walls, is the *amphitheatre** dating from the 2C AD, which could hold 5000 spectators.

A road leads inland to the pretty, old village of **Castelnuovo Magra**. In the church is a painting of the Crucifixion attributed to Van Dyck, and a large Calvary by Brueghel the Younger. The old 13C Malaspina castle here has associations with Dante.

The rest of the Magra valley, with Aulla and Pontremoli, the most important centre of the Lunigiana, lies in Tuscany (see *Blue Guide Tuscany*).

30 · Savona, Albenga and Alassio

This chapter covers part of the 'Riviera di Ponente' west of Genoa, within the province of Savona. Chaotic new building has ruined much of the coast since the last war, although the interesting town of Albenga is still well preserved.

■ **Information office.** APT 'Riviera delle Palme', 26 Viale Gibb, Alassio (tel. 0182 64711).

■ **Hotels.** There are numerous hotels in the resorts all along the coast. **Savona** has one 4-star hotel and several 3-star hotels; **Albenga** has 3-star hotels; and **Alassio** has numerous hotels of all categories (including: 4-star: *Grand Hotel Diana*, 110 Via Garibaldi; and 3-star: *Regina*, 220 Viale Hanbury and *Dei Fiori*, 78 Viale Marconi).

■ **Restaurants. Savona**: **A**: *A Spurcacciun'a*, 89 Via Nizza. **B**: *Bacco*, 17 Via Quarda Superiore. **C**: *Vino e Farinata*, 15 Via Pia. **Albenga**: **B**: *Punta San Martino*; *Cristallo*, 8 Via Cavalieri di Vittorio Veneto. **Alassio**: **A**: *Palma*, 5 Via Cavour.

SAVONA, a provincial capital (67,100 inhab.), was a maritime power and rival of Genoa up until the 16C. Its old district, overlooking the inner harbour is surrounded by the regular streets of the new town. In recent years its industries of iron founding and shipbreaking have declined.

In the main arcaded Via Paleocapa is the 16C church of **San Giovanni Battista**, with 18C paintings. The **Theatre** (1850–53) is named after the native lyric poet Gabriello Chiabrera (1553–1638), the 'Italian Ronsard'. Near a terrace of pretty Art Nouveau houses overlooking the harbour is the 14C **Torre**

Pancaldo, named after Leon Pancaldo of Savona, Magellan's 'Genoese' pilot.

Via Pia, with stone doorways, leads into the old town. The **Cathedral** was built in 1589–1605 (façade of 1886). It contains an altarpiece by Albertino Piazza, a Romanesque font, and choir stalls of 1500. A **Diocesan Museum** contains works by Lodovico Brea, and the 'Maestro di Hoogstraten'. The 17C oratory of **Santa Maria di Castello** contains a polyptych by Vincenzo Foppa and Lodovico Brea (1490). Facing the cathedral is **Palazzo Della Rovere**, begun by Giuliano da Sangallo for Julius II but never finished.

On the right of the cathedral is the **Cappella Sistina**, erected by Sixtus IV (see below) in memory of his parents, and given a harmonious Baroque interior in 1764. It contains a fine marble tomb, by Michele and Giovanni De Aria, with figures of the two Della Rovere Popes, Sixtus IV and Julius II. In Piazza del Mercato are two 12C towers. The small **Pinacoteca Civica** (open 8.30–12.30 exc. fest.) contains works by Donato de'Bardi, Vincenzo Foppa and Giovanni Battista Carlone.

The **Fortezza del Priamar**, on a hill on the southern seafront by the public gardens, was erected by the Genoese in 1542. Here Mazzini was imprisoned in 1830–31. It contains an archaeological museum, and a museum of works of art (including paintings by De Pisis and Mario Sironi) donated to the former Italian president Sandro Pertini.

Albisola Superiore, east of Savona, the birthplace of Julius II (Giuliano della Rovere,1443–1513), has been famous since the 16C for its ceramics, examples of which are displayed in a museum in Villa Faraggiana.

On the coast road west of Savona is **Zinola**, with a British Military Plot containing 104 graves, mostly from the wreck of the *Transylvania*, torpedoed off Savona in 1917. Beyond the headland of Bergeggi, with its islet offshore, is **Spotorno** with a fine sandy beach, but much ugly new building has taken place here since D.H. Lawrence's sojourn in 1926 when he wrote *Lady Chatterley's Lover*.

Noli, an important port in the Middle Ages, preserves its walls and three tall towers of brick, as well as some old houses and an 11C church.

The old village of **Finalborgo**, 2km inland from **Finale Marina**, has a church with a fine octagonal campanile (13C). It contains a 16C tomb of the Del Carretto family, whose ruined castle is nearby. In the cloister of Santa Caterina is the Civico Museo del Finale (open 9–12, 14.30–16.30; summer 10–12, 15–18; fest. 9–12; closed Mon and Jan) with finds from the many local limestone caves in which prehistoric remains have been found. On the old Roman road further inland are about a dozen Roman bridges (1C AD), five of them intact.

Pietra Ligure has a church by Fantone (1791). **Loano**, an old seaside town with palm groves, has a town hall in the Palazzo Doria (1578), which contains a 3C mosaic pavement. No. 32 Via Cavour was the birthplace of Rosa Raimondi, Garibaldi's mother.

Inland is the **Grotta di Toirano**, a remarkable stalactite cavern, with the only footprints of Mousterian man (probably Neanderthal) so far discovered, and a museum of local prehistory.

ALBENGA, an interesting old town (21,500 inhab.), was the Roman port *Albium Ingaunum*, but is now over a kilometre from the sea, since the course of the Centa river was altered in the 13C. It still has most of its medieval walls (on foundations of the 1C BC) and three 17C gates; also about a dozen 12C–14C brick tower-houses, mostly well restored. Since the 19C the town has expanded towards the sea.

The **Cathedral**, on late 4C or early 5C foundations, with an elegant campanile of 1391, was reconstructed in its medieval form in 1967. **Palazzo Vecchio del Comune** (1387 and 1421), incorporating a tall tower of c 1300, houses the **Civico Museo Ingauno** (open 10–12, 15–18 exc. Mon) with prehistoric, Roman and medieval remains. The 5C *Baptistery*, ten-sided without and octagonal within, preserves a fine Byzantine mosaic (5C or 6C) in its principal apse and 8C transennae.

The charming Piazzetta dei Leoni has three Renaissance lions brought from Rome in 1608. The former **Palazzo Vescovile** has external frescoes (15C). The **Diocesan Museum** inside contains finds from the Cathedral, and paintings by Guido Reni and Domenico Piola. Via Bernardo Ricci (the Roman *decumanus*) crosses Via delle Medaglie (*cardo maximus*) at the 13C **Loggia dei Quattro Canti**.

In Piazza San Michele is the **Museo Navale Romano** (open 10–12, 15–18 exc. Mon), containing more than 100 wine amphorae and marine fittings salvaged since 1950 from a Roman vessel sunk offshore in 100–90 BC. This is the largest Roman transport ship yet found in the Mediterranean; it was carrying more than 10,000 amphorae of wine (700 of which were recovered) from Campania to southern France and Spain. Attached to the museum is an important centre for underwater archaeology. In a fine 18C hall there is a collection of Albisola (see above) pharmacy jars. Along the river Centa are scanty remains of the Roman city.

ALASSIO (11,500 inhab.), is one of the most visited Ligurian coastal resorts, with an exceptionally mild winter climate and an excellent sandy beach. It is at the head of a wide and beautiful bay, facing nearly east. It was well known to the English by the end of the 19C—they built the church of St John's here—and is famed for the luxuriance of its gardens. While wintering here in 1904 Elgar composed his overture *In the South (Alassio)*. Carlo Levi, the writer and painter spent much time in Alassio, and a collection of his paintings are to be exhibited in the town.

Offshore is the **Isola Gallinara**, or Gallinaria (boat trips from the Porto Turistico or from Loano). Little remains of the once powerful Benedictine monastery founded here in the 8C, which at one time owned most of the Riviera di Ponente. St Martin of Tours took refuge from his Arian persecutors here in 356–360. The island is now privately owned and a protected area since 1989, with lovely vegetation and grottoes (and interesting also for its birdlife).

A short way west of Alassio is **Laigueglia**, a resort with an 18C church by Gian Domenico Baguti. Inland is **Andora Castello**, the finest medieval building on the Riviera del Ponente. Circular walls enclose a ruined castle and a late 13C church. A medieval bridge crosses the Merula.

31 · Sanremo, Bordighera, Ventimiglia and Imperia

The resorts covered here are in the province of Imperia, on the 'Riviera di Ponente'. This part of the Ligurian coast west of Genoa has a mild climate, numerous winter resorts, and luxuriant vegetation with palms, bougainvillaea and exotic plants. Now usually known as the 'Riviera dei Fiori', it has been important for its cut flower industry (especially roses and carnations) since the beginning of the century.

■ **Information office.** APT 'Riviera dei Fiori', 1 Largo Nuovoloni, Sanremo (tel. 0184 571571). IAT offices at Ventimiglia and Imperia.

■ **Hotels. Sanremo**: 5-star: *Royal*, 80 Corso Imperatrice. 8 4-star hotels, and numerous 3-star and 2-star hotels. **Bordighera**: 4-star and 3-star hotels. **Ventimiglia** and **Imperia** have 3-star and 2-star hotels.

■ **Restaurants. Sanremo**: **A**: *Da Giannino*, 23 Lungomare Trento e Trieste; *Paolo e Barbara*, 47 Via Roma; *Il Bagatto*, 145 Via Matteotti. **B**: *Nuovo Piccolo Mondo*, 7 Via Piave. **C**: *Bacchus*, 65 Via Roma; *Le Cantine Sanremesi*, 7 Via Palazzo. Near **Taggia** (Vignai): **C** *Il Vecchio Frantoio*. **Bordighera**: **A**: *La Via Romana*, 57 Via Romana; *Carletto*, 339 Via Vittorio Emanuele. **Ventimiglia**: **A**: *Baia Beniamin*, 63 Corso Europa, località Grimaldi; *Balzi Rossi*, at the Balzi Rossi. **Imperia**: **A**: *Lanterna Blu da Tonino*, 32 Via Scarincio. **C**: *Aspettando Bartali*, 9 Via dei Pellegrini; *Bistrò 56 Nannina*, 56 Viale Matteotti.

SANREMO is the largest summer and winter resort (60,100 inhab.) on the Italian Riviera, visited since the mid-19C for its superb climate. Its villas and gardens lie in an amphitheatre in a wide bay, although the sea is separated from the town by the old railway line. Edward Lear (1812–88) spent his last years at Sanremo, and built the Villa Emily (now Villa Verde) and Villa Tennyson (both named after Tennyson's wife). He died at the latter and was buried in Sanremo. Alfred Nobel (1833–96) also died here, and here in 1878 Tchaikovsky finished his Fourth Symphony and *Eugene Onegin*. The Empress of Russia, Maria Alexandrovna, consort of Alexander II, lived here, surrounded after 1874 by a large Russian colony. Among the annual festivals for which the town is famous is the International Song Contest.

Via Roma and the parallel Via Matteotti are the main streets of the modern town. In the latter, at No. 143 is **Palazzo Borea d'Olmo** (early 16C) which houses the **Museo Civico**, with an archaeological collection and pinacoteca. To the southwest surrounded by gardens, in an Art Nouveau building by Eugenio Ferret (1904–06), is the **Casinò Municipale** (always open), with celebrated gaming rooms. The *CORSO DELL'IMPERATRICE, lined with magnificent palm trees, leads past the delightful **Russian church** (San Basilio) to the **Parco Marsaglia**, in which is a monument to Garibaldi by Leonardo Bistolfi (1908). The **English Church** (All Saints) is in Corso Matuzia.

Along the shore in the other direction, Via Nino Bixio leads to the Genoese fort of **Santa Tecla** (1755) and the mole of the **old harbour**. Corso Trento e Trieste continues along the waterfront, past the harbour for private boats, to the public gardens. The old district of **La Pigna** has quaint narrow streets. The **Duomo** here is a 13C building enlarged in the 17C.

Nearby **TAGGIA** is an interesting old village in a pretty position. The 15C Gothic church of **San Domenico** contains works by Lodovico Brea. In the old walled town is a palace attributed to Gian Lorenzo Bernini and the **parish church** perhaps designed by him. A 16C **bridge** (on Romanesque foundations) of 16 arches crosses the Argentina. At the head of the pretty **Valle Argentina** is **Triora**, with remains of its fortifications and a painting by Taddeo di Bartolo in the Collegiata.

Ospedaletti, on a sheltered bay, is a horticultural centre, and has fine palms and eucalyptus trees.

BORDIGHERA (11,600 inhab.) is another winter resort with a mild climate. It became known to the English after 1855 when *Doctor Antonio* by Giovanni Ruffini, set in the town, was translated, and became a best-seller. By the end of the 19C a large English colony had been established here. It is also a centre for the cultivation of cut flowers (a market was built here in 1898), and has numerous palm trees.

Several buildings in the town were built in the 1870s by the Frenchman Charles Garnier. In Via Romana, the villa in which Queen Margherita di Savoia (widow of Umberto I) died in 1926, faces the **Museo Bicknell** (open 10–13, 15–18 exc. Mon), founded by the Englishman Clarence Bicknell in 1888, with a good local natural history collection. Here, too, is the Istituto Internazionale di Studi Liguri. At No. 30 Via Romana is the International Library, also founded by Bicknell. Northeast of the town is a British Military Cemetery, with 72 graves.

VENTIMIGLIA (25,200 inhab.) is divided by the Roia into an old medieval town on a hill to the west and a new town on the coastal plain between the railway and the Via Aurelia, at the east end of which is the site of the Roman *Albintimilium* where Agricola spent his boyhood. Since its decline in the 13C Ventimiglia has had all the characteristics of a frontier town. In the old town is the restored 11C–12C **Cathedral** with a portal of 1222; its apse adjoins the 11C **Baptistery**. In **San Michele** (open Sun only, 10.30–12), rebuilt c 1100, the stoups are made up from Roman milestones, and the Romanesque crypt is interesting. The Forte dell'Annunziata in Via Verdi houses the **Civico Museo Archeologico** (open 10–12, 15–17 exc. Mon), founded in 1900 by Sir Thomas Hanbury. It contains finds from the Roman municipium.

The lower town expanded after 1872 when it became an important station on the railway line to France. The excavations (begun in 1876) of the Roman town, which include a theatre of the 2C AD, and baths, are now isolated by modern buildings and the railway; they can be seen from a viaduct on the Aurelia.

A road runs west to **La Mortola**, where the upper road (right) leads to a wooded cape with the *****Giardino Hanbury** (open 9–19; winter 10–17 exc. Wed), a remarkable botanic garden founded in 1867 by Sir Thomas Hanbury and his brother Daniel, a botanist. The splendid garden was famous in the late

19C. It was acquired by the Italian State from the Hanbury family in 1960, and since 1983 has been run by Genoa University, who are now trying to rescue it from the grave state of abandon in which it had been left after 1979. Hanbury collected exotic plants from all over the world—particularly from Asia and Africa. There are also woods of umbrella pines and cypresses, carob trees and palms, as well as medicinal plants, citrus fruits, etc. A section of the Roman Via Aurelia was exposed here by Hanbury, and a plaque recalls famous travellers who passed along this route (including Dante, Machiavelli and Pius VII).

On the beach below the frontier village of **Grimaldi**, at the **Balzi Rossi**, are several caves where relics of Palaeolithic man were discovered in 1892. Some of these are exhibited in the **Museo Nazionale Preistorico** founded here in 1898 by Sir Thomas Hanbury. Ponte San Luigi is on the French frontier (see *Blue Guide France*).

In the flowery **Val Nervia**, inland from Ventimiglia, is the pretty village of **Dolceacqua**, beneath its splendid castle first built in the 10C–11C and transformed in the 15C and 16C by the Doria. It is now empty and in urgent need of restoration. Below the village is a single-arched 15C bridge. **Pigna** is another delightful little village (with late 15C works by Giovanni Canavesio); built on an interesting plan, it stands in a picturesque position opposite the fortified village of **Castel Vittorio**.

On the other side of Sanremo (see above) is **IMPERIA**, a double town (40,600 inhab.) created in 1923 by the fusion of Porto Maurizio, Oneglia and adjoining villages to form a provincial capital. In **Porto Maurizio**, with an old district of stepped streets, is a large church (1781–1832). **Oneglia** is at the mouth of the Impero torrent from which the province takes its name. It is an important centre of the olive-oil trade, and has a large pasta factory on the seafront. The town hall built in 1932 is between the two towns. In the eclectic Villa Grock, built in the 1930s, Grock (Adrien Wettach), the great Swiss clown died in 1959.

Diano Marina, another olive-growing town, with a sandy beach, is a summer and winter resort. **Cervo** is a very well preserved medieval borgo, which has a rich Baroque church by Giovanni Battista Marvaldi (1686).

The Veneto

The **Veneto** includes the provinces of Belluno, Padua, Rovigo, Treviso, Venice, Verona and Vicenza. In the 12C Verona, Padua, Vicenza and Treviso formed the Veronese League in imitation of the Lombard League, in an attempt to check the power of the Emperor. There followed a century in which important families, such as the Scaligeri in Verona and Vicenza, and the Carraresi in Padua and Vicenza, held courts, brilliant for literature and art. After a period of domination by the Milanese Visconti, the Venetian Republic (whose maritime expansion in the East had been checked by the rising power of the Turkish empire) turned her interests to the *terraferma*, and Treviso and Padua as well as numerous other cities came willingly under her control. By 1420 the whole territory from Verona to Udine and from Belluno to Padua was under the protection of Venice. Further extensions of the Doges' dominion, to Bergamo in the west, Rimini in the south, and Fiume in the east, provoked the jealousy of the powers beyond the Alps, and the League of Cambrai (1508) put an end to Venice's imperial ambitions. But for 300 years the Venetian dominions in Italy remained united. The Napoleonic invasion of Italy saw the dismemberment of the Veneto; in 1797 Venice itself and the area east of the Adige was ceded to Austria, who also took control of areas in the west in 1814, after a brief union with the Cisalpine Republic. In 1859 an armistice stopped the progress of Vittorio Emanuele at the Lombard frontier, and it was not until the Austrian defeat by the Prussians in 1866 that the Veneto was able by plebiscite to join the Piedmontese kingdom. In the Second World War the region was attacked from the air (notably at Treviso), and much destruction was caused by the Germans at Verona. The Allies reached Udine on the last day of the fighting in Italy (1 May 1945).

32 · Venice

☆ **For a full description of the city, see *Blue Guide Venice*.**

Venice, in Italian *Venezia*, is considered by many the most beautiful city in the world. It is built on an archipelago of islets and shoals, 4km from the mainland, in a lagoon protected from the open sea by the natural breakwater of the Lido. The buildings are supported on piles of Istrian pine, driven down beneath the water to a solid bed of compressed sand and clay, on foundations of Istrian limestone which withstand the corrosion of the sea. Torcello was one of the first islands in the lagoon to be inhabited in the 5C–6C, and Venice became an independent Byzantine province in the 9C with its centre on the islands of the Rialto. The great Venetian maritime Republic, much influenced by the Eastern Empire, flourished until 1797 under a succession of Doges, many of them remarkable rulers. The splendid monuments of the city today, contained geographically within virtually the same limits as at the height of the Republic, are testimony to her remarkable civilisation. In the total absence of wheeled transport, communications are effected by a system of some 170 canals, the main thoroughfare being the Grand Canal. The population of the historic centre is decreasing at an alarming rate, and is now only about 75,000 compared with the 200,000 it had when the Republic was at its zenith. Some measures are at last being taken to protect the city from periodic floods and to clean the polluted waters of the lagoon, and committees funded from various countries are working in conjunction with the Italian authorities on the restoration of buildings.

■ **Information offices.** APT, Palazzetto Del Selva, Giardinetti Reali (Pl. 11; tel.041 5226356). Subsidiary offices at the railway station, the Marghera exit from the Milan motorway, the airport and (in summer) on the Lido. Hotel booking facilities on arrival are run by the Associazione Veneziano Albergatori (AVA) at the above subsididary APT offices, and at the car parks at Piazzale Roma and Tronchetto.

■ **Airport** on the lagoon 9km north of Venice with international flights. Motorboat service run by Cooperativa San Marco Tel. 041 5222303) from the airport via Murano and the Lido to San Marco (Giardinetti; Pl. 11) takes 1hr 10 mins, at least every hour (more expensive than the bus but the most pleasant way of arriving in the city). Also ACTV bus No. 5 to and from Piazzale Roma at 10 and 40 minutes past the hour.

■ **Railway station.** Santa Lucia (Pl. 5), on the Grand Canal, with waterbus services and motor-boat taxis from the quay outside.

■ **Car parks.** You are strongly advised to travel to Venice by rail rather than by road. Cars have to be left at a multi-storey car parks at **Piazzale Roma** (Pl. 5) or in the garage or open-air car park at **Tronchetto** (beyond Pl. 5): there are no free car parks, and rates are per day (charges vary according to the size of the vehicle). **Parking space is very limited** since the garages are also used by Venetian residents: automatic signs on the motorway approaches indicate the space available at the time of arrival in various car parks and garages. If the car parks are full, cars have to be left on the mainland in Mestre or Marghera, both connected by frequent bus or trains services to Venice.

■ **Waterbuses (*vaporetti*).** An excellent service is run by ACTV who have an information office at Piazzale Roma (tel. 041 5287886). Another ticket office is open at Calle dei Fuseri 1810 (Pl. 11). Tickets can be bought at most landing-stages: the most convenient way is to purchase a book of 10 or 20 tickets which have to be stamped at automatic machines on the landing-stages before each journey. It is usually well worth while buying a 24-hr ticket, or a 3- or 7-day ticket, which give unlimited transport on nearly all the lines and are available at all landing stages (they need to be stamped just once at the automatic machine). Most of the services run at frequent intervals (every 10 minutes), so when a boat is particularly crowded it is worth waiting for the next one.

Up-to-date information and a free map of the system are usually available at the landing stages (there are frequent variations in the routes of some of the services, and the numbers tend to change from one year to the next), and there are summer and winter timetables. Some of the services at present in operation are as follows:

1. A comfortable *vaporetto* which runs slowly down the Grand Canal stopping at all landing stages on both banks, and providing superb views of the city. It operates every 10 minutes by day. It takes just under an hour with 20 stops between Piazzale Roma and the Lido: Piazzale Roma (car park)—Ferrovia (railway station)—Riva di Biasio—San Marcuola—San Stae (Ca' Pesaro)—Ca' d'Oro—Rialto—San Silvestro—Sant'Angelo—San Tomà (Frari)—Ca' Rezzonico—Accademia—Santa Maria del Giglio—Santa Maria della Salute—San Marco (Vallaresso)—San Zaccaria—Arsenale—Giardini—Sant'Elena—Lido.

52. Lido—Sant'Elena—Giardini—San Zaccaria—Zattere—Santa Marta—Piazzale Roma—Ferrovia—(Cannareggio)—Fondamente Nuove—Cimitero—Murano.

52 barred. Piazzale Roma—Sant'Eufemia—Zitelle—San Zaccaria—(Canale dell'Arsenale—Fondamente Nuove— Murano.

82. San Zaccaria—San Giorgio—Zitelle—Redentore—Giudecca—Sant'Eufemia—Zattere—San Basilio—Santa Marta—Tronchetto 'B'—Piazzale Roma—Ferrovia—San Marcuolo—Rialto—San Tomà, San Samuele—Accademia—San Marco.

Traghetto. The ferry (which runs all through the night) across the Giudecca canal (Zattere—Giudecca).

Regular services from the Fondamente Nuove for Murano, Burano and Torcello (as well as the minor islands of the lagoon).

Car ferry from Tronchetto via the Giudecca canal to the Lido c every hour taking 30 minutes.

23. San Zaccaria—Sant'Elena—Murano (Navagero, Faro, Colonna)—Cimitero—Fondamente Nuove—Ospedale—Celestia—Tana—San Zaccaria.

3. (Summer Service). Tronchetto—Ferrovia—Rialto—San Samuele—Accademia—San Marco—Tronchetto.

4. (Summer service). Lido—San Zaccaria—San Marco—Accademia—San Samuele—Ferrovia—Piazzale Roma—Tronchetto—San Zaccaria—Lido.

Night Service. (Every 20 mins). Lido—Giardini—San Zaccaria—San Marco—Accademia—San Samuele—San Tomà—Rialto—Cà d'Oro—San Stae—San Marcuola—Ferrovia—Piazzale Roma—Tronchetto 'B'—Zattere—Giudecca—San Giorgio—San Zaccaria.

■ **Taxis** (motor-boats) charge by distance, and tariffs are officially fixed. Taxi stands on the Grand Canal in front of the station, Piazzale Roma, Rialto, San Marco, etc. Radio taxis include tel. 5222303.

■ **Gondolas** can be hired from the gondola stands on the Grand Canal for 50-minute periods and the tariffs are fixed. A number of **gondola ferries** (*traghetti*) still operate across the Grand Canal. They are a cheap and pleasant way of getting about in Venice and provide the opportunity to board a gondola to those who cannot afford to hire one (passengers usually stand for the short journey, which costs 600 lire). *Traghetti* do not operate in bad weather and are often closed between 12 and 14. At present they run from Calle Vallaresso to the Dogana (and the church of the Salute); at Campo Santa Maria del Giglio; San Barnaba (near Ca' Rezzonico) for San Samuele; San Tomà (for the Frari); Riva del Carbon (for Riva del Vin in the Rialto area); Santa Sofia (nar Ca' d'Oro) for the Rialto markets; San Marcuola and the Fontego dei Turchi, and at the railway station.

■ **Hotels.** It is essential to book well in advance, especially in Sep and Oct, in spring, at Carnival time, around Christmas and the New Year, and on weekends (particularly those which fall near Italian public holidays). For booking facilities on arrival, see above under 'Information Offices'. A very small selection of hotels is given below.

5-star: *Danieli*, Riva degli Schiavoni; *Gritti Palace*, on the Grand Canal near San Marco. 4-star: *Cipriani*, on the Giudecca; *Europa e Regina*, on the Grand Canal near San Marco. 3-star: *Accademia Villa Maravege*, Dorsoduro; *Carpaccio*, on the Grand Canal in the district of San Polo; *Santo Stefano*, near the Accademia bridge; *Savoia e Jolanda*, on Riva degli Schiavoni. 2-star: *Seguso*, *Alla Salute da Cici*, *Agli Alboretti*, all on Dorsoduro; *La Residenza*, *Locanda Remedio* near Riva degli Schiavoni. 1-star: *Locanda Fiorita*, near Campo Santo Stefano; *Antica Locanda Montin*, Dorsoduro; *Riva*, *Gamberto*, *Silva* near San Marco; *Casa Linger*, Sant'Antonin.

■ **Youth hostel** on the Giudecca (Fondamenta Zitelle 86), in a splendid position (book in advance in writing).

■ **Restaurants**. There are numerous restaurants, many of them serving fish, all over Venice. Most of them are expensive and the general standard of Venetian cooking can be disappointing. **A**: *Harry's Bar*, Calle Vallaresso; *Taverna La Fenice*, Campiello della Fenice; and in the *Gritti*, *Danieli*, *Cipriani* and *Monaco and Grand Canal* hotels. **B**: *Madonna*, Calle della Madonna; *Cantinone Storico*, off Campo San Vio; *La Furatola*, Calle Lunga San Barnaba; *Antica Besseta*, Salizzada Zusto (near San Giacomo dell'Orio); *Riviera*, Fondamenta delle Zattere; *Altanella*, Calle dell'Erbe, Giudecca. **C**: *La Zucca*, Calle Larga, off Campo San Giacomo dell'Orio; *Alle testiere*, San Lio Calle del Mondo Novo, Castello; *Antiche Carampane*, Rio Terrà Rampani, near Campo San Polo; *Al Milion*, behind the church of San Giovanni Crisostomo.

Osterie or *bacari*, which sell wine by the glass and good simple food, include *Al Mascaron*, Calle Lunga Santa Maria Formosa; *Do Mori*, off Ruga Vecchia, San Giovanni Elemosinario; *Osteria Antico Dolo*, near Calle del Paradiso, San Polo; *Pietro Panizzolo ('Carla')*, Corte Contarina, near Piazza San Marco; *Osteria ai Postali*, Rio Marin, Santa Croce; *Osteria Enoteca Vivaldi*, San Polo; *Da Alberto* Calle Giacinto Gallina, Cannaregio. There are several *osterie* in Calle Lunga San Barnaba, Calle dei Saoneri and Rio Terrà degli Assasini.

The two most celebrated **cafés** in Venice are *Florian* and *Quadri* in Piazza San Marco, with tables outside and orchestras: customers are charged extra for their magnificent surroundings.

■ **Annual festivals.** Carnival is celebrated in the city in the week or ten days in February before Lent (when on some days the city more than doubles its population). Other popular festivals include: the Vogalonga (on a Sun in May); the Festa del Redentore (3rd Sat & Sun in July); the Festa della Salute (21 Nov); the Regata Storica (first Sun in Sep); and the Festa della Sensa (on the Sun after Ascension day).

CANNAREGIO
RIO DEL BATTELLO
RIO S. GIROLAMO
RIO MAD D'ORTO
Madonna dell'Orto
RIO DELLA SENSA
Palazzo Mastelli
FONDAMENTA DI CANNAREGIO
Ghetto
SECCA DELLA MISERICORDIA
RIO DI S. GIOBBE
S. Giobbe
Jewish Museum
RIO DE LA CREA
RIO DELLA MISERICORDIA
Scuola Vecchia
CALLE D. ANCORETTA
RIO TERRA S. LEONARDO
RIO TERRA D. MADDALENA
S. Marciliano
Palazzo Vendramin
Scuola Grande
CALLE RACCHETTA
Palazzo Labia
S. Marcuola
P. Vendramin Calergi
P. Correr
S. Fosca
RIO DI SPAGNA
CANAL GRANDE
P. Soranzo
P. Giovanelli
Palazzo Flangini
S. Geremia
P. Erizzo
S. Felice
RIVA DI BIAGIO
P. Giovanelli
Fond. d. Turchi
P. Battagia
P. Barbarigo
P. d. Giusti
Scalzi
Stazione Santa Lucia
P. Tron
P. Foscarini
STRADA NUOVA
S. Sofia
Ponte degli Scalzi
S. Giov Decollato
S. Stae
P. Pesaro (G. Arte Moderna)
Ca' d'Oro
P. Sagredo
CANALE DI S. CHIARA
FOND. S. SIMEONE PICC.
S. Simeone Piccolo
S. Simeone Grande
P. Mocenigo
P. Corner d. Regina
P. Mich d. Colonne
Ca' Da Mosto
TRONCHETTO, MESTRE
CAMPO N. SAURO
S. Giacomo dall'Orio
S. Cassiano
Pescheria
FOND. DELLA CROCE
CORTE CANAL
RIO DE S. GIUSTINA
S. M. Mater Domini
P. Querini
Tribunale
S. G. d. Rialto
Palazzo Papadopoli
CAMPO D. LANA
Scuola S. Giov. Evang.
CAMPO S. AGOSTINO
P. Soranzo
P. Albrizzi
S. Giov. Elem.
S. Aponal
P. d. Camerlengh
Car Park
PIAZZALE ROMA
Giardino Papadopoli
C. DELLA LACA
S. Giov. Evang.
C. DEI AMAI C. CHIOVERE
P. Corner Mocenigo
CAMPO S. POLO
RUGA
Ponte di Rialto
S. Silvestro
R. D'ANDREA
Archivio di Stato
S. Polo
P. Manin
S. Nicolò da Tolentini
S. Rocco
Frari
P. Centani
P. Papadopoli
P. Dandolo
P. Bembo
Teatro Goldini
R. TERRA DEI PENSIERI
C. TINTORETTO
Scuola S. Rocco
P. Bernardo
CANAL GRANDE
Municipio
S. Toma
P. Grimani
P. Grimani
R. DI SM. MAGGIORE
FOND NOVA
S. Toma
P. Pisani
P. Corner Spinelli
S. Bened
S. Luca
CAMPO MANIN
S. Pantalon
P. Persico
P. Tiepolo
Teatro Rossini
CAMPO S. MARGHERITA
P. Civran
P. Mocenigo
P. Garzoni
Mus. Fortuny
P. Cont. d. Bovolo
ACTV
P. Balbi
P. Contarini d. Figure
CAMPO S. SAMUELE
S. Fantin
Ca' Foscari
P. Moro-Lin
SAL. S. SAMUELE
P. Grassi
S. Stefano
Teatro La Fenice
Palazzo Cicogna
Scuola
P. Giustinian
Ca' Rezzonico
S. Samuele
CAMPO S. STEFANO
S. Maurizio
S. Moisè
Chiesa dei Carmini
RIO S. BARNABA
P. Contarini Michele
S. Malipiero
C. d. Duca
P. Loredan
S. Morosini
SM. d. Giglio
P. Treves de Bonfili
S. Barnaba
RIO DI ANGELO
RIO DI MALCANTON
P. Loredan
S. Vitale
P. Pisani
P. Záguri
P. Tiepolo
S. Raffaele Arcang.
S. NICOLO
P. Giustinian Lolin
(Pref)
P. Contarini
S. Sebastiano
RIO S. SEBASTIANO
Ognissanti
P. Contarini d. Scrigni
P. Cavali
Ponte d. Accademia
P. Barbaro
P. Corner d. Ca Grande
CANAL GRANDE
Galleria d. Accademia
Guggenheim Coll.
P. da Mula
Dogana di Mare
BRIDGO NISSANTI
S. Trovaso
Cini Coll.
English Church
Palazzo Barbarigo
P. Dario
S. Gregorio
Seminario
ZATTERE AL PONTE LUNGO
Palazzo Nani
S. Agnese
S. Maria d. Salute
Patriarcal
S. M. delle Visitazione
Gesuati
ZATTERE AL GESUATI
Spirito Santo
ZATTERE ALLO SPIRITO SANTO
ZATTERE AL SALON
CANALE DELLA GIUDECCA

VENICE

La Giudecca

REDENTORE

0 200 yards
0 200 metres

Cimitero
ISOLA DI S. MICHELE

Madonna dell'Orto

SACCA DELLA MISERICORDIA

Scuola Vecchia
Abbazia d. Misericordia

S. Marciliano
Palazzo Vendramin
Scuola Grande
S. Caterina
Gesuiti
Oratorio d. Crociferi
S. Fosca
P. Correr
P. Giovanelli
P. Serriman

P. Barbarigo

N

S. Felice

P. Pesaro
(G. Arte Moderna)
S. Sofia
Ca' d. Oro
P. Sagredo
SS. Apostoli
P. Corner d. Regina
P. Mich. d. Colonne
P. Valmarana
S. Canciano
Scuola di S. Marco
SS. Giovanni e Paolo
Pescheria
Ca' Da Mosto
S. M. di Miracoli
P. Sanudo
CAMPO SAN ZANIPOLO
L'Ospedaletto
BARBARIA D. TOLE
S. Cassiano
P. Querini
Tribunale
S. G. di Rialto
S. Giov. Crisostomo
S. Giov. Elem.
Teatro Malibran
S. Lorenzo
S. Francesco d. Vigna
S. Aponal
P. d. Camerlenghi
Ponte di Rialto
CAMPO S. BARTOLOMEO
S. Bart
S. Lio
S. M. d. Paradiso
Palazzo Grimani
S. Silvestro
P. Manin
S. Salvatore
SAN LIO
S. M. Formosa
P. Bembo
S. M. d. Fava
Questura
S. Giorgio d. Schiavoni
P. Papadopoli
P. Dandolo
Teatro Goldini
Palazzo Querini Stampalia
S. Antonio
CANAL GRANDE
P. Grimani
Municipio
MERCERIA
S. Giuliano
S. Giov. Nuovo
S. Giorgio dei Greci
SAL S. ANTONIO
S. Bened.
S. Luca
CAMPO MANIN
Teatro Rossini
Mus. Fortuny
P. Cont. d. Bovolo
ACTV
Palazzo Trevisan
Torre d. Orologio
Palazzo Patriarcato
C. S. Provolo
S. Zaccaria
Museo Diocesano
CAMPO BANDIERA E. MORO
S. Martino
S. Giov. in Bragora
CAMPO S. ANGELO
Teatro La Fenice
S. Fantin
P.O.
Procur. Vecchie
S. Marco
Campanile
PIAZZA S. MARCO
Mus. Correr
Procur. Nuove
Libreria Vecchia
Palazzo Ducale
Prigioni
P. te d. Sospiri
S. M. d. Visitazione
DEGLI SCHIAVONI
S. Maurizio
S. Moise
Zecca
MOLO
RIVA
RIVA CA' DI DIO
SM. d. Giglio
Giardinetti
Cap. di Porto
P. Giustinian
P. Zaguri
P. Tiepolo
P. Treves de Bonfili
ISOLA DI S. PIETRO
(Preti)
P. Contarini
P. Corner d. Ca' Grande
CANAL GRANDE
PUNTA D. SALUTE
CANALE DI S. MARCO
S. Gregorio
P. Dario
Dogana di Mare
Seminario Patriarcale
S. Maria d. Salute
BACINO
S. Giorgio Maggiore
Fondazione Giorgio Cini
CANALE DELLA GRAZIA
Teatro Verde
ISOLA DI S. GIORGIO MAGGIORE

The beauty of the city is splendidly preserved, and a walk through any of the narrow streets, known as *calli*, or along the canals (called *rii*) crossed by numerous picturesque stone bridges, through the squares (*campi*), many of them with characteristic well-heads, can be as rewarding as a visit to the great monuments of Venice. The waterbuses along the Grand Canal or in the wider Canale della Giudecca provide superb views of the buildings on the water, reflected in the changing light of the hauntingly beautiful lagoon. Piazza San Marco and its basilica and the area around the Rialto bridge can be uncomfortably crowded: it is always best to avoid these areas in the middle of the day.

PIAZZA SAN MARCO is one of the most famous squares in the world. Here are the Basilica di San Marco with its tall campanile and the Doges' Palace, the two most important buildings in Venice. The ****Basilica di San Marco (open all day), founded in 832 and Byzantine in form, was decorated with superb mosaics from the 11C onwards. Its outstanding art treasures, include the four famous bronze horses, thought to be Roman works. The ****Palazzo Ducale** (open 8.30–17 or 19), the residence of the doges, has a beautiful Gothic exterior, rebuilt in the 14C. It contains sumptuous rooms decorated in the 16C–17C by Venetian painters including Veronese and Tintoretto.

The ****Grand Canal**, which winds through the city, is bordered on either side with a continuous line of lovely old buildings including more than one hundred palaces, among which are the ***Ca' d'Oro**, the most beautiful Gothic palace in Venice (which contains an interesting museum, open 9–14, of paintings and sculpture). The Grand Canal, best seen from vaporetto No. 1, passes under the **Rialto Bridge**, a famous Venetian landmark built in 1588, with two rows of shops. The finest palaces with their façades on the Canal include the 15C Gothic Palazzo Contarini-Fasan, Ca' Foscari and Palazzo Dario; the 16C Renaissance Palazzo Corner, Palazzo Corner-Spinelli, Palazzo Grimani and Palazzo Loredan Vendramin Calergi; the 17C Ca' Pesaro and Ca' Rezzonico; and the 18C Palazzo Grassi.

The district of ***Dorsoduro** on the other side of the Grand Canal from Piazza San Marco is one of the most delightful and secluded parts of the city. Here is the famous ****Galleria dell'Accademia** (open 9–19; fest. 9–14) which contains the most important collection of Venetian paintings in existence, with Giovanni Bellini, Titian, Tintoretto and Veronese well represented.

The island of the **Giudecca** is another quiet district with very few tourists. Here is the beautiful church of the ***Redentore**, a masterpiece of Palladio. Close to the Giudecca is a small island with the church of ***San Giorgio Maggiore**, also by Palladio, in a magnificent position.

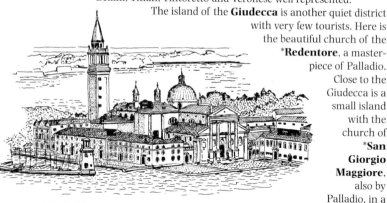

The island of San Giorgio Maggiore

Other churches in the city of particular interest include: the huge Gothic church of ***Santi Giovanni e Paolo**, with an equestrian statue outside of Bartolomeo Colleoni by Verrocchio. The church contains many funerary monuments to doges and heroes of the Republic, including Renaissance masterpieces by Pietro and Tullio Lombardo. The huge Gothic Franciscan church of the ***Frari**, with a beautiful interior, also has good funerary monuments, and paintings by Giovanni Bellini and Titian. **San Zaccaria** is a fine building of 1444–1515 (with an altarpiece by Giovanni Bellini). **Santa Maria Formosa** is interesting for its architecture and for its altarpiece by Palma Vecchio. ***Santa Maria della Salute**, the masterpiece of Baldassare Longhena, is in a splendid position and has a good collection of paintings in the great sacristy. **San Sebastiano** is decorated with superb paintings by Paolo Veronese. The charming little church of ***Santa Maria dei Miracoli** is a masterpiece of the Renaissance by Pietro Lombardo. The **Madonna dell'Orto** contains important works by Tintoretto. **La Pietà** has an 18C interior, and **San Stae**, 18C paintings.

The city also has a number of interesting buildings which belong to *Scuole*, or lay confraternities dedicated to charitable works. These include: the ***Scuola Grande di San Rocco** (open 9–17.30) which has over 50 paintings by Tintoretto, one of the most remarkable pictorial cycles in existence; the **Scuola Grande del Carmini** with beautiful frescoes by Giambattista Tiepolo; and the **Scuola di San Giorgio degli Schiavoni** (open 10–12.30, 15–18; fest 10–12.30; closed Mon), charmingly decorated with paintings by Vittore Carpaccio.

Other museums of great interest include: the **Museo Correr** (open 9–17), the city museum with historical collections and some fine paintings; the **Museo Querini-Stampalia** (good collection of Venetian paintings open 10–13, 15–18; Fri & Sat 10–13, 15–22; closed Mon); and the **Ca' Rezzonico** (open 10–17 exc. Fri) with splended 18C decorations including frescoes by the Tiepolo. The **Archaeological Museum** (open 9–14) has some fine ancient Greek sculpture. The **Peggy Guggenheim Collection** (open 11–18 exc. Tue) contains one of the most representative displays of 20C art in Europe. The **Museo Storico Navale** (open 9–13; closed fest.) is an excellent naval museum.

There are good views of the city from the top of the bell-towers of San Marco and San Giorgio Maggiore.

In the beautiful ***Venetian Lagoon** are numerous islands worth a visit. The most evocative place is the tiny island of ***Torcello**, which has a beautiful cathedral with 11C–12C mosaics. **Murano**, which has been important for its glass industry since 1292, has an excellent glass museum (open 10–17 exc. Wed), as well as a fine Byzantine basilica (Santa Maria e Donato). **Burano** has brightly painted houses on miniature canals. The **Lido**, the largest of the islands between the lagoon and the Adriatic became the most fashionable seaside resort in Italy at the beginning of this century. It is open to cars and has an atmosphere very different from that in the city of Venice itself.

VENETIAN LAGOON

JESOLO

MAZZORBO & TORCELLO

Burano

Marco Polo Airport

0 ___ 2 miles
0 ___ 4 kms

S. Francesco del Deserto

Campalto

San Giacomo in Palude

S. Erasmo

S. Giuliano

Murano

PORTO DI LIDO

MESTRE

S. Michele

Le Vignole

PORTO MARGHERA

Ponte della Libertà

La Certosa

S. Nicolò

VENICE (VENEZIA)

Tronchetto

S. Giorgio

San Servolo

Lido

PADUA

La Giudecca

La Grazia

S. Lazzaro d. Armeni

S. Clemente

Lazzaretto Vecchio

Fusina

Sacca Sessola

Santo Spirito

PUNTA SABBIONI & TREPORTI

Poveglia

ADRIATIC SEA

Malamocco

N

Alberoni

PORTO DI MALAMOCCO

San Pietro in Volta

PELLESTRINA, CHIOGGIA

33 · The province of Venice

Venice is connected to the mainland by Ponte della Libertà, a road bridge (over 3·5km long), built in 1931–32, and a parallel railway bridge (1841–42). The commercial port of **Marghera** was built on the lagoon in 1919–28, with an oil depot. The dull modern town of **Mestre** (184,000 inhab.) is incorporated in the municipality of Venice, which it has outgrown.

At the end of the Brenta canal is **Malcontenta** with the famous **Villa Foscari** (open 1 May–30 Oct, Tue, Sat and the first Sun of the month, 9–12), one of the most successful and earliest suburban villas built by Palladio (finished by 1560). The interior has frescoes by Battista Franco and Giovanni Battista Zelotti.

The **Brenta Canal** (for the boats along the canal between Padua and Venice, see Chapter 34) is lined with numerous villas built by the Venetian aristocracy, described in *Blue Guide Venice*. **Mira** is one of the most attractive places on the canal. At **Strà** is the largest of the 18C Venetian villas, with *frescoes by Giovanni Battista Tiepolo.

At the southern end of the lagoon is **Chioggia**, one of the main fishing ports on the Adriatic (particularly famous for mussels), and the most important town on the lagoon after Venice. It has a remarkable longitudinal urban structure with three canals and a parallel wide main street (described in *Blue Guide Venice*).

On the lagoon northeast of Venice is **Altino**, already settled by the 7C BC, which was the Roman *Altinum*, built at the junction of several Roman roads, and where the Dese, Sile, and Piave rivers enter the lagoon. The beauty of its country villas was admired by the Latin poet Martial; some of their fine mosaic pavements have been uncovered. A Roman road, thought to be part of the Via Claudia, has been exposed, and excavations of the city continue. The town was destroyed by Attila and the Lombards and, after floods and malaria, had been abandoned by the mid-7C. The people took refuge on Torcello and are thus directly involved with the early history of Venice (and many Roman stones from Altino were reused in the buildings of Venice, Torcello and Murano). A small museum contains mosaic pavements, stelae, Roman portrait busts (1C–2C AD), glass, amphorae and architectural fragments.

San Donà di Piave is on the Piave, a river famous as the line of Italian resistance after the retreat from Caporetto (monument on the bridge), in 1917–18. The town had to be totally rebuilt. At **Fossalta di Piave**, Ernest Hemingway, as a member of the US Red Cross, was wounded in 1918 at the age of 19 (see *A Farewell to Arms*). A memorial stele was set up here in 1979.

Eraclea, a modern village on the Piave, has taken the name of the ancient **Heraclea** (called after the Emperor Heraclius), the episcopal and administrative centre of the lagoon in the 7C–8C after the sack of Oderzo by the Lombards; its site near Cittànova, has been identified by aerial photography. It was formerly surrounded by a lagoon, and in plan it recalls Venice, with a central canal and many smaller canals. From 750 onwards the inhabitants migrated to the safer islands of Malamocco and Rialto, and a leader from Heraclea is thought to have become the first Doge of Venice. Heraclea rapidly declined as its lagoon silted up and Venice grew in importance.

Caorle is an ancient fishing village, and now a seaside resort near the mouth of the Livenza. Founded by refugees from Concordia (see below), it was a bishop's see for 12 centuries and has a cathedral of 1048 with a celebrated Venetian pala of gilded silver. The beautiful lagoon to the north (Valle Vecchia, etc.), with its fishing huts and interesting wildlife, may become a protected area.

Portogruaro is a medieval town (22,800 inhab.) with an interesting urban plan, its two main streets running parallel on either side of the river Lemene, which is still navigable from here to Caorle on the sea. The **Duomo**, with a Romanesque campanile, was rebuilt in 1793. The handsome 14C **Loggia Municipale** was enlarged in 1512. The arcaded Via Martiri della Libertà is lined with 14C–15C houses. A **museum** contains finds from the Roman station of *Concordia Sagittaria*.

The nearby present village of **Concordia** has a 15C Duomo above remains of an earlier church, and a fine 11C baptistery.

Outside Portogruaro is the Romanesque church of the early Benedictine abbey of **Summaga**.

34 · Padua

Padua, in Italian *Padova* (231,000 inhab.), is one of the most ancient cities in Italy. Above all visited for its famous frescoes by Giotto in the Cappella degli Scrovegni, it also preserves some masterpieces by Donatello and other sculptors at the great pilgrim church of Il Santo. The university here is one of the oldest and most famous in Europe, and Padua is now a lively town, crowded with young in the evenings. The three picturesque central piazzas, around Palazzo della Ragione, are filled every day with busy markets. In Italy Padua is known as the place where St Anthony of Padua lived and carried out numerous miracles, and his tomb in the Santo is visited every year by thousands of pilgrims. Although the old town has many pretty arcaded streets, the northern part of the city, rebuilt since war damage, is unattractive.

■ **Information offices.** IAT offices at the railway station and the Musei Civici agli Eremitani. The headquarters of the APT is at 8 Riviera Mugnai (tel. 049 8750655). A **cumulative ticket** for free entrance to the main museums and monuments of Padua can be purchased from these offices (or at the ticket offices of any of the museums). The APT also publishes quarterly *Padova Today* with up-to-date information for visitors. The Comune runs an information office for young people at 7 Vicolo Ponte Molino.

■ **Hotels.** 4-star: *Majestic Toscanelli*, 2 Via Dell'Arco. 3-star: *Leon Bianco*, 12 Piazzetta Pedrocchi. 2-star: *Al Cason*, 40 Via Fra Paolo Sarpi; *Al Fagiano*, 45 Via Locatelli. 1-star: *Al Santo*, 147 Via del Santo; *Bellevue*, 11 Via Belludi. **Youth hostel**: *Città di Padova*, 30 Via Aleardi. The 1-star hotels *Pace* (3 Via Papafava) and *Pavia* (11 Via Papafava) are also used by students.

■ **Restaurants**. **A**: *Antico Brolo*, 22 Corso Milano. **B**: *Trattoria ai Porteghi*, 105 Via Cesare Battisti; *Osteria dei Fabbri*, 13 Via dei Fabbri; *Isola di Caprera*, 11 Via Marsilio da Padova. **C**: *Al Pero*, Via Santa Lucia; *Nane della Giulia*, Via San Francesco (corner of Via Santa Sofia); *Cavalca*, 8 Via Manin. **Cafés**. *Pedrocchi*, Via 8 Febbraio. **Cake shop**: *Pasticceria Brigenti*, Piazza dei Signori.

■ **Picnic places.** Giardino dell'Arena (by the Cappella degli Scrovegni) and Prato della Valle (near the Basilica del Santo).

■ **Car parking.** The car parks at Prato della Valle and Via Fra Paolo Sarpi have a minibus service to Piazza dei Signori. There is also a large car park near the station.

■ **Town buses.** No. 8 from the railway station to Corso Garibaldi (for the Cappella degli Scrovegni), Riviera Businello (for the Basilica del Santo), and Prato della Valle (for Santa Giustina). No. 6 from the railway station via Viale Mazzini and Via Dante to Corso Milano (for Piazza dei Signori and Piazza del Duomo).

■ **Country buses** run by SITA depart from Piazzale Boschetti for Venice (although Venice is best reached from Padua by train); to numerous destinations in the Veneto; and to Bologna.

■ **Theatres.** *Verdi* for music and drama; *Auditorium Pollini* for music. The Orchestra di Padova e del Veneto have a concert season Oct–Apr at the Teatro Verdi and Auditorium Pollini. The Amici della Musica arrange excellent concerts Oct–Apr in the Auditorium Pollini.

■ **Daily markets** open all day in the three central piazzas (Piazza della Frutta, Piazza delle Erbe and Piazza dei Signori). The market in Piazza delle Erbe has good-value produce, while that in Piazza della Frutta also has delicacies. A weekly market is held on Saturday in the Prato della Valle.

■ **Annual festival** of St Anthony on 13 June.

■ **Boat trips on the Brenta Canal.** The Burchiello motor-launch usually operates Apr–Oct from Padua (Scalinata del Portello) along the Brenta canal to Venice in 8hrs 30mins (on Wed, Fri & Sun) with stops at Strà, Dolo, Mira, Oriago and Malcontenta (including visits to the villas at Strà, Mira, and Malcontenta). At present it is only operating from Strà (bus from Piazzale Boschetti, Padua to Strà). Bookings at New Siamic Express, 42 Via Trieste (tel. 049 660944). Other companies now also arrange trips on the Brenta (information from the APT).

History

According to the Roman historian Livy (59 BC–AD 18), the most famous native of Padua (born at Teolo, in the Euganean Hills), *Patavium* was founded by the Trojan Antenor. It is known to have been an important settlement of the Euganei and Veneti, and received full Roman franchise in 89 BC. It prospered under Byzantine and Lombard rule, and declared itself an independent republic in 1164. The foundation of the University in 1222 attracted many distinguished men to Padua, including Dante and Petrarch, as well as numerous students from England, and the city came to be known as 'la Dotta' ('The Learned'). In 1237–54 Ezzelino da Romano was tyrant of Padua, then after the suzerainty of the Carraresi (1318–1405), it was conquered by the Venetians, and remained a faithful ally of Venice until the end of the Venetian Republic.

Art

Giotto's frescoes in the Cappella degli Scrovegni gave rise to a flourishing local school of 'Giottesque' painters (Guariento, Giusto de'Menabuoi, etc). The Veronese Altichiero (c 1330–c 1395), who was active in Padua in the 1380s, was one of the most creative interpreters of Giotto's achievements before Masaccio. Renaissance art was introduced into Padua with the arrival of Donatello in 1443 to work on his equestrian statue of Gattamelata and the high altar of the Santo. He was to have a profound influence on Andrea Mantegna (1431–1506). The painter Francesco Squarcione (1397–1468) influenced a great number of followers, and in particular Mantegna, who produced a superb fresco cycle in the Ovetari chapel in the church of the Eremitani between 1454 and 1457 (almost totally destroyed in the last war). In the late 15C Bartolomeo Bellano (1434–96) and Andrea Briosco ('Il Riccio', 1470–1532) created some of the finest small bronze sculpture of the Renaissance.

The centre of the city

The centre of city life, which gravitates around the university, is VIA 8 FEBBRAIO, PIAZZETTA PEDROCCHI and PIAZZA CAVOUR, all now rather pretentiously designed pedestrian precincts, lacking in character, but free of all motor traffic. The female bronze statue by Emilio Greco dates from 1973; nearby a stele by Giò Pomodoro was set up in 1992 as an unnecessary memorial to Galileo.

The huge *CAFFÈ PEDROCCHI is one of the most celebrated cafés in Italy, and was famous in the 19C as a meeting place for intellectuals (when it was kept open 24 hours a day). It was founded by Antonio Pedrocchi and built in a triangular shape in neo-classical style in 1831 by Giuseppe Jappelli. On the Piazzetta are two protruding Doric loggias whose four lions by Giuseppe Petrelli (copies of those at the foot of the Campidoglio in Rome) are irresistible to children. The south façade has another Doric loggia, and the little wing was added by Jappelli in neo-Gothic style in 1837. It was opened to the public in 1836 and was left to the city in 1891. The ground floor has a long white and yellow main room, and two smaller red and green drawing rooms, all prettily furnished.

The **upper floor** (entered from the Piazzetta; open 9.30–12.30, 15.30–18 exc. Mon) was opened in 1842, and has recently been beautifully restored. A grand staircase, with a stuccoed apse, leads up to the Etruscan room, beyond which is the octagonal Greek room with a fresco by Giovanni Demin (1842). The charming circular Roman room has four views of Rome by Ippolito Caffi (1841–42). The Herculaneum room was decorated by Pietro Paoletti. The elaborate ballroom has a stage for the orchestra. The Egyptian room was inspired by Jappelli's friend Belzoni, actor, engineer and famous Egyptologist, and it is decorated with mock porphyry and painted stucco statues attributed to Giuseppe Petrelli and Antonio Gradenigo. Off the ballroom is the little Moorish room with good wood carvings, and beyond are the Renaissance room and the Gothic room (with paintings on glass by Demin).

Opposite the café is the **UNIVERSITY**, the second oldest university in Italy (after Bologna), founded in 1222. It was famous as a medical school, and flourished in the 15C and 16C when it was the only university in the Venetian Republic. It was nicknamed 'il Bo' (*bue*, or ox) from the sign of an inn, the most famous in the city, which used to stand on this site.

The older façade dates from 1757, and the tower from 1572; the adjoining building to the right (with the entrance) was reconstructed in 1938–39. The dignified courtyard (1552) is by Andrea Moroni. In the old courtyard (left) tickets are purchased on the ground floor for a guided tour of the university (usually on Tue & Thu at 9, 10 & 11, and on Wed, Thu & Fri at 15, 16 & 17) At the foot of the stairs is a statue of Elena Cornaro Piscopia (1646–84), who was the first woman to take a doctor's degree, in philosophy. From the upper loggia is the entrance to a room where Galileo's wooden 'cattedra' is preserved. This great teaching desk is supposed to have been made as a sign of affection by his pupils so that they could see him better: the great scientist taught physics here from 1592 to 1610, a period he looked back on as the best years of his life (one of his pupils was Gustavus Adolphus of Sweden). The Aula Magna is covered with the coats of arms of rectors, and 19C frescoes.

On the other side of the courtyard a door leads into a small museum, off which is the *anatomical theatre (1594), the most ancient in Europe, built by the surgeon Fabricius, master of William Harvey who took his degree here in 1602. Thomas Linacre (1492) and John Caius (1539) also qualified here as doctors, and among the famous medical professors were Vesalius (1540) and Fallopius (1561). Since its restoration the theatre can now only be visited from below (where the dissecting table used to be); the wooden galleries above could accommodate (standing) some 250 students.

Opposite the University, the eastern façade (1928–30) of the **Municipio** disguises a 16C building, by Andrea Moroni, that incorporates a tower of the 13C Palazzo del Podestà (seen from a side road). Behind is PIAZZA DELLA FRUTTA, a delightful large piazza with a lively daily market overlooked by the splendid *PALAZZO DELLA RAGIONE, entered from the Municipio (on Via 8 Febbraio). The immense roof was reconstructed in 1756 after storm damage. A broad flight of modern stairs in the courtyard of the Municipio leads to the *salone, on the upper floor (open 9–18 or 19 exc. Mon), one of the largest and most remarkable halls in Italy. It was built by Fra Giovanni degli Eremitani in 1306–08, and is 79m long, 27m wide and 26m high, covered with a wooden ship's keel roof. On the walls are 333 frescoes of religious and astrological subjects, divided according to the months of the year, by Nicolò Miretto and Stefano da Ferrara. These were painted shortly after a fire in 1420 which had destroyed paintings carried out by Giotto and his assistants in 1313. It is not known how closely the frescoes follow the originals by Giotto. Each month is represented by nine scenes in three tiers, representing an allegory of the month, together with its sign of the zodiac, planet and constellation. Other scenes show the labours of the month, and astrological illustrations. The hall contains a block of stone which once served as a stool of repentance for debtors, and a giant wooden horse, a copy of Donatello's Gattamelata, made for a fête in 1466. From the two terraces there are delightful views of the market squares. The hall is often used for exhibitions: its splendid proportions can only be fully appreciated when it is empty.

The palace separates Piazza della Frutta from PIAZZA DELLE ERBE, a particularly attractive square with arcaded buildings and a pretty fountain, and another daily market. At the corner of Piazza della Frutta at the Canton delle Busie is **Palazzo Consiglio** (1283) with two good Byzantine capitals. The ground floor of Palazzo della Ragione is also used as a market (with permanent stalls) which extends to a third piazza beyond (reached by Via San Clemente) called PIAZZA DEI SIGNORI, attractively enclosed by old buildings. The **Loggia della Gran Guardia** is a charming Lombard edifice begun by Annibale Maggi (1496) and finished in 1523. **Palazzo del Capitanio** (1599–1605) occupies the site of the castle of the Carraresi, of which a 14C portico survives just off Via Accademia (at No. 11). The palace incorporates a tower, adapted in 1532 by Giovanni Maria Falconetto to accommodate an astronomical clock dating from 1344 (the oldest in Italy).

Beyond the Arco dell'Orologio lies the Corte Capitaniato, with the **Liviano**, which houses the arts faculty of the university, built in 1939 by Gio Ponti. The entrance hall was frescoed by Massimo Campigli. The building incorporates the **Sala dei Giganti** with frescoes of famous men by Domenico and Gualtiero Campagnolo, and Stefano dell'Arzere (1539). These were painted over earlier 14C frescoes, including a fragment attributed to Altichiero showing Petrarch reading in his study, possibly drawn from life (Petrarch lived nearby in Arquà in 1368–74).

In Via Accademia is the beautiful **Loggia Carrarese**, seat of the Accademia Patavina di Scienze, Lettere, ed Arti. The former chapel here has frescoes of Old Testament scenes by Guariento (c 1360).

From Piazza Capitaniato, with a 16C Loggia and ancient acacias, the Corte Valaresso (fine staircase of 1607) leads under an arch of 1632 to Piazza del Duomo, with the Monte di Pietà of the 13C–14C, remodelled with a portico by Giovanni Maria Falconetto in 1530.

The **Cathedral** was reconstructed in 1552 by Andrea da Valle and Agostino Righetti to a design, much altered, of Michelangelo. The **sacristy** contains works by Nicolò Semitecolo (1367), Francesco Bassano, Giorgio Schiavone (four *saints), Gian Domenico Tiepolo, Sassoferrato and Paris Bordon. The **treasury** includes illuminated *MSS (12C and 13C), a Byzantine thurible of the 11C, a processional cross of 1228, and a large *reliquary of the Cross, of silver gilt with enamels, dating from c 1440.

The ***BAPTISTERY** (open 9.30–12.30, 15–18) was built at the end of the

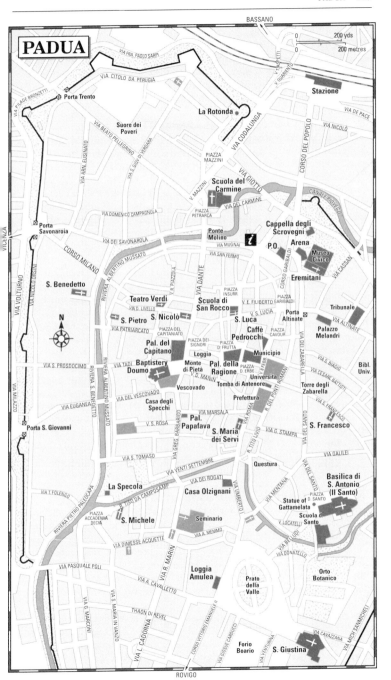

BASSANO

PADUA

0   200 yds
0   200 metres

VIA FRA. PAOLO SARPI

VIA CITOLO DA PERUGIA

VIA PILADE BRONZETTI

Porta Trento

La Rotonda

Stazione

VIA DE PACE

VIA ARN. EUSINATO

VIA S. GIOV. VERDARA

VIA BEATO PELLEGRINO

Suore dei Poveri

PIAZZA MAZZINI

VIA GIOTTO

CORSO DEL POPOLO

VIA NICOLO

VIA CODALUNGA

Porta Savonaroia

VIA DOMENICO CAMPAGNOLA

VIA DEI SAVONAROLA

CORSO MILANO

V. MAZZINI

Scuola del Carmine

VIA DEL CARMINE

PIAZZA PETRARCA

Ponte Molino

VIA MUGNAI

VIA SAN FERMO

Cappella degli Scrovegni

P.O.   Arena

Museo Civico

Eremitani

CANALE PIOVEGO

CORSO GARIBALDI

VIA CASSAN

VIA VOLTURNO

VICENZA

VIA NICOLO ORSINI

S. Benedetto

RIVIERA ALBERTINO MUSSATO

V.R. PIAZZOLA

VIA DANTE

PIAZZA INSURR.

PIAZZA GARIBALDI

Teatro Verdi

VIA D. LIVELLO

Scuola di San Rocco

V.E. FILIBERTO

V.S. LUCIA

Tribunale

VIA ALTINATE

S. Pietro

S. Nicolò

S. Luca

Porta Altinate

Palazzo Melandri

VIA PATRIARCATO

PIAZZA DEL CAPITANIATO

Caffè Pedrocchi

PIAZZA CAVOUR

VIA S. PROSDOCIMO

Pal. del Capitano

PIAZZA DEI SIGNORI

Loggia

PIAZZA D. FRUTTA

Municipio

Bibl. Univ.

VIA CESARE BATTISTI

VIA S. BIAGIO

Baptistery Doumo

Monte di Pietà

Pal. della Ragione

PIAZZA D. ERBE

VIA 8 FEBB.

Università

VIA ZABARELLA

RIVIERA S. BENEDETTO

VIA TADI

V.D. MANIN

Vescovado

Tomba di Antenore

Torre degli Zabarella

VIA DEL VESCOVADO

Casa degli Specchi

V.S. ROSA

Prefettura

R. DEL PONTI ROMANI

VIA S. FRANCESCO

VIA EUGANEA

VIA MILIZIO

Porta S. Giovanni

VIA GREG. BARBARIGO

Pal. Papafava

VIA MARSALA

VIA ROMA

S. Francesco

VIA GALILEI

S. Maria dei Servi

R. TITO LIVIO

VIA G. STAMPA

VIA DEI SANTO

VIA S. TOMASO

VIA VENTI SETTEMBRE

Questura

VIA T. FOLENGO

La Specola

VIA DEI ROGATI

Casa Olzignani

VIA UMBERTO I

VIA MONTANA

Basilica di S. Antonio (Il Santo)

R. TISO DA CAMPOSAMP.

PIAZZA ACCADEMIA DECIA

S. Michele

Seminario

VIA A. MEMMO

Statue of Gattamelata

PIAZZA S. SANTO

Scuola di Santo

V. LOCATELLI

VIA MICH SANMICHELI

VIA DIMESSE ACQUETTE

VIA BELUDI

VIA DONATELLO

VIA PASQUALE POLI

VIA R. MARIN

Loggia Amulea

VIA A. CAVALLETTO

VIA A. CAVAZZANA

Prato della Valle

Orto Botanico

VIA S. MARIA IN VANZO

THAON DI REVEL

VIA L. CADORNA

VIA G. MARCONI

CORSO VITTORIO EMANUELE II

VIA GIUSEPPE CARDUCCI

Forio Boario

S. Giustina

ROVIGO

12C. The interior is entirely covered with *frescoes by Giusto de'Menabuoi, his best work. Executed in 1378, this is one of the most interesting medieval fresco cycles in Italy. In the dome is Christ Pantocrator surrounded by a host of angels and the Blessed; in the drum, scenes from Genesis; in the pendentives, the Evangelists; and on the walls, scenes from the lives of Christ and St John the Baptist. In the apse are scenes from the Apocalypse. On the altar is a polyptych, also by Giusto.

To the south of the cathedral is the **Bishop's Palace** housing the **Museo Diocesano d'Arte Sacra**, with a frescoed *Annunciation by Jacopo da Montagnana. At No. 79 Via del Vescovado is the **Casa degli Specchi**, with tondi of polished marble, an early 16C Lombardesque building by Annibale Maggi.

Adjoining Piazzetta Pedrocchi (see above) to the north, are Piazza Cavour and Piazza Garibaldi with a Roman column surmounted by the 'Madonna dei Noli' by Antonio Bonazza. On the far side of Piazza Garibaldi opens the **Porta Altinate**, a gateway of the 13C town wall.

The church of the Eremitani

Via Eremitani leads north to the Augustinian church of the Eremitani, built 1276–1306, with a façade of 1360. It was almost completely destroyed by bombing in 1944, but has been well rebuilt. In the **interior**, on the **south side** are fresco fragments by Giusto de'Menabuoi (c 1370) and Guarltero. The *Ovetari chapel** contains all that remains of the famous frescoes by Mantegna (light on right), the destruction of which was the greatest individual disaster to Italian art in the Second World War. Mantegna worked on them between 1454 (when he was only 23) and 1457. Behind the altar, *Assumption; (left) Martyrdom of St James (recomposed from the shattered fragments) and two fragmentary frescoes by Giovanni di Camerino; (right) *Martyrdom of St Christopher (detached and removed to safety before the war). In the **sanctuary** are frescoes by Guariento. The Giottesque frescoes (very damaged) in the **Cappella Sanguinacci** include some by Giusto de'Menabuoi(1373). On the **north side** are two polychrome altarpieces by Giovanni Minello and his school (early 16C), and the mausoleum of the law professor Marco Benavides (1489–1582), by Bartolomeo Ammannati (1546).

Musei Civici and the Cappella degli Scrovegni

The convent of the church was rebuilt and modernised in 1985–91, after years of controversy, to house the Musei Civici Agli Eremitani and provide an entrance to the **CAPPELLA DEGLI SCROVEGNI** (open 9–18 or 19 exc.. Mon; inclusive ticket for the Musei Civici and Cappella degli Scrovegni). Beside the church façade is the half-built shell of an ugly new entrance, the construction of which in the 1980s was blocked by the Italian authorities; it is finally to be demolished, after years of protest. The extensive collections arranged on two floors are still in the course of arrangement.

The **Archaeological Museum**, founded in 1825, is exhibited on the **ground floor** in rooms 5–21 and the main cloister. **Rooms 5** & **6** display finds from pre-Roman and Roman tombs in Padua (including *stelae). **Rooms 7–12** contain **Roman sculpture**, mosaics, and glass; exhibits include a *bust of Silenus (2C

AD) and an imposing aedicular *tomb of the Volumnii family, dating from the Augustan period.

Rooms 13 & **14** contain **Egyptian antiquities** including two *statues of the Goddess Sekhmet in black basalt, given to the city by Giovanni Battista Belzoni in 1819, and a display relating to his activities in Egypt. Belzoni (1778–1823), born in Padua, was the first European to enter the tomb of Ramesses II at Abu Simbel, and supplied the British Museum with many of its largest Egyptian statues. **Rooms 15–18** contain Etruscan pottery, and in **room 20** are early Christian artefacts. The **cloister** contains a Roman **lapidarium**.

The **first floor** is at present reached by outside stairs from the black metal 'cloister' against the wall of the church. The **pinacoteca** is arranged chronologically in two sections. The **first section** displays works from the 14C to the early 15C. The *Crucifix by Giotto** formerly hung in the Cappella degli Scrovegni. Also here are a series of beautiful *works by **Guariento**, a *St Christopher by Giovanni da Bologna, and *polyptychs by Francesco dei Franceschi and Francesco Squarcione.

The **second section** displays works from the mid 15C to the end of the 16C. These include works by Jacopo Bellini, Lorenzo Costa (*Argonauts), Lazzaro Bastiani, Alvise Vivarini, as well as *Madonnas by Bartolomeo Veneto and Andrea Previtali, and the *Pala di Santa Giustina by Romanino. Also works by Tintoretto, Luca Longhi, and Veronese (*Crucifixion, an exquisite little work painted on slate, and *Martyrdom of Saints Primo and Feliciano).

The huge **Emo Capodilista collection** of 15C–18C paintings was left to the city by Leonardo Emo Capodilista in 1864. These include a *portrait of a man by Jan van Scorel and *St John the Evangelist by Quentin Metsys; *Leda and the Swan, and an idyllic *country scene, with figures in a landscape, two tiny works by Giorgione; two cassone *panels with mythological scenes attributed to Titian; and the *portrait of a young senator by Giovanni Bellini.

The interesting collection of **Renaissance bronzes and plaquettes** is particularly representative of northern Italian masters (Moderno, l'Antico, il Riccio, Alessandro Vittoria, Tiziano Aspetti).

The **Museo Bottacin** consists of the collection made between 1850 and 1875 by Nicola Bottacin (1805–76). It includes an important numismatic collection, Renaissance medals, and 19C works.

Sections still closed include the 17C and 18C paintings, sculpture, decorative arts (furniture, ceramics, jewellery, and lace), engravings and drawings, and a museum of the Risorgimento.

Cappella degli Scrovegni

From the ground floor of the museum a door leads out to a little garden enclosed by the ruined walls of a Roman amphitheatre (1C AD) with the **Cappella degli Scrovegni (adm. see above). This simple little chapel (also known as the Arena Chapel) was built by Enrico Scrovegni in 1303 in expiation for his father's usury (see Dante, *Inferno*, xvii. 64–75). It adjoined the Scrovegni Palace demolished in the last century. Giotto may have designed the chapel himself to contain his famous fresco cycle, painted at the height of his power (1303–05), which is the only one by him to survive intact.

Giotto's influence on all subsequent Italian painting can here be understood to the full: his painting has a new monumentality and sense of volume which had never been achieved in medieval painting. The Biblical narrative is for the first time given an intensely human significance. Bernard Berenson pointed out that his figures have remarkable 'tactile values'. The superb colouring (with strong blues) is extremely well preserved (the frescoes were last restored in 1887).

The frescoes are arranged in three bands and depict the history of Christian redemption through the lives of Mary and Christ. They were painted in chronological order: the cycle begins on the **top band** of the **south wall** (nearest to the triumphal arch). The subjects are: 1. Expulsion of Joachim from the Temple; 2. Joachim among the shepherds; 3. Annunciation to Anna; 4. Sacrifice of Joachim; 5. Vision of Joachim; 6. Meeting of Joachim and Anna at the Golden Gate. **North wall** (west end): 7. Birth of the Virgin; 8. Presentation of the Virgin in the temple; 9. Presentation of the Rods to Simeon; 10. Watching of the Rods; 11. Betrothal of the Virgin; 12. The Virgin's return home. **Triumphal arch**: 13. God the Father dispatching Gabriel; 14. Annunciation; 15. Visitation. **South wall (middle band)**: 16. Nativity; 17. Adoration of the Magi; 18. Presentation of Christ in the Temple; 19. Flight into Egypt; 20. Massacre of the Innocents. **North wall**: 21. Christ disputing with the Elders; 22. Baptism of Christ; 23. Marriage at Cana; 24. Raising of Lazarus; 25. Entry into Jerusalem; 26. Expulsion of the money-changers from the Temple. **Triumphal arch**: 27. The pact of Judas. **South wall (lower band)**: 28. Last Supper; 29. Washing of the Feet; 30. Betrayal of Christ; 31. Christ before Caiaphas; 32. Mocking of Christ. **North wall**: 33. Way to Calvary; 34. Crucifixion; 35. Deposition; 36. Angel at the empty tomb and Noli me tangere; 37. Ascension; 38. Pentecost. On the **entrance wall**, Last Judgement. The bands at the end, and separating the panels, are decorated with busts of Saints and Doctors, and Scenes from the Old Testament, mainly by Giotto's assistants. The **ceiling medallions** show Jesus, the Virgin, and the Prophets. The **lowest range** of paintings consists of beautiful monochrome allegorical figures of Virtues and Vices, also by Giotto.

In the **apse** are frescoes by followers of Giotto; on the altar are statues of the Virgin and two saints, by Giovanni Pisano. Behind the latter is the tomb of the founder, Enrico Scrovegni, by Andreolo de'Santi.

From Piazza Garibaldi (see above), Via Altinate leads east past **Palazzo Melandri** (No. 18), with a beautiful four-light window, and **San Gaetano**, a pleasant church by Scamozzi (1586), to **Santa Sofia**, the oldest church in Padua. Founded in the 9C on an earlier structure, it was rebuilt in the 11C–12C in a Romanesque style recalling earlier churches of the Adriatic exarchate. The apse is remarkable.

Going west from Piazza Garibaldi, Via Filiberto leads to the modern Piazza Insurrezione, the centre of a rebuilt business quarter. Here is the **Scuola di San Rocco** (open 9.30–12.30, 15.30–19 exc. Mon), an attractive Renaissance building of 1525 which is interesting for its frescoes illustrating the life of St Roch, attributed to Domenico Compagnola and Girolamo Tessari. They are, however, in very poor condition, and some of them have been detached. The 17C altarpiece is by Alessandro Maganza.

The **Scuola del Carmine** (open 7–12, 16–19.30), dating from 1377, has frescoes attributed to Giulio and Domenico Campagnola, notably the *Meeting of St Anne and St Joachim.

From Via 8 Febbraio (see above) Via San Francesco leads east from the university past the alleged **Tomb of Antenor**, a marble sarcophagus erected in 1233 on short columns; another sarcophagus (1309) was set up here on the 2000th anniversary of Livy's birth. The **Torre degli Zabarella** dates from the 13C (restored). Via Cesare Battisti, to the north, is a pretty road with porticoes, typical of the old town. Via San Francesco continues to the church of **San Francesco**, dating from 1416, which contains the *monument of Pietro Roccabonella, natural philosopher, by Bartolomeo Bellano and Il Riccio (1496–97), while the narrow Via del Santo leads south to the pleasant PIAZZA DEL SANTO.

The square is dominated by the great church of Sant'Antonio in front of which stands the famous equestrian *STATUE OF GATTAMELATA**, a masterpiece by Donatello (1453), and the first great Renaissance bronze equestrian monument cast in Italy. Gattamelata, or Erasmo da Nardo, was a celebrated Venetian condottiere, and protector of the Venetian Republic. He died in 1443 and had a state funeral in Venice: it is known that he desired to be buried in the Santo (see below). On the exceptionally high base are copies of the two reliefs carved by Donatello in 1447. Just out of the piazza in Via Cesarotti is the pretty **Palazzo Giusti del Giardino**, with a double loggia. It incorporates the *Loggia** and **Odeo Cornaro** (no adm.)

Statue of Gattamelata by Donatello (1453)

attributed to Giovanni Maria Falconetto and Gaultiero dell'Arzere, built in 1524 for Alvise Cornaro as the seat of a literary society. Derived from classical models, the buildings are decorated with statues attributed to Giovan Maria Mosca, and stuccoes by Tiziano Minio.

Basilica del Santo

The *Basilica del Santo (open all day, 6.30–19 or 19.30), usually called simply **IL SANTO**, was begun in 1232 as a temple for the tomb of St Anthony of Padua, and finished in the 14C. St Anthony was born in Lisbon in 1195, but on a missionary journey to Africa he was forced in a storm to land in Italy and settled at Padua, where he preached and carried out miracles under the guidance of St Francis. He was canonised the year after his death in 1231. The church is now one of the great pilgrim shrines of Italy, since St Anthony is one of the best loved saints in the country (it is estimated that some five million pilgrims visit the church every year).

The six spherical domes in the Byzantine manner, the cone of the central cupola, and the two minaret-like campanili give an oriental appearance to the **exterior** of the church. The magnificent **interior**, though Gothic in plan and detail, is Byzantine in inspiration. It contains many important sculptures. Above the main portal is a fresco by Pietro Annigoni (1985). In the **nave**, on the first north pillar is a fresco of the Madonna by Stefano da Ferrara, facing the tomb of Antonio Trombetta (died 1518), by Il Riccio. The two holy water stoups have statues of Christ, by Aspetti (left), and St John the Baptist (right), by Tullio Lombardo. Against the second north pillar is the tomb of the Venetian general Alessandro Contarini (died 1553), an elaborate work by Sanmicheli, with a bust by Danese Cattaneo and statues by Vittoria. Opposite is the tomb of Cardinal Bembo (died 1547), which has been attributed to Palladio, with a bust by Danese Cattaneo.

Basilica del Santo

South side. In the first chapel are monuments to Erasmo Gattamelata (died 1443) and his son Giannantonio (died 1455), erected by Erasmo's widow in 1458 and attributed to a certain Gregorio d'Allegretto. In the south transept is the *Chapel of St Felix (closed for restoration), designed in 1372–77 by Andriolo and Giovanni De Santi, with *frescoes by Altichiero.

The bronze gates of the **choir** are by Camillo Mazza (1661), and the four statues on the balustrade by Tiziano Aspetti (1593). The magnificent *high altar (the sanctuary gates are unlocked on request by the uniformed custodians), sculpted by Donatello and his assistants in 1446–49, has suffered many vicissitudes, and its present reconstruction dates from 1895 (it is still not fully understood how the statues and reliefs were arranged by Donatello). Above 12 reliefs of angel musicians (only four of which are by Donatello's hand) and a Pietà, are four *reliefs (two on the front and two on the back) of miracles of St Anthony, superb works by Donatello. They show the miracles of the mule, of the miser's heart, of the severed leg, and of the newborn child. At the ends are symbols of the Evangelists. The altar is crowned with the Madonna rising from her throne, in an unusual pose, holding the Child in front of her, between statues of the six patron saints of Padua. Above is a life-size bronze *crucifix, one of Donatello's masterpieces. On the back of the altar is a large stone relief of the Entombment, perhaps by an assistant of Donatello.

On the left of the altar is a bronze paschal *candelabrum, on a marble pedestal, the most important work of Il Riccio (1515). On the wall of the choir are 12 small bronze *reliefs of Old Testament scenes, ten of them by Bartolomeo Bellano (1484–88) and two by Il Riccio (1506–07). The decorations of the apse date from 1926.

In the **north transept** is the *CHAPEL OF ST ANTHONY, built to house the greatly revered tomb of St Anthony of Padua (died 1231) behind the altar. Hundreds of pilgrims come from all over Italy every day to touch the green marble sarcophagus, and many leave ex-votos in the chapel. The chapel was reconstructed in the 16C and it is one of the most beautiful works of the Italian High Renaissance, perfectly preserved. It was probably designed by Tullio Lombardo (but also attributed to Andrea Riccio) in 1499. The monumental entrance is by Falconetto (1532). High up on the entrance-screen are statues of the patron saints of Padua, among which that of Santa Justina, on the left, by Giovanni Minello, is particularly fine. The stucco ceiling of the chapel is also by Falconetto (1533).

The walls are lined with nine large classical *reliefs which commemorate the saint's miraculous powers. They were carved in 1500–77. Each panel has life-size figures in front of an architectural perspective in different marble. From left to right: Antonio Minello, St Anthony receiving the Franciscan habit (1517); Giovanni Rubino and Silvio Cosini, Miracle of the jealous husband (1524–36); Danese Cattaneo and Girolamo Campagna, Miracle of the young boy bought back to life (1571–77); Jacopo Sansovino, Miracle of the Virgin Carilla (1540–50); Antonio Minello and Jacopo Sansovino, Miracle of the young boy Parrasio (1536); Tullio Lombardo, Miracle of the miser's heart (1520–25); Tullio Lombardo, Miracle of the severed leg; Giovanni Maria Mosca and Paolo Stella, Miracle of the unbroken glass (1529); and Antonio Lombardo, Miracle of the newborn child. The altar has statues by Tiziano Aspetti (1594).

The adjoining **Conti Chapel** is dedicated to the Blessed Luca Belludi, St Anthony's companion, who is buried here. It is decorated with frescoes (recently restored) by Giusto de'Menabuoi. In the **north aisle** is the Baroque tomb of General Caterino Cornaro, by Juste le Court (1674), next to that of Antonio Roselli (died 1466), by Pietro Lombardo.

A Rococo chapel at the east end of the ambulatory houses the **treasury** (open 8–12, 14.30–19) containing more than 100 reliquaries. The ceiling painting in the **sacristy**, by Pietro Liberi (1615), shows St Anthony in Paradise. The reliquary cupboard is by Bartolomeo Bellano (1469). In the adjoining **chapter house** (closed) are fragmentary frescoes after Giotto.

To the south of the church is the large **Convent of the Santo** with four cloisters (usually entered from the right of the church façade). From the **Chiostro del Capitolo** is the entrance to the **Biblioteca Antoniana** (closed at weekends). On the steps are the original stone reliefs by Donatello from the base of the Gattamelata monument. The library contains many MSS and incunabula, including a MS of sermons annotated in St Anthony's handwriting.

In the **Chiostro del Beato Luca Belludi**, with a magnificent magnolia tree, is the entrance to the **Museo Antoniano** (open daily 9–12.30, 14.30–17 or 19), reopened in 1995 in a pretentious arrangement. It contains a marble group of four late 14C *statues by Rainaldino di Pietro di Francia (the fifth is by Giovanni Minello, 1503); paintings (removed from the choir chapels of the Santo in 1895) by Giovanni Battista Pittoni, Giovanni Antonio Pellegrini, Giovanni Battista Tiepolo (attributed) and Giovanni Battista Piazzetta; and the *navicella, an elaborate incense burner in the form of a ship made around 1500 in Nuremberg. A lunette fresco from the Santo by Mantegna (1452) is also to be exhibited here.

In another cloister, on the north side near the church, is a modest slab which marks the burial-place of the entrails of Thomas Howard (1586–1646), Earl of Surrey and Arundel, collector of the 'Arundel Marbles'.

In Piazza del Santo are the **Scuola del Santo** and the **Oratorio di San Giorgio** (inclusive ticket; 9–12.30, 14.30–17 or 19). A hand-list is lent to visitors. The Scuola, built in 1427–31 (with an upper storey of 1504), is approached by a pretty flight of stairs (1736). The paintings (1511) of the life of St Anthony are by Francesco Vecellio (Titian's elder brother), Girolamo Tessari, Filippo da Verona, Bartolomeo and Benedetto Montagna, Giannantonio Corona, Domenico Campagnola, and others. Nos 2, 12 and 13 are early works by Titian. The seated statue of the Madonna is by Il Riccio (1520). The *Oratory next door, originally the mausoleum of the Soranzo family, is entirely covered with *frescoes by Altichiero di Zevio and Jacopo Avanzo (1378–84).

In the corner of the piazza is a building of 1870–80, with an unusual façade by Camillo Boito, now used for exhibitions.

The quiet Via Orto Botanico leads out of the piazza across a canal to the *ORTO BOTANICO (open daily exc. fest. 9–13; May–Sep, also 15–18), the most ancient botanical garden in Europe, founded in 1545 and retaining its original form and structure. It is beautifully tended and all the plants are well labelled. The charming circular walled garden, with geometrical beds, is laid out around a pond with tropical water lilies. The various sections include medicinal and aquatic plants, rare species from northern Italy, flora from the Colli Euganei, and poisonous plants. Also here are a tamarisk tree, a ginkgo tree of 1750, a mimosa tree, and an ancient magnolia dating from the mid-18C. A palm tree, planted in 1585 and known as 'Goethe's palm' (he visited the garden in 1786) survives in a little greenhouse. Behind this are interesting 19C hothouses, where succulents and carnivorous plants are kept, opposite which is a row of the plants first introduced into Italy in this garden, including the lilac, first cultivated in 1565, the sunflower in 1568, and the potato in 1590. There is also a greenhouse for orchids. Trees in the arboretum surrounding the walled garden include swamp cypresses, magnolias, Chinese palm trees, cedars, pines, a plane tree dating from 1680, and ilexes.

Via Beato Luca Belludi leads past an interesting Art Nouveau house (No. 3) to the pleasant ***PRATO DELLA VALLE**, the largest 'piazza' in Italy, surrounded by a miscellany of arcaded buildings. This huge area has been used since Roman times for public spectacles, fairs, etc. (and a large market is held here on Saturday). In the centre is the Isola Memmia, encircled by a canal bordered by 18C statues of famous citizens, professors, and students of the University. Four bridges lead to the centre, decorated with fountains. On the west side of the Prato is the **Loggia Amulea**, built in 1861 in the Venetian style with two Gothic loggias in brick and marble. The statues of Giotto and Dante are by Vincenzo Vela (1865). On the south side of the square is the monumental entrance to the former Foro Boario, now used as a car park and stadium.

Santa Giustina

The Benedictine church of Santa Giustina, designed by Il Riccio in 1502 but modified, by its builder Andrea Moroni, with eight cupolas, recalls the exotic appearance of the church of Sant'Antonio. The plain façade has two marble griffins. The huge cruciform **interior** presents an epitome of 17C Venetian art. In the **south aisle** are altarpieces by Pietro Liberi, Carlo Loth and Luca Giordano.

South transept. The arca of St Matthew has reliefs by Giovanni Francesco de Surdis. Behind is a corridor which leads to a well beneath a cupola frescoed by Giacomo Ceruti. In the niches are four terracotta statues by Francesco Segala (1564–65). Beyond an unusual iron sarcophagus is a painting of the discovery of the well here by Pietro Damini and two more statues by Francesco Segala. The domed cruciform **Chapel of Santa Maria**, an oratory built c 520, has a rare contemporary iconostasis, with an inscription. Also here are a double pluteus and tympanum (both 6C). On the altar is an effigy of St Prosdocimus (1564), and above, a relief of the saint (late 5C or early 6C).

In the **sanctuary**, the *choir stalls were elaborated carved by the Norman Riccardo Taurigny, with the help of Vicentine craftsmen. The high altarpiece is by Paolo Veronese (1575). In the **south aisle** are altarpieces by Luca Giordano and Sebastiano Ricci.

Part of the **walls** of Padua survive, built by the Venetians in 1513–44, with a circumference of some 11km. The two gates to the north, the Porta San Giovanni (1528) and the Porta Savonarola (1530) are by Giovanni Maria Falconetto, their design derived from ancient Roman architecture.

35 · The Colli Euganei and the province of Padua

The **Colli Euganei** are a pretty little isolated group of hills conspicuous in the plain just to the southwest of Padua. Volcanic in origin, they reach a maximum height of 600m and are covered with extensive chestnut woods, and attractive vegetation. These unspoiled hills have, since 1989, been protected as a regional park. There are a number of paths (marked by the CAI) for walkers in the hills, and farms offering 'agriturist' accommodation. A good white wine is produced here, and wild mushrooms grow in abundance. The hills have been famous since Roman times for their hot thermal springs (70°-87°C), rich in minerals, and there are four spa towns here, most notably Abano Terme. Petrarch spent the last four years of his life in a little village in the hills, and it was here that Shelley was inspired to compose his *Lines written among the Euganean Hills* .

■ **Information offices**. APT Terme Euganee, 18 Via Pietro d'Abano, Abano Terme (tel. 049 8669055). APT Padova, 8 Riviera Mugnai (information office: tel. 049 8752077).

■ **Hotels**. The four spa towns of Abano, Montegrotto, Galzignano and Battaglia Terme have some 170 hotels with thermal pools. **Abano Terme** has 18 4-star hotels, and 35 3-star hotels, as well as numerous others. **Montegrotto Terme** has 10 4-star, and 20 3-star hotels, as well as others. **Galzignano Terme** has three 4-star and two 3-star hotels. **Battaglia Terme** has four 2-star hotels.
  At **Teolo** in the Colli Euganei: 3-star hotel *Alla Posta*. At **Montagnana**: 3-star *Aldo Moro* (with restaurant). At **Cittadella**: 4-star *Filanda* and 3-star *Due Mori*. **Youth Hostel** (open mid-Apr–mid-Oct) at Montagnana.

■ **Restaurants**. Numerous restaurants of all categories in the spa towns. At **Arquà Petrarca**: **B**: *La Montanella* (at the entrance to the village) and *Miravalle* (near the house of Petrarch). At **Montagnana: A**: *Osteria San Benedetto* . **B**: *Aldo Moro*. **C**: *Antica Tosca*. At **San Pelagio** there is a restaurant (**C**) in the Air Museum. At **Cittadella: B**: *La Speranza*; **C**: *Trattoria al Teatro*. At **Piazzola sul Brenta**, in the Villa Contarini, is *Le Cantine del Palladio*.

■ **Golf courses** at Valsanzibio (18-hole), and at Teolo and Frassanelle.

■ **Annual festivals**. The Palio of Montagnana (a horse race outside the walls) is held on the first Sun in Sep, and celebrations with fairs and markets last a week. On the third Sun in Oct the fair known as 'Fiera Franca' has been held since 1608 in Cittadella.

ABANO TERME is one of the best equipped thermal spas in Europe, with numerous hotels (catering especially for German visitors), most of them with their own thermal pools. Giuseppe Jappelli designed a number of buildings here at the beginning of the 19C, and more hotels and parks appeared at the beginning of this century. Abano is principally noted for its mud therapy, effective especially in cases of rheumatism and arthritis. In the height of the season (Mar–Oct) Abano and the neighbouring spas are crowded with visitors.

The **Abbazia di Praglia** (shown on a guided tour every half hour, 14.30–16.30) is a Benedictine abbey and church (rebuilt 1490–1548), by Tullio Lombardo. The refectory has paintings by Giovanni Battista Zelotti, and a fresco by Bartolomeo Montagna. The monks are renowned for their skill in restoring books—their laboratory is off the beautiful cloisters.

Montegrotto Terme is another important spa, with extensive remains of Roman baths, and a small Roman theatre. Above the town, a lovely park (open to the public) surrounds the neo-Gothic Villa Draghi. Nearby is the curious **Castello del Catajo** (open Tue & fest. 14.30–18; 15–19 in summer). It was built in 1570 by Andrea della Valle for Pio Enea degli Obizzi, a captain of the Venetian army. In the 19C it became the property of the dukes of Modena. It was altered in the 17C when part of the beautiful garden was created, with numerous fountains. The frescoes (1571–73) by Giovanni Battista Zelotti on the first floor depict the exploits of members of the Obizzi family, including one who accompanied Richard I of England on the Crusades, and another who perhaps fought for Edward III at Neville's Cross.

At **San Pelagio** the castle has an 'Air Museum' (open 9.30–12.30, 14–17 exc. Mon). The display is arranged chronologically from the experiments of Leonardo to the era of space travel. The exhibits include material relating to d'Annunzio's flight to Vienna in 1918, planned in the castle; a model of the first helicopter designed by Forlanini in 1877; and planes used in the Second World War.

Battaglia Terme is an attractive small, old-fashioned spa on the Canale della Battaglia, much less grand than the other neighbouring spa towns. A park laid out by Giuseppe Jappelli in the early 19C surrounds the Villa Emo Selvatico, an unusual centrally planned building with four corner towers and a dome dating from 1648. Just outside, on a byroad to Arquà Petrarca, is another Villa Emo, built in 1588 on a design attributed to Vincenzo Scamozzi. The garden (open Sat & fest. 10–19) was laid out in the 1960s and has numerous rose beds.

At **Valsanzibio** is the **Villa Barbarigo** (open 9–12, 14–19; fest. 14–19), built in the mid-17C. The fine *garden, probably laid out around 1699, has a maze, and numerous pools, fountains and statues. It is surrounded by a 19C park.

Nearby, in a pretty position in the hills, is **Arquà Petrarca**, a delightful little medieval borgo with numerous gardens, where Petrarch lived from 1370 until his death in 1374. At the top of the village is his house (open 9–12.30 and 14.30 or 15–17.30 or 19 exc. Mon) which contains visitors' books, one with Byron's signature. In the lower part of the village is the church, outside of which is Petrarch's plain marble sarcophagus with an epitaph composed by himself. Numerous *giuggiole* trees grow here, producing an orange fruit in the shape of an olive (festa on 1 Oct).

To the west of Battaglia Terme is another spa town, **Galzignano Terme**. Further north, near Torreglia, is **Luvigliano** above which is **Villa dei Vescovi** (open Mon, Wed, Fri and the 1st Sat of the month, 10.30–12.30, 14.30–18.30), built under the direction of Alvise Cornaro by Giovanni Maria Falconetto in 1532, and continued by Andrea della Valle in 1567. It contains frescoes attributed to the Netherlandish artist Lambert Sustris (1545), and is surrounded by a pretty garden. In the church is an altarpiece by Girolamo Santacroce, signed and dated 1527.

MONSELICE (17,600 inhab.) at the foot of a conspicuous hill (*mons silicis*) has a huge trachyte quarry and a ruined Rocca. It was an important Lombard city, and heavily fortified during the Middle Ages. The approach from the station (on the main line between Bologna and Padua) crosses the canal by an iron swing-bridge beside **Villa Pisani**, a Palladian building of c 1556. A stretch of 14C walls can be seen here. Via XI Febbraio and Via XXVIII Aprile continue to Piazza Mazzini, the centre of the medieval town. In Piazza Vittoria are the Duomo Nuovo (1957) and the Municipio (1965).

Via del Santuario ascends from Piazza Mazzini past the 15C Monte di Pietà to the **Castello di Monselice**, restored in 1939 for Count Vittorio Cini who transformed it into a museum of medieval and Renaissance works of art, now the property of the Veneto Region (shown on guided tours 9–12, 15–18 exc. Mon; by appointment in winter). The castle was first constructed by Ezzelino da Romano in the 12C and was transformed into a residence in the 15C. The road continues past monumental edifices including the Baroque Palazzo Nani-Mocenigo, the 13C Duomo Vecchio and the 18C Santuario delle Sette Chiese. At the top is **Villa Duodo**, a very fine building of 1597 by Vincenzo Scamozzi, with a wing added in the 18C by Andrea Tirali. It is preceded by four statues of the Seasons.

Southeast of Monselice is **Bagnoli di Sopra** where monastic buildings were transformed in the 17C by Baldassarre Longhena into the **Villa Widmann** (privately owned), with 18C frescoes. Carlo Goldoni stayed here with Ludovico Bagnoli in the 18C and put on several performances of his plays. It is surrounded by a fine garden (open Thu, 14–18) decorated with numerous statues by Antonio Bonazza (1742). Also in the piazza is the Palazzetto Widmann (owned by the Comune) with frescoes by Giovanni Battista Pittoni and Louis Dorigny.

At the southern edge of the Colli Euganei is the little town of **ESTE** (17,000 inhab.), a centre of the ancient Veneti before it became the Roman *Ateste*. Later it was the stronghold of the Este family who afterwards became dukes of Ferrara, and from 1405 was under Venetian dominion. The huge battlemented Carrarese **Castle** dates mainly from 1339 and its impressive walls enclose a public garden. Here, in the 16C Palazzo Mocenigo is the **Museo Nazionale Atestino** (open every day 9–19), illustrating the culture of the Veneti who inhabited the Veneto in the pre-Roman period, including a remarkable collection of bronzes. The museum, founded in 1888, was opened here in 1902, and many of the exhibits, arranged chronologically, come from excavations carried out in the 19C near Este. The Benvenuti *situla (c 600 BC) is decorated with bronze reliefs, and the Roman material includes a fine bronze head of *Medusa (1C AD). A Madonna and Child by Cima da Conegliano is also displayed here.

Behind the castle (Via Cappuccini) are the fine parks of several villas, including the **Villa Kunkler** (being restored) occupied by Byron in 1817–18, where Shelley composed *Lines written among the Euganean Hills*. The **Duomo** (rebuilt 1690–1708) contains a painting by Giovanni Battista Tiepolo. The Romanesque church of **San Martino** (1293) has a leaning campanile. Remains of the Roman city (including a stretch of road, houses with mosaic pavements, and fragments of a public building) have been found near the church of the Salute.

West of Este is the small town of **MONTAGNANA** (10,000 inhab.) which preserves its medieval *walls intact, nearly 2km in circumference, providing one of the most remarkable sights in Italy. The broad moat is now occupied by grassy fields. At either end of the town are two splendid fortified gate-castles, the **Rocca degli Alberi**, built by the Carrarese in 1360 and restored in 1963 as a Youth Hostel (open mid-Apr–mid-Oct; visitors are usually admitted to see the defence works of the gate and the view from the top), and the **Castello di San Zeno** (1242), recently restored for use as a library. It is well worth walking round the inside of the walls, too.

In the large central piazza with houses in the Venetian style is the **Duomo**, rebuilt in 1431. It contains two interesting late 15C frescoes on either side of the west door, works by Giovanni da Buonconsiglio, and a high altarpiece of the *Transfiguration* by Veronese.

On the main Via Matteotti is the handsome **Palazzo Magnavin-Foratti**, a 16C Venetian palace. Near the church of San Francesco, with a fine campanile, is the inconspicuous **Palazzo del Municipio**, attributed to Sanmicheli (c 1550) with an interesting staircase. Just outside Porta Padova to the east is **Villa Pisani** (privately owned; in poor condition), begun in 1552 by Palladio. The garden façade has a double open loggia with classical columns. The villa contains stuccoes in the salone by Alessandro Vittoria.

To the north there is another villa built by Palladio in 1540. Privately owned and in very poor condition, it can only be seen from the outside; it stands on the right of the road (opposite an old abbey), which leads north to **Poiana**, in the province of Vicenza. Inside are important frescoes by Bernardino India and Anselmo Canera.

In the northern part of the province is **CITTADELLA** (18,000 inhab.) built by the Paduans in 1220 as a reply to Castelfranco, fortified by Treviso some 20 years earlier. The old centre is enclosed in medieval *walls, remarkably well preserved with numerous towers and gates. The two main gates, the Porta Padova and Porta Bassano, are painted with the red coat of arms of the Carrarese family. The Porta Bassano and Porta Treviso can both be visited by appointment (made at the Municipio). The Torre Malta, built by Ezzelino III da Romano, is used for exhibitions. The moated fortifications, designed in an unusual elliptical shape, surround a simple and symmetrically planned town, which may follow the plan of a Roman town.

In the central piazza is the neo-classical **Duomo** (1820–28) by Giuseppe Jappelli, with works by Jacopo Bassano (including the *Supper at Emmaus in the sacristy). In the same square is the 19C **Municipio**. In Via Indipendenza the neo-classical **Theatre**, built by Giacomo Bauto in 1828, with a façade by Jappelli, has recently been restored. In Borgo Treviso is the interesting **Palazzo Pretorio**, with a well carved 16C marble portal, and 15C–16C frescoes. The gardens on the outside of the walls, which have a little zoo, can be entered from Porta Padova or Porta Vicenza. A weekly market is held in the town on Mondays.

To the northwest, in the locality of **Santa Croce Bigolina**, is the church of Santa Lucia di Brenta frescoed by Jacopo Bassano c 1540 (recently restored).

On the river Brenta north of Padua is the small town of **Piazzola sul Brenta**.

Here is the splendid **Villa Contarini** (open 9–12, 14–8 exc. Mon; owned by a private foundation), rebuilt in the 17C for Marco Contarini as a summer palace on the Brenta river. It is preceded by a remarkable long avenue of magnolia trees, and a monumental semicircular portico (only half built), in Palladian style, across two canals and a fountain. The façade is 180m long. The central room is the auditorium, with remarkable acoustics (the gallery in the ceiling is for the orchestra), where concerts are held in May and June. Some of the rooms in the vast interior retain their 18C decorations. The carriage entrance to the villa on a lower level has a loggia decorated with shells and pebbles. There is also a small lapidarium, with Greek and Latin inscriptions.

The park of 45 hectares can also be visited: it is surrounded by canals, and has fishponds, and a huge lake with black and white swans. To the right of the villa is the handsome stable block. A market is held in front of the villa on Fridays.

In the northeastern corner of the province is **Piombino Dese**, with the beautiful **Villa Cornaro** (open on Sat in May–Sep, 15.30–18), built for Giorgio Cornaro by Palladio in 1552. With two storeys, it has a double portico. The rooms are frescoed by Mattia Bortoloni (1716), and have stuccoes of the same date by Bortolo Cabianca. The statues in the main room are by Camillo Mariani (c 1592–94). Set beside the river Dese, it has a small garden.

To the northeast is **Levada** with the Villa Marcello (privately owned), rebuilt in the 18C, with frescoes by Giovanni Battista Crosato.

South of Piombino is **Massanzago** where the town hall in Villa Baglioni has frescoes by Gian Battista Tiepolo.

On the eastern outskirts of Padua is **Noventa Padovana** with the Villa Giovanelli, built in the 17C with a pronaos and steps on the garden front added by Giorgio Massari (1738), and the 18C Villa Valmarana, frescoed by Andrea Urbani, both now owned by institutions.

36 · Rovigo and the delta of the Po

Rovigo is a prosperous town and provincial capital (52,000 inhab.) in the Polesine, the fertile strip of land between the lower Adige and river Po. A walled town in the 12C, Rovigo was taken by the Venetians in 1482, and they held control of the town until the end of the Republic. It still has a Venetian atmosphere. In the 1930s the river Adigetto was covered over to form the Corso del Popolo.

■ **Information office.** APT, Via J. H. Dunant, tel. 0425 361481. Information Office at 3 Piazza Vittorio Emanuele II.

■ **Hotels.** 4-star: *Corona Ferrea*, 21 Via Umberto I, and others.

■ **Restaurants. C**: *Dante*, 212 Corso del Popolo; *Il Portico*, 9 Via Silvestri. **Cafés**. *Borsa*, Piazza Garibaldi (temporarily closed) and *Franchin*.

■ **Car parking** in Piazzale di Vittorio.

■ **Buses** depart from the bus station (SITA) for the Po delta.

■ **Theatre**. *Teatro Sociale*, Piazza Garibaldi (winter opera season).

■ **Annual festival**. A fair, with street markets, is celebrated on 24 Oct.

Just off the southern corner of the central PIAZZA VITTORIO EMANUELE II is **Palazzo Roncale**, a fine building by Sanmicheli (1555). In the piazza is the attractive **Palazzo del Municipio** (16C; restored in 1765) with a tower. Beside it is the 18C Palazzo Bosi which houses the civic library and the **Pinacoteca dei Concordi** (open 9.30–12, 15.30–19; Sat 9.30–12; Sun by appointment only. In Jul & Aug 10–13 exc. Sun). The Accademia dei Concordi was founded in 1580, and the origins of the pinacoteca go back to 1833. The fine collection of paintings is particularly representative of Venetian art from the 15C to 18C. It includes a *Madonna by Giovanni Bellini, works by Sebastiano Mazzoni, and *portraits by Alessandro Longhi and Giovanni Battista Tiepolo.

Opposite the Accademia is **Palazzo Roverella**, begun in the 15C on a design attributed to Biagio Rossetti. At the other end of the piazza is the **Gran Guardia**, built for the Austrians in 1854 by Tomaso Meduna.

Just to the north is PIAZZA GARIBALDI, with an equestrian statue of the hero by Ettore Ferrari, and the Caffè Borsa. The Camera del Commercio encloses the well preserved Salone del Grano built in 1934 with a remarkable glass barrel-vault. The Teatro Sociale has a neo-classical façade dating from 1819.

Via Silvestri leads out of the square past the church of **San Francesco** (with sculptures by Tullio Lombardo) to Piazza XX Settembre, at the end of which is **'La Rotonda'** or **Santa Maria del Soccorso** (open 8.30–11.30, and 15 or 16.30–18 or 19), a centrally planned octagonal church surrounded by a portico built in 1594 by Francesco Zamberlan. The campanile was designed by Baldassarre Longhena in the 17C. The interior *decoration which survives intact from the 17C consists of a series of paintings celebrating Venetian officials with elaborate allegories: the lower band includes five by Francesco Maffei, and others by Pietro Liberi. Above stucco statues (1627) is another cycle of paintings by Antonio Zanchi, Pietro Liberi, Andrea Celesti, and others. The painted dome dates from 1887. The organ by Gaetano Callido (1767) is also decorated with 17C paintings.

On the south side of Corso del Popolo, in Piazza Matteotti, is a little public park around two old towers and part of the old town defences. Nearby is the **Cathedral** of 1696. It contains altarpieces by Andrea Vicentino and Palma Giovane.

The huge convent of **San Bartolomeo**, reached off Corso del Popolo, is being restored and there are long-term plans to open the Museo Civico delle Civiltà in Polesine here.

The Polesine

■ **Restaurant** at **Lusia**: *Trattoria al Ponte* (**B**).

This flat area west of Rovigo between the Adige and Po rivers is traversed by numerous canals. At **Fratta Polesine**, facing a bridge over a canal, is *VILLA

BADOER (open 10–12, 14–17 exc. Mon), built by Palladio in 1556 for the Venetian nobleman Francesco Badoer (and now owned by the province). It is enclosed by an attractive brick wall and preceded by a green lawn with two fountains and two 19C magnolia trees. The outbuildings are linked to the house by curving porticoes, and a wide flight of steps leads up to the villa with an Ionic portico and temple pediment. The empty interior is interesting for its remarkable plan (the service rooms and servants' quarters are on a lower level) and damaged contemporary frescoes by Giallo Fiorentino.

Beside the villa is the **Villa Molin (Grimani)**, now owned by the Avezzù (open on Sat 15–16), a fine building in the Palladian style. There are more villas nearby including (on the canal) the early 18C Villa Cornoldi, and the Villa David (Franchin) preceded by two 18C statues, and the late 17C Villa Oroboni.

North of Fratta Polesine is **Lendinara**, with a few fine palaces and, in the Duomo, a painting by Domenico Mancini. The campanile, built in 1797, is exceptionally tall (107m). Here is buried Jessie White, wife of Alberto Mario, both important figures in the Italian Risorgimento. The Canozzi family of wood-carvers were born here: they produced finely carved choir stalls for a number of churches in Italy during the 15C.

West of Lendinara is **Badia Polesine** with remains of the abbey of Vangadizza, founded in the 10C and enlarged in the 11C. The attractive 12C campanile stands near two 12C tombs and the drum of the domed chapel which is all that remains of the church destroyed by Napoleon. The picturesque irregular cloister is used for concerts and the refectory is being restored. The chapel (opened on request) contains painted decoration attributed to Filippo Zaniberti and interesting stuccoes of the Cardinal Virtues (recently restored). The Museo Civico Baruffaldi contains 12C–17C ceramics. The Teatro Sociale dates from 1813.

At **Canda**, on the Bianco canal, is the Villa Nani-Mocenigo (no adm.), attributed to Vincenzo Scamozzi (1580–84), enlarged in the 18C.

The town hall of **Fiesso Umbertiano** is in a fine building by Andrea Tirali (1706).

The Delta of the Po

The **Po** is the largest river in Italy (652km), its waters now sadly polluted with chemicals. Its source is at Pian del Re (2050m) in Piedmont on the French border and it is joined by numerous tributaries (including the Ticino and the Adda) as it traverses northern Italy from west to east through Lombardy and the Veneto on its way to the Adriatic. The wide open plain—the largest in Italy—through which it runs and which separates the Alps from the Apennines, is known as the *pianura padana*. In the late Middle Ages the Po was navigable and one of the principal waterways of Europe. In 1599 the Venetian Republic carried out major works of canalisation in the delta area in order to deviate the course of the river south to prevent it silting up the Venetian lagoon. It now reaches the sea by seven different channels: the largest (which carries 60 per cent of its waters) is called the 'Po di Venezia'. The delta formed by this operation is the largest area of marshlands in Italy.

The flat open landscape with wide views over the reedy marshes and numerous wetlands (known as *valli*), channels and rivers is remarkably beautiful, whether in typical misty weather or on clear autumnal days. Rice and sugar beet were once intensely cultivated here and some attractive old farm-houses survive, although most of them have been abandoned. There seems to be a desire on the part of most of the local inhabitants to preserve this remote area from unsightly 'development', although the long-term project to make the Po delta (which falls mostly in the province of Rovigo, but also partly in that of Ferrara) into a Regional or National Park has still not been approved; those opposed to the institution of a park include local sportsmen and fishermen.

The marshes are on the migratory bird routes from northern Europe and have extremely interesting birdlife, counting some 350 species, including cormorants, herons, egrets, grebes, blackwinged stilts, wild geese and duck. Despite opposition from the naturalists, the shooting season is still open from September to January. Pila and the Po della Pila have important fisheries, and all over the delta area eels, bass, carp, tench, pike and grey mullet are caught. Clams (a new clam was imported into the delta in the early 1980s from the Philippines) and mussels are also cultivated here.

Very few boats (apart from those of the fishermen) venture into the Delta area since many of the channels are only one or two metres deep. A few characteristic bridges of boats and ferries survive (see below). The area is ideal for cyclists.

In the last few decades the delta area has sunk below sea level because of drilling operations for natural gas off the coast and quarrying in the area. In the 19C a flood submerged three-quarters of the Polesine area, and it was devastated by another flood in 1951. Pumping stations help to regulate the waters and a new canal was built in 1990 between the Po di Venezia and Po della Pila which saved the area from another disastrous flood in 1994.

Since 1982 a thermo-electrical plant near Porto Tolle (on the island of Polesine Camerini) has been in operation: it is criticised because of the atmospheric pollution it causes. Scientific studies have shown that the river (from its source over 600km away) feeds hundreds of tons of arsenic into the Adriatic every year, and according to European Community regulations, none of its waters should be used for drinking, swimming, or irrigation.

■ **Hotels. Contarina**: 3-star: *Villa Carrer*. **Adria**: 2-star: *Stella d'Italia*. **Loreo**: 3-star: *Cavalli* (with restaurant). **Taglio di Po**: 3-star: *Tessarin*. **Porto Tolle**: 1-star: *Klaus* (with restaurant) and *da Renata* (with restaurant). The two summer holiday resorts of **Albarella** and **Rosolina Mare** have hotels open in the season: two 4-star hotels at Albarella, and 3-star and 2-star hotels at Rosolina Mare.

■ **Youth Hostel**. *Rifugio Parco Delta del Po* (open all year) at Gorino Sullam (with a simple restaurant), where bicycles can be hired. **Camping sites** (four 3-star and one 2-star) at Rosolina Mare, open Apr–Sep.

■ **Restaurants**. There are a number of excellent fish restaurants in the delta area (although hardly any of them are in the cheaper category). **Gorino Veneto**: *Stella del Mare* (**A**). **Rosolina**: *Da Berto* (**B**). On the **Sacca di Scardovari**: *Marina 70* (**B**). **Adria**: *Minuetto* (**A**). **Barchessa Ravagnan**: *Ravagnan* (**A**). At **Porto Tolle**: *Trattoria da Brodon* (**B**). Near the lighthouse of **Goro** (where the Po della Donzella reaches the sea) *Rifugio al Faro* (**B**).

■ **Boat excursions** are arranged by several companies, including Marino Cacciatori (*Caparin*; tel. 0426 81508 or 0337 513818), starting from Ca' Tiepolo.

■ **Bicycles** can be hired at Taglio di Po and Ca' Tiepolo.

■ **Fish markets** at Donada and Scardovari in the morning, and in the afternoon at Pila.

ADRIA, the ancient capital (21,300 inhab.) of the Polesine, gave its name to the Adriatic (to which it is now joined only by canal). The **Museo Archeologico** (open daily 9–19) contains proof of the city's Greco-Etruscan origins. The earliest finds from the upper Polesine date from the 11C to the 9C BC. There are also Greek red and black figure *ceramics, Roman *glass (1C AD), and gold and amber objects.

Nearby is the 17C church of **Santa Maria Assunta** which incorporates some Roman masonry. Across the Canal Bianco (near which is the theatre dating from 1930), is the **Cathedral**, which has a little 6C Coptic bas-relief, and a crypt with remains of Byzantine frescoes.

A road leads east past **Loreo**, built on a canal with a parish chuch by Baldassarre Longhena, to **Rosolina** on the Via Romea, in parts a post-war revival of the long decayed Roman *Via Popilia*, which ran down the Adriatic coast from Venice to Ravenna. Nearby are conspicuous shipbuilding yards. Rosolina is on the edge of a series of typical *valli* or wetlands, which can be seen from a pretty but very narrow road leading from Chiesa Moceniga to Portesine. On a narrow peninsula facing the Adriatic, pine woods were planted and a small resort called **Rosolina Mare** built in the 1950s. At the southern end of the peninsula is a ***Botanical Garden** (open Apr–Sep, or on request), opened in 1991. This is one of the very few stretches of Adriatic coast where the vegetation of the dunes (including juniper bushes, oaks and elms) is preserved intact; it can be visited along marked paths and bridges over the marshes. On a clear day from the shore there is a spectacular view of the Alps (swimming is allowed here in summer). Further south is the **Isola di Albarella** (reached by another road from Rosolina along the Po di Levante), a well-run resort (limited access for cars; bicycles are provided) built in 1967, with a port and an 18-hole golf course. The two hotels, and residences, open Apr–Sep, are surrounded by parks and woods.

South of Taglio di Po is **San Basilio**, a simple Romanesque church beneath the pavement of which seven ancient tombs have been found. Nearby is a small museum illustrating the life of the delta.

Porto Tolle is on the **Isola della Donzella**, the largest island on the delta. The island used to have *valli* with fisheries, but was reclaimed after a flood in 1966 (a decision which met with much justified opposition), and now has ricefields. Across the Po della Donzella is **Ca' Vendramin**, an attractive old pumping station built in 1900–05 with a tall chimney stack. It is now out of use, although the pumps are preserved here and there are plans to turn it into a museum illustrating the history of land reclamation in the delta.

At **Ca' Tiepolo** there is a privately run car ferry (it carries about 20 cars and operates up to midnight) which crosses the Po di Venezia to Ca' Venier; it is soon to be replaced by a bridge under construction a short way downstream. Near the ferry station is the starting point for boat excursions on the delta, including the **Po di Maistra**, the most interesting part of the delta for naturalists, the Po della Pila, and the Po delle Tolle. The southern part of the Isola della Donzella is occupied by the **Sacca di Scardovari**, an attractive lagoon lined with fishermen's huts and boats. Mussels and clams are cultivated here, and it is inhabited by numerous birds. On its shores is a tiny protected area illustrating the typical vegetation of the wetlands which once covered this area. There are characteristic bridges of boats (with tolls) over the Po della Donzella near Santa Giulia, and over the Po di Goro near Gorino Veneto.

The Isola della Donzella is separated by the Po delle Tolle from the **Isola di Polesine Camerini**, where in 1982 a thermo-electrical plant was opened; its exceptionally tall chimney is about 250m high. Beyond Pila, with a lot of fisheries, is the easternmost island on the delta, the **Isola di Batteria**, which is gradually being engulfed by the sea. It is no longer inhabited and is the only oasis on the delta (run by the forestry commission). At the end of the delta is a lighthouse built in 1949 on land only formed some hundred years ago.

The rest of the delta area to the south, in the province of Ferrara, which includes the woods of Mesola with oak and pine trees, is described in Chapter 60.

37 · Vicenza

Vicenza is an extremely beautiful and well preserved small town. Palladio, who settled here in 1523, practically rebuilt it in his distinctive classical style, and established the fame of Vicenza, which has been greatly admired by travellers since the 18C. His most important buildings here are the Basilica, and the Teatro Olimpico and, just outside on Monte Berico, the Villa Rotonda, his masterpiece. Andrea di Pietro dalla Gondola (1508–80) was nicknamed Palladio (from Pallas, the Greek goddess of wisdom) by his patron, the poet Giangiorgio Trissino (1478–1550), and his style was later imitated in buildings all over the world. Vincenzo Scamozzi (1552–1616) followed his style and also built some fine palaces here. Vicenza is now a thriving provincial capital (116,600 inhab.) in a pleasant position beneath the foothills of the green Monti Berici.

■ **Information office.** APT, 12 Piazza Matteotti (near the Teatro Olimpico), tel. 0444 320854. The head office of the APT del Vicentino is at 5 Piazza Duomo. Provincial Tourist Board, Via Gazzolle.

■ **Hotels**. 4-star: *Campo Marzio*, 21 Viale Roma. 3-star: *Castello*, 24 Contrà Piazza del Castello; *Continental*, 89 Viale Trissino; *Cristina*, 32 Corso San Felice; and *Giardini*, 6 Via Giuriolo. In the environs (for those with a car), 4-star:*Villa Michelangelo* at Arcugnano.

4-star **camping site** *Camping Vicenza*, 241 Strada Pelosa.

■ **Restaurants. A**: *Allo scudo di Francia*, 4 Contrà Piancoli; *Cinzia & Valerio*, 65 Piazzetta Porta Padova; *Da Remo*, 14 Via Caimpenta (on the Padua road). **B**: *Agli Schioppi*, 26 Contrà del Castello, **C**: *Righetti*, 3 Piazza Duomo. In the environs at Arcugnano: **A**: *La Loggia* (in the hotel Villa Michelangelo); **B**: *Da Penacio, Da Zamboni Nogarazza*; **C**: *Moreieta*.

■ **Wine bars**: *Bere Alto* in Contrà San Biagio; and numerous others including one on the corner of Contrà Battisti Fontana and one in Contrà Lioy (near Piazza Gualdi). **Cafés**. *Pasticceria Sorarù*, Piazza dei Signori; *Offelleria della Meneghina*, Contrà Cavour, and numerous others.

■ **Picnic places**: Giardino Salvi and Parco Querini.

■ **Car parking.** Large car parks (with a mini-bus service for the historical centre) near the wholesale fruit market (north of the Verona road) and beyond the Stadium. In the centre of the town, limited space (with hourly tariff) is available off Viale Roma and Piazza Matteotti.

■ **Buses** are run by the 'Tramvie Vicentine' for places in the province. No. 18 & yellow buses (IUM) for Monte Berico. No. 8 for the Villa Rotonda, and Villa Valmarana (see below).

■ **Theatres.** At the *Teatro Olimpico*, a season of music and ballet is held in spring, and of classical theatre in September. Theatre and music performances are also given at the *Teatro Roma* and *Teatro Astra*.

■ A **market** is held in Piazza dei Signori and Piazza Duomo on Thu.

History

The Roman municipium of *Vicetia*, the successor of a Gaulish town, was destroyed during the barbarian invasions, but rose to importance again in the later Middle Ages, and became in turn an episcopal city and a free commune, and a member of the Veronese League against Barbarossa (1164). After a period of war with Verona and Padua, Vicenza reached a certain stability under the Veronese Scaligeri after 1314. As early as 1404 Verona decided to place itself under the protection of Venice, and during the century a number of pretty Venetian Gothic palaces were built in Vicenza: the Venetian dialect word *contrà* or *contrada* still replaces the more usual 'Via' in the older districts of the town. Like the rest of the Veneto, it passed under Austrian control in 1813; the insurrection of 1848 was unsuccessful, but in 1866 Vicenza was united to the Italian kingdom. The town was bombed and the centre much damaged in the Second World War.

The massive 11C **Porta Castello** is a fragment of a Scaligeri stronghold, destroyed in 1819. Here is the 17C entrance gate (open all day) to the delightful **Giardino Salvi**, which was first laid out as a botanical garden. At one end of an L-shaped canal is the **Loggia Valmarana**, a palace in Palladian style built in 1592 over the water. At the other end of the canal, here spanned by several bridges, is a loggia by Baldassarre Longhena (1649).

On the right in Piazza Castello, just inside Porta Castello, are the three huge columns of **Palazzo Breganze**, designed by Palladio in the early 1570s: he built only these two bays of what would have been a palace on a colossal scale.

Corso Palladio

Here begins the handsome *CORSO PALLADIO, the principal street of Vicenza, notable for its many fine palaces. At the beginning, on the left, No. 13 is **Palazzo Bonin**, probably by Vincenzo Scamozzi, with a good atrium and courtyard (and garden beyond). **Palazzo Pagello** (Nos 38–40) is by Ottavio Bertotti Scamozzi (1780). Opposite is the handsome neo-classical façade of the church of **San Filippo Neri** by Antonio Piovene (1824; on a design by Ottone Calderari). It contains a good 18C organ by the Favorito brothers. Beyond are two pretty 15C Venetian Gothic palaces: **Palazzo Thiene** (No. 47) and **Palazzo Brunello** (No. 67), with a portico. At No. 98 is the imposing **Palazzo del Comune**, formerly a private palace, begun by Vincenzo Scamozzi in 1592 and finished in 1662.

The Basilica

Contrà Cavour (passing a charming little old-fashioned café) leads into the huge and dignified *PIAZZA DEI SIGNORI, where the Venetian governors used to live. Here is the majestic *Basilica, one of Palladio's masterpieces. The nucleus of the building is the medieval Palazzo della Ragione. In 1549 Palladio was commissioned to replace a double loggia of 1494 on the exterior which had partly collapsed. He surrounded the building with two open colonnaded galleries, Tuscan Doric below and Ionic above, crowned with a balcony. It was finished in 1617, following his original design. Built in bright local limestone, Palladio's work shows his admiration for ancient Roman architecture, and his skill in providing a new shell to an essentially

The basilica

Gothic core. The building was formerly used as a town hall and law courts, and was called 'basilica' by Palladio to illustrate his intention of re-creating a classical public building.

On the right-hand side stairs lead up to the huge Gothic *hall of Palazzo della Ragione (open Tue–Sat 9.30–12, 14.30–17; fest. 9.30–12.30; closed Mon), with a remarkable beamed ship's keel roof. The 13C building on this site was destroyed by fire in 1444 and this beautiful hall was rebuilt by Domenico da Venezia in 1460. It is now used for exhibitions, and there are attractive old shops on the ground floor. It is in need of restoration, but an ambitious project to adapt it for use as a 'cultural centre' has met with justifiable opposition.

Near the north corner rises the unusually tall and slender **Torre di Piazza** (12C), to which additional storeys were added in 1311 and 1444. Facing the basilica is the **Loggia del Capitaniato**, commissioned from Palladio in 1571 by the town council as part of the residence of the Venetian Captain. Between the three arches on the façade are four giant semi-columns in brick which reach to the height of the attic storey. The stucco decoration by Lorenzo Rubini illustrates the Venetian victory at Lepanto in the same year. Also on this side of the square is the long façade of the **Monte di Pietà**; the left wing dates from 1500 and the right wing from 1553–57, and they are separated by the church of **San Vincenzo**, by Paolo Bonin (1614–17). The two graceful columns in the piazza bear the Lion of St Mark (1520) and the Redeemer (1640).

In the adjacent Piazza delle Biade, **Santa Maria dei Servi**, a Gothic church of 1407 enlarged in 1490, has an altarpiece by Benedetto Montagna, a Lombardesque altar, and a late 15C cloister.

PIAZZA DELLE ERBE, behind the Basilica, is a quaint market square with a medieval prison-tower, and a good view of the Basilica (here supported by vaulted shops). In the narrow streets to the southwest are several old mansions, notably—in Contrà Pigafetta—**Casa Pigafetta**, an ornate house in red marble begun in 1444 and modified in 1481, lavishly decorated with carved columns and reliefs and a French motto. On the adjacent house a plaque records Antonio Pigafetta (1491–1534), one of Magellan's company on his circumnavigation of the globe in 1519–22, who was born in Vicenza.

Contrà dei Proti (and its continuations to the west) leads to Piazza del Duomo. Here is the **Palazzo Vescovile**, rebuilt after 1944 but preserving a charming courtyard-loggia (1494) by Bernardino da Milano.

Duomo

The Gothic Duomo, largely rebuilt in the 14C–16C, was practically destroyed in 1944; the façade (1467) and some chapels remained and it was carefully rebuilt. The beautiful Renaissance tribune also survived: it was begun in 1482 by Lorenzo da Bologna, and the dome is by Battista and Francesco Della Porta on a Palladian design (1558–74). The sturdy detached campanile (11C), also at the east end, stands on a ruined Roman building.

Interior. On the **north side** are altarpieces by Bartolomeo Montagna and Antonino da Venezia (1448). In the **tribune**, the high altar, beautifully decorated with precious marbles, is by the local workshop of Pedemuro where Palladio worked as a young man (and this could be one of his earliest works). The 12 17C paintings in fine frames are by local artists including Andrea Celesti, Pietro Liberi and Antonio Zanchi. On the **south side** are a polyptych by Lorenzo Veneziano (1356) and an unusual 8C sarcophagus.

On the south side of the square, beneath Palazzo Proti, is a **Roman criptoporticus** probably part of a 1C AD palace (adm. Sat 10–11.30, or by appointment, tel. 0444 321716).

From the east end of the Duomo, Contrà Pasini leads south past the two attractive **Case Arnaldi** (Nos. 14 & 16), one Gothic, the other Renaissance. In the Contrà Carpagnon (left) is a house (No. 11) occupied by Frederick IV of Denmark in 1709. In Viale Eretenio, along the little Retrone river, facing a bridge, is the white **Casa Civena** (now a clinic), probably the first palace to be built by Palladio (in 1540–46), with an inscription to Trissino. Only the central bays are original since it was altered in the 18C and 19C. From the pretty bridge

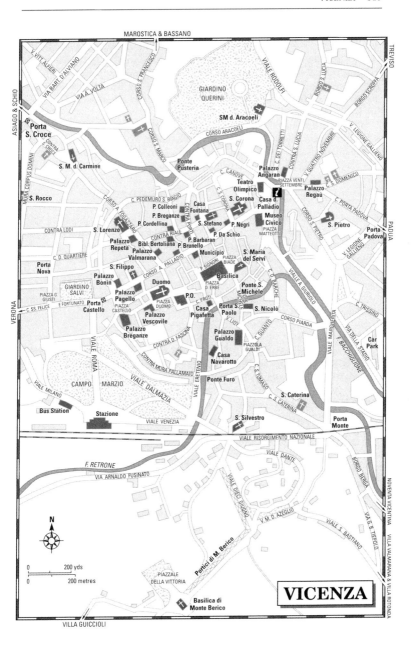

there is a good view (left) of the Basilica and Torre di Piazza, and (right) of Monte Berico. At No. 2 Piazzetta Santi Apostoli is the fine Gothic **Casa Navarotto** (14C). Opposite, the curve of the house fronts follows the shape of the Roman Theatre, which once stood on this site, and was drawn by Palladio. The road continues past the neo-classical Palazzo Gualdo (by Giovanni Miglioranza, 1838) to the **Porton del Luzzo**, a 13C gateway, and an unusual house with brick columns above a rusticated ground floor.

In Piazzola dei Gualdi are the two Renaissance **Palazzi Gualdo**. On the left, in Via Paolo Lioy, is the charming Gothic **Casa Caola**. The river may be recrossed by the hump-backed *Ponte San Michele (1620). At the end of Contrà Ponte San Michele is Contrà Piancoli with several interesting 15C houses, including one where Goethe stayed in 1786 when he came to the town to admire the works of Palladio. Contrà delle Gazzolle leads back to the centre.

In Corso Palladio (see above), beyond Palazzo del Comune, are Palazzo da Schio (No. 147), a handsome 15C Venetian Gothic palace, known as the 'Ca' d'Oro'. The church of **San Gaetano** has a neo-classical façade. Beyond the raised garden railing of Santa Corona (described below) is the simple little '**Casa del Palladio**' (Palazzetto Cogollo; Nos 165–7), which has a tall portico with two Doric columns below and two Corinthian columns above, traditionally thought to have been built by the architect for Pietro Cogollo, but now not generally ascribed to Palladio. It is in urgent need of restoration.

Museo Civico

At the end of Corso Palladio is Piazza Matteotti. Here is *PALAZZO CHIERI-CATI**, with a portico, an excellent example of Palladio's early works (1551–57), although the façade was completed a century later. Since 1855 it has housed the *Museo Civico (open 9.30–12, 14.30–17; fest. 9.30–12; closed Mon). The **Sala del Firmamento** has a ceiling with a fresco by Domenico Brusasorci and stuccoes by Battista Zelotti. The statues of Francesco Sforza and his wife Bianca Maria Visconti are by Alberto Maffiolo da Carrara (c 1494). The **Sala degli Dei** and **Sala d'Ercole** also have fine ceilings and frescoes by Zelotti. Other rooms on the ground floor display the Neri Pozza (1912–88) collection of modern art, including works by Filippo De Pisis, Gino Severini and Virgilio Guidi.

Beyond is the modern extension to the museum, the first rooms of which are designed in a severe, modern style (although the works, arranged chronologically, are well labelled). **Room I** has 13C sculptural fragments. **Room II**. Paolo Veneziano, Transition of the Virgin, signed and dated 1333. **Room III**. Works by Battista da Vicenza and Giovanni Badile. **Room IV** contains 15C works. **Room V**. Works by Pietro Lombardo and Hans Memling (*Calvary).

Room VI. Medals by Pisanello, and paintings by Francesco and Bernardino Zaganelli and Marco Palmezzano. **Room VII** contains fine *paintings by Bartolomeo Montagna. **Room VIII**. Marcello Fogolino and Giovanni Buonconsiglio.

On the other side of the stairs is the entrance to the last series of rooms. **Room IX** contains two *altarpieces by Bartolomeo Montagna and Cima da Conegliano. **Room X.** Giovanni Buonconsiglio, Bernardino Licinio and Prospero Fontana.

Room XI is the main 17C salone of the palace. Here are kept two large globes (1688). The stucco relief of the *Madonna and Child is a very fine work by

Jacopo Sansovino, in its original wood frame. Works by Alessandro Vittoria, Paolo Veronese, Valerio Belli, Tintoretto (*Miracle of St Augustine*), Il Riccio, Jacopo Bassano, Lorenzo Lotto and Francesco Maffei.

Room XII. Francesco and Leandro Bassano, Francesco Vecellio and Girolamo da Santacroce. **Room XIII**. Flemish painters: the *Three Ages of Man* by Anthony Van Dyck, and an exquisite small *Madonna and Child* in a beautiful landscape, surrounded by scenes from the Life of Christ, attributed to Jan Brueghel the Elder. **Room XIV**, with another good stucco ceiling, displays works by Pietro Vecchia. **Room XV** contains works by Francesco Maffei, and **Room XVI** works by Giulio Carpioni.

Room XVII. Early 17C works by Carlo Saraceni and Francesco del Cairo. **Room XVIII** has two works by Luca Giordano, who is also represented in **Room XIX**, together with Sebastiano Ricci. **Room XX**. Giambattista Piazzetta, Orazio Marinali, Giambattista Tiepolo. **Room XXI** has works by Francesco Pittoni and Sebastiano and Marco Ricci. **Room XXII** has fine works by Giambattista Tiepolo (an Immaculate Conception and an allegorical ceiling fresco) and his son Giandomenico. Beyond **Room XXIII**, with landscapes by Giuseppe Zais and Rosa da Tivoli, **Room XXIV** has 18C still lifes. The museum also owns 33 drawings by Palladio.

Teatro Olimpico

On the opposite side of Piazza Matteotti is **Palazzo del Territorio**, a defensive work forming part of the medieval castle of San Pietro, transformed during the centuries with a tower rebuilt since the war. Inside is the *Teatro Olimpico (open 9–12.30, 14–17; fest 9–12.30), perhaps the most famous early theatre in Italy. It was the last work of Palladio (1580) and was finished by Scamozzi. It was built for the Accademia Olimpica, founded in 1555, of which Palladio was a member and which produced numerous plays. The opening play, given in 1585, was Sophocles' *Oedipus Rex*. The classical *frons scenae*, built in wood and stucco, its architecture derived from ancient Roman buildings, has niches with statues of academicians by Agostino Rubini, Domenico Fontana and others, and reliefs of the Labours of Hercules in the attic storey. Behind the large stage is the shallow cavea, derived from Vitruvian models, surmounted by a peristyle of Corinthian columns (the former entrance to the theatre). Scamozzi designed the remarkable fixed scenery with three streets leading away from the stage in perfect perspective.

Just across the bridge over the Bacchiglione is Piazza XX Settembre with the 15C **Palazzo Angaran** (rebuilt), and in Contrà XX Settembre is the fine **Palazzo Regaù** (15C Gothic). To the right is the 14C church of **San Pietro**, with a 15C brick cloister. North of Piazza XX Settembre, at the end of Contrà Torretti, is the unusual Baroque church of **Santa Maria d'Aracoeli**. Elliptical in plan, it is perhaps based on designs by Guarino Guarini (1675–80). It stands on the edge of **Parco Querini**, pretty public gardens (open daily).

Santa Corona

Contrà Santa Corona leads north from the Corso to the Dominican church of Santa Corona (closed 12.30–14.30), early Gothic in style (1261) with a Renaissance east arm of 1482–89. In the **interior**, on the **north side**, the second altarpiece is by Bartolomeo Montagna; the third by Leandro Bassano.

The fourth altar has a late Gothic votive image of the Virgin with an early 16C landscape view of Vicenza by Fogolino. On the fifth altar, *Baptism of Christ, a superb late work by Giovanni Bellini, in a splendid altar of 1501 by Girolamo Pittoni (on a design by Rocco da Vicenza). **North transept**. Derision of Christ, by Tentorello (late 14C; restored). The colourful high altar (1669) is inlaid with marble. The choir stalls are finely inlaid (end of the 15C). In the chapel north of the sanctuary is kept the gold reliquary of the Holy Thorn (14C; displayed only on Good Friday on the high altar at the evening service).

A plaque on the nave pillar records the burial of Palladio here in 1580; his remains were removed in the 19C to the cemetery of Santa Lucia. To the south of the choir is the **Thiene chapel**, with two splendid Gothic family tombs. The chapel's altarpiece is by Giovanni Battista Pittoni (1723). The fourth south chapel is sumptuously decorated by Giovanni Battista and Alessandro Maganza. In the third chapel is Veronese's *Adoration of the Magi, with superb colouring (light; fee).

Next door (No. 4), behind a neo-classical façade of 1823, the **Museo Naturalistico-Archeologico** (part of the Museo Civico founded in 1855) has been housed since 1991 in the two cloisters of the former convent of Santa Corona. It is open 9–12.30, 14–17 exc. Mon; fest. 9–12.30.

Upstairs, arranged in the cells of the former convent, is the section devoted to natural history and geology (with special reference to the Colli Berici), with fossils, etc. Downstairs are interesting remains of the Roman theatre of Vicenza, excavated in the 19C, and more Roman and Lombard material. Across the courtyard is a room with Iron Age finds from the province, including reliefs of the 5C BC.

On the other side of Contrà Santa Corona is **Palazzo Leoni Montanari** (open Apr–Oct, Sat 10–12, 16–19), now owned by a bank which has recently carefully restored it. The building was begun in the late 17C, and has interesting architectural elements (some of which were added in 1808). The interior, with 18C decorations (frescoes by Giuseppe Alberti and Ludovico Dorigny), and neo-classical elements, includes the elaborate Baroque Galleria della Verità, and a loggia profusely decorated with stuccoes. In one room are displayed seven paintings by Pietro Longhi (and seven by his school) from the 19C collection of Giuseppe Salom.

North of Corso Palladio

Santo Stefano (open early morning or late evening), on Contrà Zanella, contains a *painting by Palma Vecchio. Opposite is the Renaissance **Palazzo Negri**, and on the right the **Casa Fontana**, a fine Gothic building.

On the left is the huge **Palazzo Thiene**, which was probably begun on a design by Giulio Romano in 1542 and may have been continued by Palladio after Giulio's death in 1546 (although it remained unfinished). Two sides of its courtyard and the east façade in the Stradella di San Gaetano are attributed to Palladio. It incorporates a second early Renaissance palace by Lorenzo da Bologna (1489) with its façade on Contrà Porti (No. 12), with rustication, a fine portal and remains of frescoes, and with a very fine stuccoed ceiling in the interior by Alessandro Vittoria.

*CONTRÀ PORTI has numerous palaces. On the left (No. 8) is the Gothic

Palazzo Cavallini (in poor repair), and on the right (No. 11), the dignified **Palazzo Barbaran da Porto** (1570–75) by Palladio, recently acquired by the state (it contains works by Lorenzo Rubini, Giovanni Battista Zelotti and Andrea Vicentino). At No. 15 Luigi Da Porto, author of the story of 'Romeo and Juliet', died in 1529. **Palazzo Porto Breganze** (No. 17) is a Venetian Gothic building with a Renaissance doorway. Beside the magnificent 15C **Palazzo Colleoni Porto** (No. 19), with a loggia overlooking a little garden, is **Palazzo Iseppo Da Porto Festa** (No. 21) built by Palladio in 1548.

Contrà Riale leads west from Contrà Porti past (No. 12; right), the sumptuous **Palazzo Cordellina** by Calderari (1776). In the former 17C convent of San Giacomo is the **Biblioteca Civica Bertoliana** (entrance at No. 5), left to the city by Giovanni Maria Bertolo in 1702. To the right is the animated Corso Fogazzaro, with **Palazzo Repeta** (1701–11), by Francesco Muttoni.

Beyond is the majestic 13C brick church of **SAN LORENZO**. The **west front** is the finest in Vicenza, with a splendid marble portal of the mid-14C. In the **interior** are the funerary monuments of General Da Porto (1661), Scamozzi (died 1616), and Volpe (the tomb was formerly ascribed to Palladio, 1575). In the **choir** and its chapels are more tombs, including a Gothic one of the Da Porto family, and an interesting large *fresco by Bartolomeo Montagna (but detached and very ruined).

In Corso Fogazzaro is **Palazzo Valmarana-Braga** (No. 16), by Palladio (1565), with giant pilasters uniting two storeys of the building.

Outside Porta Castello, Contrà Santi Felice e Fortunato leads past the Giardino Salvi (see above) to the remarkable church of **Santi Felice e Fortunato**, with a curious fortified campanile (1166) and a fragmentary mosaic pavement, partly Constantinian, partly Theodosian.

Monte Berico, Villa Valmarana and Villa Rotonda

The green hillside of Monte Berico has been preserved almost entirely without modern buildings. For those with time, the best way of visiting the basilica and the villas is on foot as described below (the return may be made by bus); the pleasant walk takes about 1hr 30mins.

■ **By bus**. The basilica of Monte Berico can be reached by a bus (IUM) from Viale Roma. The Villa Valmarana is reached in c 15 mins by bus No. 8 from Viale Roma (direction Noventa Vicentina) to Borgo Berga (request stop at Via Tiepolo, 500m below the villa); it continues along the Viale Riviera Berica to another request stop at the foot of Via della Rotonda, 200m below Villa Rotonda. If you intend to visit both villas (and not the basilica) it is best to take bus No. 8 to the stop below Villa Rotonda, and from there walk back to Villa Valmarana.

The **BASILICA OF MONTE BERICO**, conspicuous from all parts of the town, is approached by the **Portici**, a monumental portico with chapels, designed by Francesco Muttoni (1746–78), which leads up the steep hillside. There is a fine view (east) of the Villa Rotonda from just below the basilica.

The **basilica** (closed 12.30–15.30), on the site of a sanctuary built where two apparitions of the Virgin occurred (1426–28), was rebuilt, apart from the campanile, by Carlo Borella in 1688–1703. It is a pilgrim shrine (festival on 8

Sep). Lorenzo da Bologna's façade of 1476 has been re-erected alongside the present south front. The **interior** contains a *Pietà, by Bartolomeo Montagna (1500) and, in the **refectory**, *Supper of St Gregory the Great* by Veronese, repaired at the expense of the Austrian emperor Francis Joseph after having been hacked to pieces by his soldiery in 1848.

Piazzale della Vittoria, beside the church, built as a memorial of the First World War, commands a magnificent view of Vicenza, and of the mountains that once marked the front line. Viale X Giugno continues beyond the basilica to the **Villa Guiccioli**, built at the end of the 18C by Gianantonio Selva, with a beautiful park (open 9–17.30 or 18 exc. Mon) and a **Museum of the Risorgimento and Resistence** (open 9.30–12, 14.30–17; fest. 9–12; closed Mon).

From the basilica, Villa Valmarana can be reached on foot by following the Portici downhill again, and (half-way down) taking Via Massimo d'Azeglio to the right (good view of Vicenza). Just beyond a Carmelite monastery the narrow cobbled Via San Bastiano (closed to through traffic) diverges right. It leads downhill past a charming dovecote to (15 mins) **VILLA VALMARANA**, called 'ai Nani' from the dwarfs decorating its garden wall (open 15 Mar–5 Nov daily exc. fest. 14.30 or 15–17.30 or 18; Wed, Thu, Sat & fest. also 10–12; tel. 0444 543976). It consists of the *palazzina*, built in 1668, probably by Antonio Muttoni, and the *foresteria* added by Francesco Muttoni. In both buildings are remarkable *frescoes by Giovanni Battista Tiepolo and his son Gian Domenico.

The stony path (Stradella Valmarana) on the right beyond the villa continues downhill to the white *VILLA ROTONDA, or Villa Almerico-Capra (now Valmarana), the most famous of Palladio's villas (open 15 Mar–4 Nov: to the exterior on Tue, Wed & Thu 10–12, 15–18; other days usually on request; to the interior, Wed only, 10–12, 15–18; always closed Mon; tel. 0444 321793). Built as a belvedere for Paolo Almerico on a charming hilltop site, it has a central plan consisting of a circular core within a cube. The four classical porticoes complete its symmetry. Crowned with a remarkable low dome, its design is reminiscent of the Pantheon in Rome. Begun c 1551 by Palladio it was taken over at his death by Vincenzo Scamozzi and finished in 1606 for the Capra family. The Villa Rotonda had a profound influence on the history of architecture and was copied in numerous buildings, including Chiswick House, London. The domed central hall was frescoed at the end of the 17C by Louis Dorigny, and the piano nobile painted by Anselmo Canera, Bernardino India and Alessandro Maganza. The *barchessa* was designed by Vincenzo Scamozzi.

The return may be made by following Via Rotonda to the bottom of the hill (200m), where bus No. 8 can be taken back to the centre of Vicenza. From Villa Valmarana, Via Giovanni Battista Tiepolo descends to the Porta Monte, just above which is a charming little arch attributed to Palladio dated 1595. Bus No. 8 runs back along the main road into Vicenza.

The other villas on the outskirts of the town are described in Chapter 38.

38 · The province of Vicenza

■ **APT Information offices. Bassano del Grappa**: 35 Largo Corona d'Italia (tel. 0424 524351); **Marostica**: Pro-loco, Piazza Castello (tel. 0424 72127). **Recoaro Terme**: 25 Via Roma (tel. 0445 75070); **Tonezza del Cimone**: 14 Via Roma (tel. 0445 749500).

■ **Hotels. Altavilla Vicentina.** 4-star: *Genziana*. **Bolzano Vicentino**. 3-star: *Grego*. **Breganze.** 3-star: *Al Toresan*. **Grisignano di Zocco.** 4-star: *Magnolia*. **Noventa Vicentina.** 3-star: *Alla Busa* (with restaurant). **Sossano.** 3-star: *l'Alfiere dei Berici*. For Bassano del Grappa and Marostica, see below.

■ **Restaurants. Caldogno. B**: Al Molin Vecio. **Altavilla Vicentina. B**: Leoncino, Monterosso. **Montegalda. B**: Culata. **Montegaldella. A**: Da Cirillo. **Lonigo. B**: La Rocca Leonicena. **Lonedo di Lugo. B**: Torchio Antico. **Sandrigo. C**: Da Palmerino. **B**: Due Spade. **Trissino. A**: Ca Masieri. **Asiago. A**: Casa Rossa. For Bassano del Grappa and Marostica, see below.

The Ville Vicentine

The province of Vicenza is particularly rich in villas, the famous 'Ville Venete'. These were built from the 15C onwards by rich noble Venetian families who were anxious to invest in land on the *terraferma* and contribute to its fertility by the construction of canals and irrigation systems. In the early 16C Palladio invented an architecture peculiarly fitted to these prestigious villas which he also saw as places of repose and as working farms. He derived their design in part from the villas of the ancient Romans, and used classical features in their construction. He took particular care in the siting of his villas, sometimes on low hills, or near canals, and almost always surrounded by gardens and farmland. The outbuildings, known as *barchesse*, were often porticoed.

Numerous villas by Palladio survive in the province (some of them with frescoes and stuccoes by Giovanni Antonio Fasolo, Giovanni Battista Zelotti and Bartolomeo Ridolfi), and in the 17C and 18C many more villas were constructed, some of these particularly interesting for their interiors and frescoes (including some by Giovanni Battista Tiepolo and his son Gian Domenico). Architects of importance who succeeded Palladio include Vincenzo Scamozzi, Antonio Pizzocaro, Francesco Muttoni and Giorgio Massari. Orazio Marinali was responsible for the statuary in the gardens of many of the villas.

The names of the villas change with each new owner, but they generally also carry the name of the original proprietor. They are scattered widely over the province, often in remote areas outside small towns (the name of the Comune as well as the locality has been given in the description below to help with their location, since signposting is generally poor). The villas are often privately owned, and many of the interiors are closed to the public (except with special permission), but the exteriors and gardens are often their most important features. Opening times change frequently and accessibility varies; it is therefore advisable to consult the APT in Vicenza before starting a tour, or telephone to the villa for confirmation of opening times. Concerts are organised in some of the villas in July.

The most important villas (but by no means all of them) are described below by geographical areas: the outskirts of Vicenza (including those within the municipal limits); those south and west of Vicenza; and those to the north of the town. The famous Villa Rotonda and Villa Valmarana on Monte Berico are described in Chapter 37. The villas within the province in the environs of Bassano del Grappa are described on page 321. Although the province of Vicenza has most of the 'Ville Venete', others are described under the provinces of Padua, Venezia, Treviso, Verona, Rovigo and Belluno (see Chapters 35, 33, 42, 40, 36, 43).

Outskirts of Vicenza

The suburban **Villa Trissino Rigo** (1532–37) at Cricoli was designed by Palladio's first patron, Gian Giorgio Trissino. Palladio probably worked here as a young artist with the workshop of Giovanni da Pedemuro. The exterior can be visited by previous appointment (tel. 0444 922122). In località Anconetta is the **Villa Imperiali Lampertico** built in 1681, surrounded by a garden. In località **Bertisina** are a number of villas: **Villa Gazzotti Curti** built by Palladio in 1542–43; **Villa Negri Ceroni**, built in 1709 (perhaps by Carlo Borella) in Palladian style, with a park and garden; and **Villa Chiericati Ghislanzoni**, dating from 1764.

East of Vicenza at **Monticello Conte Otto** is the **Villa Valmarana Bressan**, begun in 1541 by Palladio, an austere building with a typical Palladian entrance. It is open Mon–Fri 9–2, 14–8; Sat & fest. by appointment (tel. 0444 596242). The **Villa Thiene**, owned by the Comune of **Quinto Vicentino** is another work by Palladio (c 1546), left unfinished. It is open Mon–Fri 10–12.30; Tue & Thu also 18–19; tel. 0444 357009. At **Bolzano Vicentino** (località Lisiera) is the **Villa Valmarana Zen**, on a Palladian design, with numerous statues in the garden and a pretty little chapel.

South and west of Vicenza

At **Altavilla Vicentina**, the **Villa Valmarana-Morosini** was built by Francesco Muttoni in 1724. It has been restored by the University (adm. Wed & Thu, 14.30–17.30; tel. 0444 572499). Near **Monteviale** is the **Villa Loschi Zileri Dal Verme**, attributed to Francesco Muttoni, surrounded by a fine park with exotic trees. It contains the earliest frescoes by Giovanni Battista Tiepolo (1734) outside Venice: the allegorical scenes decorate the staircase and the salone (adm. by previous appointment, tel. 0444 566146). At **Costabissari** to the west, **Villa Bissari Curti** (reconstructed in the 19C) has a loggia attributed to Ottone Calderari, and a garden with antique fragments and an amphitheatre.

The picturesque village of **Montecchio Maggiore**, a legendary stronghold of the 'Montagues' of *Romeo and Juliet*, has two restored Scaliger castles. Just outside is the **Villa Cordellina Lombardi**, by Giorgio Massari (1735), owned by the province of Vicenza and used for conferences, courses, etc. (open Apr–Oct, Tue, Wed, Thu & Fri 9–13; Sat & fest 9–13, 15–18; closed Mon; tel. 0444 399111). It has very fine *frescoes (1743) by Giovanni Battista Tiepolo in the central hall (restored in 1984). To the north of Montecchio is **Trissino**, with the **Villa Trissino Marzotto**, whose delightful park is open by previous appointment (tel. 0445 962029). Nearby is **Castelgomberto**, where the **Villa Piovene da Schio** was built in 1666, probably by Antonio Pizzocaro (chapel of

1614); it has 18C additions and is surrounded by a garden with statues by the workshop of Marinali. Inside are three early works by Giovanni Battista Tiepolo. The exterior is open by previous appointment, Jun–Sep, Sat 10–12 (tel. 0445 940052). To the west of Montecchio is **Montorso Vicentino** with the **Villa Da Porto Barbaran**, dating from 1724 with an Ionic pronaos and a pretty Ionic *barchessa*. Nearby at **Arzignano** are two more 18C villas.

At **Sarego** is the **Villa da Porto 'La Favorita'**, by Francesco Muttoni (1714–15). The little town of **Lonigo** (11,500 inhab.),at the foot of the Monti Berici, has its town hall in **Palazzo Pisani**, a very grand mansion of 1557. On the outskirts stands the **Rocca**, or **Villa Pisani** (1576), a charming work by Vincenzo Scamozzi (recalling Palladio's Villa Rotonda) on the site of an old castle, with a park (adm. by appointment, tel. 049 8757462). Outside Lonigo, in località **Bagnolo**, is the beautiful **Villa Pisani Ferri**, one of Palladio's earliest villas, built in 1542. The main entrance has rusticated arches beneath a pediment, and the villa is surrounded by farm buildings. It is open 1 Apr–4 Nov, Wed, Fri & Sun 10–12, 15–18, or by appointment, tel. 0444 831104.

At **Orgiano** is the **Villa Fracanzan Piovene**, built in 1710 and attributed to Francesco Muttoni, with an interesting garden (and *barchessa*). Open 1 Mar–30 Nov on holiday afternoons; otherwise by appointment (tel. 0444 874589). At **Noventa Vicentina** the town hall occupies **Villa Barbarigo** (early 17C; adm. Mon–Sat 8.30–12.30, or by appointment, tel. 0444 760360). Nearby, on the road to **Agugliaro** is the *****Villa Saraceno** begun by Palladio between 1545 and 1555, and surrounded by farm buildings. Acquired by the Landmark Trust of Great Britain it was beautifully restored in 1988–94, and is open 1 Apr–31 Oct on Wed at 14–16; at other times by previous appointment only (tel. 0444 891371).

On the main road at **Pojana Maggiore** is the **Villa Pojana**, built in 1540 by Palladio, with a typical Palladian arch over the entrance. It is in very poor condition, but has contemporary frescoes by Bernardino India and Anselmo Canera, and stuccoes by Bartolomeo Ridolfi. The frescoes in the atrium are attributed to Giovanni Battista Zelotti.

At **Mossano** is the **Villa Pigafetta Camerini**, a charming late 17C building attributed to Antonio Pizzocaro. The *barchesse* and chapel may be by Francesco Muttoni. Open May–Oct, Sat & fest. 9–13, 14–18, or by appointment (tel. 0444 886838). At **Longare** are two villas: **Villa Trento-Carli**, built in 1645, is attributed to Antonio Pizzocaro (adm. by appointment only); the **Ville da Schio**, with three buildings on a hillside, is surrounded by a lovely garden with sculptures by Orazio Marinali. The Villino Garzadori here, built into the hillside in 1690, has frescoes by Ludovico Dorigny. The park is open daily exc. Mon, 9.30–12.30, 15–19.

Near Grumolo delle Abbadesse, in località **Vancimuglio**, is the **Villa Da Porto Rigo** or **Villa Chiericati** (1554), almost certainly by Palladio (but left unfinished), with an Ionic portico with statues on the pediment, and in **Grisignano di Zocco** is the **Villa Ferramosca-Beggiato**, by Gian Domenico Scamozzi (c 1560). On either side of the Bacchiglione river, are Montegalda and Montegaldella. In **Montegalda** are the **Castello Grimani Sorlini**, a 12C castle adapted as a villa in the 18C (with a fine park). **Villa Chiericati Fogazzaro**, rebuilt in 1846 by

Caregaro Negrin, with a garden, and—in località Colzè—**Villa Colzè Feriani**, rebuilt in the 17C, with a chapel containing sculptures by Orazio Marinali. In **Montegaldella** is the 17C **Villa Conti Campagnolo** called '**La Deliziosa**' (altered in the 19C), its garden decorated with statues by Orazio Marinali.

North of Vicenza

At **Caldogno** is the **Villa Caldogno-Nordera** (owned by the Comune; open 1 Apr–30 Oct, Tue and Sat 9-–2, Thu 15–18; tel. 0444 585756), built in 1570 and attributed to Palladio. It is decorated with frescoes by Giovanni Fasolo, Gian Battista Zelotti and Giulio Carpioni. **Villaverla** has two fine villas: the **Villa Verlato** (1576 by Vincenzo Scamozzi), with frescoes by Girolamo Pisano and Giovanni Battista Maganza, and **Villa Ghellini** (1664–79) by Antonio Pizzocaro (now owned by the Comune; the exterior and park can be visited Mon–Sat 10–12, 15 or 16–17 or 18).

At **Thiene** (17,300 inhabitants) is the **Castello Porto-Colleoni Thiene**, a late Gothic Venetian castle perhaps begun by Domenico da Venezia and completed in 1476. It has frescoes by Giovanni Antonio Fasolo and Giovanni Battista Zelotti, a charming contemporary chapel, and a stable block attributed to Antonio Muttoni (open 21 Mar–13 Nov on Sun & fest. at 15, 16 and 17, or by appointment, tel. 041 5289274). The **Villa Beregan Cunico**, with a long, low façade and portal attributed to Antonio Pizzocaro can be visited Wed & Sat 9–12.30, 15–17 (tel. 0445 380944). At **Sarcedo** is the **Villa Capra** (1764; adm. by appointment, tel. 0424 511833).

Beyond the Astico is **Lonedo di Lugo** (in the Comune of Lonedo di Lugo). Here the **Villa Godi Valmarana**, now **Malinverni** (open Tue, Sat & Sun 15–19, winter 14–18; closed Dec–mid-Feb), is one of the earliest known works by Palladio (1540–42). The piano nobile was frescoed in the 16C by Battista del Moro and Giovanni Battista Zelotti. A wing of the palace has a representative collection of 19C Italian paintings, including works by Francesco Hayez, Tranquillo Cremona, the Indunno brothers, Segantini, De Nittis, Domenico Morelli, the 'Macchiaioli' painters, Giovanni Boldoni and Pietro Annigoni. A fossil museum has local exhibits including a palm tree 5m high. The **Villa Piovene**, close by (open 14.30–19.30, or by appointment, tel. 0445 860613), has a Palladian core, altered in the 18C by Francesco Muttoni. It is surrounded by a park designed by Antonio Piovene.

Breganze has several villas including the **Villa Diedo Basso** (1664–84, with additions), with a garden. Breganze is known for its wines (including the red 'Maculan') which can be purchased at the Cantina Sociale San Bartolomeo.

At **Dueville** are the **Villa Da Porto Casarotto**, by Ottone Calderari (1770–76; adm. to the exterior only, 9.30–11.30, 15.30–18.30), and the **Villa Da Porto del Conte**, at Vivaro, on a Palladian design (remodelled in 1855). The town hall of Dueville occupies **Villa Monza**, built in 1715 probably by Francesco Muttoni (open Mon & Wed 9.30–13; Thu 9.30–13, 16–18; tel. 0444 594060).

At **Sandrigo**, the **Villa Sesso Schiavo Nardone** (open by appointment, tel. 0444 659344) was built by a follower of Palladio in 1570 and has contemporary frescoes. At **Longa di Schiavon**, the **Villa Chiericati Lambert** was built in 1590 (and altered in the 19C); it contains 16C frescoes attributed to Ludovico Pozzoserrato.

Bassano del Grappa

Bassano del Grappa is a delightful little town (35,000 inhab.) on the Brenta, with arcaded streets, a friendly atmosphere, and lots of wine bars and good trattorie. It has an interesting town museum with a very fine collection of works by Jacopo Bassano (the Da Ponte family of painters, which included Jacopo and Leandro, were surnamed Bassano after their native town). Bassano is known for its grappa, ceramics, wrought-iron work, and cabinet-makers.

■ **Information office**, see page 315.

■ **Hotels. 4-star**: *Belvedere*, 14 Piazzale Generale Giardino. **3-star**: *Brennero*, 7 Via Torino. **2-star**: *Al Castello*, 19 Piazza Terraglio; *Victoria*, 33 Viale Diaz. **1-star**: *Al Bassanello*, 2 Via Trozzetti (with restaurant). In the environs: **4-star**: *Villa Palma*, at Mussolente, and *Al Camin* at Cassola.

■ **Restaurants. A**: *San Bassiano*, 36 Viale dei Martiri. **B**: *Al Sole*, Via Vittorelli; *Belvedere*, 1 Viale delle Fosse; *Trevisani*, 13 Piazzale Trento. **C**: *Birreria Ottone*, 50 Via Matteotti; *El Piron*, 12 Via Zaccaria Bricito, *Osteria al canese da Amedeo*, 20 Via Vendramini; *Trattoria del Borgo*, 7 Via Margnan. **In the environs**: **A**: *La Loggia* (in the hotel Villa Palma, at Mussolente). **C**: *Al Giardinetto*, 30 Via Fontanelle; Osteria *al Castellaro*, 14 Via Chiesa, San Eusebio; *Dalla Malgari*, 102 Viale Asiago; *Da Bepie e Mina*, 49 Viale Monte Grappa; *Alla Riviera*, 7 Via San Giorgio; *Alla Fratellanza*, Via Fattori, San Michele.

■ **Snack bars.** *Al Porton*, Via Gamba; *Golden Snack*, 15 Via Roma; *Pub Garibaldi*, 37 Via Bonamigo. **Cafés** and **wine bars**: *Nardini* and *Taverna degli Alpini* at either end of the Ponte Vecchio, and *Danieli* by the Museo Civico.

■ **Car parking** along Viale delle Fosse or Viale de Gasperi (with a bus service). Free parking in Prato Santa Caterina.

■ **Buses** from Piazzale Trento to Asiago, Asolo, Maser, Padua, Possagno, Treviso and Vicenza.

■ **Train services** to Padua (via Cittadella), Venice and Trent.

■ **Market**, Thu and Sat in the two piazzas.

■ **Annual festival.** An autumn fair is held on the weekend after the first Thursday of October.

History

Bassano was a dependency of Venice from the 15C onwards. Napoleon's victory over the Austrians here in 1796 was overshadowed by the campaign on Monte Grappa in 1917–18 (see below) in which the town was considerably damaged. It was again damaged in the Second World War.

In the centre of the town are two adjoining squares, PIAZZA LIBERTÀ and PIAZZA GARIBALDI. In Piazza Libertà are two columns, one bearing the lion of

St Mark and the other a statue of the patron saint Bassiano by Orazio Marinali, and pretty, old-fashioned lamp standards. Opposite the long, decorative 18C façade of the church of **San Giovanni Battista** is the small **Loggia Comunale** (1582), with a 16C astronomical clock (the mechanism dates from 1747) and a fresco of St Christopher attributed to Jacopo Bassano.

The neighbouring Piazza Garibaldi is dominated by the 13C **Torre di Ezzelino** and the campanile of the Gothic church of **San Francesco**, which contains an interesting carved wooden crucifix dating from the early 13C, with the sun and the moon carved on the two arms of the cross.

In Piazza Garibaldi is the entrance to the **Museo Civico** (open 9–12.30, 15.30–18.30; fest. 15.30–18.30; closed Mon) opened here in 1840 in the former monastery of San Francesco. The **Pinacoteca** is arranged in rooms around an 18C 'Rotonda' (described below). The earliest works (12C–15C) are in two rooms to the right, with frescoes, a terracotta relief by Giovanni Minelli de' Bardi, works by Bartolomeo and Antonio Vivarini, a *crucifix signed by Guariento (c 1332; the first documented work by this artist), and a charming *Madonna and Child by Michele Giambono.

In the room on the right of the 'Rotonda' are *works by Jacopo Bassano, showing the various phases of the development of this remarkable native artist throughout his long life (c 1510–92), including his early masterpiece, the Flight into Egypt (1534).

The large hall has 17C works by Orazio Marinali, Alessandro Magnasco (including the *Refectory of the Monks*), Giovanni Battista Piazzetta, Pietro Longhi and Gian Domenico Tiepolo (*Madonna and Child). The last room has a collection of *works by Antonio Canova (donated to the museum in 1852, and one of the most important in Italy). The library has some 7000 letters written by him, his library, and drawings.

On the ground floor are two rooms with the **Archaeological Collection**, including the Lorenzo Chini collection of vases from Puglia (6C–3C BC). At the foot of the stairs is the huge model for the statue of Goldoni in Campo San Bartolomeo in Venice by Antonio Dal Zotto. The museum also owns a fine collection of engravings for which Bassano was renowned in the 18C, and the costumes and theatrical mementoes of Tito Gobbi (1913–84), the great baritone, who was born in Bassano.

Below Piazza Libertà is Piazzotta Monte Vecchio, with the old **Monte di Pietà** (covered for restoration) on the site of the first town hall (it still bears the 14C coat of arms of the city). Built in 1454 it was used as a pawnshop until 1834. The house above the bakery has remains of frescoes by the Bassano and Nasocchio families.

Nearby is ***Ponte Vecchio** or **Ponte degli Alpini**, a famous covered wooden bridge across the picturesque Brenta river, which retains the form designed for it by Palladio in 1569. The river is subject to sudden floods, and the bridge has had to be rebuilt many times: it has been proved over the centuries that only a wooden structure (rather than stone) can survive the force of the water. There is a lovely view of the mountains upstream from the bridge and the houses on the river front are well preserved. Beside the bridge is a characteristic little wine bar, with a grappa distillery of 1769 (there is a private museum in the nearby Poli distillery illustrating the production of grappa). The bridge is called after the Alpini regiment which traversed the bridge numerous times during the campaigns on Monte Grappa and above Asiago in the First World War, and which was responsible for its reconstruction after the last war (small museum in the Taverna al Ponte, 2 Via Angarano, open 8–20 exc. Mon). The best view of the bridge is from the other side, from a lane which leads left beside a little garden on the banks of the river.

Also on the river (south bank) is the lovely 18C **Palazzo Sturm**, where the **Museo della Ceramica** (part of the Museo Civico) has recently been

Ponte degli Alpini

arranged (open Fri 9–12; Sat & Sun, 15–19). The entrance is through the attractive neo-classical courtyard overlooking the river. The entrance hall (1765) has frescoes by Giorgio Anselmi. The collection of ceramics illustrates the production of local manufactories, including Manardi ware made here in the 17C, and later pieces from Nove and Faenza. Beyond a belvedere (now enclosed) overlooking the river is the delightful little *boudoir, which preserves its original Rococo decoration intact (after a careful restoration), including very fine stuccowork.

Villas in the environs of Bassano

On the outskirts of Bassano, in località Sant'Eusebio, is the **Villa Bianchi Michiel** built in the late 17C by Domenico Margutti, perhaps on a design by Longhena. It has two wings with Doric porticoes (adm. by appointment only).

A road leads northeast out of Bassano to **Romano d'Ezzelino**, where the 17C **Villa Corner**, with an orangery by Vincenzo Scamozzi, may be visited by previous appointment. Nearby is **Mussolente** with the **Villa Negri Piovene** on a low hill approached by a flight of steps from the Asolo road, and flanked by two porticoes. It was built in 1763 by Antonio Gaidon.

To the south of Bassano is the **Villa Rezzonico**, reminiscent of a medieval castle, built in the early 18C and attributed as an early work to Longhena. It contains stuccoes by Andrea Brustolon, and has a fine park and garden (tel. 0424 524217). At **Rosà**, the park of the late 17C **Villa Dolfin-Boldù** may be visited by previous appointment. **Rossano Veneto** has two 18C villas. On the Brenta at **Cartigliano** is the eccentric **Villa Morosini Cappello** (now the town hall). It was begun in 1560 probably by Francesco Zamberlan, but left unfinished. The remarkable Ionic loggia which surrounds the building may have been added in the 17C. It is open Mon–Fri 9–13; Sat 9–12; Wed 16.30–18.30 (tel. 0424 590234). In the parish church, the chapel of the Rosary is decorated with frescoes (1575) by Jacopo Bassano and his son Francesco, and has an altarpiece by Bartolomeo Montagna.

Monte Grappa (1775m) north of Bassano was the scene of heavy fighting between Austrians and Italians in 1917–18, in three historic battles which ended in the loss of 12,615 Italian soldiers (only 2283 of whom could be identified). On the summit is a monumental cemetery built in 1935 by Giovanni Greppi, with a votive chapel dedicated to the Madonnina del Grappa. Nearby is the Austro-Hungarian cemetery with the remains of 10,295 soldiers (only 295 of whom were identified).

Marostica

Marostica is a charming old fortified townlet preserving its medieval *ramparts which connect the lower castle on the piazza with the upper castle on the green hillside above. The biennial chess game with human combatants has become a famous spectacle (see below). Marostica has a particularly pleasant climate, and excellent cherries are grown in the surroundings.

■ **Information office.** Pro-loco, Castello Inferiore, Piazza Castello (tel. 0424 72127).

■ **Hotels. 3-star**: *Europa* (with restaurant), 19 Via Pizzamano; *La Rosina*, Via Marchetti, Valle San Floriano (4km outside the town).

■ **Restaurants. B**: in the two hotels (see above); **C**: *Trattoria Da Agnese*, 23 Via Pedalto, on the road to Crosara. **Wine Bar**: *Osteria alla Madonnetta*. **Café**: *Centrale*, Piazza Castello.

■ **Annual festivals.** A chess game (*Partita a scacchi*), in which the whole town participates, takes place every two years (even years) on a Fri, Sat and Sun evening in early Sep in Piazza Castello. The match was introduced in this century to commemorate and reproduce a 'duel' fought in 1454 between Rinaldo d'Angarano (black) and Vieri da Vallonara (white) for the hand of Lionora, daughter of Taddeo Parisio, the local Venetian governor. The herald's announcements are made in Venetian dialect. At the end of the game the wedding takes place, with some 500 participants in 15C costume—flag-throwers, etc. Each year a particular 'historic' chess game is chosen to be re-enacted. The game is held at 21 (also at 17 on the last day) and tickets should be bought by June. In odd years, when the 'players' are sent abroad to perform the game, an international chess festival is held in the town.

On the last Sunday in May a Cherry Festival is held here.

History

A stronghold of the Ezzelini in the 12C–13C, Marostica was rebuilt in 1311–86 by the Scaligeri (who constructed the two castles and the ramparts). It came under Venetian control in 1404 and remained faithful to the Republic from then onwards.

The delightful PIAZZA CASTELLO, with a stone chessboard on which the chess game is played, has a superb view of the ramparts climbing the green hillside to the upper castle. In the piazza the battlemented **Castello da Basso** was built by the Scaligeri in the early 14C (restored in 1935). It can be visited on request at the Pro-loco office. In the courtyard, with a well, is an ancient ivy. Stairs lead up to the loggia with a catapult reconstructed in 1923. The Sala del Consiglio was frescoed in the 17C.

At the other end of the piazza, in a loggia beneath a bank building, chess-boards are provided for the public (and matches are often played here at the weekends). Via Sant'Antonio leads past the church of **Sant'Antonio**, which contains an altarpiece by Jacopo Bassano and his son Francesco (1574), to the

17C church of the **Carmine**. A path leads up the green hillside to the **Castello Superiore**, also built by the Scaligeri, but ruined by the Venetians in the 16C (it can also be reached by road).

Near Marostica at **San Luca di Crosara**, the parish church has an early work (c 1537) by Jacopo Bassano.

South of the town is **Nove**, known for its ceramics. The Antonibon family were active here from 1727 producing majolica and porcelain, examples of which can be seen in the Museo Civico in Palazzo De Fabris, open Tue, Wed & Thu 16–18 (15–17 in winter); Fri, Sat & Sun 10–12.30, 16–19 (winter 15–18). The collection is particularly representative of ceramics from the Veneto from the 18C onwards. There is also a ceramics museum in the Istituto Statale d'Arte per la Ceramica (founded in 1875), with a chronological display of ceramics produced in Nove from the beginning of the 18C to the present day.

Asiago and Recoaro Terme

Asiago, rebuilt since 1919 (6700 inhab.), is near the centre of the plateau of the 'Sette Comuni' (Asiago, Enego, Foza, Gallio, Lusiana, Roana and Rotzo), united from 1310–1807 in an autonomous federation (allied with Venice after 1404), the inhabitants of which were of Germanic origin (the '*Cimbri*'). Since the 1960s the area, which has a good climate, has been developed as a winter and summer resort, and there are numerous hotels in Asiago of all categories. *Asiago* cheese is produced here. The pretty old railway line (closed down in 1958) from Asiago south to Cogollo can be followed on foot.

Asiago was the scene of bitter fighting in the First World War (1916–18); a monumental war cemetery (1932–38) has the remains of 33,086 Italian and 18,505 Austro-Hungarian dead. Nearby is a museum illustrating the history of the battles. In the battle of 15–16 June 1918, the British XIV Corps was heavily engaged and the dead are buried in five cemeteries: Barenthal, Granezza, Cavalletto, Boscon and Magnaboschi.

Near Asiago is an important astrophysical observatory, administered by Padua University, which includes the largest telescope in Italy (built in 1973).

Recoaro Terme is a spa with ferruginous springs discovered in 1689 (beneficial to liver, intestine and kidney complaints), with hotels of all categories. A cable car ascends to the ski resort of Recoaro Mille (1021m).

Valdagno (28,400 inhab.) has been known since the beginning of the century for its woollen mills. Here the late 17C **Villa Valle** (now the town hall) may be visited Mon–Fri 14.30–19; Sat 14.30–18 (tel. 0445 401887).

Monte Pasubio (2235m) was hotly contested in 1916–18 and a ring of boundary-stones defines the 'Zona Sacra', dedicated to those who died here. On the Pian delle Fugazzem (1159m) is the Sacello del Pasubio, another war memorial with a battle museum.

On the other side of the lovely **Valle del Posina** is **Tonezza del Cimone**, a mountainous plateau (1000–1500m) with fine walks. Monte Cimone, also fought over in the First World War, has a war memorial and cemetery.

Schio, in a pretty position, is a town (35,000 inhab.) once important for its wool manufactures. It has a cathedral begun in 1740, a good 15C–16C church (San Francesco) and an ossuary-cloister, on the Asiago road, with 5000 graves of soldiers who fell in 1915–18.

39 · Verona

Verona is a prosperous, busy city (257,000 inhab.), and one of the most attractive in northern Italy. The wide pavements of its pleasant streets, made out of huge blocks of red Verona marble, give the town an air of opulence. The birthplace of Catullus and perhaps Vitruvius in the 1C BC, it has impressive Roman remains including the famous amphitheatre known as the Arena, a theatre, and the gateway which provided the entrance to the Roman town. Its numerous fine Romanesque and Gothic churches, including the beautiful basilica of San Zeno, contain interesting sculptures and paintings by local artists. Shakespeare's *Romeo and Juliet* was set in Verona. The Scaligeri family who ruled the town from the late 13C for over a century are commemorated by their sumptuous tombs and their castle, Castelvecchio, with its bridge over the Adige. The river is an important feature of the town, and Piazza dei Signori and the adjoining Piazza delle Erbe are two of the finest squares in northern Italy.

Verona is well equipped to receive hundreds of thousands of visitors every year, and is especially crowded during the famous opera season at the arena in July and August. Its modern commercial activity is in great part due to its position at the junction of two main arteries of transport: from Germany and Austria to central Italy, and from Turin and Milan to Venice and Trieste.

■ **Information offices.** APT, 38 Piazza Erbe. Information offices at 61 Via Leoncino, off Piazza Brà (tel. 045 592828), and at the railway station. In summer also at 42 Piazza Erbe.

◪ **Hotels.** 5-star: *Gabbia d'Oro*, 4 Corso Porta Borsari. 4-star: *Accademia*, 12 Via Scala; *Colomba d'oro*, 10 Via Cattaneo; *Due Torri Hotel Baglioni*, 4 Piazza Sant'Anastasia; *San Luca*, 8 Vicolo Volto San Luca. 3-star: *Bologna*, 3 Piazzetta Scalette Rubiani; *Antica Porta Leona*, 3 Corticella Leoni; *Giulietta e Romeo*, 3 Vicolo Tre Marchetti; *Milano*, 11 Vicolo Tre Marchetti. 2-star: *Mazzanti*, 6 Via Mazzanti; *Sanmicheli*, 2 Via Valverde; *Torcolo*, 3 Vicolo Listone; *Armando*, 1 Via Dietro Pallone. 1-star: *Arena*, 2 Stradone Porta Palio.

■ **Youth hostel.** *Ostello della gioventù*, 15 Salita Fontana del Ferro; *Casa della Giovane*, 7 Via Pigna (girls only).

■ **Camping sites.** 3-star: *Giulietta e Romeo*, 54 Via Bresciana (open Mar–Nov), on the road to Peschiera. 1-star: *Castel San Pietro*, 1 Via Castel San Pietro (open Jun–Sep).

■ **Restaurants. A**: *Dodici Apostoli*, Corticella San Marco (off Corso Portoni Borsari); *Nuovo Marconi*, 4 Via Fogge; *Il Desco*, 3/5 Via Dietro San Sebastiano. **B**: *Antica Trattoria La Pigna*, 4B Via Pigna (near the Duomo); *Maffei*, 38 Piazza Erbe; *Bottega del Vino*, Vicolo Scudo di Francia (off Via Mazzini). **C**: *La Fontanina*, Piazzetta Santa Maria in Chiavica (off Piazza dei Signori); *Osteria al Duca*, 2 Via Arche Scaligere; *Osteria Sgarzarie*, Corte Sgarzarie (off Corso Portoni Borsari). **Self-service Restaurants**: *Brek*, 20 Piazza Brà; *San Matteo*, Corso Portoni Borsari. **Snack Bar**: *Osteria Abazia* by the church of San Zeno (1 Vicolo

Abazia). **Cafés**. *Dante*, 2 Piazza dei Signori; *Mattei*, Vicolo Crocioni (off Via Cappello). **Cake Shops**: *Cordioli*, Via Cappello; *Flego*, Corso Portoni Borsari.

■ **Picnic places.** In the park near San Giorgio in Braida, in the Giusti gardens, in the small public garden off Piazza dei Signori, in the Teatro Romano, and the gardens on the far side of Ponte Scaligero.

■ **Railway station.** Porta Nuova (Pl. 13) for all main line services.

■ **Airport** at Villafranca (15km from the city centre), with daily flights to London. Bus service every 20 mins from the station.

■ **Car parking.** There are two underground car parks: 'Arena' (open 24 hours), Via Bentegodi (close to Piazza Brà) and 'Garage Cittadella', Piazza Cittadella. Free parking near the station, around the walls, at the gasometro (near the cemetery), and near the Arsenale (Lungadige Cangrande).

■ **Town buses.** From the railway station to the Arena (Piazza Brà) Nos 11, 12, and 13. From the railway station to Castelvecchio Nos 21, 22, 23 and 24. A small bus (No. 70) connects the station with Piazza Erbe. From Castelvecchio Nos 31,32 and 33 to San Zeno. From the station to the Roman Theatre Nos 70 and 72.

■ **Buses for the province** run by APT depart from Porta Nuova station (tel. 045 8004129) for the Lago di Garda, etc.

■ An **entrance ticket** for the most important churches has been introduced (cumulative ticket available) so that they can be kept open all day.

■ **Markets**. Daily market in Piazza Erbe. Tue and Fri in Piazza San Zeno; Tue in Piazza Isolo (near the Teatro Romano). Wed and Fri in Piazza Santa Toscana (Porta Vescovo); Fri in Piazza degli Arditi (Volto San Luca). A market with bric-a-brac and artisans' ware is held on the third Sat of the month at San Zeno.

■ **Theatres.** A famous opera season is held in Jul and Aug in the *Arena*, and at the same time a Shakespeare festival and ballet performances take place in the *Roman Theatre* (information from the Ente Arena, 28 Piazza Brà, tel. 045 590109). Jazz festival (Jun) at the Roman Theatre. The *Teatro Nuovo* has a theatre season from Nov to the spring, and the *Teatro Filarmonico* in Piazza Brà has opera, concerts and ballet Oct–May.

■ **Annual festivals.** Festa di Santa Lucia, with a street market in Piazza Brà and Via Roma from around 10–12 Dec. Carnival celebrations which have been held in the town since the 16C, culminate on the Fri before Shrove Tuesday (*Venerdì gnocolar*). 12 Apr is the festival of the patron saint Zeno.

History
The settlement of the Euganean tribes on this site became a Roman colony in 89 BC and, because of its position (then as now at the crossing of impor-

tant traffic routes), Verona flourished under the Roman emperors. Theodoric the Ostrogoth lived in the city; and the Lombard king, Alboin, was murdered here, in his favourite residence, by his wife Rosamunda (573). The Frankish emperors Pepin (son of Charlemagne), and Berengar I (who died here in 924) chose Verona as their seat. The free commune established here in 1107 united with Padua, Vicenza and Treviso to form the Veronese League, the model of the Lombard League. Though always in sympathy with the Empire in its struggles against the Papacy, Verona resented Germanic attempts at conquest, defeated Barbarossa in 1164, and shared in the Lombard victory of Legnano in 1176. Family feuds within the city (on which the story of Romeo and Juliet is based) were settled by the tyrant Ezzelino da Romano, who took control of the government from 1231 to his death in 1259.

In 1260 Mastino della Scala, the podestà, established his position as overlord of Verona, and his family, known as the Scaligeri, held power in the city until 1387, throughout the most brilliant period of Veronese history. Dante found a refuge in the Ghibelline city under Bartolomeo (nephew of Mastino) in 1301–04, and in the reign of Cangrande I (1311–29) Verona reached its greatest period of magnificence.

After the fall of the house of Scaligeri, Gian Galeazzo Visconti became tyrant of the city. In 1405 Verona chose to become part of the Venetian Republic. John Evelyn, who visited Verona in 1646, called it 'one of the delightfulest places that ever I came in'. In 1796 it was occupied by the French. Armed protest against the invader (the 'Pasque Veronesi', 1797) was avenged by the destruction of much of the city, and Verona was several times exchanged between France and Austria by the treaties of the early 19C, until it was finally given to Austria in 1814. During the Wars of Independence it formed the strongest point of the Austrian 'Quadrilateral' (together with Peschiera, Mantua and Legnago), but in 1866 it was united with the Italian kingdom. During the Second World War the city suffered considerably from bombing, and the bridges were all blown up. In Castelvecchio in 1944, Mussolini's puppet Republican government staged the trial of Count Galeazzo Ciano, Mussolini's son-in-law, who had been a Fascist minister but later became a leading opponent of the Duce.

Art

The beautiful church of San Zeno marks Verona as a centre of architecture in the Romanesque period. Sculpture at Verona is best represented by Pisanello, the medallist, and by Fra Giovanni da Verona, the woodcarver. In the early 15C the painters Altichiero and Jacopo d'Avanzo, and their followers, were active in Verona. Giovanni Badile, Stefano da Zevio and Pisanello were important Veronese painters and among their successors were Francesco Bonsignori, Domenico and Francesco Morone, Girolamo dai Libri (a skilful illuminator), Liberale, Francesco Torbido, Bonifazio Veronese, Antonio Badile and, most famous of all, Paolo Caliari, called Il Veronese (1528–88). There are numerous works in the city by the Veronese architect Michele Sanmicheli (1486–1559), including beautiful palaces, sculptural work, and fortifications.

Piazza delle Erbe

At the centre of the city is the delightful, irregular *PIAZZA DELLE ERBE (Pl. inset) which occupies the site of the Roman forum and is now occupied by a daily market and has numerous cafés. The centre is paved with huge blocks of red Verona marble. On a line along the centre of the piazza rise: the **Colonna Antica**, a Gothic column with a stone lantern; the **Capitello**, a tribune of four columns; a lovely, abundant **fountain** of 1368, with a Roman statue called 'Madonna Verona'; and the **Colonna di San Marco** (1523), with a Venetian lion (1886) replacing the original destroyed in 1797.

The battlemented brick **Casa dei Mercanti**, on the west side, founded by Alberto della Scala (1301), was restored in the 17C. The Madonna in the niche is by Girolamo Campagna (1595). This side of the piazza has picturesque houses with numerous balconies. The statue in the adjoining piazzetta commemorates the victims of an Austrian bomb that fell on this site in 1915. In the northwest corner rises the **Torre del Gardello** (1370), and the north end of the piazza is closed by the handsome **Palazzo Maffei** (1668), crowned with a balustrade bearing six statues.

On the east side of the square is the **Casa Mazzanti**, once a palace of the Scaligeri, which was reduced to its present size in the 16C. It has a long frescoed façade, and a terrace which runs the whole of its length. The **Arco della Costa** (named from a whale's rib hung beneath the vault) is next to **Palazzo della Ragione**, founded before 1193 but much altered; its main façade on this square was rebuilt, except for the massive **Torre delle Carceri**, in the 19C. The 12C **Torre dei Lamberti** (84m; open Wed–Sun 9.30–13.30; Sat 9.30–18.30; lift or stairs; *view) was completed with a lantern in 1464, and the Romanesque courtyard given a monumental Gothic staircase in 1446–50.

Piazza dei Signori

The Arco della Costa leads into the dignified *PIAZZA DEI SIGNORI, the centre of medieval civic life, with arches over all the streets by which it is entered. The monument to Dante dates from 1865, and the café here is the most celebrated in the city. Beneath the level of the piazza and in Via Dante, Roman paving has been revealed. An arch joins the north wing of **Palazzo della Ragione** (Romanesque and Renaissance; the Lion of St Mark was ruined in 1797) to the marble-faced **Palazzo del Capitano** with a portal by Sanmicheli (1530–31) and a crenellated tower. In the courtyard is a bizarre portal by Giuseppe Miglioranzi (1687). At the end is the **Prefettura**, originally (like the Palazzo del Capitano) a palace of the Scaligeri, restored in the original 14C style with a brick front and crenellations.

The ***Loggia del Consiglio** is an elegant Renaissance building of 1493, with arcades and a pretty balustrade. The twin windows are by Domenico da Lugo and Matteo Panteo, and the five statues of famous Romans born in Verona by Alberto da Milano (1493). Above the door an inscription records Verona's faithfulness to Venice and their mutual affection: 'Pro summa fide summus amor MDXCII'. Over the arch is a statue of the physician Girolamo Fracastoro (1559). On the last side of the piazza is the handsome **Domus Nova**, reconstructed in 1659. Through an archway (crowned with a statue of the dramatist Scipione Maffei, 1756) is the back of the Casa Mazzanti with an outside walkway and stair, and a lovely Renaissance well-head (linked to various windows with iron rods).

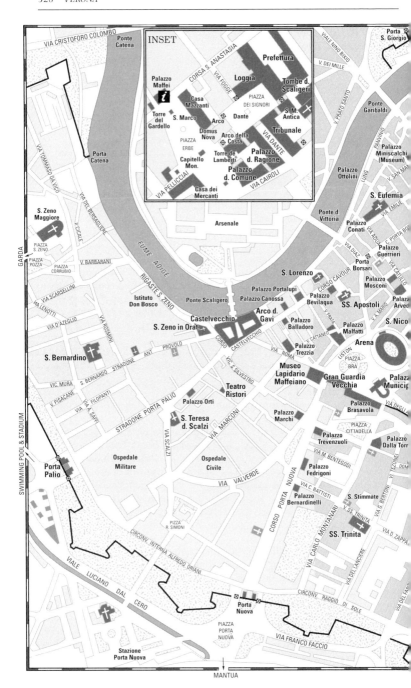

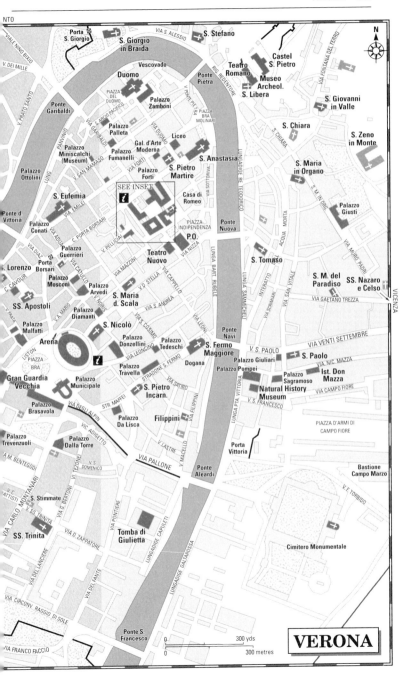

VERONA

NTO

N

VIALE NINO BIXIO

V. DEI MILLE

V. PRATO SANTO

Porta S. Giorgio

S. Giorgio in Braida

VIA S. ALESSIO

S. Stefano

Vescovado

Teatro Romano

Castel S. Pietro

Duomo

Ponte Pietra

Museo Archeol.

VIA FONTANA DEL FERRO

Ponte Garibaldi

PIAZZA DEL DUOMO

RIG REDENTORE

VIA PONTE PIE TRA

S. Libera

S. Giovanni in Valle

Palazzo Zamboni

PIAZZA BRA MOLINARI

S. Chiara

S. Zeno in Monte

PANVINIO

Palazzo Palleta

VIA DUOMO

Liceo

S. CHIARA

VIA GARIBALDI

Gal. d'Arte Moderna

Palazzo Miniscalchi (Museum)

VIA S. MAMMASO

Palazzo Fumanelli

VIA FORTI

S. Pietro Martire

S. Anastasia

S. Maria in Organo

LUNGADIGE RE TEODORICO

S. M. IN ORG.

Palazzo Ottolini

Palazzo Forti

Palazzo Giusti

LUNG.

S. Eufemia

SEE INSET

Casa di Romeo

ACQUA MORTA

VIA MURO PADRI

VIA EMILEI

PIAZZA INDIPENDENZA

Ponte d. Vittoria

C. PORTA BORSARI

Palazzo Conati

Ponte Nuova

Palazzo Guerrieri

V. PELLICIAI

P.O.

VIA ADUA

VIA DIAZ

Porta Borsari

VIA MAZZINI

Teatro Nuovo

LUNGA BART. RUBELE

S. Tomaso

S. M. del Paradiso

SS. Nazaro e Celso

VICENZA

S. Lorenzo

C. CAVOUR

Palazzo Mosconi

VIA CATULLO

Palazzo Arvedi

V. D. STELLA

VIA CAPPELLO

LUNGA SAMMICHELI

INTERRATO

VIA SAN VITALE

VIA GAETANO TREZZA

SS. Apostoli

T PRATI

V. A. MARIO

S. Maria d. Scala

VIA S. COSIMO

VIA S. ANDREA

INTERRATO

VIA SCRIMARI

Palazzo Malfatti

Palazzo Diamanti

S. Nicolò

VIA LEONI

Ponte Navi

VIA VENTI SETTEMBRE

Arena

Palazzo Donzellini

Palazzo Tedeschi

S. Fermo Maggiore

V. S. PAOLO

S. Paolo

LISTON PIAZZA BRA

VIA LEONCINO

STRADONE S. FERMO

Palazzo Giuliari

VIA NIC. MAZZA

Gran Guardia Vecchia

Palazzo Municipale

Palazzo Travella

Dogana

Palazzo Pompei

Palazzo Sagramoso

Ist. Don Mazza

VIA CAMPO FIORE

S. Pietro Incarn.

VIA SATIRO

Natural History Museum

V. S. FRANCESCO

Palazzo Brasavola

VIA DEGLI ALPINI

STR. MAFFEI

Palazzo Da Lisca

Filippini

VIA FILIPPINI

LUNGA PTA VITTORIA

PIAZZA D'ARMI DI CAMPO FIORE

Palazzo Trevenzuoli

VIC. ADIGETTO

Palazzo Dalla Torre

V. S. DOMENICO

V. LASTRE

Porta Vittoria

A M. BENTEGODI

VIA PALLONE

V. MACELLO

Ponte Aleardi

Bastione Campo Marzo

V. F. TORBIDO

V. C. BATTISTI

S. Stimmate

VIA G. BERTONI

VI. TEDONE

VIA PONTIERE

V. C. TRINITÀ

VIA CARLO MONTANARI

SS. TRINITÀ

SS. Trinità

VIA D. ZAPPATORE

Tomba di Giulietta

LUNGADIGE CAPULETI

LUNGADIGE GALTAROSSA

Cimitero Monumentale

VIA DEI LANDIERI

VIA DEL FANTE

VIA CIRCONV. RAGGIO DI SOLE

Ponte S. Francesco

0   300 yds

0   300 metres

VIA FRANCO FACCIO

Tombs of the Scaligeri

At the opposite corner of the piazza an archway leads to the *Tombs of the Scaligeri which are both historically interesting and illustrative of a century of Veronese architecture. Beside the little church of Santa Maria Antica with its 12C campanile, they are surrounded by a magnificent wrought-iron grille of the 14C in which the ladder, emblem of the Della Scala, is many times repeated. Over the side door of the church is the tomb (being restored) of Cangrande I (died 1329), by Bonino da Campione; the equestrian statue is a copy of the original in Castelvecchio. The other tombs are behind the gate (which is kept locked). Immediately on the left is the tomb of Mastino II (died 1351), and in the opposite corner that of Cansignorio (died 1375), both elaborate monuments by Bonino, with recumbent and equestrian figures. Against the wall of the church is the plain tomb of Mastino I, the first of the Scaligeri dynasty, assassinated in 1277 in Piazza dei Signori. At the back of the enclosure (protected by a roof) is the tomb of Giovanni (died 1359) by Andreolo de'Santi; nearby is the sarcophagus of Bartolomeo (died 1304) with bas-reliefs.

The church of **Santa Maria Antica** (closed 12.30–15.30) has a good early Romanesque interior with a red marble bishop's throne.

From the south side of Piazza delle Erbe (see above) Via Cappello leads to the so-called **Casa di Giulietta** (Pl. 7; open 8–18.30 exc. Mon), a restored 13C house, once an inn, with the sign 'Il Cappello' and so identified with the Cappello or Cappelletti family. Shakespeare's play of *Romeo and Juliet*, set in Verona, tells the story of Juliet Capulet (Cappello or Cappelletti) and Romeo Montague (Montecchi), an adaptation of a tale by the 16C novelist Luigi da Porto. The legend of a feud between the two families is apocryphal; in fact, it is probable that the clans were in close alliance. The romantic balcony in the courtyard was added in 1935. The spacious interior (to be restored) has its painted walls disfigured by modern graffiti. On the top floor are fine wooden ceilings, and a ship's keel roof.

VIA MAZZINI (Pl. 7), the main shopping street of Verona, connects Piazza delle Erbe with Piazza Brà. At the crossroads with Via Scala is an 18C palace by Adriano Cristofali with an old bookshop on the ground floor. The church of **Santa Maria della Scala** has an apse and campanile of 1324. It contains a Gothic tomb (1430) and frescoes by Giovanni Badile and a Baroque altar by Cristofali (1751). At the fork with Via Mario is the neo-classical Palazzo Arvedi. At the end of Via San Nicolò (left) can be seen the imposing Ionic façade of **San Nicolò**. Piazza Brà is described below.

Sant'Anastasia

A short way northeast of Piazza dei Signori is the church of *Sant'Anastasia (Pl. 3; open 9–18; fest. 13.30–18), a fine example of Gothic brickwork of two periods, 1290–1323 and 1423–81. The west front is unfinished, but the double **west door** (covered for restoration) is a beautiful work; to the right are two sculptured panels from a series of the life of St Peter Martyr. The graceful tower supports an eight-sided spire.

The **interior** is remarkable for the short space between the springing of the vault and the apex of the arcade, and has fine architectural details throughout. The splendid black, white and red marble pavement was designed by Pietro da

Porlezza in 1462. The stoups are supported by two life-like crouching figures: that on the right is by Paolo Orefice (1591) and that on the left by Gabriele Caliari (1495). **South aisle**. The first altar has a monumental marble screen by Michele Sanmicheli with statues by Danese Cattaneo (1565). The next two altars have finely carved marble frames surrounded by frescoes by Giovanni Maria Falconetto: the second altarpiece is by Pietro Rodari and the third was sculptured by Orazio Marinali. The last chapel on this side has a finely carved entrance arch, a 15C crucifix, and a carved group of the Pietà (1425).

The altarpiece in the **south transept** is by Gerolamo dai Libri. **East end**. The second chapel on the right of the sanctuary has a carved wood altar and ancona. On the right wall is a fresco by Altichiero. The tomb of Federico Cavalli has a fresco by Stefano da Zevio. The first chapel on the right of the altar, the **Cappella Pellegrini**, has its walls covered with 24 terracotta bas-reliefs by Michele da Firenze. On the jambs of the chapel, to the right, are four Apostles, by the school of Mantegna, and inside are two good Gothic family tombs, and the effigy of Wilhelm von Bibra (died 1490), ambassador of Cologne to the Vatican.

The **sanctuary** has a Last Judgement by Turone on the right wall, and on the left wall frescoes (difficult to see) by Michele Giambono around the tomb (1424–29) of Cortesia Serego, general of Antonio della Scala, by Nanni di Bartolo, with an equestrian statue (1429). In the **north transept** are three paintings by Paolo Farinati, Turchi and Liberale. In the **sacristy** (1453) is displayed a delightful fresco of *St George at Trebizond, a masterpiece by Pisanello (detached from an arch above the Cappella Pellegrini and badly damaged), but very difficult to see. The stalls date from 1490–93, and on the right wall are two paintings by Antonio Balestra. There is also a mechanical organ, an altarpiece by Felice Brusasorci, and 15C stained glass.

North aisle. The fifth chapel dates from 1585–96 and has a detached fresco attributed to Lorenzo Veneziano, and paintings by the 17C Veronese school. The organ by Domenico Farinati (1705; restored in 1967) stands over the north door. At the sumptuous fourth altar is the Descent of the Holy Ghost, by Nicolò Giolfino (1518), surrounded by statues of saints and the Redeemer (above is a fresco by Francesco Morone). In the second chapel, *St Erasmus* by Giolfino, and in the first chapel, statues and worn frescoes attributed to Morone.

Beyond the Gothic tomb of Guglielmo Castelbarco (died 1320), above the former convent-gate, is the little 14C church of **San Pietro Martire**, now used for exhibitions. It contains a large frescoed lunette of the Annunciation, a very unusual allegorical composition by Giovanni Maria Falconetto with symbolic animals and idealised views of Verona. The two German knights who commissioned the fresco are shown kneeling.

The road continues past the long neo-classical façade (in need of restoration), with Doric columns, of the **Conservatory** (1807) to cross Via Forti (left). Here in the 18C **Palazzo Forti** where Napoleon lodged in 1796–97 is the **Galleria d'Arte Moderna** (open 9–19 exc. Mon), where exhibitions are held.

Some way to the southwest (see the Plan), reached by Via Forti and its continuation Via Emilei past the Venetian Gothic **Palazzo Franchini** (No. 20), is the church of **Sant'Eufemia** (Pl. 7; closed 12–15.30). With fine tombs on the exterior, it was first built in 1262, and rebuilt in 1375. It contains works by Domenico Brusasorci, Gian Francesco Caroto, Martino da Verona and Moretto.

Duomo

The pretty Via del Duomo leads from Sant'Anastasia past several Renaissance palaces to the *Duomo (Pl. 3; open 9.30–18; Sat 9.30–16; fest. 13.30–18), whose reconstruction was begun in about 1120. The **south porch**, dating from about this time, has a double order of Roman columns, with finely carved capitals, between which are reliefs of the story of Jonah and the Whale, and a lion. The **west porch** is a beautiful work signed by Nicolò (c 1139), guarded by statues of the Paladins, Roland (identified by the name carved on the sword) and Oliver, and decorated with numerous sculptures including polychrome nativity scenes in the lunette. The campanile was continued above its Romanesque base by Sanmicheli (the bell-chamber was added in 1924–27). The beautiful **apse** can be seen in Piazza Vescovile.

Interior. The spacious **nave** has clustered pillars with interesting capitals and pointed arches. Round each chapel is a charming framework of sculptured pilasters and architectural fretwork. The walls around the first three chapels on either side are decorated with architectural frescoes by Giovanni Maria Falconetto (1503). In the **south aisle** the second chapel contains a small crowded Adoration of the Magi by Liberale da Verona, surrounded by later paintings of four saints and the Deposition, by Nicolò Giolfino (16C). By the nave pillar is a Romanesque marble stoup. The fourth chapel has delightful 18C decorations. Beyond the magnificent organ (16C; restored in the 17C and again recently) is the very damaged tomb-slab of Pope Lucius III, who died in Verona in 1185. Hanging in the aisle is a large crucifix (early 15C). At the end is the *Cappella Mazzanti**, with sculptured pilasters by Domenico da Lugo (1508); it contains the tomb of St Agatha (1353) by a Campionese master.

East end. The graceful curved *choir-screen, in pink and grey marble, is to a design by Michele Sanmicheli (1534). The dramatic *frescoes in the choir are by Francesco Torbido (1534), thought to be on cartoons by Giulio Romano. The organ, on the left, has good panels painted by Felice Brusasorci.

In the **north aisle** at the east end, the Cappella Maffei has frescoes (high up) by Giovanni Maria Falconetto. The third chapel contains a triptych of 1533 (with a predella by Michele da Verona), and near the second is a painting of the Madonna and Saints by Giovanni Caroto. Ouside the first chapel is the tomb of Galesio Nichesola (died 1527), a fine work attributed to Jacopo Sansovino. The chapel arch was elaborately decorated with sculptures and frescoes in 1468. The altar-frame, also attributed to Sansovino encloses an *Assumption, by Titian.

Off the north side of the cathedral is the entrance to a 12C vestibule with ancient columns, and part of the foundations of an early Christian basilica of the 4C. On the right is the entrance to **San Giovanni in Fonte** built in the early 12C. The huge octagonal *font hewn from a single block of marble in the late 12C has finely carved panels attributed to Brioloto. The fragmentary frescoes date from the 13C–14C. On the left of the entrance is a Baptism of Christ by Paolo Farinati (1568). From the vestibule, steps lead up to the church of **Sant'Elena** (9C; restored in the 12C) beneath which excavations have revealed remains of two early Christian basilicas (4C and 5C), with fragments of mosaic pavement. The tombs of two early bishops have also been found here. The finely carved narrow stalls date from the 16C. The altarpiece is by Brusasorci.

To the left of the façade of the Duomo, a passageway leads past the exterior portico of Sant'Elena and (opposite) the charming Romanesque **cloister** (with a double arcade on one side), also partly on the site of the 5C basilica, with remains in two places of a 6C mosaic pavement, one of which is polychrome.

In Piazza del Duomo is the **Chapter Library** (No. 21), founded by the archdeacon Pacificus (778–846) and containing many precious texts, and illuminated choirbooks attributed to Turone (c 1368).

Opposite the south door of the cathedral, a seated 14C figure of St Peter surmounts the doorway of **San Pietro in Archivolto**. In Piazza Vescovile, where can be seen the beautiful *apse of the Duomo, is the **Bishop's Palace** which has an unusual façade of 1502 with Venetian crenellations and a lovely portal decorated with statues including a delightful *Madonna and Child attributed to Fra Giovanni da Verona. The attractive courtyard with curious Romanesque capitals is dominated by the Torrione di Ognibene (1172). Next to the palace is the flank of San Giovanni in Fonte (described above), and opposite is an ancient wall (now propped up) with a gate into a neglected garden.

Nearby is Ponte Pietra over the Adige (described below), guarded by a medieval gateway.

The Stradone Arcidiacono Pacifico leads from the piazza in front of the Duomo past **Palazzo Paletta** (No. 6; with a finely carved portal) to Via Garibaldi which leads to the left. Here is the monumental neo-classical façade of **Palazzo Miniscalchi** (Pl. 3), entered from Via San Mammaso where the beautiful side *façade can be seen. This was built in the mid-15C by the Miniscalchi and has handsome marble windows and doorway. The painted decoration was carried out c 1580 by Michelangelo Aliprandi and Tullio India il Vecchio (numerous palaces in Verona once had painted façades). The **Museo Miniscalchi-Erizzo** (open Tue–Sat 16–19; fest. 10.30–12.30, 16–19) was opened here in 1990, after the last descendant of the family had left the house and collections to a foundation in 1955. It contains a miscellany of objects, all well labelled and spaciously arranged. The ground floor is used for exhibitions of the decorative arts.

The contents include: ivories, 16C–18C furniture, family portraits by Alessandro Longhi and Sebastiano Bombelli, 17C–18C majolica, a plate decorated in 1519 which belonged to Isabella d'Este, 16C ceramics from Urbino, Venetian bronzes, Murano glass, a fireplace decorated in majolica from Faenza (17C–18C), a good collection of 16C–17C drawings (mostly by Venetian masters), an armoury, 17C wooden soldiers, and curios which belonged to Ludovico Moscardo (1611–81).

Piazza Brà and the Arena

The huge PIAZZA BRÀ (Pl. 10) is so named from the German *breit*, meaning spacious. Here is the famous *Arena (Pl. 7,11), built c AD 100, the third-largest Roman amphitheatre in existence after the Colosseum and that at Capua (open 8–dusk exc. Mon; during the opera season, Jul–Aug, 8–13). Splendid vaulted passageways open into the cavea. Usually encumbered by the trappings of the summer opera festival, it is not maintained as well as it might be and is in need of restoration.

The interior is remarkably well preserved (although it has been restored many times). Of the outermost arcade, however, which originally measured 152m by 123m, only four arches, preserving their simple decoration, were left standing after an earthquake in 1183; the inner arcade (138m by 109m) of two orders superimposed is almost complete. The present circumference is made up of 74 arches (there are 80 in the Colosseum), and the floor of the arena is 73m long by 44m wide. The 44 stone stages of the cavea, restored in the 16C after they had been used in the Middle Ages as a quarry, provide space for 22,000 spectators. Goldoni's first successful play, *Belisario*, was produced here in 1834. The performance here of *Aïda* in 1913 set a new standard for the production of operatic spectacle.

On the northwest side of the piazza is the LISTON, with an exceptionally wide pavement lined with the awnings of cafés and restaurants. In the centre is **Palazzo Malfatti**, with a high rusticated portico and a balcony on the first floor, by Sanmicheli (1555). The **Portoni della Brà** (1389) is an archway which carried a covered way joining the Castelvecchio (see below) to the Visconti citadel: a pentagonal tower of the latter survives behind the **Gran Guardia**. This huge Doric building begun in 1609–14 by Domenico Curtoni dominates the west side of the piazza. It was built for military exercises and was completed in the same style by Giuseppe Barbieri in 1820. It is now used for exhibitions.

The Arena

On the other side of the Portoni della Brà is the entrance to the **MUSEO LAPIDARIO MAFFEIANO** (Pl. 10; open 8–18.30 exc. Mon). Founded in 1716 by the dramatist Scipione Maffei, (1675–1755) with material already collected in the courtyard here a century earlier, it was one of the first public museums in Italy. Goethe admired it on his visit to Verona in 1786.

The magnificent **pronaos** with six huge Ionic columns was built in 1604 by Domenico Curtoni, clearly influenced by Palladio. It was designed to be seen in conjunction with his Palazzo della Gran Guardia along the line of the medieval walls, and later served as the entrance to the Teatro Filarmonica where Mozart played in 1770. The theatre was rebuilt in 1716 by Francesco Bibiena, but this edifice burnt down and was bombed. It was only reconstructed in 1969 (and is now entered from Via Roma). In the courtyard of the museum, Alessandro Pompei added the low Doric portico in 1739–45 to display the lapidary collection: the scale has been destroyed in this century by the addition of the two floors above.

In the pronaos, the Etruscan urns were set into the wall by Maffei. Also displayed here is Roman material from Verona. In the **right portico** and on the two small modern walls and in underground rooms are inscriptions from Verona, while the **left portico** has inscriptions from Istria, Brescia, Rome, etc. From the ticket office a lift gives access to two modern rooms, well arranged, on the first and second floors. **First floor**. Some 100 Greek inscriptions from Smyrna, the Cyclades, Attica, the Peloponnese, and other places, ranging in date from the 5C BC to the 5C AD, constitute the best collection of its kind in Italy. The Greek reliefs here include the sepulchral stela of a woman (5C BC). **Second floor**. Roman sarcophagi, Etruscan cinerary urns, and Roman material from the Veneto. Steps lead up to the walkway over the Portoni del Brà, from which there is a delightful view.

On the south side of Piazza Brà is the huge **Palazzo Municipale** another impressive classical building (1838) by Giuseppe Barbieri (restored since the war).

Behind Palazzo Municipale, Via Pallone leads east, skirting an impressive stretch of the medieval city walls. Some way to the southeast (see the Plan), off Via del Pontiere in an unattractive part of the town, is the so-called **Tomba di Giulietta** and **Museo degli Affreschi** (Pl. 15; open 8–13.30 exc. Mon). In a crypt off a pretty Romanesque cloister, is an empty 14C tomb called the Tomb of Juliet. An underground room has an impressive display of Roman amphorae, found during excavations (now covered over) in the courtyard outside. Upstairs are displayed detached frescoes by Brusasorci, Bernardino India and Battista del Moro, sinopie by Altichiero, 19C sculptures by Torquato Della Torre, and 12C frescoes. The room with a fireplace was frescoed by Paolo Farinati in 1560.

Steps lead down into the church of **San Francesco al Corso**, which houses paintings by Caroto, Girolamo Bonsignori, Morone, Brusasorci, Farinati, Ludovico Dorigny, Balestra, Antonio Palma and Felice Cignaroli. Also kept here is a bronze *Annunciation in high relief by Girolamo Campagna.

San Fermo Maggiore

On the other side of Via Pallone (see above), Via Macello leads north parallel to the river past the former slaughterhouse (1859), now used as artisans' workshops. Via Filippini continues past the church of the Filippini to the old customhouse, an impressive building of 1753 with two gates. Just beyond is *San Fermo Maggiore (Pl. 7; open 9–18; fest. 12–18), really one church on top of another. The lower building retains Benedictine characteristics of 1065–1138, while the upper one was largely rebuilt by the Friars Minor c 1313 in a Gothic style; the different architectural styles are well seen from outside the east end.

Exterior. The partly Romanesque façade has a round-headed door, to the left of which is the tomb of Antonio Fracastoro (died 1368), the physician of the Scaligeri. On the north side a 15C porch protects a fine portal of 1363 (the usual entrance). The smaller apses and the campanile date from before the rebuilding.

Interior. The aisleless nave, adorned with 14C frescoes, is roofed by a very fine wooden *ceiling (1314; in urgent need of repair). Over the west doorway is a fresco attributed to Altichiero or Turone. Beyond the first south altar, *angels, a fresco by Stefano da Zevio. The marble pulpit (1396) and the tomb of the donor, Barnaba Morano (1412), in the adjoining chapel, are by Antonio da Mestre. The third south altar, beyond a 16C tomb supported by oxen, has a painting by Francesco Torbido.

The **choir** has a screen of 1573 and a fresco (1320) above the triumphal arch (being restored) depicting Guglielmo di Castelbarco offering the church to Prior Gusmerio. In the north apse are Saints, by Liberale. On the north side of the nave is a chapel containing the *tomb of Girolamo and Marcantonio della Torre, an unusual classical work in marble and bronze by il Riccio (c 1516). Also here is the elaborate Lady Chapel, with the Madonna and Saints, a good work by Caroto (1528); and at the west end the Brenzoni tomb, by Giovanni or Nanni di Bartolo (1439), with an Annunciation by Pisanello high up above (difficult to see).

Outside the church, steps lead down beneath the north porch to the **lower church**, interesting for its Romanesque architecture (with remains of frescoes). On the south side are two rebuilt cloisters, with 16C–17C frescoes.

Via Leoni leads towards Piazza delle Erbe (see above), passing the damaged remains of the Roman **Porta dei Leoni** (1C AD).

From San Fermo the Stradone San Fermo, lined with palaces, leads back towards Piazza Brà past **San Pietro Incarnario**, built on Roman foundations with a 14C campanile. The Stradone Maffei continues past **Palazzo Ridolfi**, where the great hall is frescoed by Brusasorci (showing the meeting of Charles V and Clement VII at Bologna, 1530). Opposite is the Renaissance Palazzo Maffei.

Castelvecchio

From Piazza Brà, Via Roma leads to the *CASTELVECCHIO (Pl. 6; open 8–18.30 exc. Mon), begun by Guglielmo Bevilacqua and Cangrande II della Scala in 1354, which was used by the Venetians as a citadel and from 1796 as barracks. It was inaugurated as a museum in 1925. One wing was damaged in the last war, and in 1956–64 the museum was imaginatively re-created by Carlo Scarpa.

From the drawbridge, across the courtyard, is the entrance to the Napoleonic east wing with the **sculpture galleries**. **Room I** contains a sarcophagus of 1179, a 13C male figure attributed to Brioloto, and Lombard gold ornaments. **Rooms II–IV** display **14C sculpture** including a *Crucifixion. **Room V**. **15C sculpture**, including *St Martin on horseback.

Beyond the fortress wall is the entrance to the main **keep** (1370), or *mastio*, guarding the approach road to the bridge which passes between the two parts of the fortress. From **Room VI** a stair mounts to **Room VII** with bells. A bridge leads across to the **Reggia** proper. **Room VIII** (left) contains 13C–14C frescoes and the '**Via Trezza *treasure'**, found in the city in 1938, with precious jewels dating from the 14C including a jewelled gold star, and the sword and belt found in the tomb of Cangrande I. Beyond **Room IX** with more frescoes, **Room X** displays a polyptych (1360), the only known signed work by Turone, and works by Tommaso da Modena and the school of Altichiero. **Room XI** is the only room in the palace which preserves its original painted wall decorations. Here are displayed works by Jacopo Bellini, Stefano da Zevio (*Madonna del Roseto*) and Michele Giambono, and the *Madonna della Quaglia* attributed to Pisanello. **Room XII** (left) has Flemish works, including a portrait by Rubens, and a Crucifixion by Luca di Leyden.

Room XIII, a long gallery overlooking the Adige (with a view of the Alps beyond), contains paintings by Jacopo Bellini and Giovanni Badile.

Upper floor. **Room XIV** has late 15C frescoes and works by Mocetto and Giolfino. **Room XV** contains the *Madonna della Passione* by Carlo Crivelli and a *Holy Family by Mantegna. In **Room XVI** are works by Liberale da Verona. **Room XVII**. Paintings by Francesco Bonsignori. **Room XVIII**. Francesco

Morone and Francesco dai Libri. **Room XIX**. Giovanni Bellini, *Madonna and Child. A covered passageway with a display of Lombard arms and jewels leads back to the keep. **Room XX** has 15C–17C arms and armour, and a *portrait of Pase Guarienti in a magnificent suit of armour, attributed to Domenico Brusasorci.

A second bridge leads to the upper floor of the Napoleonic wing; from the battlements the curve of the river is well seen, and from the belvedere, the *equestrian figure of Cangrande I (14C), an evocative work strikingly displayed. **Room XXI**. Cavazzola, *Passion scenes (1517) and four saints, and works by Gian Francesco Caroto. **Room XXII**. More works by Caroto, and paintings by Girolamo dai Libri (*_Holy Family with rabbits_) and Moretto. **Room XXIII**. Paolo Veronese and Jacopo Tintoretto. **Room XXIV**. Works by Domenico Brusasorci, Paolo Farinati, Alessandro Turchi. **Room XXV**. Pietro Bernardi, Bernardo Strozzi, Marcantonio Bassetti and Domenico Fetti. The collection of small paintings on stone include works by Alessandro Turchi and Marcantonio Bassetti. **Room XXVI**. Works by Claudio Ridolfi, Giulio Carpione and Spadarino, and two small paintings on copper plate by Giovanni Battista Castiglione (Il Grecchetto). **Room XXVII** displays Venetian works by Luca Giordano, Giovanni Battista and Gian Domenico Tiepolo, Antonio Balestra, Sebastiano Ricci, Guardi and Pietro Longhi.

Equestrian statue of Cangrande I

Approached through the south wing of the castle is ***Ponte Scaligero**, built at the same time as the Castelvecchio by Cangrande II. Blown up in 1945, it was rebuilt, mainly with original materials, and reopened in 1951.

The wide and busy CORSO CAVOUR (Pl. 6), lined with some very grand palaces, leads from Castelvecchio to the Porta dei Borsari. In the piazzetta beside the Castle is the **Arco dei Gavi**, a Roman arch of the 1C AD, erected astride the road in honour of the family of the Gavii, demolished in 1805, and reconstructed from the fragments in 1932. Among the fine palaces in Corso Cavour are the classical **Palazzo Canossa** (No. 44; c 1530), by Michele Sanmicheli, with an 18C screen, and Palazzo Portalupi (No. 38; 1802–04). Further on, approached through a pleasing little courtyard on the left is the finely restored Romanesque church of ***San Lorenzo** (c 1110). It has a lovely tall, narrow interior (open 9–18; fest. 10.30–18) with bands of red and white brick. Outside the west door can be seen two unusual cylindrical towers which served as approaches to the matroneum. Opposite is ***Palazzo Bevilacqua** (No. 19), an unusually ornate work by Sanmicheli (begun in 1530). In the piazza on the right is the church of the **Santi Apostoli** (1194), with a fine exterior including a Romanesque tower, apse and cloister. From the sacristy, stairs lead down to **Santi Tosca e Teuteria**, a domed cruciform shrine (5C), consecrated in 751 as a baptistery, and reduced again to a burial chapel by the Bevilacqua (two tombs and a relief) in 1427.

No. 10 is the Venetian Gothic Casa Pozzoni, and No. 11 a Renaissance palace of excellent design, which houses the study collections of the Museo Civico di Storia Naturale. No. 2 is the Baroque Palazzo Carlotti (1665). In the little piazza, No. 1 is a Renaissance house, the home of the Giolfino family of artists. The ***Porta dei Borsari** (Pl. 6,7) is a splendid Roman gateway built in the mid 1C AD, once the main entrance to the city, with a double archway surmounted by two stages of windows and niches, through which passed the Via Postumia as the *decumanus maximus*. It preserves only the outer front, though Roman masonry can be traced in the adjacent buildings. It was restored by Gallienus in AD 265 as the inscription states.

The attractive Corso Porta Borsari continues from the gate towards Piazza delle Erbe, past several palaces with frescoes, and the Romanesque church of **San Giovanni in Foro**. To the left Via Diaz leads to **Ponte della Vittoria**, a stately bridge rebuilt in 1951, with four equestrian groups, as a memorial of the First World War. The little Pilastrino dell'Agnello (16C) was erected by the Wool Guild.

San Zeno Maggiore

From Castelvecchio, buses 31, 32 and 33 run to Piazza San Zeno. On foot from Castelvecchio it is best reached by the Rigaste (quay) above the road along the river which passes the little 13C church of **San Zeno in Oratorio** (restored).

In a rather remote and less prosperous district of the town is the church of *San Zeno Maggiore (Pl. 5; open 9–18; fest. 13–18), one of the most beautiful of the Romanesque churches of northern Italy. It dates in its lower part from 1120–38 and was completed c 1225; the apse was rebuilt in 1386–98.

Exterior. The brick *campanile** was built 1045–1149, and the **Torre del Re Pipino** (c 1300), north of the church, is supposed to be a relic of the 9C palace of Pepin, but is really a fragment of the former abbey. The magnificent circular window in the upper part of the **west front**, by Brioloto (c 1200), depicts the Wheel of Fortune. The lovely **porch** (c 1138), supported on marble lions, is decorated with polychrome reliefs by Nicolò, and on either side of the doorway are scriptural and allegorical scenes by Nicolò and Guglielmo, including the Hunt of Theodoric, showing the Emperor chasing a stag headlong into Hell. In the tympanum is St Zeno trampling the Devil, and on either side is a charming row of twin arches, continued round the south side. The **doors** are decorated with remarkable bronze *reliefs of biblical subjects from the Old and New Testaments: the exact date and origin of these very unusual works is still unknown, but clearly two distinct masters were involved, one working at the beginning of the 12C and the other later in the century.

The spacious basilican **interior** has a nave separated from its aisles by simple and compound piers and covered by a trifoliate wooden ceiling (1386). Some of the capitals are from Roman buildings. On the west wall hangs a 15C crucifix. The large porphyry bowl is of Roman origin, and the large font of pink marble dates from the 12C. There are two very fine ancient stoups. The walls are frescoed in layers of varying date (13C–15C). On the **south side**, the first altarpiece is by Francesco Torbido; the second altar is made up of 'knotted' columns of red marble on a lion and a bull.

In the raised **presbytery** are a further series of very old frescoes (scribbled over in past centuries). On the balustrade are statues of Christ and the Apostles (c 1250). Above the high altar (a 12C sarcophagus), in its original frame, is a ***triptych by Mantegna** (light), the Madonna with angel musicians and eight saints, the figures influenced by Donatello. The panels of the predella are copies of the originals, now in the Louvre. The frescoes on the walls include two of the school of Altichiero (1397): the Crucifixion (left; over the sacristy door) and Monks presented to the Virgin (over the south arcade). In the north apse is a colossal painted figure of St Zeno (14C), a primitive but very striking work.

The spacious **crypt** (seen through a locked grille), supported by Romanesque columns brought from other buildings, contains the tomb of St Zeno (1889). The sarcophagus of St Lucillus has good reliefs.

On the north side of the church is the charming **cloister**, with coupled columns, built in 1123, but altered in the 14C. The tombs include those of Farinata degli Uberti (died 1348) and of members of the Scaligeri family.

Beside San Zeno is the church of **San Procolo** (open as for San Zeno), founded in the 5C, with a Romanesque interior. Below the nave, ugly modern steps lead down to remains of the early Christian church. The **crypt** has an early 16C altar and a small silver cross. In the upper church are two marble reliquary monuments (1492). The large 16C painting of Christ among the Doctors, attributed to Antonio Badile, was recently returned to the church by Princeton University. Other paintings are by Bettino Cignaroli and Giorgio Anselmi, and the seated statue of St Proculus is by Giovanni di Rigino (1392).

Some way south of San Zeno is the church of **SAN BERNARDINO** (Pl. 9), an interesting example of the transition from Gothic to Renaissance (1451–66). It is preceded by a cloister and has a Renaissance portal of 1474. On the high altar is a triptych by Benagio inspired by Mantegna's altarpiece in San Zeno.

South side. The first chapel is entirely frescoed by Giolfino, including some views of Verona; second chapel, altarpiece by Francesco Bonsignori; fourth chapel, frescoes attributed to Domenico Morone and his son Francesco. The ***Cappella Pellegrini** is a refined work of the Renaissance (1557) by Sanmicheli. The chapel at the end of the south aisle is decorated with paintings in gilded wood frames by Antonio Badile, Gian Francesco Caroto, Nicolò Giolfino and Francesco Morone.

The **north side** has a charming organ (1481) with doors painted by Domenico Morone, and a Baroque altar designed by Francesco Bibiena. The **Sala Morone** has frescoes by Domenico Morone and his pupils (1503).

To the southwest (see the Plan) are parts of the **town walls** erected by Sanmicheli in the early 16C on the lines of the older ramparts of the Scaligeri. They are the earliest example of a new type of military engineering that was later developed by Vauban. Two gates survive here, the **Porta Palio** (Pl. 9), which shows Sanmicheli's skill in combining structural beauty with military strength and, nearer the station, **Porta Nuova** (Pl. 14), dating from 1533–40.

The left bank of the Adige

The prettiest part of the river is near the church of Sant'Anastasia (Pl. 3; see above). An attractive row of houses faces the river from the church south to Ponte Nuovo: there is a narrow road skirting the river and the parallel Via Sottoriva is lined on one side by porticoes and Venetian-style houses. From Sant'Anastasia, Via Ponte Pietra leads north with some fine palaces, including one (No. 23A) with remarkable frescoes high up on its late 16C façade illustrating the various processes in cheese making and in butchering pork.

Santo Stefano

The attractive Via Cappelletta continues to *Ponte di Pietra (open to pedestrians only), guarded by a picturesque tower. It was blown up in 1945 but rebuilt in 1958 on the old lines by dredging the material (part-Roman and part-medieval) from the river. From Piazza Broilo, Vicolo Sabbionaia leads into Piazza Vescovile (described above). Across the bridge, on the left side of the Adige, is Santo Stefano (Pl. 3; open 8–12, 17–18), a venerable church rebuilt in the 12C, with a raised sanctuary. On the west wall, Christ and saints by Domenico Brusasorci (16C); in the first south chapel, built in 1620, a painting of the Forty Martyrs by Orbetto. At the end of the south and north walls are monochrome frescoes by Battista del Moro. At the top of a broad flight of steps is a colossal seated statue of St Peter in tufo, a 14C Veronese work attributed to Rigino di Enrico. Around the **apse** (with a stone episcopal throne) is an unusual raised gallery with 8C capitals and fragmentary remains of 12C painted decoration with animals. High up on the arches of both **transepts** are charming frescoes of angel musicians by Domenico Brusasorci. In the right transept is an altarpiece by Giovanni Francesco Caroto, and in the left transept, an altarpiece by Paolo Farinati. In the vaulted **crypt** is a raised semicircular gallery. Outside the apse is a tiny garden.

Across the river can be seen the cathedral, the battlemented tower of the bishop's palace, and the pretty little loggia of the chapter library.

San Giorgio in Braida

Further upstream is the large church of San Giorgio in Braida (Pl. 3), begun in 1477 on the site of a 12C church. It was completed on a design by Michele Sanmicheli, who added the cupola and who also began the unfinished campanile. The façade dates from the 17C.

In the **interior** are numerous fine paintings (although some of them are difficult to see). Above the west door, Jacopo Tintoretto, Baptism of Christ (very darkened). On the **south side**, paintings by Domenico Tintoretto, Francesco Brusasorci and Girolamo Romanino. In the **sanctuary** are two huge paintings by Felice Brusasorci and Paolo Farinati. In the apse, Sanmicheli's fine altar incorporates the *Martyrdom of St George, a masterpiece of colour and design by Veronese.

On the **north side**, below the organ, *altarpiece of Santa Cecilia and female saints by Moretto, and organ doors painted by Girolamo Romanino. In the fourth chapel, altarpiece by Girolamo dai Libri, part of another Sanmicheli altar. In the third chapel, *Saints Roch and Sebastian, and the Transfiguration, by Caroto, who also painted the two *saints, the lunette of the Transfiguration, and the predella in the triptych of the second chapel. The first altarpiece is also by Caroto.

Opposite the façade of the church is Sanmicheli's **Porta San Giorgio** (1525), in his town walls, beyond which is a little public garden on the waterfront.

Roman Theatre

On the other side of Ponte Pietra (see above) it is a short walk to the *Roman Theatre (Pl. 4; open 8–13.30 exc. Mon; during the summer drama season, 8–13.30), founded under Augustus and enlarged later. The theatre is in a superb position, built against the steep hillside on the bend of the river. It was first excavated in 1834. The cavea with its rows of seats and the arches that supported them, the scena (a third of its original height), and the two entrances all survive. In the ruins of the cavea is the little church of Santi Siro e Libera (920, altered 14C).

At the back of the theatre a lift gives access to the convent building above, which houses the **archaeological museum**, founded in 1857. The charming little collection includes Hellenistic bronzes, well-preserved glass, sculpture, mosaic fragments, and sepulchral monuments. From the windows are *views of the theatre, and the city beyond.

On the hillside high above the theatre can be seen **Castel San Pietro**, where the Austrians built their barracks on the foundations of a Visconti castle destroyed by the French in 1801.

Rigaste Redentore continues to Vicolo Borgo Tascherio which leads uphill, skirting an old convent wall, to **San Giovanni in Valle** where, in the garden, part of a small cloister survives. The charming interior, rebuilt in the 12C, has a raised presbytery, and the crypt contains two good early Christian sarcophagi (4C).

Santa Maria in Organo

Via San Giovanni in Valle leads back downhill to Via Santa Maria in Organo in which is Santa Maria in Organo (Pl. 4), a church perhaps of 7C foundation which received its present form from Olivetan friars in the late 15C. The very unusual façade is part-early Gothic, part-Renaissance, and the graceful campanile, ascribed to Fra Giovanni da Verona, dates from 1525–33.

The **interior** is frescoed all over: in the nave are Old Testament scenes by Gian Francesco Caroto (right) and Nicolò Giolfino (left), while outside the south transept are works by Caroto, Francesco Torbido and Cavazzola (Annunciation); inside is an altarpiece (Santa Francesca Romana) by Guercino.

From the apse of the north transept (with a delightful Palm Sunday figure of Christ on an ass from the mid-13C, and frescoes by Domenico Brusasorci) is the entrance to the **sacristy**, with exquisite *cupboards*, inlaid by Fra Giovanni da Verona (1519–23). The walls are frescoed with portraits of monks by Francesco Morone. Here has been placed a 14C dossal in local stone of the Madonna and saints, attributed since its recent restoration to Giovanni di Rigino.

In the main apse (unlocked by the sacristan) are *stalls* (inlaid with street scenes and musical instruments), a lectern and a candelabrum, all superb works by Fra Giovanni (1494–1500). The **crypt** (apply to the sacristan) preserves ancient capitals.

The Interrato dell'Acqua Morta continues to **San Tomaso Cantuariense** (St Thomas Becket), with a fine west front and rose window (1493). It contains Sanmicheli's tomb (1884), and a painting by Girolamo dai Libri.

Giusti Gardens

Via Carducci leads away from the river to Via Santa Maria in Organo with the entrance (through a hallway with a wooden ceiling and elaborate lantern) to the celebrated *Giusti Gardens (Pl. 8; No. 2 Via Giardino Giusti; 9–18.30 daily), the 16C green hillside pleasance of the contemporary Palazzo Giusti, praised by Coryat, Evelyn and Goethe. With ancient cypresses, and formal box hedges laid out around fountains and statues, it is beautifully kept. On the right of the cypress avenue is a labyrinth, one of the oldest in Europe, and at the end of the avenue steps lead up to a grotto beneath the rock face, at the top of which is a colossal grotesque mask. Paths lead up left through a small wood to a tower (with a spiral staircase) which gives access to the upper terrace. From the balcony above the mask there is a good view, and paths lead through the little informal garden here with lawns and pines and cypresses. On the left, beyond a locked gate, can be seen the attractive old palace with a loggia, and there is a view of the old town defences above the upper wall of the gardens.

The church of **Santi Nazaro e Celso** (Pl. 8), was built in 1463–84 near the site of a 10C shrine. The **chapel of San Biagio** has a pretty vault over the apse, an altarpiece by Girolamo dai Libri, and interesting frescoes by Bartolomeo Montagna (suffering from humidity). In the **sacristy** is a triptych by Francesco dai Libri, and part of a polyptych by Montagna. The second north altarpiece is the masterpiece of Antonio Badile.

Via XX Settembre leads back towards the river past several good palaces (including Nos. 33 and 35), as well as an amusing Art Nouveau corner house at No. 17. The church of **San Paolo** (Pl. 12) was reconstructed in 1763 and rebuilt after 1944. It contains altarpieces by Girolamo dai Libri, a *Madonna and saints by Veronese, and a high altarpiece by Giovanni Caroto.

Via San Paolo, with more fine palaces, leads to **Ponte Navi**, once a bridge of boats across the Adige. To the left, overlooking the river, is ***Palazzo Pompei** (Pl. 12), a fine early work by Sanmicheli (c 1530) housing the ***Museo Civico di Storia Naturale** (open 8–13.30; fest. 13.30–19; closed Fri), one of the most interesting natural history museums in Italy, beautifully arranged and well labelled. It has extensive collections of fossils found in the locality (1516).

40 · Soave and the Monti Lessini and Valpolicella (the province of Verona)

■ **Information office.** APT Verona, 38 Piazza Erbe (tel. 045 592828). Comunità Montana della Lessinia, 41 Via Cà di Cozzi, Verona (tel. 045 915155).

■ **Hotels. Soave**: 3-star *Regina* (at Castelcerino). **Monti Lessini**: Bosco Chiesanuova has nine hotels. **Valpolicella**: at Pescantina (Ospedaletto), 4-star *Villa Quaranta*; and at San Pietro Incariano (Pedemonte), 4-star *Villa del Quar*. Near **Gargagnago** there is a residence in the *Villa Serego Alighieri*.

The road to Soave from Verona passes the sanctuary of the *__Madonna di Campagna__, at San Michele Extra, a round church with a peristyle, designed by Michele Sanmicheli (1484–1559), who was born in the village, and __Caldiero__, which has hot springs (perhaps the Roman *Fontes Junonis*—two of the thermal pools are Roman).

__SOAVE__ is a pleasant little town (5400 inhab.), famous for its white wine, for which the district has been known for many centuries. Probably the best known Italian white wine, it is made from Garganega grapes in vineyards in a limited geographical area around the town (the estates with wine cellars welcome visitors). A wine festival is held here in September. The impressive battlemented walls, extremely well preserved, were built by the Scaligeri before 1375. In the central Piazza Antenna (named after a mast from which was flown the flag of St Mark) are Palazzo Cavalli, a Venetian Gothic palace of 1411, and Palazzo di Giustizia (1375).

From the piazza, a paved path leads up to the medieval __Castle__ (also reached by road), enlarged by the Scaligeri in 1369. The keep is defended by three courtyards, each on a different level. Privately owned (open 9–12, 15–18.30 exc. Mon), it was restored and partly reconstructed in 1892. The residence has an armoury on the ground floor, and above are rooms with neo-Gothic painted decorations and imitation furniture. There is a fine view from the battlements.

South of Soave is __San Bonifacio__ with the Romanesque abbey of San Pietro Apostolo (1131–39), recently restored.

To the north of Verona are the __MONTI LESSINI__, with the valleys of the Tredici Comuni, a high-lying district occupied by the descendants of Germanic settlers who migrated here in the 13C. Their dialect has practically died out. This pleasant remote area, part of which has been protected since 1990 as a regional park, with cherry trees and woods of chestnut and beech, has been visited for holidays by the Veronese since the begining of the century. There are winter sports facilities in the highest areas (around 1700m). The flint outcrops in the limestone hills were used in the Palaeolithic era for making tools, and remarkable fossils have been found in the volcanic and sedimentary rocks. Some of the houses still have characteristic roofs made out of slabs of stone quarried locally. This stone is also still sometimes used to form drystone walls around fields. __Bosco Chiesanuova__ is the main resort, and it has a museum illustrating the history of Lessinia.

In the central Val Pantena are __Santa Maria in Stelle__, with a Roman hypogeum (underground chamber), __Grezzana__ (Romanesque campanile) and __Stallavena__. Near here the __Riparo Tagliente__, a shelter used by Palaeolithic hunters, has revealed numerous interesting finds.

In the easternmost valley are __Roncà__, with a fossil museum, and __Bolca__, with another museum, famous for its fossilised tropical fish found in the area. The neighbouring Val d'Illasi is known for its wrought-iron craftsmen. Beyond __Illasi__, with two grand 18C villas and a fresco by Stefano da Zevio in the church, is __Cogollo__, with pretty, locally made street lights and a well-known wrought-iron workshop. At the head of the valley is __Giazza__, where a German dialect is still spoken, with a local ethnographical museum.

In a neighbouring valley are __Velo Veronese__, with interesting stone columns in its church, and __Campo Silvano__, which has a tiny geological museum housing a collection of fossils, and an interesting underground limestone cavern, the roof of which has collapsed (admission to both on request).

VALPOLICELLA, in the westernmost part of Lessinia, is a hilly district near a bend in the Adige, famous for its red wine (grown in a specific geographical area). The chief village is **San Pietro in Cariano**, which preserves the old Vicariate, the seat of the Venetian district magistrates. **Sant'Ambrogio** has quarries of 'rosso di Verona' marble. The *church of **San Giorgio** dates from the 7C and has a 13C cloister. At **Volargne** the 15C Villa del Bene (open daily 9–12, 15–18 exc. Mon) has frescoes by Domenico Brusasorci, Giovanni Francesco Caroto and Bernardino India.

At **Negrar** is the 15C Villa Bertoldi. In the valley are numerous cherry trees which blossom in May. To the north are **Sant'Anna d'Alfaedo**, with a museum of prehistory including flints, arrowheads found locally, and fossils (among them a shark 6m long), and **Fosse**, both good walking centres. On the northeast side of the **Corno d'Aquilio** (1545m), above Fosse, is the **Spluga della Preta**, a remarkable pothole in the limestone, which was first descended in 1925. Speleologists have reached a depth of about 1000m.

At **Molina** there is a lovely park with numerous waterfalls and interesting vegetation (open 8 to dusk; apply in the village at the visitors' centre or the trattoria *Du Scalini*). The visit, along marked paths, takes about 2hrs. The botanical museum in the village is to be reopened.

South of Verona is **Villafranca di Verona** which preserves a castle of the Scaligeri (1202) where there is a Risorgimento museum (open at weekends 15.30–18.30). The armistice of Villafranca was concluded here on 11 July 1859 between Napoleon III and Emperor Francis Joseph. To the west is **Valeggio sul Mincio** with another Scaligeri castle (no adm.) and, nearby, the ruins of the fortified Ponte Visconteo (1393) over the Mincio. On the Verona road is the unusual **Parco-Giardino Sigurtà** (open Mar–Nov, Thu, Sat & fest. 9–19), a park of some 50 hectares with gardens accessible only by car (7km of drives, with parking areas near footpaths).

The rest of the province of Verona on Lake Garda is described in Chapter 12.

41 · Treviso

Treviso is a bright and attractive provincial capital (90,400 inhab.) traversed by several branches of the Sile and Cagnan rivers. The canals give it an atmosphere reminiscent of Venice. Many of its narrow streets are lined with arcades and the older houses often overhang the pavement (their exterior frescoes have now mostly disappeared). The streets are decorated with numerous fountains.

■ **Information office**. APT, Palazzo Scotti, 41 Via Toniolo (tel. 0422 547632).

■ **Hotels**. 4-star: *Carlton*, 15 Largo Porta Altinia. 2-star: *Campeol*, 8 Piazza Ancillotto.

- **Restaurants**. **A**: *Alfredo al Toula*, 26 Via Collalto; *Beccherie*, 11 Piazza Ancillotto. **B**: *Osteria Bassanello*, 133 Viale Cairoli; *Toni del Spin*, 7 Via Inferiore. There are numerous *osterie* (wine bars) in the old centre, which serve good snacks.

- **Buses** run from the station to Piazza Indipendenza; also to Mestre and Venice.

- **Airport** (San Giuseppe) for charter flights.

- **Theatre**. *Teatro Comunale*, Corso del Popolo. Music festival in Oct–Jan.

History
In the Middle Ages, Treviso, as capital of the Marca Trevigiana, was well known for its hospitality to poets and artists, especially under the dominion of the Da Camino family (1283–1312). From 1389 to 1796 it was loyal to the the Venetian Republic. During both world wars it suffered severely from air raids, notably on Good Friday 1944, when half the city was destroyed in a few minutes.The city has the best works of Tomaso da Modena, a brilliant follower of Giotto.

PIAZZA DEI SIGNORI is the animated centre of the town. **Palazzo dei Trecento** (restored), the 13C council house, adjoins the **Palazzo del Podestà** rebuilt in antique style in 1874–77. Behind them, in a little cobbled piazza, is the **Monte di Pietà** (open Fri 9–12), with the charming 16C Cappella dei Rettori (works by Ludovico Pozzoserrato, Ludovico Fiumicelli, Sebastiano Florigerio and others). Beyond, through an archway, are two adjoining medieval churches: **Santa Lucia** has good frescoes by Tomaso da Modena and pupils, and a charming balustrade around the altar with half-figures of saints, probably dating from the late 14C; in **San Vito** are Veneto-Byzantine frescoes of the 12C–13C.

Duomo
The Calmaggiore, an arcaded street, leads from Piazza dei Signori to the Duomo, an attractive building founded in the 12C, with seven domes. In the **interior**, in the south aisle, is a relief by Lorenzo Bregno. The **Malchiostro chapel**, added in 1519, has frescoes by Pordenone and assistants, notably the *Adoration of the Magi (1520), and an *Annunciation by Titian. In the vestibule of the chapel are the jambs of the 12C west portal, the *Adoration of the Shepherds by Paris Bordone, the *Madonna del Fiore*, by Girolamo da Treviso il Vecchio (1487), and the tomb of Bishop Castellano (1332).

In the **retro-choir** are frescoes by Lodovico Seitz (1880), the tomb of Pope Alexander VIII (died 1691), with a remarkable portrait-statue by Giovanni Bonazza, and the *monument of Bishop Zanetto (1485), by Antonio and Tullio Lombardo (with the help of their father Pietro). On the **high altar** is the urn of Saints Teonisto, Tabra and Tabrata, with sculpted portraits attributed to Tullio Lombardo. The **chapel of the sacrament** (1501–14) has good sculptures by Giovanni Battista and Lorenzo Bregno. In the vestibule is the *tomb of Bishop Franco (1501). In the **north aisle** are a painting by Francesco Bissolo, and a sculpted St Sebastian by Lorenzo Bregno. The interesting **crypt**, beneath the choir, has 68 columns and fragmentary 14C mosaics. The so-called **baptistery**, a little rectangular church dating from the 12C, contains 13C fresco fragments and a Roman funerary stela (3C AD).

From Piazza Duomo, Via Canoniche leads under an arch to a circular Roman mosaic, an early Christian work of the early 4C AD, probably belonging to a baptistery. Beyond, the Gothic **Canoniche Vecchie** house the **Museo Diocesano d'Arte Sacra** (open Mon–Thu 9–12; Sat 9–12, 15–18) containing archaeological material; two frescoes of the Martyrdom of St Thomas Becket and Christ in Limbo (c 1260); a frescoed lunette by Tomaso da Modena; Romanesque and Gothic sculpture; church silver and vestments; a tapestry of 1500; and 17C and 18C paintings and sculpture.

Via Canova and Borgo Cavour prolong the Calmaggiore to the city wall. In Via Canova a pretty 14C building, enlarged in the 16C, houses the **Museo della Casa Trevigiana**, which has been closed for many years. It contains a collection of decorative arts, including a remarkable display of wrought-iron work, and musical instruments. In the garden (removed from nearby) is the quaint 14C Municipio.

In Borgo Cavour are the **Library** and **MUSEO CIVICO** (open 9–12, 14–17, fest. 9–12; closed Mon). On the **ground floor**, **Room 2** displays remarkable bronze ritual discs (5C BC) from Montebelluna and **Room 1** a unique collection of bronze sword-blades dredged from the Sile and its tributaries (Hallstatt period—7C–6C BC), and Roman, early Christian and Byzantine sculptures.

The **picture gallery** is on the first floor. At the top of stairs is a detached fresco by Giovanni Battista Tiepolo. The chronological display starts in the room to the right (**Room 8**). Here are exhibited sculptures by Pietro Lombardo, and paintings by Giovanni Bellini and Cima da Conegliano. **Room 9** contains works by Girolamo da Treviso and Girolamo da Santacroce. **Room 10**. Works by Paris Bordone. **Room 11**. Portraits by Titian (including Sperone Speroni) and Lorenzo Lotto (a *Dominican), and a Crucifixion by Jacopo Bassano. **Room 12**. Pordenone. **Room 13**. Frescoes attributed to Benedetto and Carletto Caliari.

In the group of rooms beyond (across the stair landing) are exhibited **16C–18C works** by Salvatore Rosa, Pietro Muttoni, Pozzoserrato (*Fire in the Doges' Palace in 1577*), Borgognone, Flemish and German painters, Giuseppe Cignaroli, Antonio Molinari, Giuseppe Zais, Francesco Guardi, Gian Domenico Tiepolo, Pietro Longhi and Rosalba Carriera.

In the last group of rooms off the stair landing is a large collection of **19C and 20C works** including paintings by Guglielmo Ciardi (1842–1917), and a good group of sculptures and charcoal drawings by the native artist Arturo Martini (1889–1947), including *La Pisana* (1930). The portrait of Canova is by Sir Thomas Lawrence.

The museum also owns the prisms with which Newton made his experiments with the refraction of light, and which passed into the hands of his disciple Count Algarotti.

At the end of the street is **Porta dei Santi Quaranta**, a town gate of 1517. To the north is the most interesting stretch of city wall, built by Fra Giocondo and

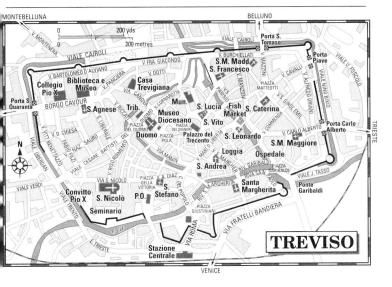

others in 1509–18, the top of which has been laid out as a pleasant walk almost as far as Porta San Tomaso, another fine gateway. The wall itself is better seen from the gardens outside.

In the southwest district is the large Dominican church of *SAN NICOLÒ*, built in brick in the 13C–14C, with a fine triple polygonal apse. The massive columns inside are frescoed with *saints by Tomaso da Modena (St Agnes, on the north side, is especially charming). On the south wall the 15C altars have good decoration. The huge fresco of St Christopher (1410) is attributed to Antonio da Treviso.

In the **apse** is an *altarpiece by Marco Pensaben and Savoldo (1521). On the right is a memorial (1693) to the great Dominican pope St Benedict XI (Nicolò Bocassino, 1240–1303), born in Treviso and the founder of the church. The tomb of Agostino d'Onigo (c 1500) has sculptures by Antonio Rizzo, and *Pages, frescoed by Lorenzo Lotto. The altarpiece in the chapel to the right of the high altar has portraits of members of the Monigo commission attributed to Lotto. On the walls are frescoes by the Sienese and Riminese schools (c 1370). The chapel to the left of the presbytery has an altarpiece by Giovanni Battista Bregno. The 16C organ by Gaetano Callido was decorated by Antonio Palma.

A door leads into the cloister of the adjoining **Seminario** (open 8–12.30, 15.30–17.30 or 19) where the chapterhouse contains delightful *frescoes of 40 leading Dominicans, by Tomaso da Modena (1352). There is also an ethnographical museum open fest. (9–12).

In Via Martiri della Libertà, leading northeast from the Corso, is the **Loggia dei Cavalieri**, a Romanesque building of 1195. Near San Leonardo, beyond remains of an old watermill beneath a modern building, is the picturesque **Fishmarket** on an island in the Cagnan. Via San Parisio continues left to **San Francesco**, a large brick church of the 13C. In the floor near the south door is the tomb slab of Francesca, daughter of Petrarch, who died in childbirth in 1384; in the north transept that of Pietro Alighieri (died 1364), the son of Dante; and in the chapel to the left of the high altar is a fresco by Tomaso da Modena (1351).

The deconsecrated church of **Santa Caterina** (open Fri, Sat & Sun 9–12, 15.30–18.30) stands a little to the east of the Fishmarket. It contains fine frescoes by Tomaso da Modena, including some detached in 1882 from a church before its demolition (the Virgin Annunciate and *Story of the Life of St Ursula).

Via Carlo Alberto leads to **Santa Maria Maggiore**, a church of 1474 containing a tomb by Bambaia and a much-venerated Madonna originally frescoed by Tomaso da Modena. The delightful Riviera Garibaldi (reminiscent of Amsterdam), alongside the Sile, returns towards the centre.

42 · The province of Treviso

The province of Treviso has a number of small towns of the highest interest, and some Palladian villas open to the public.

■ **Information offices. Asolo**: APT, Villa De Mattia, 258 Via Santa Caterina (tel. 0423 529046). **Conegliano**: APT, 45 Via Colombo (tel. 0438 21230). **Vittorio Veneto**: APT, 18 Piazza del Popolo (tel. 0438 57243). **Oderzo**: APT, Piazza Castello (tel. 0422 815251).

■ **Hotels. Castelfranco Veneto**: 3-star: *Roma*, 39 Via Filzi. **Asolo**: 4-star: *Villa Cipriani*, 298 Via Canova; *Duse*, 190 Via Browning. **Conegliano**: 3-star: *Canon d'Oro*, 129 Via XX Settembre.

At **Istrana**, west of Treviso on the Castelfranco road, the 18C Villa Lattes, now part of the Museo Civico of Treviso (open Tue & Fri 9–12; Sat & fest. 9–12, 15–18; closed Dec–Feb), has a collection of furniture, oriental art, musical boxes, 19C dolls, etc.

CASTELFRANCO VENETO (26,200 inhab.) was founded in 1199 by Treviso as a bulwark against Padua. It was the birthplace of the painter Giorgione (c 1478–1510). The old town, or **Castello**, is surrounded by a moat and a battlemented brick wall, one tower of which serves as a belfry, and the north gate of which is the **Torre Civica**. In the centre is the neo-classical **Cathedral** by Francesco Maria Preti, which contains a famous *Madonna and Child with saints (c 1500), generally attributed to Giorgione. In the sacristy are frescoes by Veronese. The so-called **Casa del Giorgione** (open Tue–Sun 9–12, 15–18) contains a small museum and a chiaroscuro frieze on the first floor thought to be by Giorgione. The 18C **Teatro Accademico**, also by Francesco Maria Preti, in Via Garibaldi (usually open weekdays 9–13, 14–18), has been restored. The lovely park of **Villa Revedin-Bolasco**, with 17C statues, in Borgo Treviso, is open to the public.

Outside the town at **Sant'Andrea**, the **Villa Corner** (now Chiminelli; open by appointment, tel. 0424 525103) has frescoes of the school of Veronese.

ASOLO is a charming little town, with numerous private villas surrounded by luxuriant gardens, and picturesque old streets with miniature arcades and a number of fountains. A bus ascends to the centre of the little town from the main road (bus stop) and car park.

The town was presented by Venice to Queen Caterina Cornaro in exchange for her dominions of Cyprus and she lived in the castle here from 1489 to 1509. From the name of this town Cardinal Bembo(who frequented Queen Catherine's court) coined the term 'asolare' (to gambol, amuse oneself at random), from which is derived 'Asolando', the name chosen by Robert Browning 'for love of the place' for his last volume of poems (1899). Browning's first visit to Asolo was in 1836, and it is the scene of *Pippa Passes*, published five years later. The actress Eleonora Duse (1850–1924), and Browning's son Pen (1849–1912) are both buried at Asolo in the cemetery of Sant'Anna. Dame Freya Stark (1893–1993), the traveller and writer, lived here for most of her life. An annual chamber music festival is held in Sep (normally in the Teatro Duse, but in San Gottardo while the theatre is being restored—see below).

By the entrance gate to the town is **La Mura**, a palace where Browning stayed on his second visit to the town and where Eleonora Duse later lived. On the right, preceded by a little garden, is the **Villa Freia** where Freya Stark lived (the house is now owned by the province). Nearby is a weaving school founded in 1840 and later run by Freya Stark's mother (usually open Mon–Sat 8–12, 16–19).

Via Browning, with delightful little arcades along one side, continues from the gate past another house where Browning stayed (plaque) to **Piazza Brugnoli**, overlooked by the grandiose **Villa Scotti**, with its impressive terraced garden. Below the piazza is the **Duomo**, rebuilt in 1747 on remains of Roman baths. It contains a copy of Titian's *Martyrdom of St Laurence*, a baptismal font by Francesco Graziolo donated to the church by Caterina Cornaro, two angels by Torretti, and two paintings of the Assumption by Jacopo Bassano (1549) and Lorenzo Lotto (1506; with an interesting predella).

The 15C **Loggia del Capitano**, with a façade frescoed by Antonio Contarini (1560), houses the **Museo Civico** (closed for restoration).

Just out of the piazza are the remains of the **Castle** where Caterina Cornaro lived (before she moved downhill to the larger Barco at Attivole). It incorporates the **Teatro Duse** which was sold to America at the beginning of this century but is now being reconstructed. At present only the battlements of the castle may be visited. Part of the large garden which surrounded the castle was purchased by Browning (despite local opposition) so that he could construct here the Villa La Torricella (in Via Sottocastello) for his son Pen. The empty **Rocca**, above the town, is open on weekends: there are fine views from the ramparts. It can be reached by a pleasant path which follows the walls from Porta Colmarion (or by car from Via Rocca). On the hills surrounding Asolo are some pretty villas with lovely gardens, including Villa Armena.

At **Maser** in a lovely setting at the foot of the hills of Asolo, is the ***Villa Barbaro** (now Villa Luling Buschetti), built by Palladio in the late 1550s for Daniele Barbaro, patriarch of Aquileia. The interior (open Tue, Sat & fest. 15–18; Nov–Feb, Sat & fest. 14.30–17) contains beautiful *frescoes (1560–62) by Veronese and stuccoes by Alessandro Vittoria. In the grounds are a nymphaeum, and a carriage museum. The little 'tempietto', a private chapel built on a centralised plan, was one of Palladio's last works (1580).

Possagno was the birthplace of the sculptor Antonio Canova (1757–1822).

His house and a museum of models and plaster casts of his works is open 9–12, 14 or 15–17 or 18 exc. Mon. The Tempio, now the parish church, was designed by Canova as his burial place.

At **Biadene**, in a deconsecrated church, a fresco has recently been attributed to Giovanni Battista Tiepolo (thought to be his earliest work in fresco).

****Villa Emo** at **Fanzolo** is open Tue, Sat & fest. 15–19; Oct–Mar, Sat & fest. 14–18. Built by Palladio (1550–60), it has frescoes by Giovanni Battista Zelotti, and a fine park.

At **Ponte della Priula**, due north of Treviso, is a votive temple commemorating the Battle of the Piave, where in 1918 the Italians withstood the last Austro-Hungarian attack and launched their successful counter-offensive. There are British war cemeteries at Tezze and Giavera.

CONEGLIANO is a wine-growing town (31,500 inhab.), noted also as the birthplace of the painter Giovanni Battista Cima (c 1459–1518), and has many attractive 16C–18C houses (notably in Via XX Settembre). The **Casa di Cima** (24 Via Cima; open Sat and Sun 16 or 17–18 or 19) has an archive dedicated to the painter. The **Cathedral** (14C–15C) contains a fine altarpiece by Cima (1492); the adjacent guildhall ('Scuola dei Battuti'; open 9.30–12, 15–19 exc. Wed) is covered with 16C frescoes attributed to Pozzoserrato, and inside are frescoes by Andrea Previtali, Jacopo da Montagnana, Francesco da Milano and Gerolamo da Treviso. In the main piazza is the neo-classical **Theatre** (1846–68). Above rises the ruined **Castello**, with a museum in one tower (open 8 or 9–12, 14 or 15.30–17.30 or 19 exc. Mon), and the Oratorio di Sant'Orsola.

VITTORIO VENETO (30,800 inhab.) was the town that gave its name to the final victory of the Italians over the Austrians in October 1918. It was created in 1866 by merging the lower (now industrial) district of Ceneda with the old walled town of ****Serravalle**. Ceneda has a museum relating to the battle (open 10–12, 15 or 16–17 or 18; closed Mon and Fri) in the former Town Hall (1537–38). In Serravalle, in the fine main piazza, is the **Loggia di Serravalle** (1462), the old town hall, with the **Museo del Canedese**, which contains local archaeological finds, paintings, frescoes, etc. (open 15–18; in winter 9–12; Sat and fest. 9–12, 15–17.30). The 14C **Duomo** (rebuilt in 1776) contains a fine altarpiece by Titian (1547). In the church of **San Giovanni Battista** (1357) are 15C frescoes (some attributed to Jacobello del Fiore), and in **Santa Giustina** the good tomb (1336–40) of Rizzardo IV da Camino.

Above Vittorio Veneto is the **Bosco del Cansiglio**, a high-lying plateau with forests of beech and fir (1120m) to the east. There is a natural history museum here (open in summer).

Oderzo was the Roman *Opitergium*, finds from which are exhibited in the Museo Civico (8–13, 15–18; Sat 10–12; closed Mon). The Duomo, founded in the 10C, was rebuilt in Gothic style in the 14C.

43 · Feltre and Belluno

■ **Information office.** APT di Belluno, Feltre, Alpago, 21 Via Psaro, Belluno (tel. 0437 940083).

■ **Hotels. Feltre**: 4-star: *Doriguzzi*, 2 Viale del Piave; 3-star: *Nuovo*, 5 Via Fornere Pazze. **Belluno**: 3-star: *Astor*, 26 Piazza Mariti, *Delle Alpi*, 13 Via Tasso; *Alle Dolomiti*, 46 Via Carrera. **2-star**: *Sole*, 11 Piazzale Marconi. In the environs: 4-star: *Villa Carpenada*, 158 Via Mier.

■ **Restaurants. Feltre**: *Osteria Novecento*, 24 Via Mezzaterra (**B**). **Belluno**: *Terracotta*, 61 Borgo Garibaldi (**C**).

FELTRE is an attractive upland town (19,700 inhab.) which was largely rebuilt after being sacked in 1510. Gateways survive at either end of the old main street in which external frescoes by the local early 16C painter Lorenzo Luzzo and his pupils decorate many houses, including the painter's own. Midway along Via Mezzaterra opens *PIAZZA MAGGIORE, with the **Castle**, the 19C **Palazzo Guarnieri**, and the 16C **Palazzo della Ragione** with a Palladian loggia (1558). Inside is a little wooden **theatre** rebuilt by Gian Antonio Selva in 1802. A 16C fountain by Tullio Lombardo stands in the forecourt of **San Rocco** (1599).

The **Museo Rizzarda** (open in summer 10–13, 16–19 exc. Mon) has a collection of superb wrought-iron work by Carlo Rizzarda left by him to the town in 1929. The **Museo Civico** (closed for restoration), contains Roman and Etruscan remains, a portrait by Gentile Bellini, a triptych by Cima da Conegliano, and works by the local artists Pietro de Marescalchi and Lorenzo Luzzo. The masterpiece of Luzzo (a Transfiguration) is in the sacristy of **Ognissanti**.

Piazza Maggiore

From Piazza Maggiore a 16C stairway descends to the Porta Pusterla (1494) and to the **Cathedral**, which has a 15C apse and a campanile of 1392, heightened in 1690. It contains works by Pietro de Marescalchi, and the tomb of Matteo Bellati designed by Tullio Lombardo (1528). A carved Byzantine cross of 542 also belongs to the church. Near the Renaissance baptistery have been found remains of the early Christian baptistery (the excavations are open in summer on Sat & Sun 10–13, 16–19).

On the outskirts of the town is **Santi Vittore e Corona**, an interesting

Romanesque church of 1100 beside a 15C monastery. **Pedavena**, north of Feltre, noted for its beer, is a climbing centre. The 17C **Villa Pasole** here has an interesting little garden (open Sun 10–17 by appointment).

Feltre is separated from Belluno by the **valley of the Piave**, in which is **Lentiai** with a fine church containing paintings by the Vecellio family, perhaps including Titian himself.

BELLUNO is an old provincial capital (34,400 inhab.) in a splendid position above the junction of the Ardo and the Piave rivers. Its large province takes in Feltre, as well as Agordo, the Cadore and Cortina d'Ampezzo (see Chapter 44). The **Duomo** by Tullio Lombardo (16C), was partly rebuilt after earthquakes in 1873 and 1936. The campanile is by Filippo Juvarra. In Piazza del Duomo are the **town hall** (1838) and **Palazzo dei Rettori**, a Renaissance building of 1492–96, to the right of which are the old town belfry and the **Museo Civico** (open Apr–Oct exc. Mon 10–12, 15–18), in a building of 1664. It has a good collection of paintings by Sebastiano Ricci, born here in 1659. In Piazza del Mercato, with a fountain of 1410 is the **Monte di Pietà** (1531).

Off Via Mezzaterra, the main street of the old town, Vicolo San Pietro leads (left) to the church of **San Pietro**. It contains carved panels by Andrea Brustolon, a high-altarpiece by Sebastiano Ricci, and paintings by Andrea Schiavone. **Porto Rugo** (12C; restored 1622) has a splendid view of the Piave valley and the Dolomites.

Santo Stefano is a fine Gothic church of 1468. It contains frescoes by Jacopo da Montagnana (c 1487) and a beautiful wooden altarpiece attributed to the Cesa, a local 16C family of sculptors.

To the east of Belluno is the hilly region of **Alpago** with a number of small resorts, including **Tambre** on the edge of the Cansiglio forest.

The **Alpe del Nevegal** (1030m), south of Belluno, is a ski resort (chair-lift to the Rifugio Brigata Alpina Cadore,1600m), with a botanical garden nearby.

Northwest of Belluno is the **Lago di Mis**, at the foot of the wild and rugged **Canale del Mis**, in an area of the Dolomites which may one day become part of the Parco Nazionale delle Dolomiti Bellunesi.

Longarone, north of Belluno, has been reconstructed after it was almost totally wiped out by a disastrous flood in 1963 when a landslide from Monte Toc (1921m) into the basin of the Vaiont dam caused a huge water displacement to sweep through the Piave valley, destroying five villages and killing 1908 people. A definitive sentence in 1997 found the hydroelectric company guilty and responsible for damages of over 55,000 million lire. The parish church (1966–76) was designed by Giovanni Michelucci.

44 · The Dolomites

■ **Information office.** APT Dolomiti, 8 Piazzetta San Francesco, Cortina d'Ampezzo (tel. 0436 3231).

■ **Hotels. Cortina d'Ampezzo** has numerous hotels of all categories. Other resorts well supplied with hotels include **San Vito di Cadore**, **Pieve di Cadore**, **Santo Stefano di Cadore**, **Sappada** and **Auronzo**.

The **Cadore** is the mountainous district surrounding the upper valley of the Piave and its western tributaries. The dolomitic mountain peaks of Marmarole (2932m), Sorapiss (3205m), Antelao (3263m) and Monte Cristallo (3221m) are among the most impressive of the Dolomites. Until 1918 only the south-eastern half of the district was Italian territory and there was heavy mountain fighting during the First World War on the old frontier-line. It now borders to the north on Trentino-Alto Adige and Austria. The Cadorini still speak Ladino, a Romance language, with Ladino-Venetian dialects in the lower valleys; but German is understood everywhere from Cortina northwards. The area is much visited for skiing and mountaineering.

PIEVE DI CADORE (878m), the chief town of the Cadore, is now a summer and winter resort beneath the southern foothills of the Marmarole. The Palazzo della Magnifica Comunità Cadorina (open in summer 9–12, 15–19), rebuilt in 1525, contains a small archaeological museum. Outside is a statue by Antonio Dal Zotto (1880) of the painter Titian who was born here c 1488. His modest birthplace has a small museum (adm. in summer 9–12, 15 or 16–19; closed Mon; ring in winter). In the parish church there is a Madonna with Saints by Titian. The 'Casa di Babbo Natale' on the hillside of Montericco receives Italian mail addressed to Father Christmas.

CORTINA D'AMPEZZO (1210m at the church) is the most important holiday resort (8500 inhab.), both in winter and summer, in the eastern Dolomites. Some of the large hotels were built in the mid-19C, and since the 1920s Cortina has been one of the most fashionable ski resorts in Europe. It lies in a sunny upland basin, and the view of the mountains on all sides is magnificent. A museum contains works by Filippo De Pisis (1896–1956), who often stayed in Cortina, and other modern Italian painters. Aldous Huxley wrote much of *Point Counter Point* here in 1926–27.

The spectacular road across the Dolomites to Canazei and Bolzano was built by the Austrians in 1901–09. The **Lago di Misurina** (1737m), northeast of Cortina, is one of the most beautifully situated lakes in the Dolomites.

In the southern Dolomites are the **Dolomiti Agordine**, visited especially by mountaineers and hikers, with the resort of **Agordo**.

Friuli-Venezia Giulia

Friuli-Venezia Giulia, at the northeastern corner of the Adriatic, consists of the provinces of Udine, Trieste, Pordenone and Gorizia. The Friuli (now in the province of Udine) was under the patriarchate of Aquileia until 1420 when, with the mountainous country of Carnia to the north and the city of Aquileia itself, it was absorbed into the Venetian Republic. Trieste, as an independent commune under her bishops, remained a rival of Venice for the seaborne trade of the Adriatic. At certain periods, Trieste—with the help of the counts of Gorizia or the dukes of Austria—held the upper hand, but on more than one occasion the Venetians captured the port. Although the Istrian coast for the most part came under Venetian influence, the hinterland and Gorizia belonged to the vassals of Austria. In the war against Austria in 1507–16 the Venetians at first made important conquests, but outside intervention forced them to withdraw their frontier west of Aquileia. Throughout the 16C, disturbed conditions on the Istrian coast were fomented by the raids of Liburnian pirates (from modern-day Croatia), nominally subject to Austria, and the power of Venice diminished. The outcome of the Napoleonic Wars here was the short-lived Kingdom of Illyria, which extended from the Isonzo to Croatia, but was shattered in 1813–14 by an Austrian army and a British fleet; and from 1815 to 1918 the whole region fell under Austro-Hungarian dominion. In the First World War prolonged and fierce fighting took place in the region between the valleys of the Isonzo and the Piave, the Italians ultimately achieving success with the aid of the British and French detachments. The frontier was extended east and south to include the whole of Istria (including Fiume, after much negotiation), with the adjacent isles and Dalmatian Zara.

In 1945 Allied forces met Marshal Tito's Yugoslav forces at Cividale del Friuli and Monfalcone; and the New Zealanders arrived at Trieste, where the occupying German force surrendered to General Freyberg. Italian and Yugoslav claims to the liberated territory came at once into conflict, and the administration of Trieste, which had been occupied by the Yugoslavs, was taken over by Allied Military Government. All territory east of the so-called 'French Line' was ceded by Italy to Yugoslavia, the ceded areas including the eastern suburbs of Gorizia and all Istria south of Cittanova. The region around Trieste, including the coast from Monfalcone to Cittanova with a portion of the hinterland, was established as a free territory, neutral and demilitarised, by the Treaty of Paris in 1947. At the same time the province of Udine was transferred from the Veneto to Venezia Giulia and the new region, under the title Friuli-Venezia Giulia, was granted special measures of autonomy. A more rational adjustment of the frontier at Gorizia was made in 1952, and in 1954 Trieste finally returned to Italian rule while the remainder of Istria was incorporated into Yugoslavia (now Slovenia).

45 · Trieste

Trieste (229,000 inhab.) is the capital of the region of Friuli-Venezia Giulia as well as the capital of a small province. In a gulf backed by the low rolling hills of the Carso, it is the most important seaport of the northern Adriatic, although its commercial traffic has diminished in recent years. For many centuries part of the Austrian empire, it retains something of the old-fashioned atmosphere of a Mitteleuropean city. Regular spacious streets were laid out around the Canal Grande at the end of the 18C when the city flourished under the enlightened rule of the Habsburg empress Maria Teresa. Its numerous monumental neo-classical and Art Nouveau buildings date from the 19C and early 20C. Now on the borders of Slovenia, the town is increasingly looking towards eastern Europe for commercial outlets. An icy cold wind (the bora) can blow northeast across the Carso plateau through the town in some seasons.

■ **Information office.** APT di Trieste, 20 Via San Nicolò (tel. 040 6796111). Information Office at the central railway station. Regional Tourist Board for Friuli-Venezia Giulia: Azienda Regionale per la Promozione Turistica, 6 Via G. Rossini (tel. 040 365152).

■ **Hotels.** 4-star: *Savoy Excelsior Palace*, 4 Riva Mandracchio; 3-star: *Milano*, 17 Via Ghega; *Nuovo Hotel Impero*, 1 Via Sant'Anastasio; *Colombia*, 18 Via della Geppa. 2-star: *Al Teatro*, 1 Piazza Bartoli. On the outskirts: 3-star: *San Giusto*, 3 Via Belli. **Youth Hostel**: *Tergeste*, in a lovely position on the sea at Miramare (bus 36 from the station). **Camping sites** open in summer (4-star) at Sistiana and Opicina.

■ **Restaurants. A**: *Suban*, 2 Via Comici; **B**: *Primo* (near San Niccolò); *Ai Fiori*, 7 Piazza Hortis; *Trieste Mia*, Piazza Silvio Benco (for fish). **C**: *Birreria Forst*, 11 Via Galatti. There are many small fish restaurants on the Riva. In the Carso, on the Slovenian border, there are a number of simple *osterie* (*gostilna*). From Apr to Sep excellent inexpensive meals (eaten outside) are provided by farm trattorie (known as *ozmizze*) in the Carso, especially in the area northeast of the city. **Cafés**: San Marco, Via Battisti 18; *Tommaseo*, 5 Riva III Novembre; *Degli Specchi*, Piazza dell'Unità; *Pirona*, 12 Largo Barriera Vecchia. **Cake Shops**: *Penso*, Via Cadorna; *La Bomboniera*, off Via San Niccolò. **Picnic places** on the hill of San Giusto. Shops are closed all day Mon.

■ **Car parking** in the centre of the town is particularly difficult; best on the Rive or on the hill of San Giusto. Multi-storey car park ('Sì silos') beside the station.

■ **Airport** at Ronchi, 35km northwest. Terminal at the railway station (coach takes 60 mins). Daily services to the principal European cities.

■ **Buses** depart from Piazza Oberdan to Miramare, Duino, etc; and from the main bus station in Piazza della Libertà to Muggia, Sistiana and Slovenia. **Rack tramway** from Piazza Oberdan to Opicina.

■ **Maritime services** for Greece (Anek lines, 4 Piazza Tommaseo, tel. 040 364386), and Turkey. **Boat tours** of the port and gulf by motor launch are organised in summer from Riva del Mandracchio.

■ **Theatres.** *Politeama Rossetti*, Viale XX Settembre. *Teatro Comunale Giuseppe Verdi* and *Sala Tripcovich*, Piazza Verdi (opera season in Nov–Mar, concerts in May and Oct, and international operetta festival in summer). Open-air theatre performances (Jul–Aug) in the Castle.

■ **Annual festivals.** 'Barcolana' on the 2nd Sun in Oct, a European regatta in which some 1000 boats take part. Antiques market during the first ten days of Nov.

■ **Honorary British Consul**, Vicolo delle Ville 16 (tel. 040 302884).

History
The settlement of *Tergeste*, already an important outlet into the Adriatic for the produce of the middle Danube and its tributaries, was absorbed into the Roman dominion early in the 2C BC. From the 9C to the 13C the city was ruled by its bishops. Rivalry with Venice for the commerce of the Adriatic began at the beginning of the 13C, with the rise of the independent Commune of Trieste, and continued for many centuries. In 1382 Trieste came under the protection of the Austrian Emperor Leopold III, and in 1463 the city was saved by Pius II from a Venetian blockade; it was then rebuilt by Frederick III. Charles VI declared Trieste a free port in 1719, and it flourished under the rule of Maria Teresa (1740–80). Despite the increased prosperity brought about by the opening of the Suez Canal (1869), Trieste became the centre of Irredentism, and the desire for liberation from Austrian rule was fulfilled when Italian troops entered Trieste in 1918 and the city, together with the Carso and Istria, was ceded to Italy by treaty in 1920. These territories fell in 1945 to Yugoslav forces and the Carso was incorporated into Yugoslavia. By the Italian peace treaty of 1947 Trieste and Istria were created a Free Territory, with Anglo-American trusteeship of the city and a Yugoslav zone in Istria, until in 1954 the existing frontier was agreed at a further four-power conference. Trieste remains a free port.

Literary associations
The traveller and writer Sir Richard Burton was consul here from 1872 until his death in 1890. At the Albergo Obelisco in Villa Opicina he completed the translation of the *Thousand and one Nights*. James Joyce (1882–1941) lived in the city in 1904–15 and 1919–20, with his wife Nora Barnacle, and their two children were born here. They lived at No. 4 Via Donato Bramante (near Piazza Vico, on the far side of the hill of San Giusto) where Joyce wrote part of *Ulysses*. While here he befriended the native writer Italo Svevo (Aron Hector Schmitz; 1861–1928). The poet Umberto Saba (Umberto Poli; 1883–1957) was also born in Trieste.

The centre of the city

The life of Trieste centres on the handsome PIAZZA DELL'UNITÀ D'ITALIA, open to the sea, with pretty old fashioned lamp-standards and tall flagstaffs, laid out at the end of the 19C by Giuseppe Bruni. Facing the sea is **Palazzo Comunale** built by Bruni in 1875. On the left is **Palazzo del Governo** (1904–05) by the Austrian architect Emil Artmann, and on the right the huge offices built in 1883 by the Austrian Heinrich Ferstel for the **Lloyd Triestino Shipping Company**, founded in 1830. The **Caffè degli Specchi**, one of the city's famous cafés, was established in the square in 1840.

The **harbour** is fronted by the broad quay, or Riva. The name of Riva Mandracchio is derived from *mandraki*—in Greek 'sheepfold'—which often denotes an ancient galley port (as at Rhodes, Kos, and also Hvar). On the seafront is the neo-classical Greek Orthodox church of **San Nicolò**. The **Molo Audace** commemorates the name of the destroyer from which the first Italian troops landed on 3 November 1918 to liberate the city from Austrian rule. On the Molo Bersaglieri, the former maritime station (1930) is now a congress centre.

Behind the neo-classical **Teatro Verdi**, opened in 1801, is the triangular Piazza della Borsa, with the **Tergesteo** (1840), a neo-classical building, and the Borsa Vecchia (1806, by Antonio Molari). A bronze statue of Leopold I (1673) faces up the busy CORSO ITALIA, the main street with elegant shops.

The Cittavecchia and hill of San Giusto

To the west of Piazza dell'Unità d'Italia is the dwindling area of the **Cittavecchia**, the old town, the heart of which is now PIAZZA CAVANA, partly demolished and partly abandoned. Only a few buildings here have been restored, despite the fact money has been made available to carry out some of the work. To the east, in Via del Teatro Romano, demolitions in 1938 revealed the remains of a **Roman Theatre** endowed in the late 1C by a certain Q. Petronius Modestus. Behind the theatre rises the hill of San Giusto, reached by narrow lanes and and two flights of steps up to Androna dei Gricioni. Here is the little Evangelical and Waldensian church of **San Silvestro** (open Thu and Sat 10–12, Sun at 11) with an 11C exterior. Beside it is the Baroque church of **Santa Maria Maggiore**, begun in 1627, with an unusual façade, and an altar-piece attributed to Francesco Maffei.

To the right of San Silvestro, in an area of half demolished and derelict buildings, is the **Arco di Riccardo**, a remarkably well preserved vaulted Roman arch erected in honour of Augustus in AD 33; its name survives from the traditional belief that Richard I was imprisoned here after his return from the Holy Land. It served as a city gate and one side is now supported by a house. To the right is the busy Piazza Barbacan on the corner of which is the fine neo-classical **Casa Panzera** (by Matteo Pertsch, 1818), with a curving façade.

Via della Cattedrale leads steeply uphill past another derelict house (keep right), and there is a view, looking back, of the port. An attractive short avenue lined with trees continues up to San Giusto (its façade visible at the top of the hill), past (No. 15), the **MUSEO CIVICO DI STORIA ED ARTE** (open 9–13 exc. Mon), which has been undergoing rearrangement for years: only the archaeological section of the museum is at present displayed here. In the garden is the Roman **lapidarium**. Also here is the cenotaph of the archaeologist J.J.

Winckelmann (1717–68), who was murdered at Trieste under the assumed name of 'Signor Giovanni' by a thief whose cupidity he had excited by displaying some ancient gold coins. The chapel has recently been restored and contains Greek and Roman inscriptions.

On the ground floor of the **museum** are statues from the Roman Theatre, and a room of Egyptian and Gandhara material. Upstairs are prehistoric finds from the Carso and upper Isonzo valley, and Roman material (glass, small bronzes). The other sections of the museum (at present closed) contain Greek red-figure and black-figure vases; finds from Tarentum (5C BC) including a silver-gilt *rhyton, in the form of a deer's head, and a bronze *wine-vessel; and some 250 drawings by Tiepolo.

The avenue continues up to the top of the hill, and with fine views out to sea. The *CATHEDRAL OF SAN GIUSTO (closed 12–15) is a venerable building of irregular plan and in several styles. Between the 5C and the 11C two aisled basilicas were built here, one dedicated to San Giusto, the other (smaller) dedicated to Santa Maria Assunta. A third Romanesque church, to the left, is now the baptistery. In the 14C the two larger churches were made into one and dedicated to Justus, a Christian martyr who was thrown into the sea during Diocletian's persecution.

Exterior. The irregular *façade incorporates five Roman Corinthian columns and Roman friezes in its projecting campanile (1337), and the pillars of the main doorway are fragments of a Roman tomb, with six busts. Above the latter are three modern busts of bishops of Trieste (including Pope Pius II) and a splendid rose-window. Over the campanile door is a 14C statue of St Justus.

Interior. The nave is made up of the north aisle of San Giusto and the south aisle of the Assunta and has a 14C roof. The **central apse**, disfigured in 1842, has a mosaic by Guido Cadorin (1932). The two aisles on the right preserve the dome of San Giusto and in the first south chapel is a small carved polychrome *Pietà (early 15C). The **south apse** has a 13C *mosaic of Christ between St Justus and St Servulus upon a gold ground with a beautifully decorated border. Below is preserved the old choir-bench and some pretty little Byzantine columns with 6C capitals, between which are very worn early 13C frescoes of the Life of St Justus. In the little side apse to the right are more very worn frescoes, and a finely carved 9C pluteus with doves. In the main nave can be seen fragments of the original old polychrome mosaic pavement. In the **north apse** is a splendid 12C *mosaic of the Veneto-Ravenna school with the Madonna enthroned between two Archangels above the Apostles, with another beautifully decorated border. In the side apse to the left is a sculptured wooden group of the Pietà (16C). Next to this is the **treasury**, protected by a fine iron gate (1650), with remains of 15C frescoes. Here are preserved a 13C painting on silk of St Giusto, a cross donated to the church in 1383, and precious reliquaries.

Off the north aisle, an inconspicuous door (above which is a Madonna and Saints by Benedetto Carpaccio, 1540) leads into the **baptistery**, which has a 9C immersion font, and five frescoes detached from the south apse, illustrating the life of St Giusto (1350), in good condition.

In the piazza outside is a column of 1560, and at the end of a cypress avenue is an impressive **war memorial** of 1935 by Attilio Selva. Above rises the castle, in front of which are the paved floor and column bases of a large **Roman basilica**

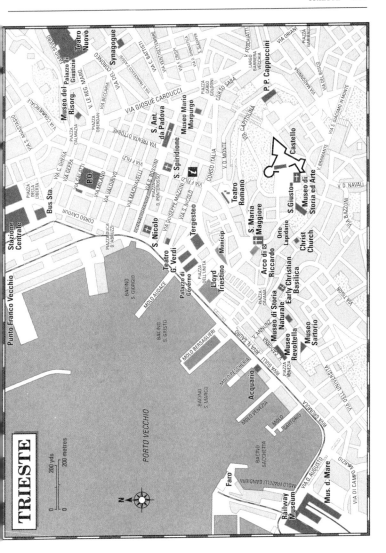

of c AD 100. The 15C–16C **CASTLE** (open during daylight hours), approached by a little drawbridge, was begun by the Venetians in 1368 and later altered and enlarged by the Austrians. In summer plays are given in the courtyard. To the right of the atrium is the Cappella di San Giorgio with a wooden 15C statue of the saint. The castle contains part of the **Museo Civico** (open 9–13 exc. Mon). A staircase, rebuilt in the 1930s, leads up to the **Sala Veneta**, which is the reconstruction of a 17C room in a private palace with its furniture and 16C Flemish tapestries. The good wooden ceiling has a painted allegory of Venice by Andrea Celesti. More stairs lead up to the (covered) battlements with a large collection of arms. The old kitchen and a loggia can also be visited here. From the courtyard near the entrance (see above) there is access to the walkways above the ramparts from which there are good views of the entire city.

The Città Nuovo (Borgo Teresiano)

The centre of the 18C–19C district of the city, which was laid out during the rule of Maria Teresa, is the **Canal Grande**, designed as a harbour and now used by small boats. At its north end in PIAZZA SANT'ANTONIO (formed by filling in part of the canal) stands the large neo-classical church of **Sant'Antonio** (1827–47, by Pietro Nobile), with an impressive interior. The Serbian church of **San Spiridione** also has a fine interior (1869, by Carlo Maciachini and Pietro Palese). A daily market is held in Piazza Ponterosso on the canal.

The Canal Grande

Via Dante leads past an elaborate building (No. 6) with balconies and statues, to Piazza della Repubblica with two impressive early 20C buildings. Via Mazzini continues north to Via Imbriani where at No. 5 is the entrance to the small **Civico Museo Morpurgo** (open 9–13 exc. Mon). This is an interesting example of a late 19C private apartment which has been preserved intact with its elaborate gloomy furnishings, including enamelled terracotta stoves. Its contents include Japanese prints, 19C paintings, glass, ceramics and porcelain, all collected by Mario Morpurgo and left to the the city on his death in 1943. On the first floor the **Civico Museo Teatrale** (open 9–13 exc. Sun) is provisionally displayed, with an extremely interesting collection and archive including 19C musical instruments and documents relating to the production of operetta, for which Trieste has been famous since the 19C. The museum was founded in 1924 in the Teatro Verdi with the collection of Carlo Schmidl.

The northern districts of the city are centred around PIAZZA OBERDAN, laid out in the 1930s. The **Museo del Risorgimento** (9–13 exc. Mon) is arranged in a fine palace by Umberto Nordio (1934), which incorporates the cell of Guglielmo Oberdan, hanged in 1882 by the Austrians in the old barracks on this site. Here also is the station of the Opicina tramway—the line, first opened in 1902, was rebuilt in 1978. **Palazzo di Giustizia**, in the Foro Ulpiano, was built by Enrico Nordio in 1933. In Via San Francesco, the **Synagogue**, built by the local architect Ruggero Berlam and his son Arduino (1910), is one of the finest in Europe. On the outskirts of the town, on the Opicina road are the buildings (1940–50, by Umberto Nordio and Raffaello Fagnoni) of the **University**, founded in 1919 and particularly noted for its scientific faculties.

The western districts with the Museo Revoltella

From Piazza dell'Unità d'Italia, Riva del Mandracchio leads west along the seafront. Beyond the Molo dei Bersaglieri, on another jetty is the **Pescheria** (fish market) with its spacious market hall (1913, by Giorgio Polli) open to the sea, and a clock tower. At the side is the entrance to a fine **Aquarium** (open 9–19; winter 9–13 exc. Mon), founded by the municipality in 1933, with fish from the Adriatic and tropics, as well as three penguins.

In Piazza Venezia (left) is the **MUSEO REVOLTELLA** (open 10–13, 15–20; fest. 10–13; closed Tue; entrance at No. 27 Via Diaz) in a palace built by Friedrich Hitzig in 1850 for the businessman Pasquale Revoltella (1795–1869) as a museum for his art collections and as an art institute. It has retained some of its interesting furnishings, handsome ceilings, inlaid wooden floors and enamelled terracotta stoves. In the **atrium** is an allegorical fountain by Pietro Magni. On the **ground floor** are 17C and 18C landscapes, a room of portraits by the local artist Giuseppe Tominz (1790–1866), the panelled library, and a statue of Napoleon as Mars by Antonio Canova (the model for his colossal statue in Apsley House, London). On the **first floor** is an elaborate allegorical statuary group representing the Suez canal by Pietro Magni (Revoltella was vice-president of the company responsible for the cutting of the canal), and paintings by Vincenzo Cabianca, Girolamo Induno, Giovanni Fattori, Filippo Palizzi and Francesco Hayez. On the **top floor** are four more allegorical statues by Magni, and the handsome dining room.

The adjacent palace was bought by the city in 1907, and its restoration was begun by Carlo Scarpa in 1960. It displays a large collection of modern art acquired through funds left for the purpose by Revoltella. Artists represented include: Urbano Nono, Domenico Trentacoste, Leonardo Bistolfi, Medardo Rosso, Giuseppe De Nittis, Felice Carena, Felice Casorati, Giorgio Morandi and Giorgio De Chirico. The large collection of works by local artists includes paintings by Pietro Marussig. Frequent exhibitions are held on the fifth floor, and there are fine views of Trieste and the port from the sixth floor.

In Piazza Attilio Hortis, with a little public garden, is the **Museo Civico di Storia Naturale** (open 8.30–13.30; fest 9–13; closed Mon) in a palace built in 1816 by Pietro Nobile. Founded in 1846, it has a very fine and well displayed natural history collection, particularly rich in material from the Carso and Venezia Giulia. On the third floor are mammals, fish, shells, insects, an Egyptian mummy, and a botanical section (with lovely watercolours of plants which grow in the region). On the floors below are sections devoted to mineralogy, palaeontology, birds and reptiles. There are extensive study collections and a specialised library.

Nearby, in Via Madonna del Mare, are remains of an **early Christian basilica** (usually closed).

Via Duca d'Aosta leads uphill to the **Museo Sartorio** (open 9–13 exc. Mon) with a collection of decorative arts arranged in 19C period rooms (including one in neo-Gothic style). It has especially interesting 16C ceramics, local majolica produced in Trieste, a recently restored triptych attributed to Paolo Veneziano and his school, and works by Magnasco and Tiepolo.

At the end of Riva Grumula, in Via Campo Marzio (see the Plan), is the **Museo del Mare** (9–13 exc. Mon) with sections devoted to harbours, navigation and fishing. In the old railway station of Campo Marzio (entrance at No. 1 Via G. Cesare) is a **Railway Museum** (open 9–13 exc. Mon) which illustrates the history of railways in the region, and preserves some old locomotives. Beyond is the modern port area.

On the outskirts of the town on the Muggia road, at 43 Ratto della Pileria, is the **Civico Museo della Risiera di San Sabba** (open 9–13 exc. Mon), originally an industrial building of 1913 where rice was prepared. It was turned into a prison and then (in 1943) used as a concentration camp by the Germans. An internal railway was used for the deportation of prisoners, and the cremation oven here—the only one set up by the Germans in Italy—was blown up as they retreated. Since 1965 this Nazi lager has been preserved as a museum.

Environs of Trieste

MIRAMARE is the most interesting place to visit near Trieste. The road (taken by bus no. 36 every half hour from Piazza Oberdan and the station; journey time 20–25mins) follows the railway line for several kilometres, and then passes public gardens on the seafront. The **Faro della Vittoria** is a beacon erected in 1927 by Arduino Berlam in memory of the victims of the First World War who died at sea.

There are three entrances to the **park of Miramare** (open daily as public gardens). The nearest one to Trieste is on the sea (at a road fork), but from this entrance it is a good 20 minutes' walk to the castle. The entrance closest to the castle is on the main road before the two tunnels which precede Grignano, and the third entrance is by the bus terminus at **Grignano**, near the Castelletto.

On the edge of the sea surrounded by a wooded park is the **Castle of Miramare**, a grand building in white Istrian stone designed in an eclectic style by Karl Junker for Archduke Maximilian of Austria in 1856–60. The Archduke (younger brother of the Habsburg emperor Francis Joseph) was married to Charlotte of Saxony, and in 1864 became Emperor of Mexico, where he was shot in 1867. The castle is now very well maintained, and the rooms preserve much of their original furniture and panelling in Gothic style. Notices in each room describe the contents which include (in the gaming room) a painting of celebrations in Venice in honour of Maximilian and Charlotte by Ippolito Caffi, portraits (in Room XVI) of Maximilian and Charlotte by Heinrich, and a sculpture of Daedalo and Icarus by Innocenzo Fraccaroli. The huge throne room has an elaborate ceiling in Gothic style.

The **park** has some fine trees, and an Italianate garden. The **Castelletto**, where the Archduke lived during the construction of the castle, is now used as a visitors' centre by the Worldwide Fund for Nature who have preserved this stretch of the coastline as a marine park since 1973. The path which leads back along the seafront towards Trieste passes a fine stable block, being restored as a museum of applied arts, and the Trieste Youth Hostel. In Jun–Sep son-et-lumière pageants are held in the evenings at Miramare (including performances in English).

Sistiana, on a delightful bay known to the Romans as *Sextilianum*, is used as a harbour for private boats. A path (known as the Sentiero Rilke) follows the rocky coast from here to Duino for nearly two kilometres, through interesting vegetation, with fine views.

Duino is a fishing village with the ruined Castello Vecchio. The imposing Castello Nuovo on a rocky promontory above the sea was built in the 15C on the ruins of a Roman tower (which has been partly reconstructed). The poet Rainer Maria Rilke stayed here as a guest of Maria von Thurn und Taxis in 1910–14. Since 1964 part of the castle has been occupied by the United World College of the Adriatic, one of eight international schools all over the world for scholarship students between the ages of 16 and 18. The other part of the castle, rebuilt since damage in the First World War, is still owned by the Della Torre Tasso family.

At **San Giovanni al Timavo** is the mouth of the river Timavo, which emerges here from an underground course of over 38km. The six springs here have been sacred since Roman times. The province of Gorizia is described in Chapter 46.

A tramway (5km) and funicular runs from Trieste (Piazza Oberdan) to **Villa Opicina**. In the Carsic hills between Opicina and Sistiana a good dark red wine known as *terrano* is produced. Near Opicina is the **Grotta Gigante** (open Apr–Sep 9–12, 14–19; in winter 10–12, 14.30–16.30; closed Mon), the largest single cave yet discovered in the Carso (280m long, 107m high). It was first opened to the public in 1908 and is famous for its stalactitic formations. From **Monrupino** there is a superb view of the **Carso** (German *Karst*, Slav *Kras*), a curiously eroded limestone plateau, now mostly in Slovenian territory. It was the scene of the most violent struggles in the Austro-Italian campaign. Vast trenches and veritable caverns were easily constructed by widening the existing crevasses in its surface; and although large-scale operations were made difficult by the nature of the ground, immense concentrations of artillery were brought up by both sides for the defence of this key position. It was the Duke of Aosta's stand here with the 3rd Italian Army that averted complete disaster after Caporetto (October 1917). A local ethnographical museum at Rupingrande is open on holidays.

MUGGIA, across the bay south of Trieste, is reached by bus No. 20 from the station in 30 mins. It is a charming little old fishing-port, with brightly painted houses, the only Istrian town which has remained within the Italian border. For centuries a faithful ally of the Venetian republic, it retains a remarkably Venetian atmosphere (the roads are called *calli*). The **harbour**, with its fishing boats, is also used by numerous yachts, and there are a number of simple fish restaurants here. Above can be seen the 14C **castle**. Near the inner basin (or *mandracchio*) is the main piazza with the **Duomo**, a 13C foundation with a 15C Venetian Gothic façade and an interesting treasury, the **Municipio**, and the **Palazzo dei Rettori** (rebuilt after a fire in 1933), once a palace of the patriarchs of Aquileia who controlled the town in the 10C. Opposite the town hall an archway leads into VIA DANTE with interesting old houses. There is a particularly pretty Venetian Gothic palace at No. 25 Via Oberdan.

On the hillside above (reached in 10 minutes by bus No. 37 from Porto

Vecchio) are the ruins of the Roman and medieval settlement of **Muggia Vecchia**, destroyed in 1356 by the Genoese for having taken the side of Venice in the battle of Chioggia. The basilica here is a 9C building with an ambo of the 10C, transennae in the Byzantine style, and remains of early frescoes.

46 · Gorizia

Gorizia (39,000 inhab.) is a provincial capital standing in an expansion of the Isonzo valley hemmed in by hills on the Slovenian border. It is a particularly pleasant and peaceful little town with numerous public gardens and pretty buildings, in Austrian style.

■ **Information office.** APT, 16 Via A. Diaz (tel. 0481 533870).

■ **Hotels.** 3-star: *Palace hotel*, 63 Corso Italia. 1-star: *Sandro*, 18 Via Santa Chiara.

■ **Restaurants. B**: *Lanterna d'oro*, Borgo Castello. **C**: *Al Sabotino*, 4 Via Santa Chiara; *Ai Tre Amici*, 11 Via Oberdan; *Alla Luna*, 13 Via Oberdan; *Da Gianni*, 10 Via Morelli; *Primozic Vito*, 138 Viale XX Settembre; *Rosenbar*, 98 Via Duca d'Aosta, and numerous other small and simple trattorie. **Cafés** and **Cake shops**: *Bar Ferigo*, Corso Italia; *Bisiach Donaldo*, 15 Via Mazzini.

■ **Picnic places** on the castle hill and in the public gardens.

■ **Market**. On Thu in the public gardens in Corso Giuseppe Verdi. On the second Sun of the month a market of artisans' ware, etc. is held in Via Ascoli.

■ **Annual festivals**. Theatre and cinema festival in summer at the Castle. International folklore festival for a week in Aug.

History
After the fall of the independent counts of Gorizia in the 15C, the city remained an Austrian possession almost continuously from 1509 to 1915. In the First World War it was the objective of violent Italian attacks in the Isonzo valley, and was eventually captured on 9 August 1916. Lost again in the autumn of 1917, it was finally taken in November 1918. The Treaty of Paris (1947) brought the Yugoslav frontier into the streets of the town, cutting off its eastern suburbs, but in 1952, and again in 1978–79, more reasonable readjustments were made, including a ten-mile (16km) wide zone in which local inhabitants may circulate freely.

The attractive, wide CORSO ITALIA, lined with trees and some Art Nouveau villas, leads up from the railway station into the centre of the town. Via Garibaldi diverges right to the **Palazzo Comunale**, built by Nicolò Pacassi in 1740, with a public garden. Via Mazzini continues to the **Duomo**, a 14C building much restored, with a pleasant interior including galleries and stucco decoration. It contains a pulpit of 1711, a high altarpiece by Giuseppe Tominz, and a precious treasury brought from Aquileia in 1752.

Viale Gabriele d'Annunzio leads uphill to the pleasant and peaceful **Borgo Castello** (approached on foot by steps up through the walls and past a garden). The castle was built by the Venetians in 1509, and within its wards are the **Musei Provinciali di Borgo Castello** (open 10–13, 15–19 exc. Mon), well arranged in two 16C palaces. On the **ground floor** are late 19C paintings by local painters, including works by Giuseppe Tominz (1790–1866). On the **upper floor** there is a display illustrating the history of silk production in the town from 1725 to 1915, including a wooden 18C twisting machine, looms, samples of silks, and costumes showing Balkan influence. Another section of the museum has delightful reproductions of local artisans' workshops, and a street of reconstructed shops. Downstairs is the *Museo della Grande Guerra**, one of the most important museums in Italy dedicated to the First World War, founded in 1924. Excellently displayed in ten rooms it includes the reconstruction of a trench, material illustrating both the Italian and Austrian fronts in the Carso campaign, and a room dedicated to General Diaz.

The **Museo di Storia e Arte** next door is closed for restoration. The unusual little church of **Santo Spirito**, with the copy of a 16C crucifix outside, dates from 1398. The **Castle** (open 9.30–13.30, 15–19.30 exc. Mon), was built by the counts of Gorizia, and remodelled in 1508. Important exhibitions are held here. From the rampart walk there is a good view towards Slovenia, and the interesting interior has some 17C and 18C furniture and paintings. The park on the castle hill is to be opened to the public.

Below the hill, off Viale Gabriele d'Annunzio, the pretty Via Rastello, with arcades along one side and some old shop fronts, leads to PIAZZA DELLA VITTORIA (or PIAZZA GRANDE) with a fountain designed in 1756 by Nicolò Pacassi and the 17C–18C church of **Sant'Ignazio** (1654–1747) with eccentric oriental domes on its two bell-towers. Beyond the far end of the piazza, Via dell'Arcivescovado and Via Seminario lead to Via San Giovanni, another nice street. Its continuation, Via Ascoli, passes several houses with attractive balconies and windows, including Palazzo Ascoli (with a garden), next to San Giovanni; the church, founded in 1587, is set back from the road behind two cedars of Lebanon. At the end of Via Ascoli is the little yellow **Synagogue** (open Thu 19–20), first built in 1756 and restored in the 19C and 20C (the façade dates from 1894) . Beyond on the right is **Palazzo Attems**, a fine building by Nicolò Pacassi (1745), with a library and archive.

From Via Giuseppe Verdi (in which, on the corner of Via Boccaccio, is a pretty market building of 1927), Via Santa Chiara and Viale XX Settembre lead to the late 18C gateway (removed from Palazzo Attems) at the entrance to **Palazzo Coronini**, left to the city by Guglielmo Coronini Cronberg in 1990 (to be opened to the public after restoration). It is surrounded by a fine *park laid out in the 19C, with evergreen trees, statues by Orazio Marinali, and a sculpture of Hecate, which may date from the 2C AD. Built in 1597 by Giulio Baldigara, the palace was purchased from Marshall Radetzky in 1820 by the Coronini. Charles X Bourbon of France died here in exile of cholera in 1836. It has a 19C wing and portico, and a 17C family chapel. The 30 rooms are preserved intact and contain

18C furniture, paintings and porcelain. The library has some 15,000 volumes, including illustrated manuscripts and incunabula.

Viale XX Settembre continues to the Isonzo river across which is the Parco Piuma (public gardens).

Environs of Gorizia

Across the Isonzo, northwest of Gorizia at **Oslavia**, a 'Gothic' castle (open 9–11.45, 15–17.30 exc. Mon) holds the graves of 57,000 men of the 2nd Army who fell in 1915–18.

To the north is the hilly area of **Collio**, famous for its excellent wine. At **San Floriano del Collio** there is a wine museum (open weekdays 8–17), and the attractive little town of **Cormòns**, an ancient seat of the patriarchs of Aquileia, has a few hotels, and good restaurants.

South of Gorizia on the Isonzo is **Gradisca**, an old Venetian fortress still preserving many of its 15C watchtowers and some good Baroque mansions. In the 17C–18C Palazzo Torriani, the Civico Museo Gradiscano (open Tue, Thu and Fri 17–19) contains Roman material. The county of Gradisca was ceded to Austria in 1511, and in 1615–17 it caused a war between Austria and Venice.

Monte San Michele was a ridge hotly contested in the Carso campaign. At Sagrado a museum (open 8–12, 14–7 exc. Mon) commemorates the battle.

Further south is **Redipuglia** with the huge war cemetery of the 3rd Army, containing over 100,000 graves, including that of the Duke of Aosta (1869–1931), the heroic defender of the Carso. There is also a small museum here dedicated to the First World War. Nearby is a war cemetery with the graves of 14,550 Austro-Hungarian soldiers. **Ronchi dei Legionari**, with the airport of Trieste, is on the edge of the Carso and the region of the battlefront of 1915–17. Guglielmo Oberdan (1858–82), the patriot, was arrested here by the Austrians in 1882 before his execution, and from here in 1919 the poet and nationalist Gabriele D'Annunzio set out to occupy Fiume.

47 · Udine and Cividale del Friuli, and the province of Udine

Udine

Udine, with 100,700 inhabitants, the historical centre of Friuli and capital of a large province, is a delightful, lively town. Its attractive old streets, most of them arcaded, fan out round the castle hill. Some splendid examples of Tiepolo's work are preserved here. The streets are often full of soldiers since there are numerous barracks in or near the town.

■ **Information office.** APT, 7 Piazza I Maggio (tel. 0432 295972).

■ **Hotels.** 4-star: *Astoria Hotel Italia*, 24 Piazza XX Settembre. 3-star: *Principe*, 51 Viale Europa Unità. 2-star: *Ramandolo*, 28 Via Forni di Sotto.

- **Restaurants. A**: *Astoria Italia*, 24 Piazza XX Settembre; *Il Vitello d'Oro*, Via Valvason. **B**: *Alla Concordia*, Piazza I Maggio; *Alla Giaccaia*, Via Zanon. **C**: *Al Vecchio Stallo*, Via Viola; *All'Allegria*, Via Grazzano. **Wine Bar**: *Ai Piombi*, Via Manin. **Cafés and cake shops**: *Cantarena*, Piazza del Comune; *Volpe Pasini*, Via Cangiani; *Sommariva*, Via Rialto. **Picnic places** on the castle hill.

- **Car parking** in Piazza I Maggio.

- **Buses** depart from the bus station next to the railway station to all destinations in the province.

- **Market** on Sat mornings in Piazza I Maggio.

- **Annual festival.** 25 Nov, Festa di Santa Caterina, with a fair and market for three days in Piazza I Maggio.

History

A Roman station called *Utina* is alleged to have occupied the site of Udine, and a 10C castle here is recorded as part of the domain of the patriarch of Aquileia. In the 13C Udine, appointed the seat of the patriarch, became a rival of Cividale, but the attacks of the counts of Gorizia and Treviso (c 1300) and of Philip of Alençon (c 1390) unified the Friuli. In 1420, after nine years' resistance, Udine surrendered to Venice, and from then on remained under her influence. It was occupied by Napoleon's marshals Bernadotte in 1797, and Massena in 1805. In the First World War it was Italian General Headquarters until October 1917, and then was held by the Austrians for a year. In the Second World War, after considerable destruction from air raids, it was entered by South African troops on 1 May 1945, the day before the official end of the campaign. The castle hill was damaged in the 1976 Friuli earthquake and is still partly under restoration.

*PIAZZA LIBERTÀ is the picturesque main square of the town, with an unusual medley of buildings. The particoloured **Palazzo del Comune**, a typical Venetian Gothic building, dates from 1448–56 and was rebuilt after a fire in 1876; the statue of the Madonna at the corner is by Bartolomeo Bon. Opposite is the Renaissance **Porticato di San Giovanni** (1533), with a chapel that has been converted into a war memorial, and the **Torre dell'Orologio**, by Giovanni da Udine (1527; the *mori* on the

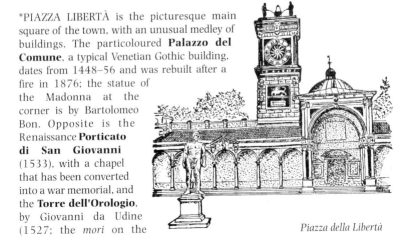

Piazza della Libertà

clock, which strike the

hours, are 19C). In the piazza are a fountain of 1542, two columns with the Lion of St Mark and Justice, and colossal statues of Hercules and Cacus (called by the Udinese 'Florean' and 'Venturin') from a demolished 18C palace. The statue of Peace (with a sarcastic inscription) commemorates the Treaty of Campo Formio, by which Napoleon ceded Venice to Austria in 1797.

Beyond the **Arco Bollani**, a rusticated triumphal arch by Palladio (1556), a road lined with a delightful Gothic portico (1487) and steep steps climb up the **CASTLE HILL**. The 13C church of **Santa Maria di Castello** (unlocked on request at the museum; often used for weddings at weekends) has been beautifully restored after the 1976 earthquake. The campanile dates from 1540. It has fine 13C frescoes, and a seated wooden statue of the Madonna. Next to the church is the 15C **Casa della Confraternità** restored in 1929. The summit of the hill has a green with two wells, from which there is a fine view stretching as far as the Alps on a clear day. The **Casa della Contadinanza**, with a double loggia was reconstructed in this century.

The **Castle**, the seat of the patriarchs and Venetian governors, was destroyed by an earthquake in 1511. The present building, the rear façade of which faces the green, is a handsome palace designed in 1517 by Giovanni Fontana with a double stair and loggia on the ground floor. It houses various museums, but was damaged in the 1976 earthquake, and only the **GALLERIA D'ARTE ANTICA** is at present open (9.30–12.30, 15–18 exc. Mon and Sun afternoon). The fine collection is beautifully arranged chronologically.

Room I contains 14C Emilian frescoes. **Room II**. Works by Battista da Zagabria, Domenico da Tolmezzo and Fiorenzo di Lorenzo. **Room III**. *Christ with the instruments of the Passion* by Vittore Carpaccio. **Room IV**. *Annunciation and organ doors by Pellegrino da San Daniele. **Room V** has two fine works by Giovanni Antonio da Pordenone. **Room VI**. Francesco Floreani and Palma il Giovane. **Room VII**. Portrait by Bronzino, and *St Francis Receiving the Stigmata*, thought to be by Caravaggio.

The huge **Salone**, designed by Giovanni da Udine, has classical and historical frescoes by Pomponio Amalteo and Gian Battista Grassi. The very damaged monochrome frieze below is partly the work of Giovanni Battista Tiepolo. **Room VIII**. Works by Antonio Carneo, Fra' Galgario and Sebastiano Bombelli. **Room IX**. Frieze with Roman triumphs by Francesco Maffei, and a portrait by Luca Giordano.

Room X contains works by Giovanni Battista Tiepolo including a delightful small painting of the *Consilium in Arena* (with the help of his son Gian Domenico). **Room XI**. Alessandro Longhi, Giovanni Battista Piazzetta and Marco and Sebastiano Ricci. Beyond **Room XII** with works by Nicola Grassi, **Room XIII** displays works by Giuseppe Bison, Odorico Polito and Giovanni Paglierini.

The **Archaeological Museum** (closed) was founded in 1866 and contains material from Aquileia, and a valuable numismatic collection (some 60,000 pieces). The fine collection of **Prints and Drawings** is also at present closed.

Duomo

From Piazza Libertà (see above) Via Vittorio Veneto leads to the Duomo, which was consecrated in 1335 and completed in the mid-15C. Much altered later, it retains a heavy octagonal campanile of 1441 above the 14C baptistery. On the

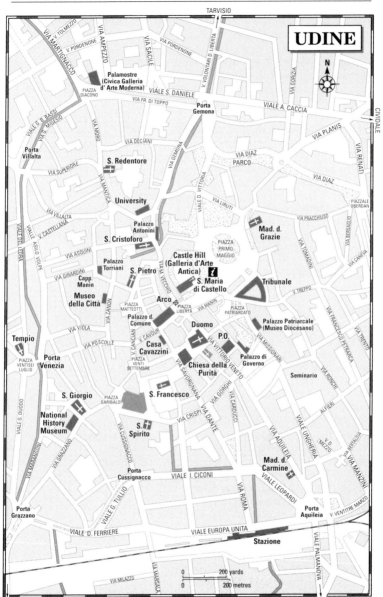

east side (seen from Via Vittorio Veneto) are two statues (the Annunciation) of the 14C. By the door of the baptistery is a blocked portal dating from the late 13C. The brick west front dates from the late 14C.

Interior. The first three altars on either side of the nave were designed by Giorgio Massari, and the vaults painted by Andrea Urbani. In the **south aisle** are altarpieces by Giovanni Battista Tiepolo, paintings by Pomponio Amalteo, sculptures by Giuseppe Torretti, and small paintings on the organ by Giovanni Antonio da Pordenone.

In the Baroque **presbytery** and **choir**, designed by Abondio Stazio, the unusual high altar is by Giuseppe Torretti. The two side altars have angels by Orazio Marinali. The carved dossals are attributed to Andrea Brustolon. The vault is frescoed by Lodovico Dorigny, who also decorated the choir with paintings and frescoes. The 18C **sacristy** contains paintings by Giovanni Antonio da Pordenone, Franz Hals and Giovanni Battista Tiepolo.

In the **north aisle** are altarpieces by Pellegrino da San Daniele and Giovanni Martini. The **Museo del Duomo** (closed indefinitely) is in a chapel frescoed by Vitale da Bologna in 1349, and in the 14C baptistery (containing the 14C tomb with the relics of St Hermagoras and St Fortunatus).

The **CHIESA DELLA PURITÀ**, on the south side of Piazza del Duomo, is opened on request at the sacristy of the Duomo (preferably 16.30–18.30). The ceiling fresco of the *Assumption is by Giovanni Battista Tiepolo, who also painted the altarpiece of the *Immaculate Conception. The grisaille biblical *scenes on a gold ground on the walls are by his son Gian Domenico.

Via Lovaria leads east to **Palazzo Patriarcale**, reconstructed in the early 18C by Domenico Rossi and Giorgio Massari, and decorated in 1726 by Giovanni Battista Tiepolo. Since 1995 it has housed the **MUSEO DIOCESANO E GALLERIE DEL TIEPOLO** (open 15.30–18.30; Thu, Fri, Sat & Sun also 10–12; closed Tue). On the **first floor** is an interesting collection of 13C–18C wood sculpture from churches in Friuli, arranged chronologically.

A pretty spiral staircase, with a fresco by Nicolò Bambini, leads up to the **second floor**, or piano nobile, with splendid *frescoes carried out in 1726 by Giovanni Battista Tiepolo for the partriarch Dionisio Delfino. Beyond the **blue room**, with ceiling frescoes by Giovanni da Udine, the **red room** contains the *Judgement of Solomon and four *Prophets in the lunettes by Giovanni Battista Tiepolo. The *Galleria** is entirely frescoed with delightful Old Testament scenes (the stories of Abraham, Isaac and Jacob) by Tiepolo, using remarkable pastel colours. On the stairs is another splendid fresco by him of the *Fall of the Rebel Angels.

Near Piazza Libertà is the attractive Via Mercato Vecchio, and in Via Gemona, on a corner site, is the handsome **Palazzo Antonini** by Palladio (1554–56), near a pretty canal. PIAZZA MATTEOTTI is a large arcaded marketplace with attractive houses and a fountain by Giovanni da Udine (1542). Near the church of **San Giacomo**, with an early 16C Lombard façade, is a well by Tommaso Lippomano (1487; being restored). A passageway leads from the piazzetta to Via Zanon, on a picturesque canal overhung with willows. Here the **Museo di Città**, which incorporates the tower of the 13C town walls, is being restored as an exhibition centre. The Baroque **Cappella Manin**, attributed to Domenico

Rossi, is closed for restoration.

Behind the Municipio in Piazza Libertà, Via Savorgnana leads south. At No. 5 is the **Casa Cavazzini** left to the municipality by Dante Cavazzini, with an apartment on the first floor containing murals (1939) by Corrado Cagli and Afro. The large building is to be restored, and the Astaldi collection of modern art, at present displayed in Piazzale Diacono (see below), may be moved here. Further south, in Piazza Venerio, the church of **San Francesco** has been restored to its 13C appearance for use as an auditorium. To the southwest, beyond Piazza Garibaldi, in Palazzo Giacomelli in Via Grazzano, is the **Museo Friulano di Scienze Naturali** (open 9–12, 15–18 or 16–19), with an important natural history collection.

In Via Vittorio Veneto which leads south from Piazza Libertà is **Palazzo Tinghi** (No. 38), first built in 1392 with a wide ground-floor portico. The façade of 1532 has very faded frescoes by Pordenone.

At the north end of the town, in Piazzale Diacono (see the Plan) is the modern Palamostre, which houses a theatre. The large **Civica Galleria d'Arte Moderna** (open 9.30–12.30, 15–18 exc. Mon and fest. afternoons) is temporarily housed here. It includes the *Astaldi collection, representative of Italian art from 1920 to 1960 (Alberto Savinio, Gino Severini, Giorgio De Chirico, Carlo Carrà, Felice Carena, Mario Sironi, Filippo De Pisis, Mario Mafai, Sciltian, Renato Guttuso, Giovanni Colacicchi, Onofrio Martinelli, Francesco Trombadori and Amerigo Bartoli).

Cividale del Friuli

Cividale del Friuli is a very old town (11,000 inhab.) and one of the most interesting in the Friuli, with peaceful streets and attractive houses. It was the first Lombard duchy in Italy: important relics from this period include the Tempietto Lombardo and numerous treasures which are preserved in its excellent museum. The Natisone river runs through the town in a deep gorge.

■ **Information office.** APT, 4 Largo Boiani (tel. 0432 731398).

■ **Hotel.** 2-star: *Locanda al Pomo d'oro*, Piazza San Giovanni. At Fortino, 3-star: *Al Castello.*

■ **Restaurants.** *Zorutti* (**A**); *Alla Frasca* (**B**). **Wine Bar**: *Enoteca dell'Elefante,* Piazza Diacona.

■ **Train services** from Udine every hour taking 15 minutes.

History

Founded as *Forum Iulii*, probably by Julius Caesar, the town gave its name to the Friuli. The first Lombard duchy in Italy, it later became the capital of a free duchy of which Berengar I, afterwards King of Italy (888–924), was the most distinguished lord. From the 8C until 1238 Cividale was the chief seat of the patriarchs of Aquileia. From the 16C onwards it became subject to the Venetian Republic. The town was badly shaken in the earthquake of 1976.

From the station and the main road from Udine, Viale Libertà leads east to Corso Alberto which continues south to the pleasant large PIAZZA DIACONO, scene of a daily market, with an old-fashioned café and a house traditionally taken to be on the site of the birthplace of Paul the Deacon (Warnefride; 723–799), historian of the Lombards. The fountain is surmounted by an 18C statue of Diana.

CORSO MAZZINI, the main street of the town, leads past **Palazzo Levrini-Stringher**, with remains of 16C frescoes on its façade, to PIAZZA DEL DUOMO. The **Duomo** was begun in its present form in 1453 and continued in 1503–32 by Pietro Lombardo. It contains a magnificent 12C silver-gilt *altar (set within the Baroque high altar), the most important work of its date in Friuli. The monument to the Patriarch Nicolò Donato is by Antonio da Carona (1513).

The **MUSEO CRISTIANO** (entered from the Duomo, or from behind the bell-tower on Sun; open 9.30–12, 15–18) contains an octagonal *baptistery (8C) reconstructed from Lombard fragments, the marble patriarchal throne (9C–11C), which was used from 1077 to 1412 (the feet were added in the 17C), the altar of Duke Ratchis (744–49) with sculptured panels, and detached frescoes.

In the handsome **Palazzo dei Provveditori Veneti**, begun in 1565 and attributed to Palladio, is the ***MUSEO ARCHEOLOGICO NAZIONALE** (open daily 9–14; fest 9–13; summer: 8.30–19; Mon 8.30–14), founded in 1817. The important collection, especially famous for its early medieval treasures, is beautifully displayed.

The **ground floor** displays Roman and early Christian mosaic pavements (2C-4C AD), and medieval and Renaissance architectural fragments. **Room VIII** and the **courtyard** contain a lapidary collection from Dalmatia, and Jewish tombstones (13C–17C).

Piano nobile. In the **portego** are displayed three Roman bronzes excavated in the forum of Zuglio (see below) at the beginning of the 19C, including a *portrait head. Also here are paintings by Pellegrino da San Daniele and Pordenone, and a rare embroidered linen *altar cover (c 1400).

The other rooms on this floor contain a superb display of ***Lombard finds** (late 6C to early 9C) from Cividale and the Friuli, arranged partly according to type, and partly according to the way they were found in each individual tomb. **Room C**. In Case 8 is the material found in a knight's tomb at Cella (early 7C) including a gold leaf disk showing a mounted knight. In **Room D** is a sarcophagus (mid-7C) with its contents, including a fine cross, a signet ring, an enamelled gold fibula, a glass bottle, and a tiny *box with polychrome enamels in the shape of a bird. In **Room E** is an ivory casket (Case 2), a cross with a stag (Case 4), and exquisite *clasps in gilded silver (Cases 9 and 11). Also here are the contents of a warrior's tomb, including his arms, gold and silver ornaments, and ivory chessmen.

Room F contains Roman Byzantine works, including a remarkable filigree disk (Case 6). **Room G** has late Lombard works including a large cross (9C), and the Psalter of St Elizabeth of Hungary with a beautiful cover (Case 4). In Case 6 is the *pax of Duke Orso (8C) with a relief of the Crucifixion in a jewelled silver frame. Also here are two *reliquary boxes (8C–9C) from the treasury of the Duomo.

Stairs lead up to the **upper floor** where finds from recent excavations are displayed including very fine glass (1C–2C AD), and a hoard of 15C ceramics.

From the ground floor, stairs lead down to the **basement** where walkways provide a view of excavations showing various levels from the late Roman period (3C AD) to the 16C.

Other material belonging to the museum may one day be exhibited in the 16C **Palazzo Nordis**, the former seat of the archaeological museum, also in Piazza del Duomo, which is undergoing a lengthy restoration. **Palazzo Comunale**, opposite the Duomo, was reconstructed in the 16C and heavily restored in this century. The modern extension dates from 1970. The bronze statue of Julius Caesar is a copy of a Roman original.

Corso Ponte d'Aquileia leads down to the ***Ponte del Diavolo** (15C; rebuilt after 1917) crossing the impressive limestone gorge of the Natisone river. On the left bank a flight of steps leads down from the parapet to the river. There is a good view of the bridge from near the church of San Martino. Just before the bridge the pretty VIA MONASTERO MAGGIORE, once the main street of the town and attractively paved with cobblestones in 1990, leads east. At No. 2 is the so-called **Ipogeo Celtico** (key at the tourist office or Bar del Ponte exc. Sat & Sun). Steep stairs lead down to a few underground caverns excavated in the rock with, above the entrances, three primitively carved masks. It is thought this may have been a Celtic burial place or a prison of the Roman or Lombard period.

Further on the road passes the **Pozzo di Callisto**, a well-head behind the apse of the Duomo. Near **Porta Brossana**, a Roman or medieval arch in Stretta Santa Maria di Corte, is an old medieval house. Beyond Porta Patriarchale (surmounted by a Romanesque house) opens the Piazzetta San Biagio on the banks of the Natisone.

A raised walkway above the river leads to the celebrated ***TEMPIETTO LONGOBARDO** (open daily 10–13, 15.30–17.30 or 18.30), one of the most interesting and evocative early medieval sacred buildings in Italy. Thought to date from the mid-8C, and damaged over the centuries by earth-

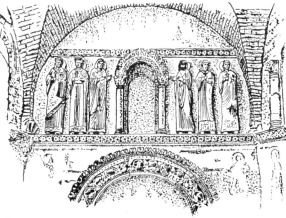

Detail of the interior of the Tempietto Longobardo

quakes, it is in a peaceful corner of the town from which only the sound of the river can be heard. The present entrance is through the **presbytery** of the little church, with an iconostasis consisting of a marble screen and two very unusual columns (5C–6C) beneath three small barrel vaults, the central one of which has 14C frescoes. The beautifully carved stalls also date from the 14C.

The little quadrangular **nave** preserves remarkable *stucco decoration on the end wall (formerly the entrance wall) with the monumental figures of six female saints and beautifully carved friezes, thought to be by the hand of an artist from the east and contemporary with the building (c 760). The two side walls would have had similar decorations. Fragments of the original frescoes also survive.

From Piazza Paolo Diacono (see above), Via Ristori leads to Piazza Diaz where the **Theatre**, first built in 1815, is named after the tragedienne Adelaide Ristori (1821–1906), born here, who is also commemorated by a monument in Foro Giulio Cesare. In the Piazzetta Terme Romane are scant remains of **Roman Baths**, below the level of the pavement. Beyond **Porta San Pietro** (used by the Venetians as a store) is the church of **San Pietro**, with a good altarpiece by Palma Giovane.

The **Natisone valley**, northeast of Cividale, is Slovene-speaking in its upper reaches. Across the Slovenian border, 30km from Cividale, is **Caporetto**, memorable for the disaster inflicted on the Italian armies in October 1917.

The province of Udine

■ **Information offices.** APT della Carnia, 15 Via Umberto I, Arte Terme (tel. 0433 929290. APT del Tarvisiano, 10 Via Roma, Tarvisio (tel. 0428 2135).

■ **Hotels. Buttrio**: 3-star: *Alle Officine*, 58 Via Nazionale, località Camino. **Codroipo**: 3-star: *Ai Gelsi* (near the Villa Manin). **Gemona**: 3-star: *Glemone Park Hotel*, località Piovega, and *Pittini*. **Latisana**: 3-star: *Bella Venezia*. **Magnano in Riviera**: 4-star: *Green Hotel*, località Colli. **San Daniele del Friuli**: 3-star: *Alla Torre*. **San Giovanni al Natisone**: 3-star: *Wiener*. **Tolmezzo**: 3-star: *Roma* (with restaurant). **Venzone**: 3-star: *Carnia*, località Arzin di Sore. Agriturist accommodation in the hills between San Daniele del Friuli and Tarcento, and in the Carnia area.

■ **Restaurants. Venzone** has a number of small *trattorie*, and the **Café** *Vecchio* in the piazza. **San Daniele del Friuli**: *Al Cantinon* (**A**). **Café**: *Toran*.

■ **Transport.** Gemona and Venzone are accessible by train on the pleasant line from Udine to Tarvisio. There is an attractive branch line from Gemona across the Tagliamento to Sacile, in the province of Pordenone. Other railway lines run to Palmanova, and Codroipo. There are also bus services from Udine to all the main places in the province.

The road, railway and motorway for Austria lead north from Udine through an area which was the epicentre of an earthquake in May and September 1976. The communes of Gemona, Tarcento, San Daniele, Maiano, and many others were devastated. Earth tremors continued for two years and the final toll was nearly 1000 dead, and over 70,000 homeless. Reconstruction where possible has now been all but completed, and the most spectacular monument to the skill and determination of the local people is the splendidly reconstructed little town of Venzone.

The small town of **San Daniele del Friuli**, famous for cured ham (celebrated with a festival at the end of August), has been largely rebuilt at the foot of its hill. In the former church of Sant'Antonio Abate are *frescoes (1487–1522) by Pellegrino da San Daniele. The Duomo is by Domenico Rossi (1725). The Guarneriana library, founded here in the 15C, has some precious incunabula and illuminated manuscripts. There is also a Museo Civico.

GEMONA was one of the worst hit towns in the 1976 earthquake when over 300 people lost their lives. The town has been rebuilt with colourful new buildings and a modern railway station in the plain below (from which it is half an hour's walk uphill to the centre). The town has lost some of its atmosphere since reconstruction.

The fine Romanesque and Gothic *Cathedral** has been carefully restored. Its tall 14C **campanile** had to be entirely reconstructed (using the same materials). The **façade** (redesigned in 1825) bears an inscription (above and to the left of the door) dated 1290 with the name of the architect and sculptor 'Magister Johannes', in charge of work on the building, and responsible for the portal. There is a gallery with niches, and statues representing the Epiphany (c 1350) include the delightful seated statues of the weary Magi, and a groom holding their three horses. The colossal statue (7m high) of St Christopher dates from 1332, and the superb rose-window from 1334.

In the beautiful **interior** the pilasters have been strengthened but left leaning out of line. The choir arch and dome over the sanctuary are particularly beautiful. The 12C font incorporates a Roman altar of the 1C or 2C AD with a delightful relief of a dolphin ridden by a putto. Beneath the sacristy is the shrine of St Michael with 14C frescoes. The church owns a rich treasury including a superb 15C *monstrance made by Nicolò Lionello and eight illuminated choir books (late 13C and early 14C).

The tiny medieval town of *VENZONE**, on the Tagliamento enclosed by high hills, is first documented in 1001. It became a free commune in 1381, and part of the Venetian Republic in 1420. It has been exquisitely reconstructed after it was reduced to rubble by the earthquake in 1976. The stones of its monuments were numbered and reused and its *genius loci* remains. Local limestone and sandstone has been used to pave the streets. The town is surrounded in part by medieval walls. The railway station is five minutes' walk from Porta di Sotto (1835), on the site of the 14C town gate. The beautiful *Duomo**, consecrated in 1338, was carefully reconstructed in 1988–95. Partly Romanesque and partly Gothic, it appears to have been designed by Magister Johannes, who was also responsible for the sculptural details (inscription, with the date 1308 above the north door) and who also worked on the cathedral of Gemona. Above the main door is a bas-relief of the Crucifixion, a fine work of the mid-14C. Between two bell-towers (one never completed) at the east end is the lovely apse in the Cistercian style. In the beautiful **interior** is a 14C fresco by the school of Vitale da Bologna showing the consecration of the Duomo. Only fragments now remain of the early 15C frescoes in the Cappella del Gonfalone, and other works of art are still being restored.

In the pretty piazza with a 19C fountain is the Gothic **Palazzo Comunale** (also entirely reconstructed) which dates from 1410. The church of **San Giovanni Battista** has been left as a ruin. The **Torre di Porta San Genesio** is inserted in the 13C double walls (well seen from here, defended by a moat).

Northeast of Venzone is **Tarvisia,** the Valle di Dogna, dominated by the Iôf di Montasio (2754m), the highest peak in a forested area of c 40,000 hectares, a protected park which extends north to the Austrian border and east to the Slovenian border. The Valcanale is a Slovene-speaking region. **Tarvisio** is a ski resort close to the Austrian frontier.

Carnia

Tolmezzo is the chief centre of Carnia, damaged in 1976. It has a museum of local handicrafts (open 9–12, 14–18 exc. Mon). To the west are summer resorts in the Carnic Alps. Nearby is the village of **Zuglio**, the ancient *Iulium Carnicum* which guarded the Roman road (the Via Iulia Augusta) from Aquileia over the Monte Croce pass. A fortified settlement established here in 50 BC became a Roman colony in the following century. It was important throughout the Imperial period, and was seat of a bishop up to the 8C. Excavations were carried out here in the early 19C and in the 1930s: the Roman forum and its basilica, as well as an early Christian basilica with mosaics, have been exposed. An archaeological museum contains finds from the site. The little church of San Pietro di Carnia is the oldest in the district (possibly 14C).

On the main road between Udine and Pordenone is **Codroipo** which was the Roman *Quadrivium*, on the Via Postumia. Nearby is **Passariano** with the vast **Villa Manin** (altered c 1650 perhaps by Giuseppe Benoni, and later by Domenico Rossi) which belonged to Lodovico Manin, last of the Venetian doges. It was restored by the region, and is now a cultural centre, and the seat of a restoration school. The interior (open 9–12.30, 15–18; winter 9–12, 14–17; exc. Mon) has frescoes by Ludovico Dorigny and Amigoni, a chapel with sculptures by Giuseppe Torretti, a carriage museum and an armoury. The fine **park**, the most important in the region, first laid out in the 18C, is open from Easter to October on weekends. The villa was occupied by Napoleon in 1797 when he concluded the shameful treaty of Campo Formio, which sacrificed Venice to Austria. The village after which it is named is now called **Campoformido** and is a few kilometres west of Udine.

South of Udine is **Palmanova** a Venetian fortress town, the plan of which is remarkably well preserved. It was built in 1593 on a star-shaped regular plan probably designed by Giulio Savorgnan, with symmetrical brick bastions, moated and grassy, and a hexagonal central piazza. The three chief gates are by Vincenzo Scamozzi, and the Duomo begun in 1603 may have been completed by Baldassarre Longhena after 1639.

Villa Vicentina was built by Elisa Bonaparte Baciocchi in 1815 (here in 1869–70 Pasteur saved the silk industry of Italy, as he had that of France). Near **San Giorgio di Nogaro** is the tiny Ausa river which marked the Austro-Italian frontier from 1866–1918.

48 · Aquileia and Grado

■ **Information office.** APT Grado e Aquileia, 72 Viale Dante Alighieri, Grado (tel. 0431/899220). Apr–Nov an information office (tel. 0431/919491) is open at Aquileia in Piazza Capitolo.

■ **Hotels. Aquileia**: 3-star: *Patriarchi*, 12 Via Giulia Augusta. 1-star: *Aquila Nera*, 5 Piazza Garibaldi. The sea resort of **Grado** has about 83 hotels of all categories, including (3-star) *Antares*, 4 Via delle Scuole. **Camping sites** at **Grado** and **Belvedere** (4-star and 2-star).

■ **Restaurants. Grado**: **A**: *Canevon*, 11 Calle Corbatto; *All'Androna*, 4 Calle Porta Piccola; *De Toni*, 47 Piazza Duca d'Aosta; *Vittoria*, Piazza della Vittoria. **B**: *Alla Borsa*, 1 Via Conte di Grado; *Da Silvio*, 4 Piazza Duca d'Aosta.

■ **Bus services** are run by APT from Gorizia to Aquileia (bus stop a few metres from the basilica) and Grado.

Aquileia

*Aquileia preserves magnificent and evocative remains of its great days both as a Roman city and as an early medieval capital, including some splendid mosaics. One of the last colonies founded by the Romans as a military outpost, it became an important city and it is estimated that its population had reached between 70,000 and 100,000 by the end of the Roman empire. It is is now a village of some 3000 inhabitants, in a fertile plain. There are still large areas of the Roman city being excavated.

History
Aquileia was founded as a Roman colony in 181 BC and soon rose to prominence. In 10 BC Augustus was in residence here and received Herod the Great. In AD 238 the 'Emperor' Maximinus was murdered by his troops when besieging the city, and in 340 Constantine II was killed on the banks of the Aussa (a little to the west) by his brother Constans in their struggle for imperial power. The bishopric or patriarchate was founded soon after 313, but civil wars and barbarian incursions, culminating in the Lombard sack of 568, led to the transference of the see to Grado, which had become the foreport of Aquileia. After 606 there were two rival patriarchs, but in 1019 Poppo united the sees and rebuilt the basilica, and the town had a second period of splendour which lasted up to the 14C. In the following centuries its importance declined because of malaria. In 1420 the civil power passed to Venice, and in 1509 Aquileia was seized by the Austrians. The patriarchate was merged in the archbishoprics of Udine and Gorizia in 1751.

The approach road follows exactly the line of the Roman *cardo*. There is a car park off the main road or by the Basilica.

Basilica

The **Basilica (open daily 8.30–12.30, 14.30–18; in summer 8.30–dusk), built soon after 313 by the first patriarch Theodore, was the scene of a historic council in 381, attended by St Ambrose and St Jerome. It was extended soon afterwards and was reconstructed in its present form by the patriarch Poppo in 1021–31.

A portico, probably dating from the beginning of the 9C, extends from the west front to the 'Chiesa dei Pagani' (now used as a shop), a rectangular 9C hall for catechumens (Christian converts under instruction) with remains of 13C frescoes, to the much altered remnants of the **baptistery**. Beneath the font, an earlier octagonal font was discovered in 1982 above part of a Roman house.

The tall leaning **campanile** (73m) was built by Poppo; the upper part dates from the 14C, the bell-chamber and steeple from the 16C. On a Roman column facing it is a figure of the Capitoline Wolf, presented by Rome in 1919.

Interior. The arcades surmounting the fine Romanesque capitals date from the patriarchate of Markward (1365–81), the nave ceiling from 1526. The huge colourful mosaic *pavement (700 square metres), discovered at the beginning of this century, dates from Theodore's basilica. It is the largest antique mosaic pavement known, and one of the most remarkable early Christian monuments in Italy, combining Christian images (like the Good Shepherd, fish, birds in trees) with pagan symbols such as the cock fighting the tortoise, the Seasons, and a winged figure of Victory holding a crown and palm branch. Other panels contain the portrait heads of donors, and numerous animals and birds, including two waders catching a serpent and frog. At the east end is one large mosaic representing the sea filled with a great variety of fish, with twelve putti fishing from boats and rocks. The story of Jonah is illustrated here in three scenes: the prophet is thrown from a boat into a sea monster's mouth (the praying figure in the boat probably represents him before his martyrdom); the prophet is regurgitated safely on shore by the monster; and Jonah rests after his adventures beneath a pergola. In the centre of the sea is a circular inscription recording Theodore.

In the **south aisle** is the Gothic chapel of St Ambrose, built by the Torriani in 1298, with family tombs and a polyptych by Pellegrino da San Daniele (1503) in a fine frame. The chapel on the right of the presbytery has a 9C–10C transenna, and frescoes. To the left of the chapel is the sarcophagus of Pope St Mark (14C, Venetian Gothic), and in front of the tomb is a fragment of 5C mosaic pavement (discovered in 1972).

Presbytery. The central Renaissance tribune and the altar to the right of it, with a good Pietà, are the work of Bernardino da Bissone. The high altar was carved by Sebastiano and Antonio da Osteno (1498). In Poppo's apse are faded frescoes, with a dedicatory inscription (1031), showing the patriarch (with a model of the church), the Emperor Conrad II with Gisela of Swabia and Prince Henry (later Henry III) before the Madonna and six patron saints. The bishop's throne is probably somewhat earlier. In the chapel to the left of the presbytery are interesting frescoes and (north wall) a bas-relief with Christ between St Peter and St Thomas Becket, sculptured soon after St Thomas's martyrdom at Canterbury in 1170. Outside the chapel is a bust of Christ (1916) by Edmondo Furlan. In the **north aisle** is the **Santo Sepolcro**, an 11C reproduction of the Holy Sepulchre at Jerusalem.

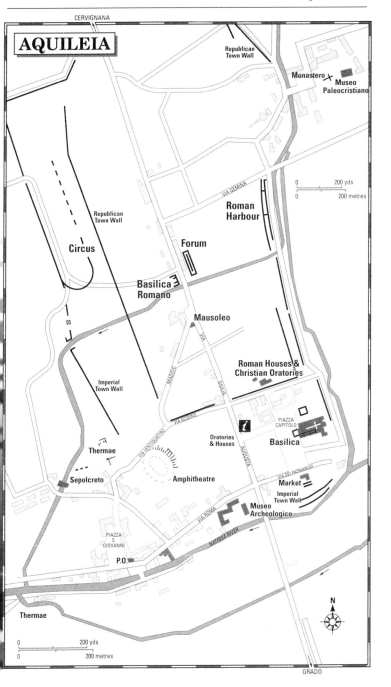

AQUILEIA

CERVIGNANA

Republican Town Wall

Monastero

Museo Paleocristiano

VIA GEMINA

Roman Harbour

0   200 yds
0   200 metres

Republican Town Wall

Circus

Forum

Basilica Romano

Mausoleo

Roman Houses & Christian Oratories

Imperial Town Wall

VIA MAGGIO

VIA GIULIA

VIA ACIDINO

Thermae

VIA VENTIDIATRO

Oratories & Houses

PIAZZA CAPITOLO

Basilica

VIA AUGUSTA

Sepolcreto

Amphitheatre

VIA DEI PATRIARCHI

Market

Imperial Town Wall

Museo Archeologico

PIAZZA S. GIOVANNI

VIA ROMA

P.O.

NATISSA RIVER

N

Thermae

0   200 yds
0   200 metres

GRADO

The **Cripta degli Affreschi** (the ticket includes admission to the Cripta degli Scavi), beneath the presbytery, has frescoes of great interest, thought to date from around 1180. They depict scenes from the life of Christ (including a fine Deposition) and that of the Madonna, and scenes relating to Saints Hermagoras and Fortunatus.

The **Cripta degli Scavi** is entered from beside the Santo Sepolcro. It is remarkable for three levels of *mosaics: those of a Roman house of the Augustan period (to the left on entering); the magnificent floor of a second basilica of the time of Theodore, encircling the foundations of Poppo's campanile; and parts of the floor of the late 4C basilica, as well as its column-bases.

Archaeological Museum

The *Archaeological Museum (open daily 9–14; sometimes for longer in summer) is reached by the main road (Via Giulia Augusta) and Via Roma (right). Founded in 1882, it has a good collection of finds made in and around Aquileia.

Ground floor. **Room I** contains an interesting collection of portrait busts of the Republican era, an inscription with the name of L. Manlius Acidinus, one of the city's founders; and a bas-relief relating to the elevation of Aquileia to a Roman colony in the first century AD. **Rooms II–IV** contain Roman sculpture.

First floor. **Room V** (to the left) contains semi-precious gems (mostly of local make), cameos, intaglios (fine Farnese bull), objects in amber and gold (notably the golden *flies, ornaments from a lady's veil). **Room VI**. Egyptian fragments and a bronze chandelier (late 4C AD). **Rooms VII–IX**. Terracotta vases, reliefs, votive statuettes, small bronzes, and a fine collection of *glass, with some unique specimens.

Second floor (still in the course of arrangement). An unusual bronze *relief of a head in profile, a Hellenistic work or a Roman imitation (very well preserved), and the gilded bronze *head of a man dating from the 3C AD, and amber.

The extensive **lapidarium** is arranged beneath porticoes and around a quadriporticus. It has an impressive collection of architectural fragments, funerary altars, mosaics, stelae, inscriptions, large sculptures and sarcophagi. A room houses a Roman ship of the late 2C AD, recovered from the sea in one of the most successful operations of underwater archaeology in recent years. Also here is an exquisite little *mosaic panel with 20 different fish (late 1C AD) . On the south side of the quadriporticus are more Roman mosaics, including one depicting a *vine-branch and a ribbon tied in a bow, dating from the Augustan age.

The last four porticoes display inscriptions from the Republican and Imperial periods, mosaic pavements, some with marble intarsia, etc.

The *EXCAVATIONS are open daily from 9 to one hour before sunset. Near the Basilica, across Via dei Patriarchi (see the Plan) are the foundations of late Roman **market-halls**, and, beyond, along the river, the foundations of a stretch of two circuits of the **town walls**. The inner walls were built c 238 and the outer walls at the end of the 4C.

On the other side of the Basilica, reached from Piazza Capitolo, are the remains of **Roman houses and Christian oratories** with superb *mosaic pavements. To the east, a path, clearly marked by a noble avenue of cypresses, follows the Natissa stream north. It is lined with architectural fragments of the 1C–4C AD found here. The little **Roman harbour** has a finely wrought quay which still skirts the greatly diminished waters of the Natissa, once a navigable river as far as Grado.

Across Via Gemina a road leads past a group of modern houses to a quiet little piazza (with a fragment of Roman road) in front of the former Benedictine Monastery of Santa Maria. Here is the **Museo Paleocristiano** (open daily 9–14; sometimes for longer in summer), housed in a huge long early Christian **basilica** (5C AD), which has another remarkable *mosaic floor, with polychrome geometrical decorations and Greek and Latin inscriptions. At the west end modern stairs lead up to a balcony on which (on three levels) are displayed a good collection of sarcophagi, transennae and mosaic panels, showing the transition of art from the classical Roman period to the new Christian era.

Via Gemina leads right to the busy Via Giulia Augusta, which passes several Roman monuments on its way back towards the Basilica. On the right can be seen a fine stretch of Roman road, and beyond are traces of the **circus**. On the left of the road, a row of fluted composite columns belongs to the **forum**. The sculptural fragments include a fine Gorgon's head. The west and east porticoes, as well as part of the pavement, have been uncovered, and on the other side of the road are the foundations of the Roman basilica of the Forum.

At the road fork is the **grande mausoleo**, an imposing (reconstructed) family tomb (1C AD). Further on, on the right of the main road (opposite the church), is a large area still being excavated of **Roman houses and early Christian oratories** (2C–4C AD) with good pavements (especially near the vineyard). The polychrome mosaic floor under cover belonged to an oratory. Via Acidino leads west past (left) the scanty remains of the **amphitheatre** and (right) the site of the **thermae** (still being excavated) towards the **sepolcreto** (key at No. 17), a row of five family tombs of the 1C–2C. Via XXIV Maggio returns south to Piazza Giovanni, the village square.

Grado

The road from Aquileia continues towards the sea for just over 4km to Belvedere at the start of a causeway nearly 7km long which leads across a beautiful *lagoon to the island-city of Grado, which was the foreport of Aquileia after the 2C. The tiny old town has been suffocated by a large seaside resort (10,000 inhab.) with a very popular sandy beach equipped with thermal and sand baths, holiday flats and numerous hotels (mostly closed in winter). An ugly raised concrete esplanade lines the seafront—only the beaches at the extreme west and east end are free.

The picturesque old **castrum**, later a fishing village, preserves a few old houses, some of them poorly restored and others derelict. Here three interesting 6C early Christian buildings stand close together.

The ***DUOMO** (Santa Eufemia) was founded as the seat of the patriarchate of Nova Aquileia by Patriarch Elias in 579; after the union of the sees these rival patriarchs moved to Venice, and in 1451 the title was finally abolished. It has a beautiful **exterior** and the **campanile** is crowned by a statue of St Michael (1462). The basilican **interior** of the Ravenna type preserves 20 different columns with Byzantine capitals. The splendid 6C mosaic ***pavement** (being restored) has charming geometrical patterns and stylised waves, connected and interlinked with a knot frieze, incorporating numerous inscriptions of donors. Near the west door is a dedicatory inscription in honour of Elias.

The charming *ambo is made up of numerous 11C fragments, with symbols of the Evangelists and an oriental cupola. On the east wall behind the high altar is a Venetian altar frontal of beaten silver (1372).

Off the right side of the basilica is a rectangular room with another fine mosaic pavement (and inscription of Elias). Here has been placed the cast of the bishop's throne donated to Grado by the Emperor Heraclius in 630 (the original was taken to Venice after 1451, and is still there—in the treasury of the Basilica of San Marco).

The **lapidarium** has Roman sepulchral inscriptions (1C–3C AD), 4C–5C early Christian fragments, sarcophagi of the 2C–3C AD, architectural fragments (1C–6C), liturgical fragments (8C–9C), and Carolingian reliefs.

The **treasury** (only open in summer) contains some splendid works, many of them made by local craftsmen, including little silver reliquary boxes (6C and 7C), a 12C Byzantine evangelistery cover, and the silver reliquary urn of St Hermagoras and St Fortunatus, an early 14C Venetian work.

The octagonal **BAPTISTERY** dates from the late 6C (restored in 1925). It is approached by a path lined with three monumental sarcophagi, and contains another mosaic pavement, a pretty wooden roof, and an hexagonal font.

Nearby is **SANTA MARIA DELLE GRAZIE**, another basilica of the 4C–5C, rebuilt in the 6C on a small scale, with an even more miscellaneous assortment of ten columns, a restored marble transenna, and an apsidal bench and throne with passage behind. In the presbytery is a marble intarsia pavement, and excavations have revealed some good 6C floor-mosaics (seen below the level of the floor on the right side).

Remains of another early Christian basilica have been found in Piazza della Vittoria, to the southeast (the excavations are fenced off). In a little garden are remains of its baptistery. The line of the old walls of the castrum can be seen in Via Gradenigo.

On the modern esplanade on the seafront a former school building is being restored as the seat of a **Museum of Underwater Archaeology**, where the remains of the *Julia Felix* , discovered in the sea between Grado and Marano in 1986, is to be exhibited. The ship, built at the end of the 2C or beginning of the 3C AD, and about 16m by 5m, was carrying wine and fish sauce in amphorae and a wooden barrel full of pieces of broken glass (for recycling). It has been recovered from the sea bed using all the latest scientific methods.

In the lagoon, to the northeast, is the islet of **Barbana**. It can only be reached (in 30–40 mins) by hiring a private boat in Grado (usually available every hour daily in summer, and on weekends in winter; the boatman will wait while you visit the island). The church, built in 1593, and rebuilt since 1918, contains a venerated statue of the Virgin (annual procession of boats on the first Sun in July).

At the mouth of the Laguna di Marano is **Lignano Sabbiadoro**, a huge planned tourist resort with some 400 hotels along a sandy spit. Across the mouth of the Tagliamento is **Bibione**, another resort.

49 · Pordenone and its province

Pordenone

Pordenone is a very pleasant provincial capital (50,000 inhab.), with a delightful long Corso. Modern buildings, some of them by Gino Valle, have been successfully integrated into the town. There are pretty parks on the banks of the river Noncello. The river used to be navigable down to the Adriatic, and Pordenone was for centuries important as a port. Cotton factories were established here in 1840, and it is still the industrial centre of Friuli. The town was the birthplace of the painter Giovanni Antonio de' Sacchis (c 1483–1539), called 'Il Pordenone', many of whose works survive in the town and province.

■ **Information office.** APT, 38 Corso Vittorio Emanuele (tel. 0434 21912).

■ **Hotels.** 4-star: *Villa Ottoboni*, 2 Piazza Ottoboni (with restaurant). 3-star: *Park Hotel*, 43 Via Mazzini; *Minerva*, 5 Piazzale XX Settembre.

■ **Restaurants. B**: *La Vecia Osteria del Moro*, 2 Via Castello. **C**: *Centrale*, 19 Piazza XX Settembre; *Britannia*, 20 Piazza della Motta. **Cafè**: *Caffè del Municipio*.

■ **Car parking** in Via Coda Fora (beyond the town hall).

■ **Annual festival** of silent movies in Oct.

The long undulating *CORSO VITTORIO EMANUELE, which winds through the old centre, is lined on either side by arcades and has interesting houses from all periods. Beyond some 13C and 14C palaces is the neo-classical façade of the former theatre. A side road leads to the **Chiesa del Cristo**, with two fine 16C portals, one by Pilacorte. The monumental Palazzo Gregoris (No. 44) in the Corso has masques in the Venetian style. No. 52 has faded frescoes attributed to Pordenone, and No. 45, the former Palazzo dei Capitani, has good fresco decoration (also on its side façade in Via Mercato). Palazzo Montereale-Mantica (No. 56) has a fine interior with Baroque stuccoes (recently restored).

Via Castello and Via della Motta lead to **Palazzo Mantica** with a fresco attributed to Pordenone. In Piazza della Motta is the **Museo delle Scienze**, with an unusual collection, arranged on three floors, some of it in old-fashioned showcases. Opposite, the former church of **San Francesco**, with damaged 15C frescoes, is used for exhibitions. Also in the piazza are the 18C civic library (with the Lion of St Mark over the door) and the 13C **Castle** (now a prison).

At No. 51 in the Corso is **Palazzo Ricchieri**, which houses the **Museo Civico** (expected to reopen soon after years of closure). The palace dates from the 15C and has fine painted wooden ceilings and some remains of mural paintings. The collection consists mainly of 16C–18C works by regional artists including Giovanni Caroto, Pordenone and Luca Giordano. It also contains a 15C seated wooden Madonna attributed to Andrea Bellunello, a wooden crucifix by the circle of Donatello, and an altar frontal in gilded and painted wood of c 1508.

The Corso ends in front of the delightful **Palazzo Comunale** which has a projecting clock tower in a Venetian Renaissance style (16C) at odds with its 13C Emilian Gothic core.

Beyond is Piazza San Marco with pretty houses, some with frescoes. The **Duomo** has a Romanesque *campanile and good west portal by Pilacorte (1511). In the light interior are altarpieces by Pordenone (*Madonna of the Misericordia*, 1515), Marcello Fogolino and Pomponio Amalteo. The **treasury** of the Duomo contains 16 precious Gothic reliquaries (at present not on view).

At the other end of the Corso, beyond Piazza Cavour, is CORSO GARIBALDI, with two grand palaces in the Venetian style facing each other. A side road leads to the 16C church of **San Giorgio** with one of the most eccentric bell-towers in Italy, consisting of a giant Tuscan column (1852).

The province of Pordenone

■ **Information office.** APT Piancavallo, Piazza Duomo, Aviano (tel. 0434/651888). Comune di Valvasone, tel. 0434/89081.

■ **Hotels. San Vito al Tagliamento**: 3-star: *Patriarca* (with restaurant).

■ **Restaurants. Spilimbergo**: *La Torre*, in the Castle (**A**). **Cordovado**: *Osteria al Tiglio* (**C**).

The most interesting places in the province are on its eastern border near the Tagliamento. Numerous monuments have been carefully restored since the 1976 earthquake.

SPILIMBERGO has a pleasant, spacious green on which is the flank of its large **Duomo**, with a side door by Zenone da Campione (1376). The organ by Bernardo Vicentino (1515) has doors painted by Pordenone. The presbytery is covered with 14C frescoes attributed to the school of Vitale da Bologna. The second south altar has a sculpted balustrade by Pilacorte.

At the end of the piazza is the entrance (across the dry moat, now a garden) to the 12C *Castle (reconstructed after a fire in 1511) which encloses a pleasant medley of 16C–18C palaces (restored since 1976), notably one with restored frescoes on its façade attributed to Bellunello. There is a fine view of the Tagliamento valley. An important **mosaic school** was founded in 1922 in Spilimbergo and is one of four in Italy (visitors are welcome by appointment).

To the north are the small village churches of **Vacile** (with apse frescoes by Pordenone), **Lestans** (frescoes by Pomponio Amalteo), and **Valeriano**, where two churches side by side (recently restored) both have frescoes by Pordenone.

To the south of Spilimbergo, **Provesano** has a church with lovely *frescoes in the sanctuary by Giovanni Francesco da Tolmezzo, and a stoup and font by Pilacorte. Further south is **Valvasone** where the Duomo has a splendid *organ (recitals in Sep) dating from 1532 and restored in 1974, with doors painted by Pordenone in 1538 (completed by Pomponio Amalteo). Nearby the church of

San Pietro has a tiny Venetian 17C organ and frescoes by Pietro da Vicenza. The Castle which encloses an 18C theatre is in very poor condition. A medieval pagaent is held here in September.

SAN VITO AL TAGLIAMENTO is an interesting little town with a pleasant long piazza in front of its **Duomo** and tall campanile. It contains some important works by Pomponio Amalteo. Also in the piazza is Palazzo Fancello with a painted façade and next to it the 15C Palazzo Rota (the town hall) with a fine garden (a public park). At the end of the piazza is the Torre Raimonda, seat of the town library and (on the top floor) of the **Museo Civico** (ask for admission at the library). It contains prehistoric and Roman finds from the area, as well as Renaissance ceramics from Palazzo Rota and 15C frescoes detached from Palazzo Altan.

To the south, on the border with the Veneto, is **SESTO AL REGHENA** with the former Benedictine abbey church of **Santa Maria in Sylvis** (open 8–17), founded in 762 and fortified and surrounded by a moat in the 9C (the walls were demolished in 1939). Beautifully restored in 1989–92, it has an unusual plan, preceded by a vestibule and large aisled atrium. On the left of the entrance a little **loggia** has a fragment of a fresco with courtly scenes (12C). On the right, steps lead up to the **salone** with a fine wooden ceiling, and delightful painted decoration in pastel shades in imitation of curtains with flowers above. The fragment of the head of St Michael is the oldest fresco to have survived in the abbey (12C).

The **vestibule** has frescoes of Paradise and (very ruined) of Hell, traditionally attributed to Antonio da Firenze. On the right the little **refectory** has more fresco fragments. The large **atrium** has sculptured fragments, a detached lunette of St Benedict, and an unusual scene of three figures on horesback and three coffins thought to date from 1316. The **church** has a remarkable *fresco cycle in the presbytery (including scenes from the life of St Benedict) dating from the early 14C by the bottega of Giotto. The **crypt**, rebuilt at the beginning of this century, contains the splendid reliquary urn of St Anastasia, adapted in the late Middle Ages from an 8C abbot's throne. Also here is a late 13C sculpted diptych of the Annunciation (with a view of the fortified abbey in the background) and a stone 15C Pietà. On the lawn outside can be seen the foundations of the first Lombard early Christian church.

To the east of Sesto is the tiny, well preserved little town of **Cordovado** which was a fortified borgo on the southern border of Friuli. The delightful old centre has one street between the two gates and narrow alleys on either side. Opposite Villa Freschi, with a garden with statues, is Villa Marrubini. Outside the walls is the ocatagonal church of Santa Maria delle Grazie next to the town hall. The spring of Venchiaredo, mentioned by Ippolito Nievo in his *Confessioni di un italiano* (1867) is nearby.

Just to the west of Pordenone is the old town of **Porcia** which has an interesting old centre. From Sacile, further west, there is a pretty branch railway line which leads northeast and crosses the Tagliamento to Gemona, see Chapter 47.

Trentino-Alto Adige

Trentino-Alto Adige (841,000 inhab.; 13,613 sq. km), the mountain territory of the upper Adige valley and south Tyrol, incorporating the modern provinces of Bolzano and Trento, is a semi-autonomous region. Most characteristic among the mountains of this region are the fantastic pinnacles of the **Dolomites**, the strangely shaped limestone mountains disposed in irregular groups between the Adige and Piave valleys. The region of Trento is almost entirely Italian speaking, while in that of Bolzano (the Alto Adige) the native language of Ladin has, except in the more remote valleys, been overlaid by the official language of the ruling power: German until 1918 and, since then, Italian or German.

The two provinces represent respectively the old ecclesiastic principalities of Trento and Bressanone (or Brixen), both of which in the Middle Ages paid nominal allegiance to the Empire. In the 14C–15C the prince-bishops held the balance between the rising power of Venice on the south, and the Counts of Tyrol on the north, while in the 16C, under the great bishops Clesio of Trento and Madruzzo of Bressanone, the valleys were practically independent. The decay of local powers prevailed here as elsewhere in the 17C–18C, and the Trentino and southern Tyrol became more closely attached to the Empire. During Napoleon's campaigns the region was transferred first to Austria, then (in 1803) to Bavaria; the insurrection of Andreas Hofer in 1809 led to a return to Austria in 1814. Austrian misgovernment in the 19C caused great discontent in the Trentino, and a movement for absorption into the Veneto. The successful outcome of the First World War brought the Trentino under Italian power, and the extension of the frontier northward to the strategic line of the Brenner was an inevitable consequence, though the mountain warfare in the region produced little result for either side. In the Second World War the road and railway over the Brenner Pass, the main channel of communication between Italy and Germany, was heavily attacked from the air.

50 · Trento and Rovereto

■ **Information offices.** APT del Trentino, 3 Via Sighele (tel. 0461/914444). APT di Trento, 4 Via Alfieri (tel. 0461/983880). APT di Rovereto, 63 Via Dante (tel. 0464/430363).

■ **Hotels. Trento**: 4-star: *Buonconsiglio*, 16 Via Romagnosi; 3-star: *America*, 50 Via Torre Verde. **Rovereto**: 3-star: *Rovereto*, 82 Corso Rosmini (with restaurant); *Leon d'oro*, 2 Via Tacchi.

■ **Restaurants. Trento**: A: *Osteria a le due Spade*, 11 Via Don Rizzi; *Chiesa*, Via San Marco; *Orso Grigio*, 19 Via degli Orti. **B**: *Locanda Gius Port'Aquila*, 66 Via Cervara; *Semprebon*, 7 Piazza Centa; **C**: *Al Vo*, 11 Vicolo del Vo. **Rovereto**: A: *Al Borgo*, 13 Via Garibaldi; *Novecento* (in Rovereto hotel) **C**: *La Lanterna*, 12 Piazza Malfatti.

Trento

Trento is a cheerful town (91,700 inhab.), capital of its province and of the autonomous region of Trentino-Alto Adige. It is encircled by spectacular mountain ranges. Though it remained in Austrian hands until 1918, it is a typically northern Italian city and entirely Italian speaking. It has a number of fine palaces and churches as well as the Castello di Buonconsiglio, famous seat of the prince-bishops of Trento.

History

Trento, the Roman *Tridentum*, owed its importance throughout the Middle Ages to its position on the main road from the German Empire into Italy; and in the 10C the bishops of Trento acquired the special privileges from the Emperor (probably Conrad the Salic) which they held until 1796 practically without a break. Early in the 15C the citizens rebelled against the overwhelming power of the bishops, but local unrest came to an end with the threat of a Venetian invasion, Venice having secured control of the Val Lagarina as far up as Rovereto (1416). The Tridentines asked for help from the Count of Tyrol, the Venetians were defeated in 1487, and in 1511 Austria established a protectorate over the Trentino. In the 16C the city rose to prominence under Bishop Bernardo Clesio and Bishop Cristoforo Madruzzo, and during the episcopate of the latter the famous Council of Trent met here (1545–63). The last prince-bishop escaped from the French in 1796, and the Austrians took possession of the town in 1813, holding it until 1918 through a century of great unrest.

Via Roma and its continuation VIA MANCI, the chief street of the old town, runs east and west. From its north side, between the Baroque church of **San Francesco Saverio** and **Palazzo Galasso**, built by the banker Georg Fugger in 1602, Via Alfieri runs north, across the old course of the Adige, to the public gardens and the station. To the left is a good monument to Dante (1896, by Cesare Zocchi), behind which rises the tower of the Romanesque church of **San Lorenzo**, a fine example of 12C monastic architecture.

In Via Belenzani, opening opposite San Francesco, is the 16C **Palazzo del Municipio**, with frescoes by Brusasorci in the Sala della Giunta. **Palazzo Geremia**, in the Venetian Renaissance style, has charming frescoes of the early 16C showing the Emperor Maximilian, who stayed here in 1508–09, and members of his court. Vicolo Colico (right) leads to the graceful Renaissance church of **Santa Maria Maggiore**, by Antonio Medaglia (1520). The great portal of the façade dates from 1535; on the south side is a 16C Lombardesque portal. In the interior were held several sessions—including the last—of the Council of Trent. It contains altarpieces by Giovanni Battista Moroni (1551), Cignaroli, Unterberger and Falconetto. The *organ gallery, richly carved, is by Vincenzo Grandi (1534).

Piazza Duomo is a pretty square with the handsome 18C Neptune fountain, the frescoed **Palazzo Cazuffi** (16C), and the **Torre Civica**, on the site of a Roman enceinte tower (one of the 'Trenta Torri'—Thirty Towers—from which Trento is erroneously supposed to have taken its modern name). **Palazzo Pretorio**, once the episcopal palace, now houses the **Museo Diocesano Tridentino** (open 9.30–12.30, 14.30–18 exc. fest.), with a fine collection of paintings and sculpture from local churches, objects from the cathedral treasury, and a superb series of Flemish *tapestries by Pieter van Aelst (1497–1532).

The *Duomo, a handsome Romanesque building, entirely of marble, was begun by Adamo d'Arogno (died 1212), and not completed until 1515. The beautiful exterior of the east end has galleries, and three apses, next to the Castelletto (the rear part of the adjoining Palazzo Pretorio). In the interior clusters of tall columns carry the arcades, surmounted by a diminutive clerestory, and unusual arcaded staircases lead up to the galleries. It contains numerous tombs of bishops, 13C–14C frescoes (some attributed to Tomaso da Modena), paintings by Carlo Loth, a 13C statue of the Madonna, and two 13C marble reliefs of St Stephen. The crucifix, before which the decrees of the Council of Trent were promulgated, is the work of Sixtus Frei of Nuremberg (1510–12).

The 18C Palazzo Sardagna houses the Museo Tridentino di Scienze Naturali (open 10–12.30, 14.30–18 exc. Mon), with interesting natural history collections. Near the charming Renaissance Palazzo Tabarelli is the picturesque Cantone, once the chief crossroads in the town.

Castello del Buonconsiglio

The *Castello del Buonconsiglio (open 9–12, 14–17 exc. Mon) was the stronghold of the medieval prince-bishops of Trento from the 13C onwards, and is the most important monument in the region. The Castelvecchio, dating from the 13C, occupies the northern wing, and the southern part is the Renaissance Magno Palazzo, built under Bishop Clesio in 1528–36. The well arranged Collezioni Provinciali include 15C music manuscripts (French, German and Italian), paintings, sculpture, majolica and porcelain, as well as prehistoric, Roman and Lombard finds.

The rooms of the castle are frescoed by Dosso and Battista Dossi and Girolamo Romanino. The great hall has a good fireplace by Vincenzo Grandi, and the Sala degli Specchi is an 18C Rococo room.

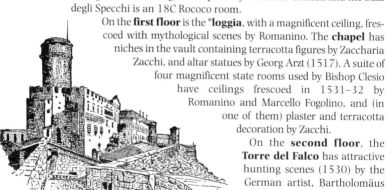

On the first floor is the *loggia, with a magnificent ceiling, frescoed with mythological scenes by Romanino. The chapel has niches in the vault containing terracotta figures by Zaccharia Zacchi, and altar statues by Georg Arzt (1517). A suite of four magnificent state rooms used by Bishop Clesio have ceilings frescoed in 1531–32 by Romanino and Marcello Fogolino, and (in one of them) plaster and terracotta decoration by Zacchi.

On the second floor, the Torre del Falco has attractive hunting scenes (1530) by the German artist, Bartholomäus Dill, and the Torre dell'Aquila *frescoes of the Months (c 1400), with delightful contemporary rural scenes, probably by a Bohemian painter. The apartment of

Castello del Buonconsiglio

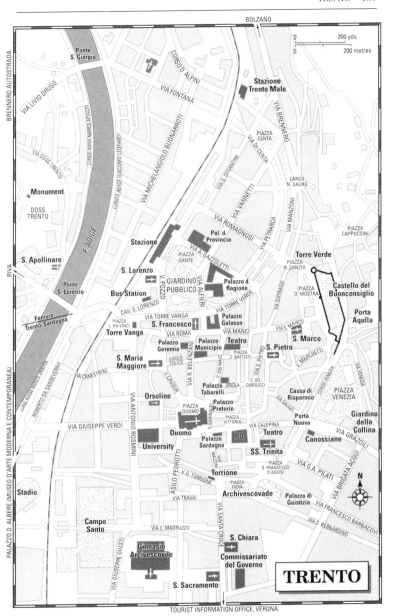

BOLZANO

TRENTO

Bernardo Clesio includes the large **library**, in the coffered ceiling of which are 18 Sages by Dosso Dossi.

In a former carpenters' workshop is the **Museo Storico**, with a copious collection illustrating the history of the Trentino from the Risorgimento to the Resistence (including the Cesare Battisti archives).

On the Adige is the 16C **Palazzo delle Albere**, a suburban villa with frescoes by Marcello Fogolino, which now houses the **Museo d'Arte Moderna e Contemporanea** (open 9–12.30, 14.30–18 exc. Mon), which includes works by the Italian Futurists.

On the plateau of **Viotte** is a renowned alpine **Botanic Garden** (open Jun–Sep, 9–12, 14.30–18). A cableway mounts to the summit of Monte Bondone (1875m).

To the south of Trento is the **Val Lagarina**, a deep valley covered with woods and vineyards. At **Mattarello**, near the airport of Trento, is the **Museo Aeronautica 'Gianni Caproni'** (open 9–13, 16–18 exc. Mon), an interesting aircraft museum which displays 20 planes built between 1910 and 1980. Near Calliano is the **Castel Beseno** (open Apr–Oct 9–12, 14–17.30 exc. Mon) which controlled the valley south of Trento. The hill was inhabited in the Iron Age, as well as in the Roman and Lombard periods. The castle dates from the 12C, and was owned by the Castelbarco from 1303 until the 15C when it was given to the Trapp family who donated it to the province in 1973. It has recently been restored and includes two large courtyards within its impressive walls. A room of the castle preserves 16C frescoes of the Months.

Rovereto

Rovereto is the chief town (29,600 inhab.) of the Val Lagarina. The **Museo Civico** (open 9–12, 13–17.30 exc. Sun & Mon), first opened to the public in 1855, houses the collections of the archaeologist Paolo Orsi (1849–1925), who was a native of the town, and a natural history section. The Accademia degli Agiati was foundeded in 1750. The **Galleria Futurista Depero** (open 9–12, 14.30–18 exc. Mon) contains numerous works by the Futurist artist Fortunato Depero (1892–1960). The tapestries, furniture, mosaics, paintings and graphic works were all produced here in Depero's 'Casa d'Arte' between 1920 and 1942.

The **Castle**, enlarged in the 15C, contains a large **Museum of the First World War** (open 8.30–12.30, 14–18 exc. Mon), the most important in Italy. The war is commemorated by the **Sacrario** (1936) and

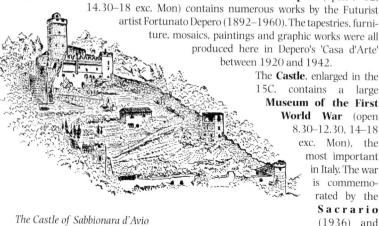

The Castle of Sabbionara d'Avio

the **Campana dei Caduti**, the largest bell in Italy, which tolls every evening for the fallen of all nations. The front line of 1916–18 was in the valley south of the town.

South of Rovereto, in a fine position on a hillside with woods and cultivated terraces above the Adige, is the picturesque **Castello di Sabbionara d'Avio**, the home of the Counts of Castelbarco since the 14C. It was the first monument in Italy to be donated (in 1977) to the FAI (Fondo per l'Ambiente Italiano, founded in 1975 on the model of the British National Trust) who restored it (open 10–13, 14–17 or 18 exc. Mon, and in Jan). The Casa delle Guardie has remarkable frescoes (1345–60) of battle scenes. The well preserved keep which dominates the fortress, dates from the 11C–12C. On the fourth floor, the Stanza d'Amore preserves fragments of 14C frescoes with courtly scenes. In front of the tower is the Palazzo Baronale with remains of its chapel.

51 · The Adamello-Brenta group, with Val di Non and Val di Sole

This chapter describes some of the finest country in the Italian Alps, including the Val di Non and Val di Sole and the Presanella and Brenta mountain groups, forming part of a protected area to the east of Monte Adamello (3539m).

■ **Information offices.** APT del Val di Non, 14 Piazza San Giovanni, Fondo (tel. 0463/830133). APT delle Valli di Sole, 7 Viale Marconi, Malè (tel. 0463/901280). APT Madonna di Campiglio, 4 Via Pradalago (tel. 0465/42000).

■ Numerous **hotels** and **restaurants** in all the resorts.

In the **Valli Giudicarie**, between **Stenico** and **Tione**, is the *Gola della Scaletta, a narrow winding gorge of the Sarca. The **Castello di Stenico** (open 9–12, 14–17 exc. Mon), dating from the 12C, was a stronghold of the prince-bishops of Trent. It is now owned by the province and has been restored. Inside are frescoes including battle scenes and female allegorical figures, as well as arms, furniture, and archaeological material.

To the north of Stenico is the lovely peaceful *Lago di Molveno, 6.5km long, lying under the lee of the Brenta mountains. Spectacular walks can be taken in the area.

The lovely *VAL DI NON, with its woods and ruined castles, is known for its apples: the landscape is particularly beautiful in spring when the trees are in blossom. A scenic branch railway line runs from Trento via Cles to Malè. The most important place in the valley is **Cles**, whose castle was the ancestral home of the famous episcopal Clesio family, rebuilt in the 16C. Standing at the foot of Monte Peller (2319m), the northern peak of the Brenta group, it has a good Renaissance church and old houses.

Sanzeno is a pleasant village with a large 15C church built on the site of the martyrdom in 397 of Sisinio, Martirio, and Alessandro from Capodoccia. Above is the sanctuary of *San Romedio, a pilgrim shrine on a steep rock.

To the northwest of Cles is the **VAL DI SOLE**, the upper glen of the Noce (now used for canoeing and rafting). **Malè**, the main village in the valley, has a local ethnographical museum (Museo della Civiltà Solandra).

MADONNA DI CAMPIGLIO (1522m) is a famous winter and summer resort, in a wooded basin in the upper valley of the Sarca, below the Brenta mountains. It has excellent ski facilities. The Brenta mountains, an isolated dolomitic group between Madonna di Campiglio and the Adige valley, are for expert climbers only, but there are many easier walks (marked by coloured signs) in their foothills. A path (or chair-lift) ascends Monte Spinale (2104m), from which there is a splendid circular view of the Brenta, Adamello, Presanella and Ortler mountains. To the south is the magnificent **Val Brenta**.

Pinzolo, another ski resort and climbing centre, is in a splendid position at the junction of the two main upper valleys of the Sarca.The church of *San Vigilio has a remarkable external fresco of the Dance of Death, by Simone Baschenis (1539). A similar painting (1519) by the same artist decorates the exterior of the church of **Santo Stefano** (which also contains frescoes by him inside).

The **Val di Genova** is a magnificent valley, thickly wooded in parts and with several waterfalls, which is the main approach to the Presanella and Adamello groups from the east. The **Presanella** (3556m) was first ascended by the English alpinist Douglas Freshfield (died 1929) in 1864.

52 · The Val di Fiemme and San Martino di Castrozza

■ **Information offices.** APT Valle di Fiemme, 60 Via Fratelli Bronzetti, Cavalese (tel. 0462/241111). APT San Martino di Castrozza e Primiero, 165 Via Passo Rolle, San Martino di Castrozza (tel. 0439/768867).

■ Numerous **hotels** and **restaurants** in the resorts.

Cavalese is the main village in the **Val di Fiemme**, the middle course of the Avisio. Like many of the valleys of the Pyrenees, this glen has preserved something of its medieval independence, and the 'Magnifica Comunità', installed in the ancient palace of the bishops of Trent, still administers the valuable communal lands. The palace contains a museum (open Jul & Aug and at Christmas, 16.30–19), illustrating the history of the valley.

Predazzo (1018m) has an interesting collection of local geological specimens in the Museo Comunale (open 15–18 exc. Sat & fest.; also 10–12 in summer). The Ladin-speaking **Val di Fassa** is in the heart of the Dolomites; between Pozza di Fassa and Canazei it forms part of the Strada dei Dolomiti (see Chapter 56). The main village is **Vigo di Fassa** (1382m), a winter sports resort, where the Museo Ladino records the history of the valley. The fantastic **Torri del Vaiolet** is typical of the dolomitic mountains.

To the east of Predazzo is the **Parco Naturale Paneveggio-Pale di San Martino**, a protected area noted for its magnificent forest, wild flowers and wildlife (deer, mountain goats, etc.). Much of the wood used to build the

Venetian Republic's fleet came from here. **San Martino di Castrozza** (1444m) is the most popular summer and winter resort in the southern Dolomites. It lies in an ample basin of the Cismon valley, with wooded slopes leading up to the towering peaks of the Pale di San Martino.

53 · Bolzano

Bolzano, in German *Bozen* (105,800 inhab.), is the largest town in the upper basin of the Adige, and has been the capital of the province of Bolzano-Alto Adige (mainly German speaking) since 1927. It has the character of a German rather than Italian town, although its population is now mainly Italian speaking. The old town, with its low-pitched Tyrolean arcades and Gothic architecture has a somewhat grim appearance. Lovely walks can be taken in the neighbourhood, though in summer the heat can be oppressive.

■ **Information offices.** APT Alto Adige, 11 Piazza Parrocchia, Bolzano (tel. 0471 993808). APT Bolzano, 8 Piazza Walther (tel. 0471 970660).

■ **Hotels.** 4-star: *Parkhotel Laurin*, 4 Via Laurin (with Belle Epoque restaurant, **A**). 3-star: *Città-Stadt*, 21 Piazza Walther. 2-star: *Lewald*, 17 Via Maso della Pieve.

■ **Restaurants. B**: *Gostner Floras Bistro*, Piazza delle Erbe. **C**: *Ca de' bezzi Batzenhausl*, 30 Via Andreas Hofer; *Vogele*, 3 Via Goethe.

History
An Iron Age necropolis has been found beneath the city, and a bridge is believed to have been built across the Isarco by Drusus in the 1C BC somewhere in the neighbourhood of Bolzano. Bolzano became an important market in the Middle Ages, and was contended between the bishops of Trent and the counts of Tyrol until 1276. With the rest of Tyrol it was handed to the Habsburg family in 1363. Andreas Hofer led a rebellion against the Bavarian invasion from 1796 to 1809. In 1810–13 it was part of the Napoleonic kingdom of Italy, and from then until 1918 it belonged again to Austria. The town was damaged by bombing in the Second World War.

In the central Piazza Walther is the **Duomo**, a Gothic church of the 14C–15C with a fine tower of 1501–19, by Johann Lutz. The former **Dominican Monastery** has frescoes with interesting Giottesque figures (1330–40), a Gothic cloister, and a chapel with 14C–16C frescoes. The 14C church of **San Francesco** contains a fine carved wooden altarpiece by Hans Klocker (1500), and an entertaining frieze of celebrated Franciscans (16C).

The **Museo Civico** (open 9–12, 14.30–17.30; fest. 10–13) has an interesting local collection. The **Castello Mareccio**, a 13C building with five later towers, is now a congress centre. The **Talvera Bridge**, with a good view, leads across the river to a triumphal arch by Marcello Piacentini (1928).

In the garden suburb of **Gries**, the parish church (15C–16C) contains a carved wooden altarpiece (1471–80), by Michael Pacher. The **Passeggiata Sant'Osvaldo** is a fine terraced walk.

A cableway leads up from Bolzano (Via Renon) to the high plateau northeast of Bolzano, with its *views of the Dolomites.

North of Bolzano, in the **Valle Sarentina**, is **Castel Roncolo** (1237) which contains remarkable frescoes (shown on a guided tour Mar–Nov 10–17 exc. fest. & Mon).

On the other side of the Adige is the ruined *Castle of Appiano, founded in the 12C, which retains a Romanesque chapel with murals (open Apr–Oct exc. Tue). **Appiano sulla Strada del Vino** has several fine 17C–18C houses in a Renaissance style peculiar to the district. At **Caldaro**, on the Lago di Caldaro, there is a wine museum.

54 · Merano and Tirolo

MERANO, in German *Meran*, is an ancient town (34,200 inhab.) famous as a climatic resort and spa, and also a climbing centre and ski resort. Together with **Maia Alta** and **Maia Bassa** (*Obermais* and *Untermais*) on the opposite bank of the torrent, it consists mainly of monumental hotels and villas, many of them built at the turn of the century by Austrian architects, surrounded by luxuriant gardens in a sheltered valley. Spring and autumn are the fashionable seasons for visiting Merano. The inhabitants are mainly German speaking.

■ **Information office.** APT Merano, 45 Corso Libertà (tel. 0473/235223).

■ Numerous 4-star and 3-star **hotels**.

History

Although it is probable the area was already inhabited in Roman times, the name *Mairania* appears for the first time in 857. After the town came into the possession of the Counts of Venosta in the 13C it gradually assumed importance and by 1317 it had been designated a municipality. After 1836, under Austrian rule, its good climate began to attract visitors and it developed into one of the most celebrated climatic resorts in Italy. The thermal centre here uses radioactive springs.

The old main street of the medieval town is the dark and narrow VIA DEI PORTICI. Beneath its low arcades are excellent shops and the town hall (1930). Behind this is the **Castello Principesco** (open 9.30–12, 14–18; Sat 9–12; closed fest.), one of the best preserved castles in the region, built by Archduke Sigismund in 1445–80 and containing contemporary furnishings. The arms of Scotland alongside those of Austria recall the marriage of Sigismund with Eleanor, daughter of James I of Scotland. Also in Via Galilei, is the **Museo Civico** (open 10–12, 15–18 exc. Mon & fest.), with local collections.

At the end of Via dei Portici is the **Duomo**, a Gothic church of the 14C–15C, with a curious battlemented façade, a tall tower (83m), and 14C–16C tomb-reliefs. Inside are two 15C altarpieces by Martin Knoller. Along the river Passirio extend gardens and promenades laid out at the turn of the century. The cheerful CORSO LIBERTÀ, with the most fashionable shops, was laid out before the First World War. It passes the Kursaal (1914), the neo-classical theatre, and several elaborate hotels.

In Maia Bassa is the hippodrome (1935), run in conjunction with a famous national lottery.

TIROLO to the north, a village given over to tourism, is especially favoured by Germans on walking holidays. Ezra Pound stayed in the **Castel Fontana** (reconstructed in 1904), which contains mementoes of the poet as well as a local ethnographical museum (open Apr–Nov 9.30–12, 14–17 exc. Tue). On the opposite side of a ravine, in a superb position, is *Castel Tirolo** (open Mar–Nov 10–17 exc. Mon), the 12C castle of the counts of Tyrol which gave its name to the region. With the abdication of Margaret Maultasch, the 'ugly duchess', in 1363, the castle and province passed to the Habsburgs. Damaged by a landslip in 1680, the castle was restored in 1904.

The castle of **Scena**, on the hill northeast of Maia Alta, is a 14C building, restored by the Count of Liechtenstein in 1700. It is privately owned but shown to visitors from Easter to Nov at 10.30, 11.30, 14, 15, 16 & 17 exc. Sun. There is an armoury, and rooms with Renaissance furniture.

In the pastoral **Val Passiria** is **Maso della Rena**, the birthplace of Andreas Hofer (1767–1810), the Tyrolese patriot who led the successful insurrection of 1809 against Bavaria. There is a little private museum in his house (now a hotel).

55 · The Val Venosta

The Val Venosta, or *Vinschgau*, is the wide and fertile upper valley of the Adige to the west of Merano, near the Austrian and Swiss borders. It has numerous small summer and winter resorts and fine mountain scenery. Part of the valley lies in the Stelvio National Park.

■ **Information office.** APT Alto Adige, 11 Piazza Parrocchia, Bolzano (tel. 0473 830600). At Trafoi, tel. 0473 611677.

At the summer resort of **Naturno** is the little Romanesque church of San Procolo which contains remarkable mural paintings (8C).

The **Val di Senales** is a long mountain valley dominated by the great pyramid of the Similaun (3597m), on the Austrian frontier. The **Val di Fosse** is a beautiful side valley in front of **Monte Tessa**, a protected area (33,000 hectares), with deer and other wildlife.

The **Val Martello** is within the **Stelvio National Park**, designated a protected area in 1935 and now some 134,600 hectares, an area of great natural beauty around the Ortles-Cevedale mountain ranges. Mountain goats, deer and eagles are among the wildlife to survive here. The administrative centre of the park is now at Bormio in Lombardy (see Chapter 7), but there are information centres at Prato allo Stelvio and Cogolo. In the last few decades the beauty of the park has been threatened, especially in the area within the Province of Bolzano: hunting has been allowed, as well as the building of roads, hotels, ski-lifts, etc. **Morter** in the Val Martello has a triapsidal Romanesque church, and an aviary for falcons.

The main place in the Val Venosta is **Silandro**, the upper limit (722m) of the vine. In the **Val di Solda**, in the Stelvio National Park, **Solda** (1907m) is one of the most important climbing centres in the upper Adige and a holiday resort. Above rise Monte Cevedale (3769m) and the *****Ortler** (or *Ortles*, 3905m), a magnificent peak, defended by the Austrians throughout the First World War.

Trafoi (1543m) is a summer and winter resort with a magnificent panorama of the Ortler group. The **Stelvio Pass** (2758m), the second highest road-pass in the Alps (12m lower than the Col d'Iseran) is generally open only Jun–Oct. It is visited for summer skiing (chair-lift to 3174m). Until 1918 this was the meeting-place of the frontiers of Italy, Switzerland and Austria. There is a good view from the **Pizzo Garibaldi** (2838m), in German called Dreisprachenspitze ('three languages peak') from the meeting of the districts where Italian, Romansch and German are spoken. The **Umbrail Pass** or **Giogo di Santa Maria** (2502m) is on the Swiss frontier.

Above **Sluderno** is the **Castel Coira**, or *Churburg*, the 13C castle of the bishops of Coire, restored in the 16C by the Counts Trapp (interesting armoury). To the west is **Glorenza**, a typical old Tyrolean town, particularly well preserved, with medieval and 16C ramparts and three gates. In the Val Monastero (Münster-Tal) is the Calven gorge, where in 1499 the Swiss defeated the Austrians and won their practical independence of the Empire. **Tubre** (1240m), or *Taufers*, on the Swiss border, has a Romanesque church (good 13C frescoes).

Malles Venosta (1051m) is an old mountain town (4700 inhab.) with its churches rebuilt in the Gothic style. San Benedetto dates from the 9C or earlier (important Carolingian fresco cycle). The large Benedictine abbey of **Monte Maria**, outside the town, mainly rebuilt in the 17C–19C, preserves frescoes of c 1160.

At the north end of the Lago di Resia, below the source of the Adige, stands **Resia** (1525m), with a splendid view down the valley of the Ortler group. It was rebuilt when its original site was submerged. The Austrian frontier lies just beyond the **Passo di Resia** (1507m).

56 · The Strada delle Dolomiti (Val di Fassa)

The famous *****Strada delle Dolomiti** (N241) from Bolzano to Cortina, one of the most beautiful roads in the Alps, is a magnificent feat of engineering.

■ **Information office.** APT Alto Adige, 11 Piazza Parrocchia, Bolzano (tel. 0471 993808).

From Bolzano the road enters the wild and romantic gorge of the **Val d'Ega**, passing the *Ponte della Cascata. It then passes the resorts of **Nova Levante**, or Welschnofen (1182m), and **Carezza al Lago** (1609m), dominated by the two most typical

Dolomite mountain groups with their characteristic battlemented skyline, the **Látemar** (2842m) and the **Catinaccio** (2981m), especially famous for its marvellous colouring at sunrise (from which it takes the German name *Rosengarten*).

The road-summit is reached at the Passo di Costalunga (1745m), with a splendid view ahead of the Val di Fassa and the Marmolada and San Martino mountains. The **Marmolada** (3342m), the largest and highest group of mountain peaks in the Dolomites, is approached by the Avisio and Contrin valleys, by cableways and chair-lifts.

A winding descent into the province of Belluno in the Veneto through high pastures brings the road into the Val Cordevole, with the villages of **Arabba** (1601m), and **Pieve di Livinallongo** (1475m). The **Val Pettorina** is the main approach to the east side of the Marmolada. The Cortina road beyond Pieve leaves the Cordevole and begins a long ascent beneath the ruined castle of Andraz. The **Passo di Falzarego** (2105m) was a hotly contested strongpoint in the First World War. The road descends to Cortina d'Ampezzo, described in Chapter 44.

57 · Bolzano to the Brenner Pass (Val Gardena)

This is the main route to the Brenner Pass into Austria, for many centuries one of the most important routes over the Alps. There are numerous castles defending the Isarco valley. The side valley of Val Gardena has beautiful scenery and spectacular views of the mountains. The inhabitants still speak Ladin and there are many small resorts here.

■ **Information office.** APT Alto Adige, 11 Piazza Parrocchia, Bolzano (tel. 0471 993808).

To the north of Bolzano, in the Isarco valley, **Ponte Gardena**, or *Waidbruck*, stands at the mouth of the Val Gardena. The **Castel Forte Trostburg** is a 12C castle of the Wolkenstein, with a 16C hall (open Easter–Oct exc. Mon at 10,11, 14, 15 & 16). **Castelrotto**, or *Kastelruth* (1060m), is an ancient village with a 17C town hall and an 18C belfry, now visited for skiing in summer and winter. **Siusi** (998m), or *Seis am Schlern*, is a well-known resort near the **Alpe di Siusi**, a wide upland plateau. At **Fiè a Sciliar** is the 13C **Castel Presule Colonna**, rebuilt in 1517 (open Apr–Oct at 11, 14 & 15 exc. Sat).

The *VAL GARDENA is a Ladin-speaking valley, at the centre of which is **Ortisei** (1234m) or *St Ulrich* (4000 inhab.), another fine resort. The 18C **church** contains good examples of woodcarving for which Ortisei is noted. The **Museo della Val Gardena** has a collection of local interest.

The resort of **Selva di Val Gardena**, or *Wolkenstein in Groden* (1563m), stands at the foot of the Vallunga, which penetrates the heart of the Puez and Gardenaccia mountains to the northeast. The **Passo Sella** (2213m) has a splendid view, perhaps the finest in all the Dolomites, which takes in the Sasso Lungo (northwest), Sella (northeast) and Marmolada (southeast).

Beyond Ponte Gardena (see above) the Brenner road passes the ancient small town of **Chiusa**, or *Klausen*. The chapel of the Madonna di Loreto contains a precious treasury. The fine *****Castel Velturno**, built in 1577–87, is now owned by the province (shown on guided tours Mar–Nov at 10, 11, 14.30 & 15.30 exc. Mon).

BRESSANONE, in German *Brixen*, is a pleasant old episcopal city (16,000 inhab.), for many centuries the capital of an independent state in continual dispute with the counts of Tyrol. Via Mercato Vecchio is a characteristic old street. The tall *bell-tower of **San Michele** (1459) is known as the 'White Tower'. In the attractive Piazza Duomo, the **Cathedral** was completely rebuilt in 1745–54; it has a façade in a strange mixture of styles. Inside are carved alter-pieces, vault frescoes by Paul Troger, and paintings by Francesco and Cristoforo Unterberger. The Romanesque *****cloister** has 14C–15C frescoes. In the 11C **Baptistery** was held the council instigated by Henry IV in 1080 to depose Hildebrand (Pope St Gregory VII) and elect the antipope Clement III.

The **Palazzo dei Principi Vescovi**, first built in the 13C but later altered, has a handsome exterior with its windows decorated in terracotta. It contains the cathedral treasury and the **Diocesan Museum** (open Mar–Oct 10-17 exc. fest.) with a collection of locally carved *presepi* (cribs). The handsome courtyard of the palace has terracotta statues by Hans Reichle (1599). Also in Piazza Duomo is **Palazzo Pfaundler**, built in 1581, and behind the town hall are typical old houses in the arcaded Via dei Portici.

Just outside the town is the **Abbey of Novacella**, in a low site near the Isarco. The church and cloister are open all day, but the library and pinacoteca are only shown on guided tours at 11 and 15 (or by appointment). The abbey was founded in 1141/42 and now belongs to priests of the Agostinian order. A characteristic wooden bridge leads over the river to the entrance beside the curious round castellated chapel of **San Michele**, dating from the 12C (rebuilt in the 16C). Beyond a courtyard with a little 'tempietto' protecting the well, is the elaborate 18C **church**. The **cloister** has fragments of 14C–15C frescoes. The Rococo **library** has a good collection of illuminated MSS and incunabula. The **pinacoteca** contains an altarpiece by Michele Pacher and a Crucifixion of c 1380.

Above Bressanone are the fortifications (1833–38) of **Fortezza**, or *Franzensfeste*, **Castel Tasso**, or *Reifenstein* (open Easter–Nov exc. Fri on guided tours at 9.30, 10.30, 14 & 15), dating from the 12C–16C, with late Gothic decorations, and **Castel Pietra** (or *Sprechenstein*) in the open vale of Vipiteno.

VIPITENO, or *Sterzing*, takes its Italian name from a Roman post established here. The town owed its importance to the mines which were worked in the side-valleys until the 18C. The **Palazzo Comunale** is an attractive building of 1468–73, and around the tall **Torre di Città** are 15C–16C *mansions, many with battlements, built by the old mine-owning families. The **Casa dell'Ordine Teutonico**, with the **Museo Civico** and **Museo Multscher** (open May–Oct 10–12, 14–17 exc. fest.) contains maps, prints, artisans' products, and paintings by Hans Multscher (1458). The 15C **Palazzo 'Jochelsthurn'** houses the Museo Provinciale delle Miniere (open Apr–Oct, 10–12, 14–17 exc. Sun & Mon), which illustrates the history of mining in the area.

North of Vipiteno the valley narrows and its higher slopes are covered with pine forests. **Colle Isarco** (1098m), or *Gossensass*, is a resort at the foot of the wooded Val di Fléres, once famous for its silver mines.

Brennero (1375m) is the last Italian village, just south of the stone pillar (1921) which marks the Austrian frontier on the **Brenner Pass** (Passo di Brennero; 1375m). This is the lowest of the great Alpine passes, and the flat broad saddle of the Brenner, first mentioned with the crossing of Augustus in 13 BC, was the main route of the medieval invaders of Italy. From here to Innsbruck, see *Blue Guide Austria*.

58 · The Val Pusteria

The Val Pusteria, the valley of the Rienza, is one of the most beautiful districts in the South Tyrol. In the attractive, brightly coloured villages many of the churches have bulbous steeples, and often contain good local woodcarvings. The breadth of the valley allows splendid views of the mountains at the head of the side-glens on either side. In the main valley German has replaced Ladin as the language of the inhabitants, but in one side-valley the old language has been preserved. It now has good skiing facilities for cross-country skiing as well as downhill skiing. There are numerous small family-run hotels in the valley.

■ **Information office.** APT Alto Adige, 11 Piazza Parrocchia, Bolzano (tel. 0474 913156)

Near **Rio di Pusteria** is **Castel Rodengo** (open May–Oct exc. Mon at 10, 11 & 15), a well preserved castle dating from 1140 (altered in the 16C). It contains secular frescoes of c 1200. **Casteldarne** (*Ehrenburg*) has a fine Baroque 16C castle (open in summer, exc. fest., on guided tours). The convent of Castel Badia (*Sonnenburg*; in part restored as a hotel), with a 12C chapel, can be seen on the left on the approach to **San Lorenzo di Sebato**, a village on the site of the larger Roman *Sebatum*, partly excavated (the walls are conspicuous). The 13C church contains good carvings.

The **Val Badia** is a Ladin-speaking valley, and has a number of winter resorts. **BRUNICO**, or *Bruneck*, is the picturesque capital (10,100 inhab.) of the Val Pusteria. It stands in a small upland plain with fir trees, and is overlooked by the castle of Bishop Bruno of Bressanone (1251). Brunico is the native town of Michele Pacher (c 1430–98), whose sculpted wooden crucifixes can be found in the churches of the region. The attractive, long main street with numerous shops leads from the church to the town gate.

The **Val di Tures** provides access to a group of thickly wooded mountain glens lying beneath the peaks and glaciers of the Alpi Aurine on the Austrian frontier. **Campo Tures**, or *Sand in Taufers*, is the main centre in these valleys, visited by climbers and skiers. It is dominated by the 13C–15C castle (shown on guided tours) of the barons of Tures. In the **Valle Aurina** is **Pratomagno** (1623m), the northernmost village in Italy. The peak of the Vetta d'Italia (2912m) is the northern point of the frontier. The Picco dei Tre Signori (3498m) further east marked the junction of the counties of Tyrol, Salzburg and Gorizia.

The Val Pusteria opens out at Rasun and the three picturesque villages of

Valdaora, each with a church. At the head of the **Val di Anterselva** (or *Antholzer Tal*) is the lake of Anterselva (1642m). In the lovely **Val Casies** is the picturesque 12C castle of Monguelfo, with a tall tower, and **Tesido**, a pretty village on the lower sunny slopes of the hillside with two delightful churches, one Baroque, with a pink exterior, and the other—older—with a large external fresco of St Christopher.

The village of Valdaora

The ***Lago di Braies**** (1493m) is a vividly green mountain lake in a remarkable position surrounded by pine woods. It is a summer resort as it is totally frozen over in winter.

Dobbiaco (1256m), or *Toblach*, has a large church and a castle built in 1500 for the Emperor Maximilian I. Gustav Mahler stayed here in 1908–10 (small museum open in summer).

SAN CANDIDO (1175m), or *Innichen*, is a lovely little summer and winter resort, with a Baroque parish church. The 13C *****Collegiata** (tower 1326) is dedicated to St Candidus and St Corbinian, who are depicted in the fresco above the south door, by Michele Pacher. It is the most important Romanesque monument in the Alto Adige, with interesting sculptural details. The 15C atrium protects the main portal with Romanesque carvings. In the interior is a splendid Crucifixion group above the high altar (c 1200). The remarkable frescoes in the cupola date from about 1280. The crypt has handsome columns.

San Candido is 7km from the Austrian frontier on the road to Lienz (see *Blue Guide Austria*).

Emilia Romagna

Emilia Romagna as the name of a district dates only from the Risorgimento (c 1860) but its use is derived from the Via Emilia, the great Roman road built in 187 BC by M. Aemilius Lepidus, as a military thoroughfare from which to guard the newly conquered lands of Cisalpine Gaul. Emilia occupies the region between the middle and lower Po, the Apennines and the Adriatic. The modern provinces are those of Bologna, Ferrara, Forlì, Modena, Parma, Piacenza, Rimini, Ravenna and Reggio Emilia; Bologna is the chief town. The eastern and southern part of the region, coinciding roughly with the modern provinces of Ravenna, Forlì and Rimini, is known as the **Romagna**, while the western and northern part including Bologna, Ferrara, Modena, Reggio Emilia, Parma and Piacenza forms **Emilia**.

All the principal towns except Ferrara and Ravenna lie along the line of the Via Emilia at the foot of the Apennines; the climate here is subject to extremes, and the summers are often unpleasantly hot.

Ravenna was the capital of the western Roman Empire from 402, after the fall of Rome, until it was taken by Odoacer who, like his successor Theodoric, made it capital of a short-lived Gothic Empire. It was conquered by the Byzantines in 540, and was governed by Exarchs of the Eastern Empire for two centuries. In 757 the Romagna came into possession of the Popes, who maintained at least a nominal suzerainty here until 1860; in the 13C–15C, however, the effective rule of the Da Polenta clan gave Ravenna a pre-eminent position in the world of learning. Parts of historic Romagna are now included in the modern regions of Tuscany and the Marches.

Emilia was invaded in the 5C–8C by the Goths, Lombards and Franks. In the early Middle Ages Guelfs and Ghibellines struggled for power in the region, although Piacenza and Parma came under the influence of Milan. The dominion of the Este family at Ferrara in the 13C extended over Modena and Reggio, while the Pepoli and Bentivoglio at Bologna, the Ordelaffi at Forlì, and the Malatesta at Rimini held temporary rule before the 16C. Papal power was later firmly established in Romagna and at Ferrara and Bologna, while the Farnese family, descended from the son of Pope Paul III, made Modena the capital of a new duchy and the centre of a court of some pretensions. The ex-Empress Marie Louise (wife of Napoleon) became Duchess of Parma, with Piacenza and Lucca in Tuscany also subject to her rule; the rest of Emilia went to Austria, as successors of the Este dynasty, and Romagna remained papal land. In 1860 Emila and Romagna were united with Piedmont. Emilia, and especially the Romagna, played an important part in the Second World War: the Romagnole partisans were particularly active in 1945.

59 · Bologna

Bologna (390,434 inhab.) is the capital of Emilia and one of the oldest cities of
Italy, the seat of a famous university. The old town, built almost exclusively of
red brick, is remarkable for its attractive porticoes which line each side of almost
every street. With numerous Romanesque and Gothic churches, and interesting
civic museums, Bologna is one of the most beautiful cities in northern Italy,
often unjustly left out of the usual tourists' itinerary. The important Bolognese
school of painting is well represented in its picture gallery. The city stands at the
southern edge of the plain of the Po, at the northeastern foot of the slopes of the
Apennines.

- **Information offices.** IAT, 6 Piazza Maggiore (Pl. 10; tel. 051/239660), and
  at the station and airport.

- **Hotels.** The city has numerous hotels of all categories, but they are often all
  full when big trade fairs are being held (especially in spring and
  autumn).There is a scheme called 'Bologna non solo week-end' which offers
  good rates at certain hotels at weekends, and in the summer. 4-star: *Grand
  Hotel Baglioni*, 8 Via Indipendenza; *Corona d'Oro*, 12 Via Oberdan; *San Donato*,
  16 Via Zamboni. 3-star: *Orologio*, 10 Via IV Novembre; *Cavour*, 4 Via Goito; *Dei
  Commercianti*, 11 Via Pignattari. 2-star: *Touring*, 1 Via Mattuiani.

- **Youth hostels**: *San Sisto* and *Due Torri*, 14 and 5 Via Viadagola.

- **Camping site** (3-star) in Via Romita.

- **Restaurants.** Bologna is full of excellent restaurants. **A**: *Battibecco*, 4 Via
  Battibecco; *Cesarina*, 19 Via Santo Stefano; *Diana*, 24 Via Indipendenza;
  Franco Rossi, 3 Via Goito; *Grassilli*, 3 Via del Luzzo; *Le Maschere*, 5 Via Zappoli;
  Al Montegrappa da Nello, 2 Via Montegrappa; *Pappagallo*, 3 Piazza Mercanzia;
  Re Enzo, 79 Via Riva di Reno; *Torre de' Galluzzi*, 5 Corte de' Galluzzi. **B**: *Anna
  Maria*, 17 Via Belle Arti; *Cambusa*, 8 Via Mascarella; *Circolo della Stampa*, 8 Via
  Galliera; *Gianni*, 18 Via Clavature; *Osteria del Palazzo Malvezzi*, 24 Via
  Zamboni; *Trattoria della Santa*, 7 Via Urbana; *Serghei*, 12 Via Piella. **C**: *Boni*, 88
  Via Saragozza; *Bottega del Vino Olindo Faccioli*, 15 Via Altabella; *Cantina
  Bentivoglio*, 4 Via Mascarella; *Moretto*, 5 Via San Mamolo.

- **Picnic places** in the Giardini Margherita (Pl. 16).

- **Car parks.** The centre of the city is closed to traffic (except for those with
  special permits) every day including holidays from 7 to 20, and cars are
  controlled electronically. Access is allowed to hotels by arrangement with the
  hotel. The large free car park outside the historic centre in Via Tanari has a
  mini-bus service every 15 mins to the station (from there Piazza Maggiore is
  reached by buses 25 and 30). Car parks in the historic centre (with hourly
  tariff and limited space) include Piazza Roosevelt, and Piazza 8 Agosto (exc. on
  Fri & Sat).

■ **Buses** are run by ATC (tel. 051/350301). Nos 25 or 30 from the railway station to Via Ugo Bassi (for Piazza Maggiore). Bus 30 continues to San Michele in Bosco. Bus 29 from Via Ugo Bassi for San Mamolo; and bus 14 for the Certosa. Bus 20 from Via Indipendenza to Villa Spada (and from there mini-bus every 30 mins to the Madonna di San Luca). Buses 38 & 91 from Via Marconi via the station to the Quartiere Fieristico (trade fair centre).

■ **Bus station** at Piazza XX Settembre (Pl. 3) with excellent services to nearly all places of interest in the region, as well as long-distance coaches to other Italian regions and international services.

■ **Airport** (Marconi) at Borgo Panigale, 7km northwest, with international services (including daily flights to London; tel. 051/311578). Airport bus No. 91 to and from the station at 41 minutes past the hour. 'Aerobus' every 30 mins to and from the airport via Via Ugo Bassi and Via dell'Indipendenza to the station, and the trade fair ground.

■ **Theatres.** *Comunale*. Opera and ballet and concerts late Oct–May. Plays and concerts are also held in Palazzo dei Congressi (Sala Europa) in the Quartiere Fieristica. For theatre: *Duse*, *Testoni*, *Arena del Sole*, and *Dehon*.

■ **Markets** are held on Fri & Sat in Piazza 8 Agosto (Pl. 7). Daily food markets in Via Ugo Bassi and Via Pescherie Vecchie.

■ **Annual festivals.** San Petronio, the patron saint, is celebrated on 4 Oct with a fair in Via Altabella.

■ **British Council**, 18 Corte Isolani.

History
Felsina, an important Etruscan city on the site of Bologna, was overrun by the Gauls in the 4C BC. They named their settlement *Bononia*, and the name was retained by the Romans when they conquered the plain of the Po in 225–191 BC. After the fall of the Western Empire, Bologna became subject to the Exarchs of Ravenna, and later formed part of the Lombard and Frankish dominions. In 1116 it was recognised as an independent commune by the Emperor Henry V. Its university first became prominent at about this time.

One of the foremost cities of the Lombard League (1167), it reached the height of its power after the peace of Constance (1183), and sided with the Guelfs. Taddeo Pepoli founded a lordship here c 1337 which was held in turn by the Visconti, the Pepoli and the unlucky Bentivoglio, under the last of whom (Giovanni II Bentivoglio; 1463–1506) Bologna reached great fame and prosperity.

In 1506 Pope Julius II reconquered the city, and for three centuries Bologna was incorporated into the Papal States, except for a brief interval (1796–1814) when it was part of Napoleon's Cisalpine Republic. In 1814 Bologna was occupied by a British force under General Nugent, in support of the Austrians against Napoleon. Unsuccessful insurrections broke out in

1831 and 1848 (the latter inspired by the eloquence of Ugo Bassi), and from 1849 until the formation of the Kingdom of Italy in 1860 the town was held by an Austrian garrison. In the Second World War Bologna was for months the focal point of German resistance, but it escaped serious artistic damage. It was entered on 21 April 1945, by the Polish Second Corps.

Art

In the architecture of Bologna the predominant material has always been brick, for both constructional and decorative purposes, and the late Gothic buildings of the 14C show the height attained by local skill in brick designing. Sculptors who left important works in the city include Nicolò Pisano, Jacopo della Quercia and Giambologna. The wealthy court of the Bentivoglio attracted the painters Franceso Cossa, Ercole de'Roberti and Lorenzo Costa from Ferrara (c 1490). Francesco Francia was the founder of the Bolognese school of painting which had an important revival at the end of the 16C with the Carracci (Lodovico and his cousins Annibale and Agostino). Their influence extended into the 18C, through Francesco Albani, Guido Reni, Domenichino and Guercino.

Piazza Maggiore

In the centre of the city is the large and peaceful *PIAZZA MAGGIORE (Pl.11), known simply as the 'Piazza' to the Bolognese. It is adjoined by Piazza Nettuno, and both are surrounded by splendid public buildings. ***Palazzo del Podestà** (Pl. 11) was begun at the beginning of the 13C, but remodelled in 1484. At the centre of the building is the tall tower (Arengo) of 1212: two passageways run beneath it and in the vault are statues of the patron saints of the city by Alfonso Lombardi (1525).

Fronting Via dell'Archiginnasio is the handsome long façade of **Palazzo dei Banchi** (1412) remodelled by Vignola (1565–68), once occupied by moneylenders. On street level is the Portico del Pavaglione, and two tall arches that give access to side streets. Above the roof of the palace can be seen the dome of Santa Maria della Vita and the top of the Torre degli Asinelli.

On the other side of San Petronio is **Palazzo dei Notai**, the old College of Notaries, part of which was begun in 1381 and the rest completed by Bartolomeo Fieravanti (1422–40).

San Petronio

*San Petronio (Pl. 11), the most important church in Bologna, even though never the cathedral, is one of the finest brick Gothic buildings in existence. Founded in 1390 on designs by a certain Antonio di Vincenzo, it is dedicated to St Petronius, bishop of Bologna 431–450 and patron saint of the city. Houses and churches were demolished on this site so that the huge church could take its place at the political centre of the city and it soon became a symbol of civic pride and independence. Designed to have been twice the size, its construction went on until the mid-17C, when the nave-vault was completed.

Exterior. The immense incomplete brick **façade** has a beautiful pink-and-white marble lower storey with three canopied doorways on which exquisite reliefs illustrate Biblical history from the Creation to the time of the Apostles. The **central doorway** is famous for its ***sculptures by Jacopo della Quercia**, his masterpiece begun in 1425 and left unfinished at his death in 1438. On the pilasters are ten bas-reliefs, mostly by assistants, illustrating the Story of Genesis, and a frieze of half-figures of Prophets.The architrave bears five scenes of the Childhood of Christ. In the lunette are statues, also by Jacopo, of the Madonna and Child with St Petronius (the St Ambrose was added in 1510). Above them the archivolt is decorated with panels of prophets (1510–11); the central figure is by Amico Aspertini.

The two lateral doorways (1524–30) have sculptures by Nicolò Tribolo, Alfonso Lombardo, Girolamo da Treviso, Amico Aspertini and others. The two sides of the building have a high marble basement beneath the large Gothic traceried windows.

Interior (open all day, 7.30–17 or 18.30). The great white and pink nave, 41m high, is lit by round

San Petronio

windows, and is separated from the aisles by ten massive compound piers. Because of its orientation (north to south), the church is unusually light. The splendid Gothic *vaulting of the nave dates from 1648; it is a masterpiece by Girolamo Rainaldi who adapted the 16C designs of Terribilia and Carlo Cremona. The side chapels are closed by beautiful screens, many of them in marble dating from the late 15C, others in ironwork. Outside the chapels have been placed four 11C–12C crosses which marked the limits of the late medieval city.

South aisle. First chapel, *Madonna della Pace* (German, 1394), framed by a painting by Giacomo Francia. Second chapel, polyptych by Tommaso Garelli (1477), and early 15C frescoes. Third chapel, frescoed polyptych of the school of the Vivarini. Fourth chapel, early 16C crucifix, and more 15C frescoes; the stained glass is by Jacob of Ulm (1466). Fifth chapel, Amico Aspertini, Pietà (1519). Sixth chapel, Lorenzo Costa, St Jerome. Eighth chapel, carved and inlaid *stalls, by Raffaello da Brescia (1521). Ninth chapel, Statue of St Anthony of Padua, and monochrome frescoes by Girolamo da Treviso (1526). The design of the stained glass is attributed to Pellegrino Tibaldi. The screen of the tenth chapel is particularly beautiful (c 1460). The altarpiece is by Bartolomeo Passarotti. The eleventh chapel has a framed high relief of the *Assumption, by Nicolò Tribolo (with 18C additions) on the left wall. Beneath the organ, opposite, is a *Lamentation group by Vincenzo Onofrio (1480).

The **choir** contains carved stalls by Agostino de'Marchi (1468–77). The organ on the right was built by Lorenzo di Giacomo da Prato in 1470–75. Before the high altar, Charles V was crowned emperor in 1530 by Clement VII.

North aisle. At the east end is a small **museum** (open 10–12 exc. Tue & Thu). It contains numerous drawings for the completion of the façade of the church, submitted right up to 1933 (including works by Baldassarre Peruzzi, Domenico Tibaldi and Palladio), and 16C–17C plans and models of the church (Girolamo Rainaldi, etc.). Also 17C–18C church vestments, reliquaries, church silver, and illuminated choir books (some by Taddeo Crivelli).

In the eleventh chapel are two large painted panels by Amico Aspertini from the 15C organ. Ninth chapel, *St Michael*, by Denys Calvaert (1582), and the Barbazzi monument with a bust by Vincenzo Onofrio (1479). Eighth chapel, *St Roch*, by Parmigianino. In front of the monument of Bishop Cesare Nacci, by Vincenzo Onofrio (1479) begins the meridian line, nearly 67m long, traced in 1655 by the astronomer Gian Domenico Cassini. It has since been several times adjusted; a hole in the roof admits the sun's ray. The seventh chapel has a particularly fine screen attributed to Pagno di Lapo. The altarpiece is by Lorenzo Costa (1492). Here are neo-classical funerary monuments of Felice Baciocchi and his wife Elisa Bonaparte by Cincinnato Baruzzi (1845; with two putti by Lorenzo Bartolini), and of their children. Sixth chapel, Assumption by Scarsellino and a statue of Cardinal Giacomo Lercaro by Giacomo Manzù (1954). The huge wooden pulpit of unusual design is attributed to Agostino de'Marchi (c 1470). The fifth chapel was decorated in 1487–97. The *altarpiece is a late 15C Ferrarese work, and the paintings are by Francesco Francia and Lorenzo Costa. The stalls date from 1495, and in the pavement is enamelled tilework by Pietro Andrea da Faenza (1487). Between this chapel and the next is a fine statue of St Petronius in gilded wood (late 14C).

The fourth chapel (**Cappella Bolognini**) has another fine marble balustrade. The gilded polychrome wood Gothic *altarpiece was painted by Jacopo di Paolo in 1410. The remarkable *frescoes are by Giovanni da Modena. Outside is an 18C clock. The second chapel is a Baroque work by Alfonso Torreggiani (1743–50) with a fine grille, and the tomb of Benedict XIV. Outside the chapel are frescoes by Lippo di Dalmasio, and a Madonna attributed to Giovanni da Modena, who also executed the allegorical frescoes in the first chapel. Above the right door on the inside façade are Adam and Eve, attributed to Alfonso Lombardi.

Piazza Nettuno

In PIAZZA NETTUNO (Pl. 11) is the ***Neptune Fountain**, designed by Tommaso Laureti and decorated with a splendid figure of Neptune and other bronze sculptures by Giambologna (1566). Fronting both Piazza Nettuno and Piazza Maggiore is the long façade of the huge **Palazzo Comunale** (Pl. 11), which incorporates **Palazzo d'Accursio**, and is made up of several buildings of different dates, modified and restored over the centuries. The entrance gateway is by Galeazzo Alessi (c 1555), and the bronze statue above it of Pope Gregory XIII (Ugo Buoncompagni of Bologna, the reformer of the calendar), is by Alessandro Menganti (1580). To the left, under a canopy, is a *Madonna in terracotta by Nicolò dell'Arca (1478).

PALAZZO D'ACCURSIO, to the left, with a tower (and clock of 1773), was acquired by the Comune in 1287 from Francesco d'Accursio on his return from the court of King Edward I of England. The loggia was used as a public granary. In 1336 Taddeo Pepoli began to unite various palaces on this site as a town hall, and in 1425–28 Fieravante Fieravanti rebuilt the palace to the right of the main entrance. In the 16C the whole edifice was fortified by the papal legates as their residence: the impressive battlemented walls (restored in 1887) extend along Via Ugo Bassi and Via IV Novembre.

From the courtyard the grand **staircase**, a ramp ascribed to Bramante, leads up to the **first floor**, where the **Chamber of Hercules** contains a colossal terracotta statue by Alfonso Lombardi, and a Madonna by Francesco Francia (1505). On the **second floor** the **Sala Farnese** has a good view of the piazza. It contains frescoes by Carlo Cignani and a copper statue of Pope Alexander VII (1660). The **Cappella Farnese** has 16C frescoes by Prospero Fontana. Here is the entrance to the **COLLEZIONI COMUNALI D'ARTE** and the **MUSEO GIORGIO MORANDI** (both open 10–18 exc. Mon). The former is a well displayed collection of paintings and furniture in 20 rooms of a wing of the Palazzo d'Accursio, used by the Cardinal legates of the city from 1506 up to the 19C. The long gallery was decorated in the 17C by the papal legate Pietro Vidoni. Other rooms have good 16C ceilings, late 18C decorations by Giuseppe Valliani and Vincenzo Martinelli (Room 16), and (Room 17) trompe l'oeil frescoes by Dentone, Angelo Michele Colonna, and Agostino Mitelli.

The contents (in the course of rearrangement) are well labelled, and include works by Carlo Francesco Nuvolone, Artemisia Gentileschi, Ubaldo Gandolfi, Donato Creti (mostly painted in 1710–20), Jacopo di Paolo, Simone da Bologna, Vitale da Bologna, Francesco Francia (*Crucifixion*), Guido Cagnacci, Amico Aspertini, Lodovico Carracci, Giuseppe Maria Crespi, Francesco Hayez (*Ruth*), Giovanni Boulanger and Pelagio Pelagi.

The **Museo Morandi** (open as for the Collezioni Comunali d'Arte: separate or cumulative ticket) contains the most representative collection in existence of works by Giorgio Morandi (1890–1964), a native of Bologna, donated by his family to the city. Well displayed chronologically, it includes many of his paintings, watercolours, drawings and etchings. There are also works of art owned by the painter and a reconstruction of his studio.

Adjoining Palazzo del Podestà in Piazza Nettuno is the battlemented **Palazzo di Re Enzo** built in 1246 which was the prison of Enzo (1225–72), King of Sardinia and illegitimate son of the Emperor Frederick II, from his capture at Fossalta in 1249 until his death in 1272. The palace was radically restored in 1905–13.

Museo Archeologico

Via dell'Archiginnasio skirts the left flank of San Petronio. Beneath the marble paved Portico del Pavaglione, with elegant uniform shopfronts, the windows enclosed in tall wooden frames, is the entrance to the *Museo Civico Archeologico (Pl. 11), founded in 1881 and especially notable for its Etruscan material and Egyptian section (open weekdays 9–14, exc. Mon; Sat & Sun 9–13, 15.30–19).

In the **basement** the *Egyptian Collection** is one of the most important in Europe. The first room has delicately carved limestone *reliefs from the tomb of Horemheb (1332–23 BC). The next section has a chronological display of

BOLOGNA

Stazione Centrale

VIALE PIETRAMELLARA

VIA BOVI CAMPEGGI

VIA LOD. BERTI

VIALE PIETRAMELLARA

VIA CESARE BOLDRINI

VIA DELLE LAME

PIAZZA VENTI SETTEMBRE

Porta Galliera

VIA MILAZZO

VIA MILAZZO

VIA CAROLI

VIA GRAMSCI

V. PIER DE' CRESCENZI

VIA DON MINZONI

Porta Lame

PIAZZA SETTE NOVEMBRE 1944

PIAZZA DEI MARTIRI 1943-1945

VIA DEI MILLE

S. Benedetto

VIA DEL PORTO

Seminario

VIA I. MALVASIA

VIALE ANT. SILVANI

VIA GRAZIANO

VIA DELLE LAME

VIA S. CARLO

VIA POLESE

Pal. Tanari

Palazzo dello Sport

APT

MODENA & AIRPORT

Porta S. Felice

VIA G. MARCONI

Pal. Palavicini

V. D. ORSO

VIA RIVA DI RENO

S. Maria Maggiore

VIA RIVA DI RENO

Pal. Montanari

VIA S. FELICE

S. Giorgio

VIA S. GIORGIO

VIA VOLTURNO

VIA DELLE LAME

VIC. O. COLONNE

Liceo

VIA PARIGI

Mad. di Galliera

Pal. Benelli

S. Gregorio

Mus. Civico Medievale (Pal. Ghisilardi Fava)

Duomo

VIA MONTE

VIA ALTABELLA

VIA DEL PRATELLO

VIA UGO BASSI

GRAPPA

Pal. di Re Enzo

CERTOSA

V. COSTA

Porta Sant' Isaia

S. Francesco

Pal. Marescalchi

PIAZZA ROOSEVELT

Pal. Comunale

Pal. d Podes

PIAZZA NETTUNO

Porta Colonna della Nuova Immacolata

Casa Castaldini

V. 4 NOVEMBRE

Prefettura

PIAZZA GALILEO

S. Salvatore

Palazzo dei Notai

PIAZZA MAGGIORE

VIA S. ISAIA

S. Petronio

Palazzo Salina

VIA BARBERIA

S. Giov. Batt.

Archiginnasio

PIAZZA GALVANI

Spirito Santo

Collegio di Spagna

S. Paolo

Palazzo Bevilacqua

Pal. Marsigli

Porta Saragozza

VIA SARAGOZZA

VIA SARAGOZZA

CAPRAMOZZA

Corpus Domini

S. Procolo

VIA D. TOVAGLIE

VIALE ANTONIO ALDINI

VIA SOLFERINO

Istituto d'Ingegneria

Coll. S. Luigi

VIA MIRA SOLE

Porta San Mamolo

VIALE ENRICO PANZACCH

S. S. Annunziata

S. MICHELE IN BOSCO

0   200 yds

0   200 metres

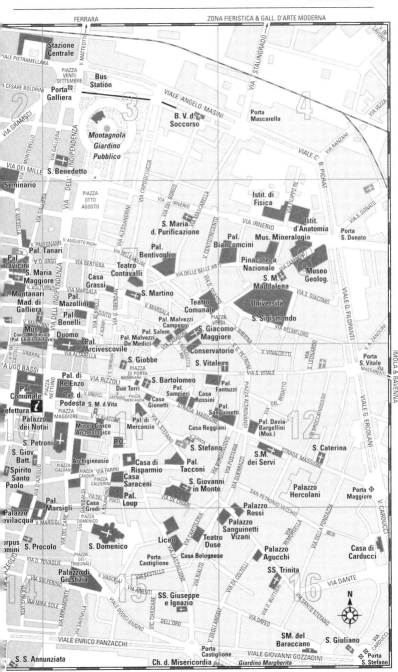

FERRARA — ZONA FIERISTICA & GALL. D'ARTE MODERNA

Stazione Centrale
VIALE PIETRAMELLARA
PIAZZA VENTI SETTEMBRE
Bus Station
Porta Galliera
VIALE ANGELO MASINI
B. V. d. Soccorso
VIA STALINGRADO
Porta Mascarella
VIA C. B. PICHAT
VIA LAURO
VIA VEZZA
VIA RANZANI

VIA CESARE BOLDRINI
VIA GRAMSCI
VIA MONTEBELLO
VIA GALLIERA
VIA DELL'INDIPENDENZA
Montagnola Giardino Pubblico
VIA DEI MILLE
S. Benedetto
Seminario
VIA GALLIERA

PIAZZA OTTO AGOSTO
VIA CAPODIFIUCA
VIA DEL BORGO
VIA MASCARELLA
VIA IRNERIO
Istit. di Fisica
Istit. d'Anatomia
Mus. Mineralogia
VIA FILIPPO RE
Porta S. Donato
VIA S. DONATO

V. ATTESTA
V. PALEGNAME
V. AUGUSTO RIGHI
Pal. Tanari
V. D. ORSO
S. Maria Maggiore
V. VOLTURNO
Pal. Palavicini
Pal. Montanari
Mad. di Galliera
Pal. Mazzolini
VIA MARSALA
VIA ALBIROI
VIA G. OBERDAN
Pal. Benelli
V. MANZONI
Mus. (Civica Medievale Pal. Ghisilardi Fava)
Duomo
GRAPPA
VIA UGO BASSI
Pal. Arcivescovile
VIA ALTABELLA
S. Maria d. Purificazione
Pal. Bentivoglio
VIA CENTOTRECENTO
VIA DELLE MOLINE
Teatro Contavalli
Casa Grassi
S. Martino
VIA DELLE BELLE ARTI
VIA DEL GUASTO
Pal. Biancomcini
Pinacoteca Nazionale
S. M. Maddalena
VIA ZAMBONI
Museo Geolog.
VIA S. GIACOMO
VIALE O. FILOPANTI
Università
S. Sigismondo
VIA BELMELORO
Teatro Comunale
PIAZZA VERDI
Pal. Malvezzi Campeggi
V. MARSALA
S. Giacomo Maggiore
Pal. Salem
Pal. Malvezzi De'Medici
S. Giobbe
Conservatorio
S. Vitale
VIA S. VITALE
V. VINAZZETTI
Porta S. Vitale
VIA MASSARENTI
IMOLA & RAVENNA

PIAZZA DI PORTA RAVEGNANA
Pal. di Re Enzo
VIA RIZZOLI
S. Bartolomeo
Due Torri
Pal. d. Podestà
S. M. d.Vita
Pal. Sampieri
Casa Rossini
Pal. Fantuzzi
Casa Gionetti
STRADA MAGGIORE
Pal. Sanguinetti
Pal. Davia-Bargellini (Mus.)
S. Caterina
VIA DE BRIATO
VIALE G. ERCOLANI
VIA BROCCAINDOSSO
Casa Reggiani
S.M. dei Servi
Palazzo Hercolani
Porta Maggiore
VIA CARDUCCI

Pal. Comunale
Prefettura
Palazzo dei Notai
PIAZZA NETTUNO
PIAZZA MAGGIORE
Museo Civico Archeologico
P.O.
Pal. di Mercanzia
S. Stefano
S. Petronio
S. Giov. Batt.
Spirito Santo Paolo
Archiginnasio
PIAZZA GALVANI
Casa di Risparmio
Casa Saraceni
Pal. Loup
Pal. Tacconi
S. Giovanni in Monte
VIA DE CHIARI
Palazzo Rossi
Palazzo Sanguinetti Vizani
SAN PETRONIO VECCHIO

Palazzo Bevilacqua
Corpus Domini
S. Procolo
V. D. TOVAGLIE
VIA MARSILI
Pal. Marsigli
Casa Gradi
PIAZZA S. DOMENICO
S. Domenico
PIAZZA DEI TRIBUNALI
Liceo
Porta Castiglione
Teatro Duse
Casa Bolognese
Palazzo Agucchi
SS. Trinità
VIA DANTE
Casa di Carducci
VIA DELLA FONDAZZA

Palazzo di Giustizia
VIA SOLFERINO
VIA MIRA SOLE
VIA SAFFI
VIA VASCELLI
VIA FESTELLO
VIA RIALTO
SS. Giuseppe e Ignazio
VIC. CHIUDARE
DELL'ORO
VIA DODICI GIUGNO
VIA DEI COLTELLI
VIA DEI BUTTERI
VIA SANTO STEFANO
VIA ORFEO
SM. del Baraccano
S. Giuliano
Porta S. Stefano

S. S. ANNUNZIATA
ICHELE IN BOSCO
VIALE ENRICO PANZACCHI
Porta Castiglione
Ch. d. Misericordia
VIALE GIOVANNI GOZZADINI
Giardino Margherita

funerary stelae, sarcophagi, objects in wood, bronzes, jewellery, etc., starting with the Old Kingdom (including a seated statuette of Neferhotep I). At the end of the hall are works from the Ptolomaic and Roman periods. The second wing has exhibits related to writing and the cult of the dead.

The **courtyard** contains a Roman lapidarium, and the **gipsoteca** has casts made at the end of the 19C of famous classical Greek masterpieces.

First floor. The first door on the right leads into a room with a fine display of **Villanovan finds** (7C BC) from Verucchio (see Chapter 68), including beautiful amber, a reconstructed wooden throne, tables, and foot-rests.

Rooms I and **II** (still with their old-fashioned arrangement) contain prehistoric finds. The chronological display continues in the huge **Room X** with a vast collection of Villanovan and Etruscan *finds from the burial-grounds of *Felsina*, the Umbro-Etruscan predecessor of Bologna. The **long gallery**, decorated in the 19C with copies of Etruscan painted tombs, contains tomb-furniture illustrating the development of the Umbrian (9C–6C BC) and Etruscan (6C–mid-4C) civilisations. The Umbrian tombs contain urns with scratched, painted, and (later) stamped geometric decoration, while the Etruscan tombs bear reliefs in sandstone, and contain fine Attic vases (the so-called 'Etruscan' ware) and various objects of daily use in bronze, bone, etc. In Case 20 is a beautiful bronze *situla (6C BC), with exquisite reliefs of a ceremonial procession. Against the wall is a fine display of funerary stelae. At the end of the gallery are ivory and glass objects from the Tomba dello Sgabello (Case 33) and splendid finds from the Tomba Grande (5C BC) in Case 34. At the other end of the gallery is the entrance to **Room XV** with a hoard of bronze fragments.

Off Room IX (see below) is **Room VI** with Greek works of art, including a *head of Minerva, said to be a copy of the Athene Lemnia of Phidias and the 'Cup of Codrus', a fine red-figured Attic vase. Beyond **Room VII** with Roman sculpture, **Room VIII** contains Etruscan Bucchero ware, and engraved bronze mirrors (notably the 'patera cospiana'). **Room IX** contains Roman glass, bronze statuettes, utensils, and early Christian ivory reliefs.

In the narrow road to the left of the museum, next to the indoor market, is the church of **Santa Maria della Vita** (open all day), rebuilt in 1687–90 with a cupola. It contains a dramatic *Lamentation over the Dead Christ, in terracotta, a superb work by Nicolò dell'Arca, thought to date from 1463.

The Archiginnasio

Further along the Portico del Pavaglione is the Archiginnasio (Pl. 11), built by Antonio Morandiin 1562–65 for the University, which had its seat here until 1800. The upper floor is shown by the porter on request (9–13 exc. Sun). The wooden *Anatomical Theatre** was built in 1637 by Antonio Levanti. By the 14C the university had acquired notoriety as the first school where the dissection of the human body was practised. The baldacchino over the reader's chair is supported by two remarkable anatomical figures by Ercole Lelli (1734). In the Aula Magna, Rossini's *Stabat Mater* was given its first performance under the direction of Donizetti. From here can be seen the long series of school rooms, now part of the **Biblioteca Comunale** with c 700,000 volumes and 12,000 MSS.

In front of the building is a monument commemorating the physicist Luigi

Galvani (1737–98). Across Via Farini, Via Garibaldi (left) continues to the cobbled PIAZZA SAN DOMENICO (Pl. 15). Here are tall columns bearing statues of St Dominic (1627) and the Madonna (1633), and the canopied tombs of Rolandino de'Passeggeri (1300) and Egidio Foscherari (1289).

San Domenico

The church of *San Domenico (Pl. 15; open 7–20) was dedicated by Innocent IV in 1251 to St Dominic, founder of the order of Preaching Friars, who died here in 1221 two years after establishing the convent on this site. It is still one of the most important Dominican convents in Italy, with about 40 monks. The church was remodelled by Carlo Francesco Dotti (1728–31).

Interior. The **Chapel of San Domenico** was rebuilt in 1597–1605 (and restored in the 19C). The *arca di San Domenico, the monumental sarcophagus of St Dominic, is a masterpiece of sculpture. It was carved with scenes from the saint's life in high relief in 1267 on a design by Nicola Pisano, mostly by his pupils, including Fra Guglielmo and Arnolfo di Cambio. The lid of the sarcophagus is decorated with statuettes and festoons by Nicolò dell'Arca who took his name from this work. After Nicolò's death in 1492, Michelangelo—who was staying for a year in the city in 1495 (at the age of 20) with Gianfrancesco Aldovrandi—carved three statuettes: the right-hand angel bearing a candelabrum (the other is by Nicolò dell'Arca), St Petronius holding a model of Bologna, and (behind) St Proculus (with a cloak over his left shoulder). Girolamo Corbellini carved the last statue (St John the Baptist) in 1539. The sculpted scenes in relief below the sarcophagus and between the two kneeling angels are by Alfonso Lombardi (1532). The altar beneath dates from the 18C. Behind the tomb in a niche is a reliquary by Jacopo Roseto da Bologna (1383) which encloses the saint's skull. In the apse of the chapel is the *Glory of St Dominic, by Guido Reni. Also here are two paintings by Alessandro Tiarini and Lionello Spada.

South transept, Guercino, St Thomas Aquinas. Here marquetry doors by Fra Damiano Zambelli (1538) lead into the **sacristy**. The **museum** (open 10–12, exc. fest.) contains damaged figures from a Pietà group by Baccio da Montelupo; a *bust of St Dominic (1474), a very fine work in polychrome terracotta by Nicolò dell'Arca; paintings and frescoes by Lippo di Dalmasio, Lodovico Carracci and Bernardino Luini; intarsia panels by Fra Damiano; and books of anthems. On the floor above, another room contains 13C–15C reliquaries, including one made in France in the 13C, and a large chest of drawers with vestments (17C and later).

The **choir** has *stalls in marquetry by Fra Damiano Zambelli (1541–51). The painting of the Magi is by Bartolomeo Cesi. A marquetry door opposite the sacristy (usually unlocked) leads into the charming **Cloister of the Dead**, its fourth side closed by the exterior of the apse and cupola of the chapel of San Domenico. Here foreigners who died in Bologna were buried, including students and professors from the university. A simple tomb slab opposite the apse of the Chapel of St Dominic marks the burial place of the English.

Off the Chiostro Maggiore is **St Dominic's Cell** (normally shown on request by a monk), with relics of the saint and a 13C painting of him.

In the little chapel to the right of the choir (light on the right), *Marriage of St Catherine, signed by Filippino Lippi (1501). **North transept**, inscription (1731) marking the tomb of King Enzo (see page 407). In the adjoining chapel is a 14C wall monument (altered in the 16C) to Taddeo Pepoli, and a painted crucifix signed by Giunta Pisano (removed for restoration). In the Chapel of the Relics at the end of the transept is the tomb of Beato Giacomo da Ulma (Jacob of Ulm), the painter on glass, who died in Bologna in 1491.

North aisle. In the chapel opposite the chapel of San Domenico is an altarpiece of 15 small paintings of the Mysteries of the Rosary by Lodovico Carracci, Bartolomeo Cesi, Dionigi Calvaert, Guido Reni and Francesco Albani. The painters Reni and Elisabetta Sirani are buried in this chapel (inscription on the left wall). In the porch leading to the side door is the funerary monument of Alessandro Tartagni by Francesco Ferrucci (1477). On the second altar, *St Raimondo* by Lodovico Carracci.

To the south of San Domenico, at the end of Via Garibaldi is **Palazzo di Giustizia** occupying Palazzo Ruini, with an imposing Palladian façade and courtyard (1584).

To the north of San Domenico is Via Rolandino, with the 15C–16C **Casa Gradi**. The **Casa Saraceni** (No. 15 Via Farini) is another fine late 15C building. VIA CASTIGLIONE (Pl. 11,15) is a handsome old street which leads away from the centre of the city to a city gate, past (No. 47) the 15C **Casa Bolognesi**.

The Due Torri

PIAZZA DI PORTA RAVEGNANA is dominated by the famous *Due Torri (Pl. 11), two leaning towers one of which is exceptionally tall. At one time some 180 towers existed in the city. The *Torre degli Asinelli**, thought to have been built by the Asinelli family, or by the Comune (1109–19), is 97·5m high and leans 1·23m out of the perpendicular. The masonry at the base was added in 1488. A flight of 500 steps leads up to the top (open every day 9–17 or 18). The *Torre Garisenda**, built by the Garisendi family at the same time as the other, was left unfinished owing to the subsidence of the soil, and was shortened for safety in 1351–60. It is now only 48m high and leans 3·22m out of the perpendicular; but it was higher when Dante wrote the descriptive verses (*Inferno*, xxxi, 136) inscribed at the base of the tower.

No. 1 in the piazza is the **Casa dei Drappieri** (1486–96), with a balcony added in 1620. The narrow Via dell'Inferno which leads out of the piazza is on the site of the **Ghetto** of Bologna (the synagogue was at No. 16).

Five old roads lead from Piazza di Porta Ravegnana out of the city; each one ends in a gate on the line of the old city walls. The towers are now isolated by traffic; especially busy is the wide Via Rizzoli, one of the least attractive streets in the centre of Bologna. The subway beneath preserves Roman mosaics found during its construction. Adjoining Piazza di Porta Ravegnana is Piazza Mercanzia with the *Palazzo della Mercanzia**, arguably the best preserved example of ornamented Italian-Gothic in the city. It was built in 1382–84 from the plans of Antonio di Vincenzo and Lorenzo da Bagnomarino.

VIA SANTO STEFANO (Pl. 11,16) is lined by some fine 15C–16C *mansions, notably Nos 9–11 Palazzo Salina-Bolognini, begun in 1525 in the style of Formigine, and Nos 16–18 Palazzo Isolani by Pagno di Lapo Portigiani (1455). In Via de'Pepoli (right) is the 17C **Palazzo Pepoli-Campogrande** (with frescoes by Donato Creti and Giuseppe Maria Crespi) which houses some 18C paintings from the Pinacoteca, open Jul–Aug. Adjoining is Palazzo Pepoli (Nos 6–10 Via Castiglione), a huge Gothic building begun in 1344 by Taddeo Pepoli and restored in 1925.

Santo Stefano

The street opens out in front of an attractive piazza (recently redesigned), in a peaceful corner of the town, with the basilica of *Santo Stefano (Pl. 11; closed 12–15.30), an ancient and picturesque group of monastic buildings, mentioned as early as 887 and dedicated as a whole to St Stephen the Martyr. Three churches face the piazza: Santi Vitale e Agricola, the oldest ecclesiastical building in the city, San Sepolcro, and the Crocifisso, with a 12C pulpit on its front.

The **Crocifisso**, restored in 1924, has a painted crucifix by Simone dei Crocifissi (c 1380) hanging in the raised choir. The crypt has some 11C details and a jumble of capitals. The 18C Pietà is the work of Angelo Piò, and the Aldovrandi tomb dates from 1438.

On the left is the entrance to the polygonal church of **San Sepolcro**, perhaps founded as a baptistery in the 5C, but dating in its present form from the 11C. It has a brick cupola and interesting architectural details. The imagined imitation of the Holy Sepulchre at Jerusalem is partly hidden by the Romanesque pulpit and a stair and altar placed against it in the 19C. In the centre, behind a grille, is the tomb of St Petronius.

To the left again is the church of **Santi Vitale e Agricola**, a venerable building perhaps of the 5C, with massive columns and capitals, incorporating many fragments of Roman buildings. The three apses (rebuilt in the 8C and 11C) are lit by tiny alabaster windows. The altars in the side apses are 8C or 9C Frankish sarcophagi enclosing the relics of the 4C martyrs St Vitalis and St Agricola (see page 415).

From San Sepolcro is the entrance to the **Cortile di Pilato** (12C); in the middle of this open court is 'Pilate's Bowl' (8C) bearing an obscure inscription relating to the Lombard kings Luitprand and Ilprand. The beautifully patterned brickwork of the exterior of San Sepolcro can be seen here. On a pillar in a little window is a delightful cockerel sculpted in the 14C.

Off the court is the church of the **Martyrium**, with a façade reconstructed in 1911. The chapel has good capitals and remains of 14C–15C frescoes. In the left chapel (light) is a charming group of wooden statues of the Adoration of the Magi painted by Simone dei Crocifissi (c 1370). The chapel of San Giuliano, also off the courtyard, has 14C frescoes. A door from the court leads into the *cloister*, which has two beautiful colonnades, the lower one dating from the 11C, and the upper from the 12C, with fine capitals. Here can be seen the Romanesque campanile.

There is a small **museum** off the cloister (open 9–12, 15.30–17.30), in poor condition. It includes works by Jacopo di Paolo, Michele di Matteo, Simone dei Crocifissi and Lippo di Dalmasio. In the Cappella della Benda, are reliquaries including that of St Petronius by Jacopo di Roseto, 1370.

San Giovanni in Monte

Across Via Santo Stefano and Via Farini, on a little hill, stands the church of
*San Giovanni in Monte (Pl. 11; closed 12–15.30). Of ancient foundation, in its
present form it is a 13C Gothic building with extensive 15C additions. The
façade has a great portal by Domenico Berardi (1474), and above it an eagle in
painted terracotta by Nicolò dell'Arca. The campanile dates from the 13C–14C.

In the pleasant **interior** the columns are partly decorated with frescoes by
Giacomo and Giulio Francia. On the west wall the stained glass tondo is by the
Cabrini on a design by Lorenzo Costa or Francesco del Cossa (1481). The
Romanesque cross on an inverted Roman pillar capital bears a figure of Christ in
fig wood attributed to Alfonso Lombardi.

In the **south aisle** are altarpieces by Girolamo da Treviso, Bartolomeo Cesi,
Pietro Faccini (*Martyrdom of St Lawrence*), Lippo di Dalmasio (fresco) and
Lorenzo Costa (*Madonna enthroned with saints, 1497). In the sacristy is a
precious collection of reliquaries, church silver, vestments, etc.

Choir. The inlaid stalls are by Paolo Sacca (1523). The *Madonna in Glory on
the east wall is another fine work by Lorenzo Costa, and the *crucifix is by
Jacopino da Bologna. The **North transept** is a good architectural work of 1514
built for the blessed Elena Duglioli Dall'Oglio (1472–1520) who is buried here.
She also commissioned the famous St Cecilia altarpiece for the chapel from
Raphael (now in the Pinacoteca), substituted here by a poor copy still enclosed
in the original frame by Formigine.

In the **north aisle** are works by Francesco Gessi, Luigi Crespi and (second
chapel) Guercino.

Vicolo Monticelli descends to Via Castiglione, described above.

The Strada Maggiore

From the Due Torri, the STRADA MAGGIORE (Pl. 11,12), one of the most
attractive old streets of the city, runs southeast on the line of the Via Emilia.
Beside the Due Torri is the church of **San Bartolomeo** (Pl. 11). The rich decoration by Formigine (1515) of the **portico** has been worn away (although it was
restored in 1993). A 16C portal is in better condition. The ornate **interior**, with
small domes over the side aisles, is largely the work of Giovanni Battista Natali
(1653–84). In the fourth chapel of the south aisle is an *Annunciation by
Francesco Albani (1632). The tondo of the Madonna in the north transept is by
Guido Reni.

Further on in the Strada Maggiore is a series of characteristic Bolognese
mansions of all periods from the 13C to the 19C, some of them restored. Among
the finest are the **Casa della Fondazione Gioannetti** (No. 13), with Gothic
windows and polychrome decoration; **Casa Gelmi** (No. 26), built for the
composer Gioacchino Rossini, from designs by Francesco Santini (1824–27);
Casa Isolani (No. 19), a characteristic 13C house (restored), with a tiny upper
storey on tall wooden brackets; **Palazzo Sanguinetti** (No. 34) with a rich 16C
cornice; and **Casa Reggiani** (Nos 38–40), a large 15C mansion with an
arcaded court.

Beyond opens Piazza dei Servi (Pl. 12), with its porticoes. Here at No. 44 is
Palazzo Davia-Bargellini, built in 1638, with two atlantes flanking the
gateway. The fine staircase dates from 1730. It contains the **Museo Civico
d'Arte Industriale e Galleria Davia-Bargellini** (open 9–4; fest. 9–13; closed

Mon), founded in 1924 by Malaguzzi Valeri and still preserving the character of its original arrangement. It includes domestic artefacts, wrought-iron work, ceramics, an 18C puppet theatre, a dolls' house, woodcarvings, Emilian furniture, and paintings by Vitale da Bologna, Bartolomeo Vivarini, Giuseppe Maria Crespi, Marcantinio Franceschini, Marco Meloni, Joseph Heintz the Younger, Bartolomeo Passarotti (portraits of the Bargellini family) and Prospero Fontana. There is also a good collection of terracottas by Giuseppe Maria Mazza and Angelo Piò.

The four porticoes of Piazza dei Servi, built in a consistent style at various periods from the 14C to 1855, are a continuation of the wide arcades in the Strada Maggiore alongside the church of **SANTA MARIA DEI SERVI** (Pl. 12). Begun in 1346 and enlarged after 1386, this is one of the most attractive Gothic buildings in Bologna.

Interior (very dark). **South aisle**. Fourth chapel, Denys Calvaert, *Paradise* (1602). On the left pillar outside the sixth chapel is a fresco fragment attributed to Lippo di Dalmasio. The finely carved **main altar** is the work of Giovanni Angelo Montorsoli (1558–61). The **choir**, entered by a door off the ambulatory, contains good Gothic stalls (1450; completed in 1617). Outside the door into the sacristy are frescoes by Vitale da Bologna which survive from the 14C church. In the **ambulatory** are a polyptych by Lippo di Dalmasio (in very poor condition), and a delightful high relief in terracotta by Vincenzo Onofri. In the chapel to the left of the east chapel, Cimabue *Madonna enthroned (light) and a 15C fresco by Pietro di Giovanni Lianori. On the choir wall is the Grati monument by Vincenzo Onofri.

North aisle. Sixth chapel, Annunciation, by Innocenzo da Imola (in a frame by Formigine); and fifth chapel, Byzantine Madonna and Child (c 1261). Around the side door, elaborate monument to Cardinal Gozzadini (died 1536) by Giovanni Zacchi. Second chapel, Noli me tangere, by Francesco Albani.

In Via Guerrazzi to the south are (No. 13) the **Accademia Filarmonica**, founded in 1666, to which Mozart was elected in 1770 at the age of 14, and (No. 20) the **Flemish College** (1650).

At No. 5 in Viale Carducci, on the right beyond Porta Maggiore, is the **Casa di Carducci** and **Museo del Risorgimento** (open 9–13 exc. Mon), where the poet Giosuè Carducci lived from 1890 to 1907. There is a collection of MSS, and a library of over 40,000 volumes. Outside is a monument by Leonardo Bistolfi (1928).

Piazza Aldrovandi, with chestnut trees and a street market, leads north to Via San Vitale. Here on the left, beyond an old city gate (11C–12C), is the church of **Santi Vitale ed Agricola** (Pl. 12), rebuilt in 1824, except for its 12C crypt. It is dedicated to two saints martyred under Diocletian in the Arena, thought to have been in this area. Inside are works by Alessandro Tiarini, and frescoes attributed to Giacomo Francia and Bagnacavallo.

Opposite is the long, oddly proportioned façade of **Palazzo Fantuzzi** (begun in 1517), decorated with two elephants in relief, and with a Baroque staircase.

It is a short way back from here, by Via San Vitale, to the Due Torri.

From the Due Torri, Via Zamboni (Pl.11,7 & 8) leads away from the centre of the city. A short way along opens PIAZZA ROSSINI (Pl. 7) with the **Conservatorio Giovanni Battista Martini** where Rossini studied in 1806–10, with one of the most important music libraries in Europe, and a portrait gallery. Opposite is Palazzo Malvezzi de'Medici, by Bartolomeo Triachini (1560).

On Via Zamboni, also facing the piazza, is **Palazzo Magnani** by Domenico Tibaldi (1577–87). In the salone (adm. freely granted when not in use) is a beautiful frescoed frieze of the Founding of Rome by the Carracci (1588–91). Also here are paintings by Tintoretto, Lodovico Carracci, Simone Cantarini, Domenico Induno, Giuseppe Maria Crespi and Guercino. Next door is **Palazzo Malvezzi-Campeggi** (No. 22), by Formigine, with a good courtyard.

San Giacomo Maggiore

The Romanesque church of *San Giacomo Maggiore (Pl. 7), was begun in 1267 (restored in 1915). The top of the façade has majolica decoration.

Interior (closed 12–15.30). The aisleless **nave** is surmounted by a bold vault of unusually wide span. The side chapels are crowned by a terracotta frieze of statues and urns (by Pietro Becchetti, 1765). On the **south side** are altarpieces by Bartolomeo Passarotti (1565), Innocenzo da Imola (in a frame by Formigine) and Lodovico Carracci. The eleventh chapel was designed by Pellegrino Tibaldi, who also painted the frescoes.

Ambulatory. On the left wall, Jacopo di Paolo, large painted crucifix (c 1420). Second chapel, Lorenzo Veneziano, polyptych (1368; removed for restoration). The damaged frescoes of the life of St Mary of Egypt are by Cristoforo da Bologna. Third chapel, Jacopo di Paolo, polyptych, and crucifix, signed by Simone de' Crocifissi (1370). In the fourth chapel are detached late 13C frescoes (very damaged) from the façade. Opposite, on the choir wall, is the funerary monument of a philosopher and a doctor, both called Nicolò Fava, by a follower of Jacopo della Quercia.

The **Cappella Bentivoglio** (light switch on the floor), at the end of the north aisle, was founded in 1445 by Annibale Bentivoglio, and enlarged for Giovanni II, probably by Pagno di Lapo Portigiani. Its *altarpiece is by Francesco Francia (c 1488). The *frescoes from the Apocalypse, of the Triumph of Death, and of the Madonna enthroned with charming portraits of Giovanni II Bentivoglio and his family, are all by Lorenzo Costa. The relief of Annibale I on horseback dates from 1458, the worn floor-tiles from 1489.

Opposite the chapel is the *tomb of Anton Galeazzo Bentivoglio, father of Annibale, one of the last works of Jacopo della Quercia (1435; with the help of assistants). The Madonna in Glory in the last chapel is by Bartolomeo Cesi.

The **Oratory of Santa Cecilia** (entered from No. 15 under the side portico of the church) has interesting *frescoes by Francesco Francia and Lorenzo Costa, and their pupils, including Amico Aspertini. They were painted in 1504–06 by order of Giovanni II Bentivoglio. The altarpiece is also by Francia.

Along the side of the church, a delightful vaulted portico of 1477–81, with good capitals and decorated with terracotta, perhaps by Sperandio, connects Piazza Rossini with Piazza Verdi. Here is the best view of the fine brick campanile (1472). The **Teatro Comunale** by Antonio Bibiena (1756; façade 1933), occupies the site of the great palace of the Bentivoglio, which was destroyed in a riot in 1507 and left in ruins until 1763 ('il Guasto'—'The Ruin').

The University

Beyond, Via Zamboni is now lined with buildings used by the various faculties of the University (the 'Studio'), the oldest in Italy, founded in the second half of the 11C and already famous just a century later. Its headquarters have been installed since 1803 in **Palazzo Poggi**, (No. 33; Pl. 8), built by Pellegrino Tibaldi (1549). The courtyard is ascribed to Bartolomeo Triachini. The palace contains frescoes of the story of Ulysses by Pellegrino Tibaldi.

> Irnerius taught here between 1070 and 1100. He revived the study of the Roman system of jurisprudence, which his disciples spread over Europe—in 1144 Vacarius, founder of the law school at Oxford,was sent to England. In return, many Englishmen and Scotsmen served as rectors at Bologna. Here Petrarch was taught, and Copernicus started on the study of astronomy; and in 1789 the university became renowned for the discovery of galvanism. The number of its female professors is remarkable, among them being the learned Novella d'Andrea (14C), Laura Bassi (1711–88), mathematician and scientist, and mother of 12, and Clotilde Tambroni, professor of Greek 1794–1817.

The **University Library** (No. 35 Via Zamboni) contains over 800,000 volumes and 9000 MSS and autographs and has a fine 18C reading-room. Here Cardinal Mezzofanti (1774–1849), who spoke 50 languages and was called by Byron 'the universal interpreter', was librarian, and his own library is added to the collection.

The **Museo Storico dello Studio**, and numerous other scientific collections belonging to the University can be seen by previous appointment. The Torre dell'Osservatorio dates from 1725.

Pinacoteca Nazionale

On Via delle Belle Arti is the **Accademia di Belle Arti** installed in an old Jesuit college, with a handsome courtyard. In this building is the *Pinacoteca Nazionale, (Pl. 8) one of the most important collections of paintings in northern Italy (open 9–14; fest. 9–13; closed Mon). The gallery, especially important for its pictures of the Bolognese school, also has paintings by artists who worked in Bologna (including Giotto, Raphael and Perugino). Acquisitions have augmented the 17C and 18C works. The paintings are arranged by period and school. The rooms are unnumbered but have been numbered in the description below according to the Plan on page 418.

At the top of the entrance stairs three galleries (**4**) around the cloister display works by the **14C Bolognese school** including Vitale da Bologna (*St George and the Dragon*), Jacopino da Bologna, Giovanni da Modena and Simone de'Crocifissi. In **Room 5** are works by **Giotto** and Lorenzo Monaco. In **Rooms 7–10** the **15C Bolognese school** is represented by Michele di Matteo and **Vitale da Bologna** (detached *frescoes and sinopie).

The most important works of the 15C–16C are displayed in the **Long Gallery** (**11**). In the first section (**A**) the **Venetian school** is represented by Antonio and Bartolomeo Vivarini, Cima da Conegliano (*Madonna) and Marco Zoppo.

PINACOTECA
NAZIONALE
Bologna

Beyond is the **Ferrarese school** (**B**), with **Francesco del Cossa** (*Madonna enthroned). **Section C**: Ercole de'Roberti (*St Michael Archangel), Lorenzo Costa and Marco Palmezzano. **Bolognese school** (**D** and **E**). **Francesco Francia** (*Felicini altarpiece). **Section F**: Amico Aspertini. At the end (**G**), **Raphael**, *Ecstasy of St Cecilia*, one of his most famous works. Also here are works by Perugino, Giulio Romano, Franciabigio and Giuliano Bugiardini. **Section K**: Parmigianino (*Madonna and Saints) and works by the 16C Emilian mannerists, including Bartolomeo Passarotti, Camillo Procaccini and Pellegrino Tibaldi. **Section M**: **15C–16C foreign schools**, including El Greco. The fragment from a Crucifixion is by Titian.

Return to the entrance, from which **Room 12** can be reached. It contains fine works by **Guido Reni**, including the large *Pietà dei Mendicanti*, with a model of Bologna. **Room 13** has large *works by **Annibale**, **Lodovico** and **Agostino Carracci**, including the *Madonna Bargellini* by Lodovico and the *Last Communion of St Jerome* by Agostino. **Room 14** contains works by Giorgio Vasari and Federico Barocci.

The long corridor (**Room 15**) off Room 12 displays **Bolognese 17C–18C paintings**, including works by Francesco Albani. The small rooms off the gallery (**16–19**) contain works by Guercino, Domenichino, Francesco Albani, Giuseppe Maria Crespi, the Gandolfi and Donato Creti.

The hall (**20**) at the end is hung with seven huge altarpieces by Domenichino, Guercino, Francesco Albani, Lodovico Carracci and Carlo Cignani.

Near the other end of Via delle Belle Arti is (No. 8) the majestic **Palazzo Bentivoglio** (No. 8; Pl. 7), built to a design perhaps by Bartolomeo Triachini in 1550–60. Further on, Via Mentana (left) leads to the basilica of **San Martino** (Pl. 7), founded in 1217. It was remodelled in the mid-15C, and the façade rebuilt in 1879.

Interior. On the **south side** are altarpieces by Girolamo da Carpi and Amico Aspertini, and a fragment by Vitale da Bologna. In the sanctuary, the pretty organ by Giovanni Cipri dates from 1556. **North side**. Beside the sacristy door are fresco fragments by Simone de'Crocifissi. The altarpieces are by Lorenzo Costa, Lodovico Carracci and Bartolomeo Cesi. The first chapel, built in 1506, contains paintings by Francesco Francia and Amico Aspertini. The statue of the Madonna is attributed to Jacopo della Quercia. Here also is a fresco fragment of the Nativity, recently uncovered and attributed to Paolo Uccello (very difficult to see).

The interesting Via Marsala, across Via Oberdan, has good medieval houses, one with high wooden brackets. At No. 12 is Casa Grassi (late 13C).

The Cathedral (see below) is a short way to the south (see the Plan).

The Cathedral

From Piazza Nettuno and Via Rizzoli (Pl. 11), VIA DELL'INDIPENDENZA, the busy, long main street, opened in 1888, leads north towards the railway station.

A short way up on the right, is the Cathedral (Pl. 7). Probably founded before the 10C, it was rebuilt several times after 1605, and is now essentially a 17C Baroque building, with an elaborate west front by Alfonso Torreggiani (18C). The nave is by Floriano Ambrosini, and the choir is the work of Domenico Tibaldi (1575). The crypt, campanile and two delightful red marble lions survive from the Romanesque building.

In the second chapel of the south aisle is preserved the skull of St Anne, presented in 1435 by Henry VI of England to Nicolò Albergati. Above the inner arch of the choir is an Annunciation, frescoed by Lodovico Carracci. On the high altar is a 12C Crucifixion group carved in cedar wood.

Museo Medievale

The area behind the cathedral is an interesting survival of medieval Bologna, with many old houses and remains of the towers erected by patrician families.

On the opposite side of Via dell'Indipendenza is the Hotel Baglioni with interesting frescoes and remains of Roman buildings. Via Manzoni leads to Via Galliera past the **Madonna di Galliera**, a church remodelled in 1479, with a Renaissance façade. Opposite, beneath a raised portico is the entrance to **Palazzo Ghisilardi-Fava**, begun in 1483. Here is the ***MUSEO CIVICO MEDIEVALE E DEL RINASCIMENTO** (Pl. 6; open 9–14; Sat & Sun 9–13, 15.30–19; closed Tue), an important collection of medieval and Renaissance sculpture and applied arts, beautifully arranged.

Ground floor. Rooms 1 & 2 illustrate the origins of the collections in the 17C and 18C, prior to the founding of the Museo Civico in 1881. On the other side of the courtyard (which has 16C Jewish tombstones) is **Room 4** with 14C tombs by the Dalle Masegne. The second courtyard (on Via Porta di Castello) has a medieval lapidary collection. **Rooms 5 & 6** display medieval metalwork and ivories including a bronze 13C Mosen *ewer in the shape of a horse and rider. In

Room 5 can be seen remains of the Imperial palace in the first city walls, destroyed in 1116. **Room 7** is dominated by the over life-size bronze and beaten copper statue of Pope Boniface VIII by Manno Bandini (1301), formerly on the façade of Palazzo Pubblico. The 14C *cope is one of the finest works ever produced in opus anglicanum (English medieval embroidery). It includes scenes showing the martyrdom of St Thomas Becket.

Stairs lead down to the **lower ground floor**. **Room 9** has a statuette of St Peter Martyr by Giovanni di Balduccio. **Room 10** has remains of a Roman building on this site, and charming 14C tombs of university lecturers. In **Room 11** is the red marble tomb slab of Bartolomeo da Vernazza (died 1348). **Room 12**. *Triptych of the Madonna and Child with saints, carved in bas-relief by Jacopo della Quercia (and his bottega), and a terracotta Madonna in high relief also by Jacopo. The interesting recumbent image of a saint in stuccoed and painted wood is by Antonio Federighi. **Room 13** displays several 15C floor tombs, and the tomb of Pietro Canonici (died 1502) attributed to Vincenzo Onofrio.

First floor. **Room 15** has a major collection of bronzes which include the *model for the Neptune fountain by Giambologna, the first version of the famous *Mercury by the same artist, *St Michael and the Devil, by Alessandro Algardi, and a bronze bust of Gregory XV by Gian Lorenzo Bernini. **Rooms 17–22** contain the collection of applied arts. Among the more notable items are: a ceremonial sword and sheath given to Lodovico Bentivoglio by Pope Nicholas V (**Room 17**); a collection of European armour (**Room 18**); an ivory parade saddle (German, 15C) in **Room 19**; and Turkish armour and *bronzes from the 13C–15C (**Room 20**). In **Rooms 21 & 22** are northern European ivories, and Venetian and German glass, including a rare blue glass *cup with a gilt enamelled frieze, perhaps from the Barovier workshop in Murano (mid-15C), and two vessels probably made for the wedding of Giovanni Bentivoglio and Ginevra Sforza in 1464. Another room (**16**) has a fine display of illuminated choir books (13C–16C).

The rooms in Palazzo Fava are frescoed by the Carracci. The collection of musical instruments, and the museum's celebrated holdings in majolica are to be displayed here.

Via Manzoni enters *VIA GALLIERA (Pl. 6,3), the main north–south artery of the city before Via dell'Indipendenza was built. It has been called, from the splendour of its palazzi, the 'Grand Canal' of Bologna. A short way to the right is Palazzo Montanari (1725) next to the church of **Santa Maria Maggiore**, with two 16C statues of Mary Magdalen and St Roch attributed to Giovanni Zacchi. In the other direction Via Porta di Castello ascends through an archway across Via Monte Grappa into the busy Via Ugo Bassi. Straight across, a road skirts the interesting exterior of the huge Palazzo Comunale (described above) into Piazza Roosevelt.

In Via Val d'Aposa is the charming façade of **Santo Spirito** (Pl. 10), a gem of terracotta ornament, in very good condition (well restored in 1893). Beyond is the church of **San Paolo**, by Giovanni Magenta (1611). The *__Collegio di Spagna__ (Pl. 10,14; adm. only with special permission) was founded by Cardinal Albornoz in 1365 for Spanish students, the last survivor of the many colleges, resembling those at Oxford and Cambridge, which existed in Bologna in the Middle Ages. It still has a high scholastic reputation. Among its famous students were Ignatius Loyola and Cervantes. The main building is by Matteo Gattapone (1365); the gateway (1525) is probably the work of Bernardino da Milano. The handsome courtyard has a double gallery; the chapel has an altarpiece by Marco Zoppo.

Via Urbana follows the delightful garden wall of the College (part of the external painted decoration on the building can be seen from here), back to Via Tagliapietre. Here on the right is the church of **Corpus Domini** (Pl. 14) built in 1478–80, with a terracotta portal by Sperandio. It contains frescoes by Marcantonio Franceschini in the cupola. In a 17C chapel (opened by a closed order of nuns) are preserved the relics of St Catherine de'Vigri (died 1463), an erudite ascetic of Bologna, greatly venerated.

Nearby, at No. 54 Via d'Azeglio, is **San Procolo** (Pl. 14), a church of ancient foundation, with a Romanesque façade. In the choir is an interesting Roman sarcophagus, probably decorated in the late 15C. **Palazzo Bevilacqua** (Nos 31–33; Pl. 10) is a good example of the imported Tuscan style of 1474–82, with a splendid courtyard. The Council of Trent held two sessions in this building in 1547 having moved to Bologna to escape an epidemic. Beyond Via Farini, the attractive and peaceful Via d'Azeglio, one of the few old main streets without arcading, continues back to Piazza Maggiore.

In Piazza Roosevelt (see above) is the enlarged Palazzo della Prefettura (No. 26), of 1561–1603, perhaps by Terribilia. Via IV Novembre continues left past Palazzo Marescalchi (No. 5), in an early 17C style, and (No. 7) the birthplace of Guglielmo Marconi. Opposite is the huge classical exterior of the flank of **San Salvatore** (Pl. 10), with its façade on Via Battisti, by Giovanni Magenta and Tomaso Martelli (1605–23). The church contains the tomb of Guercino, and works by Lippo di Dalmasio, Girolamo da Treviso, Girolamo da Carpi, Vitale da Bologna, Innocenza da Imola, Carlo Bononi and Garofalo.

San Francesco

Via Portanuova continues from here to emerge beneath the **Porta Nuova**, one of the old city gates, into the long Piazza Malpighi beside the Colonna dell'Immacolata, with a copper statue designed by Guido Reni. Here is the church of *San Francesco (Pl. 10), in many ways the most attractive church in Bologna. In the churchyard are the **tombs of the Glossators**, Accursio (died 1260), Odofredo (died 1265) and Rolandino de'Romanzi (died 1284), restored in 1904. The church is in a more or less French Gothic style, begun in 1236, completed early in 1263, but considerably altered since. The façade (c 1250) has two carved 8C plutei and 13C–14C majolica plaques in the pitch of the roof. The smaller of the two towers was completed in 1261; the larger and finer, the work of Antonio di Vincenzo (1397–c 1402), is surrounded by decorative terracotta.

Interior. In the north aisle is the terracotta tomb of Pope Alexander V, completed by Sperandio (1482), and in the south aisle is the Fieschi tomb (1492). The choir has a marble *reredos by Jacobello and Pier Paolo dalle Masegne (1388–92). On the sanctuary walls are frescoes by Francesco da Rimini. In the east chapel of the ambulatory hangs a crucifix attributed to Pietro Lianori.

At No. 23 Via dei Gombruti (off Via Portanuova) the 'Old Pretender' stayed during several visits to Bologna.

The most pleasant way back to Piazza Maggiore is to return along Via Portanuova and Via IV Novembre.

Via dell'Indipendenza ends at the **Montagnola** (Pl. 3), a public garden laid out around the mound formed over the ruins of the citadel of Galliera. Beyond it is Porta Galliera (1661). The **railway station** (Pl. 2) is just to the west. A bomb placed by right-wing terrorists in the station waiting-room in August 1980 killed 85 people and wounded 200 others. On the other side of the railway is the **Sacro Cuore**, a large church in the Byzantine style, begun in 1877 and completed in 1912; the dome was rebuilt in 1934.

The outskirts of Bologna

In the southern part of the town are the pleasant **Giardini Margherita** (Pl. 16), laid out in 1875. The church of **Santa Maria della Misericordia** (Pl. 15), enlarged in the 15C, has stained-glass windows by Francesco Francia. The little church of the **Madonna del Baraccano** (Pl. 16) has a good fresco by Francesco Cossa. Further south, reached by Via Murri, at 19 Via Toscana is the **Villa Aldovandi** which has an 18C theatre (open on the 1st and 3rd Thu of each month at 15).

On a hill to the southwest (bus 30) stands the former Olivetan convent of **San Michele in Bosco** (beyond Pl. 14), with a splendid view of Bologna. It was here on 1 May 1860 that the meeting took place between Cavour and Vittorio Emanuele II at which approval was given for the sailing of the 'Thousand' to Sicily. The church, rebuilt since 1437 and completed in the early 16C, has a façade ascribed to Baldassarre Peruzzi (1523). It contains the tomb of the condottiere Armaciotto de'Ramazzotti, by Alfonso Lombardi (1526). The frescoes on the triumphal arch are by Domenico Maria Canuti. In the cloister are the remains of an important fresco cycle by Lodovico Carracci, Guido Reni and others. The primitive church of **San Vittore**, on the next hill to the south (at No. 40 Via San Mamolo), dates from the 11C, enlarged in the 12C. It was altered in 1864, and later partly restored.

Just outside the Porta San Mamolo (bus 29 from Via Ugo Bassi) stands the Observantine church of the **Annunziata** (Pl. 14). A Renaissance portico precedes the austere basilica of c 1475. Above is the **Osservanza** convent (1811–16), and the public park of **Villa Ghigi**.

The sanctuary of the **Madonna di San Luca** is a famous viewpoint. It is reached by bus No. 20 from Via Indipendenza to the public park of **Villa Spada** (which contains a museum dedicated to fabrics, open 9–13 exc. Mon) in Via Saragozza (Pl. 13) at the foot of the hill of San Luca. From here a mini-bus (every 30 mins) ascends the hill. The church is connected with Porta Saragozza (Pl. 13), just over 3km away, by a *portico of 666 arches (1674–1793). Where the portico begins the ascent of the hill is the Arco del Meloncello, by Carlo Francesco Dotti (1718). The sanctuary, built by Dotti in 1725–49, contains a Noli me tangere by Guercino, and paintings by Calvaert.

To the west, in the Comune of **Zola Predosa**, is Palazzo Albergati with an unusual plain rectangular exterior built in 1659–94 on a plan by Giovanni

Giacomo Monti. The huge salone has stuccoes by Gian Filippo Bezzi, and other rooms have elaborate 17C–18C frescoes.

Outside Porta Sant'Isaia (Pl. 9), is the huge sports stadium built in 1926, and the **Certosa** (bus 14), founded in 1334, suppressed in 1797, and consecrated in 1801 as the public cemetery of Bologna. It was much admired by Byron. The 14C–16C church contains marquetry stalls (1539) and frescoes by Bartolomeo Cesi. Near a statue of Murat, by Vincenzo Vela (1865) is the tomb of Carducci. The Etruscan necropolis of *Felsina* was discovered in the precincts of the Certosa in 1869.

In the northeast part of the town (buses 38 or 91 from Via Marconi via the station) is the **Quartiere Fieristica**, where important trade fairs are held. It has permanent exhibition halls, a conference centre and a theatre. The international Children's Book Fair is held here annually in spring. Here, too, is the **Galleria d'Arte Moderna** (open 10–13, 15–9 exc. Mon), with 20C works by artists from the region, most of which have been donated by the artists themselves. .

Off the Via Emilia, 5km southeast of Bologna, is a **British Military Cemetery**.

The province of Bologna

Southwest of Bologna, on the Via Emilia, is the town of **IMOLA** (57,200 inhab.), on the site of the Roman *Forum Cornelii*, founded by L. Cornelius Sulla in 82 BC. It still preserves the main outlines of its Roman plan.The **Cathedral** was entirely rebuilt in the 18C. The early 14C **Castle** was rebuilt by Gian Galeazzo Sforza, whose daughter Caterina married Girolamo Riario, lord of Imola, and held the fortress after his death until her defeat by Cesare Borgia (1500). It contains a collection of arms and armour. In the **Pinacoteca** is a painting by Innocenzo Francucci (da Imola; 1494–1550).

On the road from Imola to Florence, which ascends the valley of the Santerno, is **Castel del Rio**, dominated by its huge 13C castle (of the Alidosi; containing a War Museum), with a 16C palace (now the town hall) of the same family. Near **Moraduccio** is a British Military Cemetery. There are quarries of pietra serena (a dark grey sandstone) in the hills, which have interesting rock formations. The road continues into Tuscany (see *Blue Guide Tuscany*).

The Pistoia road which leads south from Bologna passes **Pontecchio Marconi**. Here is the mausoleum (by Marcello Piacentini) of Guglielmo Marconi (1874–1937), whose first experiments in the transmission of signals by Hertzian waves were made at his father's Villa Griffone above the town. In the park is preserved a relic of the boat *Elettra* from which, while at anchor in the port of Genoa in 1930, Marconi lit up the lights of Sydney. At **Marzabotto**, in the park of Villa Aria, are remains of an Etruscan city, thought to be *Misa* (6C–4C BC). Excavations have revealed traces of houses, temples and two necropoli. The road continues south to **Porretta Terme**, a little spa on the Reno, with warm springs of sulphurous and alkaline waters, beyond which it enters Tuscany (see *Blue Guide Tuscany*).

60 · Ferrara and its province

Ferrara (130,000 inhab.) is one of the most pleasing towns in northern Italy, apparently well administered and with a peaceful atmosphere, cycling being the main means of getting about. The city is divided into two distinct parts: the southern district retains many attractive cobbled streets and medieval houses, while the area to the north, defined by Jacob Burckhardt as the first modern city of Europe, was laid out with spacious streets and fine palaces in the 15C by Ercole I d'Este. Ferrara is famous as the residence of the Este dukes, whose court was one of the most illustrious of the Italian Renaissance. Its 15C walls are among the most extensive and interesting in Europe, and the huge Este castle survives right in the centre of the town. There are also numerous gardens and good museums, and important exhibitions and concerts are often held here. The town lies in a fertile plain near the right bank of the Po: extensive land-reclamation operations in the delta area brought back to Ferrara much of its old prosperity, and it is now an important market for fruit.

■ **Information offices.** Ufficio informazione (Comune di Ferrara), 21 Corso Giovecca (tel. 0532/209370), and (open in summer) at 2 Via Kennedy. Assessorato del Turismo della Provincia di Ferrara, Castello Estense (tel. 0532/299308).

■ **Hotels.** 4-star: *Ripagrande*, 21 Via Ripagrande; *Annunziata*, 5 Piazza Repubblica; *Duchessa Isabella*, 68 Via Palestro. 3-star: *Touring*, Viale Cavour; *Carlton*, 93 Via Garibaldi. 2-star: *San Paolo*, 13 Via Baluardi.
    The **youth hostel** near Palazzo dei Diamanti is being restored. **Camping site** (3-star), Via Gramicia (open Apr–Oct).

■ **Restaurants. A**: *La Provvidenza*, Corso Ercole I d'Este. **B**: *Centrale*, 8 Via Boccaleone; *La Romantica*, 36 Via Ripagrande. **C**: *Osteria degli Angeli*, 4 Via Volte; *Osteria dei Borgia*, 26 Via Borgoleoni. **Sandwich bar** in Piazza Savonarola (beside the castle). **Cafés**: *Roverella* and *Europa*, Corso Giovecca.

■ **Picnic places** in Parco Massari, Parco Pareschi, and on the walls (especially pretty near the Baluardo San Tommaso).

■ **Car parks.** Large car park in Via Kennedy (Pl. 10). Cars with foreign number plates are allowed to park in Piazza Castello and on Corso Portareno (Pl. 10,11). Other car parks on Corso Ercole d'Este, near Plazzo Schifanoia, and the station.

■ **Bicycles** can be hired on Corso Giovecca (next to the tourist office).

■ **Buses.** Nos 1 & 9 from the station to the Castello. Services for the province (including Comacchio) depart from the bus station on Corso Isonzo (Pl. 6).

■ **Theatres.** *Comunale* (opera and concert season Nov–May, and theatre performances). There is a summer festival of music, and concerts are sometimes held in palace courtyards. Ferrara is the seat of the European Youth Orchestra.

■ **Annual festival.** The Palio of Ferrara (San Giorgio) is held at the end of May with races (horses, mules, etc.) in Piazza Ariostea.

History

Originating probably as a refuge of the Veneti in the marshes of the Po, Ferrara first became important under the Exarchate of Ravenna (6C). The Guelf family of Este, after a decisive defeat of the Ghibellines by Azzo Novello at Cassano in 1259, here established the earliest and one of the greatest of the northern Italian principalities. Ferrara remained under the sway of the Este dukes until 1598, and their court attracted a great many poets, scholars and artists, while trade and commerce flourished, and 'Ferrara blades' rivalled the swords of Toledo. Nicolò II (1361–88) gave hospitality to Petrarch; Alberto (1388–93) founded the university; Nicolò III (1393–1441) was the patron of Pisanello, and in his city (1438) the eastern Emperor John VI Palaeologus met Pope Eugenius IV for the ecumenical council, later transferred to Florence; Lionello (1441–50) inaugurated the age of artistic pre-eminence that Borso (1450–71) continued; Ercole I (1471–1505) laid out the northern district of the city; Alfonso I (1505–34), husband of Lucrezia Borgia, was the patron of Ariosto and Titian; Ercole II (1534–59) exiled his wife Renée, the daughter of Louis XII of France and the protectress of John Calvin, who lived for a while in Ferrara under the assumed name of Charles Heppeville; Alfonso II (1559–97) was the patron of Tasso and began the reclamation of the marshes.

In 1598 the city was annexed to the States of the Church on the pretext that Cesare d'Este, heir apparent to the duchy in a collateral line, was illegitimate, and the city soon lost importance. It suffered widespread bomb damage in the Second World War.

Art

Ferrara had a productive school of painting, including Cosmè Tura, 'the Mantegna of Ferrara', Francesco del Cossa, Ercole de'Roberti, Lorenzo Costa, Dosso Dossi and his brother Battista Luteri, and Il Garofalo, pupil of Raphael. Ferrara was the birthplace of a great sculptor, Alfonso Lombardi (1497–1537), and of a great architect, Biagio Rossetti (c 1447–1516). The composer Girolamo Frescobaldi (1583–1643) was also born here. At the end of the 16C the 'concerto delle donne' at the Este court had an important influence on the development of the madrigal. Robert Browning wrote several poems about Ferrara, and *My Last Duchess* (written in 1842) probably refers to Alfonso II and his wife. The writer Giorgio Bassani was born in Ferrara in 1916 (and his novel *Il Giardino dei Finzi Contini* is set here).

The Castello Estense

In the centre of the city rises the *Castello Estense (Pl. 7; open 9.30–16.30 or 17.30 exc. Mon), the former palace of the dukes, a massive quadrilateral surrounded by a moat (still filled with water) and approached by drawbridges. It houses the administrative offices of the province.

The castle was begun in 1385 by Bartolino da Novara for Duke Nicolò II; he incorporated the 13C 'Torre dei Leoni' into the northern corner of the fortress, and added three more identical towers. It was altered by Girolamo da Carpi in the 16C.

There is a lovely **courtyard**, off which is the entrance to the rooms open to the public. **Ground floor**. The **Sala del Caminetto** has three frescoes (1577) of Este princes on a design by Pirro Ligorio (the only ones to have survived of the hundred which once decorated the courtyard). Steps lead down through a room with a detached 15C fresco of an Este prince in profile, to the **kitchens**. At the end of a corridor, wooden steps lead down to the grim **dungeons** beneath the 'Torre dei Leoni', where Parisina, wife of Nicolò III, and her lover Ugo, his illegitimate son, were imprisoned and murdered; the cells were last used for political prisoners in 1943.

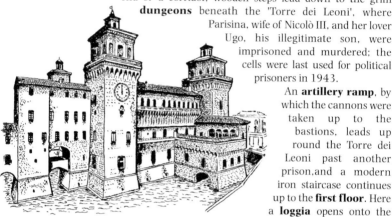

Castello Estense

An **artillery ramp**, by which the cannons were taken up to the bastions, leads up round the Torre dei Leoni past another prison, and a modern iron staircase continues up to the **first floor**. Here a **loggia** opens onto the **Giardino degli aranci**, a charming little walled hanging garden designed by Girolamo da Carpi for the Este duchesses (with delightful views of the town). The **Camerino dei Baccanali** is beautifully frescoed by Camillo Filippi and his sons Cesare and Sebastiano (Il Bastianino). The **Chapel of Renée de France** was one of the few Calvinist chapels in Italy to survive the Counter-Reformation. The **Sala dell'Aurora**, **Saletta dei Giochi** and **Sala dei Giochi** have delightful ceiling *frescoes by the Filippi (in the last two, around the walls, are copies made in 1911 of the frescoes in Palazzo Schifanoia). The tiny *Stanzina delle Duchesse** was entirely decorated with *grotteschi* by the Filippi c 1555–65.

In the piazzetta on the west side of the castle stands the chapel of **San Giuliano** (1405). Off Corso Martiri della Libertà is a monument to the great reformer, Savonarola, born in Ferrara in 1452, by Stefano Galletti (1875). **Palazzo del Comune** (Pl. 7), built for Azzo Novello (1243), was considerably altered in the late 15C by Pietro Benvenuti and Biagio Rossetti. The bronze statues of Nicolò III and Borso, on the classical arch (on a design attributed to Leon Battista Alberti) and column in front, are reproductions (by Giacomo Zilocchi; 1926) of the 15C originals destroyed in 1796. The arcaded courtyard has a fine staircase by Pietro Benvenuti (1481).

Cathedral

The *Cathedral (Pl. 11), begun in 1135 by the architect Wiligelmo and the sculptor Nicolò, was almost complete by the end of the 13C. The very fine **west front** has a projecting **west portal**, with beautiful carving by Nicolò (1135), crowned with an elaborate *tribune**. In the tympanum is the Last Judgement in high relief executed by an unknown Romanesque sculptor in the mid-13C. In the loggia beneath is a statue of the Madonna and Child by Cristoforo da Firenze (1427). To the right of the side door is a statue of Alberto d'Este (1393). The south side is partly obscured by a charming little portico of shops added in 1473. The massive **campanile**, southeast of the church, was built from 1412 to 1514.

The **interior** (open 7.30–12; 15–18.30), remodelled in 1712–18, is preceded by a **narthex** with a 5C sarcophagus and the original pilasters from the main portal. On the west wall are two detached frescoes by Garofalo. In the north aisle are altarpieces by Garofalo (1524) and Francesco Francia. In the transepts are terracotta busts by Alfonso Lombardi, and in the south transept a Martyrdom of St Laurence by Guercino (1629), and the *altar of the Calvary, composed in 1673 from large 15C bronze groups of statuary by Nicolò and Giovanni Baroncelli and Domenico di Paris. Below is the effigy tomb of Bishop Bovelli (died 1954). In the apse is the Last Judgement, by Bastianino (1580–83).

The **Museo della Cattedrale** (in a room entered from the narthex up a long staircase) is open 10–12, 15–17 (exc. Sun and fest.). It contains good Flemish tapestries and illuminated choir books; St George and an *Annunciation, by Cosmè Tura (1469); *Madonna of the Pomegranate, and a statuette of St Maurelius, both by Jacopo della Quercia (1408); and charming *reliefs of the Months, from the old south doorway.

At 32 Via Cairoli the **Seminario** occupies the 16C Palazzo Trotti, which contains two rooms frescoed by Garofalo (1519–20), with remarkable perspectives.

In the piazza south of the cathedral are the Torre dell'Orologio and a department store in an ugly building of 1957 on the site of the 14C Palazzo della Ragione. The pretty arcaded Via San Romano leads south through an interesting medieval part of the town. The street ends at Porta Reno (or Porta Paolo), built in 1612 on a design by Giovanni Battista Aleotti.

Before the gate the pretty Via delle Volte (Pl. 11), which runs beneath numerous arches, leads left. It crosses Via Scienze in which (No. 17) is **Palazzo Paradiso** which houses the **Biblioteca Comunale Ariostea**. The building dates from 1391, and has a façade of 1610 by Giovanni Battista Aleotti. The courtyard contains Roman and Renaissance marbles, and in the library are the tomb of Ariosto, MS pages of the Ariosto's epic poem Orlando Furioso, and autographs of Ariosto and Tasso. Nearby in Via Mazzini is the **Synagogue** in the area which was the **ghetto** of Ferrara from 1627 to 1848, although a large Jewish community from Spain had lived freely in the town during the period of the Este dukes.

Well preserved old houses of the 15C city and little churches can be seen in the narrow lanes lying between Via Scienze and Via Borgo Vado (Pl. 11). At 31 Via Gioco del Pallone is the house which belonged to Ariosto's family.

The attractive Via Voltapaletto (Pl. 11), east of the Cathedral, leads past the handsome **Palazzo Costabili** (No. 11; 17C), decorated with busts and trophies, to the spacious church of **San Francesco** (open 7.30–11, 15.30–19), partly rebuilt in 1494 by Biagio Rossetti. The frescoes above the arches (Franciscan saints) and on the vault are good Ferrarese works of the 16C. In the north aisle is a fine fresco of the seizure of Christ in the Garden (1524) by Garofalo, and an altarpiece by Scarsellino.

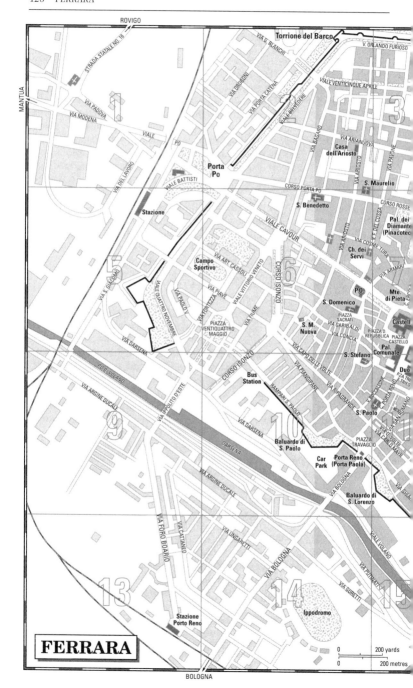

FERRARA

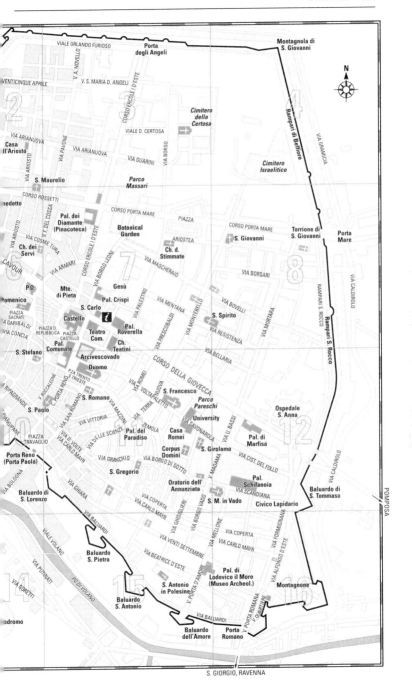

Casa Romei

Via Savonarola continues to the *Casa Romei (Pl. 11; No. 30; open 8–14, Sat & Sun 8.30–19.30). Begun c 1442 it retains two graceful courtyards, its original ceilings, and (in a room off the second courtyard) delightful contemporary mural paintings and a fine fireplace. The *grotteschi* decorations on the upper floor are by the Filippi. It houses 13C–15C sculptures and detached frescoes. On the opposite side of Via Savonarola is the seat of the **University**, founded in 1391.

The church of **San Girolamo** (1712) faces the house (No. 19) where Savonarola passed the first 20 years of his life. The church of **Corpus Domini** (closed for restoration), with a 15C façade, contains the floor tombs of Alfonso I and II d'Este and of Lucrezia Borgia (died 1519) and two of her sons. Via Savonarola ends at the severe Palazzo Saracco.

To the left, Via Ugo Bassi leads to Corso della Giovecca (see below), where No. 174 is the **Palazzina di Marfisa d'Este** (Pl. 12; open 9–12.30, 14 or 15–17 or 18). Built in 1559 it was restored in 1939. It has good ceilings and contemporary furniture, a supposed portrait of James I of England, and a damaged bust in profile of Ercole I d'Este, by Sperandio. The 'loggia degli aranci' in the garden has a vault painted with trellised vines and birds.

To the right, Via Madama continues as Via Borgo Vado, where the church of **Santa Maria in Vado**, another work of Rossetti (1495–1518), has a handsome interior. Nearby, at No. 47 Via Borgo di Sotto, is the **Oratorio dell'Annunziata** (Pl. 11; ring for adm. at the convent at No. 49, 10–12, 15–17 exc. Sat & fest.) decorated in 1548 with frescoes attributed to Camillo Filippi, Pellegrino Tibaldi and Nicolò Rosselli, and trompe l'oeil perspectives by Francesco Scala. On the altar wall is a Resurrection with members of the Confraternità della Morte (who assisted the condemned), and on the opposite wall an Assumption signed by Lamberto Nortense.

Palazzo Schifanoia

In Via Scandiana is **PALAZZO SCHIFANOIA** (entrance at No. 27; Pl. 12; open daily 9–19), begun in 1385 and enlarged in 1391, 1458, and in 1469 by Pietro Benvenuti and Biagio Rossetti. Stairs lead up to the *Salone dei Mesi, decorated for Duke Borso d'Este with delightful frescoes of the Months, one of the most renowned fresco cycles of the Renaissance of profane subjects (now in rather poor condition). They were painted by Francesco Cossa, with the help of Ercole de'Roberti and other (unidentified) masters of the Ferrarese school.

The frescoes follow a complicated decorative scheme referring to the months of the year in three bands: above are 12 scenes illustrating the triumph of a divinity; the middle band has the sign of the zodiac for that month, flanked by two symbolic figures, and the lower part of the walls are decorated with scenes from the court of Duke Borso.

The present entrance (formerly on the long north wall) is on the **west wall**. The scenes illustrating **January** and **February** are very ruined. The **east wall**, opposite the present entrance, is the best preserved and is known to have been decorated by Francesco Cossa. **March**: Triumph of Minerva, showing her on a chariot drawn by two unicorns; the sign of Aries; hawking scenes. **April**: Triumph of Venus (her chariot drawn by swans); Taurus; Duke Borso returning from the hunt and the Palio of St George. **May**: Triumph of Apollo; Gemini; fragments of farming scenes.

North wall. June: Triumph of Mercury; Cancer; scenes of the Duke in a land-scape. **July**: Triumph of Zeus; Leo; the Duke receiving visitors, and scenes of women working hemp. **August**: Triumph of Ceres; Virgo. The scenes for **September** are usually attributed to Ercole de'Roberti: Triumph of Vulcan, with Vulcan's forge, and a love scene in bed thought to represent Mars and the vestal virgin Silvia, from whom Romulus and Remus were born; Libra; Borso receiving Venetian ambassadors. The **south wall** with the last three months is almost totally obliterated. There is a display of illuminated manuscripts here.

The ***Sala dei Stucchi**** (1468–70) has a delightful ceiling attributed to Domenico di Paris. The adjoining room has another good ceiling, and a display of 14C–15C ceramics.

The main staircase leads back downstairs. Half-way down is the entrance to rooms which contain material from the **Museo Civico**, including (in the first room) Egyptian works, two Greek red-figure vases, and Roman glass. The next three rooms on a mezzanine floor (with remains of painted decoration on the walls) display 15C–16C ceramics. On the floor below are exhibited: ivories and scenes of the Passion in alabaster made in Nottingham in the early 15C; 15C intarsia stalls; plaques and medals by Pisanello, Matteo de'Pasti, and Sperandio; sculptures including a bust by Guido Mazzoni and two Madonnas attributed to Domenico di Paris; 16C bronzes (Giovanni Francesco Susini, Giambologna and Duquesnoy), 18C marble busts, and a portrait of Cicognara by Canova (1822).

Across the road is the **Lapidario Civico** (adm. as for Palazzo Schifanoia), arranged in the 15C former church of Santa Libera. The collection of Roman works was formed in 1735 by Marchese Bevilacqua. Among the funerary stelae and sarcophagi are those of Annia Faustina and of the Aurelii (both dating from the 3C AD).

At No. 124 Via XX Settembre is ***Palazzo di Lodovico il Moro** (Pl. 15), a masterpiece by Biagio Rossetti, which he left unfinished in 1503. There is a beautiful courtyard and a room decorated by Garofalo. It houses the ***Museo Archeologico Nazionale di Spina** (closed since 1987). Founded in 1935, this contains a superb collection of objects discovered in the necropolis of Spina, near Comacchio, a Greco-Etruscan port that flourished in the 6C–3C BC. The collection consists principally of vases, including many made in the 5C BC, and splendid jewellery of the 4C BC. There are also two dug-out canoes.

At No. 152 is the house built for himself by Biagio Rossetti (destined to become a museum). Gardens crown the ramparts of **Montagnone** (Pl. 16), and a park extends north above the walls built by Alfonso I (1512–18). Paths continue from here for c 5km around the walls as far as Porta Po (see the Plan), only inter-rupted at Porta Mare. The walls are described in greater detail below.

Via Porta Romana leads south through the walls and across the Po di Volano canal to the church of **San Giorgio** (beyond Pl. 16), which was the cathedral of Ferrara in the 7C–12C, then rebuilt in the 15C and partly renovated in the 18C. The campanile is by Rossetti (1485). Inside is the magnificent *tomb of Lorenzo Roverella, physician to Julius II and afterwards Bishop of Ferrara, by Ambrogio da Milano and Antonio Rossellino (1475), and the pavement tomb of Cosmè Tura.

From Porta Romana there is a path along a good stretch of walls built by Alfonso II. Near Palazzo di Lodovico il Moro, off Via Beatrice d'Este, is the convent of **Sant'Antonio in Polesine** (ring for adm. 9.30–11.30, 15–17 exc. fest.) with 13C–15C frescoes.

The northern district of the town

The area of the city north of the Castello and the broad and busy Corso della Giovecca (Pl. 7,11, & 12), was planned by Ercole I in the early 15C with wide thoroughfares and fine palaces and gardens.

In Corso Giovecca, No. 37 is a fragment of the old **Arcispedale Sant'Anna** where Tasso was confined as a lunatic in 1579–86; behind is a 15C cloister of the former Basilian convent. The fine church of **San Carlo** is by Giovanni Battista Aleotti (1623). On Via Borgo Leoni is the church of the **Gesù** (Pl. 7), which contains a *Pietà in terracotta by Guido Mazzoni (1485). On Corso Giovecca, **Palazzo Roverella** (No. 47) has a beautiful terracotta façade (1508), attributed to Biagio Rossetti. Nearby, at 24 Via De Pisis, is the **Museo Civico di Storia Naturale** (open Tue 9–13, Wed–Sun 9–13, 15–19). On the other side of Corso Giovecca is the church of the **Teatini** (1653) which contains a Presentation in the Temple by Guercino. The **Teatro Comunale**, without a monumental façade, is attributed to Antonio Foschini (c 1780).

The handsome cobbled CORSO ERCOLE I D'ESTE (Pl. 7,3) leads north past several palaces and garden walls to **PALAZZO DEI DIAMANTI** (Pl. 7) begun by Rossetti for Sigismondo d'Este c 1492 and remodelled around 1565. It takes its name from the diamond emblem of the Estes, repeated 12,600 times on its façade. The palace contains the **PINACOTECA NAZIONALE** (open 9–14; fest 9–13; closed Mon), especially notable for its paintings of the Ferrarese school. Important exhibitions are often held here.

The rooms are unnumbered, but the works are all labelled. The Vendeghini-Baldi collection (displayed in a room to the left) includes works by Garofalo, Michele Coltellini, Bartolomeo Vivarini, Andrea Mantegna, Ercole de'Roberti, Jacopo and Giovanni Bellini, and Gentile da Fabriano. Another series of rooms displays works by the 'Maestro di Figline', Simone de'Crocifissi, Ercole de'Roberti, Giuseppe Mazzuoli, the school of Piero della Francesca, and Cosmè Tura.

Early and mid-16C painters represented include Giovan Francesco Maineri, Michele Coltellini, Domenico Panetti, Bastianino, and Lodovico and Agostino Carracci. The 17C and 18C works include paintings by Scarsellino, Guercino and Pietro della Vecchia.

The works from the Collezione Sacrati Strozzi which were assigned to the city in 1992 include Madonnas by Biagio d'Antonio and Francesco Bianchi Ferrari, two 15C *Muses, Christ in the Garden attributed to Dosso Dossi, and two interesting 16C views of Ferrara.

The **salone** has a fine wooden ceiling of 1567–91. Here are displayed frescoes by Serafino Serafini (*Apotheosis of St Augustine*) and Garofalo, and huge late 13C frescoes. Also here are two works of 1565 by Camillo Bastiani and Bastianino.

The rooms beyond, part of the apartment of Cesare and Virginia d'Este, preserve their 16C decoration. Here are displayed a painting by Vittore Carpaccio, and works by 16C painters from Ferrara (Ortolano, Mazzolino, Bastianino, Scarsellino and Carlo Bononi), with Garofalo and Dosso Dossi especially well represented. The gallery also owns a good collection of etchings and engravings. **Palazzo Prosperi Sacrati**, on the opposite side of the Corso, with an elaborate 16C portal, is to be used as an extension to the gallery.

Beside Palazzo dei Diamanti, at No. 19, is the entrance to the well arranged **Museo del Risorgimento e della Resistenza** (open 9–14, 15–19; fest. 9–12,

15.30–18.30). At No. 17 is the **Museo Michelangelo Antonioni** (open 9.30–13, 15.30–19), with a collection documenting the work of the film director, who was born in Ferrara.

At the end of Corso Ercole I d'Este is the former **Porta degli Angeli** (Pl. 3) in the *WALLS of Ercole I. This was the gate by which the Este left Ferrara in 1598, and it was closed the following year. The walls (see Plan) were begun in 1451 at the southern limit of the city, and in 1492 Biagio Rossetti was commissioned to build the walls here around Ercole I's extension to the city. Alfonso I and Alfonso II strengthened the fortifications and more work was carried out on them by the popes in the 17C and 18C. Their total length is c 9·2km, and paths and avenues surmount them for some 8·5km.

To the left of Porta degli Angeli, eight semicircular towers survive and at the northwest angle is the Torrione del Barco. The most interesting and best preserved stretch of the walls (followed by a picturesque walkway open to cyclists) is from the Porta degli Angeli to the Porta Mare (Pl. 8). The view north extends across the former 'Barco', the ducal hunting reserve, as far as the Po, an area of some 1200 hectares destined to become a park. Inside the walls can be seen the orchards which surround the Certosa (see below) and the Jewish Cemetery, and in the distance are the towers of the Castello.

From Palazzo dei Diamanti, Corso Porta Mare leads east. At No. 2 is the **Botanical Garden** (open 9–13, exc. Sat & fest.). Beyond is the Parco Massari where the Palazzine dei Cavalieri di Malta provides a fit setting for the **Museo Boldini** (Pl. 7; open 9.30–13, 15.30–19), devoted to works by the Ferrarese painter Giovanni Boldini (1842–1931). The **Museo Civico d'Arte Moderna e Contemporanea** (open as for the Museo Boldini) displays works by Ferrarese artists of the 19C and 20C (including Giorgio De Chirico). The Metaphysical school of painters was founded in Ferrara c 1917, and De Chirico (1888–1978) spent much time in the city. An important collection of works by De Pisis was donated to the gallery in 1996.

Further on, on the right is Piazza Ariostea (Pl. 7), with two Renaissance palaces, and a statue of Ariosto (19C) on a column which in turn has carried statues of Duke Ercole I, Pope Alexander VII, Liberty and Napoleon.

Via Borso leads north to the **Certosa** (Pl. 3; 1452–61), with interesting cloisters, now occupied by a cemetery. The adjoining church of **San Cristoforo**, begun in 1498, probably by Rossetti, has good terracotta decoration. Off Via Borso, Via Guarini and Via Aria Nuova lead due west to the **Casa dell'Ariosto** (Pl. 2; No. 67 Via Ariosto), the house built for himself by the poet, who died here in 1533.

The province of Ferrara

Ferrara has a small province, most of which is to the east of the town in the southern part of the Po delta where the Po di Volano reaches the sea in a partly protected area. The main delta of the Po is described in Chapter 36. The most important monument in the province is the abbey of Pomposa.

■ **Information offices.** Assessorato Turismo Provincia Ferrara, Castello Estense, Ferrara (tel. 0532/299308). Offices are open in summer at Comacchio, Pomposa and at the Lidi resorts.

■ **Hotels. Argenta**: 4-star:*Villa Reale*, 16 Viale Roiti. **Cento**: 4-star: *Al Castello*, 57 Via Giovannina. Numerous hotels (3- and 2-star), many only open in summer, at the Lidi.

■ **Public transport.** Pomposa is not accessible by public transport. Buses from Ferrara (see above) to Comacchio.

The once marshy country between Ferrara and the sea, where the Po enters the Adriatic, has many times been the subject of land-reclamation schemes since the time of Alfonso II d'Este. The dunes in the Po di Goro delta are of great interest to naturalists. The **Gran Bosco della Mesola** on the Volano, one of the last wooded areas in the Po delta, has been designated a nature reserve (open fest., 8–dusk). On the Po di Goro is the splendid **Castello di Mesola**, a hunting lodge of Alfonso II, built in 1583 by Antonio Pasi (on a design by Giovan Battista Aleotti), now used for exhibitions.

The isolated Benedictine *ABBEY OF POMPOSA was founded in the 7C–8C on what was then an island and gradually deserted in the 17C because of malaria. It is still one of the most evocative sites on the delta, marked by its fine *campanile 48m high. The **Church** (closed 12–14) dates from the 8C–9C, and was enlarged in the 11C. It is preceded by an atrium with beautiful Byzantine sculptural decoration. The fine basilican interior (good capitals) is covered with charming 14C frescoes, some attributed to Vitale da Bologna (including the Christ in Glory in the apse). Most of the mosaic pavement survives. The monastic buildings include the **chapterhouse** and **refectory**, both with important frescoes of the Bolognese school. There is a small **museum** above the refectory. Guido d'Arezzo (c 995–1050), inventor of the modern musical scale, was a monk here. The **Palazzo della Ragione** (abbot's justice court) is a beautiful 11C building (altered in 1396).

To the south are fields where rice is cultivated, and the marshes of the **Valle Bertuzzi** (visited by migratory birds). **COMACCHIO** is an interesting little town which grew to importance because of its salt-works, and is now important for fishing and curing eels—the huge shoals of eels which make for the sea in Oct–Dec are caught in special traps. The town was continuously attacked by the Venetians and destroyed by them in 1509. The pretty canal-lined streets are crossed by numerous bridges, notably the 17C Trepponti, which traverses no less than four canals. The Loggia dei Mercanti, Duomo and Loggiata dei Cappuccini all date from the 17C.

In the drained lagoon northwest of Comacchio the burial-ground of the Greco-Etruscan city of **Spina** yielded a vast quantity of vases and other pottery (kept in the archaeological museum in Ferrara). Founded c 530 BC, it was a port carrying on a lively trade with Greece, but it barely outlasted the 4C BC. Part of the city itself, laid out on a regular grid plan with numerous canals, was located by aerial survey in 1956 and excavations continue.

The dwindling **Lago di Comacchio** is now more than two-thirds drained to the detriment of the egrets, herons, stilts, terns and avocets that were once found here in profusion. It has, however, now become a protected area. At **Porto Garibaldi** (formerly Magnavacca) the Austrian navy captured the last 200 'Garibaldini', leaving Garibaldi alone with Anita and his comrade Leggero. Anita died at **Mandriole**, on the southern shore of the lake (monument), now in the province of Ravenna near the vast pine woods of San Vitale which hide the view of the sea.

On the sandy coast are a line of popular resorts, including **Lido delle Nazioni** and **Lido degli Estensi**, known as the **Lidi Ferraresi**, with numerous hotels and camping sites, crowded with tourists in summer.

At **Argenta** on the western side of the Valli di Comacchio, there is a **Marsh Museum** (open 9.30–13, 15–17.30 exc. Mon), which documents land reclamation here over the centuries as well as the interesting flora and fauna of these wetlands.

On the western border of the province is the little town of **CENTO**, the birth-place of Isaac Israeli, great-grandfather of Benjamin Disraeli, and of Guercino whose painting is well represented in the **Pinacoteca Civica**. The church of the **Rosario** contains a chapel built for Guercino and a fine Crucifixion by him. Above the town rises the 14C **Rocca**.

At **Pieve di Cento** is a small Pinacoteca Civica in the main square, with paintings by the Bolognese and Ferrarese schools (15C–19C), a wooden 14C Madonna,and 18C reliquaries.

61 · Modena and its province

Modena is an extremely prosperous provincial capital (171,000 inhab.) which has figured prominently in Italian history. It has a very beautiful cathedral built by Lanfranco with remarkable early 12C sculptures by Wiligelmus and later works by Campionese sculptors. A number of churches in the town have expressive works dating from the early 16C by the local sculptor Antonio Begarelli. The Galleria Estense has a very fine collection of paintings formed by the Este family in the early 16C, and the Musei Civici, recently well restored, have interesting local collections. The name of Modena is also associated with the Maserati motor works here and especially with the Ferrari works founded by Enzo Ferrari (1898–1989) outside the town at Maranello.

■ **Information office.** IAT, 17 Piazza Grande (tel. 059/206580).

■ **Hotels.** 4-star: *Canalgrande*, 6 Corso Canalgrande. 3-star: *Libertà*, 10 Via Blasia; *Centrale*, 57 Via Rismondo; *Roma*, 44 Via Farini. 2-star: *La Torre*, 5 Via Cervetta.

■ **Restaurants. A**: *Borso d'Este*, 5 Piazza degli Estensi; *Fini*, Piazzetta San Francesco; *Oreste*, Piazza Roma. **B**: L'*Aragosta*, Largo Muratori, *Gargantua e Pantagruel*, 10 Vicolo Frassone; *Osteria Toscana*, 21 Via Gallucci; *La Francescana*, 22 Via Stella. **C**: *Antica Masone*, 16 Via Masone; *La Cantina del Baccanale*, 5 Piazza Torti, *Cervetta*, 7 Via Cervetta, *Trattoria alla Redecocc*a, 8 Piazzale Redecocca, *Ermes*, 89 Via Ganaceto.

■ **Picnic places** in the public gardens behind Palazzo Ducale.

■ **Railway stations.** Piazza Dante for all main line services of the FS. Piazza Manzoni for local trains to Fiorano and Sassuolo run by the Ferrovie Provinciali.

■ **Car parking.** Free parking outside the historic centre at Parco Novi Sad, Viale Vittorio Veneto, Viale Berengario, Viale Fontanelli and Viale Sigonio. Pay parking in Piazza Roma.

■ **Public transport.** Trolley-bus No. 7 from the station to the museums and Via Emilia (for the Duomo). ATCM also run services to localities in the province (including Maranello) from the bus station in Via Molza.

■ **Theatres.** *Storchi* (theatre season) and *Comunale* for music.

■ **Annual festivals.** San Geminiano (patron saint), 31 Jan with a fair. Carnival celebrations on the Thu preceding Shrove Tuesday.

History
The Roman colony of *Mutina*, established in the 2C BC on a site already inhabited by Gauls and Etruscans, diminished in importance under the Empire, and the present city dates its prosperity from the time of Countess Matilda of Tuscany (died 1115), who supported the Guelfs and the Pope's authority. After her death Modena became a free city and, in rivalry with Bologna, inclined more to the Ghibelline faction. In 1288 the Este family gained control of the city, and the duchy of Modena was created for Borso d'Este in 1452. It lasted until 1796, and was reconstituted in 1814–59 through an alliance of the Este with the house of Austria. Mary of Modena (1658–1718), queen of James II of England, was the daughter of Alfonso IV d'Este. The town suffered damage from air raids in 1944.

VIA EMILIA is the main thoroughfare of the city, and at its centre, behind the Torre Ghirlandina and the Duomo is the cobbled PIAZZA GRANDE. The splendid Romanesque ***DUOMO** was begun in 1099 on the site of two earlier churches built over the tomb of St Geminianus (died 397), patron saint of the town. The architect Lanfranco worked together with Wiligelmus, who here produced some remarkable Romanesque sculptures. The work was continued by Campionese artists in the 12C–14C. The sculptures were beautifully restored and cleaned in 1972–91.

On the ***façade**, the ***west portal** is a splendid work by Wiligelmus (the two lions are restored Roman works). On the left of the door is the foundation stone of the church, to which was added a dedication to Wiligelmus. Across the front of the façade are four bas-reliefs with stories from Genesis also by Wiligelmus (1100; they were formerly all aligned, but two were moved up when the side doors were added). Above the loggia, with finely carved capitals by the school of Wiligelmus and Campionese artists, is a large rose window by Anselmo da Campione (1200).

On the **south side**, which flanks the Piazza Grande, are more beautifully carved capitals by Wiligelmus and his school. The first door is the **Porta dei Principi**, also by Wiligelmus, with six very fine bas-reliefs of the life of San Geminianus. The lion on the right is a copy made in 1948 after damage to the porch. Above to the right is a very damaged bas-relief of Jacob and the Angel. The **Porta Regia** is by the Campionese school (1209–31). In the last arch on the south side (covered for restoration) are four reliefs of the Life of St Geminianus by Agostino di Duccio (1442). The exterior of the apse is also very fine, and there is another inscription here of the early 13C recording the foundation of the church by Lanfranco. On the

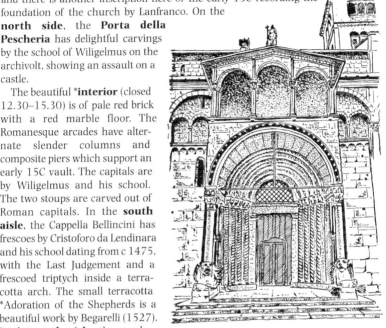

north side, the **Porta della Pescheria** has delightful carvings by the school of Wiligelmus on the archivolt, showing an assault on a castle.

The beautiful **interior* (closed 12.30–15.30) is of pale red brick with a red marble floor. The Romanesque arcades have alternate slender columns and composite piers which support an early 15C vault. The capitals are by Wiligelmus and his school. The two stoups are carved out of Roman capitals. In the **south aisle**, the Cappella Bellincini has frescoes by Cristoforo da Lendinara and his school dating from c 1475, with the Last Judgement and a frescoed triptych inside a terracotta arch. The small terracotta **Adoration of the Shepherds* is a beautiful work by Begarelli (1527). In the **north aisle**, the wooden statue of St Geminianus probably dates from the 14C. The elabo-

The Porta Regia of the Duomo

rately carved terracotta ancona is attributed to Michele da Firenze, and the detached fresco of the Madonna della Piazza to Cristoforo da Modena (late 14C). The pulpit is by Enrico da Campione (1322). The second altarpiece is by Dosso Dossi. On the stairs is a wall monument to Claudio Rangoni (died 1537) on a design by Giulio Romano.

The **rood-screen*, supported by lions and crouching figures, forms the approach to the raised choir. The coloured sculptures are splendid works by Anselmo da Campione (1200–25). They represent the Evangelists (on the pulpit), and scenes of the Passion. Above hangs a wooden crucifix in high relief (1200).

In the **choir**, a screen of slender red marble coupled columns in two tiers by Campionese artists surrounds the beautiful altar table. In the apse is a restored statue in bronze and copper of St Geminianus by Geminiano Paruolo (1376). The stalls are by Cristoforo and Lorenzo da Lendinara. In the left apse is a polyptych by Serafino Serafini. There is more inlaid work by Lendinara in the **sacristy** (being restored). In the **crypt** (with remarkable capitals, some attributed to Wiligelmus) is the tomb of St Geminianus, and an expressive group of five terracotta statues known as the 'Madonna della Pappa' by Guido Mazzoni (1480). The tiny organ here by Domenico Traeri dates from 1719.

The north side of the Duomo is connected by two Gothic arches to the *Torre Ghirlandina, the beautiful detached campanile of the cathedral, 86m high and slightly inclined. It was begun at the same time as the cathedral, the octagonal storey being added in 1319; the spire was rebuilt in the 16C. The interior can be visited on fest. (10–13, 15–19). Nearby is the Museo Lapidario (at present closed) which contains sculpture from the cathedral, including eight 12C metopes from the south side.

In Piazza Grande is the Palazzo Comunale, with an arcaded ground floor and a clock tower, founded in the 12C, but dating in its present form from a reconstruction of 1624. The Sala del Fuoco has fine frescoes (1546) by Nicolò dell'Abate.

From Piazza della Torre beside the Torre Ghirlandina, Via Emilia runs west through the centre of the town past the domed Chiesa del Voto built in 1634 (with 17C works by Francesco Stringa and Lodovico Lana) and the church of San Giovanni Battista which contains a life-sized polychrome *Descent from the Cross by Guido Mazzoni (removed for restoration). On the other side of Via Emilia is the church of Sant'Agostino with a sumptuous interior designed by Giovanni Giacomo Monti in 1664. The *Deposition here with stucco figures bearing traces of polychrome is the masterpiece of Antonio Begarelli (1524–26). The detached 14C fresco of the Madonna and Child is by Tommaso da Modena.

Next door is the huge Palazzo dei Musei, built in 1771 as a poor house. Since 1884 it has been the seat of the city's interesting museums. In the atrium and courtyard is a lapidary collection founded in 1828. On the top floor is the *GALLERIA ESTENSE (open 9–14; Tue, Fri & Sat 9–19; fest. 9–13; closed Mon), a fine collection of pictures put together by the Este family in the early 16C, notable especially for its works by the 15C–17C Emilian schools; it was first opened to the public in 1854. The most important part of the collection was sold to Dresden in the 18C. The rooms are not numbered, but the collection is displayed in roughly chronological order (although the paintings are often moved around). The room numbers given below correspond to the plan of the gallery on display. Beyond the atrium is a marble *bust of Francesco I d'Este, founder of the collection, by Gian Lorenzo Bernini (1652).

The long gallery is divided into nine small rooms. Room 1 contains 14C–15C works including paintings by Tommaso da Modena and Barnaba da Modena. Room II, works by Cristoforo da Lendinara, Agnolo and Bartolomeo Erri and Bartolomeo Bonascia. Room III is devoted to Francesco Bianchi Ferrari and Marco Melonio. Room IV, Lombard, French, Spanish, and Byzantine sculptures in ivory and marble. Bronzes by L'Antico (including the Gonzaga vase), and a relief of Mars by Antonio Lombardo. Room V, Works by Francesco Botticini (*Adoration of the Child), and Giuliano Bugiardini. Room VI contains Flemish works by Albrecht Bouts and Madonnas by Joos van Cleve and Mabuse. Room VII, *Deposition by Cima da Conegliano, and works by Vincenzo Catena and Giovanni Cariani. Room VIII, Filippo Mazzola and Francesco Maineri. Room IX, detached frescoes by Lelio Orsi, the *Madonna Campori by Correggio (being restored), and works by Lelio Orsi. The room at the end (X) displays terracotta works by Antonio Begarelli.

Room XI displays works by the Ferrara school, including Girolamo da Carpi

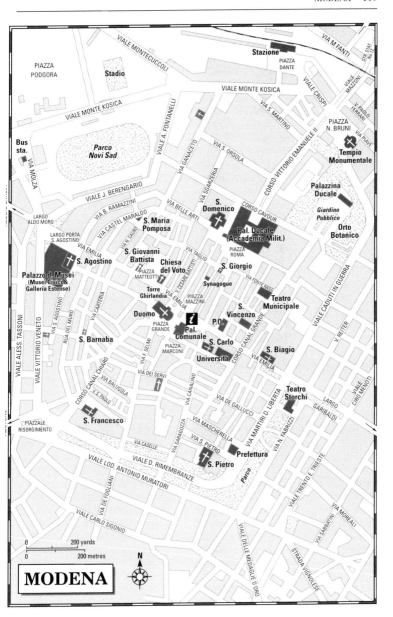

PIAZZA
PODGORA

Stadio

VIALE MONTECUCCOLI

Stazione

PIAZZA
DANTE

VIA M FANTI

VIALE MONTE KOSICA

VIALE CRISPI

VIA PAOLO FERRARI

V. PAOLO FERRARI

PIAZZA
N. BRUNI

VIA PAVE

Tempio
Monumentale

VIALE MONTE KOSICA

VIA A. FONTANELLI

VIA S. MARTINO

CORSO VITTORIO EMANUELE II

Bus
sta.

VIA MOLZA

Parco
Novi Sad

VIA GANACETO

VIA S. ORSOLA

Palazzina
Ducale

VIALE J. BERENGARIO

VIA SGARZERIA

S.
Domenico

CORSO CAVOUR

Pal. Ducale
(Accademia Milit.)

Giardino
Pubblico

Orto
Botanico

LARGO
ALDO MORO

VIA B. RAMAZZINI

VIA CASTEL MARALDO

VIA BELLE ARTI

S. Maria
Pomposa

LARGO PORTA
S. AGOSTINO

VIA EMILIA

VIA N. SAURO

S. Giovanni
Battista

Chiesa
del Voto

VIA TAGLIO

PIAZZA
ROMA

S. Giorgio

VIALE CADUTI IN GUERRA

S. Agostino

Palazzo d. Musei
(Musei Civici &
Galleria Estense)

VIA CARTERIA

PIAZZA
MATTEOTTI

Torre
Ghirlandia

VIA CESARE BATTISTI

VIA EMILIA

Synagogue

PIAZZA
MAZZINI

S.
Vincenzo

VIA FONTE RASO

Teatro
Municipale

V. REITER

VIA S. AGOSTINO

RUA DEL MURO

Duomo

PIAZZA
GRANDE

Pal.
Comunale

P.O.

VIALE ALESS. TASSONI

VIALE VITTORIO VENETO

S. Barnaba

VIA F. SELMI

PIAZZA
MARCONI

S. Carlo

Università

CORSO CANAL GRANDE

S. Biagio

VIA EMILIA

CORSO CANAL CHIARO

VIA BALUGOLA

V. S. PAOLO

VIA DEI SERVI

VIA CANALINO

VIA DE GALLUCCI

VIA MARTIRI D. LIBERTA

Teatro
Storchi

LARGO
GARIBALDI

VIALE CIRO MENOTTI

S. Francesco

PIAZZALE
RISORGIMENTO

VIA CASELLE

VIA SARAGOZZA

VIA MASCHERELLA

VIA S. PIETRO

VIA N. FABBRIZI

Prefettura

S. Pietro

VIALE LOD. ANTONIO MURATORI

VIALE D. RIMEMBRANZE

Parco

VIALE DE FOGLIANI

VIALE CARLO SIGONIO

VIALE DELLE MEDAGLIE D'ORO

VIALE TRENTO E TRIESTE

VIA MOREALI

VIA SABBATINI

STRADA VIGNOLESE

0   200 yards
0   200 metres

N

MODENA

and Dosso Dossi. Also here is the Estense harp, beautifully decorated at the end of the 16C. **Room XII**, 16C ceramics from Urbino, bronzes, and a *portable altar—an early work by El Greco. **Room XIII** displays 16C Emilian paintings including works by Garofalo. **Room XIV** displays 16C–18C portraits, notably the *portrait of Francesco I by Velazquez. **Room XV** has a collection of medals including some by Caradosso, Pisanello, Moderno, Bonacolsi and Giovan Cristoforo Romano. The marble head of a veiled lady is by Francesco Duquesnoy. **Room XVI** contains a carving by Grinling Gibbons.

The last four large rooms contain 16C–17C works. **Room 1**, works by the Venetian school, including Tintoretto, Il Padovanino, Veronese (*Saints), Palma il Giovane, Pietro Liberti and Jacopo Bassano. **Rooms 2 & 3**, Emilian school: Guercino (*Martyrdom of St Peter), Guido Reni, Lodovico Carracci, Prospero Fontana (*Holy Family), Carlo Bononi, Scarsellino, Pier Francesco Cittadini (still lifes) and Carlo Cignani (*Flora). **Room 4**, 17C works by Camillo and Giulio Cesare Procaccini, Pomarancio, Il Cerano, Rosa da Tivoli, Salvator Rosa, Nicolò Tournier, Domenico Fetti, Daniele Crespi and Charles Le Brun.

On the floor below is the entrance to the **MUSEO D'ARTE MEDIEVALE E MODERNA** and the **MUSEO ARCHEOLOGICO ETNOLOGICO** (open Tue–Sat, 9–12; Tue & Sat also 16–19; fest. 10–13, 16–19; closed Mon). Both form part of the Museo Civico founded in 1871 and recently sensitively restored, retaining its 19C appearance with old-fashioned showcases. The contents include the terracotta *Madonna di Piazza* commissioned from Begarelli in 1523 for the façade of Palazzo Comunale; reliquary crosses; musical instruments including a harpischord by Pietro Termanini (1741) and flutes made by Thomas Stanesby (1692–1754) in London; scientific instruments including the microscope of Giovanni Battista Amici; ceramics; and arms.

Room 8 preserves its furnishings of 1886, when it was opened to display the Gandini *collection of ancient fabrics, textiles and embroidered silks (with about 2000 fragments dating from the 11C to the 19C). The large hall (**10**) displays the **Museo Archeologico**, arranged chronologically from the palaeolithic era onwards. There is an important section devoted to *Mutina*, Roman Modena. The **Museo Etnologico** is arranged in **Rooms 11, 12 and 13**, with material from New Guinea, pre-Columbian Peru, Asia, South America and Africa. The last room (**14**) displays the Matteo Campori (1857–1933) collection of paintings with 17C and 18C works, and a collection of cameos.

Also on the first floor is the Archivio Storico Comunale (Mon–Sat 8.30–13; Tue and Thu also 15–17.30; closed fest.) and the **Biblioteca Estense** (9–13; closed fest.), with illuminated MSS, notably the *Bible of Borso d'Este, illuminated by Taddeo Crivelli and Franco Russi; a 14C edition of Dante; and the missal of Renée of France, by Jean Bourdichon (16C).

Via Sauro leads north from the Via Emilia (see Plan) to **Santa Maria Pomposa** where Lodovico Antonio Muratori (1672–1750), provost of the church from 1716 and 'father of Italian history', is buried. He lived and died in the adjacent house, now the **Museo Muratoriano** (open 17.30–20), which preserves his autograph works and other mementoes.

Via Cesare Battisti, on the left further on, leads to the church of **San Domenico**, rebuilt in 1708–31. In the baptistery is a colossal terracotta statuary *group by Begarelli, thought to represent Christ in the house of Martha. The huge ***Palazzo Ducale** (used as a military academy), was begun in 1634 for Francesco I on the site of the old Este castle. The interesting interior (open on 4 Nov and sometimes in Jul) has a fine courtyard and a monumental 17C staircase. In the state apartments, with numerous portraits and frescoes by Francesco Stringa, the Salone d'onore has a ceiling fresco by Marco Antonio Franceschini, and the Salottino d'oro elaborate decorations dating from 1751. There is also a museum illustrating the history of the military academy founded in 1669.

Behind the palace (entered from Corso Cavour) are pleasant **public gardens** laid out in 1602. The **Palazzina dei Giardini**, a garden pavilion begun in 1634 by Gaspare Vigarani (and altered in the 18C), is used for exhibitions by the Galleria Civica. It adjoins the **Botanical Gardens** (adm. on request at the Istituto Botanico of the university) founded by Francesco III in 1758. Beyond the other end of the gardens is the huge **Tempio Monumentale**, a war memorial built in an eclectic style by Achille Casanova and Domenico Barbanti in 1929.

From Piazza Roma in front of Palazzo Ducale a narrow road leads south past the Baroque church of **San Giorgio** by Gaspare Vigarani on a Greek-Cross plan, to Piazza Mazzini with the **Synagogue**, built in 1869–73 (adm. by appointment, tel. 059/223978), which adjoins the Via Emilia.

In the southern part of the town, reached from the Duomo by the arcaded Corso Canal Chiaro, is the church of **San Francesco** (1244; altered in the 19C), which contains a terracotta *Descent from the Cross (1530–31), by Begarelli. To the east is the Baroque church of **San Bartolomeo** with paintings by Giuseppe Maria Crespi, and others. Further east is the church of **San Pietro** (rebuilt in 1476), with a well ornamented brick front. It contains sculptures by Antonio Begarelli, an organ with 16C paintings, and a good painting by Francesco Bianchi Ferrari. Beyond the church is a pleasant park, with a war memorial of 1926 and the **Teatro Storchi**, built in 1886 and important for drama performances. Further west, near the Via Emilia is the **University**, founded c 1178, in a building of 1773. North of Via Emilia is the 17C church of **San Vincenzo**, with Estense tombs, and paintings by Matteo Rosselli and Guercino.

The province of Modena

The most interesting place in the province of Modena is the town of **CARPI** (60,000 inhab.), with an attractive centre and some fine palaces, but now surrounded by extensive industrial suburbs. From 1327 to 1525 it was a lordship of the Pio family, famous as patrons of the arts, who after 1450 were called Pio di Savoia. The huge ***Piazza**, laid out in the 15C–16C, with a lovely portico, is particularly handsome. Here the Pio **Castle** houses the **Museo Civico**, founded in 1914, which contains works by Bernardino Loschi, Vincenzo Catena, Mattia Preti, Scarsellino and Mastelletta, as well as some fine works in *scagliola*, a material made from selenite which is used to imitate marble and pietre dure (the town was famous in the 17C–18C for its production of *scagliola* works). There is also a museum which commemorates the victims deported to Nazi concentration camps in Germany in the last war. The largest Nazi internment camp set up in Italy in 1944 was at Fossoli, 5km outside Carpi; it was described at the beginning of *Se Questo è un'uomo* by the writer Primo Levi who was deported from here to Auschwitz.

Beneath the portico in the piazza is a 19C pharmacy. The **Duomo**, begun by Baldassarre Peruzzi in 1514, contains terracottas and sculptures by Antonio Begarelli, and paintings by Luca Ferrari, Giacomo Cavedoni and Sante Peranda. The **Teatro Comunale** (with a fine interior) dates from 1857–61. The **Portico del Grano** dates from the end of the 15C.

Behind the castle is the pieve of **Santa Maria in Castello** (known as La Sagra), with its tall campanile. The 12C church was greatly reduced in size in 1514. It contains the sarcophagus of Manfredo Pio (1351), a marble ambone attributed to Nicolò (12C) and two frescoed*chapels of the early 15C. On Corso Manfredo Fanti is the late 17C church of **Sant'Ignazio** which contains a fine high altar in *scagliola* (1696) and a large 17C painting by Bonaventura Lamberti. To the south is the church of **San Nicolò**, built on a central plan in 1494 (the nave was added in 1516 by Baldassarre Peruzzi). It also contains fine *scagliola* *altars. Further south are the Rococo church of the **Crocifisso** (with a Madonna by Begarelli) and **San Francesco**, with the tomb of Marco Pio attributed to the school of Jacopo della Quercia, and a fresco of the Madonna Enthroned attributed to Giovanni da Modena. Via Giulio Rovighi is on the site of the **Ghetto**, where the Jewish community was forced to live between 1719 and 1796. The synagogue at No. 57 was in use until 1922.

NONANTOLA, with two 14C towers, is famous for its abbey, founded in 752 and rebuilt in brick in the 13C. The portal has reliefs by the school of Wiligelmus (1121). The church contains the tombs of Popes St Sylvester and Adrian III. In the refectory are fresco fragments dating from the early 12C.

MIRANDOLA (21,600 inhab.) was a principality of the Pico family, the most famous member of which was Giovanni Pico (1463–94), noted for his wide learning, a typical figure of the Italian Renaissance. There are family tombs in the church of San Francesco, and scanty remains of the Pico ducal palace in the main piazza. The Baroque church of the Gesù is also of interest.

At **San Felice sul Panaro** is a castle of the Este built in the 14C–15C, now the seat of an archaeological museum. **Finale Emilia** is a pretty little town with a 14C castle, numerous fine palaces, and interesting 16C–17C paintings in the Collegiata. In the Palazzo Comunale are 18C paintings by Fra Stefano da Carpi.

South of Modena on the Panaro is **Vignola**, a fruit-growing centre, famous for its cherries. It was the birthplace of the architect Jacopo Barozzi, called Il Vignola (1507–73). The fine castle was built by Uguccione Contrari between 1401 and 1435. The chapel has very interesting late Gothic frescoes by an unknown artist.

At **Maranello**, next to the Ferrari works, is a museum (open 9.30–12.30, 15–18 exc. Mon), with mementoes of Enzo Ferrari, vintage cars, etc.

At **Sassuolo** is the important Palazzo Ducale (being restored) rebuilt for the Este in 1634, with an interesting park. It contains decorations by Jean Boulanger (and by Angelo Michele Colonna and Agostino Mitelli in the Salone).

On the road to Abetone across the Apennines is **Pavullo nel Frignano**, the 19C residence of the Dukes of Modena, and the resorts of Fiumalbo, Sestola and Pievepelago below **Monte Cimone** (2165m; skiing facilities).

62 · Reggio Emilia

Reggio Emilia (or Reggio nell'Emilia) is the large and flourishing centre (134,800 inhab.) of an important agricultural area. It is one of the richest cities in Italy, where the inhabitants have a particularly high tenor of life, and there is an efficient local administration. Excellent Parmesan cheese (*parmigiano-reggiano* or *grana*) is produced here. It was the Roman *Regium Lepidi* and is still divided in two by the Via Emilia: the southern part of the town retains a medieval pattern, while to the north are broad streets and open squares. The most settled period of Reggio's turbulent history was under the Este domination (1409–1796).

■ **Information office.** IAT, 5 Piazza Prampolini (tel. 0522/451152).

■ **Hotels.** 4-star: *Posta*, 4 Piazza del Monte. 3-star: *Reggio*, 7 Via San Giuseppe; *Scudo d'Italia*, 5 Via del Vescovado. 2-star: *Ariosto*, 12 Via San Rocco.

■ **Restaurants. B**: *Lo Scudo d'Italia* (see above); *Canossa*, Via Roma.

■ **Picnics** in the public gardens by the theatre.

■ **Car parking** (free) in the former Caserma Zucchi near the bus station.

■ **Buses.** Mini-bus A from the station to Piazza del Monte. Bus station for the province in the former Caserma Zucchi.

■ **Theatres.** *Municipale*, with a renowned winter opera season, and *Ariosto*, for music and theatre.

■ **Market** on Tue and Fri in Piazza Prampolini and Piazza San Prospero.

In the centre of Via Emilia is the little Piazza del Monte. Here is the altered 14C **Palazzo del Capitano del Popolo**, part of which is the Palazzo dell'Albergo Posta, transformed in the 16C into a hospice and restored in an eclectic style in 1910. It adjoins the central Piazza Prampolini. The altered Romanesque **Duomo** has an unfinished façade added in 1555 by Prospero Sogari, who also carved the statues of Adam and Eve above the central door. The unusual tower bears a group of the Madonna and donors, in copper, by Bartolomeo Spani (1522), who also carved the tomb of Valerio Malaguzzi, uncle of Ariosto, in the interior. The tomb of Bishop Rangone and the marble ciborium are by Sogari.

In **Palazzo Comunale**, begun in 1414, the green, white and red tricolour of the Revolution was proclaimed the national flag of Italy in 1797. The Sala del Tricolore has a small museum, shown on request.

A passageway leads into the piazza in front of the church of **San Prospero**, guarded by six red marble lions. It was rebuilt in 1514–27, with a choir frescoed by Camillo Procaccini and fine inlaid stalls.

On the other side of Via Emilia is the huge Piazza Martiri del 7 Luglio with the **Musei Civici** (open 9–12, exc. Mon; fest. also 15–18), various collections, still with their charming old-fashioned displays. The **Museo Spallanzani**, founded in 1772 and bought by the Comune in 1799, is a delightful natural history collection (including a room of fossils). Upstairs is the **Galleria Fontanesi**, founded in 1893, with pictures by Emilian painters from the 15C to the 19C, and the **Museo Chierici**, with archaeological material (including Etruscan finds), arranged for study purposes. The numismatic collection has examples from the Reggio mint. The prehistoric finds from the locality include a 5C treasure dug up in 1957 (with a fine gold fibula). The **Museo del Risorgimento e della Resistenza** is at present closed.

Across the garden, with a harrowing bronze monument (1958) to Resistance martyrs, is the elegant **Teatro Municipale** (1852–57), with a high theatrical reputation. Behind the theatre are extensive **public gardens** in which has been placed a Roman family tomb of c AD 50. In Piazza della Vittoria, beside the **Teatro Ariosto**, designed in 1741 by Antonio Cugini (and rebuilt after a fire in 1851), is the neo-Gothic spire of the **Galleria Parmeggiani** (closed for restoration), with a fine 16C Hispano-Moresque doorway brought from Valencia. The eclectic collections include medieval metalwork and 14C–16C paintings of the Flemish and Spanish schools, including The Redeemer by El Greco.

Off the south side of Via Emilia (reached from the broad Corso Garibaldi) is the splendid Baroque church of the *****Madonna della Ghiara** (1597–1619), with a well preserved interior (restored in 1996), its vaults and domes beautifully decorated with *frescoes and stuccoes by early 17C Emilian artists including Alessandro Tiarini, Lionello Spada and Camillo Gavasseti. An altarpiece by Guercino has been removed for restoration. A museum displays the cathedral treasury (open Sun 15.30–18.30).

The province of Reggio Emilia

The **Mauriziano** (reached by bus No. 2; adm. by appointment only) was the country villa of the Malaguzzi family, where the poet Lodovico Ariosto (1474–1533), born in Reggio Emilia, often visited his relatives.

Correggio was the birthplace of the painter Antonio Allegri (1489–1534) surnamed Correggio, whose house (reconstructed) is in Borgovecchio. The Palazzo dei Principi, begun in 1507, contains the Museo Civico with 12 Flemish tapestries (16C) and a tempera head of Christ by Mantegna. The Teatro Asioli (18C) has been restored. San Quirino (1516–87) has an interesting interior.

Novellara has a castle (now town hall) of the Gonzaga, dating in part from the 14C. It contains a small museum (open 9–12) with detached frescoes of the 13C–16C, and a remarkable series of ceramic jars made for a pharmacy in the 15C–16C.

Gualtieri has the vast *Piazza Bentivoglio as its main square (with a garden in the centre). It was begun in 1580 by Giovanni Battista Aleotti. Palazzo Bentivoglio, also by Aleotti, has 17C frescoes in the Salone dei Giganti.

Guastalla was once the capital of a duchy of the Gonzagas. In the square is a statue of the condottiere Ferrante Gonzaga (died 1457), by Leone Leoni. The Basilica della Pieve is an interesting Romanesque church.

Brescello is a town of Roman origins. In the central piazza is a copy of a statue of Hercules by Jacopo Sansovino (the original is kept in the Museo Comunale). Sir Anthony Panizzi (1797–1879), librarian of the British Museum, was born in the town. The church of Santa Maria Maggiore (1830–37) was used as the setting of the film of *Don Camillo* (based on the book written in 1950 by Giovanni Guareschi), and there is a little museum with mementoes of the film.

The ruined **Castle of Canossa** (open 9–12, 15–18.30; 9–15 in winter; closed Mon) was the home of the Countess Matilda of Tuscany, who was responsible for the submission of the Emperor Henry IV to Pope Gregory VII in 1077. Only the foundations of the castle of that time remain; the ruins above ground date from the 13C and later.

63 · Parma and its province

Parma is the second city of Emilia (175,000 inhab.), and has some very fine works of art and important buildings, all grouped close together in the centre of the city. There is a beautiful Baptistery, and delightful frescoed domes by Correggio (who arrived in the city around 1520) grace the Camera di San Paolo, the Cathedral and the church of San Giovanni Evangelista. The huge Palazzo della Pilotta has at last been restored so that the splendid Farnese theatre can now be visited as well as the Galleria Nazionale with a large collection of paintings of the highest interest, including masterpieces by Correggio and fine examples of the later Emilian schools. Parma is a gastronomic centre, famous for Parmesan cheese and Parma ham. Unattractive new buildings were constructed in the town after damage in the last war.

■ **Information office.** IAT, 3 Piazza Duomo (tel. 0521/234735).

■ **Hotels.** 4-star: *Grand Hotel Baglioni*, 14 Viale Piacenza; *Park Hotel Stendhal*, 3 Via Bodoni; *Park Hotel Toscanini*, 4 Viale Toscanini. 3-star: *Torino*, 7 Via Mazza.

■ **Restaurants.** The standard of cuisine in Parma is high, but restaurants are not cheap. **A**: *Angiol d'Or*, 1 Vicolo Scutellari; *Charly*, 89 Via Lepido; *Isa Filoma*, 15 Via XX Marzo. **B**: *Al Tramezzino*, 5 Via Del Bono; *Croce di Malta*, 8 Borgo Palmia; *Gallo d'Oro*, 3 Borgo Salina; *Il Cortile*, 3 Borgo Paglia; *Parizzi*, 71 Via Repubblica; *Parma Rotta*, 158 Via Langhirano. **Cafés** in Piazza Garibaldi, including *Le Bistrò* and *Orientale.*

■ **Picnics** in the Parco Ducale.

■ **Car parking.** In Viale Mentana (free); underground car parks: 'Toschi' on the river by Palazzo della Pilotta, and 'Goito', Strada Farina.

■ **Buses** from the bus station in Via IV Novembre (Palazzo della Pilotta) to the main places in the province.

■ **Theatre.** *Regio*, famous for its music (opera season Nov–Mar).

■ **Market** on Wed & Sat in Piazzale della Pilotta.

History

There was a Roman station here, on the Via Emilia. In the 12C–14C the town had a republican constitution, but from c 1335 onwards it was ruled by a succession of ducal families: the Visconti, Terzi, Este and Sforza. In 1531 it became a papal dominion and in 1545 Paul III made it over, along with Piacenza, to his illegitimate son Pier Luigi Farnese, with the title of duke. The house of Farnese, and their heirs, the Spanish house of Bourbon-Parma, held the duchy until 1801. In 1815 the Vienna Congress assigned Parma to the ex-Empress Marie-Louise, but in 1859 the widow of her son Charles III was obliged to hand it over to the King of Italy. It was heavily bombed in the Second World War.

The Baptistery

The peaceful cobbled Piazza Duomo is dominated by the pink-and-white *Baptistery (open 9–12.30, 15–18), one of the finest in Italy. It is a splendid octagonal building in red Verona marble, of extremely interesting design, showing the influence of French Gothic architecture as well as ancient Roman buildings. Begun in 1196 by Benedetto Antelami, it was completed after 1216 by Campionese masters (and consecrated in 1270).

Exterior. The three *portals bear splendid carvings by Antelami. The **north door** has a lunette with the Madonna, Adoration of the Magi and the Dream of Joseph. In the architrave beneath: Baptism of Christ, Banquet of Herod, and the Beheading of the Baptist. In the door jambs are the genealogical trees of Jacob and the Virgin. The **west door** depicts the Last Judgement in the lunette and architrave, and the **south door** illustrates the Legend of Baarlam and Josaphat. Between the doors are blind arches with classical columns, and a frieze of 79 small panels carved with stylised reliefs, fantastic animals, etc. which almost girdles the edifice. Above are four delicate galleries, with small columns.

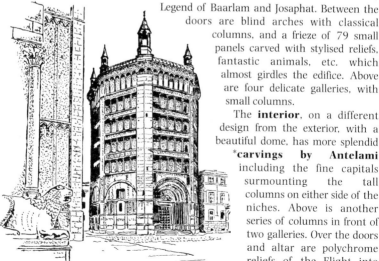

The **interior**, on a different design from the exterior, with a beautiful dome, has more splendid *carvings by Antelami including the fine capitals surmounting the tall columns on either side of the niches. Above is another series of columns in front of two galleries. Over the doors and altar are polychrome reliefs of the Flight into Egypt, David, and the Presentation in the Temple.

Baptistery

Between them are angels and the Annunciation figures in the apses of the niches. Above in the lower gallery have been placed 14 figures of the Months, and Winter and Spring (some with reliefs of the signs of the zodiac below). The red porphyry altar is carved with the figures of John the Baptist, a priest and a Levite. In the centre is a font, and against the wall a stoup supported by a lion, also carved by Antelami. Displayed around the walls are six statues formerly in niches on the exterior.

The cupola has lovely tempera *paintings of 1260–70, in Byzantine style, with the story of Abraham, the life of St John the Baptist, Christ and the Prophets, and the Apostles and the symbols of the Evangelists. The painted decoration of the lunettes below dates from the same period. The lower part of the walls has 14C votive frescoes, including two attributed to Buffalmacco.

Duomo

The *Duomo (closed 12–15) is a splendid 11C church, modified by Antelami in the 12C. The projecting pink-and-white porch supported by two huge lions has reliefs of the Months added around the arch in 1281. The doors themselves date from 1494. The *campanile was built in 1284–94.

In the **interior** (being restored), with finely carved 12C capitals, the Romanesque structure is still clearly visible, although it was entirely covered in later centuries by frescoes in the vault, nave, aisles and west end. High up on the **inner façade** is a fresco of the Ascension by Lattanzio Gambara (1573; with the help of Bernardino Gatti). Above the matroneum in the **nave** are frescoes of the Life of Christ, also by Gambara. The vault is frescoed by Girolamo Mazzola Bedoli (1557). The statue of the Archangel Raphael (formerly on the campanile) dates from c 1294.

In the **cupola** (light in the south transept) is the celebrated *Assumption by Correggio (1526–30), one of the most remarkable frescoed domes in existence. In the spandrels are the four patron saints of Parma, and above—between the round windows—are the colossal figures of the Apostles, in a crowd behind a balustrade. Above the clouds and angels surrounding the Madonna, Christ descends from a golden Heaven to greet His mother. It is said that when Titian saw the dome he commented that if it were to be turned upside down and filled with gold, Correggio would still not receive the recompense he deserved for such a masterpiece.

The **south aisle** (under restoration) has frescoes in the vaults by Alessandro Mazzola. In the last chapel is a Crucifixion with saints by Bernardino Gatti. In the **south transept** is a relief from the pulpit of the *Deposition by Antelami, his earliest known work, signed and dated 1178 and surrounded by niello decoration.

A sarcophagus carved by Campionese sculptors serves as **high altar**. The **choir** (difficult to see) and apse have frescoes by Girolamo Mazzola Bedoli. The beautiful stalls are signed by Cristoforo da Lendinara, and the bishop's throne is by Benedetto Antelami. The **crypt** has good capitals and two fragments of Roman pavement. The last chapel in the north aisle was entirely frescoed in the 15C.

Opposite the Duomo is **Palazzo Vescovile**, first built in the 11C, with a well-restored façade which shows successive additions of 1175 and 1234. The court-

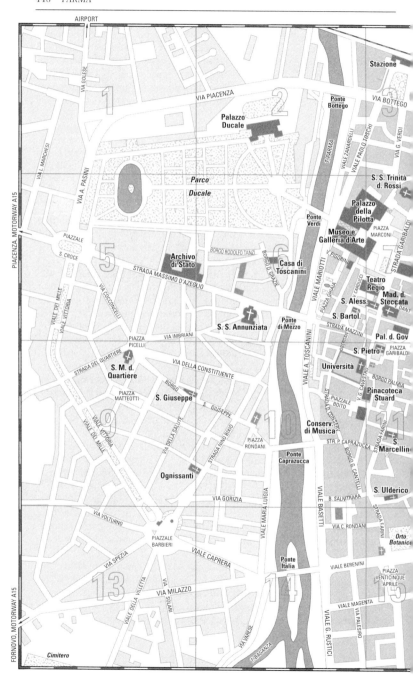

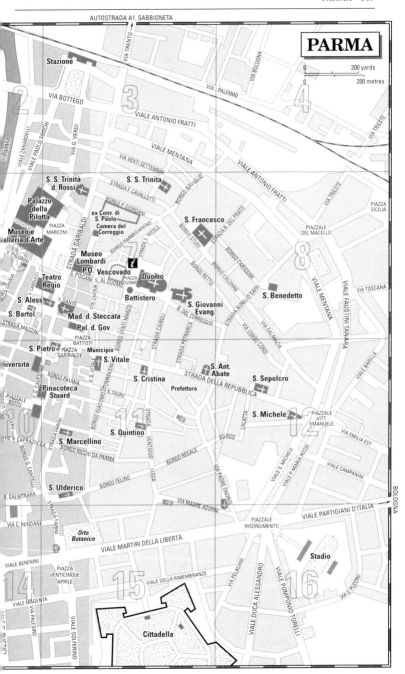

yard dates from the 16C. Just out of the piazza is a red palace on the site (plaque) of the birthplace of the chronicler Frate Salimbene (1221–c 1290). On the south side of the Duomo is the 16C **Seminario**, with a double blind arcade, and the early 20C doorway of a pharmacy.

San Giovanni Evangelista

Behind the Duomo (facing its pretty apse) is the church of San Giovanni Evangelista (closed 12–15.30), rebuilt in 1498–1510, with a façade of 1604–07. It contains in its dome another splendid ***fresco by Correggio** (1521), the Vision of St John at Patmos (light in the north transept), showing Christ surrounded by the Apostles appearing to St John at his death. In the spandrels are the Fathers of the Church, and over the sacristy door in the north transept is a lunette fresco of the young St John writing, also by Correggio. The walls of the **nave** have a beautiful frieze by Francesco Maria Rondani (on cartoons by Correggio) of Prophets and Sibyls. The **vault** is frescoed by Michele Anselmi.

In the first, second and fourth **north chapels** the entrance arches have lovely frescoes by Parmigianino: the first chapel has a font made out of a Roman urn, and delightful frescoed putti, and the fourth chapel has an altarpiece by Girolamo Mazzola Bedoli. The frieze in the transepts dates from the late 15C or early 16C. In the **south transept** are statues by Antonio Begarelli. The Coronation of the Virgin in the **main apse** is a copy made in 1587 by Cesare Aretusi of a larger work, formerly here, by Correggio. On the **high altar** is a Transfiguration by Girolamo Bedoli Mazzola. The stalls date from 1513–38. In the sixth chapel in the north aisle is Christ Carrying the Cross by Michele Anselmi.

At the side of the façade of the church is the entrance to the **Benedictine monastery** (used by 20 monks; open 9–12, 15–18) with three lovely cloisters, a chapterhouse and a library (only open on fest.).

The **Spezeria di San Giovanni** (open 9–13.45), founded in 1298 and in use up to 1881, preserves its 16C furnishings (entrance at No. 1 Borgo Pipa). In the three rooms are 17C vases, mortars, pharmaceutical publications, etc.

From Piazza Duomo, Via al Duomo leads to the Strada Cavour, the main shopping street. It leads left to Piazza Garibaldi with the 17C Municipio and Palazzo del Governatore, and a number of cafés.

Camera di San Paolo

In the other direction, the Strada Cavour ends at a war memorial tower. Just to the left, approached by an avenue of japonica trees, is the entrance to the *Camera di San Paolo (open 9–13.45) in the private apartment of the abbess Giovanna Piacenza in the former Benedictine Convent of San Paolo. Beyond several rooms with paintings by Alessandro Araldi, is the little room with celebrated ***frescoes by Correggio**, commissioned by the abbess in 1518/19 (the artist's first commission in Parma). The Gothic umbrella vault is decorated with a dome of thick foliage supported by wickerwork (canes cover the ribs of the vault). In the centre is the abbess' coat of arms surrounded by drapes off which hang festoons of fruit. Through 16 oculi in the arbour can be seen groups of putti at play, against the open sky. The monochrome lunettes below have painted trompe l'oeil statues and reliefs of mythological subjects, and below is a frieze of rams' heads with veils stretched between in which are hung plates and pewter-ware (which may signify that the room was used as a refectory). Over the fire-place is Diana returning from the hunt, also by Correggio.

The significance of these remarkable Humanistic frescoes, in which the artist uses a careful play of light, is uncertain: the abbess was a particularly cultivated lady who lived in the convent for 17 years and was unsuccessful in her attempt to prevent it from becoming a closed order in 1524. The frescoes remained unknown to the outside world until the 18C, which probably accounts for their excellent state of preservation.

The room next door has another vault adorned with *grotteschi* by Alessandro Araldi painted four years earlier.

Strada Pisacane continues Via del Duomo to Via Garibaldi which runs through one side of the huge untidy Piazza della Pilotta. At No. 15 Via Garibaldi is the **Museo Glauco Lombardi** (open 9.30–12.30, 15 or 16–17 or 18; fest. 9.30–13; closed Mon) with a collection relating to the Empress Marie Louise. Just to the left is the **Teatro Regio** (adm. by appointment), which opened in 1829 with Bellini's *Zaira*. It is one of the most famous opera houses in Italy. The conductor Arturo Toscanini (1867–1957), who was born in Parma, played in the orchestra.

The Madonna della Steccata

Also in Via Garibaldi is the church of the *Madonna della Steccata, (closed 12–15) built in 1521–39 on a Greek-cross plan by Bernardino and Giovanni Francesco Zaccagni. The very fine **exterior** includes an elegant dome surrounded by a balustrade, and 18C statues on the roof.

The **interior** has superb frescoes by the Parma school all carried out between 1530 and 1570. On the barrel vault between the dome and apse are six tempera *figures of the Virgins*, the last work of Parmigianino. The fresco of the Assunta in the dome is by Bernardino Gatti (inspired by Correggio). The side apses and arches are frescoed by Girolamo Bedoli Mazzola. The Coronation of the Virgin in the apse is by Michelangelo Anselmi (on a design by Giulio Romano). The organ doors are early works by Parmigianino (the organ itself was built in 1574 by Benedetto Antegnati, and restored by Negri Poncini in 1780). The tomb of Field-Marshal Count Neipperg (1775–1829), second husband of Marie Louise, is by Lorenzo Bartolini (1840). The Sagrestia Nobile (1670) has cupboards by Giovanni Battista Mascherone.

On the other side of Strada Garibaldi, on the bank of the river, is **Palazzo della Pilotta**, a gloomy and rambling palace built for the Farnese family c 1583–1622, but left unfinished; it was badly bombed and half of it demolished. It contains the Museo Archeologico Nazionale, Teatro Farnese and Galleria Nazionale (all of them open daily 9–13.45, although the archaeological museum is closed on Mon; adm. with separate tickets). The entrance is under the portico towards the river.

Museo Archeologico

On the first floor is the well arranged Museo Archeologico Nazionale, founded in 1760, interesting chiefly for its finds from Veleia (see page 460). **Room I** displays

Roman statues from the Farnese and Gonzaga collections. **Room II** has the Egyptian collection. **Room III**, Roman copy of the Eros of Praxiteles, and a head of Zeus. **Room IV** (kept locked) contains the numismatic collection. **Room V** displays a fine group of Roman statues from Veleia. **Room VI**, finds from Veleia including the tabula alimentaria, the largest Roman bronze inscription known, and the bronze head of a boy (1C BC). **Room VII**, Greek, Italiot and Etruscan ceramics, and the relief of the head of an African river god in onyx (2C). **Lower floor**. **Room I**, palaeolithic finds from the region around Parma. **Room II**, material from the pile-dwellings of Parma and the lake-villages of Castione dei Marchesi, Castellazzo, etc. **Room IV**, lapidary collection, and **Room V**, Roman bronzes. Beyond **Room VI** with amphorae, **Room VII** displays Roman mosaic pavements.

Teatro Farnese

Stairs continue up to the wooden portal at the entrance to the Teatro Farnese and Galleria Nazionale. The huge *Teatro Farnese was built in 1617–18 in wood and stucco by Giovanni Battista Aleotti for Rannuccio I, Duke of Parma. It has a U-shaped cavea, which could seat 3000 spectators. Above are two tiers of loggias, with typical Palladian arches, modelled on Palladio's theatre at Vicenza, although the stage in this theatre had movable scenery. Used only nine times after its inauguration in 1628 (when it was flooded for a mock sea-battle), it fell into ruins in the 18C, and was almost entirely destroyed by a bomb in the last war. It has been beautifully reconstructed. Most of the painted decoration (including the ceiling fresco) has been lost, although two painted triumphal arches survive at the sides, with stucco equestrian statues of Alessandro and Ottavio Farnese.

Galleria Nazionale

From the stage of the theatre is the entrance to the *Galleria Nazionale, founded by Philip of Bourbon-Parma in 1752. A walkway leads into the Romanesque section, with 10C–11C wooden doors from San Bertoldo, and three **capitals carved by Benedetto Antelami**. Beyond are exhibited early Tuscan works (Agnolo Gaddi, Nicolò di Pietro Gerini, Spinello Aretino, Fra Angelico); inlaid stalls by Bernardino di Lendinara; and local 15C works (St Peter Martyr and stories from his life, by the circle of Agnolo and Bartolomeo degli Erri). Beyond paintings by Francesco Francia and Cima da Conegliano (*Madonna and Child with saints) is an exquisite *Head of a girl ('La Scapiliata') by Leonardo da Vinci (c 1508), owned by the Gonzaga in 1531. The two marble bas-reliefs are by Giovanni Antonio Amadeo.

Beyond a corridor with tiles made in Faenza in 1482 is a room with **16C Emilian works** by Cristoforo Caselli, Filippo Mazzola, Garofalo and Dosso Dossi. Stairs lead up to another room with 16C Emilian works (Michele Anselmi), and works by Giulio Romano, Holbein (portrait of *Erasmus*), Sebastiano del Piombo and Bronzino. On the balcony above are interesting works by Girolamo Bedoli Mazzola and El Greco, and large works by the Carracci. The room below displays works by Guercino and Gian Lorenzo Bernini (two marble busts of Rannuccio II). At the end: portraits by Frans Pourbus the Younger; portrait of Isabella Clara Eugenia and Madonna and Child, both by Van Dyck; Flemish landscapes; and works by Canaletto and Bernardo Bellotto.

A walkway, with early maps and prints of Parma and 19C views of the city, leads back to the Teatro Farnese. Beneath the cavea is the entrance to the last section of the gallery, displayed in the small rooms of the Rocchetta, with the **masterpieces of Correggio and Parmigianino**. The works by Correggio include several frescoes and the *Madonna della Scodella* (his finest work, c 1525–30), *Madonna and Child, with St Jerome, an angel, and Mary Magdalene* (1527–28), *Deposition (1524), and the Martyrdom of four saints. Parmigianino is represented by a superb portrait known as the *Turkish Slave*, his self portrait, and a fine collection of drawings.

In an oval room nearby are two colossal basalt statues dating from the 2C AD from the Orti Farnesiani on the Palatine in Rome, and a large neo-classical hall exhibits 18C and 19C works including portraits by Zoffany and Jean Marc Nattier, and a seated statue of Maria Luigia by Canova. The last room has smaller 18C works (Zoffany, Maria Callani and Vigée Lebrun).

The **Palatine Library** houses about 600,000 volumes, with editions and matrices of Giovanni Battista Bodoni, the printer, who set up his office in the palace in 1768–1813, and a section with musical MSS.

On the other side of the river, across Ponte Verdi, is the entrance to the **Parco Ducale**, created in 1560, now pleasant public gardens with fine trees (chestnuts, beeches and plane trees), usually crowded with people. There is a second entrance on Viale Pasini. **Palazzo Ducale** (open 8–12 exc. fest.) was built as a summer residence for Ottavio Farnese by Giovanni Boscoli in 1564. A wing is furnished in the neo-classical French style.

A pretty road leads south from Ponte Verdi towards Borgo Rodolfo Tanzi, where at No. 3 is the simple **birthplace of Toscanini**, now a small museum with mementoes of the conductor (open Tue–Sat 10–13, 15–18; fest. 10–13; closed Mon). The church of the **Annunziata**, in this part of the town, is an impressive Baroque building (1566), beyond which the graceful **Ospedale della Misericordia**, begun c 1214 and enlarged in the 16C, houses the state archives, with the archives of the Duchy.

In the southern part of the town, on the right bank of the river is the **University**, in a 16C building ascribed to Galeazzo Alessi and Vignola. Nearby, at No. 14 Via Cavestro, is the **Pinacoteca Stuard** (closed for restoration) with 14C–19C paintings (including works by Paolo di Giovanni Fei, Bernardo Daddi, Paolo Uccello, Lanfranco and Guercino). To the east, on the Strada della Repubblica, is the church of **Sant'Antonio Abate**, begun by Francesco Bibbiena in 1712, and finished in 1766.

On the southern outskirts of the town, in Via San Martino, is the **Museo Cinese ed Etnografico** (open Wed & fest. 15–18), founded in 1900. In the **Villetta Cemetery**, further south, the embalmed body of Paganini rests beneath a classical canopy.

The province of Parma

■ **Information offices. Fidenza**, IAT office in Piazza Duomo.

■ **Restaurants.** At **Soragna**: *Locanda del Lupo* (**B**). At **Colorno**: *Al Vedel* (**C**); and nearby at Torrile, *Romani* (**B**).

FIDENZA (23,000 inhab.) is the most important town in the province of Parma. Known as Borgo San Donnino from the 9C to 1927, it occupies the site of the Roman *Fidentia Iulia*, where St Domninus was martyred by the Emperor Maximian in 291. It was on the Via Francigena, the pilgrim route from Britain and France to Rome, and there are several carvings of pilgrims on the façade of its cathedral.

The *Cathedral, built during the 13C, has a façade with particularly interesting Romanesque *sculptures, by Antelami and his school. On the left tower are two reliefs, one showing Herod enthroned, and the other the three kings on horseback. **Left portal**. In the tympanum are Pope Hadrian II and St Domninus, with Charlemagne on the left and a miracle of St Domninus on the right. The arch is carved with figures of animals. The column on the right has a capital ingeniously carved with a scene of Daniel in the lions' den. On either side of the **central portal** are fine *statues of David and Ezekiel, both by Antelami. The portal has beautifully carved capitals, and a relief of the Martyrdom of St Domninus in the architrave, with Prophets, Apostles and Christ in the lunette. On the right of the door is a relief showing an angel leading a group of poor pilgrims towards Rome. The **right portal** is crowned by the figure of a pilgrim, and beneath in the tympanum is St Domninus. The lunette is carved with figures of animals. On the right tower is another frieze showing a group of pilgrims. The exterior of the apse is also interesting.

In the beautiful **interior** (closed 12–15), on the first right pillar (above the capital) is the figure of Christ with a relief of a battle of angels below, both by Antelami. **South aisle**. The fourth chapel (1513) has good terracotta decorations and frescoes. The stoup by the school of Antelami includes the figure of Pope Alexander II. In the last chapel is a wooden statue of the Madonna and Child of 1626, and remains of very early frescoes. In the raised **choir**, high up between the apse vaults, are good sculptures including a figure of Christ as Judge by Antelami, and a fresco of the Last Judgement dating from the 13C. The **crypt** has interesting capitals including one of Daniel in the lions' den. Here is displayed a seated statue of the Madonna and Child by Antelami (damaged in 1914) and the Arca of St Domninus with carved scenes of his life (1488). Nearer the altar is a 3C Roman sarcophagus.

Just off the piazza is the medieval **Porta San Donnino** where excavations are in progress. In the main Piazza Garibaldi is the restored town hall and the **theatre** dating from 1812. At the end of Via Berenini is Palazzo delle Orsoline in which is the **Museo del Risorgimento** (entered from the road on the left, at No. 2; open 10–12, 16–18 exc. Mon & fest.), with an interesting collection relating to the period from 1802–1946, excellently displayed. The huge **Jesuit college** and **church** dates from the end of the 17C.

From the Roman era until the mid-19C salt was extracted from the waters of **Salsomaggiore Terme**. After 1839 it became one of the most famous spas of Italy, and its saline waters are used in rheumatic, arthritic and post-inflammatory disorders. The Grand Hotel des Thermes (now a congress centre) was opened in 1901 and bought in 1910 by Cesare Ritz. It contains Art Nouveau works by Galileo Chini, who also decorated the spa building opened in 1923. There are still a number of Art Nouveau and Art Deco buildings in the town.

On the Parma river south of Parma is **Mamiano**. Here, surrounded by a beautiful park, is the Villa Mamiano, seat of the **Fondazione Magnani-Rocca**. This was the residence of the connoisseur, musicologist and art historian Luigi Magnani until his death in 1984. His remarkable private museum here is open Mar–Nov exc. Mon 10–18. The *paintings include works by: Dürer (Madonna and Child); Carpaccio (Pietà); Filippo Lippi (Madonna and Child); Gentile da Fabriano (St Francis receiving the Stigmata); Van Dyck (equestrian portrait of Giovanni Paolo Balbi); Titian (Madonna and Child with St Catherine, St Dominic and a donor, c 1512/14); and Goya (Allegorical family portrait of the Infante Luis de Bourbon, a conversation piece of 1789). The later paintings include works by Monet, Renoir, Cézanne and Giorgio Morandi.

On the eastern outskirts of Parma is the **Certosa di Parma**, first built in 1282, which gave its name to Stendhal's famous novel (*La Chartreuse de Parme*). The present church contains frescoes by Sebastiano Galeotti, Francesco Natali, and others.

The province is rich in feudal strongholds. **Fontanellato** has a moated 13C *castle of the Sanvitale family (guided tours Oct–Mar, 9.30–11.45, 15–17 exc. Mon; Apr–Sep daily 9.30–11.45, 15–18. It contains a little room with delightful *frescoes by Parmigianino (1524), as well as 16C–18C furnishings, ceramics, etc.

The Rocca Meli Lupi at **Soragna** has 16C works of art (guided tours daily 9–11, 14 or 15–16 or 18). The synagogue, with a Jewish museum, is open on fest. (9.30–12.30, 15–18).

Nearer the Po are the fortresses of the Rossi family at **Roccabianca** and **San Secondo Parmense** (open Mon–Sat 8–13), with frescoes by the Campi.

Montechiarugolo has a good castle of 1406 (guided visit Sat & fest. 15–18), and **Montecchio Emilia** preserves parts of the old ramparts.

Torrechiara has the finest *castle (open 8.30–14 exc. Mon) in the province, built for Pier Maria Rossi (1448–60), with its 'golden room' frescoed by Benedetto Bembo (c 1463). Other rooms are decorated by Cesare Baglione and his followers.

At **Roncole Verdi** is the simple birthplace of the composer Giuseppe Verdi (1813–1901). His house is open Apr–Nov, 9.30–12, 14.30–17 or 19 exc. Mon. **Busseto** is a charming small town, which was the lordship of the Pallavicini in the 10C–16C. It has many buildings decorated with terracotta in the Cremonese style. The battlemented castle contains the town hall and the little Teatro Verdi (1868), and the Villa Pallavicino (attributed to Vignola) houses the Museo Civico with mementoes of Verdi (open Apr–Nov, 9.30–12, 14.30–17 or 19 exc. Mon).

Sant'Agata di Villanova sull'Arda, with another Verdi villa is described in Chapter 64.

Colorno has a grand ducal palace of the Farnese (adm. by appointment only), with a park and orangery. The church of San Liborio (begun in 1777) and several 18C oratories are also of interest.

In the broad valley of the Taro south of Parma is Sala Baganza near which are the **Boschi di Carrega**, a beautiful wooded area (now protected). The village of

Fornovo di Taro, was the scene of a battle in 1495, in which the retreating Charles VIII of France defeated the Milanese and Venetians. The Romanesque church has fine 13C sculptures on its façade: Fornovo was on the **Via Francigena**, the medieval pilgrimage route to Rome, which ran south via **Berceto** (where there is a 13C church) and across the Apennines by the Passo della Cisa (1039m) to descend into the Magra valley (see *Blue Guide Tuscany*).

64 · Piacenza and its province

Piacenza, an important centre (106,900 inhab.) of internal trade, situated at the strategic point where the Via Emilia touches the Po, possesses a beautiful cathedral and several fine churches, as well as some interesting museums. Its name (the French for which is *Plaisance*) is derived from the Latin *Palacentia*.

■ **Information office.** IAT, 7 Piazzetta Mercanti, off Piazza Cavalli (tel. 0523/329324).

■ **Hotels.** 4-star: *Grande Albergo Roma*, 14 Via Cittadella. 3-star: *Milano*, 47 Viale Risorgimento.

■ **Restaurants. A**: *Antica Osteria del Teatro*, 16 Via Verdi; **B**: *Peppino*, 183 Via Roma. **C**: *La Pireina*, 137 Via Borghetto.

■ **Car parks** near the station and Piazza Milano.

■ **Country buses** from Piazza Cittadella to places in the province and cities in Emilia.

■ **Markets** on Wed and Sat in Piazza Cavalli, Piazza Duomo and Chiostri del Duomo.

History
The peace negotiations ratified at Constance (1183) between Frederick Barbarossa and the Lombard League were conducted in the church of Sant'Antonino. In 1545 Pope Paul III created the dukedom of Parma and Piacenza for his illegitimate son Pier Luigi Farnese. Alessandro Farnese (1545–92), the 'Prince of Parma' was governor of the Low Countries from 1578 until his death. Piacenza was the first city to join Piedmont by plebiscite in 1848.

The centre of the old city is PIAZZA CAVALLI, named after its pair of bronze equestrian *statues of Duke Alessandro (1625) and his son and successor, Ranuccio Farnese (1620). The latter commissioned these fine works from Francesco Mochi, who also designed the pediments. *Palazzo del Comune is a fine Gothic building begun in 1280, built of brick, marble and terracotta.

Via XX Settembre leads out of the square, past **San Francesco**, a church begun in 1278 with a transitional façade. The fine Gothic interior has a pretty apse with an ambulatory.

At the end of the street stands the ***DUOMO**, an imposing Lombard Romanesque church (1122–1240). **Exterior**. The beautiful polychrome ***façade** in sandstone and red Verona marble has recently been restored. The left porch and door are attributed to the school of Wiligelmus. The central door was heavily restored at the end of the 19C by Camillo Guidotti, but the original elements include the archivolt with signs of the zodiac, the two telamones (supporting male figures), and capitals above. The lions were replaced in the 16C. The right door is by a certain Nicolò, and has finely carved panels of the Life of Christ including three unusual scenes of the Temptations in the Desert.

From the piazza on the south side can be seen the exterior of the drum, and the 14C **campanile** crowned by a gilded angel, a weather vane placed here in the early 14C by Pietro Vago. Beyond the Chiostri del Duomo can be seen the exterior (from the Strada della Prevostura) of the early 12C apse, a carved window with four figures and pretty loggias above.

In the beautiful **interior** (closed 12–16) massive cylindrical pillars divide the nave and aisled transepts. Set into the pillars are little square reliefs by local sculptors (c 1170) showing the work of the guilds which paid for the erection of each column. Above the arches are 12C figures of saints and the Madonna (left) and Prophets (right). At the west end are two capitals attributed to Nicolò, one with the story of Saul and David, and one showing the stoning of St Stephen. On the west wall are paintings by Camillo Procaccini and Lodovico Carracci. On a nave pillar are three votive frescoes (14C–15C) of the Madonna.

The architecture of the **transepts** is particularly fine, and there are interesting remains of frescoes here (c 1390). The frescoes in the vault of the **central octagon** were begun by Morazzone, but he only completed two sections before his death. The *frescoes in the rest of the vault (and the lunettes below) were completed by Guercino. A lunette over the entrance to the sacristy has a Giottesque Madonna. The two ambones are 19C reconstructions.

In the raised **choir** the high altar has a sculpted gilded reredos (late 15C), behind which are good stalls of 1471. The two large 18C neo-classical paintings are by the local painter Gaspare Landi. The apse fresco is by Camillo Procaccini, and those in the side aisles are by Lodovico Carracci.

Via Chiapponi leads to the church of **Sant'Antonino**, rebuilt in the 11C with an octagonal lantern tower, which dates in part from the 10C, supported inside on a group of massive pillars. The huge north porch was added in 1350. The large paintings in the sanctuary are by Roberto De Longe (1693). A small museum contains parchments, illuminated codexes, and 15C–16C paintings.

Nearby is the **Teatro Municipale** (1803–10) with a little museum (ring for adm. at 41 Via Verdi). At 13 Via San Siro is the ***GALLERIA RICCI ODDI**, with a representative collection of Italian 19C–20C painting (open 10–12, 14 or 15–16, 17 or 18 exc. Mon). The collection was begun in 1902 by Giuseppe Ricci Oddi (1868–1937), and donated by him to the city in 1924. The charming building, with excellent natural lighting, was built by Giulio Ulisse Arata for the collection, which is arranged in 25 rooms by schools and regions. Artists represented include: Vito d'Ancona, Telemaco Signorini, Giovanni Boldini, Giovanni Fattori, Giuseppe Abbati, Vincenzo Cabianca, Antonio Fontanesi, Francesco Hayez, Girolamo Induno, Vincenzo Gemito, Federico Zandomeneghi, Antonio Mancini, Filippo Palizzi, Edoardo Dalbono, Domenico

Morelli, Ettore Tito, Felice Casorati, Bruno Cassinari, Mario Cavaglieri and Gustav Klimt.

Via Sant'Antonino is prolonged by the busy Corso Garibaldi in which are (right) the 12C front of **Sant'Ilario**, with a relief of Christ and the Apostles on the architrave, and (at the end of the street) **Santa Brigida**, also 12C. A little to the left is **San Giovanni in Canale**, a 13C and 16C church, well restored. Nearby in Via Taverna, at the Collegio Morigi, is a **Natural History Museum** (open 8.30–12.30 exc. fest.).

Via Campagna leads northwest from beyond Santa Brigida to (15 mins' walk) the church of the **MADONNA DI CAMPAGNA** (closed 12.30–15), a graceful Renaissance building by Alessio Tramello (1522–28). On a Greek-cross plan, it has four little domed corner chapels. The central *dome, beautifully lit by small windows in a loggia, has frescoes by Pordenone (1528–31). The decoration of the drum and the pendentives was completed by Bernardino Gatti (1543). There are more works by Pordenone in other parts of the church, including a corner chapel with *scenes from the life of St Catherine. The paintings are by Camillo and Giulio Cesare Procaccini, Guercino and Camillo Boccaccino.

Via Sant'Eufemia leads northeast past the church of **Sant'Eufemia**, with an early 12C front (restored); straight ahead is **San Sisto**, another pretty church by Tramello (1499–1511), preceded by a courtyard. It was for this church that Raphael painted his famous '*Sistine Madonna*', sold by the convent to the elector of Saxony in 1754, and now at Dresden. On the north choir pier is the monument of Duchess Margaret of Parma (1522–86), governor of the Netherlands from 1559 to 1567; the fine stalls date from 1514.

Via Borghetto leads back towards the centre: on the left, in Piazza Cittadella, is the huge **PALAZZO FARNESE**, which houses the **MUSEI CIVICI** (open 9–12.30; Thu, Sat & fest. also 15.30–18; closed Mon). The palace was begun for Duchess Margaret in 1558 by Francesco Paciotto and continued after 1564 by Vignola, but left only half finished. It has a grand if plain exterior, divided in three floors by protruding cornices and numerous well proportioned windows. Adjoining to the left is the smaller 14C Rocca Viscontea. In the courtyard can be seen the 15C loggia of the castle, and a huge double loggia with niches of the Palazzo Farnese. It is still in the process of restoration.

Room 2 displays 16C paintings by Malosso, Girolamo Bedoli Mazzola and Camillo Boccaccino. **Rooms 3 & 4** display 16C–18C ceramics and Venetian glass (16C–19C). **Rooms 6–8** are decorated with paintings by Sebastiano Ricci and Carlo Draghi illustrating the life of the Farnese Pope Paul III. In Room 6 is displayed a tondo by Botticelli, and in Room 7 Farnese portraits. The large **Room 9** contains 14C frescoes. **Rooms 10–14** display 12C–18C sculpture. **Room 15** has a very fine display of arms and armour, mostly dating from the 16C and 17C.

On a mezzanine floor is the **Risorgimento Museum**, which documents the history of the city during the wars of independence against Austria. In the **basement**, in remarkable vaulted rooms, once used as kitchens and storerooms, is a fine collection of 50 *carriages dating from the 18C and 19C. Here can be seen a remarkable spiral staircase designed by Vignola which ascends to the top of the palace. On the **second floor** is the deconsecrated ducal *chapel, built on an octagonal design in 1598. In a wing of the palace, underground rooms are to exhibit the **archaeological section**, which includes the celebrated 'Fegato di Piacenza', an Etruscan divination bronze representing a sheep's liver, marked with

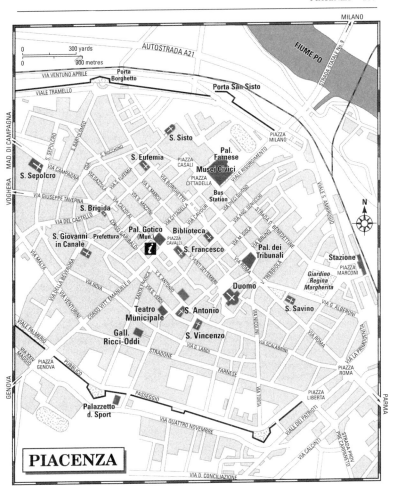

PIACENZA

the names of Etruscan deities. The **Pinacoteca**, approached through a beautiful iron *gate with the Farnese arms, at the foot of the stairs, is to be reopened on the second floor in rooms frescoed with episodes from the life of the Farnese.

Near the palace are scanty remains of the Roman amphitheatre. **Palazzo dei Tribunali** is a 15C building with a good sculptured doorway and a pretty garden. The **Biblioteca Comunale Passerini-Landi** has over 170,000 volumes and 3000 MSS (interesting psalters and codexes). **San Savino** is a 12C church with two mosaics of the 13C or earlier. Nearby is a pleasant public park in front of the railway station.

Beyond the southern outskirts of the city, at **San Lazzaro Alberoni**, is the

Collegio Alberoni, with an important collection of works of art (open by appointment, tel. 0523/63198), including Christ at the Column by Antonello da Messina; 18 Flemish tapestries; Flemish paintings (Mabuse, Provost, and still lifes); church silver and vestments; engravings by Piranesi; and scientific instruments. These belonged to Giulio Alberoni (1664–1752) who was a gardener's son who rose to be a cardinal and the able minister of Philip V and Charles III of Spain.

The province of Piacenza

On the northern border of the province, on the Po, is **Monticelli d'Ongina**, with a 15C castle (adm. on request) with frescoes by Bonifacio Bembo and an ethnographical museum illustrating life on the Po (open fest. 15–18.30).

At **Sant'Agata di Villanova sull'Arda** is the Villa Verdi built by Verdi in 1849 as a summer residence. The Verdi Museum here is open Apr–Oct, 9–12, 15–19 exc. Mon; it contains relics and a bust by Vincenzo Gemito.

The abbey of **Chiaravalle della Colomba** (open 9–12, 14–18) has a Romanesque church and a 13C Gothic *cloister, with coupled columns.

In the pretty Arda valley is **Castell' Arquato**, a picturesque hill-town with double walls. In the attractive piazza stand the Palazzo Pretorio of 1293 and the Romanesque Collegiata with a 14C cloister, off which is a museum (open 10–12, 15–18) with church silver, sculpture and paintings. The Rocca Viscontea can also be visited. Near the 16C Torrione Farnese is a geological museum with marine fossils, etc.

Near Lugagnano Valdarda, in pretty countryside, is **Veleia** (open daily from 9 until 1hr before sunset; Mon & Wed 9–15), the picturesque ruins of a small Roman town which flourished in the 1C BC, first excavated in the 18C. There is a small archaeological museum here.

Grazzano Visconti is a village rebuilt in medieval style at the beginning of this century.

Near Gazzola, above the Trebbia river, is the medieval **Castello di Rivalta** (privately owned; open at weekends or by appointment, tel. 0523/978104), enlarged in the 15C and 18C, which retains its original furnishings and paintings by Pordenone.

Bobbio, in the southwest corner of the province, is noted for its learned monastery founded in 612 by the Irish Saint Columbanus, who died here in 615. The basilica, a 15C–17C building, has a crypt with some traces of the primitive church and the tomb of St Columbanus (1480). The museum (open 16.30–18 exc. Mon & Thu) contains a remarkable ivory Roman bucket with a representation of David in high relief (4C). The castle is being restored.

65 · Ravenna and its province

Ravenna (131,900 inhab.) is unique in western Europe for the profusion of its Byzantine remains. Now 10km from the sea, it was once a flourishing Adriatic port and the capital of the Byzantine exarchs, whose semi-oriental power is reflected by the magnificently coloured mosaics and imperial tombs. In the quiet old centre (most of the residents use bicycles to get about) are numerous basilican churches with cylindrical bell-towers of the 9–10C. The Museo Nazionale has a particularly interesting collection. The modern town is without distinction and is surrounded by extensive industrial suburbs.

■ **Information office.** 8 Via Salara (tel. 0544/35404).

■ **Hotels.** 4-star: *Bisanzio*, 30 Via Salara. 3-star: *Centrale Byron*, 14 Via IV Novembre.

■ **Youth hostel**: *Dante*, 12 Via Nicolodi.

■ **Restaurants. C**: *Ca' de vén*, 24 Via Ricci; *Giamba e Cocò*, 34 Via Pasolini; *La Gardela*, 3 Via Ponte Marino.

■ **Picnic places** in the public gardens of Rocca Brancaleone, or on the lawns around the Mausoleo di Teodorico.

■ **Car parks** (with hourly tariff and limited space) in the centre of the city.

■ **Buses.** Nos 4 and 44 run on weekdays from the station to the basilica of Sant'Apollinare in Classe. Buses run to places of interest in the province, including Bagnacavallo, Lugo and Brisighella, and to the resorts on the coast. Faenza is best reached by train from Ravenna.

■ **Annual festivals.** Music festival in Jul, and international organ music festival in Aug with concerts every Mon in the basilica of San Vitale.

■ The monuments of Ravenna have unusually long **opening hours**: San Vitale, the Mausoleum of Galla Placidia, the Battistero Neoniano, Museo Arcivescovile, Sant'Apollinare Nuovo and Santo Spirito have a cumulative ticket (available at any one of the six monuments). They all have the same opening times (9–19; 9.30–16.30 in winter), except for Santo Spirito (see p 469).

History

The importance of Ravenna begins with the construction, by Augustus, of the imperial port of *Classis*, to which the town was united by the Via Caesarea. Its greatest period, however, began in 401 when Honorius moved the imperial court and civil administration from Milan to Ravenna, and it became the capital of the Western Empire. His sister, Galla Placidia, was the first to adorn the city with splendid monuments. Its importance continued under the successor of Honorius, Valentinian III.

The town also flourished under the German king Odoacer (473–93), who took up residence here. He was killed by the Ostrogoth Theodoric (493–526), who captured the city in 493 and proved to be a strong and effective ruler, respecting the traditions of Rome. In 540 Belisarius conquered Ravenna and there followed a period of prosperity under the Eastern Empire, when Justinian and his empress Theodora constructed some magnificent buildings here in the capital of the new Exarchate.

Although the province passed into the hands of the Church in 757, Ravenna was still able to proclaim its independence as early as any town in Italy (1177). In the 13C–14C the city was governed by the Da Polenta family (of which Francesca da Rimini was a member), distinguished for their hospitality to Dante. From 1441 to 1509 Ravenna prospered as part of the Venetian Republic, but the renewal of papal domination and the sack of the city in 1512, after the battle between Louis XII of France and the Holy League outside its walls, marked the beginning of its final decline. In 1849 Garibaldi found a brief refuge in the pine forest near the town, though his wife Anita died from the hardships of her flight from the Austrians; and in 1860 the city was finally united with the Kingdom of Italy. It was captured from the Germans in December 1944. Since the war, a busy industrial district has been built beyond the railway and the port is again flourishing (the Candiano canal links the inner harbour of Ravenna with the sea at Marina di Ravenna).

Art

Ravenna is unequalled in western Europe as a centre for the study of Byzantine architecture, sculpture and mosaic. The plan of the churches had a wide-spread influence on later buildings in Italy, and the storeyed capitals at San Vitale are equal to the finest work in Constantinople itself. The mosaics show a progressive movement from the naturalism of the earlier work inspired by classical ideals (Tomb of Galla Placidia, the Baptisteries, Sant'Apollinare in Classe) to the hieratic decorative quality of the purely Byzantine style (San Vitale, and the processional mosaics in Sant'Apollinare Nuovo).

In the central PIAZZA DEL POPOLO are two Venetian columns with bases (much worn) decorated by Pietro Lombardo (1483) and now bearing statues of St Apollinaris and St Vitalis (1644). On the left of the crenellated **Municipio** is a portico of eight 6C columns (four bearing the monogram of Theodoric). In **Palazzo Guiccioli**, at No. 54 Via Cavour, Byron lived with the Count and Countess Guiccioli, and wrote the end of *Don Juan*, *Marino Faliero*, and other poems.

Just off Via San Vitale, beyond a 17C archway, is the garden surrounding San Vitale and its former convent. **San Vitale, the Mausoleum of Galla Placidia and the Museo Nazionale** are now all approached through one entrance in Via Fiandrini, where there are two ticket offices (one for the combined ticket to San Vitale and the Mausoleum of Galla Placidia and one for the Museo Nazionale).

Museo Nazionale

The *Museo Nazionale (for adm. see p 461), which occupies the former Benedictine Monastery of San Vitale (founded in the 10C), contains an excellent and varied collection of treasures. The monastic collections were taken over by the municipality in 1804, and in 1887 the Museo Nazionale was founded. Recent archaeological finds from the territory are kept here.

The three cloisters contain interesting sculptural fragments. In the 18C **third cloister** is a statue of Alexander VII (1699), and in the **second cloiste**r, by Andrea da Valle (1562) is a seated statue of Clement XII by Pietro Bracci (1738). The **refectory** contains detached *frescoes from Santa Chiara by Pietro da

Rimini (mid-14C). In the **first cloister**, which dates from the early 16C, are Roman epigraphs and funerary stelae. From the little Renaissance portico near the east end of San Vitale can be seen the terracotta frieze on the wall below the campanile.

A staircase by Benedetto Fiandrini (1791) leads up to the **first floor** and the rooms around the second cloister. On the landing is a fine Byzantine capital probably made in Constantinople. A room with a pretty vault has a fine display of small 16C **bronzes** and **plaquettes**, and—at the end—a late 18C pharmacy has been reconstructed (the ceramics date from the 17C–18C).

In the little vaulted rooms to the right of the landing are displayed **Bronze Age ceramics**, and **Roman finds** from excavations in this century in Ravenna and Sant'Apollinare in Classe, including portrait heads and glass. Another room displays four **Roman herms** found offshore, and an early Christian sarcophagus of a child.

A long hall displays 6C **transennae**, including a relief of Hercules and the stag, and the cross from the top of San Vitale. The next room contains marble reliefs from the so-called Palazzo di Teodorico. Among the fine display of **fabrics** are some precious examples from the tomb of St Julian at Rimini, and the so-called 'Veil of Classis' with embroideries of Veronese bishops of the 8C–9C. The *ivories include a relief of Apollo and Daphne (530 AD), a 6C diptych from Murano, and evangelistary covers. On the last side of the cloister are five small rooms of 16C–18C **furniture**.

Off the room with finds from the palace of Theodoric (see above) is a room with a large **sinopia** found beneath the apse mosaic in Sant'Apollinare in Classe. Beyond is an L-shaped hall with an interesting collection of **icons** of the Cretan-Venetian school, dating from the 14C to the 17C and arranged iconographically by type.

In the large hall (once part of the dormitory of the monastery) is a splendid display of **Coptic fabrics**, including a 7C Egyptian tunic. At the end are models of buildings in Ravenna and finds from excavations in the church of Santa Croce. Small rooms off the hall contain **ceramics** (Ravenna, Deruta, Faenza, Urbino, Castelli, etc.) and some detached frescoes (including one from San Vitale dating from the 13C).

A modern staircase leads down to a mezzanine floor where a splendid collection of *coins is beautifully displayed in chronological order from the Roman period onwards. The stairs continue down to a hall with a marble statue of Venice by Enrico Pazzi (1884), the first director of the museum, and recent donations. A large room displays funerary **stelae** (1C BC–1C AD), many of them belonging to sailors, and finds (6C–5C BC) from the necropolis of San Martino in Gattara including a large Greek krater. A corridor beyond contains four **mosaics** decorated with birds. The collection of 16C–17C **armour** is at present closed.

San Vitale

In the third cloister is the narthex of **San Vitale (for adm. see page 461; the best light in which to see the mosaics is usually between 12 and 13), the most precious example of Byzantine art extant in western Europe. Founded by Julianus Argentarius for Bishop Ecclesius (521–34), the church was consecrated in 547 by Archbishop Maximian. The narthex, which stands obliquely to the church, was formerly preceded by an atrium. The octagonal building is surrounded by a double gallery and surmounted by an octagonal cupola.

The impressive **interior** is famous for its decoration in marble and mosaics (partly under restoration). The remarkable plan, two concentric octagons with seven exedrae or niches and an apsidal choir, may have been suggested by SS Sergius and Bacchus at Constantinople. The eight pillars which support the dome are encased in marble (largely renewed), and are separated by the exedrae with their triple arches. Higher up is the matroneum, or women's gallery, and above all is the dome, built—for lightness—from two rows of terracotta tubes laid horizontally and fitting into one another. The vault-paintings are of the 18C; the intended mosaic decoration was probably never executed.

A capital in San Vitale

The chief glories of the church are in the ***choir** and ***apse**. On the triumphal arch are mosaics of Christ and the Apostles with St Gervasius and St Protasius, the sons of the patron saint. On either side are two constructions of antique fragments patched together in the 16C–18C, including four columns from the ancient ciborium (the first on the left is of rare green breccia from Egypt), and a fragment with putti of a Roman frieze known as the 'Throne of Neptune'. Within the arch, on either side, are two *columns with lacework capitals beneath impost blocks bearing the monogram of Julianus. In the lunettes are mosaics: on the right, Offerings of Abel and of Melchizedech; in the spandrels, Isaiah and the Life of Moses; on the left, Hospitality and Sacrifice of Abraham; at the sides, Jeremiah and Moses on the Mount. The upper gallery has magnificent capitals and mosaics of the Evangelists, and the vault mosaics of Angels and the Paschal Lamb amid foliage are also very fine. The stucco decoration beneath the arches is beautiful. In the centre is the altar, reconstructed, with a translucent alabaster top (usually covered).

The apse (partly under restoration) has the lower part of its walls covered with marble inlay, a modern reconstruction from traces of the original plan. In the centre of the *mosaic, in the semi-dome, Christ (beardless) appears between two angels who present St Vitalis and Bishop Ecclesius (with a model of the church). On the side walls are two fine processional friezes: on the left, *Justinian with a train of officials, soldiers and clergy, among whom are Archbishop Maximian and Julianus Argentarius or Belisarius; on the right, *Theodora with her court. In front of the apsidal arch are Jerusalem, Bethlehem and two angels.

To the right of the apse, beyond an apsidal chamber, is the Sancta Sanctorum (kept locked). Further on is the former entrance to the campanile (originally one of the staircase towers giving access to the matroneum); beneath an adjoining arch are some fine stuccoes. On the other side of the narthex is the second stair-case tower, still preserving some original work, with a stair ascending to the matroneum. Some early Christian sarcophagi are kept in the church.

Tomb of Galla Placidia

From the north side of San Vitale a pathway leads across a lawn to the charming **Tomb of Galla Placidia (for admission, see page 461), a small cruciform building erected by the sister of Honorius towards the middle of the 5C. The plain exterior is decorated with blind arcades and pilasters. The interior, lit by alabaster windows, is famous for its magnificent, predominantly blue *mosaics, especially interesting for the classic character of the figures and for their excellent state of preservation (although they are restored periodically).

Over the entrance is the Good Shepherd; in the opposite lunette, St Laurence with his gridiron; in the side lunettes, stags quenching their thirst at the Holy Fount. The vaults and arches of the longer arm of the cross are decorated to represent rich hangings and festoons of fruit. In the shorter arm are four Apostles; the other eight are on the drum of the cupola. In the pendentives are the symbols of the Evangelists, and—above all—the Cross in a star-strewn sky. The three empty sarcophagi are no longer considered to have held the remains of Placidia, Constantius and Valentinian III; only one of them is of 5C workmanship.

The church of **Santa Maria Maggiore** (525–32, rebuilt 1671) preserves Byzantine capitals above Greek marble columns, and a tiny cylindrical campanile (9C–10C). The small church of **Santi Giovanni e Paolo** (locked), rebuilt in 1758, retains another 10C campanile. Nearby, in Via d'Azeglio, a 4C–7C palace with interesting mosaic pavements was found in 1993.

The Cathedral

The Cathedral, founded early in the 5C by Bishop Ursus and often known as the *Basilica Ursiana*, was almost totally destroyed in 1733, but immediately rebuilt. The columns of the central arch of the portico and those on either side of the central door are from the original church. The round campanile, many times restored, dates from the 10C. In the nave is the 6C *ambo of St Agnellus, pieced together in 1913. In the south transept chapel are two huge 6C *sarcophagi. In the ambulatory is a good relief of St Mark in his study (1492, ascribed to Pietro Lombardo). The north transept chapel has an altarpiece and frescoes by Guido Reni and his school.

Battistero Neoniano

Adjoining the cathedral is the octagonal *Battistero Neoniano (or *degli Ortodossi*, open as for San Vitale), converted from a Roman bath-house, perhaps by Bishop Neon (mid-5C), perhaps 50 years earlier. The plain exterior is decorated with vertical bands and small arches. The remarkable interior is entirely decorated with mosaics and sculptural details which blend with the architectural forms. The original floor is now more than 3m below the present surface.

Eight corner columns support arches decorated with mosaics of Prophets. In the niches and on the wall-spaces which are arranged alternately beneath the arches are mosaic inscriptions and marble inlaid designs from the original Roman baths. Each arch of the upper arcade encloses three smaller arches; the stucco decoration is very fine. In the dome, built from hollow tubes like that of San Vitale, are mosaics of the Baptism of Jesus (the old man with the reed represents the Jordan), the Apostles, the Books of the Gospel, and four thrones, remarkable for their contrasting colours. The font is of the 12C–13C. In the niches are a Byzantine altar and a pagan marble vase.

Museo Arcivescovile

Nearby, on the first floor of the Arcivescovado, is the little **MUSEO ARCIVESCOVILE** (open as for San Vitale), with some exquisite works, and incorporating a little chapel with beautiful early 6C mosaics. In the first room is a lapidary collection, with fragments and mosaics from the original cathedral and from San Vitale; the silver **Cross of St Agnellus*, probably dating from 556–69 and restored in the 11C and 16C; a headless 6C porphyry statue thought to be Justinian; and the marble pulpit from Santi Giovanni e Paolo (596). The so-called chasuble of St John Angeloptes may be a 12C work.

On the left is a **chapel* built by Bishop Peter II (494–519), and preceded by an atrium with a barrel vault covered with a delightful **mosaic of birds*. The chapel also contains beautiful **mosaics* in the vault. In the end room is the famous ivory **throne of Maximian*, an Alexandrine work of the 6C, exquisitely carved with the story of Joseph, the Life of Christ, and figures of St John the Baptist and the Evangelists, and a 6C Paschal calendar incised on marble.

The **Biblioteca Classense* (entered from Via Baccarini), in a 16C–17C building, contains the former monastic library of the monastery of Sant'Apollinare in Classe, founded in 1515 and augmented by Pietro Canneti (1659–1730). The **Aula Magna*, designed by Giuseppe Antonio Soratini, with stuccoes and a frescoed ceiling and carved bookcases, can be visited on request (8–19 exc. Sat afternoon and fest.). The important library, owned by the municipality since 1803, has some 600,000 volumes, with 749 valuable codexes, including a 10C text of Aristophanes, illuminated manuscripts, choir books, works relating to Dante, and a collection of Byron's letters.

San Francesco

The church of San Francesco, built by Bishop Neon in the 5C, and remodelled in the 10C, was almost entirely rebuilt in 1793. The 10C campanile was restored in 1921. The lovely basilican interior has 22 columns of Greek marble. In the **north aisle** are three sarcophagi (including one with Christ and the Apostles dating from the 5C), and the tombstone of Ostasio da Polenta (1396) in red marble (with his death mask). Beyond the tomb of Luffo Numai, by Tommaso Fiamberti (1509), the 4C **tomb of St Liberius* serves as high altar. Beneath it steps lead down to an opening which provides a view of the 9C–10C **crypt** (light outside), partly flooded. Here can be seen the foundations of an earlier church with its restored mosaic pavement. The first chapel on the south side has carved pilasters by Tullio Lombardo (1525).

Tomb of Dante

On the left of San Francesco is the so-called Cappella di Braccioforte (1480, restored in 1920), containing several early Christian sarcophagi. To the left again by a little memorial bell-tower (1921) is the Tomb of Dante (open 8–19; Oct–Mar,

9–12, 14–17). Exiled from Florence and harried by his political enemies, the poet found refuge, in 1317, with the Da Polenta family of Ravenna, and with them he spent his last years, finishing the *Divina Commedia*. He died on the night of 13–14 September 1321. The mausoleum was commissioned from Camillo Morigia by Cardinal Luigi Gonzaga in 1780 to enshrine an older tomb, with a relief by Pietro Lombardo (1483), and an epitaph by Bernardo Canaccio (1357). This in turn covers the antique sarcophagus in which the poet's remains were originally interred in the old portico of San Francesco. The bronze doors by Lodovico Pogliaghi, and the polychrome marble in the interior were added in 1921.

The **Museo Dantesco** (entered through a restored 15C cloister at No. 4 Via Dante; open 9–12, 15–18; Oct–Mar, 9–12; closed Mon), first opened in 1921, has mementoes of the poet and material relating to various memorials to him. The room decorated by artists influenced by the Arts and Crafts movement in England was intended as a homage to Dante.

At the corner of Piazza San Francesco and Via Ricci stood Palazzo Rasponi,

Byron's first home in Ravenna (1819). Further south is the 5C basilican church of **Sant'Agata Maggiore**, which has a squat round campanile completed in 1560, and sarcophagi on the lawn outside. The basilican interior, similar to San Francesco, contains Roman and Byzantine capitals, a very unusual fluted 7C pulpit, an early Christian sarcophagus used as a high altar, and two Renaissance baldacchini over the altars at the east end.

Via Cerchio, to the left, ends opposite **Santa Maria in Porto**, a church begun in 1553, with a sumptuous façade by Morigia (1780). It contains fine stalls by Mariano (1576–93), and other French craftsmen, and (over the altar in the north transept), a marble Byzantine relief called '*La Madonna Greca*' (probably 11C). In the public gardens behind is the early 16C Loggetta Lombardesca.

Adjoining the church, the former monastery of the Canonici Lateranensi houses the **Accademia di Belle Arti**. The fine large **Pinacoteca Comunale** here (open 9–13, Tue & Thu also 14.30–17.30) is spaciously arranged around a pretty cloister in the well lit rooms of the convent. It includes works by Taddeo di Bartolo, Paolo di Giovanni Fei, Lorenzo Monaco, Marco Palmezzano, Bernardino Zaganelli, Ludovico Brea, Antonio Vivarini, Gentile Bellini, Luca Longhi, Nicolò Rondinelli, Francesco di Santacroce, Palma Giovane and Paris Bordone. The effigy of Guidarello Guidarelli, killed at Imola in 1501, is the work of Tullio Lombardo (1525). The 19C–20C section includes works by Armando Spadini, Felice Carena, Giuseppe Abbati and Arturo Moradei. Off the cloister there is also an **ornithological museum**.

In Via di Roma, to the north, is the building known as the '**Palazzo di Teodorico**', really the ruined church of **San Salvatore** (entered from Via Alberoni, open 8.30–19). Exhibited here on the walls and on an upper floor (approached by a spiral stair) are fine mosaics and part of a marble intarsia floor found in 1914 in a palace nearby.

Sant'Apollinare Nuovo

The church of *Sant'Apollinare Nuovo (entered through a little garden on the right; open as for San Vitale) is one of the finest in Ravenna. It was built by Theodoric in the early 6C; the mosaics are partly of this time, partly of the mid-6C. Dedicated originally to Jesus and later to St Martin, the church passed from the Arians to the orthodox Christians under Archbishop Agnellus. Its present dedication dates only from the 9C. The façade with its portico was rebuilt in the 16C; adjacent is a fine 10C **campanile**.

Interior. The floor and the 24 Greek marble columns were raised in the 16C and are surmounted by a panelled ceiling of 1611; the arcades bulge noticeably to the north. Along the nave walls are two magnificent bands of *mosaics (partly under restoration): that on the north side represents the port of Classis, with a procession of 22 virgin martyrs preceded by the Magi who offer gifts to the Infant Jesus seated on His mother's lap between four angels. On the south side are Ravenna, showing the façade of Theodoric's palace, and a procession of 26 martyrs approaching Christ enthroned. Above, on either side, are 16 Fathers of the Church, or Prophets; higher still, 13 scenes from the Life of Christ.

The stucco decoration of the arches is very fine. The ambo in the nave dates from the 6C. In the apse, reconstructed in 1950 (and being restored), are the recomposed altar, transennae, four porphyry columns, and a marble Roman chair.

At the corner of Viale Farini, leading to the station, is Piazza Anita Garibaldi, with a monument to the martyrs of the Risorgimento (with amusing lions). Here the 14C marble portal of the church of **San Giovanni Evangelista** has been reconstructed on a new wall which encloses a little garden in the church precincts. The church was built by Galla Placidia in fulfilment of a vow made in 424 during a storm at sea. It was well restored after most of the façade and the first four bays were destroyed and the notable galleried apse, as well as the aisles, seriously damaged in the Second World War. The 10C–14C **campanile** survives (leaning to the west); two of the bells date from 1208. In the basilican **interior** some columns, with their capitals and impost blocks, are original. Round the walls are displayed mosaics from the 13C floor, their naïve designs illustrating episodes from the Fourth Crusade. In a chapel off the north aisle are fresco fragments of the 14C Riminese school. At the end of the south aisle the chapel has a little 8C carved altar.

Battistero degli Ariani

To the left, beyond the crossroads, is Via Paolo Costa. The first lane on the left (Via degli Ariani) leads to the church of **Santo Spirito** (open 9–12.30, 14–18.30; winter 12–14), converted, like Sant'Apollinare, to the orthodox cult by Agnellus in the mid-6C. Fourteen columns and an ambo from the original church were retained after a rebuilding in 1543. Beside it is the tiny little *Battistero degli Ariani (now Santa Maria in Cosmedin; open 8.30–19), built by Theodoric in the early 6C. It contains splendidly preserved *mosaics of the Baptism of Christ and of the Apostles in the dome.

In Via Costa, No. 8 is the **Casa Stanghellini**, a charming 15C Venetian house, and at the end is the leaning 12C Torre Comunale. From here Via Rossi (right) leads to the church of **San Giovanni Battista**, with a cylindrical campanile; the interior, a 17C reconstruction, retains its ancient marble columns.

The Mausoleum of Theodoric

At the north end of Via di Roma is Porta Serrata, a gate of 1582. The Circonvallazione alla Rotonda leads east through unattractive suburbs past the rugged bastions of the Venetian **Rocca di Brancaleone**, which now enclose delightful public gardens. Beyond the railway (a rather unpleasant walk of c 20 mins along a busy road), in a clump of trees to the left, is the *Mausoleum of Theodoric (open 8.30–19.30; bus 2 from the station, every 30 mins). This remarkable two-storeyed tomb, is unique in the history of architecture, and its solid structure shows the influence of Syrian buildings as well as Roman models.

Begun by the great Ostrogoth himself in c 520, it was built of hewn Istrian stone without mortar and crowned by an unusual monolithic roof. It was never finished, and for a time, until 1719, it was used as a monastic church (Santa Maria al Faro).

The ten-sided lower storey has a deep recess on every side. The upper floor, which is decorated with unfinished arcading, was approached by two 18C staircases, which collapsed in 1921. The monolithic cupola of Istrian limestone from Pola has a diameter of 11m and weighs about 300 tons. The crack, which is clearly visible, was probably the result of a harsh knock received during its installation. It is not known how the monolith was transported here. Inside is a porphyry bath which was used as the royal sarcophagus.

Sant'Apollinare in Classe

About 5km south of Ravenna and reached either by rail (Classe station, on the Rimini line), or—better—by road (buses 4 and 45 from Ravenna station) across the Ponte Nuovo (1736) and the sit^ of Classis, is the basilica of *Sant'Apollinare Classe (open 9–12, 14–19), built for Bishop Ursicinus by Julianus Argentarius in 535–38, and consecrated by Archbishop Maximian in 549. The narthex, which preceded the church, has been reconstructed. The magnificent late 10C *campanile is the tallest and most beautiful of all the towers of Ravenna (covered for restoration).

The wide bare **interior** has 24 lovely Greek marble veined columns with square Byzantine bases and beautiful capitals. In the centre of the nave is the altar of Archbishop Maximian, restored in 1753. At the west end of the church are eight columns from the two original ciboria, and a fragment of the original mosaic floor. In the aisles are a series of magnificent sarcophagi, complete with lids, dating from the 5C to the 8C. At the end of the north aisle is a 9C ciborium and an interesting altar with a 5C relief of Christ and the Apostles.

The *mosaics of the apse are extremely interesting, though much altered. On the outside arch are five rows of symbolic mosaics, with figures of saints, palm trees, sheep, and Christ in a roundel with the symbols of the Evangelists. In the apse itself is a cross on a blue ground with the symbol of the Transfiguration; below is a field of flowers and trees with birds and sheep and St Apollonius in prayer in the centre. Below, to the right and left, are two large scenes, with the sacrifices of Abel, Melchizedech and Abraham, and Constantine IV granting privileges for the church of Ravenna to Archbishop Reparatus in the 7C. Between the windows are the figures of the four bishops Ursicinus, Ursus, Severus and Ecclesius (6C). The arches of the windows are also decorated with columns in mosaic.

The **Pineta di Classe**, east of the basilica beyond the railway, whose sylvan grandeur was celebrated in poetry by Dante and Byron, is now sadly diminished. Although designated a nature reserve it is threatened by the industrial development on the outskirts of Ravenna.

The province of Ravenna

■ **Information offices.** Provincial tourist office, 8 Via Salara, Ravenna. IAT offices at Brisighella (6 Via De Gasperi, tel. 0546/81166) and at the coastal resorts.

■ **Hotels. Lugo**: 4-star: *Ala d'Oro* and *San Francisco.* **Brisighella**: 2-star: *Gigiolé* and *La Rocca.* (3-star hotels at the spa). Numerous hotels in the Adriatic coastal resorts.

■ **Restaurants. Bagnacavallo**: C: Osteria in Piazza Nuovo. **Lugo**: A: *Antica Trattoria del Teatro.* C: *La Zambra.* **Brisighella**: A: *Osteria La Grotta.* C: *La Casetta.* **Sarna**: C: *La Cantina.* **Ponte Vico** (località Russi): C: *Trattoria da Luciano.* **Strada Casale**: A: *Trattoria di Strada Casale,* 22 Via Statale.

BAGNACAVALLO is a small town with, in its central piazza, a charming **Theatre** (1855). In Via Garibaldi, next to a 13C tower, is the **convent of San Giovanni** where Allegra, daughter of Byron and Claire Claremont, died in 1821 at the age of five (plaque). In another former convent (the orchard of which is now a pretty public garden) are a **Pinacoteca** with paintings by Bartolomeo Ramenghi (1484–1542), called 'Il Bagnacavallo' after his native town, a local ethnographical museum, a library, and a natural history museum. The Collegiata and Carmine also have paintings by Bagnacavallo. **San Francesco**, next to its huge convent, has a small Flemish painting and the tombstone of Tiberio Brandolini. Piazza Nuova is a charming little 18C oval cobbled marketplace surrounded by porticoes. The church of **San Pietro in Silvis**, just outside the town (open 9–11.30, 15–17.30; fest. 9–11.30; ring at the house next door), has a lovely basilican interior of the Ravenna type probably dating from the early 7C, with a raised presbytery above the crypt. It has *frescoes in the apse by Pietro da Rimini c 1323 (being restored). At **Villanova**, on the river Lamone, is an interesting local museum illustrating life on the wetlands in the district, with handicrafts made from the reeds which grow in the marshes.

The pleasant little town of **LUGO** (34,600 inhab.) has interesting 18C architecture. The *Teatro Rossini** was begun in 1757–59 by Francesco Petrocchi, and Antonio Bibiena designed the boxes, stage and three backcloths in 1761. It is built entirely of wood (with excellent acoustics), and the stage is the same size as the auditorium, which seats 500. Important opera productions were given here in the 18C, and concerts are now held in spring. The huge neo-classical **Paviglione** was built at the end of the 18C on the site of a marketplace in use since 1437; the arcading on one side dates from the early 16C. Beneath the porticoes are attractive shops with uniform fronts, and a market is held here on Wednesdays. Opera performances took place here in 1598 and again in the 17C. The colossal incongruous monument (intended for another site) dedicated to Francesco Baracca, a First World War hero, was inaugurated here in 1936 by Mussolini. The Estense **Rocca** (the seat of the Comune; open daily exc. fest.) dates in its present form from the 15C–16C. In the well restored courtyard is a 15C well-head. Upstairs is the Salotto Rossini with a portrait by Haudebourt Lescot (1828) of the composer, who lived in the town in 1802–04 as a child. The hanging garden is now a public park. The church of the **Carmine** preserves an organ by Gaetano Callido (1797) used by Rossini. At 65 Via Baracca is the **Museo Francesco Baracca** (open 10–12, 16–18) with mementoes of the pioneer aviator (1888–1918), born in Lugo, including his plane used in the First World War. There was an important Jewish community in the town from the 15C onwards, and their cemetery survives.

BRISIGHELLA is a charming little town in the foothills of the Apennines, beneath three conical hills—one crowned by a clock-tower of 1290 (rebuilt in 1850), another by a 14C Manfredi **castle** with two drum towers (restored by the Venetians in the 16C; inside is a local ethnographical museum), and the third by a 17C sanctuary; all are reached by pretty paths. A delightful medieval pageant is held by candlelight in June and July in the town. Excellent olive oil is produced in the vicinity. Above the main street runs the **Strada degli Asini**, a picturesque covered lane with a wooden vault and arches. The **Museo**

Ugonia(open 15–18.30 exc. Mon; weekends also 10–12) contains a very interesting collection, beautifully displayed, of lithographs and watercolours by Giuseppe Ugonia (1880–1944). The town hall is in an imposing neo-classical building of 1828. The church of the **Osservanza** contains fine stuccowork of 1634 and a painting by Marco Palmezzano.

Just outside the town, beyond the 16C **Villa Spada** (with an 18C façade), surrounded by a large garden and containing a remarkable private art collection, is the ****Pieve del Thò** (ring for adm. at the house on the right). This ancient church, first mentioned in 909, is thought to be on the site of a Roman building. The interior has primitive columns and capitals, on one of which is an inscription mentioning four late Roman emperors. It is thought that 'Thò' may come from '*ottavo*', referring to the eighth mile on a Roman road from the Adriatic. Roman remains can be seen beneath the church.

The stretch of Adriatic coast which lies within the province of Ravenna has numerous resorts, with hotels of all categories. They include **Marina di Ravenna**, which developed round Porto Corsini (1736), and **Cervia**, to the south near pine woods, a small walled town built in 1698 on a regular plan, later surrounded by a large seaside resort and spa (with an 18-hole golf course).

In the **Pineta di San Vitale**, one of the few wooded areas left along the coast of Italy, is **Garibaldi's Hut**, a reconstruction of the hut where the great patriot lay in hiding in 1849; the original was burned in 1911. The Colonna dei Francesi (1557) on the Forlì road, marks the spot where Gaston de Foix fell mortally wounded in 1512 in the battle between the French and Julius II.

There are British and Canadian military cemeteries northwest of Ravenna and at Alfonsine: this area saw a lot of fighting during the Second World War during the 8th British Army's advance on the Po.

66 · Faenza

Faenza is a pleasant old town (54,700 inhab.) on the Lamone river, in the province of Ravenna, which has long been famous for its manufacture of the glazed and coloured pottery known as majolica or 'faience'. There are still some 60 working potteries in the town. The street names are indicated by faience plaques, and several houses have ceramic decoration. The town, still with its Roman plan, is divided into two by the Via Emilia (Corso Mazzini and Saffi).

■ **Information office.** IAT, Piazza del Popolo (tel. 0546/25231).

■ **Hotel.** 4-star: *Vittoria*, 23 Corso Garibaldi.

■ **Restaurants**. C: *Baia da Re*, 71 Via Marcucci; *Osteria del Mercato*, 13 Piazza Martiri della Libertà; *Entoteca Astorre*, 16 Piazza Libertà. **Wine Bar**: *Conti*, 16 Corso Matteotti.

   On the outskirts: **B**: *La Cantena*, 221 Via Sarna; *La Pavona*, 45 Via Santa Lucia; *Trattoria del Tiglio*, 171 Via Santa Lucia.

■ **Theatre.** *Comunale*, with a theatre and ballet season.

■ **Annual festival.** The 'Palio del Niballo', a Renaissance tournament, takes place in June. At certain periods of the year (usually between June and Oct) a portable kiln (with a wood fire) is set up outside the Duomo, and pottery is fired on the spot to be sold for charity.

History

From the early 13C until 1501 the powerful Manfredi family played a leading part in Faentine affairs, though they did not prevent the city from being severely damaged in 1241 by Frederick of Hohenstaufen and again sacked in 1376 by the mercenary soldier Sir John Hawkwood, then in the papal service. In 1501 Cesare Borgia took the town and killed the last of the Manfredi, and from 1509 Faenza was included in the States of the Church. It was damaged in the Second World War.

The great period of Faentine majolica was 1450–1520, when the most famous of 40 potteries in the town was that of the brothers Pirotti (the Ca' Pirota). The earliest authenticated specimen (in the Cluny Museum in Paris) is a votive plaque dated 1475, though its manufacture is already documented in 1142. Baldassare Manara (first half of the 16C) and Virgilio Calamelli (Virgiliotto da Faenza; later 16C) both produced distinguished work. The art had a second revival in the early 18C.

In the broad Viale Baccarini, which connects the station with the town, is the ***MUSEO INTERNAZIONALE DELLE CERAMICHE** (open in summer: 9–19; fest. 9.30–13; winter: 9–13.30, Sat also 15–18), the best and most extensive collection of Italian majolica in Italy. Founded in 1908, it covers all periods, and is beautifully displayed and well labelled (an excellent catalogue is also available). The lower floor is currently being rearranged. The museum includes superb examples of 15C–16C Faentine ware and ceramics from all the major Italian manufactures. It also has pre-Columbian, Minoan, Greek and Etruscan ceramics, and a small Oriental and Middle Eastern collection. The 20C works include pieces by Picasso and Matisse. The study collections are complemented by an excellent library and photographic collection.

The impressive large PIAZZA DELLA LIBERTÀ, with arcades and a fountain of 1619–21 (by Domenico Paganelli), is at the centre of the town. The **DUOMO**, begun by Giuliano da Maiano in 1474, is a Renaissance building with an unfinished front. It contains good sculpture including a Bosi monument by the local sculptor Pietro Barilotti (1539), the reliquary urn of St Terenzio with beautiful *carvings in very low relief, and the *tomb of St Savinus (first bishop of Faenza, early 4C), with exquisite reliefs by Benedetto da Maiano (1474–76). An altarpiece by Innocenzo da Imola has been removed for restoration.

On the other side of the Via Emilia is the picturesque arcaded PIAZZA DEL POPOLO with a clock tower, by Domenico Paganelli (reconstructed in 1944), **Palazzo del Podestà** (partly of the 12C), and the **Municipio**, once the palace of the Manfredi. The **Voltone della Molinella** is a shopping arcade with a beautiful frescoed vault and *grotteschi* by Marco Marchetti (1566). Here the Bottega dei Ceramisti Faentini exhibits and sells ceramics made in the town. In a pleasant cobbled courtyard is the neo-classical ***Teatro Comunale Masini**, reopened in

1989. Designed by the local architect Giuseppe Pistocchi (1780–87) it has a charming interior with statues and reliefs by Antonio Trentanove.

Via Severoli leads right to the town **PINACOTECA** (closed since 1982), with an interesting collection of works of art, including sculptures by Fra Damiano, Alfonso Lombardi and Donatello or his school (wooden statue of *St Jerome), and paintings by Marco Palmezzano. The church of **Santa Maria dell'Angelo** (1621, by Girolamo Rainaldi) has a Spada tomb by Francesco Borromini, and busts by Alessandro Algardi.

Further southwest, reached by Via Cavour, is ***PALAZZO MILZETTI** (open 8.30–13.30 exc. fest.; Thu also 14–17), a fine building by Giuseppe Pistocchi (1794–1802), with a good neo-classical interior on two floors, and its decoration and furnishings intact. Many of the rooms have delightful tempera paintings by Felice Giani. On the piano nobile is an impressive octagonal room designed by Giuseppe Antonio Antolini with stuccoes by Antonio Trentanove.

Nearby rises the 10C campanile of Santa Maria Vecchia. In Corso Mazzini, with a number of 18C and early 19C buildings, **Palazzo Mazzolani** may one day house a local archaeological museum. In Borgo Durbecco, beyond the Lamone bridge, is the small Romanesque church of the **Commenda**, with a remarkable fresco by Girolamo Pennacchi the Younger (1533). The next road to the right, beyond the Barriera, leads to a British Military Cemetery.

67 · Forlì and Cesena

Forlì

An undistinguished provincial capital (104,900 inhab.) and agricultural centre, Forlì takes its name from the Roman *Forum Livii*, a station on the Via Emilia, which bisects the town. Its urban architecture suffered under the influence of Mussolini, born nearby.

■ **Information office**. 9 Piazza Morgagni (tel. 0543/714335)

In the central piazza is the church of **San Mercuriale** (12C–13C but altered later), dedicated to the first bishop of Forlì. It has a fine contemporary *campanile, 76m high, a high relief of the school of Antelami above the west door, and a graceful cloister. In the red-brick interior are paintings by Marco Palmezzano and the *tomb, by Francesco Ferrucci, of Barbara Manfredi (died 1466) wife of Pino II Ordelaffi. Beneath the apse are remains of the 11C church and the crypt of 1176.

Palazzo del Municipio, dating from 1459, was altered in 1826. Corso Garibaldi, with some 15C–16C mansions, leads to the **Duomo**, mainly an elaborate reconstruction of 1841, but preserving a huge tempera painting of the Assumption, the masterpiece of Carlo Cignani (1681–1706). The campanile, in Piazza Ordelaffi, was formerly the watchtower of the Orgogliosi, a rival family to the Ordelaffi, who ruled the town from 1315 to 1500.

At the south end of the town is the **Rocca di Ravaldino** (1472–82; now a prison), where Caterina Sforza was besieged by Cesare Borgia in 1499–1500.

It was the birthplace of her famous son Giovanni delle Bande Nere (1498–1526).

In Corso della Repubblica, the former hospital (1772) houses the **Pinacoteca Comunale Saffi** (open Tue–Fri 9–14; Sat 9–13.30; fest. 9–13; closed Mon), first opened to the public in 1846, and in this location since 1922. It is one of few museums in Italy to have preserved its old-fashioned arrangement, but is in urgent need of restoration. The gallery possesses only one work (the *pestapepe*, a druggist's street sign) attributed to the famous local painter Melozzo da Forlì (degli Ambrogi; 1438–95), but it contains a fine collection of paintings by his most important follower, Marco Palmezzano (including an *Annunciation), as well as paintings by Fra Angelico (two tiny panels of the Nativity and Christ in the Garden), Cavalier d'Arpino, Livio Agresti, Lodovico Carracci, Carlo Cignani, Francesco Albani, Andrea Sacchi, Guido Cagnacci, Lorenzo Costa, Lorenzo di Credi, Bartolomeo Ramenghi and Silvestro Lega. It has sculptures by Bernardo and Antonio Rossellino, and Pier Paolo and Jacobello delle Masegne. On the upper floor is an ethnographical collection, and below is an archaeological collection.

There is a museum of musical instruments in Palazzo Gaddi. In the church of **Santa Maria dei Servi** the tomb of Luffo Numai (1502) has good reliefs by Tommaso Fiamberti.

In the Rabbi valley outside the town is a British Military Cemetery.

The town of **Predappio** was the birthplace of Benito Mussolini (1883–1945). The village, originally a hamlet called Dovia in the commune of Predappio Alta, received communal rank in 1925, and many new public buildings were erected. In the cemetery are Mussolini's remains, finally interred there in 1957, and those of his wife 'Donna Rachele' (Rachele Guidi), buried there in 1979. Predappio was taken from the Germans by Poles of the 8th Army in October 1944. There is an Indian and British Military Cemetery nearby.

Cesena

Cesena is a town (86,500 inhab.) which now lacks distinction, although it enjoyed a period of brilliance under the Malatesta family (1379–1465).

■ **Information office.** IAT, 11 Piazza del Popolo (tel. 0547/356327).

The most interesting building is the ***Biblioteca Malatestiana** (open 9–12.30, 15–18; or 16–19; fest. 10–12.30). In the vestibule are displayed two Roman silver plates (early 5C AD) with banquet scenes in gold and niello. A handsome doorway, with a relief of the Malatesta heraldic elephant, leads into the perfectly preserved *old library, a beautiful aisled basilica built in 1447–52 by Matteo Nuti for Domenico Malatesta Novello. Some precious old books, in their original presses, are still kept chained to the reading desks. The opaque windows look onto the cloister. Another room contains a display of some of the the 340 valuable MSS, including some with 15C illuminations, and 48 incunabula, which belong to the library.

Near the 15C **Palazzo del Ridotto** (rebuilt in 1782) is the church of the **Suffragio**, with a late Baroque interior and a high altarpiece by Corrado Giaquinto (1752). The **Cathedral**, begun in 1385, contains 15C sculpture. The **Theatre** was opened in 1846 (being restored).

The central Piazza del Popolo has a pretty fountain of 1583, opposite which steps lead up to the public gardens surrounding the 15C **Rocca Malatestiana** (open 9.30–12.30, 15–19 exc. Mon) which was a prison until 1969 and has been heavily restored. It contains 17C tournament armour and a Garibaldi collection. From the battlements are views of the coast, including the tower of Cesenatico, and inland to the Apennines. In one of the towers, in the former prison cells, is a local ethnographical museum.

From Piazza del Popolo, Viale Mazzoni leads round the foot of the castle hill to **San Domenico** with 17C paintings. In Via Aldini is the **Pinacoteca Comunale** with works by Sassoferrato, Antonio Aleotti and Giovanni Battista Piazzetta.

Outside the town is the **Madonna del Monte**, a Benedictine abbey rebuilt in the 15C–16C with a collection of ex-votos, and a Presentation in the Temple by Francesco Francia. A British Military Cemetery northeast of Cesena recalls the heavy fighting in this area in October 1944 by the 8th Army.

Cesenatico was the port of Cesena, designed in 1502 by Leonardo da Vinci for Cesare Borgia, from which Garibaldi and his wife Anita set sail on their flight towards Venice in August 1849. It is now the biggest of the numerous popular seaside resorts here, which stretch for some 30km south to Rimini and Pesaro. Near Gatteo a Mare is the mouth of the **Rubicone** river, the fateful Rubicon which Caesar crossed in defiance of Pompey in 49 BC. A Roman bridge (c 186 BC) survives over the river inland at **Savignano sul Rubicone**.

68 · Rimini and its province

Rimini (118,400 inhab.), capital of a new province created in 1995, was first visited for its bathing beaches in 1843, and it was the largest seaside resort on the Adriatic by the 1950s. Its beaches, especially popular with German, French, British and Eastern European holidaymakers, extend along the shore in either direction; some 16 million tourists visit this coast every year (there are 2800 hotels in the province). The old city, over a kilometre from the sea front, is separated from it by the railway. Although Rimini is a somewhat characterless town, it contains the famous Tempio Malatestiano, one of the most important Renaissance buildings in Italy. It also has a good local museum, and preserves a splendid Roman arch and bridge.

■ **Information office.** Agenzia di Informazioni Turistiche della Provincia di Rimini, 28 Piazza Malatesta (tel. 0541/716371).

■ **Hotels.** There are about 1400 hotels within the city limits, nearly all of them near the sea (and many with their own beaches). The *Grand Hotel* (5-star) was first opened on the seafront in 1908. In the old centre: *Hotel Duomo*, 28 Via Giordano Bruno (4-star).

■ **Restaurants.** The best fish restaurants are in the fishing village of Borgo San Giuliano (including *Da Tonino* and *Il Lurido*, both **B**). **Cafés** and **cake shops**:

Bar Dovisi, Piazza Tre Martiri; *Pasticceria Vecchi*, Piazza Cavour.

■ **Car parking.** Across Ponte d'Augusto e Tiberio, or in Largo Gramsci.

■ **Public transport. Trolley-buses** depart from Piazza Tre Martiri to the station and the shore, from where there are frequent services via Bellariva and Miramare to Riccione. **Buses** run to Ravenna, Faenza, San Marino, Ancona, etc.

■ **Airport** at Miramare, c 6km south with summer charter flights from all over Europe.

■ **Market day** on Wed & Sat around the Castle.

History

Rimini occupies the site of the Umbrian city of *Ariminum*, which became a Roman colony c 268 BC and was favoured by Julius Caesar and Augustus. In the 8C it became a papal possession, and was contended between the papal and imperial parties in the 12C–13C. Neri da Rimini produced some beautiful illuminated manuscripts here from 1300 to 1323.

Malatesta di Verucchio (1212–1312), Dante's 'old mastiff', was the founder of a powerful dynasty of Guelf overlords, most famous of whom was Sigismondo (1417–68), a man of violent character, but an enthusiastic protector of art and learning. Malatesta's son, Giovanni the Lame, was the husband of the beautiful Francesca da Rimini (died 1258), whose love for her brother-in-law Paolo inspired one of the tenderest passages in Dante's *Inferno* ('we read no more that day'). Pandolfo (died 1534) surrendered the town to Venice, but after the battle of Ravenna (1512) it fell again into papal hands. Rimini, bombarded from sea or air nearly 400 times, was the scene of heavy fighting between the Germans and the 8th Army, and was captured by Canadians in September 1944. The film director Federico Fellini was a native of Rimini and some of his films were inspired by the town.

In the centre of the old town is the arcaded Piazza Tre Martiri, with the little **Oratory of St Anthony** on the spot where the saint's mule miraculously knelt in adoration of the Sacrament.

Via IV Novembre leads south to the ****TEMPIO MALATESTIANO** (open 7–12, 15.30–19), one of the outstanding monuments of the Italian Renaissance, built in Istrian stone. The original building (on the site of a 9C church) was a late 13C Franciscan church, used by the Malatesta family in the 14C for their family tombs. In 1447–48 Sigismondo Malatesta transformed this into a personal monument, as his own burial place. He commissioned Leon Battista Alberti to redesign it, with the help of Matteo de'Pasti in the interior, and had Agostino di Duccio decorate it with exquisite sculptural reliefs. The decline of Sigismondo's fortunes caused the suspension of the work in 1460, and the Franciscans completed the building.

Exterior. The ***façade**, on a high basement and inspired by the form of the Roman triumphal arch (and the nearby Arch of Augustus), is one of the master-pieces of Alberti. It had a lasting effect on 16C and 17C church architecture in Italy. The upper part is incomplete. The two sides have wide arches surmounting

Tempio Malatestiano, tomb of Isotta degli Atti, wife of Sigismondo Malatesta

the stylobate, beneath which (on the south side) are seven plain classical sarcophagi containing the ashes of eminent members of Sigismondo's court. Latin and Greek inscriptions record Sigismondo and his victories.

The ***interior** is being beautifully restored. The spacious nave is flanked by a series of deep side chapels connected by remarkably fine ***sculptural decoration by Agostino di Duccio**, and closed by fine balustrades in red-and-white veined marble. The walls are covered with beautiful sculptural details (including the vaults and window frames). On the right of the entrance is the tomb of Sigismondo, whose armorial bearings (the elephant and rose) and initials (SI) recur throughout the church.

South side. In the **first chapel** is a seated statue of St Sigismund supported by elephants' heads, and very low reliefs of angels, all elegant works of Agostino di Duccio. In the niches, statues of the Virtues and armour-bearers. The little **sacristy** (formerly the Chapel of the Relics), preserves its original doors surrounded by marble reliefs including two putti on dolphins. Inside is a damaged *fresco (above the door) by Piero della Francesca (1451), representing Sigismondo kneeling before his patron, St Sigismund of Burgundy, and relics found in Sigismondo's tomb. The **third chapel** has a frieze of putti at play on the entrance arch and (over the altar) St Michael, by Agostino. Here is the tomb of Isotta degli Atti, Sigismondo's mistress and later his third wife. The crucifix was painted for the church by Giotto before 1312. The **fourth chapel** has more superb decoration representing the planetary symbols and signs of the zodiac, also by Agostino.

North side. The **fourth chapel** is the masterpiece of Agostino, with reliefs representing the Arts and Sciences. The **third chapel** has particularly charming putti. In the **first chapel** (of the Ancestors) are figures of prophets and sibyls, a tiny Pietà (15C, French), above the altar, and the Tomb of the Ancestors, with splendid reliefs by Agostino.

The end chapels and presbytery do not belong to the original Malatesta building: it is thought that the original design incorporated a dome at the east end. It was completed by the Franciscans (and rebuilt in the 18C and again after the Second World War). Since 1809 the temple has served as the cathedral of Rimini.

Behind the temple and across Largo Gramsci, in a residential area with a children's playground, can be seen the impressive ruins (fenced off) of the **Roman Amphitheatre**; only two brick arches remain above the foundations.

From Piazza Tre Martiri, Corso d'Augusto leads west to the ugly Piazza Giulio Cesare, in which stands the ***ARCO D'AUGUSTO**, a single Roman archway (c

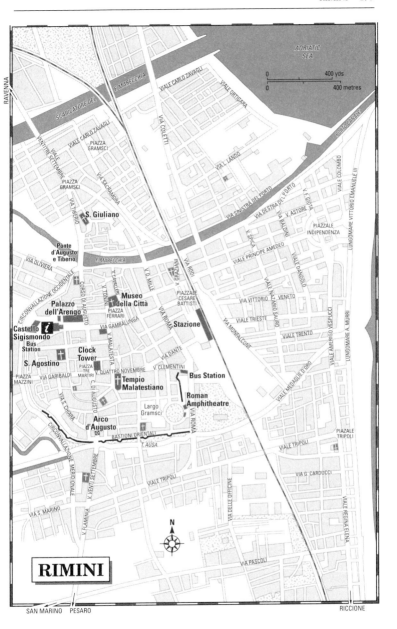

RIMINI

27 BC; restored) with composite capitals, marking the junction of the Via Emilia with the Via Flaminia. It was later inserted into the medieval walls. At the opposite end of the Corso is the ***PONTE D'AUGUSTO E TIBERIO**, a five-arched bridge across the Marecchia begun by Augustus in the last year of his life and finished by Tiberius (AD 21). It is remarkably well preserved (and used by cars and pedestrians), with its handsome dedicatory inscriptions still in place in the centre of the bridge. The north arch was rebuilt after the Goths destroyed it in order to cut Narses off from Rome in 552.

In Corso d'Augusto is the **Cinema Folgor** built in the 1920s often visited by Fellini as a child (destined to become a study centre dedicated to him). The Corso runs through the south end of Piazza Cavour, with a fountain of 1543 incorporating Roman reliefs, and a seated 17C statue of Paul V. Here are two restored Gothic buildings: the battlemented **Palazzo dell'Arengo** (1204), now used for exhibitions, and the 14C **Palazzo del Podestà**, now the town hall. At the end is the neo-classical façade of the **Theatre**, built in 1857 by Poletti, which hides the foyer (used for exhibitions): the theatre itself was bombed in the war and is still in ruins behind.

The **Castello Sigismondo**, which dates from 1446, is the seat of the **Museo delle Culture Extraeuropee**, founded by Delfino Dinz Rialto (1920–79) in 1972 (open 8–13.30; Tue & Thu also 15.30–18; closed fest.). It contains a remarkable ethnological collection. The first section is dedicated to Oceania, on the lower floor is material from pre-Columbian America, and on the upper floor material from Africa.

In Via Sigismondo is the Romanesque church of **Sant'Agostino**, with a fine campanile and remarkable 14C frescoes (very damaged) by local artists, including Giovanni da Rimini, and a huge painted 14C crucifix.

Via Gambalunga leads from Piazza Cavour past the town library to Piazza Ferrari where excavations of a Roman house are in progress. Beyond the church of the Suffragio, at 1 Via Tonini, in the ex-Jesuit college built by Alfonso Torreggiani in 1746–55, is the ***MUSEO DELLA CITTÀ** (open 8–13.30; Tue & Thu also 15.30–18; Sat 8.30–12.30, 15.30–18; fest. 10–13, 15.30–18). Founded in 1871, the museum is being beautifully rearranged. It is particularly interesting for its works of art produced by Riminese artists.

In the first corridor are **Roman mosaics** (including one, dating from the early 2C, showing boats in the port of Rimini). On the **ground floor** is a Roman lapidarium and a large 14C fresco by the Riminese school.

On the **first floor** are paintings by the **14C Riminese school**, including a fine crucifix by Giovanni da Rimini. In the **corridor** is a Last Supper by Bartolomeo Coda. In the room on the right at the end of the corridor are the two masterpiece of the collection: ***Giovanni Bellini's** *Dead Christ with four angels*, commissioned by Sigismondo Pandolfo Malatesta c 1460, and ***Domenico Ghirlandaio's** *Pala of St Vincent Ferrer*, commissioned by Pandolfo IV, with portraits of the Malatesta family. Other rooms display 15C and 16C paintings, nine 17C Flemish **tapestries**, a bronze bust of Michelangelo attributed to Giambologna, and 14C–16C majolica.

On the **second floor** are displayed **17C Riminese paintings**, three works by **Guercino**, a painting by Guido Reni, 18C and 19C works including portraits, and a painting of the Roman bridge of Rimini by Richard Wilson.

The prehistoric and archaeological collection has not yet been arranged: it includes Etruscan tomb-furniture of the Villanovan period, with a remarkable axe-mould, and coins from the mint of *Ariminum*.

The church of **San Giuliano**, in the suburb beyond the bridge, contains a fine Martyrdom of St Julian painted by Paolo Veronese. The pleasant public **Parco XXV Aprile** occupies the former bed of the river Marecchia (now channelled to the north).

Viale Principe Amadeo was laid out in the 19C to connect the old town with the sea. It is lined with pretty Art Nouveau villas with their gardens. By the railway line is the only skyscraper in the city. The sandy beaches along the coast north-west and southeast of Rimini, ruined by uncontrolled new building begun in the 1950s, attract millions of holidaymakers every year from all over Europe. There is a continuous line of resorts, including **Riccione**, with numerous hotels.

The province of Rimini

■ **Information offices.** open in summer at **Santarcangelo di Romagna** (5 Via Cesare Battisti) and at **Verucchio** (15 Piazza Malatesta).

■ **Restaurants. Villa Verucchio**: *Rò e Bunì, Casa Zani, Le Case Rosse* (all **C**). **Verucchio**: *Ristorante La Rocca* (**C**). There are numerous good *osterie* in **Santarcangelo di Romagna**, including *La Sangiovesa* (**C**). **Montebello**: *Pacini* (**C**); *Armeria dell'Albana* (**B**). **Torriana**: *Osteria del Povero Diavolo* (**B**).

■ **Annual festivals.** The Fiera di San Martino is held in Santarcangelo di Romagna in Nov.

In the pleasant wide **Marecchia valley**, with hilly outcrops, is **Villa Verucchio**, with a Franciscan convent which may date from 1213. The church contains a 14C Riminese fresco. **VERUCCHIO** is an attractive hill-town from which the Malatesta clan set out to conquer Rimini. Its site, on a low hill where the river Marecchia emerges into the plain, has been of strategic importance since earliest times, and an Etruscan centre flourished here in the 7C BC. At the foot of the hill is an ancient pieve. From the pretty Parco dei 9 Martiri an old walled mule path (to be reopened to the public) leads up to the Rocca. A lane descends to the former convent of Sant'Agostino, beautifully restored as the seat of the **Museo Civico Archeologico** (open in summer 9.30–12.30, 14.30–19.30; otherwise on request at the IAT office). Here are displayed finds from an important Etruscan and Villanovan necropolis (9C–7C BC) excavated at the foot of the hill since 1894. Particularly beautiful *amber and gold jewellery was found, as well as textiles and wooden objects (other material is displayed in the archaeological museum in Bologna).

The **Rocca** (open as for the Museo Civico) has a splendid view of the Adriatic coast (Rimini and Cesenatico marked by their two skyscrapers) and inland to the Marche. In the **Collegiata** hangs a 14C Riminese painted cross, and in the north transept is an early 15C cross attributed to Nicolò di Pietro.

MONTEBELLO is a delightful little hamlet with just one street, from which steps lead up to the entrance to the **Castello dei Guidi di Romagna**, still privately owned by the Guidi (open 14.30–18.30 or 19.30; in winter at week-ends only). The old church is now used as a wine bar. There are fine views over the beautiful river valley and the former estate (now a nature reserve), in which is the castle of Saiano (reached by a path) with a church perched on an outcrop of rock. San Marino is also prominent. The courtyard is part 12C (with a tower built onto the rock), and part Renaissance. The interior, interesting for its archi-tecture, has particularly good furniture in the Renaissance wing. In the medieval part of the castle a pretty angle room has an interesting collection of *cassoni* (marriage chests), including three dating from the 13C and 14C, an old oven, and a painted Islamic panel thought to date from the 11C. The family still owns a private archive dating from 980. There is a small garden inhabited by peacocks inside the walls. The castle was used for a time as German headquarters in the last war, and during a battle here 386 Gurkhas (part of the British 8th Army) lost their lives; their military cemetery is on the San Marino road south of Rimini.

SANT'ARCANGELO DI ROMAGNA is a pleasant small town. In the lower town is the Sferisterio below the walls built for ball games (and now used for the game of *tamburello*). In Via Cesare Battisti is the fish market of 1829 and the Collegiata with a Venetian polyptych. Also in this street is an old family-run shop where fabrics are still printed by hand (the wheel dates from the 17C); all the old books of samples have been preserved. Uphill is Piazza delle Monache where a local museum of paintings and archaeology is to be opened in a well restored 17C palace. Also in the piazza is the entrance to a grotto (opened on request at the tourist office), used as a wine cellar since the 16C. A passageway leads to a remarkable underground circular room with an ambulatory and niches carved in the tufa rock, possibly a pagan temple. There are many other similar grottoes beneath the town. Further uphill is the picturesque old borgo with three long straight streets of low houses leading from the neo-Gothic clock-tower to the 14C–15C Rocca (still privately owned by the Colonna), recently restored and to be opened to the public.

The diminutive **REPUBLIC OF SAN MARINO** (61 sq.km; 20,900 inhab.) lies a few kilometres south of Rimini (reached by an ugly fast road), on the border with the Marche. The Republic is famous for having preserved its independence for more than 16 centuries, since its alleged foundation c 300 by Marinus, a pious stonemason from Dalmatia, who fled to the mountains to escape Diocletian's second persecution. Most of its territory consists of the peaks and slopes of the limestone **Monte Titano** (739m).

The capital, **San Marino** (4600 inhab.), is totally given over to the tourist trade. The three medieval citadels (Rocca, Cesta and Montale) are connected by a splendid *walkway which follows the crest of the hill and has fine views of the Adriatic coast. The church of San Francesco has a St Francis by Guercino and a Madonna and Child attributed to Raphael. The Palazzo del Governo dates from 1894. The legislative power is vested in a Council General of 60 from whom ten (the Congress of State) are chosen as an executive, and 12 as a Council that functions as a Court of Appeal; the chiefs of state are two 'regent captains' who hold office for six months (investiture Apr and Oct). San Marino has its own mint, postage stamps, police force, and an army of about 1000 men.

Historical Introduction

By John Law

To the visitor, northern Italy can appear as part of a united nation. Italian is the predominant language. Roman Catholicism appears as the established religion. Certain social mores are common throughout: a seemingly well-ordered existence; a resigned deference to bureaucracy; the conspicuousness of family life; café society; the *passeggiata* (the fashion-conscious parade—on wheels or heels—around noon or in the early evening); the flourishing state of small—often family—businesses in shops, restaurants and bars; the interest in sport (above all in football) and in the byzantine complexities of the political situation. Good and bad taste vie for predominance: carefully preserved town centres and appalling urban sprawl; exquisite craftsmanship and sordid neglect.

The legacy of Rome

Behind such initial impressions more fundamental signs of unity present themselves. Throughout, the legacy of Rome is apparent in place names and the layout of cities, in civic monuments and the direction of roads. The region of Friuli is called after the Roman colonies established in the first century BC, like Forum Iulii (now Cividale). The street plan of central Verona is predominantly Roman while buildings, like its Arena or Roman amphitheatre, are still in use. The modern Via Emilia follows the line of the Roman Via Aemilia from the Adriatic through Bologna to Piacenza.

Moreover, the legacy of Rome should be understood in terms of an ongoing influence. This influence was probably at its most intense and fruitful during the Renaissance, from the mid-14C to the mid-16C. This was the period when artists, architects and scholars—and their patrons—sought a rebirth, or 'renaissance' of ancient Rome. Hence the delight of the poet Francesco Petrarch (1304–74) when he discovered a neglected collection of letters of Cicero in the cathedral library in Verona. Hence the almost archaeological interest in Antiquity displayed by the painter Andrea Mantegna (1431-1506).

But the impact of Rome can be detected both earlier and later. Virgil, from Mantua, was revered in the Middle Ages as a prophet and a magician before his poetry was subjected to a more scholarly appreciation in the Renaissance. Roman Law shaped the statutes of the medieval communes and provided the law curriculum at the university of Bologna, one of the earliest of medieval Europe, founded in the 12C. Roman architectural designs and ornament influenced all periods of architecture down to the 20C, only seriously challenged by the Gothic from the 13C to the 15C. The expansion of Rome, its military and political strength, influenced the political aspirations of many regimes, from the Holy Roman Empire to Fascism.

This historical introduction is dedicated to the memory of Harry Hearder, 1924-96

Diversity in Language, Religion and Art

The Fascist period (1922–45) was noted for the effort made to foster a sense of Italian unity, but this was a process begun with the *Risorgimento*, the unification —but literally the renewal or revival—of Italy in the 19C. It is a process which continues to the present, and it can heighten the impression of unity: the monuments to the heroes of the *Risorgimento*; the street names and memorials to the First World War which defended and extended Italian unity; the presence in major cities of a large military establishment and grandiose public buildings; the standardised lay-out of railway stations and the far-reaching railway network; the superbly engineered *autostrade*

But on closer scrutiny, the homogeneity of northern Italy can appear more superficial. The survival of regional and even local dialects shows little sign of weakening; in some areas Italian can reveal the influence of foreign languages, as is the case with French in Piedmont. German is the majority language in the province of Bolzano in the region of the Alto Adige, acquired by Italy from Austria only in 1919. In the same region, a distinct romance language, Ladino, also survives. And linguistic survivals from German immigration in the Middle Ages can still be detected in the Dolomites, as well as in Friuli, where pockets of Slavonic can also be found.

Again, while Catholicism is certainly the predominant religion, Piedmont is the centre for the earliest surviving 'protestant' church, that of the Waldensians (la Chiesa Evangelica Valdese). This owed its origins to a 12C reformer, Peter Waldo, his followers finding sanctuary from persecution in the valleys of the Alps; one particularly savage wave of persecution inspired Milton's sonnet *Avenge, O Lord, thy slaughtered saints* (1655). At a time of tension between the papacy and the House of Savoy, the Waldensians finally received royal recognition (1848), and the 19C also saw increased support from other protestant churches; J.C. Beckwith, a veteran of the battle of Waterloo, established Waldensian schools and encouraged the use of Italian rather than French in services. The Church has established small congregations elsewhere, for example in Milan and Venice.

Diversity can also be detected in architecture and the arts. In the Alpine valleys, stone and wood are used to a much greater extent than in the Lombard plain where brick, terracotta and marble are more prevalent. In artistic terms, regional schools can be detected in the medieval and Renaissance periods. Because of long political and commercial connections with the eastern Mediterranean, Venetian art and architecture registers a strong Byzantine influence, seen strikingly in the church of S. Marco; the embellishment and maintenance of that building encouraged the art of mosaic to survive more vigorously and for longer than in the rest of northern Italy. Again, in Piedmont and Friuli, the Middle Ages and Renaissance saw the creation of elaborately carved wooden altarpieces, familiar enough in northern Europe, but largely unknown in the rest of Italy.

Finally, the monumental presence of the state in public buildings and works exists in a creative tension with strong regional, provincial and communal autonomy. For example, the Val d'Aosta, whose strategic importance at the foot of the St Bernard Passes had secured it privileges in the Middle Ages, enjoys regional status in modern Italy. In 1972, the state gave special powers to the region of the Trentino and Alto Adige and to its provinces of Trent and Bolzano to assuage separatist opinion. However, from the 1980s the issue of greater regional autonomy has been rather overtaken by movements demanding the separation—though how completely?—of the North—though within which frontiers?—from the rest of Italy.

Unification

That the nature of the Italian state is still a matter of debate is hardly surprising: the unification of the country is relatively recent. The House of Savoy, ruling the kingdom of Sardinia, comprised of that island and the mainland regions of Liguria and Piedmont, acquired Lombardy from the Austro-Hungarian empire in 1859 and most of the rest of the Peninsula in 1860. The first national parliament was held in Turin in 1861 and the Kingdom of Italy was proclaimed on 14 March. The Veneto was added in 1866, while the First World War brought the acquisition of the Trentino, the Alto Adige, Venezia Giulia and Istria.

This is the period of the **Risorgimento**, and while it still retains a prominent place in national history and mythology, it was not a story of unalloyed victory and patriotic fervour. The first attempt by the House of Savoy to expand its frontiers (1848/9) met with heavy defeat from Austro-Hungary, despite the valiant siege of Venice. The successes of 1859/60, 1866 and 1919 were in part due to developments on the European stage, for example, French intervention assisted in the acquisition of Lombardy. But there were losses as well as gains. French support was paid for, in 1861, with the cession of Savoy—the ancestral lands of Italy's ruling house—and Nice—the birthplace of Giuseppe Garibaldi, the patriotic military genius who won Sicily and southern Italy for the new kingdom. The ill-judged participation of Italy on Germany's side in the Second World War led to the loss of territory to the former Yugoslavia. In northern Italy itself, the record of plebiscites—still commemorated in central *piazze*—can suggest overwhelming support for the national cause. However, as some foreign observers noted, Austro-Hungarian rule was not as oppressive or unpopular as Italian patriots claimed; indeed some believed that conditions in Venice had improved since the overthrow of the noble oligarchy that had ruled the city down to 1797. In fact, the *Risorgimento* was driven by a minority of committed enthusiasts and skilful opportunists, and their vision of a united Italy ranged widely, from support for the House of Savoy, to solutions of a republican or federalist nature. Camillo Cavour, prime minister of the Kingdom of Sardinia from 1852 and a principal architect of the successes of 1859/60, preferred to speak French rather than Italian, while his actions reveal him to have been a shrewd pragmatist rather than a visionary patriot.

The northern boundaries reached by Italy at the end of the First World War are close to those established by the reign of the first Roman emperor, Augustus (27 BC–AD 14); this has more to do with natural frontiers imposed by the Alpine chain than historical precedent. Roman expansion began in the late 3C BC and continued after Hannibal's invasion in the early 2C BC, encompassing (from west to east) the Ligurians, the Celts and the Veneti. Romanisation was both signalled and encouraged by the planting of colonies (e.g. Aquileia and Aosta), the construction of roads, the elevation of urban centres to the privileged status of *municipium*, the spread of Roman Law and the Latin language.

This was the longest period of stable political unity the north was to experience; it was brought to an end by waves of barbarian invaders and settlers from north of the Alps. For example, the Ostrogothic kingdom of Italy lasted from 493 to 553, and was at its height under Theodoric the Great (493–526). After his death, his successors were overwhelmed between 535 and 553 by the armies of the eastern Roman, or Byzantine, empire with its capital at Constantinople. This 'Roman' recovery was virtually destroyed by the invasions of the Lombards whose kingdom encompassed much of the north between 568 and 774. In turn, it succumbed to another northern conqueror, the Franks under Charlemagne (768–814). His imperial coronation by the pope in Rome (800) incorporated the kingdom of Italy within a western empire, known from the 13C as the Holy Roman Empire. Ruled by the Habsburg dynasty from the 15C, this empire lasted —at least in name—down to 1806 when Francis II surrendered the title under pressure from Napoleon.

At the height of Napoleon's power—as king of Italy (1805–14)—all of northern Italy was either directly under his rule or dependent on the French empire; after the battle of Waterloo, there appeared to be an emphatic return to the status quo, with the reinstatement of the principal powers in the region. The House of Savoy was restored and added Genoa to its dominions. The Habsburgs added the Trentino and the Veneto to Lombardy and client states were set up in Parma and Modena. Papal authority was restored in Emilia Romagna.

However, the Revolutionary and Napoleonic periods had far-reaching consequences. They encouraged radical political and social ideas. They had seen constitutional experiments, for example the setting up of a more democratic Ligurian Republic in Genoa (1798–1800). They had brought about the abolition of customs barriers and the remnants of the feudal system, as well as a massive reduction in the property of the Church. There had also been a reaction against the demands made upon Italy by foreign, French, rulers, but in general old orders had been seriously questioned and a new mood was prevalent, if only among elements of the political class. These changes contributed to the movement for independence which saw the whole of northern Italy come under the House of Savoy.

The issue of unity in Italian history

Why did the periods of unity in Italy prove—on the whole—to be either fragile or superficial? In part, the answer lies with the incorporating states themselves: they could not maintain the resources necessary to impose their authority in the area or defend themselves from external enemies. Hence the efforts of the Hohenstaufen emperors, Frederick I (Barbarossa) (1123–90) and his grandson Frederick II (1194–1250) to make good imperial authority were thwarted by a combination of internal resistance and the hostility of the papacy. The popes were anxious to defend their position in Rome and the States of the Church, and that introduces geo-political explanations for the disunity of the north. It lay across some of the principal routes to Rome, a secular and religious capital that for centuries attracted aspiring conquerors. For the north itself, the Alps presented a formidable barrier, but they were pierced by passes, while the rivers and lakes of northern Italy—and the great Lombard plain itself—facilitated the movement of armies; an attempt to counteract this can be seen in the system of heavy defences built by the Habsburgs on the borders of the Veneto and Lombardy in the early 19C—the 'Quadrilateral' based on Mantua, Peschiera, Verona and Legnago. And lastly, northern Italy was a prize in itself in terms of its communications, its natural resources and its large number of taxable cities.

Many of these points can be illustrated from the early history of Venice. The lagoons had had only peripheral importance in the Roman Empire, but they became a haven for refugees trying to escape the barbarian invasions. These settlements were protected not only by the lagoons, but also by Byzantine naval power, the head of the Adriatic remaining under that empire long after its authority had been driven from the rest of northern Italy. However, as the Venetians grew in prosperity—as fishermen, salt manufacturers and traders—the Byzantine Empire declined. The balance of power between capital and frontier province changed. From the early 9C the Venetians began to supply ships to defend the empire, in return securing commercial privileges. And, the Venetian duke—or doge—began to lose the character of a Byzantine representative and to assume that of a Venetian official.

The rise of the communes

The emergence of Venice can also be seen in its rejection of the authority of the western empire, and this introduces a further reason for the failure of powers seeking to unify northern Italy—the resistance of the north Italians themselves, with the rise of the communes. As with Venice, these were urban based associations which owed their political and social prominence to the recovery of the Italian economy in the 10C and 11C. The aims of the communes included the protection and advancement of the interests of their members—their citizens—and resistance to the feudal nobility, the bishop or the emperor and his representatives.

In Italian historiography, the rise of the communes in the 11C and 12C has been seen in heroic terms, and coupled with such grand issues as the defeat of feudal and foreign power and the rise of capitalism and the bourgeoisie. In the 19C and early 20C, the communes were seen as prototypes for modern Italy, democratic and free from foreign rule; the great—and patriotic—composer Giuseppe Verdi captured this spirit in his opera *La Battaglia di Legnano* (1849) which celebrated the victory of the Lombard communes over Frederick Barbarossa in 1176.

Inevitably historians have sought to tone down this view. The communes were not early experiments in democracy; real power was always held by a narrow, if changing, élite of wealthy landowners, entrepreneurs and professional men— and noble families were never totally excluded. Their political tolerance was low: critics faced heavy taxation, loss of office, exile, execution. From the 13C to the end of the Middle Ages, the communes could be dominated by a relentless conflict between two parties, the Guelfs and the Ghibellines operating—albeit opportunistically—under the banners of pope and emperor respectively. Shakespeare's *Romeo and Juliet*—in any case drawn from Italian literary sources —was a not too distant reflection of a world of vendetta.

Finally, a preoccupation with the history of the communes can disguise the fact that most of northern Italy in the late medieval and Renaissance periods was ruled by different types of regime. Most cities came under the rule of signorial, or lordly, dynasties, generally from powerful local families who seized or acquired power to dominate or manipulate the republican constitutions of the communes they ruled. The leading examples here are the Este of Ferrara (1209–1598), the Della Scala of Verona (1260–1387), the Gonzaga of Mantua (1329–1708), the Carrara of Padua (1337–1405), the Visconti of Milan (1277–1447) and the Sforza of Milan (1450–1499). To some contemporaries, and to later historians, the *signori* are seen to conflict, in political and ideological terms, with the communes they came to rule, but the majority of the *signori* did not rule from behind fortifications, as aloof and capricious dictators. Rather they needed and sought the cooperation of at least an élite of the citizenry and generally sought to project their governments as legitimate and mindful of the welfare of their subjects. Moreover, in other areas of the north, where urban life was less advanced, princely governments of various types had even earlier and longer histories. For example, the prince-bishopric of Trent was established by the western emperors in the 11C and lasted until 1801.

Foreign intervention and rule

The number and diversity of north Italian states had profound consequences. For historians of the nation state these can appear in a negative light; the economic resources and political will of the northern cities may have defeated the Hohenstaufen in the 12C and 13C, but the on-going divisions of the region encouraged intervention from France, the Empire and Spain in the late 15C and early 16C, the period of the 'Italian Wars': Italy became—and remained— caught up in the rivalries of the major powers. At the time, this was seen as a disaster, and in the main the Italian historical tradition has continued to see it in this light, seeking to pin blame on individual rulers, the state system, methods of government, military organisation.

However, the impact of foreign intervention and rule should not be exaggerated. It did not involve the settlement of foreign peoples as had occurred with the collapse of the Roman Empire. On the whole, foreign rule was not savagely enforced; repression of that kind was not experienced until the **Second World War** (1943–45) as the Third Reich delayed the advance of the Allies northwards, but then the situation was compounded by a vicious civil war between those who remained loyal to Mussolini and anti-Fascist partisans. Earlier, foreign rule could prove temporary: the lands of the House of Savoy were largely under French rule from 1536 to 1559, but the dynasty recovered its duchy and skilfully exploited its position on the frontier between French and Imperial spheres of influence, attaining royal status with the acquisition of Sardinia in 1720.

And the hegemony of foreign powers could be exploited in other ways. The merchants and bankers of Genoa were able to profit from Spanish conquests in the New World. The Genoese statesman and admiral Andrea Doria (1466–1560) used an alliance with the Habsburgs to rule the city, virtually as prince after 1528. Alessandro Farnese, duke of Parma and Piacenza (1545–92) brought fame and fortune to himself and his dynasty by serving Philip II of Spain in the Mediterranean and the Low Countries.

Finally, of the northern states only Milan and central Lombardy remained constantly under direct foreign rule; its last Italian duke, Francesco II Sforza, died in 1535 and the duchy was annexed to the Habsburg Empire. Otherwise, the north Italian states long retained at least nominal independence, if their freedom of action on the international stage was restricted. Thus the Gonzaga ruled Mantua to 1708. The Venetian Republic survived down to 1797 in a state of watchful neutrality protected by skilful diplomacy and massive fortifications.

Cultural heritage

The fall of the Republic was symbolised by the transport of the famous bronze horses from the façade of S. Marco to Paris. They were returned, but war and invasion have contributed to the destruction, damage and dispersal of the 'cultural heritage' of northern Italy. An earlier French invasion, in 1498, led to the removal of the fine library built up by the Visconti and Sforza dukes of Milan; Allied bombing severely damaged Mantegna's fresco cycle, the *Martyrdom of St James*, in the Ovetari Chapel, Padua. But much has survived intact and in place, and undoubtedly the political divisions of northern Italy contributed to enriching its 'cultural heritage'. Major cities—Venice, Milan, Genoa—did of course act as magnets, but the north had no traditional, effective, central capital with a first call on men of talent and their patrons: the sense of the 'provincial' is largely absent from the cities of northern Italy. So, for example, in Verona— subject to Venice from 1405 to 1797—an intense interest was maintained from the Renaissance in the geology, flora and fauna, antiquities, history and musical and literary traditions of the area, finding expression in the founding of such institutions as the Accademia Filarmonica in the 16C and the Accademia di Scienze, Lettere ed Arti in the 18C. A similar phenomenon can be detected in smaller centres: an academy was established in Rovereto in the Trentino in 1750. The conscious maintenance of such traditions helps to account for the present rich and varied cultural activity of the towns and cities of northern Italy, from folklore to festivals of music and film, from pageantry to art exhibitions and the celebration of local saints.

Architecture provides another, older and more continuous, expression of political diversity. City walls and fortresses were built to protect republican and princely governments. Churches—like S. Antonio in Padua—were embellished to celebrate local cults. Ruling dynasties like the Visconti of Milan and the Gonzaga of Mantua built palaces to proclaim their authority and magnificence. As that suggests, political and cultural competition within states could be mirrored by rivalries within them; from the end of the Middle Ages, the Grand Canal in Venice, some islands in the lagoons—like Murano—and some areas of the mainland—as on the banks of the Brenta—became prized sites for families to demonstrate their wealth and nobility in the construction of palaces, villas, gardens.

But explanations for the rich heritage of the north lie in more than political diversity. Historically, the region has been of great economic importance, even if its wealth has not been evenly spread in geographical or social terms. Christianity, however, has been and religious observance has contributed vitally to the cultural life of the region. This can be seen in the patronage of parish, monastic and friary churches—and the chapels and altars within them—as well as in the support of hospitals, for the spiritual good of an individual, a family or a collective, like a guild or confraternity.

Motives could also be utilitarian, as seen in the construction of bridges, fountains, markets, halls—*palazzi*—for the conduct of government. And cultural patronage could also seek to delight or instruct a more restricted circle of courtiers or cognoscenti, for example in the tapestry-like frescos depicting the labours and pleasures of the months painted for the prince-bishop of Trent around 1400, or the collection of antiquities established by the Veronese scholar Scipione Maffei in 1714.

However, it would be misleading to insist on single or predominant motives behind cultural patronage. Three members of the Della Scala, the rulers of Verona, had free-standing tomb monuments built in the centre of the city in the 14C to commemorate and celebrate the dynasty, to express its piety, to proclaim its authority, aims enhanced by their employment of innovative and gifted Gothic sculptors. In 1456, Francesco Sforza, duke of Milan, appointed the highly regarded architect and sculptor Antonio Filarete to design a major hospital for the city; the project was intended to improve the welfare of his subjects while enhancing the duke's reputation for good government. The stone bridge at the Rialto in Venice was designed by Antonio da Ponte (1588–91) to impress; it also served a very practical function at the commercial heart of the city. When in 1729 Vittore Amedeo II of Savoy commissioned Filippo Juvara to build a palace, the Stupinigi, near Turin it was intended as a hunting lodge and a rural retreat; he was also seeking to emulate the magnificence of the French crown.

Travellers to Italy

Palaces and villas, often enhanced by gardens and collections of antiquities and works of art, drew generations of admiring and envious foreign visitors. But northern Italy had long attracted foreigners: from mercenary soldiers to pilgrims heading for Rome or the Holy Land (via Venice); from merchants and diplomats to musicians seeking to benefit from the taste for northern singers and composers in the courts of Renaissance Italy; from students frequenting the great universities of Padua and Bologna to refugees from political and religious persecution—the later categories being particularly marked in the 15C and the 16C with the spread of Islam and Protestantism. Cultural tourism probably has its origins in the curiosity of pilgrims and the enthusiasm of scholars and collectors; from the 15C pilgrim guides and accounts are increasingly descriptive while from the 16C impressions left by the traveller seeking to broaden his education—like Sir Philip Sidney (1554–86)—become steadily more numerous.

Drawn to court societies and concentrations of Roman antiquities, participants in the Grand Tour tended to head further south, but Venice due to its remarkable site, its reputation as a more open society, the achievements of such widely regarded artists as Titian (1490–1576) and architects as Andrea Palladio (1508–80) ensured that Venice remained a magnet for travellers, as the demand for painters like Canaletto (1697–1768) and Guardi (1712–93) demonstrates. From the late 18C, an appreciation of the scenery of the Alps and the northern lakes—an appreciation which had existed since Roman times as is suggested by the villa, associated with the poet Catullus, at Sirmione on Lake Garda—was heightened with Romanticism. The Alpine passes and the northern lakes became major subjects for artists like John Turner (1773–1857) and their followers and assistants like James Hakewill (1778–1843). The following century was to see a growing interest in the art and architecture of medieval Italy, which heightened the interest of travellers and scholars, like the Scottish historian and collector James Dennistoun (1803-55) in the northern cities.

The succession of European wars from the French Revolution to the *Risorgimento* did little to deter, for long, foreign travellers; indeed sympathy with Italian Unification—together with the development of the railway network—increased the number of foreign visitors. Both a cause and an effect of this was the growth in guide books and accounts. The first Murray guide (by Sir Francis Palgrave) appeared in 1842, the first Baedeker (in English) in 1870. As early as 1840 the *Edinburgh Review* was complaining about the anodyne character of many accounts of the country, if the *Quarterly Review*—in a more charitable mood in 1847—welcomed further descriptions of Italy. Not all travellers were consistently impressed. Wordsworth complained that 'improvements' to the Simplon Pass made on the orders of Napoleon had ruined its natural beauty. Most of northern Italy, with the exceptions of Venice, Verona and—eventually—Genoa, seems to have depressed Charles Dickens on his tour of 1844–45. Ruskin's fascination for Venice was tinged with reservations and disappointments; he was certainly critical of the railway bridge linking it to the mainland and of the insensitive restoration of its principal monuments.

Hans Christian Anderson (1835) and Thomas Mann (1912) were among those who detected a sinister quality to Venice, but that did not prevent a sizeable foreign community from establishing itself in the course of the 19C, drawn by the advocacy of Ruskin and others, as well as by its art market, low rents and cosmopolitan—and apparently tolerant—society. Even earlier a much larger foreign community settled on the Riviera whose climate was highly regarded. Its history and legacy are remarkable. For example, an English entrepreneur, Sir Thomas Hanbury, established a botanical garden near Ventimiglia in 1867 while in 1888 another Englishman, Clarence Bicknell, founded an archaeological museum at Bordighera. Edward Lear, and his cat Foss, set up home in San Remo in 1871.

An insight into these foreign communities is provided by the career of the Scottish Presbyterian minister Alexander Robertson who lived in Italy from 1882 to 1933. He first settled at San Remo where he ministered to a Presbyterian congregation; that this was only one of a number of flourishing Protestant churches on the Riviera is suggestive—together with the presence of libraries, clubs and consulates—of the large and varied foreign community. From 1888 Robertson was in Venice, where he again established a church—again one of several Protestant churches in the city—and where he wrote prolifically on Venetian and Italian affairs. Though now largely forgotten as a writer, the 'pastore scozzese' made himself known and useful to a large number of visitors to Venice, one of whom—Ezra Pound—affectionately mimicked the sound and fury of his sermons in his *Cantos*. Pound is now buried near to Robertson in the cosmopolitan Protestant section of the cemetery island of S. Michele in the Venetian lagoons.

Further Reading

E. Baudo, *The Charm of the Western Riviera* (Genoa, 1995).

A. Cole, *Art of the Italian Renaissance Courts* (London 1995).

C. Duggan, *A Concise History of Italy* (Cambridge, 1994).

D. Hay (ed.), *The Longman History of Italy* (London, 1980–).

H. Hearder, *Italy: a Short History* (Cambridge, 1990).

M. Hollingsworth, *Patronage in Renaissance Italy* (London, 1994).

D. Mack Smith, *Italy and its Monarchy* (London, 1992).

J. Morris, *Venice* (London, 1983).

T. Parks, *Italian Neighbours* (London, 1993),

T. Parks, *An Italian Education* (London, 1994).

J. Pemble, *The Mediterranean Passion* (Oxford, 1988).

J. Pemble, *Venice Rediscovered* (Oxford, 1995).

D.P. Waley, *The Italian City-Republics* (London, 1978).

Italian place names

Many of the place names in Italian towns and cities have ancient origins. The names assigned to public buildings, market places, towers, bridges, gates and fountains frequently date back to the Middle Ages; this is strikingly so with the *rii* (canals), *calli* (alleys) and *fondamente* (quays) of Venice. But the practice of formally naming all streets and squares began in the 19C. Frequently local—even parochial—patriotism determines the choice as the community celebrates its own history and its own political, literary, religious, artistic and scientific figures, as well as famous foreign visitors.

On the other hand, some individuals transcend the local and are widely commemorated. For example, **Dante Alighieri** (1265–1321), **Francesco Petrarch** (1304–74) and **Giovanni Boccaccio** (1303–75), pioneering masters of the Italian language, emerge as national heroes. And events and issues of national history are also prominently represented. Thus a united republican Italy can be celebrated in terms of concepts (e.g. **Via della Repubblica**, **della Libertà**, **della Vittoria**), events (e.g. **Via del Plebiscito** recalling the vote that preceded a region uniting with the Kingdom of Italy), or by drawing on the gazetteer of Italian rivers, mountains, seas and cities.

Broadly speaking the national figures and events chosen tend to be representative of four phases in recent Italian history. Probably the most emotive and frequently commemorated is the ***Risorgimento*** (the Resurgence), the movement that led to the unification and independence of Italy in the 19C; among the battles commemorated are: **Custoza**, **Lissa**, **Solferino**, **Magenta**, **Montebello**, **Mentana**. For some historians, Italy's entry to the First World War represents the final phase in the pursuit of national unity; the battles and campaigns between Italy and her allies and the Central Powers are also frequently recorded in place names: the **Isonzo**, **Monte Pasubio**, **Caporetto**, **Monte Grappa**, **the Piave**, **Vittorio Veneto**. Opposition to Fascism and the ending of the Second World War are also commemorated, as are the statesmen and events associated with the country's reconstruction, economic development and membership of the EC. Casualties in Italy's successful struggle against political terrorism (**Aldo Moro**, murdered by the Red Brigades in 1978) and the less successful war against organised crime (**Alberto della Chiesa** killed by the Mafia in 1982) are also entering the pantheon.

Of course, the political climate changes. So the **Arce della Pace** in Milan was originally intended as part of a neo-classical complex celebrating Napoleon's victories, but appropriated by the Austro-Hungarian Empire it came to celebrate his defeat. Largely censored and deleted from the more recent record are the events and personalities closely linked to **Fascism**, Italy's empire and the reigns of the last two members of the House of Savoy, Vittorio Emanuele III (1900–46) and Umberto II (1946). However, the keen-eyed observer might be able to identify traces of Fascist insignia and the Fascist system of dating (1922, when Mussolini was invited to lead the government, is year 1) on public buildings and monuments, and some street names still recall territories once ruled from Rome (e.g. **Dalmazia, Albania, Libia**).

Below is listed a selection of the more prominent figures and events from recent Italian history the traveller is likely to encounter time and again.

People

Vittorio Alfieri (1749–1803), poet and dramatist

Cesare Balbo (1789–1853), political thinker and historian

Cesare Battisti, Italian patriot, executed by the Habsburg regime in Trent, 12 July 1916

Cesare Beccaria (1738–94), legal theorist and political economist

Don Bosco (the Blessed Giovanni, 1815–88), educationalist and founder of the Salesian Order

Giosuè Carducci (1835–1907), patriotic poet and literary critic

Camille Cavour (1810–61), statesman and cautious architect of Italian unification

Francesco Crispi (1818–1901), statesman

Gabriele D'Annunzio (1863–1938), poet, novelist, dramatist, nationalist

Massimo D'Azeglio (1798–1866), painter, man of letters, patriot

Armando Diaz (1861–1928), leading Italian general of the First World War

Ugo Foscolo (1778–1827), poet and patriot

Giuseppe Garibaldi (1807–82), inspirational political and military leader in the *Risorgimento*

Vincenzo Gioberti (1801–52), political thinker, philosopher

Antonio Grasmsci (1891–1937), political thinker, Marxist, opponent of Fascism

Daniele Manin (1804–57), Venetian patriot and statesman, defender of that city against the Habsburgs, 1848–49

Alessandro Manzoni (1785–1873), poet and novelist

Guglielmo Marconi (1874–1937), electrical engineer and radio pioneer

Margherita of Savoy (1851–1926), wife of Umberto I, noted for her piety, good works and cultural patronage

Martiri della Resistenza (or **Della Libertà**), opponents of Fascism and German occupation (1943–45)

Giacomo Matteotti (1885–1924), socialist politician, assassinated by Fascists

Giuseppe Mazzini (1805–82), leading republican figure of the *Risorgimento*

Guglielmo Oberdan (1858–82), patriot executed by the Habsburg regime in Trieste

Bettino Ricasoli (1809–80), Florentine statesman, instrumental in securing Tuscany's adherence to the Kingdom of Italy in 1860

Aurelio Saffi (1819–1890), man of letters and hero of the *Risorgimento*

Umberto I of Savoy, King of Italy, 1878–1900

Giuseppe Verdi (1813–1901), prolific opera composer whose output was often associated with the cause of a united Italy. His surname could be read as the initials of 'Vittorio Emanuele Re d'Italia'

Vittorio Emanuele II of Savoy, King of Sardinia-Piedmont from 1849, King of Italy 1861–78

Events

XI Febbraio: 11 February 1929, formal reconciliation between the papacy and the Kingdom of Italy

XXIX Marzo: 29 March 1943, armistice between Italy and the Allies

XXVII Aprile: 27 April 1945, Benito Mussolini captured in northern Italy. The Fascist leader was quickly tried and executed on 28 April

XXIV Maggio: 24 May 1915, Italy enters the First World War

II Giugno: 2 June 1946, referendum designed to favour a republican constitution

XX Settembre: 20 September 1870, Italian forces enter Rome, overthrowing papal rule

IV Novembre: 4 November 1918, proclamation of the armistice between Italy and Austria

Glossary

Ambo (pl. *ambones*), pulpit in a Christian basilica; two pulpits on opposite sides of a church from which the gospel and epistle were read

Amphora, antique vase, usually of large dimensions, for oil and other liquids

Ancona, retable or large altarpiece (painted or sculpted) in an architectural frame

Arca, wooden chest with a lid, for sacred or secular use. Also, monumental sarcophagus in stone, used by Christians and pagans

Architrave, lowest part of an entablature, horizontal frame above a door

Archivolt, moulded architrave carried round an arch

Atrium, forecourt, usually of a Byzantine church or a classical Roman house

Attic, topmost storey of a classical building, hiding the spring of the roof

Badia, *Abbazia*, abbey

Baldacchino, canopy supported by columns, usually over an altar

Basilica, originally a Roman building used for public administration; in Christian architecture, an aisled church with a clerestory and apse, and no transepts

Borgo, a suburb; street leading away from the centre of a town

Bottega, the studio of an artist: the pupils who worked under his direction

Bozzetto, sketch, often used to describe a small model for a piece of sculpture

Broletto, name often given to the town halls of North Italy

Bucchero, Etruscan black terracotta ware

Bucrania, a form of classical decoration—heads of oxen garlanded with flowers

Campanile, bell-tower, often detached from the building to which it belongs

Canopic vase, Egyptian or Etruscan vase enclosing the entrails of the dead

Cantoria, singing-gallery in a church

Cartoon, from *cartone*, meaning large sheet of paper. A full-size preparatory drawing for a painting or fresco

Caryatid, female figure used as a supporting column

Cassone, a decorated chest, usually a dower chest

Cavea, the part of a theatre or amphitheatre occupied by the row of seats

Cella, sanctuary of a temple, usually in the centre of the building

Cenacolo, scene of the Last Supper (often in the refectory of a convent)

Chalice, wine cup used in the celebration of Mass

Chiaroscuro, distribution of light and shade, apart from colour in a painting

Ciborium, casket or tabernacle containing the Host

Cipollino, onion-marble; a greyish marble with streaks of white or green

Cippus, sepulchral monument in the form of an altar

Crenellations, battlements

Cupola, dome

Diptych, painting or ivory panel in two sections

Dossal, an altarpiece

Duomo, cathedral

Ex-voto, tablet or small painting

expressing gratitude to a pagan god or saint

Fresco (in Italian, *affresco*), painting executed on wet plaster. On the wall beneath is sketched the *sinopia*, and the *cartone* (see above) is transferred onto the fresh plaster (*intonaco*) before the fresco is begun either by pricking the outline with small holes over which a powder is dusted, or by means of a stylus which leaves an incised line on the wet plaster. In recent years many frescoes have been detached from the walls on which they were executed

Gonfalon, banner of a medieval guild or commune

Graffiti, design on a wall made with an iron tool on a prepared surface, the design showing in white. Also used loosely to describe scratched designs or words on walls

Greek-cross, cross with the arms of equal length

Grisaille, painting in various tones of grey

Grotesque, painted or stucco decoration in the style of the ancient Romans (found during the Renaissance in Nero's Golden House in Rome, then under-ground, hence the name, from 'grotto'). The delicate ornamental decoration usually includes patterns of flowers, sphinxes, birds, human figures, etc., against a light ground

Iconostasis, high balustrade with figures of saints, guarding the sanctuary of a Byzantine church

Impost block, a block with splayed sides placed above a capital

Intarsia (or *tarsia*), inlay of wood, marble, or metal

Intrados, underside or soffit of an arch

Krater, Antique mixing-bowl,

conical in shape with rounded base

Latin-cross, cross with a long vertical arm

Lavabo, hand-basin usually outside a refectory or sacristy

Loggia, covered gallery or balcony, usually preceding a larger building

Lunette, semicircular space in a vault or ceiling, or above a door or window, often decorated with a painting or relief

Matroneum, gallery reserved for women in early Christian churches

Medallion, large medal; loosely, a circular ornament

Monochrome, painting or drawing in one colour only

Monolith, single stone (usually a column)

Narthex, vestibule of a Christian basilica

Niello, black substance used in an engraved design

Oculus, round window

Opera (del Duomo), the office in charge of the fabric of a building (i.e. the Cathedral)

Pala, large altarpiece

Palaeochristian, from the earliest Christian times up to the 6C

Palazzo, any dignified and important building

Pendentive, concave spandrel beneath a dome

Pietà, group of the Virgin mourning the dead Christ

Pietre dure, hard or semi-precious stones, often used in the form of mosaics to decorate cabinets, table-tops, etc.

Pieve, parish church

Plaquette, small metal tablet with relief decoration

Pluteus (pl. *plutei*), marble panel, usually decorated; a series of them used to form a parapet to precede the altar of a church

Polyptych, painting or panel in more than three sections

Predella, small painting or panel, usually in sections, attached below a large altarpiece, illustrating the story of a Saint, the life of the Virgin, etc.

Presepio, literally, crib or manger. A group of statuary of which the central subject is the Infant Jesus in the manger

Pronaos, porch in front of the cella of a temple

Putto (pl. *putti*), figure of a boy sculpted or painted, usually nude

Quadratura, painted architectural perspectives.

Reredos, decorated screen rising behind an altar

Rhyton, drinking-horn usually ending in an animal's head

Rood-screen, a screen below the Rood or Crucifix dividing the nave from the chancel of a church

Scagiola, a material made from selenite, used to imitate marble and pietre dure

Schiacciato, term used to describe very low relief in sculpture, where there is an emphasis on the delicate line rather than the depth of the panel

Scuola (pl. *scuole*), Venetian lay confraternity, dedicated to charitable works

Sinopia, large sketch for a fresco made on the rough wall in a red earth pigment called sinopia

(because it originally came from Sinope on the Black Sea). By detaching a fresco it is now possible to see the sinopia beneath and detach it also

Situla, water-bucket

Soffit, underside or intrados of an arch

Spandrel, surface between two arches in an arcade or the triangular space on either side of an arch

Stele, upright stone bearing a monumental inscription

Stemma, coat of arms or heraldic device

Stoup, vessel for Holy Water, usually near the west door of a church

Tessera, a small cube of marble, glass, etc., used in mosaic work

Thermae, Roman Baths

Tondo, round painting or bas-relief

Transenna, open grille or screen, usually of marble, in early Christian church

Triptych, painting or panel in three sections

Trompe l'oeil, literally, a deception of the eye. Used to describe illusionist decoration, painted architectural perspectives, etc.

Villa, country house with its garden

The terms **quattrocento**, **cinquecento** (abbreviated in Italy '400, '500), etc., refer not to the 14C and 15C, but to the 'fourteen-hundreds' and 'fifteen-hundreds', i.e. the 15C and 16C, etc.

Artists' index

General index

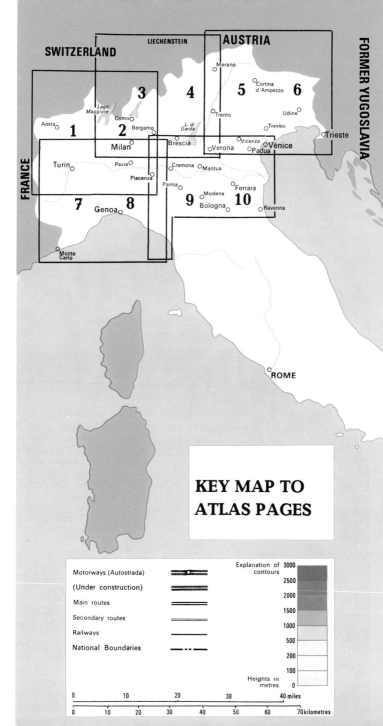

Motorways (Autostrada)	
(Under construction)	
Main routes	
Secondary routes	
Railways	
National Boundaries	

Explanation of contours

Heights in metres

3000
2500
2000
1500
1000
500
200
100
0

| 0 | | 10 | | 20 | | 30 | | 40 miles |
| 0 | 10 | 20 | 30 | 40 | 50 | 60 | | 70 kilometres |

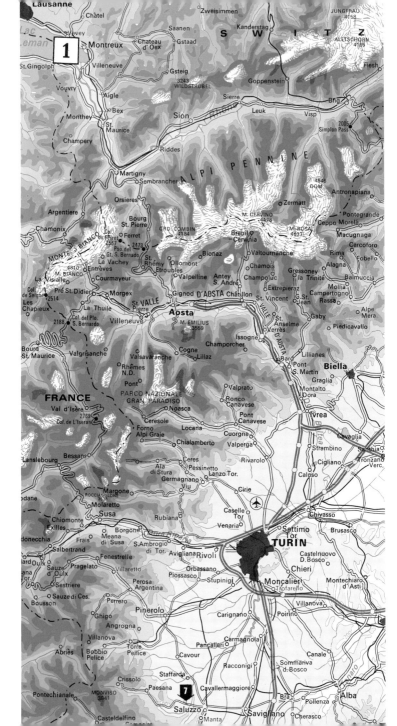

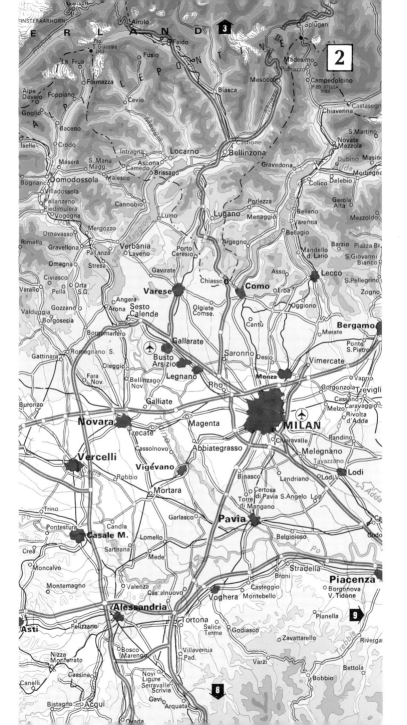

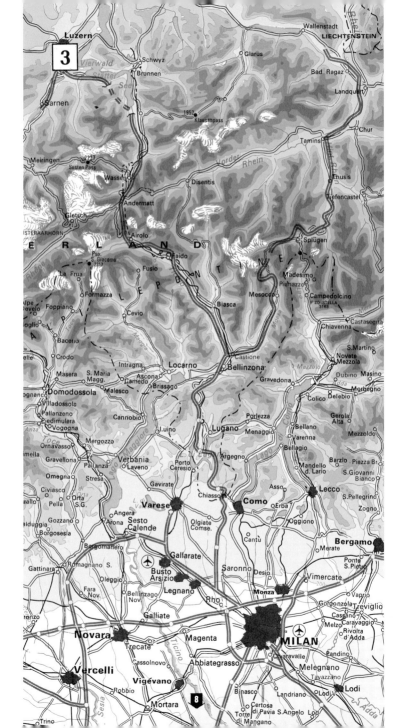

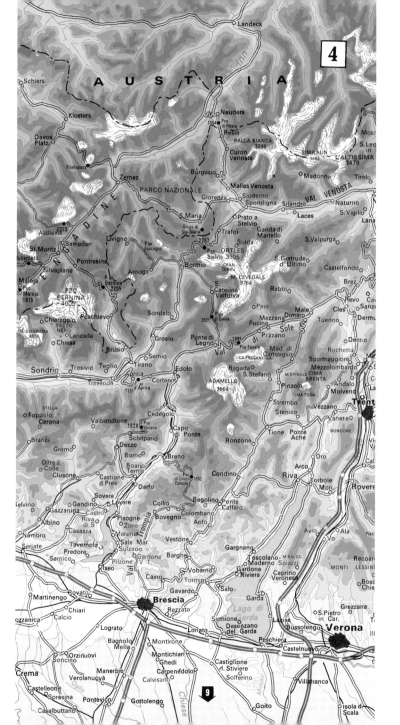

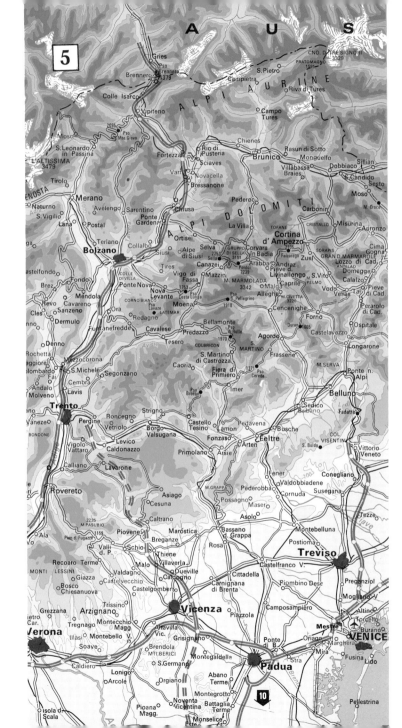

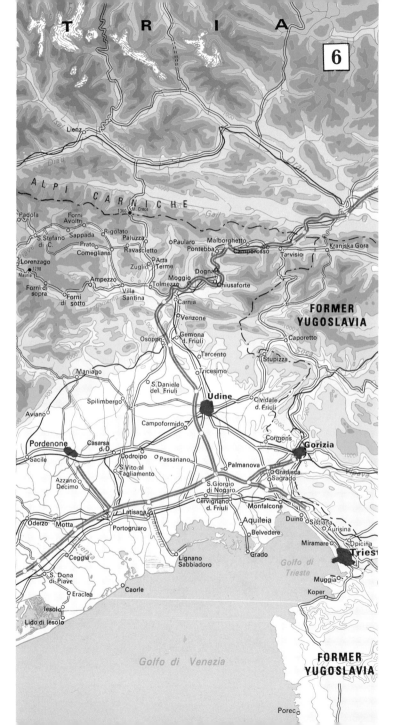

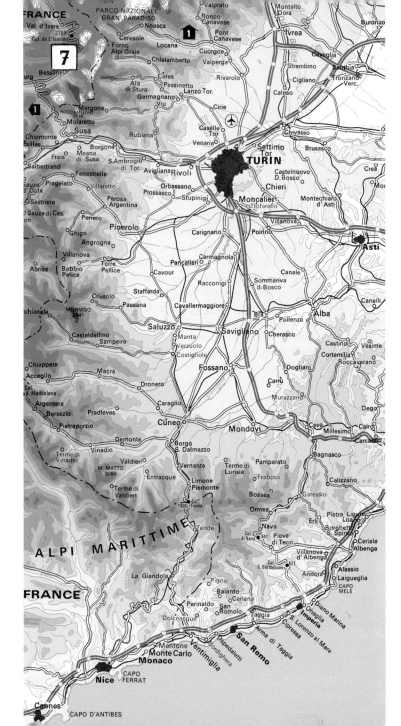

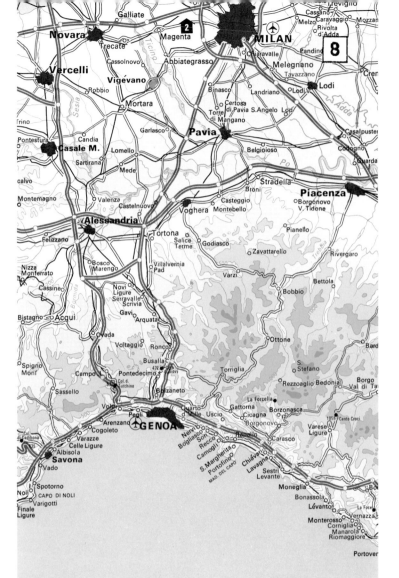

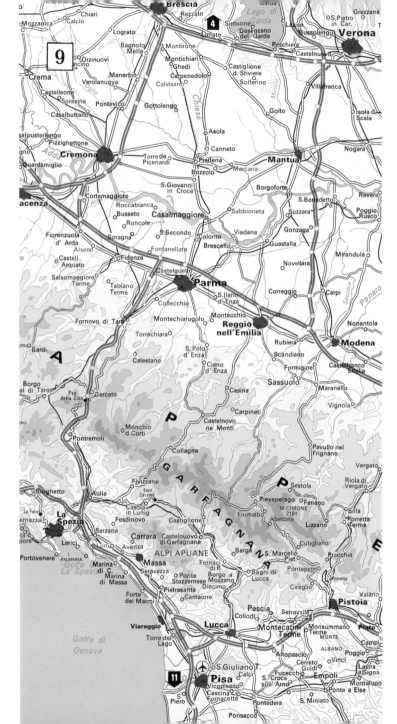

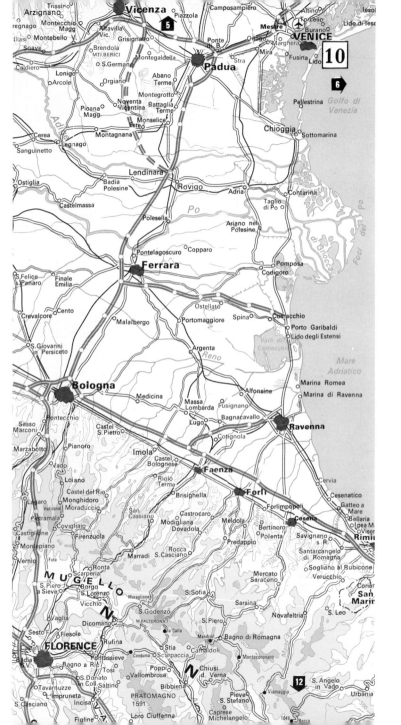